D0754407

The Boast of Heraldry the Pomp of Power,
And all, that Beauty, all that Wealth, e'er gave
Awaits alike th' inevitable Hour.
The Paths of Glory lead but to the Grave.

Forgive ye Proud, th' involuntary Fault,
If Memory to these no Trophies raise,
Where thro' the long-drawn Isle, & fretted Vault
The pealing Anthem swells the Note of Praise.

Can storied Urn, or animated Bust,
Back to its Mansion call the fleeting Breath?
Can Honour's Voice awake the silent Dust,   provoke
Or Flattery sooth the dull cold Ear of Death?

Perhaps in this neglected Spot is laid
Some Heart once pregnant with celestial fire,
Hands, that the Reins of Empire might have
Or waked to Ecstasy the living Lyre:

Some Village   Breast

The little Tyrant of his Fields withstood;
Some mute inglorious Tully here may rest;
Some Caesar, guiltless of his Country's Blood.

But Knowledge to their Eyes her ample Page,
Rich with the Spoils of Time, did ne'er unroll;
Chill Penury had damp'd their noble Rage,
And froze the genial Current of the Soul.

Full many a Gem of purest Ray serene
The dark unfathom'd Caves of Ocean bear:
Full many a Flower is born to blush unseen
And waste its Sweetness on the desert Air.

Th' Applause of listening Senates to command,
The Threats of Pain & Ruin to despise,
To scatter Plenty o'er a smiling Land
And read their Histry in a Nation's Eyes.

Their Fate forbad: nor circumscribed alone
Their struggling Virtues but their Crimes confined;
Forbad to wade thro' Slaughter to a Throne,
And shut   Mercy on Mankind

Thomas Gray

THOMAS GRAY

A Life

Robert L. Mack

Yale University Press
New Haven and London

For my parents

Published with the assistance of the Annie Burr Lewis Fund

Designed by Adam Freudenheim
Set in Sabon by Best-set Typesetter Ltd., Hong Kong
Printed in China through World Print, Ltd.

Library of Congress Card Number 00–104461

A catalogue record for this book is available from the British Library
10 9 8 7 6 5 4 3 2 1

Endpapers: The Eton College Manuscript of Gray's *Elegy*, entitled 'Stanza's
Wrote in a Country Church-Yard', c. 1742–50

CONTENTS

PLATES

SOURCES OF ILLUSTRATIONS

The author would like to thank the following sources for permission to reproduce illustrations:

Front Jacket and Plate 17, The National Portrait Gallery, London; End-papers and Plates 7, 11, 24, 25, 47, 49, Eton College Library, Eton College, Windsor; Plate 5, The Fitzwilliam Museum, University of Cambridge; Plates 2, 6, 29, 30, 31, 32, 33, 48, British Library; Plates 8, 9, 10, 13, 14, 45, The Bridgeman Art Library; Plates 3, 4, Guildhall Library, London; Plates 15, 16, 18, 19, 21, The Paul Mellon Centre for Studies in British Art, London; Plate 20, Castle Museum, Nottingham; Plates 23, 27, 34, 36, 37, 46, Oxford University Press; Plates 26, 28, 35, Cambridge University Press Plates 12, 38, 39, 40, 41, 42, 43, 44, Courtauld Institute of Art Plates 1 and 22 are from the author's own collection.

ACKNOWLEDGEMENTS

My indebtedness to the following institutions and individuals is gratefully acknowledged: the Librarians of the Berg Collection in the New York Public Library; Ms. Pauline Birger, Bayer PLC, Stoke Court, Stoke Poges; the Librarians and staff of the Bodleian Library, Oxford; Mr. Tony Coia of Byer's Green (for information regarding the history of the Wharton estate at Old Park, Durham); Durham District Land Registry Office; the Librarians of the Firestone Library, Princeton University; Mrs. Linda Fowler, Assistant Librarian of Eton College; Mr. John Gaze, Parish Clerk, St. Michael's, Cornhill; Dr. W. Grimstone, Pembroke, Cambridge; The Keeper of Manuscripts, the Keeper of Prints and Maps, and the staff of the Guildhall Library, Corporation of London; Dr. R. P. H. Green, Glasgow University; Mrs. Penny Hatfield, Eton College Archivist; the Librarian and staff of the Huntingdon Library, San Marino, California; Ms. Kerry Howles, Burnham Beeches Hotel, Burnham, Buckinghamshire; Mrs. P. Judd, of Pembroke College Library, Cambridge; Ms. Mary Kerrell, Crane Davies, the Manor House, Stoke Poges; Mr. James Kilvington and the Librarians of the National Portrait Gallery, London; Ms. Hilary Laurie, formerly editor of the 'Everyman' Library; Ms. Emma Lauze, Photographic Archivist, Paul Mellon Centre for Studies in British Art; Mr. Julian W. S. Litten of Walthamstow, London (for information about burial practices in eighteenth-century England); Ms. Clare Van Loenen, Keeper of Art, Castle Museum, Nottingham; the London Public Record Office; Dr. R. W. Lovatt, Perne Librarian, Peterhouse, Cambridge; Ms. Judith Luna, Oxford University Press; Mr. Alan Marshall, of the British Library Picture Library; Dr. Rosiland K. Marshall, Assistant Keeper of the Scottish National Portrait Gallery; Mr. Michael Meredith, Librarian of Eton College; Ms. Sylvie Merian of the Pierpont Morgan Library, New York; the National Trust (in particular Mr. Edward Gibbons and the staff of the Photographic Library); Mrs. Josie Royce, of the British Library Reproductions and Permissions Department; Mr. David Scrace and the staff of the Fitzwilliam Museum, Cambridge; Spennymoor Library and the Spennymoor Local History Society; Mr. Peter Stevens, the Worshippful Co. of Scriveners; the Robert Taylor Collection, Princeton University; the Revd. Canon Peter Wright, Rector of Aston, Yorks.; Ms. Erica Wylie, Essex County Record Office, Chelmsford, Essex.

Throughout my research I have necessarily relied on the advice and the practical support of a number of my professional colleagues, foremost among them Vereen Bell, Barbara Bowen, Ann Cook, Thadious M. Davis, Roy Gottfried, Laurence Lerner, and Leonard Nathanson. I also owe a profound debt to the unstinting attention of Mr. Paul Burch, Mrs. Sarah Corbitt, and Mrs. Carolyn Levinson; particular and heartfelt thanks are due to Mrs. Janis May, whose firm and unflagging encouragement contributed at least as much as any research grant could have done to the ultimate (if not quite so timely) completion of this project.

I have also enjoyed the unflagging friendship and practical assistance of a great many friends both in England and in America. I would like particularly to express my deepest gratitude to Angela Burdick, Stefan Chmelik, Ruth Gavin (an especially valued friend and adviser), and Haidee Schofield. I wish also and especially to thank the Marquis of Cholmondoley for inviting me to spend time at his home at Houghton not merely as a scholar, but as a guest, and for so kindly offering me such free access to Sir Robert Walpole's personal library and archives. To my oldest and dearest friend in England, Allegra Huston, I owe something far more valuable than can ever truly be reckoned in words. Together, as undergraduates, Allegra and I first tasted something of the genuine excitement inherent within the grandest tradition of learning – first tasted something, perhaps, of the enabling *achievement* of scholarship – even as we studied, ensconced at opposite ends of the same table, beneath the elaborately painted arms and panels of Duke Humphrey's Library. I drew then on Allegra's strength of character for the support of my own resolve; I rely to this very day – as I expect to rely far into the future – on the solid sense of her judgement, on the gift of her keen and unerring sense of humour and, quite simply, on the invaluable generosity of her friendship.

Also in London I would like to express my gratitude to Ms. Stephanie Cabot, of the William Morris Agency, and to Mr. John Nicoll and Adam Freudenheim at Yale University Press.

In the United States and Canada I would like to acknowledge some similarly long-standing debts – intellectual, material, and (on occasion) inspirational – to Deborah Barker and Ivo Kamps, John Bomhoff, the Bouldin family (Dr. Mel, Marshall Bouldin III, Bo, Annette, Jamie, Mahlon, Jason, and Alicia), Kathy Eden, Sam and Scottie Girgus, Allan Hepburn, Gene Jennings, Thomas P. Roche, Jr., Marcia Rosh, and Matthew Santirocco. I wish to take this opportunity also to acknowledge the encouragements both of my brother, René Allen Mack, and of my sister-in-law, Phyllis Mack.

I doubt if any biographer could have discovered a more sympathetic reader or, for that matter, could ever have recognized a more committed advocate than I have the privilege of acknowledging in John Halperin. My indebtedness to Margaret Anne Doody – whom I likewise and with gratitude regard not merely as a teacher or mentor, but as a personal friend – is no less incalculable. Had I not first been exposed to Margaret's own, often electrifying enthusiasms, I would most certainly never have had the opportunity to determine the direction or even the essential nature of my own; and although I can only hope some day to approach the level of her insight, I could never really have gone very far astray in looking to emulate the achievement of Margaret's intrepid intelligence, or in attempting (as best I might) to approach not simply literature, but life itself with some reflection of her own insatiable and uncompromising spirit – a spirit motivated by an irrepressibly vital sense of engagement and of joy. It is no exaggeration for me to assert that had it not been for Margaret Anne Doody, this biography would never have been written; whatever might be thought best in it, is best thanks to her. In recollection of John Dryden, it was yours, Margaret, before I could call it my own.

Finally, I would like to thank Sarah Zimmerman, a colleague since graduate school days whose support has sustained me throughout this project, and (not incidentally) a Romanticist who has by now been compelled to listen to far more about Thomas Gray (and to spend far more time in the eighteenth-century, generally) than she could ever conceivably have bargained for. I am as undeserving of the benefit of Sarah's judgement and as thankful for the patient confidence implicit in her criticisms as I am grateful for that affection which I can only attempt – inadequately, perhaps, but with pure and genuine intent – somehow and always to return.

AUTHOR'S NOTE

Samuel Johnson observed in one of his *Rambler* essays that even in books that 'best deserve the name of originals', there is often 'little more beyond the disposition of matters already provided'. However much the present volume hopes to make its own original contribution to the tradition of criticism which has grown up around Gray's writing, I remain keenly aware of my profound indebtedness to the work of those twentieth-century scholars and editors whose painstaking research and whose often passionate diligence resulted in meticulous and authoritative editions of Gray's poetry and correspondence throughout the twentieth century. The present biography would have been inconceivable had it not been for the immense achievement of individuals such as William Powell Jones, H. W. Starr and J. R. Hendrickson, Paget Toynbee, and Leonard Whibley; the monumental accomplishment of Yale University Press's multi-volume edition of the correspondence of Horace Walpole likewise provides for the modern reader a similar and seemingly unfathomable mine of information and interpretation. I have also benefitted immeasurably from the comprehensive work of one of Gray's most enthusiastic and sympathetic editors in the twentieth century, Roger Lonsdale, of Balliol College, Oxford. Among the many modern and contemporary critical studies of Gray's work to which I owe a sustained and thorough-going obligation, I would like particularly to acknowledge my indebtedness to the work of Lord David Cecil, Robert F. Gleckner, Donald Greene, George E. Haggerty, Jean H. Hagstrum. G. S. Rousseau, and Bruce Redford. My central purpose in these pages has been to tell the story of Gray's life in such a manner as to draw together the separate insights of such critics into a single and coherent narrative. I would also be remiss if I did not here also acknowledge my reliance on the following volumes detailing general information concerning historical events and social customs throughout the period covered by this biography: Jeremy Black and Roy Porter, eds., *The Penguin Dictionary of Eighteenth-Century History* (London and Harmondsworth, Middlesex, 1994); Paul Langford, *A Polite and Commercial People: England 1727–1783* (Oxford, 1992); Gerald Newman, ed., *Britain in the Hanoverian Age, 1714–1837: An Encyclopedia* (New York and London, 1997); Ben Weinreb and Christopher Hibbert, *The London Encyclopedia* (London, 1983; 1993).

All quotations from Gray's poetry are taken from *The Poems of Thomas Gray, William Collins, Oliver Goldsmith*, edited by Roger Lonsdale (New York: Longman, 1969); lengthier references to this volume will documented parenthetically in the text as *PTG* and page number. Although translations in the text from Greek and French are my own, the English versions both of Gray's Latin poetry and of his few attempts at Italian translation are based with only few substantial changes on the excellent prose paraphrases included in Lonsdale's volume; note, however, that any extended references to Lonsdale's own criticisms of Gray's work contained within his edition will be acknowledged individually (e.g. Lonsdale, *PTG*, 34).

Quotations from Gray's letters are from *Correspondence of Thomas Gray*, edited by Paget Toynbee and Leonard Whibley, with Corrections and Additions by H. W. Starr, 3 volumes (Oxford: Clarendon Press, 1971); all extended references to Gray's correspondence in the text will be to *CTG* and page number (the three volumes of Gray's correspondence are paginated consecutively). Citations from the letters of Horace Walpole not contained in the Toynbee and Whibley edition of Gray's *Correspondence* are from *The Yale Edition of the Correspondence of Horace Walpole*, edited by Wilmarth S. Lewis, 48 volumes (New Haven: Yale University Press, 1937–83), and when quoted at length are documented in the text as *WC*, volume and page number. Some few, obvious misspellings in the correspondence of Gray and his friends have been silently amended, and the long 's' has been eliminated throughout. I have also modernized abbreviations (e.g. wch for *which*, th^t for *that*, etc.) and have regularized the spelling of words in some few instances in which the writers used macrons to double letters. Otherwise, the texts of letters are printed as Gray or his correspondents wrote them; apart from the exceptions noted above, idiosyncracies of orthography, punctuation, capitalization, and abbreviation – all of which contribute significantly to the tone of epistolary exchange – have been reproduced as they were originally written. The sources mentioned above are indispensable to further knowledge and understanding of Gray and his circle; the footnotes, chronological tables, and genealogical charts included in Toynbee and Whibley's edition of the poet's correspondence are particularly recommended to the reader's attention. The same edition's twenty-six appendices further make available for general study material relating to Gray (such as the documents in the case submitted to Dr. Audley, the letters relating to the poet's last illness and death, Walpole's Memoir of Gray, and Norton Nicholls's *Reminiscences*, etc.) with a thoroughness and precision close to impeccable.

In the effort to tell the story of Gray's life and writing as fluidly as possible, reference notes in the present volume have been kept to a minimum; only extended references to and quotations from outside sources have been documented in the text itself. However, care has been taken to provide a precise and thorough Bibliography at the end of the volume, so that the work of critics, scholars, and historians explicitly referred to in the narrative can in all cases with very little effort be traced back to their original sources. In addition to the abbreviations of the major reference sources already noted above, other frequently cited authorities are referred to in the text as follows:

Ausonius	Ausonius, *Ausonius I*, trans. H. G. Evelyn White. The Loeb Classical Library (London, 1919; 1988).
Cecil	Lord David Cecil, *Two Quiet Lives: Dorothy Osborne and Thomas Gray* (London, 1948).
Downey and Jones	*Fearful Joy: Papers from the Thomas Gray Bicentenary Conference at Carleton University*, James Downey and Ben Jones, eds. (Montreal, London, 1974).
Gleckner	Robert F. Gleckner, *Gray Agonistes: Thomas Gray and Masculine Friendship* (Baltimore and London, 1997).
Gosse	Edmund Gosse, *Gray* in English Men of Letters Series (London, 1882; 1889).
Hutchings and Ruddick	*Thomas Gray, Contemporary Essays*, W. B. Hutchings and William Ruddick, eds. (Liverpool, 1993).
Mason (1775)	*The Poems of Mr. Gray, to which are prefixed Memoirs of his Life and Writings by W. Mason* (York, 1775).
Mason (1807)	William Mason, *The Works of Thomas Gray . . . to which are added Memoirs of His Life And Writings*. 2 vols. (London, 1807).
Mitford	John Mitford, *The Poetical Works of Thomas Gray, Edited, With a Life by Rev. John Mitford*. Boston: Little Brown and Co., 1853.
Powell Jones	William Powell Jones, *Thomas Gray, Scholar: The True Tragedy of an Eighteenth-Century Gentleman* (New York, 1965).
Rothstein	Eric Rothstein, *Restoration and Eighteenth-Century Poetry 1660–1780* (London, 1981).

*

The author wishes finally to acknowledge the following sources for permission to quote from copyrighted books:

Longmans, Green and Co Ltd – for quotations from *The Poems of Thomas Gray, William Collins, and Oliver Goldsmith*, ed. Roger Lonsdale.

Oxford University Press – for quotations from *Correspondence of Thomas Gray*, ed. Paget Toynbee and Leonard Whibley.

Yale University Press – for quotations from *The Yale Edition of Horace Walpole's Correspondence*, ed. W. S. Lewis. *Correspondence.*

*

A section of the Introduction was published as part of an essay in *Journal X*, Volume 4, No. 2 (Spring, 2000); a section of Chapter Eight appeared as 'From Eton to Ranelagh: Context and Meaning in an Early Parody of Thomas Gray's "Ode on a Distant Prospect of Eton College" in *ELN* Volume XXXVI, No. 1 (September, 1998), and is reprinted by permission of the Regents of the University of Colorado.

Who then but must conceive disdain,
   Hearing the deed unblest
Of wretches who have dared profane
   His dread sepulchral rest?

> – William Cowper, 'Stanzas on the
> Late Indecent Liberties Taken With the Remains
> of the Great Milton'

'We lay him bare. We serve him up. What is it called? We give him to the world.'

. . . 'And why shouldn't we?'

'Because we don't know. There are natures, There are lives, that shrink. He mayn't wish it. We never asked him'.

> – Henry James, *The Real Right Thing*

We desire to understand human beings with a comprehension entirely different from that of the movement of electrons or the habits of birds. Why? Because we know that for these more delicate inquiries we have at our disposal the instruments of a more perfect process, the process of confronting another's emotions with our own.

> – André Maurois, *Aspects of Biography*

INTRODUCTION

NEVER AND ALWAYS

Stoke Poges, Buckinghamshire

If, today, a traveller journeys west from central London toward the village of Stoke Poges in the southernmost corner of Buckinghamshire, the trip is unlikely to be a particularly enjoyable or relaxing one. Having perhaps first wound their way out of the increasingly embattled financial centre of the City, and having then cut through the seemingly interminable chaos of traffic that so often clogs the West End to the Marylebone Road, drivers are momentarily lifted by the Westway flyover above the no-man's land of roads and tangled rail lines which insuperably divides the still genteel placidity of Maida Vale and Little Venice, to the north, from the rather more self-conscious aspirations of areas such as Notting Hill and Holland Park, to the south. On either side of the motorway stretches the determinedly dreary – if still diverse and culturally vibrant – landscape of west London. The sheer panoramic extent of this landscape manages somehow to remain impressive. Drivers are fortunately vouchsafed only the most fleeting glimpse of the fragmented remnants of flats, shops, and severed streets over which the convenient arc of the flyover now carries them. Acres of windswept and unweeded railroad yards splay within an easy distance of the monumental bulk of Paddington Station, once the terminus of the Great Western Railway and one of the four great railway stations of the metropolis. Along the changeable precincts of the rail-yards, walls of soot-blackened London brick stand sentinel within the shadows of the gargantuan tower blocks that hover ominously in the steely skies above the Golborne and Harrow Roads.

Though typically whisked north of Shepherd's Bush and with any degree of luck carried with equal speed past the vaguely sepulchral eminence of the BBC studios at White City, travellers quickly find themselves deposited once again and with little ceremony among the congested lanes of the A40. Only at this point do motorists begin more determinedly to inch their way to the north-west on the main road leading toward High Wycombe, Oxford, and beyond. After passing through nearly twenty miles of suburban sprawl, the bland monotony of which is enlivened only rarely by anything of either architectural or historical interest (the Art Deco magnificence of the old Hoover building west of Park Royal near Perivale, for instance, or the site of the old 'Aerodrome' at Northolt), drivers finally cross the Grand

Union Canal past Uxbridge, where the slight climb into the Chilterns gradually begins.

Rather than pursuing the gentle ascent of the motorway and cross-ing the range of chalk downs, however, drivers heading for Stoke Poges swing south at the Denham roundabout, where they then turn onto the secondary road that leads in the direction of Slough. By this stage of their journeys, travellers have already passed south of Harrow and through the modern borough of Hillingdon. They are now well within the range of London's so-called Green Belt, the encompassing ring of which was intended originally to forestall the otherwise insatiable geo-graphic appropriation of the urban environment. And, indeed, its fore-sighted attempt at metropolitan containment has not been entirely without result. The world now blurring beyond the frame of the automobile windows seems to have become a little more verdant, if not with woodland then at least with golf courses; the immediate fore-ground, too, appears noticeably less cluttered with the more egregious debris of urban development. The simple perception that one has finally succeeded in shaking off some of the concerns of the city and has at least begun to trespass within the demesne of the modern countryside is itself the kind of realization that is often experienced with dramatic suddenness – a suddenness the nature of which, moreover, prompts a visceral awareness of a sort that rarely fails favourably to impress even the most hardened city-dweller. Although the scrupulously tidy fields and hedge-rows that typify this affluent junction of Berkshire, Buckinghamshire, and Surrey are obviously and by any truly rural measure far too neat and trim ever to be mistaken for *real* country, and for all that this is today very much a stolidly suburban landscape, the antiquity of the region's oldest settlements – the living experience intractably embodied in the contoured memories of its long tamed and subdued countryside – remains as genuine and as distinctive a feature of its history as any modern innovation or development might ever hope to be. Having once left the faceless tyranny of the motorway behind them, travellers are at the very least afforded some small opportunity of uncovering something of the rich and compellingly human traditions inherent in their surroundings. Even today, beyond or just beneath the manicured verges of the putting greens, the dust here is not the dust of the quick and hasty footstep. It is, in some very real sense, the dust of the past.

Drivers are now within minutes of Stoke Poges. Well-prepared travellers are likely already to have taken note of some few of the region's other, small claims on their attention as well. Just over five miles to the north, in the small town of Chalfont St. Giles, rather more patiently thorough pilgrims of literary history will find their efforts rewarded by the sight of the 'pretty box' of a house in which John Milton, having fled London during the Great Visitation of the plague in 1665, completed *Paradise Lost*. Purchased by public subscription in 1887, Milton's cottage is the only house long lived in by the poet to have survived into the twenty-first century. The neighborhood surrounding the small cluster of villages sometimes collectively referred to as 'the Chalfonts' – particularly considering the near proximity of larger urban centres such as Slough and Beaconsfield and the close conjunction of two of London's major through-roads with the encompassing ribbon of the M25 – has managed somehow to remain a surprisingly green and leafy enclave.

The town of Stoke Poges itself is located roughly four miles south of the quiet, residential suburb of Gerrards Cross. The small scattering of buildings that today make up the modern village at Stoke lies just to the east of Burnham Beeches, the fragile remains of the vast beech forests that once blanketed the area, and which for many generations supplied the raw materials for the region's native industries of joinery or furniture-making. The name 'stoke' (from the Old English *stoc*) can be translated variously as 'hamlet', 'outlying farmstead', 'stockaded place' or, even more simply, 'place'. The local manor house had been noted in the Doomsday survey as 'Stoches Ditton' or Stoke Ditton. At that time, of course, the property had only recently passed from the hands of its earlier tenant, a vassal of King Harold's known rather forbiddingly as 'Sired the Saxon', into those of the Norman Baron William Fitz-Ansculf. The new owner is unlikely to have developed any great personal attachment to the area, however; Fitz-Ansculf appears to have been granted a further sixteen manors in Buckinghamshire, twelve more in Berkshire, and an astounding sixty-eight properties elsewhere in the kingdom. Even so, the manor remained in the Baron's family for some eight generations, and both he and his descendants came in time more precisely to style themselves by such names as William 'Stoches' and Walter 'de Stoke'. When, late in the thirteenth century, the heiress of the manor house, then one Amicia of Stoke, was married to a knight of the shire for Edward I's parliament by the name of Robert Pogis (from the family of *le Pugeis*), the Great House and the area immediately surrounding its property were together dubbed 'Stokepogies' or 'Stoke Poges', a place-name that – for all the blunt and pointedly straightforward statement of its designation – would nevertheless have served to alert all comers to the fact that they were at that particular stage of their journeys passing through and among the 'place' or 'hamlet' of the Pogeys family.

The old parish church of St. Giles at Stoke Poges is today situated on the edge of some fifteen acres of preserved fields. The church, not surprisingly, is convenient rather to the ancient manor house itself (the most recent manifestation of which still stands some 200 yards away) than to those structures which constitute the modern centre of the still small community. The earliest church had been established on the same site in 1086, and some portions of the present building (most notably the north wall of the chancel, which preserves a small Norman window) date from as far back as the twelfth or even the eleventh century. The better part of today's chalk and flint church, though not quite so ancient, can still lay claim to an impressive and extended architectural history. Many of its defining features had already been set out by the fourteenth century. Fragments of brickwork and masonry – integral supports and structures of old timber – stand in place today, much as they might already have been found standing in place several hundred years ago. The once slender and famously 'ivy-mantled' tower of the church, however, was granted no such longevity. Doomed to suffer an altogether more igno-minious fate, the last such structure (though aesthetically beyond reproach) was in the earliest years of the twentieth century judged to be too unsound to remain any longer in place. Dismantled in 1924, the spire of St. Giles has never been rebuilt.

A visitor's first impression of the Stoke Poges church itself is likely to be somewhat unprepossessing. The red brick and stone-mullioned windows of a Tudor addition to the building (the Hastings chapel, built in the angle of the chancel and the south aisle by Lord Hastings of Loughborough, son of the first Earl of Huntingdon and the lord of the manor in 1558) can first strike the eye as undistinguished and even slightly commonplace. The facade of the stone buildings that today constitute the chapel and the chancel, particularly when taken with the ghostly outline of the almshouse which for many years buttressed the south side of the church, appear at first to huddle rather too closely about the nave and cropped tower, the latter of which is today capped only by a squat and unremarkable roof. Nevertheless, even as one makes one's way through the churchyard toward the building's entrance on the south side of the nave (an elegant porch supported by oak timbers over seven hundred years old), the degree to which the structure's several architects have each, in their own manner and across the span of cen-turies, judiciously consulted the native 'genius of the place' slowly becomes obvious. There inheres within both the church and its grounds, the inescapable aura of sheer authenticity that seems only rarely to have found expression in the overly-enthusiastic creations of such nineteenth-century revivalists who, in the words of the *fin-de-siècle* nov-elist John Meade Falkner, 'wouldn't have known an aumbry from an abacus'. An accoutered, frowsty barn to some, the church of St. Giles at Stoke Poges manages, nevertheless, modestly to convey to its more receptive visitors the depth of its own quiet seriousness of purpose – the reverence inherent, even, within its own venerable sanctity of space.

Guidebook in hand, our visitor enters the church porch and, swinging open the heavy, outer door that turns easily on its hinges, first examines the south aisle and the nave. The white walls are cold and damp. The dates and names on many of the flagstone monuments have been worn away by years of curious footsteps. The air inside the church is redolent of polished wood and brass, workaday fragrances of the ecclesiastical world, proper and professional – aromas that mingle on appropriate occasions with the lingering scent of spruce asters, or perhaps with the dusky aroma of Sunday's September roses. The atmosphere within the church seems also to savor, though less precisely, of that visible silence in which prayer and meditation seem more readily to recognize their desired effect.

Much of what the modern visitor first observes inside St. Giles is likely to be the product of late nineteenth- or early twentieth-century reconstruction; many features of the original structure had already been eliminated or otherwise obscured by repairs on the church undertaken from 1702 to 1734. The interior roof-beams, for example, the heavy timbers of which so often strike the taste of today's observers as elegantly interwoven and impressively bare and rough-hewn, were until as late as 1897 hidden from general view by a flat and unremarkable ceiling. The chancel arch, too, as some more scrupulous visitors to the church might point out with a murmur of righteous disapproval, dates only from the early Victorian era, when the original Norman structure was altered in a misguided attempt to widen the passage between the chancel and the nave. A private entrance connecting the church to the manor house still passes through the 'cloister' of the north aisle, opposite the porch entrance, but the passage would appear now to be used only as a storage space. Having persisted in the face of such mild aesthetic setbacks as these to undertake a reasonably thorough examination of the brasses, monuments, and memorials around the main alter and in the Hastings chapel, most visitors are soon ready to forsake the insidious chill of the church's interior, compelled instead – perhaps with a renewed sense of spiritual awareness and energy, though perhaps just as frequently betraying the hasty formality of decorous retreat – toward the warmth of the sunlight that appears suddenly and with unwonted vitality to splash across the building's tiny entrance. The bright, discernable shafts of sunshine, particularly when glimpsed from within the comparative darkness of the church itself, appear typically to have transformed themselves into an iridescent gateway, a vaguely supernatural portal opening onto an altogether different environment. And, as some visitors have no doubt had the presence of mind to reflect as they exit the building and begin to walk among the tombstones, such a move can indeed resemble the eerie sensation of having effected a brief moment of contact with another world. The churchyard at Stoke Poges retains the potential to remind its visitors of some of the more fundamental aspects of their own participation in an extended human past, much as it maintains its power to communicate to those same visitors some rather more obvious intimations of their inevitable participation in the collective human future.

The churchyard, too, the visitor soon notices, appears to have undergone some significant changes in recent years. Even more meticulously tended and groomed than in former times, the tidy precincts of St. Giles remain a cool and silent retreat, participating, some might think with a touch of irreverence, or with the discomfiting twinge that accompanies the increasingly rare perception of sacrilege, at least as much in the character of a formal park or garden as in that of a burial ground. Yellow beeches, laurels, oaks, horse-chestnuts, cedars, and tender young elm trees strategically dot the graveyard; a stately progress of Royal William rose bushes – each shrub carefully planted, marked, and maintained – lines the pathways. In actual fact, the churchyard is today bordered on its south side by one of the first planned 'memorial gardens' in England, an early publicity pamphlet for which, not surprisingly, had attempted to fill space within the park by emphasizing its envied proximity to St. Giles. 'Melodious notes are struck in the surroundings of the world-famous church', one anonymously written, 1937 advertisement for the development rhapsodized, 'and the gardens, connected by a private entrance thereto, are in perfect harmony with the quietude and beauty'. Some of the more recent graves in the Stoke Poges cemetery itself, their plots contained within the meticulous precision of individual stone copings, seem strangely impersonal – oddly devoid of the resonance of any lived or historical existence. Yet the better part of the soil here has been sanctified not merely by the hand of man, but by the considerably more authoritative hand of time. An ancient yew tree still shades the moss-blackened headstones of dead years in the older part of the churchyard, and visitors passing among the lichen-coloured tombs in autumn might find the stone slabs stained crimson with the juice of its fallen, waxy berries. Beyond the older alter-tombs near the church itself, the line of graves extends along the path that leads visitors back toward the wicket gate and the main entrance to the grounds.

On the weathered surface of one of the prominent pair of tombs set very close to the windows on the eastern exterior of the Hastings Chapel, the careful visitor will have little trouble in making out the following inscription:

In the Vault beneath are deposited,
in Hope of joyful Resurrection,
the remains of
MARY ANTROBUS
She died unmarried, November 5, 1749
Aged 66.
In the same pious confidence,

beside her friend and sister,
here sleep the remains of
DOROTHY GRAY
Widow, the careful tender mother
of many children, one of whom alone
had the misfortune to survive her.
She died March 11, 1753
Aged 67.

Only a small and unobtrusive tablet set within the wall opposite the inscription records that the poet Thomas Gray – the child who, in his own words, quoted above, 'alone had the misfortune' to outlive his 'tender mother' Dorothy – was laid to rest in the same vault following the event of his own death on 30 July 1771.

*

It was some thirty years after the poet's death before the memorial, affixed first to the now graffiti-scarred bricks of the tomb itself, was moved to the sill outside the chapel window. In his Last Will and Testament – a document drawn up just over one year before his final illness – Gray had gone out of his way carefully to specify his desire that his body be placed in this same grave ('in the vault made by my late dear Mother in the church-yard of Stoke-Pogies' [sic]), close to the remains of his mother and his aunt. Gray had also made a particular point of requesting that he be buried modestly, 'in a coffin of season'd oak neither lined nor cover'd'.[1]

The simple fact that he had been the renowned author of the *Elegy Written in a Country Church-yard* lends no small degree of interest to the circumstances that surrounded the poet's final interment at Stoke Poges in 1771. By the time of Gray's death, the *Elegy* had already long enjoyed a reputation among many of its readers as one of the most moving and effective meditations on death ever to have been written in English. Addressing in its lines such compelling subjects as the shared lot of human mortality, the pain of loss and bereavement, and the puzzling web of impulses that would appear perennially to mingle the ache of memory with the unanswerable compulsions of desire, Gray's *Elegy* seemed instantly to have struck a powerfully sustained chord among its eighteenth-century audience. The stunning popularity of the poem

---

[1]   The full text of the poet's Last Will and Testament is included as Appendix X in *CTG* (1283–86); letters relating to Gray's last illness and death exchanged among Brown, Mason, Nicholls, Cole, Stonhewer, Wharton and Walpole are included in the same volume (1269–82) as Appendix W.

was not merely a result of its writer's oddly fortuitous choice of genre or sentiment, however. Such stuff, as Gray himself would have been among the first to acknowledge, was as old as poetry itself. As one early commentator on Gray, John Young, had soon observed of the poet's 'matter' in the *Elegy*:

> Meditation upon death is, and ever has been, the occasional business or pastime of mankind; and though, like devotion, it cannot admit of the sublimer flights of poetry, yet, when the mind is fairly clung to the subject with its sensibilities awakened, and their expressions within call, nothing that is thus produced will be totally void of interest. The views, if not striking from novelty, will be commanding from serious-ness; and even mediocrity in the sentiment will be a passport to general correspondence.[2]

Far more integral than what Young here characterizes as the 'occasional pastime' of Gray's poem to the unrivaled popularity of the *Elegy* through-out the latter half of the eighteenth century was Gray's successful creation, within the sometimes troubled arc of the poem's narrative, of a fully rounded and fully imagined poetic persona – a persona intimately related, as we shall see, to the Thomas Gray of history, but a being who grew also, in the course of time, to assume a life (and, for that matter, a death) of his own. Many of the *Elegy*'s earliest readers were impressed by its speaker's ability to express apparently familiar thoughts in a paradoxically new and powerfully realized language of consolation. The *Elegy* seemed perfectly to fulfill the standard of Alexander Pope, whose criterion had been expressed earlier in the century in his own *Essay on Criticism* (1711), and who had then famously judged the art of true poetic wit to lie in its writer's ability successfully and naturally to express 'what oft was *Thought*, but ne'er so well *Exprest*'.[3] Much the same prin-ciple, of course, was to inform Samuel Johnson's widely celebrated (if otherwise contextually qualified) praise of the *Elegy* as abounding with 'images which find a mirrour in every mind, and with sentiments to which every bosom returns an echo'.[4] The sympathetic persona of the *Elegy* seemed for many to speak in an unpremeditated and spontaneous language of private meditation – a language of direct devotion – and, in so doing, seemed likewise to articulate a form of prayer that effected a

---

[2]   John Young, *A Criticism of the Elegy written in a Country Church-Yard. Being a Con-tinuation of Dr. J———n's Criticism on the Poems of Gray* (London, 1783) 3.
[3]   Alexander Pope, 'Essay on Criticism' (l. 298) in *The Poems of Alexander Pope*, ed. John Butt (London: Methuen, 1963) 193.
[4]   Samuel Johnson, 'Gray' in *Lives of the English Poets*, ed. George Birkbeck Hill, 3 vols. (Oxford: Oxford University Press, 1905) iii.441.

forceful combination of secular, stoic candor, on the one hand, with the unflinching honesty which would appear to be demanded of true Christian belief, on the other. The voice of Gray's poem, in other words, seemed almost instantly to possess a rhetorical authority that moved beyond any merely formal or calculated intellectual engagement with its subject matter, an authority which confronted some of the imminently real yet at the same time oddly intangible issues that continue still to lie just beneath our talk of death and dying – subjects as ambitiously speculative as the nature and 'meaning' of death itself, the relative worth of our existence as embodied human beings, and the possibly dubious value of all gestures of remembrance and commemoration.

The simple fact that the terms of Gray's own will suggest that he bestowed considerable attention on the event of his own death and burial – attention which resulted in precise instructions regarding the manner of his interment – is not, in itself, all that unusual. Nor, for that matter, was the poet's obvious attempt within those same instructions to balance the decorum required of the occasion of his burial with an equal regard for the financial burden imposed by funeral expenses, generally, in any way out of keeping with the accepted practice of the day. From the earliest decades of the century the growing funeral trade in England had looked increasingly to add basically unnecessary (if highly profitable) elements of pomp and panoply to the event of burial. Such additions on the part of an industry that was soon commonly known only as 'the Trade' eventually prompted those of their prospective clients who were more socially aware, or who were simply more alive to the commercial motivation behind such frankly exploitative tactics, instead to request interments of extreme simplicity. Be that as it may, an individual of Gray's standing – i.e., a prominent person of the middle or upper middle class – would still typically (if only for reasons of hygiene) have been buried within a triple coffin consisting of alternating layers of wood, lead, and, finally, wood again. Gray, of course, had his own particular reasons for requesting an especially modest and unremarkable burial. It would hardly have been appropriate for the author of the *Elegy* – whose work was thought so pointedly to have celebrated the life of quiet, rural retirement, and one whose most popular verses had so memorably eulogized 'the short and simple annals of the poor' – to have been buried with any great or conspicuous flourish of ceremony. Even in death, Gray felt the need to exercise a particular care, lest he inadvertently draw too much attention to himself.

The precise instructions included in the poet's will, however, had needed in the event slightly to be modified. It so happened that Gray died rather suddenly in Cambridge in high summer. Both the warm weather of the season and the distance between his university home and the churchyard at Stoke Poges (the heavily laden funeral carriage,

which left Cambridge early on Sunday morning, did not arrive at
its final destination until Tuesday, having rested overnight first at
Hoddesdon and then at Salt Hill) necessitated that his coffin be sheathed
in a heavy, protective covering of lead. So much, then, for the understated simplicity of a plain wooden coffin. Gray was to be only slightly
more fortunate in some of his other final requests. He had asked in his
will that at least one of his executors personally see him laid to rest in
the grave, a 'melancholy task' which, as events turned out, fell to his old
Cambridge friend, the Reverend James Brown. The will's co-executor,
William Mason, to whom the poet left all his books and papers, had
departed for his summer holiday only days before Gray's death; he
would not receive the news of his friend's passing until 7 August, when
his forwarded letters reached him in a cluster at the seaside resort of
Bridlington.

    The funeral itself must have been a somber affair. Of Gray's other
close friends and colleagues, it is possible that only Richard Stonhewer
– a Fellow of Peterhouse who had been spending part of the long academic vacation in London, and who had hurried from the city to visit
the poet in the final days of his illness at Cambridge – might have been
able to meet Brown as he arrived at the churchyard, having accompanied Gray on this last journey to Stoke Poges. The bell in the tower of
St. Giles tolled regularly as the hearse approached the churchyard, followed by the mourning coach. The manifest grief of at least one of Gray's
Cambridge relatives (Mary Antrobus, who attended the service in the
company of her sister's husband, a Cambridge shopkeeper) and perhaps
of such mourners as his long-time manservant, Stephen Hempstead,
is likely to have lent an understated dignity to the ceremony. An
unidentified young gentleman 'of Christ's College, with whom Mr. Gray
was said to be very intimate', was also noted by some later chroniclers
to have attended the ceremony.[5] The tiny group, dressed in the heavy
black crape required on such occasions, stood in stark contrast to the
lush August landscape. The measured intonations of the burial service
would have been punctuated occasionally by the lazy cawing of the
rooks that sheltered within the shade of the heavy trees bordering the
churchyard. Only the softest of summer noises – the somnolent bleating
and lowing of the flocks and herds in the fields nearby – could
have intruded upon the prayers of Gray's friends and family. The
heat that August was unusually oppressive, and it is unlikely that few
even of the elderly parish poor, to whom Gray had left the sum of
£10 to be distributed in charity, would have been tempted from their

---

[5]   See, for example, Appendix C ('Miscellaneous Extracts from the manuscript Papers
of the Rev. William Cole, of Milton in Cambridgeshire, relating to Gray; now in the
British Museum') in Mitford, xcix; see also Gosse, 207.

own shady retreats and into the withering glare of the late summer sun as spectators.

Glancing from time to time beyond the walls of the churchyard and in the direction of the peaceful, rural scene that lay just outside its borders, the official mourners could not help but have comforted themselves by recalling the lines of Gray's own *Elegy* – by repeating quietly or within their own thoughts the several consolations that the poet had himself offered, over twenty years earlier, when contemplating the inevitable toll of precisely such a loss. The *Elegy* had suddenly and unavoidably become eerily re-integrative of its own, already powerful resonance for those who actually witnessed the consignment of the poet to his grave. The poem's purposefully modest 'Epitaph' – lines which had until that very afternoon constituted merely a speculative and self-consciously literary conclusion – trembled for the very first time with the power of a new and rawly specific meaning:

> Here rests his head upon the lap of earth
> A youth to fortune and to fame unknown.
> Fair Science frowned not on his humble birth,
> And Melancholy mark'd him for her own.
>
> Large was his bounty and his soul sincere,
> Heaven did a recompense as largely send:
> He gave to Misery all he had, a tear,
> He gained from Heaven ('twas all he wish'd) a friend.
>
> No farther seek his merits to disclose,
> Or draw his frailties from their dread abode,
> (There they alike in trembling hope repose),
> The bosom of his Father and his God. (*PTG* 138–140)

Solemn witnesses to the interment of Gray's body within the vault at Stoke Poges, most of the mourners in the churchyard could not help but have felt that with Gray's death some kind of circle had been completed – that some rare form of prophecy had finally and inevitably been fulfilled.

Brown surely regretted that the oldest of Gray's childhood friends yet living, Horace Walpole, had been prevented by circumstances from attending this, the formal ceremony that marked the closing moment of the poet's life. Walpole, who had only days before left England for France, was to learn of Gray's passing in the worst possible way. Casually turning over the pages of a newspaper some few days after the funeral, he encountered a blunt and public announcement of his friend's death. 'I started up from my chair when I read the paragraph', he would later confide to William Cole, further recalling of his shock on the

occasion, '– a cannon-ball would not have surprised me more!'[6] Also
absent from Brown's side at Stoke Poges, for various reasons, were
almost all of Gray's other closest friends and correspondents: William
Mason, Thomas Wharton, Norton Nicholls, William Cole, as well as
the romantic protegé whose admiration and lively personality had lent
an unexpected poignancy to the poet's final years, Charles Victor de
Bonstetten. Turning again to observe the pitiably small group of friends
and relations who stood near him at the grave site, Gray's executor may
very well have pondered the irony of circumstances which dictated that,
although the poet's loss was felt strongly and sincerely by his many dear
friends and colleagues, so few had been able actually to be present as he
was finally laid to rest. Too few, Brown must surely have felt, to bear
witness to the seeming inevitability of Gray's final interment within the
very churchyard he had, a seeming lifetime before, immortalized the
world over in his most famous work.

For let us make no mistake: the churchyard of St. Giles at Stoke Poges
must inevitably and for all practical purposes stand as *the* churchyard
of Gray's *Elegy*. However eager the proponents of some few, other sites
have been over the years to advance their own claims to having provided Gray with the inspiration for the 'actual' physical location of the
Elegy (the possible contenders stretch from as near as neighboring
Burnham to as far away as Durham), the provenance of St. Giles is very
close to irrefutable. Some of Gray's modern readers still feel that the
much touted universality of his poem argues *against* a specific setting for
the work. It has often been protested that the *Elegy* ought itself to be
thought of not so much an expression of novel or original thought, but
as a perfectly adequate (but by no means singularly worthy) re-presentation of widespread popular feeling. Gray's *Elegy*, such a view contends,
is an essentially unremarkable collection of previously uttered general-
izations (or, as the critic John Guillory has put it, 'an anthology of literary clichés available to every minimally educated reader') at once far
too vague and far too aphoristic ever to maintain a tenable, historical
connection to any one place or time.[7] The *Elegy* is an allusively derivative poem – so much so, in fact, that it might be said to stand as a convenient summation of the entire elegiac tradition. The poem's unusually
prominent position in the traditions of literary history and influence is
thus itself the direct result of the *Elegy*'s status as a veritable 'anthology'
of the western language of mourning. Gray's poem is thus, and as a
necessary consequence of its own practical nature as an easy handbook

---

[6]   WC i.228.
[7]   John Guillory, *Cultural Capital: The Problem of Literary Canon Formation* (Chicago
and London: University of Chicago Press, 1993) 87.

to the tropes of death and dying in European culture, topographically and temporally imprecise.

To be sure, some of Gray's critics have advanced more theoretically sophisticated critiques of any attempt to situate the *Elegy*'s churchyard within the physical spaces of the 'real' world. Yet even while such critics maintain that speculation regarding the actual location of Gray's churchyard is at best 'idle', some of those same scholars who would otherwise disparage any practical attempt to situate the *Elegy* (either in Stoke Poges or elsewhere) rather grudgingly concede that, given the fraught tension between 'particular' and 'universal' place which on some very fundamental level actually motivates the poem, the impulse that so often prompts readers to root Gray's work within the real world of our shared human history and experience is an excusable one. One such critic, Marshall Brown, has best expressed the manner in which such an impulse is fostered among the *Elegy*'s reader by the very diction, imagery, and argument of the poem itself. In the famous opening stanzas of Gray's *Elegy*, as Brown has observed:

> the repeated possessives drive towards local dominions, and so indeed do the definite articles. At twilight the private consciousness faces dormancy unless it is rescued by positioned singularities ('Save where,' 'Save that from yonder ivy-mantled tow'r'). Dominion is ubiquitous: in the owl's 'solitary reign,' the children's envied sire, the war to subdue nature to cultivation. It is not by chance that the three model figures named in the fifteenth stanza were all politically involved in bloody tyranny, nor that the body politic provides the standard for judging the village's emulation or privation.... If nothing else survives, the heaving turf of line 14 remains a literally posthumous assertion of territoriality. In country and city alike, action stratifies mankind into levels of domination, and, dis-comfortingly, identity remains conceived as place in the scale of being. Hence the promptings from the poem itself towards finding the church-yard. It has no power if it has no location, and no reality or truth if it has no power.

Brown suggests that the status of the *Elegy* as a 'work of art' – its status as a meticulously crafted, poetic artefact – ultimately transforms these initial conditions. 'The indefinite articles of the Epitaph', he concludes with reference to the three final stanzas of the poem, quoted above, 'should teach us at least how precise is the indefinite article of the title'.[8]

Brown's careful analysis of churchyard space in the *Elegy* is a valid

---

[8] Marshall Brown, *Preromanticism* (Stanford, California: Stanford University Press, 1991) 42–48.

one and, as such and taken on its own terms, holds its own against a great many other possible readings of the poem. It remains the task of the literary biographer, however, to locate the work as far as possible within the life – to situate the public achievement of the writer within the comprehensive and culturally-specific narrative of his or her personal history. Poetic 'countries of the mind' such as Gray's church-yard, as Maynard Mack once observed (noting that one would need to extend such an observation to include, among such 'countries', physically precise locations as diverse and varied as Wordsworth's Lake District, Emily Dickinson's New England, Thomas Hardy's Wessex, Robert Frost's New Hampshire, Robinson Jeffers's California, or Dylan Thomas's Wales), even while they remain *essentially* 'retreats of the imagination', tend nevertheless and over time to resemble, in the traditions of English and American poetry, 'more and more some actual locality'.[9] Even the vaguer Arcadias postulated as occupying some 'place' within the shared traditions of English literature have demon-strated a tendency to become 'rooted' in precise and specific locations. As we shall see, it was to this very burial ground at Stoke Poges that Gray often retreated in the traumatic and eventful summer of 1742. And, in subsequent years, as the *Elegy* slowly evolved and moved towards its final shape within his mind, it was often within the shade of these trees and in the shadow of this church's spire that the full moment and the final commitment of its lines must slowly have grown clear to him. It was here, at Stoke Poges, that his own mother and the closest of his maternal aunts had been buried; it was here, at Stoke Poges, that Gray knew he was eventually to be buried himself. It was in the church-yard at Stoke Poges that Thomas Gray chose deliberately and with great care to set the scene of his most personal and revealing poem – a poem which, even with the passing of centuries, manages to intimate the inter-section of its own, deepest meanings within the ever-changing language of the living. It is in the churchyard at Stoke Poges that the *Elegy* finds, if not its very birthplace, then at least its long and abiding home in this world.

*

Since Gray's death in 1771 the churchyard of St. Giles has twice been enlarged. A new burial ground, immediately adjacent to the old, was consecrated in 1911. Predictably, and when once the poet's own modesty had ceased to be heeded in the matter, little time was lost in raising some permanent memorial to Gray's achievement near the site of his grave (a

[9]   Maynard Mack, *Alexander Pope: A Life* (New Haven and London: Yale University Press, 1988) 144.

cenotaph, designed by John Bacon, was likewise soon placed in West-minster Abbey, immediately under that of Milton). At Stoke, a monu-mental stone sarcophagus, which sits upon a raised pedestal some fifteen feet high, and on the smooth surface of which are inscribed verse-stanzas from both the *Elegy* and the *Eton Ode*, still stands about one hundred yards outside the precincts of the churchyard. The monument's setting remains a suitable one. The fields immediately adjacent to the memo-rial are likely to be covered in spring by a profusion of wild flowers. A variety of birds – doves, hedge-sparrows, and common wagtails – might in the same season be glimpsed among the surrounding trees and bushes. Designed by the prolific architect James Wyatt and erected not long after the poet's death (in 1799), the massive structure of the monument itself, however, is in almost every respect wildly inappropriate to Gray's own wishes (no 'frail memorial', this). Yet the deeper urge to commemora-tion that the monument rather clumsily represents – the defiant asser-tion of perpetuity that such structures seek to advance – maintains some of its power to speak to us today. The identical impulse that at once fostered the erection of Wyatt's sarcophagus, and which at the same time facilitated the preservation from development of the nearby fields in the name of Gray's poetry, bespeak a tendency to which we still, as a culture, seem very much to respond. Had it not been for the addi-tional efforts of local residents earlier this century, the entire churchyard and the area surrounding Gray's final resting place would almost cer-tainly have been transformed beyond recognition. The three acres beside the church in which the Gray monument now stands (officially desig-nated as 'Gray's Fields') were originally purchased by private indivi-duals and presented to the National Trust in 1921. A public subscrip-tion helped to provide the financial wherewithal to acquire an additional ten acres of the neighboring field just three years later. It is thanks almost entirely to the efforts of such early twentieth-century preservationists, in fact, that today's visitor to Stoke Poges can still, with the help of only a little imagination, recreate the environment of the churchyard much as Gray himself might have known it. The footsteps of plodding ploughmen may long ago have stopped sounding on the nearby lawns and meadows, and even owls are increasingly hard to come by in these fallen, suburban days. But if one closes one's eyes and listens hard enough and long, the fraternizing bells of a slow-moving herd might still be discerned tinkling drowsily in some distant field, and the sound of a droning airplane high in the midsummer sky, rather oddly, intrudes on the elegiac mood only slightly, if at all. For a moment, at least, the world is as it used to be.

It is no mere accident of circumstance that the most significant efforts to preserve the environment of the Stoke Poges churchyard took place in the years immediately following the Great War. The preemptive actions of the many local and individual preservationists who saved the fields from development in the 1920s formed a preludial part of the government's larger and, in time, more carefully organized response to the unprecedented growth of greater London in the third and fourth decades of the twentieth century. The population of Middlesex, grew by almost a third between 1921 and 1931 – a rate that raced as much as five times ahead of the average national increase. The centrifugal migration from the old City boroughs had begun even by the earliest decades of the century to reach well into the surrounding Home Counties – Hertfordshire, Essex, Kent, and Surrey – and further into the west. 'For anyone who wants to live practically in London and yet away from its frenzy', one fashionable character can be found opining in George Gissing's 1897 novel *The Whirlpool*, the 'uplands towards Buckinghamshire' provided some ideally situated and 'convenient' ground.

The dispassionate analysis of social geography can tell us only part of the story, however. Following the unprecedented cataclysm of the First World War – in the wake of the incomprehensible loss of an entire generation, and imbued with the inconsolable grief of its stunned and shaken survivors – Gray's *Elegy* had itself acquired powerful new meanings. The poem's longstanding connections to the literary landscape of England, in general, and its ties to Stoke Poges, in particular, found themselves being redefined. Such a confrontation – such redefinition – was inevitable. In a manner similar to nearly all truly great works of literature, Gray's *Elegy* is best thought of as timeless not so much in its capacity to communicate to its readers any one, specific meaning that remains unaltered and unchanged *through* time, but, rather, in its broad and receptive ability to respond *to* and change its significance *with* time.

Universal relevance is always, to some extent, a matter of perceived applicability. That having been said, in the aftermath of the Great War Gray's poem suddenly was called upon to commemorate the depth of a disaster that amounted in many minds to the brutal extermination of an entire world of innocence and promise. The familiar, half-muttered verses of Gray's *Elegy*, once memorized in childhood and repeated in snatches and fragments throughout a lifetime of retrospectively mild tribulation, returned home suddenly, and to a country bled white by the cost of its sacrifice, with a force and a unity of feeling greater than they had ever before possessed. The 'invisible power' that had for so long been the object of mere 'lip-worship' and 'lip-resignation', as George Eliot (recalling the gospel of Matthew) once wrote of the nature of such spiritual transformations as occur only in moments of profound personal or cultural revaluation, 'became visible' – and Gray's poem seemed capable somehow of addressing the manifestation of precisely such an awful power with a genuine and heartfelt intensity. In the sepia distances of the early twentieth century, mothers read the *Elegy* in mourning for the sons they had so fondly surrendered to the dark, arterial trenches of the western front. The widows of war looked at the same time to find within Gray's long familiar consolations the grain of some small and temporary explanation – the foundation for some numbing rationalization, possibly – that might begin to help them make sense of their own, personal loss.

The ground around the Stoke Poges churchyard also grew with sad significance. Almost side by side with the 'rude forefathers' of the village's distant and increasingly irretrievable past was commemorated a younger generation – a generation sacrificed before its time, immolated even in the promise of its youth. Of the many men and boys who left Stoke Poges for the front in the dark years that followed and were measured from August 1914, forty-eight were never to see their Buckinghamshire home again, a high cost for a village which counted only 1,500 souls. Most of those who fell in the War, of course, were destined never even to be returned to English soil ('Alas, alas for England', lamented one of the many elegists of the period of these soldiers, 'They have their graves afar'). A tablet inscribed with the names of those lost to Stoke Poges and erected by public subscription was unveiled on the north wall of the Chancel of St. Giles in January 1920. As time passed, the survivors of war turned their footsteps to the church and to its burial ground in their search for some sense of closure and in their hope of dumb forgetfulness; the same individuals turned their hearts and their minds to the *Elegy* for the articulation of meaning, and the respectful tribute of attention. Modern gestures were exchanged for ancient ones, and Thomas Gray's most famous poem was once again transformed.

The fundamental experience of those individuals who, reading and re-reading the *Elegy* in the wake of the Great War, together infused Gray's poem with the force of new and specific meanings was, at least to the degree that such revaluations themselves constitute a recognizable response of interpretive practice, far from unique. Every generation of readers has to some greater or lesser extent been compelled to reinterpret, to recreate, and on occasion even to rewrite Gray's poetry in its own image. And while much the same observation might be made with reference to the work of any artist whose reputation has withstood the changeable tests of time or with regard to any poet whose work has survived the various readings and mis-readings of generations of professional critics, the degree to which such critics, students, and readers of poetry in general have been compelled to return to and constantly to re-interpret nearly all of Thomas Gray's poetry, in particular, remains in many significant respects strikingly peculiar.

Readers have always found it necessary – and will, no doubt, long continue to find it necessary – to ground their responses to the literary past in the soil of their own perceptions and experiences; yet the long-standing status of Gray's poetry as a body of work comprising some uniquely accessible touchstones of literary taste, genre, style, and expression has in his case resulted in a diverse range of such responses. The significance of all poetry and the gesture of all language obviously change over time. The various meanings attributed to Gray's poetry in general and to the *Elegy* in particular, however, seem often to have been provoked by what can only be described as some uniquely reflexive or dialectically provocative capability inhering within that poetry itself.

The compulsion of each generation to revise and to respond to Gray's work in some new or distinctive manner, it very soon becomes clear, is at once both a privilege and a burden. The *Elegy* once read by the Romantic poets, for instance, seems to bear only a passing resemblance to the *Elegy* we read today. For a writer such as William Wordsworth, to turn at once to the most obvious example, Gray was to be regarded as an immediate and problematic predecessor. Much has been written over the years regarding Wordsworth's influential rejection of Gray's language and vocabulary, as set out in a passage included by that poet in the Preface to the second edition of the *Lyrical Ballads* in 1800 (Wordsworth's criticisms were exemplified by Gray's early *Sonnet* on the death of Richard West, but were easily extended to his later poetry as well). In attempting to 'widen the space of separation between Prose and Metrical composition', Gray, Wordsworth sought to convince his readers, was 'more than any other man curiously elaborate in the structure of his own poetic diction'.[10] Wordsworth, of course, defined his own style and his own choice of 'poetic diction' in opposition to Gray's own and, in so doing, made it abundantly clear that he considered his predecessor's work to be Φωνᾶντα συνετοῖσιν or 'vocal to the intellect alone' in ways that the earlier poet had never deliberately intended it to be. Gray's audience, as Wordsworth himself might have put it, was truly but only unintentionally 'fit though few'.

Such, at least, has constituted received opinion. At least one recent writer on the subject, however, Angus Easson, has emphasized the underlying truth that 'in terms of theme and attitude', Wordsworth's response to Gray's poetry in general was (both in theory and in practice) 'far more complex than that of mere rejection'. Wordsworth may on some level and on some occasions have looked to push Gray's supposedly ornate poetic language to one side in his own attempts to distill the idiom and

---

[10]   *The Prose Works of William Wordsworth*, ed. W. J. B. Owen and Jane Worthington Smyser, 3 vols. (Oxford: Oxford University Press, 1974) i.32.

power of the simpler diction which he supposed was 'really used by men'; yet Wordsworth could just as readily, when it served his own purpose to do so, turn to his predecessor's work as 'a recurrent point of reference and a source of sympathetic feeling'. Simply put, Wordsworth could respond with great vitality and even enthusiasm to many of the substantive and *thematic* concerns articulated throughout Gray's work – to aspects of loss and memory explored in his poetry, for instance, or as Easson has argued, to 'the ability of the mind to retain what has been suffered and to organize that suffering' – while succumbing, at the same time, to a compelling need to transcend and to supersede the earlier poet in particularly defined and circumscribed matters of style, diction, vocabulary, and expression.[11]

The members of the so-called second generation of Romantic poets – Byron, Shelley, and Keats most prominently among them – naturally responded to Gray's poetry in an entirely different manner. Byron, in particular, was to experience a more problematic (if rather less critically celebrated) engagement with Gray's work than even Wordsworth himself. As one of Byron's critics, Bernard Beatty, has pointed out, Byron was on certain occasions in his own writing clearly drawn to Gray's 'sentiment'. He was, moreover, 'equally drawn to the self-consciousness of Gray's diction as a means of expressing feeling, manifesting energy, and voicing the void in a calculated mix of metaphysics and fiction'.[12] The result of this peculiar dynamic between the two poets, the critic W. B. Hutchings further concludes, helped ultimately to provide Byron himself with 'a texture of language which demonstrates a particular energy of feeling characteristic of Gray, rather than of the poets of the "Romantic" generations'.[13] Still later in the nineteenth century, the Victorians, even while they perpetuated the popularity and established what some would call the 'canonicity' of the *Elegy* within the nascent traditions of English literary history, rejected much of Gray's other verse out of hand. Matthew Arnold, foremost among Gray's mid-nineteenth-century critics, memorably criticized Gray's output (describing him as 'the scantiest and frailest of classics in our poetry') and his supposed timidity; in an attempt further to underscore his point Arnold wagged a chastening, critical finger at the elegist's supposedly constitutional and debilitating reticence ('*He never spoke out*' – a frequently repeated 'criticism' of Gray's work and temperament, incidentally, that is rooted

[11] On Wordsworth and Gray see Angus Easson, '"A Man of Genius": Gray and Wordsworth', in Hutchings and Ruddick, 205–23.
[12] On Byron and Gray see Bernard Beatty's 'Unheard Voices, Indistinct Visions: Gray and Byron' in Hutchings and Ruddick, 224–247.
[13] Hutchings comments on Beatty's essay are made in his essay 'Past Criticism and the Present Volume' in Hutchings and Ruddick, 10.

in an arguably perverse misinterpretation of an anecdote referring specifically to the circumstances of Gray's final illness, and an observation having little if any bearing on Gray's literary style or output).[14] We should not be surprised that Arnold's assessment of Gray's achievement, much like those of his predecessors, appears likewise, on closer examination, only to have reflected the particular fears and anxieties of his own generation. Arnold elsewhere deplored the 'vague' and indeterminate qualities he discerned as failings in his own poetry. Suffering as he did from a notoriously acute case of *mal de siècle*, Arnold thus predictably criticized Gray for the very same failings – or at least pointed in his work to some of the very same weaknesses – that he already recognized as characteristic of his own work, and of his own era.[15]

Gray's poetry has never lacked its share of supporters, however. Gerard Manley Hopkins, for one, demonstrated himself an able defender. Hopkins on one occasion commented simply, in a letter to his fellow clergyman and poet Richard Watson Dixon, that the supposedly 'evident' criticisms of commentators on Gray's poetry, Wordsworth's among them, were 'not so, nor true'.[16] Arguing for what he perceived to be the rhythmical beauty and grace of Gray's *Sonnet* on the death of Richard West, Hopkins dismissed the Romantics' own devaluation of Gray's diction as self-serving and 'rude at best'. Seemingly more comprehensive criticisms of that same sonnet's structure, Hopkins continued, were equally quite beside the point, since, he reasoned, 'in a work of art having so strong a unity as a sonnet, one part which singly is less beautiful than another may be as necessary to the whole effect, like the plain shaft in a column, and so on'.[17]

And so on, indeed. Such conflicting responses to the work of a poet so genuinely popular and so widely read in his own day are, again, perhaps only to be expected. One possible measure of the true 'quality' inherent in any work of art, after all, might be said to find its standard precisely in the relationships that connect and correlate the inherent power of the creative artefact, on the one hand, with both the multiplicity and the depth of passion evinced in the critical responses of its several and ever-changing audiences, on the other. Both the Romantics

---

[14] Matthew Arnold, 'The Study of Poetry' and 'Thomas Gray' in *The Complete Prose Works of Matthew Arnold*, Vol. IX: *English Literature and Irish Politics*, R. H. Super, ed. (Ann Arbor: University of Michigan Press, 1973) 181;189–204.

[15] On the criticisms of Matthew Arnold and Gerard Manley Hopkins on Gray see Malcolm Hicks, 'Gray Among the Victorians' in Hutchings and Ruddick, 248–70.

[16] Hopkins, *The Correspondence of Gerard Manley Hopkins and Richard Watson Dixon*, edited with notes and an introduction by Claude C. Abbott, 2 vols. (London: Oxford University Press, 1935;1970) ii.137.

[17] Ibid.

and the Victorians tended to approach Gray, to adopt the phraseology
of the great art historian Erwin Panofsky, not historically but pragmat-
ically – as 'something far-off yet, in a sense, still alive and, therefore, at
once potentially useful and potentially dangerous'.[18]

Although it might be comforting to think that we have ourselves,
today, at least begun to achieve the distance so often found wanting in
our predecessors' judgements of Gray's work, such is almost certainly
not the case. The responses of Gray's readers in the twenty-first century,
no less so than those of earlier generations, will be rooted in the possibilities of their own histories and defined by the governing compulsions
of their age. As for present judgement, we would at the very least do
well to keep in mind that we, too, have only recently passed through a
remarkable age of elegy. While there is some truth in the observation
that the subjects of death and loss, of mourning and memory, may sound
the eternal notes of sadness in the established traditions of English
poetry, ours has been (and continues to be) a peculiar lot. The earlier
generations of the twentieth century seem in retrospect to have struggled their way through unimaginable war and economic depression, only
then to face a war still more incomprehensible in its thoroughgoing brutality, and so briefly to achieve the breathing space of comparative peace.
In England and America, at least, there was a window in time when a
generation of youth was not led wholesale to slaughter on the battlefields
of Europe, an historical moment when the anthems that sounded
seemed to sing not of death and loss, but of reconciliation and possibility, the fragments of an era in which the passing bells rang most frequently for those who had at least begun to live long and natural lives.
The shadow of a plague was soon cast across the final decades of the
twentieth century, however, and we continue to live within the darkness
of that shadow. The work of poets such as Robert Boucheron, Mark
Doty, Thom Gunn, Adam Johnson, Paul Monette, Reynolds Price, and
a great many other AIDS elegists commemorates the fact that the lives
of too many individuals had once again, in the closing decades of
the twentieth century, been cut short by disease and death. These and
other poets, many of whose immediate forefathers had rejected the
apparent constraints and boundaries imposed by traditional poetic
forms as unmodish and unworkable, found themselves compelled to
return to the very same forms and cadences they had once disparaged,
discovering in their patterns, rhythms, and orderings of language
the only possible articulations of structure and coherence – the only
intimations of any carefully informed design – that might in turn confer
a momentary meaning on the incomprehensible. A providential pattern

[18] Erwin Panofsky, *Renaissance and Renascences in Western Art* (New York: Harper
and Row, 1969) III.

in human affairs is perhaps too much for many of us to discern this late in the shambles of our collective history, yet we appear still to seek some consolation in the face of perpetual and often self-sown (if otherwise unmerited) catastrophe. Noting the late twentieth-century proliferation of AIDS memoirs, plays, novels, and poetry, the critic Jahan Ramazani has remarked, 'some future historian – let us hope – will be able to write about [such work] as a body of literature whose occasion has ended'.[19] Such a task still remains, however, well beyond our grasp.

*

Perhaps a more practical way for us to approach Gray's life and writing would be to begin by addressing the central issue of influence, and then move on to confront with equal candor the related issue of that preeminence which has generally been granted his work within the most accepted narratives of English literary history. The judgements most often reprinted with Gray's poetry seem invariably to make use within their praise or their criticisms of words like 'immortal', 'essential', 'timeless', and 'transcendent'. Johnson's assessment of what might today be called the 'recognition factor' at work in the *Elegy* has done its work well. Within the traditions of Western poetry, it has not infrequently been asserted, Gray's churchyard *Elegy* manages to give voice to the hopes, the fears, and the anxieties that are as close to being genuinely universal as those expressed by any poet, in any language. 'Everyone', as Leslie Stephen, writing of Gray in the earliest years of the twentieth century commented, 'knows his poetry by heart'. 'The *Elegy* has so worked itself into the popular imagination', Stephen memorably contended, 'that it includes more familiar phrases than any poem of equal length in the language'.[20] Thomas Gray did not, of course, invent the elegy (the honour of that distinction is traditionally bestowed on the Greek poet Theocritus). Nor, even, did he effect any significant revolution in elegiac sentiment or style. Even so, and for well over two centuries, Gray's name has been practically synonymous with the form. One prominent American academic, who, in his late maturity, claimed still vividly to recall having been set the task of memorizing the *Elegy* as a child, confessed to me on one occasion that he had passed well into his elementary education before he realized

---

[19] Jahan Ramazani's remarks on elegies and AIDS are quoted from his *Poetry of Mourning: The Modern Elegy from Hardy to Heaney* (Chicago, 1994) 361–65.
[20] Leslie Stephen's comments on the popularity of the *Elegy* were first included in his 'Hours in a Library, No. XXI – Gray and His School' in *Cornhill Magazine*, 40 (1879) 70–91.

that the casual, aural title 'Gray's *Elegy*' (sounding in his ears something like 'Grazelegy') comprised two separate words – that 'Gray' and 'Elegy' should or even *could* be orthographically and conceptually distinguished from each other.

Such a misapprehension was neither so unique nor so childishly naive as he may at first have believed it to be. As another critic, Ian Jack, conceded, 'we have always known Gray's poem as an elegy – as *the* Elegy'.[21] Gray's *Elegy* is easily to be counted among the most popular and widely memorized poems of all time – and, as such, it has carried as part of its legacy a tradition of oral recitation and performance that further sets it apart from most modern poetry. The roughest of counts shows over fifty separate editions of the *Elegy* in the first half century following its initial publication in February, 1751, not to mention scores of unauthorized appearances in newspapers, magazines, and other journals. Perhaps more than any other poem in English, the *Elegy* seems almost from the moment of its first appearance to have become an inextricable part of the very language itself (though, of course, it was quickly translated into French, German, Latin, Italian, Spanish, and Portuguese; the nineteenth century was to witness appearances in Armenian, Dutch, Hebrew, Hungarian, Japanese, Russian, and Welsh). The years immediately following Gray's death in fact produced nearly as many parodies and imitations of the *Elegy* as they did editions of the original poem.

Gray's more general popularity – facilitated, of course, by the apparent ubiquity of his churchyard *Elegy* – seemed only to increase with the passing of time. When, in Jane Austen's *Emma* (1816), the character of Mrs. Elton prefaces a brief quotation from the *Elegy* with a comment to the novel's heroine, 'I dare say you have heard those charming lines of the poet', she is pointedly and condescendingly insulting Emma; anyone with the slightest degree of education would not only have 'heard those charming lines', but would have been able no doubt him or herself to quote them as well. In the work of novelists such as Ann Radcliffe, whose popular gothic romances Austen herself so much enjoyed, and an author whose work the novelist was eventually to burlesque with such open affection, Gray's verses were within only years of his death likewise being introduced as the work of *the* poet – a privileged and singular designation till then more often reserved by English writers for Shakespeare, Milton or, at least, Pope. Gray appears already, by the end of the eighteenth century, routinely to have been invoked

[21] Ian Jack, 'Gray's *Elegy* Reconsidered' in *From Sensibility to Romanticism: Essays Presented to Frederick A. Pottle*, eds. Frederick W. Hilles and Harold Bloom (New York: Oxford University Press, 1965) 140.

simply as 'The Poet', author of 'The Elegy'. Characters in popular mid-nineteenth-century novels as diverse as Charles Dickens's *David Copperfield* (1849–50), Charlotte Yonge's *The Heir of Redclyffe* (1853), Mary Elizabeth Braddon's *Lady Audley's Secret* (1862), Anthony Trollope's *Can You Forgive Her?* (1864–65), and George Eliot's *Middlemarch* (1871–72), among a great many others, seem unhesitatingly to include the specific language of Gray's verses as a natural and intrinsic part of their own thoughts, speech, and writing. (In Dickens's novel, the straightforward sentiments of the *Elegy* are even quoted in a letter by the imperturbably grandiloquent and notoriously circumloquacious Wilkins Micawber.) Thomas Hardy's *Far from the Madding Crowd* (1874) of course acknowledges its author's debt to Gray's language in its very title. The *Elegy*, one soon concludes, appears on a remarkable number of occasions to have constituted the common language of a multitude of authors who otherwise spoke in a babel of tongues; moreover, Gray's poems managed with equal power and authority to address several generations of writers – writers who otherwise typically expressed themselves in a range of voices or literary styles far from similar to one another.

Nor was Gray's influence and presence as a literary touchstone to flag all that much with time. Prominent writers throughout the twentieth century continued to refer to Gray's poetry in their own work. Fragments both of the *Elegy* and of the *Eton Ode* were likely to turn up adapted for use not only as titles of works of fiction (as in the case of Willa Cather's 1932 *Obscure Destinies*, or Joyce Cary's 1949 *Fearful Joy*), but also of critically acclaimed films (such as Stanley Kubrick's 1957 *Paths of Glory*, based in turn on a novel of the Great War by Humphrey Cobb), and even critical studies (Cleanth Brooks's immensely influential collection *The Well-Wrought Urn* may owe the exact debt of its name to the language of John Donne's 'The Canonization', but the 'storied urn' of Gray's *Elegy* is slyly invoked in the study's title as well). Snatches of Gray's work continued to be echoed and embedded almost unknowingly in the speech of characters in 'serious' fiction, but were no less likely to feature prominently within the pages of the work of comic novelists such as P. G. Wodehouse and Barbara Pym. Any comprehensive list of the indirect parodic and imitative descendants of the *Elegy* in verse would demand to include works of major significance, such as Edgar Lee Master's 1915 *Spoon River Anthology*, Wallace Stevens's 'Dutch Graves in Bucks County', the 'Little Gidding' section of T. S. Eliot's 1944 *Four Quartets*, and even, to some degree, *The Wasteland* itself. It was while he was hard at work on early drafts of the latter poem that Eliot, casually inspecting the graves on a country visit to a churchyard at Padworth, in Berkshire, observed to his friend Richard Aldington that 'if a contemporary poet . . . would concentrate all his

gifts on one such poem [as the *Elegy*], he might achieve a similar success'
to the overwhelming popularity with which Gray had been rewarded
in his own day.[22] More recent poets, Seamus Heaney and Colum
McCartney among them, have continued to confront the achievement
and the legacy of Gray's verses within the language of their own, necessarily derivative, elegiac poetry. Other major poems, such as Tony
Harrison's controversial 1985 threnody *V.*, explicitly rely upon the
reader's familiarity with the *Elegy* to inform their own meanings, or to
contextualize the measures of their own lament.

Parodies, echoes, and imitations, of course, seem typically and by
the very textual promiscuity of their nature to engender only more
imitations, echoes, and parodies. Masters's original *Spoon River* volume
was followed up not only by the author's own sequel or 'revisitation'
to the fictional Midwestern cemetery in 1924, but by a frequently
reprinted parody (J. C. Squire's 'If Gray Had to Write His Elegy in
the Cemetery of Spoon River Instead of Stoke Poges') that explicitly
called attention to the formal and thematic ties which connected
the eighteenth-century work with its twentieth-century derivation.
Parodies of T. S. Eliot's poetry are of course legion, but many of those
same burlesques – Henry Reed's 'Chard Whitlow' ('As we get older we
do not get any younger'), for example, or A. M. Sayer's 'It Always Seems'
('It always seems to me that Thomas Gray / In praise of lowly folk was
led astray') – made a similar point of emphasizing the implicit if often
complicated relationship that linked the memory and desire of the
modern poet's spiritual wasteland to the earlier elegist's thoughts in the
churchyard at Stoke Poges, or to the figure of Gray himself. Still other
writers – most notably G. K. Chesterton, in works ranging from the
obviously titled 'Elegy in a Country Churchyard', to his quiet 'The
English Graves' – exorcized their own particular demons by drawing
explicit and sometimes savagely satirical connections between the sentiments expressed in Gray's poem, and reaction to the tragedy of the Great
War itself.

At the very least, the continuing echoes of the page and the oddly
remorseless insistence of such patterns of literary reference seem strongly
to suggest that the *Elegy* inescapably *haunted* the work of later writers
both in England, in America, and elsewhere in the English-speaking
world. The astounding summary of Gray's achievement in the poem
appears often to have stood directly in the path of poetic creativity in
general; its ubiquity, to say nothing of the acceptance or approval of its
sentiments, certainly frustrated any possible innovations constitutive of

---

[22] T. S. Eliot's reflections on the possibility of writing a twentieth-century 'Elegy' are
included in Peter Ackroyd's biography of the poet, *T. S. Eliot: A Life* (New York: Simon
and Schuster, 1984) 110.

structural or thematic novelty within the form of the elegy itself. Both
the substance and the precise textual patterns and language of Gray's
Elegy presented monumental and unavoidable precedents to any poet
who looked to address in his or her work such fundamental subjects
as fame, death, war, loss, remembrance, and the apparently inelimi-
nable yearnings of humankind. The editors of a recent edition of the
Oxford Dictionary of Quotations, paying scant attention to their own
qualification that a phrase or passage suitable for inclusion in the volume
'should be able to float free from its moorings, remaining buoyant when
detached from its original context', cite no less than fifteen of the
Elegy's thirty-two stanzas – thirteen of them in full. The verse stanzas
of Gray's *Elegy*, to further the editors' parlous nautical metaphor, seem
not only to remain 'floating' and 'buoyant', but appear also to insist,
when quoted, on dragging the rest of the poem into the sea of literary
reference after them – pier, moorings, hawsers, and all.[23]

*

Despite Gray's pervasive influence in English, and despite the fact too
that a great many professional critics tend still to repeat the well-worn
commonplace that the *Elegy* remains the 'best known' poem in the
English language (or, as the compilers of popular classroom anthologies
of English literature sometimes snobbishly put it, the English poem best
known and loved by 'unsophisticated' readers), it is far from certain that
many people would today recognize an allusion to Gray's most famous
poem as a matter of course. To whatever extent the *Elegy* may still be
thought of as a work familiar to students of English literature or to
readers of poetry in general, there is no denying that Gray's poem is for
the most part no longer read and memorized by younger schoolchildren
to the extent that it once was. Individuals who can today quote even the
poem's opening stanzas with any confidence usually date themselves as
having completed their grammar school educations just prior to the cultural upheaval ironically celebrated in Philip Larkin's *annus mirabilis* –
the year 1963. Throughout the later decades of the twentieth century,
Gray's *Elegy* was increasingly replaced as a set text within the English
school curriculum largely (and in many ways appropriately) by the work
of poets such as Thomas Hardy and Wilfred Owen. In American class-
rooms, the *Elegy* was no less likely to be pushed to one side by the work
of native New Englanders, such as Emily Dickinson, or by the decep-

[23]   The criteria of the editors of the *Oxford Dictionary of Quotations* are set out by
Angela Partington in her 'Preface to the Fourth Edition' of that same undertaking
(Oxford: Oxford University Press, 1992) vii–xi.

tively simple narratives and lyrics of the California-born laureate, Robert Frost. However one chooses finally to account for such a change, the fact remains that for modern readers on both sides of the Atlantic, the reiterated sentiments and the linguistic specifics of the *Elegy* seem finally to be growing distant and unfamiliar.

Such a shift in status, however – a shift itself a consequence (at least in part) of the sweeping canonical revaluations encouraged by the methods and priorities of the analytical criticism so fashionable since the mid-1960s – need not necessarily be accepted as demonstrable 'proof' that the *Elegy* or, for that matter, Gray's other popular poems have slipped entirely from our collective poetic consciousness, either as readers or as writers. Hardy and Owen, Dickinson and Frost were all themselves dramatically influenced by Gray's work; Gray's popularity, it should once again be emphasized, had been so widespread as to render any confrontation with his legacy close to unavoidable. We do not find it at all surprising, for example, to find Dickinson casually and with apparent spontaneity quoting a phrase from the *Elegy* in a letter written to a friend while she was yet a very young woman. Dickinson also appears to have shared Gray's ambivalence regarding the act of publication; she would certainly have sympathized with her predecessor's anxieties when faced with the possible indiscretion and public exposure of private experiences and emotions in print. Thomas Hardy, too, was one with his generation in knowing his predecessor's work so well and in holding it so highly in esteem as to be able extemporaneously to repeat aloud to himself a passage from one of Gray's lesser-known poems (the *Ode on the Pleasure arising from Vicissitude*) when feeling fully and for the first time his recovery from the effects of a near-fatal illness. Although a philosophical pessimist such as Hardy is unlikely ever to have been able to accept the spiritual reality of the deity to whose judgement the *Elegy*'s speaker finally resigns both the virtues of his merits and the transgressions of his frailties, the precise articulations of Gray's language sounded no less familiarly in his ears (and were to be echoed no less clearly in his writing) than they did for any other author in the nineteenth or early twentieth century.

The sort of casual indebtedness to Gray's poetry that a reader might thus recognize at work within the writings of Dickinson or of Hardy constituted for such authors merely one of the unnegotiable *circumstances* of poetic composition. Intelligent and historically aware or historically responsible poets, for all their protestations of originality and native genius, necessarily follow in the textual footsteps and inevitably retrace the generic trails of those who have gone before them. We too often forget that the response of the creative artist (if not that of the critic) when confronted with the material achievement of the past or with the aesthetic parameters of influence and tradition is not always, exclusively or inevitably, a response of debilitating anxiety or indebtedness.

There are some, to be sure, who move to acknowledge this debt of precedence more willingly or more graciously than others. Wilfred Owen's recollections of Gray's work were in many respects far more consequential than those of his two predecessors mentioned above. Gray was granted an enviable pride of place among the very few eighteenth-century poets included by Owen in his own personal and exclusive pantheon of 'dead and gone bards'. In 1911, shortly after he first arrived at Dunsden in Oxfordshire, where he had accepted a post as lay assistant to the local vicar, Owen wrote in a tone approaching religious awe of the enthusiasm and of the palpable, physical excitement he felt whenever he reflected on the simple fact that he was finally, himself, living within the very same area of the country which had earlier played host to so many of England's greatest writers. Shelley, Tennyson, and Matthew Arnold, Owen recalled in a spirit of topographical reverence, were just a few of those figures who had passed their time – and who had written some of their best poetry – in these edenic surroundings. Perhaps Owen was aware that Edmund Waller, too, had once lived here. (On a slightly more prosaic note, the Irish Edmund Burke had purchased an estate at nearby Beaconsfield in 1768, and was thus buried not far away; the novelist G. K. Chesterton had only three years earlier bid farewell to his familiar haunts in Kensington and along Fleet Street to begin renting a property in the same town.) And just 'to eastward' of his own situation, as Owen particularly remembered,

> A churchyard sleeps, and one infirm old yew,
> Where in the shadows of the fading day,
> Musing on faded lives, sate solemn Gray.
> There to majestic utterances his soul was wrought,
> And still his mighty chant is fraught
> With golden teachings for the world, and speaks
> Strong things with sweetness unto whoso seeks.
> Yet can I never sit low at his feet
> And, questioning, a gracious answer meet.
> For he is gone, and his high dignity
> Lost in the past . . .[24]

Owen's lines underscore the simple fact that although the personal essence of Gray's 'high dignity' had irretrievably been 'lost in the past', his 'majestic utterances' were still to be regarded as a living presence for the

---

[24] Wilfred Owen's references to Gray can be found in Sven Bäckman, *Tradition Transformed: Studies in the Poetry of Wilfred Owen* (Lund, 1979) 42–43.

twentieth-century writer. Gray was one of those rare poets who, in Owen's estimation at least, had most perfectly fulfilled the classical maxim of combining within the golden measures of his 'mighty chant' the useful and the pleasurable – of speaking, as the modern poet put it, 'strong things with sweetness'. Gray's *Elegy* would return even more forcefully to Owen's mind some six years later, when, toward the end of the War and only months before his own untimely death, he was to write 'The Send-Off', a poem that describes the departure of a group of young soldiers heading vaguely in the direction of the western front from an unidentified country railway station. Owen's masterful 'Anthem for Doomed Youth', of course, would even more pointedly rely on the precedent of the *Elegy* to provide the subtextual poignancy that motivates the awesome sense of inadequacy which lies at the heart of its own, central conceit.

Only a few years before Wilfred Owen delighted in finding himself in the same countryside that seemed only naturally to have produced so much memorable poetry, Robert Frost had already, himself, been waking up to inspired mornings in Buckinghamshire. Frost had crossed the Atlantic with his wife and family in 1912, and it was not in America but in England that he eventually published his first volumes of poetry. Although Frost appears to have professed at the time of his own residence near Stoke to discount the possibility that there might really exist, for the writer, any practicable or demonstrable 'virtue in Location' (maintaining, instead, that poetry ought properly to emanate solely from 'within' the writer), he too, anticipating Owen's rather more confident assertions of the osmotic possibilities of the landscape, could not help but comment on the fact that he was in some ways ideally situated to 'devise' poetry. 'Here we are', Frost wrote from his country cottage, 'between high hedges of laurel and red-osier dogwood, within a mile or two of where Milton finished *Paradise Lost* on the one hand and a mile or two of where [Gray] lies buried on the other. . . .'.[25] This might for any lesser poet have been an overwhelming experience. Yet perhaps Frost's own instincts were in this particular instance mistaken. Perhaps there really can exist – on the right occasion and for almost every writer – precisely such a certain if imperceptible 'virtue in Location'. As matters so turned out, the two volumes of verse which Frost was to publish while still living in England – *A Boy's Will* (1913) and *North of Boston* (1914) – were themselves to be singled out by his earliest English reviewers for some of the very same features that had for so long been perceived as being characteristic of Gray's own work. In fact, Frost's poems, much like Gray's, would often be admired for the apparent 'universality' of

---

[25] Robert Frost's letter from Buckinghamshire is taken from *Selected Letters of Robert Frost*, ed. Lawrance Thompson (New York, 1964) 52.

their themes and praised for the deceptively straightforward simplicity
– the easy accessibility – of their language. As the American critic Mark
Van Doren once observed, Frost (much like Gray himself) would in his
best work demonstrate an uncanny ability memorably to formulate in
the space of only a few, simple words 'more than the volumes of ordinary rhetoric could express'.[26] Both excelled in the linguistic arts of
economy and compression, and both betrayed a seemingly natural
instinct for a peculiar sort of verbal precision that is far too often dismissed as the result of mere lapidary craftsmanship. The poet who would
only a little later in his career turn his hand to such quietly moving mas-
terpieces as 'Home Burial' and 'The Death of the Hired Hand', at least,
learned somewhere to value and to commemorate the obscure destinies
of such seemingly unremarkable individuals whose existence would
otherwise pass unremembered and unmourned. Other works by Frost –
'Acceptance' and 'The Wood Pile', for example – echo Gray even more
specifically.

The specific dynamics of all such influence and the precise motivations
determining all such allusions – however one chooses to describe the
kinetics of textual recollection at work within the poetry of Dickinson or
of Hardy, of Owen or of Frost – remain, for the moment at least, quite
beside the point. Far more relevant to the larger purpose of this biography is the fundamental contention that, armed merely with a necessary
patience and possessing only such admittedly rudimentary skills as are
needed to do so, any reader might themselves demonstrate the degree to
which nearly *all* of those poets who have since carved their own places
within the traditions of English and American poetry can be shown similarly to have owed some measure of formal, stylistic, or thematic debt to
Thomas Gray. The *Elegy* alone, taken as an historically and biographically situated structure of language and meaning, has exercised a prolific,
textual influence close to unparalleled in the shared traditions of our literature; viewed from a rather different angle as an indisputably central
and quintessentially human and *humanist* affirmation of the inalienable
value of an individual life in the face of time and mortality, the *Elegy* has
likewise compelled a response of sustained and sympathetic recognition
far too vital, far too dynamic, and far too persistently relevant to the
human experience ever very easily to be taken lightly or, for any truly substantial length of time, neglected or ignored. Routinely rejected or even
despised by modern critics, the standard by which Johnson himself finally
measured the success of Gray's *Elegy*, or the success of failure of any
poem, would seem still to govern the judgements of most modern readers;

[26] Mark Van Doren quoted in *Robert Frost's Poems*, with an introduction and commentary by Louis Untermeyer (New York: Washington Square Press, 1967) 8.

as Johnson wrote of the *Elegy*: 'I rejoice to concur with the common reader; for by the common sense of readers uncorrupted with literary prejudices, after all the refinements of subtlety and the dogmatism of learning, must be finally decided all claim to poetical honours'.[27]

Our own age of elegy would appear to situate Gray's most famous poem in a position to speak to us with renewed voice and meaning, and to address the generations of yet another century with all the force such change can give. The succinct recapitulation within Gray's lines of an entire tradition of meditative and reflective verse – a tradition stretching as far back as Theocritus and Propertius, yet at the same time comprehending predecessors in English extending from Milton's *Lycidas* (1637) to lesser works, such as Edward Young's influential *Night Thoughts* (1742–45) and Robert Blair's *The Grave* (1743) – stands once again in need of sympathetic reinterpretation. The generic summation of the *Elegy* demands no less forcefully than it has in the past to be retranslated, retransmitted, and reinterpreted to and for its contemporary audiences.

What I have here characterized as the elegiac impulse of our own era, bound as it is with the indisputable centrality of Gray's unshakeable position in the history of elegiac form and meaning in English, has not passed unnoticed. After a lapse of nearly three decades, both scholars and critical theorists have begun once again and with a renewed vigor and sophistication to turn their attention to Gray's poetry, and to his influential prose writings as well. The closing years of the twentieth century witnessed the publication of several book-length studies and collections of essays devoted to Gray's work and reputation. Some of these studies emphasized the remarkable generic and linguistic diversity that characterizes Gray's otherwise limited output as a poet. Others paid more specific attention to the influence of individual works, such as the *Elegy*, the *Eton Ode*, or the later Pindaric *Odes*. Still others made use of Gray's poetry as a means to explore larger and more comprehensive issues of ideology and cultural production. Suvir Kaul's *Thomas Gray and Literary Authority* (1992), for example, undertook closely to examine 'the cultural and self-representational authority of the gentleman poet' in Gray's work; Eugene B. McCarthy's 1997 *Thomas Gray: The Progress of a Poet* looked in a similar manner 'to explore the control [Gray] exercised over his career through consciousness of both his personal and poetic problems'.[28] Volumes such as Henry Weinfeld's *The*

---

[27] Johnson, 'Gray', in *Lives of the English Poets*, iii.441.
[28] Suvir Kaul, *Thomas Gray and Literary Authority* (Stanford, California: Stanford University Press, 1992) 8; Eugene B. McCarthy, *Thomas Gray: The Progress of a Poet* (London: Associated University Presses, 1997) 11.

Poet Without a Name: Gray's Elegy and the Problem of History (1991)
and John Guillory's *Cultural Capital: the Problem of Literary Canon
Formation* (1993) attempted even more ambitiously to situate Gray's
poetry as cultural 'product' within the frameworks of larger sociological debates. Guillory's study, for example, made use of Pierre Bourdieu's
notion of 'cultural capital' to address the issue of literary canon formation; Gray's *Elegy* provided a particularly nice example of the kinds of
socially privileged forms of language that are imposed on students as
'canonical' texts within the establishment.

Despite such attention to Gray's work, however, and to the unique
role which that work has played in the established and institutional traditions of English literary history, the need for a new, full-length and
biographically-based study of the poet has long remained unmet.[29]
Wyndham Ketton-Cremer's 1955 *Thomas Gray: A Biography* has long
stood as the only generally available volume for readers who wish
further to explore the legitimacy of their own intuitions regarding the
possible points of connection between the private events of Gray's life
and the public achievement (and the often wily indirection) of his poetry.
As adequately as Ketton-Cremer's narrative has served its readers, many
critics – most persistently G. S. Rousseau and, subsequently, George E.
Haggerty – have observed that the sustained absence of any genuine consideration of the relevance of Gray's sexuality to the narrative of his life
and writing has tended to render even the most thoughtful and perceptive of later analyses primitive, evasive, and ultimately dishonest. Years
have now passed since these critics first voiced the opinion that Gray's
biography stood in need of a fully modern rewriting – a rewriting that
would include within its narrative a more comprehensive and far less
prudish discussion of Gray's romantic attachments to childhood friends

---

[29] The biographical accounts of Gray's life referred to in the Introduction most
prominently include: R. W. Ketton-Cremer, *Thomas Gray: A Biography* (Cambridge:
Cambridge University Press, 1955); A. L. Lytton Sells, *Thomas Gray: His Life and
Works* (London: George Allen & Unwin, 1980); Morris Golden, *Thomas Gray: Updated
Edition* (Boston: Twayne Publishers, 1988). Among those critics whose work has either
directly or indirectly called for a revaluation of Gray's life have been G. S. Rousseau,
both in his 'The Pursuit of Homosexuality in the Eighteenth Century: 'Utterly Confused
Category' and/or Rich Repository', *Eighteenth-Century Life* 9 (1985) 132–68, and
in 'Love and antiquities: Walpole and Gray on the Grand Tour' in *Perilous
Enlightenment: pre- and post-modern discourses, sexual, historical* (Manchester
and New York: Manchester University Press, 1991) 172–74; G. S. Haggerty, ' "The Voice
of Nature" in Gray's *Elegy*', in *Homosexuality in Renaissance and Enlightenment
England: Literary Representations in Historical Context*, ed. Claude Summers
(Binghamton, New York: Harrington Park Press 1992) 199–213; Peter Watson-Smyth,
'Elegy written in St. Peter's Churchyard, Burnham', in *The Spectator* (31 July 1971)
171–74; see also Jean H. Hagstrum's important essay, 'Gray's Sensibility', in Downey and
Jones, 6–19.

such as Horace Walpole and Richard West, and of his unexpected infatuation in the years just before his death with the young Charles Victor
de Bonstetten. 'Beyond any shadow of doubt', as G. S. Rousseau has
argued, '. . . Walpole and Gray were essentially homosexual throughout
their lives'; as Rousseau has further written with reference to the friendships of Gray, Walpole, and their circle: 'Future biographers of these
figures will no doubt assemble [the] record . . . and in the case of Gray
will no doubt reconsider his entire life and works in the light of his
preponderant sexuality'.[30]

In his own biography of Gray, Ketton-Cremer alluded darkly to the
unspoken 'secrets of his own nature' that had been reawakened for
Gray in the wake of Bonstetten's visit to England, but declined to pursue
the implications of such an intuition with any vigor. He merely noted,
cryptically, that Gray 'knew the existence of temptations which could
not for one moment be contemplated, by one who had been, all his life
long, a strict observer of the laws of God and the laws of men'.[31] Robert
F. Gleckner, on the other hand, has more recently asserted that Gray's
homosexual desires 'and the fears deriving therefrom' were dramatically
enacted and played out in the products of his poetic imagination.[32]
Gleckner's clear-sighted and refreshingly corrective study (a partial portrait that the author himself qualifies early on as 'something *like* a psy-
chobiography') warrants the close attention of any reader interested in
the deeper, motivating subtexts of Gray's poetry. Taking as his own starting point the compelling notion that all of Gray's verse is fundamentally
autobiographical, Gleckner has argued persuasively that the poet 'opted
for the only alternative available to him as a poet to give us his self,
. . . the insistent yet hidden, occluded, and secret sub-text that to
date has been as largely unrecognizable and signally memorable'.[33]
Thanks to William Mason's conscious and thorough-going bowdlerization of the poet's surviving correspondence, Gleckner has further
suggested, Gray's poems themselves remain the 'only alternative' to an
understanding of his inner, emotional life. The nature of Gray's poems
as painstaking and more often than not lovingly constructed artefacts,

---

[30] Rousseau, *Perilous Enlightenment*, 174.
[31] Ketton-Cremer, 251.
[32] Robert F. Gleckner's valuable analyses of Gray's poetry are included in his important
study, *Gray Agonistes: Thomas Gray and Masculine Friendship* (Baltimore and London;
John Hopkins University Press, 1997); Gleckner makes his own case for the need for a
new life of Gray in his 'Introduction' (1–18). Gleckner also reprints some of William
Epstein's comments on same sex intimacy and the question of biographical (or physical
or textual) evidence from Epstein's own 'Assumed Identities: Gray's Correspondence and
the "Intelligence Communities" of Eighteenth-Century Studies', in *The Eighteenth
Century: Theory and Interpretation*, 32 (1991) 279.
[33] Gleckner, 17.

in other words, testifies to their unique ability to clear the best possible path for those who wish honestly to explore the psycho-sexual origins of Gray's troubled 'temperament' – and so to delve, with patient sympathy, into the roots of his near-mythical and chronically misunderstood 'melancholy'.

The very nature of Gray's 'temptations', 'fears', and 'desires', as Ketton-Cremer routinely referred to the poet's homosexual impulses in his biography, would seem themselves at best to position Gray as an unwilling and intentionally uncooperative subject for a thorough, literary biography. With the possible exception of the famous admonition carved on the stone slab that covers the mortal remains of William Shakespeare at Stratford – an epitaph that enjoins readers and playgoers now and forever to 'forbeare' to dig the dust of his grave, and which goes so far as to curse anyone who would ever consider disturbing his final resting place – few English writers have articulated in their own work a more emphatic or explicit injunction that they not in any way be 'exhumed' by later generations. The language of the *Elegy*'s 'Epitaph' – 'No farther seek his merits to disclose, / Or draw his frailties from their dread abode' – memorably looks to deflect any and all attention away not only from the poet's physical remains, but from the legacy of his lived, personal history as well.

Yet, even in the face of such an unassailable request, the urge to uncover the human and personal sources of Gray's 'melancholy' seems to have exerted a force among his most sympathetic readers which can only be described as very close to irresistible. But let's not beat about the bush: Gray's chronic depression – his so-called 'melancholia' – was itself surely an incidental symptom of his response to the perception of his own sexual impulse. Few readers of Gray's poetry fail to respond to the sub-texts of confusion, guilt, and anxiety that lie just beneath the surface of his work. Few of those same readers – once they have been introduced to the narrative of Gray's personal history, at least – fail likewise to acknowledge the deeper roots of such sub-texts within the poet's often uneasy perception of the exact nature of his own sexual and emotional impulses (many would in fact agree with Rousseau's bluntly confessional admission, as a reader, that 'about Gray's homosexuality there never seemed any doubt to [him]').[34] Apart from his close relationship with his mother, and with the further exception only of his family ties to his maternal aunts and to his female cousins, Gray was at no point in his life ever to maintain any deeply sympathetic (much less physical) relationship with a woman. His strongest attachments linked him almost exclusively to a small and carefully circumscribed circle of friends of his

---

[34]   Rousseau, *Perilous Enlightenment*, 172.

own age and sex, or drew him similarly to the society of younger men, many of them university undergraduates. Admittedly, we possess no evidence – no proof of overt behaviour – to suggest that Gray ever (either as a child or as an adult) engaged in intimate, sexual relations of any kind. We do know that in the earliest years of his life, Gray developed a romantic attachment to his school-fellow at Eton, Horace Walpole. We also know that he attempted to maintain that relationship long after the two men had left school. Following a traumatic and seemingly final break with Walpole shortly after the two men had left university, Gray appears to have reignited his affections for another of his old school friends, Richard West. West's death in 1742 came close to overwhelming him completely. Apparently celibate and romantically unattached through his early middle age, Gray in the closing years of his life succumbed to a sudden passion for a young visitor to England from Switzerland, Charles Victor de Bonstetten. Although the relationship between Gray and Bonstetten was to remain platonic, Gray, at least, was abundantly aware of the volatile erotic fire that fueled their friendship. The conventional evidence of Gray's natural life, then – particularly when taken with the muted testament of his poetry – would appear overwhelmingly to suggest that, had the poet lived in our own era, he would probably have been identified by others or would even have identified himself as in some significant sense 'homosexual'. Moreover although there is no incontestable evidence that Gray's homoeroticism led at any point in his life to same-sex intimacy, the possibility of such intimacy should not be precluded. What must be acknowledged is that the events of Gray's daily existence – no less than the formal and stylistic obsessions of his verse, no less than the meticulous patterns of his scholarly research – were shaped and even determined by his life-long confrontation with and management of his own physical and emotional desires. Both in his letters and in his poetry, as in his life, Gray demonstrated a keen awareness of the pressure of such psychic forces as he wished somehow to express, and always to control.

But what, really, does it mean for us to describe Gray as a homosexual, or, as readers, to approach his writing as the work of a homosexual poet? What, if anything, do we stand to gain by imposing the restless categories of our own culture on the past, or by applying the ever-shifting designations of our own discourse on the alien eighteenth-century subject? The fine and anxious distinctions outlined by the sexual labels of the late twentieth century would obviously have meant nothing to Gray himself.

A conspicuous amount of recent criticism, of course, has focused on the issue of the 'construction' of sexual identity – of the structures of masculinity and femininity – in the early modern period in Europe. Michel Foucault, in the introduction to his proposed six-volume history of human sexuality (1976), most persuasively stressed the need to understand our own, modern notions of sexuality not as expressions of biological truth, but rather as 'inventions' or 'social constructions'. The supposed distinction which positions sexuality (biological or 'natural' sex) against gender (sexual identity as determined by the ideological forces of culture and society) has with the wider dissemination of Foucault's ideas become one of the most reiterated commonplaces of modern critical practice.[35] Foucault's arguments are far from incontestable, yet the extent of his influence has been undeniable. The practical activity of 'reading for gender' when confronting the literature of the eighteenth century in England, however, has proven to be particularly problematic. Definitions of masculinity throughout the period, as critics such as Philip Carter and Susan Amussen have observed, appear to have been founded at least as much in an appreciation and assessment of conspicuous social qualities as they were in explicitly sexual activity.[36] Any definitions of 'masculinity' or even of 'homosexuality' are especially difficult to formulate when dealing with a society that was itself already inclined to debate 'changing notions of acceptable and unacceptable male conduct in an urban environment given over to socializing facilitated by displays of politeness'.[37] Perhaps the most vigorous line of critical inquiry into eighteenth-century representations of homosexual behaviour, as critics such as Tim Hitchcock have commented with reference to the work of Louis Crompton and A. N. Gilbert,

[35]   Michel Foucault's work on the history and construction of human sexuality is well known; *Histoire de la sexualité, vol I: La volonté de savoir* (Paris, 1976) and translated into English as *The History of Sexuality*, vol. I (New York: Pantheon, 1978).
[36]   On definitions of masculinity in eighteenth-century English culture, see, for example, Philip Carter, 'Men About Town: representations of foppery and masculinity in early eighteenth-century urban society', in Hannah Barker and Elaine Chalus, eds. *Gender in Eighteenth-Century England: Roles, Representations and Responsibilities* (Harlow, Essex: Longmans, 1997); Susan Dwyer Amussen, ' "The Part of a Christian Man": the cultural politics of manhood in early modern England', in Susan Dwyer Amussen and Mark Kishlansky, eds., *Political Culture and Cultural Politics in Early Modern England* (Manchester: Manchester University Press, 1995) 227. Note also editor Robert P. Maccubbin's important collection, *'Tis Nature's Fault: Unauthorized Sexuality in the Enlightenment* (Cambridge: Cambridge University Press, 1987), and George S. Rousseau and Roy Porter, eds. *Sexual Underworlds of the Enlightenment* (Manchester: Manchester University Press, 1987). Tim Hitchcock's observations on the history of sexual representation in the period are made in his very useful *English Sexualities, 1700–1800* (London: Macmillan, 1997); particularly useful is Hitchcock's fifth chapter, 'Subcultures and Sodomites: The Development of Homosexuality', 58–75. The traditions of the foundational work of Louis Crompton and A. N. Gilbert referred to by critics such as Hitchcock can best be sampled in Crompton's *Byron and Greek Love: Homophobia in 19th-Century England* (London: GMP Publications Ltd., 1985;1998) and Gilbert's 'The "Africane" Courts-Martial: A Study of Buggery in the Royal Navy', *Journal of Homosexuality* I (1974) 111–22.
[37]   Carter, 34.

has been 'less concerned to describe a uniquely homosexual culture, and more interested in charting the treatment of homosexuals by the courts and the state'.[38]

Yet even if the work of critics has been more concerned to demonstrate 'the existence of a continuing anti-homosexual strand within Western culture, which in its most extreme formulations has been characterized as a type of genocide' than it has been to identify or to explore a possibly fruitful, homosexual tradition in European literature, few such studies have confronted the terminological or conceptual dilemma that faces any modern critic of the homosexual 'tradition' with greater candour or with greater practicality than Crompton himself.[39] 'Accorded an honored place in Greek, Latin, Islamic, and Far Eastern Literature', Crompton has argued, 'love poems addressed by males to other males have generally been taboo in postclassical Western civilization. . . . In light of this tradition, interpreters have often refused to find a homosexual meaning in poetry unless conclusive biographical evidence has been forthcoming, and this, for obvious reasons, has often been the most incomplete part of the personal record'.[40] Moreover, as readers such as Eve Kosofsky Sedgewick have observed, class lines could further cloud the shape and discretion of the male homosocial spectrum; of Gray's friend Horace Walpole ('whose life', she notes, is 'staggeringly well-documented'), Sedgewick comments, 'we cannot tell how far he was homosexual, because of the close protective coloration given by the aristocratic milieu'.[41] As Crompton himself has observed: 'In treating homosexuality in an historical context, whether the subject is biography or social history, a serious dilemma invariably faces any writer.'[42] Faced in his own work, as a practicing critic of Byron's poetry, with the seemingly unnegotiable terminological and conceptual gap that separates modern notions of sexual identity from the self-stylizations of an earlier era, Crompton wisely decided against using the modern designation 'gay' with reference either to Byron's own sexuality or to his writing. In the particular case of Byron, at least, a viable alternative was available in the connotations of the term 'Greek love'. As Crompton reasoned: 'If homosexual and gay are both words which would have puzzled Byron's contemporaries, the expression *Greek love* . . . would have been intelligible to them and would have carried resonant historical and literary associations'.[43]

---

[38] Hithcock, 59.
[39] Ibid.
[40] Crompton, 6.
[41] Eve Kosofsky Sedgwick in *Between Men: English Literature and Male Homosocial Desire* (New York: Columbia University Press, 1985) 92–93.
[42] Crompton, 9.
[43] Ibid, 11.

In my own attempts to describe the possible emotions and the activities of figures such as Thomas Gray himself, or of Horace Walpole, Richard West, John Chute, Horace Mann, or any number of other subsidiary actors in the drama of Gray's life, I have thought it best to avoid the anachronism imposed by modern terminologies as much as possible. Neither can Thomas Gray himself nor can any of his work be described as 'gay' or 'queer' in any critically meaningful (or even useful) way – certainly not in any of the senses with which we currently employ those terms. To describe a poet of such extensive appeal as a 'gay' poet, in any event, quite apart from the anachronism of such a label, accomplishes very little, and arguably works to limit his appeal to readers rather than to enhance it. 'Homosexual' and 'Homosocial', though each no less problematic in their own manner, are at least terms which, when used judiciously and with great care, might suggest to the modern reader the possibly erotic depths of such relationships as would otherwise demand to be labeled merely as close or romantic 'friendships'. Gray and his friends did, of course, imbibe some profoundly determining notions regarding the nature of male affection and homosexual attachment while at school. They read and enjoyed the work of writers such as Catullus, Horace, Virgil, and Suetonius; they would have been familiar with the commendatory account of male–male love in Plato's *Phaedrus*. It is decidedly more than probable, too, that they encountered as young men either at Eton or at Cambridge (or at both) some more practical manifestations of such 'friendships'. 'Among the chief men in some of the colleges', wrote one Oxford diarist in the period, 'sodomy is very usual, [so] that [it] is dangerous sending a young man that is beautiful to [university]'.[44] Even discounting the possibility of such encounters, the bonds of male desire, as we shall see, were to form the motivating sub-text of almost all of Gray's own poetry, and of many of his letters as well. The nature of the homoerotic connection between Gray's poetry and his correspondence has been well summarized by Gleckner, who has argued convincingly that 'the Gray–West correspondence [at least] is in fact an interpsychic scripting of their deepest selves, their mutual homosexual desires and the fears deriving therefrom, replete with precisely the same private fantasies Gray's poetry dramatically plays out in his poetic imagination'.[45] With regard to Gray's autumnal infatuation with Charles Victor de Bonstetten, oddly enough, the autobiographical remarks of the modern writer T. H. White, as related by his biographer Sylvia Townshend Warner, arguably capture the emotional tenor of that late-life relationship. 'It would have been unthinkable to make [him] unhappy with

[44]   The entry of Oxonian Dudley Ryder in his 1715 diary is reprinted in Hitchcock, 64.
[45]   Gleckner, 18.

the weight of this unpracticable, unsuitable love', White wrote of just such an attachment, '. . . Besides, I love him for being happy and inno-cent, so I would be destroying what I loved. . . . It has been my hideous fate to be born with an infinite capacity for love and joy with no hope of using them'.[46] Had the mind and the language of his own era per-mitted him to do so, Gray, sadly, might have said much the same thing himself.

One of the most thought-provoking studies of Gray's character and personality and the most compelling reconstruction of the manner in which that character was formed by the circumstances of his life and reflected in the seemingly fragile beauty of his poetry first appeared almost seventy years ago. The French scholar Roger Martin's monu-mental *Essai sur Thomas Gray* (1934) ended up tracing much of Gray's constitutional peculiarities – his 'désordres fonctionnels' – to the poet's father (Martin was among the first critics uncompromisingly to insist that Thomas Gray 'était un enfant d'alcoolique'.[47] As we shall see for ourselves, there is reason enough to contend that Philip Gray did indeed play an important and even determining role in the development (or lack thereof) of his son's psychological sense of health, temperament, self-worth, and well-being. The 'Thomas Gray' who emerges from the pages of Martin's study, however (if one can even conceive the possibility that Martin's Gray would ever, in life, have had the audacity to 'emerge' from anything), is close to being a hypochondriacal aberration. Having begun by recapitulating the perceived sources of Gray's chronically melancholic temperament and having then rooted them in the particularities of his family history, Martin compared the poet to both Alexander Pope and Samuel Johnson, and concluded (my translation):

> Drawing together these general symptoms of nervous debility, such con-ditions of anguish and submission to fate throw a decisive light on Gray's development. Weakened from the moment of his birth in the universal struggle that pits the body against the material world, carrying within him the seeds of a disease that might at any moment in his life destroy him, Gray found himself entrenched in a position that was eminently unstable – a constant state of uncertainty and of dubious, spectral secu-rity. Such a position is a neurosis. . . . The invasive illness that Gray inherited was a mental disorder. Pope, suffering and deformed, wrapped in his fine cloth jacket, was nevertheless able to conquer his sickness and,

[46] Sylvia Townshend Warner reprinted T. H. White's thoughts on his own homosexual attachments in her biography of the writer, *T. H. White* (New York: Viking Press, 1968) 277–78.
[47] Roger Martin, *Essai sur Thomas Gray* (Paris, Les Presses Universitaires de France, 1934) 9.

embittered as he was, retain a lively moral strength and a tireless zeal for
his work. Johnson, similarly threatened by madness, his face horribly
disfigured by scrofula, awed his circle of friends, directed his energies
towards physical exertion, and had only scorn for those who succumbed
to their weaknesses. Gray's illness, however, destroyed his very will
power. Rather than stimulating him, it crushed him. The result was a
refusal even to engage in life.[48]

Joseph Wood Krutch was undoubtedly correct when he commented that
such an insistence on locating 'the ultimate source of Gray's peculiarities in the physical constitution of his possibly alcoholic father' was a
flaw in Martin's study.[49] The *Essai* mistakenly judged Thomas Gray,
finally, to have been a truly unhappy and pitiable figure; for Martin, at
least, the often subtle, parodic resonance of Gray's allusive language had
too often been lost in the translation.

Other elements of Gray's general psychological environment,
however, will need to be taken into consideration when discussing the
development of his personality and the course of his life. The particular
psychological impulse that prompted Gray to deal with his disturbing
sense of his own sexuality in his writing through processes such as
deflection, evasion, and the ventriloquism of parody, can be traced in
many other aspects of his life as well. Even the poet's unusually intense
and life-long fear of fire, once we attempt to view such pyrophobia as
a possibly figurative representation of his fear of any frightening
outburst of emotion, can be linked to Gray's chronic anxiety regarding
the culturally 'unspeakable' nature of his own, deepest impulses as a
human being.

*

Where, then, are we to start? As always, it would be best for us to
begin at the very beginning. If we wish not merely to retrace the narrative journey of Gray's life, but desire ultimately to gain some deeper
understanding of the psychic drama that propelled and motivated
that life (and that minted the achievement of its living mind into the
formal artefacts of poetry), it will be necessary for us first to reacquaint
ourselves with the world into which Gray was born. As we prepare
to do so, we will need to muster all the historical knowledge at our
disposal in a focused attempt to re-envision the changing, dynamic

[48]   Martin, 18–19.
[49]   Joseph Wood Krutch, 'Introduction' to *The Selected Letters of Thomas Gray*
(New York: Farrar, Straus, and Young, 1952) xxvii.

culture of England and its capital city in the earliest years of the eighteenth century. Even more pressingly, we will need to bring an unusual quality of imaginative intensity to bear upon our subject. The novelist Henry James once cautioned: 'To live over people's lives is nothing unless we live over their perceptions, live over the growth, the change, the varying intensity of the same – since its was *by* those things they themselves lived'.[50]

James's concise observations on the genre suggest that he, too, was unusually alive to the decisive role so often played by the near-fictional element of sympathetic identification in the comparative success or failure of any written life; the novelist clearly recognized the forceful intensity of readerly involvement – of emotional effort – demanded by good biographical writing. I suggest that it is only by openly and boldly accepting the immense imaginative challenges implicit in James's definitional observation that we can hope to make any significant progress in the task that lies ahead; that it is only *by* and *through* the inescapable processes of our own, several attempts as embodied readers to (as James puts it) 'live over' the life of the biographical subject that we can ever expect to gauge the distance of that life – or begin to measure the unique experience and achievement of its history – from our own. It is only by means of the intensity of such engagement that we can arrive at some better appreciation of the individual participation of *any* life within the pattern of our own; and it is only by the light of such commitment that can we assess the continually changing significance of that life within our culture and so, perhaps, finally, achieve some sense of its transformative role in the larger world we all inescapably perpetuate and share.

*

One final note of caution is perhaps in order here. For most of us, the notion that a poet such as Thomas Gray was to some degree the unknowing product of his earliest domestic environment needs little if any methodological justification. Some few readers, however, will place considerably less faith in the basic premises of psychoanalytic criticism. Still others will have serious reservations regarding the validity of the linguistic model of Freudian psychology in general, or may more particularly object to the manner in which the language of human psychology is typically put to use in works of literary biography. Readers

---

[50] Quoted by Stephen B. Oates in his 'Prologue' to the second edition of Paul Murray Kendall's *The Art of Biography* (London: W. W. Norton & Co., 1965;1985) v.

are here warned, therefore, that without pretending to undertake a rigorously Freudian or even a consistently 'psychoanalytical' reading of Gray's life and writings, this narrative tends implicitly to accept and to reflect the general assumption that 'ignored or well-informed, our culture has found Freud's vision of mind compelling enough to live with it, whether comfortable or not'.[51] That these pages may appear finally to focus rather more intensely on the events of Gray's early life and childhood at the possible expense of the institutional achievement and reputation that characterized his later years is to a significant degree merely the incidental yet unavoidable result of the historical narrative of the poet's own life. The events of those years that witnessed Gray's passage from childhood and adolescence and his emergence into early adulthood were peculiarly significant to his later life; indeed, even to the extent that we today operate within a culture where such a model of psychological development is a generally accepted norm, much of Gray's entire adult life demands to be read as an unusually intense and sustained response to the tensions that shaped and motivated his earliest environments. As we set out to explore the shape of this response, we would do well always to keep in mind that the English poet who was eventually and most famously to eulogize the often desirable placidity and moral safety of a circumscribed, rural life – the man who, in the outward disposition of his own existence, appears contentedly to have reaped the modest rewards of the academic *vita contemplativa* – was himself by birth an urban child, a city man, a Londoner. Gray's poetry, in other words, to the extent that it might be said to stand in some relation to the events of his life, is quite literally eccentric.

In order to begin our imaginative journey into Gray's life, then, we need first to be reborn into his world. We need to conceptualize for ourselves his own first, most vivid and broad impression of the identity of things. We need to walk in the path of his childhood footsteps; to reimagine what his daily life in the City would have been like; to trace the alleys and lanes, and to explore the streets and buildings of his earliest years. We need to reconstruct the probable pattern of his days and of his nights. We need as fully as possible to immerse ourselves in the psychologically formative years of his youth and beginning adolescence – to envision the sights he saw, to peek over his shoulder at the books he read, to recreate as best we can the experiences and sensations through which he lived. We need, if possible, to imagine ourselves as capable of breathing in the very air that he breathed. We need finally, in the words of George Eliot, comprehensively and rigorously to train our minds

---

[51] Peter Gay, 'Introduction', *The Freud Reader* (London: W. W. Norton & Co., 1989) xiii.

to be like the ghosts of the ancients, 'wandering about the world, and trying mentally to construct it as it used to be, in spite of ruin and confusing changes'. We begin, therefore, with an exploration of the city which Gray dimly perceived to be growing up around him as a child. We begin – as ghostly revenants – at the very heart of the ruin and confusing changes of a London only recently and catastrophically transformed by fire.

PART ONE

CHAPTER ONE

THE GLORY OF THE WORLD IN A MOMENT

London and Cornhill
1716–1725

I. A Childhood in Troynovant

By the morning of Monday, 3 September 1666 – a day that promised to be fair and very warm but still considerably windy – the Great Fire of London had begun to engulf the City in earnest. Since almost two o'clock the previous morning the blaze had steadily burnt its way from Pudding Lane, in the east, toward the warehouses that lined Upper Thames street; it soon encompassed the whole of Cannon street, to the northeast, and stretched as far south as the well-known waterside tavern of Three Cranes in the Vintry on the Thames itself. The fire threatened now, with the help of a constant and seemingly treacherous 'Belgian Wind' blowing from the southeast, to double back upon itself and consume the very heart of the capital. Students as far away as Eton had already been alerted to the City's plight by the heavy snow of ashes and blackened papers, lifted toward Windsor by the prevailing winds, that had begun falling noiselessly in the school's courtyards. Further afield, those who had yet to receive any official news regarding the extent of the fire curiously observed the rays of the sun to be tinged red by the blaze. Visible even from beyond the Chilterns, a bleak and ominous cloud had begun to hover over the lower Thames Valley. The heavy smoke slowly stretched to the north and to the west, into both Buckinghamshire and Berkshire. 'A black darkness', as William Taswell would later recall of the seeming apocalypse, 'seemed to cover the entire hemisphere'.[1]

Closer to home, the unprecedented extent of the London fire was fast becoming matter for serious alarm. By Monday morning King Charles had already decided personally to take command of the situation. There seemed little, however, that the Crown's hastily appointed authorities could actually do in their efforts to halt the blaze. The physically arduous task of pulling down (and blowing up) houses and other structures, the calling in of militia from the Home counties, the establishment of fire posts – all of these otherwise practically minded procedures required

---

[1] William Taswell, 'Autobiography and Anecdotes by William Taswell, D. D.', ed. G. P. Elliott, *Camden Society Miscellany* (1853) ii.13.

resources in the way of time and equipment not readily available to the King's makeshift army of servants and volunteers. As the fire moved with pyrotechnic confidence into the power of its second and third days, its self-fueled destruction began to advance at a truly furious pace. To the north of the already devastated Cannon Street, the fate of the increasingly vital centre of London's commercial life – the roughly triangular area bounded to the north by Threadneedle Street, to the south by Lombard Street, and through the tip of which the broad expanse of Cornhill emptied into the Poultry near St. Mary Woolchurch – seemed ever more certain. The south-easterly wind continued to blow as the fire crept to the north and the west throughout that Monday morning. The venerable fruit, herb, and vegetable markets on Gracechurch Street were quickly consumed by the flames; the proud exteriors of the numerous Companies' Halls in Thames Street and Clock Lane were summarily leveled; countless churches and ancient Inns were similarly dispatched in a mere matter of hours. Presenting to fleeing residents a spectacle close to Biblical in its aspect of dread certainty, the City's plague of fire began to blow so strongly and with such a destructive heat that there seemed to be no alternative but simply to stand by in awe as the inferno carried all before it.

And so, ever greedy for more, the fire licked and leapt and howled its way in the direction of the City's choicest spoils. By early afternoon, the large, timber-framed homes and the shops of the wealthy merchants in Lombard Street, and with them the normally crowded businesses and offices in Cornhill, had also begun crashing to the ground. The organic simplicity of the City's street-plan – the medieval logic of which had been borne of the particular needs and matched to the precise conveniences of London's practically advantageous situation as an active river port – seemed suddenly and with Sinon-like treachery to have invited a catastrophe of total destruction. The myriad alleys that had since the City's earliest recorded history snaked their way between Lombard Street and Cornhill – close and sinuous passageways crammed with shops and taverns, arterial paths likely to curl with surprising suddenness into the tortured cul-de-sacs which played host to the first of the City's coffee houses – worked only to facilitate the now deafening fire. The narrow streets began now to draw the searing wind and flames up their sheltered conduits toward the most potent symbol of the nation's commercial wealth and prowess, Sir Thomas Gresham's grand 1568 Royal Exchange.

By the time the Exchange was threatened, even the most blindly optimistic of Londoners must have been overwhelmed by the scale of events. Almost every surviving eye-witness account of the Great Fire is marked by its author's dramatically humbled apprehension of the sublime *immensity* of the scene being witnessed. Much to their horror, the foot-soldiers and local parishioners who had persisted in their attempts to halt the spread of the blaze by pulling down the old wooden halls and houses that stood in its path must soon have realized that their efforts had in actual fact helped only to further the conflagration. The tremendous mounds of rubble left by their preventive demolitions had effectively resulted in the creation of actual bridges of flammable material in the streets; the same litter left behind by these well-intentioned fire-fighters formed piles of ready tinder – heaps of debris by means of which the fire could conveniently stretch and leap across even the widest of the City's major avenues, and so carry its destruction further to the north.

For days following the fire, the scent of the many spices that had been imported by the East India Company and which had been stored in the large underground crypts of the Royal Exchange (not even the building's basement vault survived the blaze) continued to pour their sacrificial fragrance into the darkened air. The smoldering stores, as Samuel Crouch would later write, seemed 'to burn incense to the incensed Powers'.[2] The incense imposed an odd and at times over-poweringly exotic perfume on what was already an eerie and un-familiar scene. The diarist and naval administrator Samuel Pepys, attempting to walk along Cornhill and then down the expanse that had formerly been Lombard Street two days after their destruction (his feet still, as he observed, 'ready to burn walking through the town among the hot coles [sic]'), noted the once-opulent district to be 'all in dust', and commented sorrowfully that the formerly glorious Exchange building had itself been reduced to a 'sad sight'.[3] By the morning of Thursday, 6 September, when the winds finally shifted decisively to the south (thus urging the fire back upon those areas which it had already consumed, and so eventually leaving it to spend itself out) no less than one third of the City lay in ruins. 'You can compare London (were it not for the rubbish)', wrote one observer sadly, 'to nothing more than an open field'.[4] Having so predictably consumed Cornhill and the Exchange by mid-afternoon Monday, the blaze had swiftly moved on to demolish with equal thoroughness such landmarks as the Guildhall, Newgate, and old St. Paul's, extending its wrath as far north as Cripplegate, and measuring its ruin from Fetter Lane, in the west, to the Tower, in the east. A total of over 400 acres – within which had stood some 13,200 houses – had been transformed within less than a week

[2] See W. G. Bell, *The Great Fire of London in 1666* (London, John Lane, The Bodley Head, 1920) 66.
[3] Samuel Pepys, *The Diary of Samuel Pepys*, ed. R. C. Latham and W. Matthews, 11 vols. (London: G. Bell and Sons, 1970–83) vii.276.
[4] See S. Weston, 'Copy of a Letter from Sir Robert Atkyns ... Written from London during the Great Fire 1666' in *Archaeologia*, 19 (1821) 105–8.

into a scene of chaotic, urban wreckage. The City's homeless refugees –
roughly 100,000 of them – gathered forlornly in the makeshift camps
which had been established by authorities just to the north of the old
City walls. Contemporary observers estimated the total cost of the
damage to stand above a staggering £7,000,000.

*

For all the devastation occasioned by the fire, however, there seemed
no question but that London would rebuild itself. Within only a few
weeks of the destruction, the same City tradesmen who had initially
sought temporary accommodation at Gresham House in Bishopsgate
(one of the few ancient structures spared by the fire) had begun again
to set up shop within the still-smoking ruins of the Exchange. The
makeshift pavement on which they now carried on their business had
hastily but efficiently been assembled from among the stones carted
down from the demolished Guildhall. Builders mixed their bricks from
the earth and from the very ashes of the ruins. The ready imagery of the
regenerate Phoenix (an image of rebirth which already, thanks largely to
the careful iconography of Tudor propaganda, resonated as a potent
political symbol among the English) came very quickly to be associated
not only with the comparable 'rebirth' of the City of London as a
whole, but also and with more specific reference to the equally miraculous rejuvenation of the most important of the many public structures
and institutions leveled by the fire. St. Paul's, the Guildhall, the Customs
House, the Royal Exchange: all of these inexpressibly important social
and political nexuses were to be rebuilt on a scale even grander than
before. The 'Arabian Bird' of the metropolis, as a least one poet
described the City in its rejuvenation, was destined not merely to rise
unscathed from the ashes of its own destruction, but 'to live again in a
more vigorous birth'.[5]
Everything about the new City was to be bigger and better than it
had been prior the fire; every aspect of its irrepressible inner life was to
be allowed to reveal itself in a manner and a style more impressive and
more vital than ever before. John Evelyn, Robert Hooke, Valentine
Knight, and Christopher Wren were just a few of the individuals who
submitted elaborate plans for the rebuilding of London. Most such plans
suggested that the re-envisioned capital be constructed on a tremendous
and imposing new continental model (the young and comparatively

---

[5] From 'Ecclesia Restaurata', quoted in Robert A. Aubin, *London in Flames, London
in Glory* (New Brunswick: Rutgers University Press, 1943) 276.

inexperienced Wren managed to submit the first of his own schemes for the rebuilding even while the ashes were still hot, and less than a week before the fire had begun in all areas to burn itself out). According to such schemes, broad boulevards and highways – their easy transits varied and interrupted by elegant, open parades and by such social spaces as piazzas, fountains, and riverfront squares – were to replace the older City's tangled jumble of narrow streets and noisome alleyways. The dimensions of the cramped medieval community that had grown only haphazardly and by fits and starts in the centuries before the fire were to be dispensed with entirely. The unsanitary disorder of the old urban environment would be replaced instead by a clean, streamlined, and elegantly organized City. This new London was to be worthy of the tenacity of its own citizens. Even more emphatically, it was to be a London the potent grandeur of which was calculated to be a manifestation of its own deepening awareness that it stood poised, in the decades to come, to secure its own unique place in history among the few truly great capitals of the modern world.

Such visionary plans for the 'mighty handsome' new City, not surprisingly, found favour in the eyes of the King. Yet the enormous cost of such comprehensive plans, involving as they did the need for the government to purchase large tracts of private land and entailing myriad difficulties in the way of sorting out inheritance rights or compensation and reimbursements, rendered such designs utterly impracticable to a government already impoverished by the Dutch War of 1652–54, and one which, even as the architectural plans were being drawn up, was to be crippled even further by another on-going conflict with Holland (a war that would not be brought to its close for yet another year). Other difficulties were likewise soon acknowledged. In the case of some City properties, the very title deeds and leases that would have specified the exact siting and extent of individual properties were documents which had themselves been lost or destroyed in the fire. Officials encountered considerable difficulties in their attempts simply to decide precisely which properties belonged to which owners and tenants. In the immediate aftermath of the fire, honesty seemed in many cases to be in short supply. Surveyors who had carefully measured and staked out their land claims in the daylight hours might very well return the next morning to find that their own painstaking markings indicating areas and frontages had been altered overnight, having typically been shifted by other property owners looking dishonestly to claim more acreage than that to which they were legitimately entitled.

The City planners were compelled finally to face the facts. The grand utopian schemes were soon pushed to one side, and more immediate and practical concerns just as quickly took their place. While some few basic changes and improvements could be effected in the City (such as widening certain principal streets and avenues, providing public areas with better paving, and building with brick rather than wood), much about the urban environment would necessarily need to remain the same. In time, even the tortuous street patterns of the old London – retaining almost every twist and turning of their arcane and labyrinthine complexity – began inevitably to reassert themselves. Indeed, the 'new' City must have been regarded by many of those who had known London in its previous incarnation actually to constitute a kind of strange and geographically precise imitation of – a perverse and stubbornly material allusion to – its own former self. The same streets, the same alleys, the same shops, the same residents and merchants, the same public institutions: all these elements began to reappear in a London superficially familiar and knowable, yet at the same time transmuted and transformed. The landmarks of London reappeared in a city strange yet at the same time oddly familiar; a landscape intimately known, yet often and quite literally uncanny. The experience must for many Londoners have been similar to that of once again meeting a dear old friend who, in the course of time, rather than growing frail with care and age, appears not only to have recovered the spring of their youth, but seems also (and even more mysteriously) somehow to have gained the hard-earned wisdom of experience. Or perhaps, more simply, it was a meeting that engendered a feeling akin to the sensation of encountering an old soul in a youthful body – of recognizing the habits and traits of the parent in the impulses and inclinations of the growing child.

Still, if there was necessarily a great deal that was old about this re-built London, contemporary writers were determined to find much to celebrate that was new. Each public monument, each of the new parish churches (to be constructed under the supervision of Wren, who eventually acted as a chief architect of the project) was accorded due praise in the form of numerous poetic tributes. Wren's plans for the glorious new cathedral of St. Paul's – the 'Mother-Bird' or 'Phoenix Paulina' that nested at the centre of his project – were singled out for particular attention. Other works were written specifically with reference to the rebuilding of the Royal Exchange and to 'the future advancement of Trade' to be conducted therein. Poems such as Henry Duke's 1688 'London's Nonsuch', systematically set about describing each of the shops that were eventually to be granted a space within the rebuilt structure. Hosiers, milliners, linen and lace shops, coatsellers, 'Silkmen', goldsmiths, button sellers, mercers, mourning shops, 'bauble' shops, glassmakers, booksellers, watchmakers, stationers, scriveners: all were to assume their rightful places among the elegant walks and arcades of the City's new and efficiently centralized hub of commerce.

The structure of the new Exchange, it was soon decided, was to be designed and built by Edward Jernam. The builders began clearing the ground in February, 1667, and the first stone was laid in October of that same year. In obvious imitation of its predecessor, Jernam's Exchange fronted onto Cornhill, the broad and spacious thoroughfare that had since the earliest years of the City's history served as a bustling and dynamic centre of commercial activity. Sloping down one of the twin hills of London – facing Ludgate Hill to the west across the valley of the Walbrook, and thought by some to have been named, as the anti-quarian John Stow recorded in 1598, after 'a corn market time out of mind there holden' – the street bears one of the oldest recorded names in the City's history.[6] As early as Chaucer's day, Cornhill had already long established itself as the principal highway leading from the great meat and fish market of Cheap toward Aldgate and to the furthest, eastern extremities of the City. The Tun – a stout, round building of stone first constructed as a reservoir in 1282 – was by the fourteenth century being used as a prison and holding pen for the area's 'night-walkers'. Even as early as the late 1300s, Cornhill boasted everything from blacksmiths' shops and poulterers' stalls to the venues of more prosperous tradesmen – retailers who looked to provide the City's increasingly wealthy citizens with a wide variety of luxury goods. London stood at the centre of the country's trade routes, and Cornhill, in turn, stood at the concentrated centre of London. By the mid-seventeenth century the highway was as busy and as prosperous a thoroughfare as one could hope to find any place in the ever-growing metropolis. 'Here if anywhere', the Revd. Samuell Rolle had written in his proud description of Cornhill and the Royal Exchange in the years immediately before the Great Fire, 'might a man have seen the glory of the world in a moment'.[7] The old water-standard which had long marked the interstices of Cornhill, Gracechurch Street, Bishopsgate, and Leadenhall Street had ceased to be of any practical use decades before, but the support was still generally regarded as the marker of London's 'ground zero' – the utterly central point at which distances to and from the City were traditionally reckoned and measured.

The Cornhill that emerged following the destruction of the fire, like so many of London's other rebuilt 'landmarks', was deliberately designed to be even more impressive than the near-medieval street that had crumbled so swiftly into the ashes of history. Many Georgians would eventually and as the new era took shape forsake the City (and the supposedly bourgeois obsessions of the native 'Cit') for the increasingly fashionable neighborhoods of the West End. As the

---

[6] John Stow, *The Survey of London* (London: J. M. Dent, 1912; 1987) 168.
[7] Samuell Rolle, '[The] Burning of London', quoted in Bell, *The Great Fire of London in 1666*, 65.

historian Simon Jenkins has written: 'The wealthy and the well-born had now endured two disorders [the plague and the fire] in as many years, and during reconstruction they inevitably had to find somewhere else to live'. 'For poorer people', Jenkins added, 'the new buildings may have been handsome constructions, blessed at least with some sort of drainage, but they were far more expensive than the old tenements had been'.[8] Indeed, throughout the late seventeenth and early eighteenth centuries residential dwellings in the area along Cornhill and in the streets around the Exchange were still among the most expensive in the City. Directly across from Jernam's towering new structure, and along the familiar passages and by-ways of Pope's Head Alley, Exchange Alley, Birchin Lane, George Yard, and St. Michael's Alley that once again angled their way between Cornhill and Lombard Street, there soon arose a proud new series of shops and storefronts. Such structures – within the scope of their own, admittedly more modest ambitions – constituted a tribute to the renewed and strengthened commercial vigor of the City no less powerful than the building of the Royal Exchange itself. Early eighteenth-century engravings of the area show the expanse of Cornhill to have been a broad, cobble-stoned street, bounded on either side by clean and (by contemporary standards) comparatively wide pavements for the movement of pedestrians. Tradesmen's signs hung from the second storey of many buildings, but the graded and orderly range of their intrusion into the streetscape would have created little if any sense of clutter or confusion. The newly instituted construction regulations forbade the use of timber framing, or of building materials such as rubble or thatch; safety laws required that the new structures be made of fire-resistant brick, stone, slate, and tile. Similar regulations dictated that along principal streets such as Cornhill, all structures be a uniform four storeys high. No longer, in other words, were buildings with jettied fronts allowed to 'oversail' the street, thrusting their roofs haphazardly into the air above the roadway. The ominous effect of having the visibly heavy second and third storeys of structures hovering above the heads of passing pedestrians – their outer walls seeming to lean across the street in an aggressive effort to touch their counterparts on the opposite side of the highway – was generally eliminated, and replaced instead by a greater sense of order, openness, and uniformity. The vista presented along the lengthy perspective of the street was a prospect of clear and unbroken lines. The overall impression of Cornhill from contemporary prints is one of an admirably well-maintained and well-frequented neighborhood thoroughfare, crisp and

[8]   Simon Jenkins, *Landlords to London: The Story of a Capital and Its Growth* (London: Constable, 1975) 34.

assured even in the simple and intrinsic strength of its confident verticality.

On Cornhill itself, in what the *Gentleman's Magazine* would later in the eighteenth century describe as 'a stately row of buildings' distinguished by the prosperous regularity of their flush facades, sash windows, and pleasant entryways, book-sellers, milliners, drapiers, haberdashers and hosiers set up shop. Along the area's side streets, bakers, barbers, button makers, and shoe-makers, as well as numerous coffee houses and ale houses, soon opened their doors for business. The unofficial designation following the fire of Cornhill (along with the Poultry and Lombard Street) as a 'High Street', and the demolition of the unwholesome 'Stocks' or ramshackle meat market at the junction of Cornhill and the Poultry, also and for the first time created what some historians of the period have described as 'a regular "City" quarter'; as Jenkins notes of the area: 'it began [now] to acquire many of its present-day characteristics as a central business district'.[9] 'The City in modern parlance – a financial centre', as Roy Porter likewise asserts, '... emerged after the Restoration'.[10] Moreover, even in the earliest years of the eighteenth century the first of the era's 'Improvement Acts' had begun to make living conditions in the most crowded urban areas generally more hygienic (much as the era's many 'Reformation Societies', which were to flourish a little later in the period, from about 1690 to the late 1730s, would seek in a similar manner to 'improve' manners and morality). The interiors of the retail shops may still by any modern standard have been cramped and poorly lit, but their plenteous goods and proud exteriors proclaimed a renewed and unmistakable faith in the area as the City's central marketplace. By day, the streets echoed not only with the constant hammering and pounding of new building and construction, and of the distinctive 'cries' of the London peddlers – the lively shouts, too, of butchers, fishmongers, poulterers, and fowlers – but carried on their urban breezes the whispered deals and bargains of the exchange merchants who once again made Cornhill their professional home. By night, lamps and tapers could be glimpsed shining in the windows of the neighborhood's ale houses and coffee houses – establishments often couched at odd angles in Cornhill's internal courtyards, or in the damp and darkness of its alleyways – and the boisterous noise of the taverns' occupants would echo through the narrow passages to the broader streets beyond. Various establishments in the quarter catered to various clientele. The Swan and Rummer Coffee House in Finch

[9]   T. F. Reddaway, *The Rebuilding of London after the Great Fire* (London: Jonathan Cape, 1940) 294; Jenkins, 35.
[10]   Porter, *London: A Social History* (Cambridge, Massachusetts: Harvard University Press, 1995) 146.

Lane was a popular venue for Masonic Lodge meetings. Merchants in the service of the East India Company, whose headquarters lay just to the east, in Leadenhall Street could most often be found gathering in the Jerusalem Coffee House. Seamen tended rather to patronize the Fleece, while the George and Vulture in nearby George Yard specialized in catering to large dinners and suppers. John's Coffee House, in Swithin's Alley by the Royal Exchange, was well-known in the early decades of the eighteenth century as a popular haunt among 'projectors' looking to attract new investors. The Golden Fleece Tavern hosted meetings of insurers and of the employees of the Hudson Bay Company. Other merchants were likely to be found clustering, even on Sundays, on the southern side of the Exchange, or at Batson's Coffee House, a lively and popular establishment which also attracted medical men. Lloyd's Coffee House, later in the century to develop into the commercial institution still known today as 'Lloyd's of London', was soon a feature of the neighborhood, having been founded in about 1691 on the south side of Lombard Street. Thomas Garraway, the entrepreneur who opened his own coffee house in Exchange Alley in 1669, was the first man in England to sell and retail tea, a beverage which he originally promoted and marketed as 'the cure for all disorders'. The Jamaica Coffee House in St. Michael's Alley took its name from its connections with those businessmen interested in the highly profitable trade with the Crown's West Indian plantations; the city streets were touched by the exoticism of indigo, sugar, and cacao, to say nothing of being tainted by the colonies' enormously lucrative slave trade, the darkness of which could extend even into this very heart of London. An advertisement posted in the *Daily Journal* for 8 August, 1728 alerted local readers: 'Ran away from her master at Blackheath, a negro woman, aged about 25 years, pretty fat (went by the name of Caelia) . . . and has several years to serve. . . . Whoever secures her and gives notice at the bar of the Jamaica Coffee House so that she be brought to justice shall have two guineas reward, but whoever entertains her shall be prosecuted with the utmost rigor'.

Obviously, there was a darker side to all this bustle and activity. The great Augustan satirists – Jonathan Swift, John Gay, and the artist William Hogarth among them – would all, on occasion, give further voice and testament to the often noisome squalor of the metropolis. The very same ale houses and coffee houses that provided the cheering light of fellowship to the passing pedestrian, might just as easily conceal within their walls the haunts of gamblers, thieves, sharpers, and prostitutes. City-dwellers were faced always with the possibility that danger and the threat of violent crime lurked around every corner. The central thoroughfares may have been broader and cleaner than they had been before the fire, but as the evening darkness descended on the City, the 'Hotch-Potch' of 'serpentine narrow streets, close, dismal, long Lanes, stinking Allies, dark, gloomy Courts and suffocating Yards' that stretched into the coal-darkened gloom on either side of those main streets could ensnare the unwary in any number of ways.[11] Even by the bright light of day, the City streets held their perils. When Daniel Defoe, writing in the first decades of the eighteenth century, chose to depict his young hero 'Colonel' Jack as committing his earliest robberies within the very shadow of the Royal Exchange, he was only drawing on the obvious wealth of possibilities daily presented to any gang of enterprising young thieves or pickpockets by a crowd of busy and preoccupied merchants and shoppers. Defoe knew the area about which he was writing well; he had himself, as a young man, operated a hosier's shop not far from Cornhill in nearby Freeman's Court.

And yet for all such qualifications – for better or for worse – the 'phoenix' of London had by the earliest years of the eighteenth century securely resuscitated the pulses and the rhythms that flowed from and within its vital financial heart. London was once again, as Joseph Addison would write, 'a kind of *Emporium* for the that Earth'.[12] From the ashes of the Great Fire, there had risen an astounding testament to the determination and tenacity of the craftsmen and shopkeepers of London. With the Royal Exchange standing as the jewel in the crown of its own, uncompromising preeminence, Cornhill, as Richard Steele was to put it in 1712, was without doubt and without rival, 'the centre of the City, and the centre of the world of trade'.[13]

*

To be born into and to grow up surrounded by the spectacular activity of this dynamic new 'centre' of metropolitan life could be both daunting and inspiring. Everybody could come to London – and, it so often seemed, everybody *did* come to London – in the eighteenth century. 'The poorest 'squire, as well as the richest peer', Tobias Smollett's Matthew Bramble would grumble later in the period, 'must have his house in town, and make a figure with an extraordinary number of domestics'.[14] Craftsmen, writers, artists, self-proclaimed philosophers

[11]   Joseph Massie quoted in Porter, *London: A Social History*, 97.
[12]   Joseph Addison, *Spectator* No. 69 (19 May 1711) in Richard Steele and Joseph Addison, *Selections from The Tatler and the Spectator*, ed. Angus Ross (London: Penguin, 1982) 437.
[13]   Richard Steele, *Spectator* No. 454 (11 August 1712) in *Selections from the Tatler and the Spectator*, 309.
[14]   Tobias Smollett, *The Expedition of Humphrey Clinker*, ed. O. M. Brack, Jr. with an Introduction and Notes by Thomas R. Preston (London and Athens, Georgia: University of Georgia Press, 1990) 87.

and ambitious politicians: all forsook the dunghill and peace of rustica-
tion and flocked to the metropolis in their search for wealth, pleasure,
fame, and the myriad opportunities dropped by the hand of a peculiarly
urban Fortune. Not a few bewailed every minute they were compelled
to spend away from town. A new cult of the written word – a new
configuration of print, authorship, and authority (both moral and
political) – also adhered to this new environment of the City. 'It is a
harmless fiction', Pat Rogers has commented, 'that eighteenth-century
life was equally rich and sustaining in remote parts of the country as in
London, but the truth is that the real allegiance of contemporary intellectuals lay in a London-based culture'.[15] Few of those professionals who
journeyed to London in the eighteenth century, of course, would have
required any assistance in articulating such a splendid realization for
themselves. 'The truth is', as the Scotsman James Boswell was to write
of his adoptive City later in the century, 'that by those who from sagac-
ity, attention, and experience, have learnt the full advantage of London,
its pre-eminence over every other place, not only for variety of enjoyment, but for comfort, will be felt with a philosophical exultation'.[16]

Throughout the eighteenth century London dominated the cultural
life of England as no other capital city has dominated the intellectual
life of its country before or since. It remained the superior and inalienable birthright of the native Londoner, moreover, to be at least one step
ahead of everyone else. For a poet such as Alexander Pope, for example,
who was to spend his very earliest years in nearby Plough Court (located
on the south side of Lombard Street, just west of Gracechurch Street),
the environment of the City and the sight of its many spectacles proved
in time to be a constant and almost invariably positive source of
creative, poetic inspiration. Although most often recognized by modern
readers when posed as a poet devoted to the pastoral retirement of
his Thames-side retreat at Twickenham – a latter-day Horace secluded
within the privacy of his artificial 'grot' – Pope and almost all of
his major writings were to be touched in some obvious way by the
memory of the diurnal images and by the recollection of the noisy
activities which he had first soaked in as a young child living in this
very heart of London.

Until he was about nine years old, Thomas Gray, much like
Alexander Pope a generation before him, was to awake each morning
with the throbbing and tolling of the City's many new church bells

---

[15] Pat Rogers, 'Introduction: The Writer and Society' in *The Context of English
Literature: The Eighteenth Century*, ed. Pat Rogers (New York: Holmes & Meier, 1978)
23.
[16] James Boswell, *Life of Johnson*, ed. R. W. Chapman (Oxford: Oxford University
Press, 1953; 1980) 1014.

ringing in his ears. For a campanologist the neighborhood around Cornhill was a very heaven. St. Michael's Cornhill, St. Edmund's, St. Clement's Eastcheap, St. Magnus, St. Mary ab-Church: all combined their chimes with the music of the tremendous bells of the new St. Paul's Cathedral (the final stone of which had been set in place in 1710) just one half-mile to the west. A veritable army of peddlers, so-called 'basket people', and other itinerant tradesmen trundled their barrows through the busy streets, constantly crying their wares as they made their way within the urban bazaar. To the south, the crafts of experienced Thames watermen and fishermen jostled against each other as they navigated the dangerous waters around London Bridge. Like Pope, Gray also drank in Cornhill and its activity almost every day of his young life. Jernam's Royal Exchange stood practically opposite the windows of his parent's home, and his own nursery and bedroom must inescapably have looked out on one of the busy City streets, more than likely facing onto Cornhill itself. Gray, like Pope, must surely have been present in Cornhill on several Lord Mayor's Days, the one holiday when the City's residents, rather than escaping to the fields and countryside which still bordered the growing metropolis, spilled instead into the quarter's streets – crowding the shops, filling the windows, and clambering along the rooftops – to watch as the pageant and procession passed by. Other holidays, such as 5 November (Guy Fawkes Day) and 29 May (the day of Restoration or Oak Apple Day) provided less spectacular but similarly jubilant opportunities for public celebration. On the latter festival, boughs and branches of Oak (commemorating that same tree which Gray would later, in one of his Latin school exercises, describe as 'nostrae felix tutela coronae' or 'the happy preserver of our crown') would be ranged along the avenues and hung with flags, flowers, and ribbons; young boys, Gray perhaps among them, would typically blow horns or bang drums. Some would even collect strings of wild birds' eggs to decorate the City's impromptu and incongruous arbors. On such occasions, the urban environment of the streets must have appeared suddenly to have been transformed into a saturnalia of parks and greenery, its normally sober promenades made verdant and trimmed with foliage. The Pope burnings and bonfires of Guy Fawkes Day or Gunpowder Plot Day were largely a thing of the past by the reign of George I, but that holiday might still, too, be counted on to provide the diversions and distractions of a day of noisy, public celebration.

As a young man, Gray was to take an active part in London's life and amusements. He frequented the theatre and the opera, and undertook excursions to such places of popular resort as the pleasure gardens at Ranelagh and Vauxhall, and on many occasions even betrayed an easy familiarity with lesser-known venues, such as Cupid's Gardens in

Bermondsey. Some people might call such 'curiosities' of the capital city 'dissipations', he would write only half-jokingly in 1746, 'but to me they appear Employments of a very serious Nature, as they enlarge the Mind, give a great Insight into the Nature & Genius of a people, keep the Spirits in an agreeable Agitation, and . . . amazingly fortify & corroborate the whole nervous System'. There can be little doubt that Gray knew the various topographies of the city well; nor, indeed, is it seriously open to question that he possessed the peculiar intuition of the urban native in his response to the centrality of the capital not merely as a physical space, but also as a dominating cultural entity.

Yet casual sentiments of the kind expressed by Gray in the passage quoted above were only rarely, in his surviving correspondence, allowed to be given full voice. For all the time he would throughout his life spend in his native 'Cornhillshire' and 'Lunnon' (and his adult years were to be punctuated by regular and extended stays in town) Gray seems to have had remarkably little to *say* about the city. He typically refrains from commenting about the business, the bustle, or even the trappings of London life. While particular locations are mentioned with no small degree of specificity in his letters, such references tend to appear only perfunctorily – as inconsequential, short-hand necessities (usually to close friends such as Horace Walpole), serving only to indicate precisely where he has been, or precisely what he has been doing. Gray's best-known poems, of course, are all to some degree recognizably pastoral works. By very definition, such poems acknowledge the presence of the city, but they do so only as part of their generic desire emphatically to situate themselves away from and against the urban environment; the *Eton Ode* and the *Elegy* – and even, to some extent, *The Progress of Poesy* and *The Bard* – are all the products of a creative sensibility that has carefully considered and then judiciously rejected the daily business and activities of the 'madding crowd' in favour of the grander, cosmic cycles of nature and of the seasons – rejected them, it would seem, in favour of the rather more comprehensive patterns of growth, maturation, decline, and eventual renewal of the natural world. In stark contrast to Pope, Gray rarely permits the spectacle and the pageantry of the renewed, early eighteenth-century city openly to enter – much less metaphorically to inform – his poetic work. For Pope, even the smallest details of his London youth were indelibly engraved in his memory and then reimagined his work; but for Gray, his entire early childhood would appear to have been obliterated. It is from the boundaries and from the borders of the ever-encroaching metropolis – from the comparative distance of Windsor and Cambridge, not London; from the personally informed perspective of Stoke, not Cornhill – that Gray chooses ultimately to observe the relationship between the individual and society, and within which he positions his most celebrated poetic persona, in the *Elegy*, as a solitary and inconsolably melancholy commentator on the interlaced pattern of values, opportunities, abilities, and rewards which determine our lives. Only by such a measure is Gray quite legitimately described as in any sense a marginal or liminal poet.

At least part of the key to understanding the persistence of such a distancing stance in Gray's poetry lies in understanding precisely why Gray himself felt it necessary to relegate his lived experience of the city and its resonances – or, even more simply, to relegate the narrative of the earliest years of his life – to such an inconspicuous place in the drama of his own personal history. That he was able to effect such a shift at all must in itself be counted as an impressive psychological maneuver. The nineteenth-century essayist Charles Lamb, who was likewise a London native and who would himself recall witnessing, as a child, the 'solemn processions through the City and Easter, with the Lord Mayor's largesse of buns, wine, and a shilling', once observed that having been (as he put it) 'born in a crowd', he had inescapably imbibed 'an entire affection for that way of life, amounting to an almost insurmountable aversion from solitude and rural scenes'.[17] It was much easier for most individuals to embrace the charms and diversions of the urban environment than to reject them. In putting Cornhill behind him, Gray looked at the same time to disassociate himself as much as possible from the domestic violence and abuse which, as we shall see, had formed the determining and unavoidable condition of life in the Cornhill household. Gray's eventual rejection of the paths of glory in the *Elegy* – his dissatisfaction, in fact, both with the aristocratic and with the mercantile or political high roads to worldly success ('the boasts of heraldry' . . . 'the pomp of power') – is a rejection which constitutes not merely the rhetorical gesture of a poet seeking to reinsert the familiar humanist traditions of the *memento mori* within some vague revaluation of the concept of 'melancholy' that appears to have taken place in mid-eighteenth-century poetry. Nor, it need hardly be added, does the poet's rejection of the city's majesty betray any particular dullness of soul. Gray's shift in creative focus as a young man to the topographical and thematic landscapes of an idiosyncratically redefined pastoral mode is to some degree the legacy of his own earliest experiences in London. It is a shift that was, at least in part, a result of a domestic legacy which would forever haunt and inform the deepest and most traumatized aspects of both his personality and his art.

[17]   Charles Lamb qouted in Edward Thomas, *A Literary Pilgrim in England* (Oxford: Oxford University Press, 1980) 25–26.

II. An Exchange Broker of Reputation and Fortune

Thomas Gray was born in Cornhill to Philip and Dorothy Gray (née Antrobus) on Wednesday, 26 December 1716. The birth was almost certainly a difficult one. At least two of the infants to whom the 31-year-old Dorothy Gray had already given birth had died very shortly after being brought into this world; two more of her children were to die within months of Thomas's own birth. Several of Dorothy's children appear to have been stillborn. Many years later, the fragile child who was himself introduced to life on that cold December morning in those last, waning days of 1716, would write a Latin poem that was to include a startlingly vivid description of the trauma endured by an infant even as it is being born:

> Necdum etiam matris puer eluctatus ab alvo
> Multiplices solvit tunicas, et vincula rupit:
> Sopitus molli somno, tepidoque liquore
> Circumfusus adhuc: tactus tamen aura lacessit
> Iamdudum levior sensus, animamque reclusit.
> Idque magis simul ac solitum blandumque calorem
> Frigore mutavit caeli, quod verberat acri
> Impete inassuetos artus: tum saevior adstat,
> Humanaeque comes vitae Dolor excipit: ille
> Cunctantem frustra, et tremulo multa ore querentem
> Corripit invadens, ferreisque amplectitur ulnis.
> Tum species primum patefacta est candida Lucis
> (Usque vices adeo Natura bonique, malique,
> Exaequat, iustaque manu sua damna rependit)
> Tum primum, ignotosque bibunt nova lumina soles. (*PTG* 324;330)

> [Even before the child has struggled from his mother's womb and broken through his many layers of covering and burst his bonds; while he is still drugged with soft sleep and bathed with warm fluid, a slight breath has already simulated his sense of touch and released his soul. This happens all the more at the moment when he exchanges the familiar soothing warmth for the cold of the atmosphere, which strikes at his unaccustomed limbs with a bitter onslaught. Then, yet more cruelly, Pain, the companion of human life, is waiting to receive him and tears out with violent hands the child who in vain delays and utters many querulous cries, clasping him in its iron embrace. Then, for the first time, the bright face of Light is revealed (in such a way does Nature balance good and evil by turns and with just hand make amends for the harm she inflicts); and then it is that the newborn eyes first drink in the sunlight unknown before.]

Gray's lines offer a grim recapitulation of just some of the ideas concerning perception and the natural senses which had first been advanced in John Locke's influential *Essay Concerning Human Understanding* (1689). Gray would in fact appear in this passage essentially to have been versifying some of the observations put forth by Locke in Book II of his *Essay* ('I doubt not but *Children*', Locke had written, 'by the exercise of their Senses about Objects, that affect them *in the Womb, receive some few Ideas*, before they are born').[18] The *Essay* would prove in time to be one of the most influential books Gray was ever to read; much of his mature poetry, as the modern critic S. H. Clark has observed, 'can fairly be designated as reactive, a series of rigorous meditations on the Lockean self, the premises of which remain prior to the text and largely unchallenged'.[19]

We should not, however, discount the possibility that Gray's description of the newborn's simultaneous birth into human life and human suffering in this passage – his grim reportage of the sanguine baptism of the senses in a 'bitter onslaught' that combines the commencement of perceived experience with a frank and unflinching, not to say pitiless, assurance of the certainty of sempeternal pain – may itself owe something to the accounts of the events that accompanied his own introduction into the world. As a boy, he no doubt listened to such accounts himself. Children are to this day typically fascinated by their parents' fond and wonderfully detailed (and often lovingly embellished) accounts of precisely 'what happened' on the day on which they were born; these are accounts which tend, in time, to assume the status of serious and oft-repeated family lore and legend. Such tales form the peculiar and unique *epyllia* of each and every domestic world. The one 'event' in which we have all participated as human beings remains – frustratingly and paradoxically – the very experience about which we can almost certainly remember nothing. We need to be told the story of our own becomings by others, and we seek whenever possible to hear that story from the lips of those individuals who actually witnessed or in some way participated in the events themselves. Frequent retellings of the natal saga serve to reassure the child of his or her own integral place in and importance to the family unit, just as they tend likewise to insist on the fact that there was at least one moment in time when the centrality of that importance was paramount to all other concerns.

Gray may have been informed of the circumstances which surrounded his own delivery either by his mother herself, or by one of his aunts, or

[18] Locke, 144.
[19] S. H. Clark, '"Pendet Homo Incertus": Gray's Response to Locke' in *Eighteenth-Century Studies* 24 (1990/91) 274.

even by one or more of household servants who would in various ways have assisted in the birth, and who are likely to have remained, as he grew older, in the family's employ. That such accounts would not normally have hesitated to include within their narratives some of the more clinical details involved in such procedures should come as no great surprise to the modern reader; Gray's own lines appear specifically to refer to the recently redesigned forceps – 'ferreisque amplectitur ulnis' – that were only just beginning commonly to be used in England. The men and women of early eighteenth-century England were in many ways far less squeamish and fastidious about such things than we tend to be today; the 'facts of life' were for most of them much more factual and much less lively (or at least much less shrouded in a deceptively lively veil of mystery) than they were throughout the better part of the twentieth century. Gray himself as a small boy may have witnessed at least some portion of the births of one or more of his less fortunate siblings, and so, in the lines quoted above, may, as the critic Eugene McCarthy has noted, 'have created the scene from memory'.[20] There is certainly no reason why he should ever have been shielded from the fact that his own delivery had been fraught with danger, or that both he and his mother had come close to dying in the process. Dorothy Gray may even at times have looked to emphasize the physical pain she had endured in bringing him into the world. The midwife who handed the tiny bundle to its mother on that cold December morning, in any event, surely did so with a grim awareness that this first encounter between parent and child outside the womb was a meeting that once again partook in its mortal uncertainty as much in the character of a leave-taking, as in that of a greeting or welcoming consecration and benediction.

It is likely that Thomas held onto life only barely. Dorothy, despite her own weakness, no doubt sheltered the newborn within a protective embrace that would have attempted, if possible, to fend off the threat even of death itself. As the events of her own later life indicate, Dorothy Gray drew strength from the very fact of her child's existence. Her son, in turn, and in the hours immediately following his birth, perhaps likewise drew some vague and primal resource from his mother's uncompromising insistence on his own vitality. Throughout his entire life Gray was to enjoy a close and unbroken relationship with his mother. If, as Lord David Cecil has written, the other circumstances of his home environment would work to implant in Gray 'an irradicable sense of insecurity about human existence in general', Dorothy's love and support must at least have counterbalanced that insecurity to some extent, and there is no evidence that Gray was ever to take that sustaining support

---

[20]   Eugene B. McCarthy, *Thomas Gray: The Progress of a Poet*, 77.

for granted.[21] 'He seldom mentioned his mother without a sigh', William Mason would write of Gray many years later, observing that after the poet's own death Dorothy's 'gowns and wearing apparel were found in a trunk in his apartments just as she had left them; it seemed as if he could never take the resolution to open it, in order to distribute them to his female relations, to whom, by will, he bequethed them'.[22]

Throughout the chill December afternoon, the fate of the newborn's life may very well have hung in the balance. Dreadfully fearful for her child's health, Dorothy Gray insisted that her son be baptized in St. Michael's Church that very same day. Dorothy's outwardly simple gesture of faith may subconsciously have signaled a profound sense of surrender or resignation on her part; representations of St. Michael dating from the Middle Ages and early Renaissance often depicted the archangel in his capacity as the leading power opposed to the adversarial forces of evil – the captain of the heavenly host – sometimes in the very act of weighing individual souls and so determining their fate in the life to come. Hard experience had perhaps already taught Dorothy that the decision as to whether her son was to live or die was no longer her own to shape. Once reassured that her child's spiritual salvation was beyond question, she must nevertheless have continued to pray that this one of her children, at least, be spared an early death. So, even, was the birth of the poet who would in time be remembered most for his sober estimation of the lot of mankind, and whose work would most memorably give voice in the English tradition to the fears and anxieties that haunt and accompany the simple fact of human existence, itself shrouded within the looming shadows of mortality.

*

Beyond the frosted panes that formed the windows of Dorothy's busy and by-now overheated Cornhill bedroom, the world went on much as usual. Thomas Gray had been born into a city that was still in the midst of a period of dynamic and unprecedented growth. The swelling boundaries of the metropolis extended now as far north as Shoreditch, and crept across the river past Southwark and Bermondsey toward George's Fields and Kennington. London had sprawled in recent years so as first to touch and then completely to overwhelm the city's remaining fields from as far as Westminster to Whitechapel; Wapping, Ratcliff, Shadwell, and Limehouse were likewise all in the process of being built over. The issue of the *London Gazette* covering the day of Gray's birth detailed

---

[21] Cecil, 83.
[22] Mason (1807) ii.307.

the expected selection of domestic news and bankruptcy notices; in its final issue for the year, the *Post Boy* advertised for workers needed for 'the Propagation of the Gospel in Foreign Parts' for their new college in Barbados. Papers such as the *British Gazetteer* and the *Daily Courant* highlighted international news. King George I had succeeded to the throne just over two years earlier, and a comfortable Whig majority (the Tories having been soundly disgraced in the eyes of the King by the ill-fated Jacobite rebellion in the year following his accession) had settled into the new Parliament of 1715. The nation as a whole was soon to begin a generally prosperous period of growth and commercial expansion under the 'Robinocrisy' of Sir Robert Walpole. Britain, France, and the Netherlands were to form the Triple Alliance in January 1717, an agreement that would be transformed into a so-called Quadruple Alliance in August 1718, by the adherence of the Emperor Charles VI. One practical result of the treaty was to give Britain an unprecedented voice in European affairs. The financial and political debacle of the South Sea Bubble still lay ahead, but that crisis would help ultimately only to strengthen Walpole's position as the 'Great Man' in the face of a factious Whig Opposition. Despite repeated setbacks, Walpole was to remain in power until 1742, when he would finally be driven from office by his political enemies.

The growing power and wealth of the nation seemed for some to be reflected in its very appearance. Throughout the countryside elegant and in many cases tremendous new homes and estates were built in the fashionable, Palladian style then being advanced by architects such as Colen Campbell. Designers and horticulturists including William Kent and Stephen Switzer were already hard at work reshaping and redesigning the English landscape itself. Palaces and gardens seemed in some cases to have emerged fully conceived and grown around the aristocracy and among the more prominent members of the new Whig governing class. Lord Burlington, who had returned from his (first) Grand Tour of the continent in 1714–15, had just begun designing his Chiswick House, modeled after and inspired by Andrea Palladio's own Villa Capra near Vicenza. The structure was to prove a fashionable meeting place for the literary and artistic *cognoscenti* of the era. Chiswick House would eventually house paintings by the likes of Sir Godfrey Kneller and Guido Reni; it would be completed in 1729. Older buildings, too, were often gutted and dramatically remodeled to suit the dictates of the new taste. Rousham House, for example, an old, castellated Oxfordshire mansion that had been requisitioned as a Royalist garrison in the preceding century, was carefully redecorated, its grounds laid out with striking, Italianate gardens. Within easy distance of Rousham lay Vanburgh's baroque masterpiece, Blenheim Palace, the 'gift of the nation' of John Churchill, first Duke of Marlborough. Blenheim's magnificent courtyards and formal gardens (patterned after the original designs of Le Nôtre) set out to rival even the most impressive of their continental models. Never one to be outdone, Sir Robert Walpole would soon construct his own version of the magnificent home; the result was his surprisingly somber and dignified estate at Houghton (although even the glorious Palladian style was deemed by some of the Minister's less objective critics to have lost something of its sunny splendor when adapted to the mists and sands of Norfolk).

The commercial heart of the City of London, meanwhile, seemed busier than ever. A pall of wood and coal smoke, fed by fires in the sprawling factories that had begun already to line the Thames, hung heavy over the City and the East End. As an exhausted Dorothy Gray lay in Cornhill (even she would not have been able to brave the dank chill of the winter's late afternoon to carry her tiny bundle into St. Michael's Alley to the baptismal font just across the street), merchants and retailers took a brief rest from their own affairs to celebrate the season around the hearth fires in the coffee houses that stood a few doors down from the church. From the narrow streets and alleys to the south of Cornhill came the sounds of other revelers, many of them already drunk from too much steaming-hot punch, or from brandy, cider, and ale. In the larger inn-yards of the George and Vulture and the Swan, waiters might be glimpsed balancing heavy platters of food and dinners on their shoulders, as they skillfully passed and repassed one another in their bustle and haste. The celebratory sounds of shrill wooden pipes and thumping drums wound their way through Castle court and White Lion Yard to Birchin Lane. Even on the day after Christmas, however, the speculators beat the snow from their hats, and shook its chill powder from their fashionable, full-bottomed wigs; stockjobbers clustered in Jonathan's and Batson's on Exchange Alley, eager as always to discuss their financial plans and schemes. Although the newspapers were careful to report the latest foreign news, England seemed for the first time within recent memory comfortably to be at peace with her continental rivals. The mood among the businessmen in the City's taverns and coffee houses was generally confident and optimistic.

Just over two miles away, in London's increasingly fashionable West End, those in search of less consequential pastimes and entertainments had their choice of holiday fare. Despite the fact that one of the greatest dramatists of the late seventeenth century, William Wycherley, had died earlier that same year, and although the vogue for the Restoration 'comedy of manners' had slowly given way to what some were already beginning to call the 'comedy of sensibility', theatre-goers that December were still eager to see Wycherley's *The Plain Dealer* at Lincoln's Inn Fields. Audiences were entertained between the acts of the play by novel displays of dancing, singing, rope-walking, and ballet. A revival of Nicholas Rowe's *Tamerlane* at the nearby Drury Lane theatre was also proving very popular that season, as were Susannah Centlivre's *The Cruel Gift* and Shakespeare's *Henry VIII*; John Gay and Alexander Pope's *Three Hours After Marriage* was to premiere the following month at the same theatre. The coming year would also see the publication of Pope's *Poems* (those in the literary world knew that he was already well along in his translation of the *Iliad*), and would witness the first appearance of Thomas Parnell's translation of the Homeric burlesque, 'The Battle of the Frogs and the Mice'. Although it may be something of an exaggeration to agree with Lord David Cecil's assertion that, by the early eighteenth century, England had 'settled down to an epic of prosperous stability' that was 'undisturbed alike by bloodshed or by spiritual yearnings', it is still true that, taken all in all, the European world at the end of 1716 seemed for once, at least from the point of view of an English merchant, to be in a pretty flourishing state.[23] The Russian Czar Peter the Great was that very winter touring the continent and planning to emulate its architectural and cultural achievements back home, and just a few months earlier, in his native Venice, the Italian composer Antonio Vivaldi had put the finishing touches on a new series of concerti that he had decided to call 'Le Quattro Stagioni' or 'The Four Seasons'.

*

The house in which Gray was born, No. 41 Cornhill, was owned by his father. The building stood on the corner of Cornhill and St. Michael's Alley, about fifteen doors down and on the opposite side of the street from Jernam's Royal Exchange. The structure would eventually be destroyed by a fire which would again devastate Cornhill in March 1748. At that time, a payment of £485, on a policy of £500, was paid directly to Dorothy Gray (though the care of the property had by then already passed into the hands of her son). The site – home now, as No. 39 Cornhill, to the Union Discount Company of London – is marked by a plaque quoting the first line of the *Elegy* and a bronze medallion featuring Gray's profile designed by F. W. Pomeroy. The 1748 fire also damaged the old church of St. Michael's itself, an Anglo-Saxon foundation that had already been rebuilt by Wren in 1670–77, and the ancient tower of which had undergone further extensive repairs in the years immediately surrounding Gray's birth. Although not damaged in the Second World War, St. Michael's had by

[23] Cecil, 78.

the twentieth century already suffered a drastic 'reconstruction' at the hands of Sir George Gilbert Scott in the mid-nineteenth century, and so today bears little resemblance to the ancient and heavily scaffolded church Gray would have known as a small child (though visitors to the site will still find some of the interior furnishings – including a late seventeenth-century oak alter table and the font in which the poet was baptized – still on view).

The human scale of the street-scape around St. Michael's Cornhill is today so dwarfed by the post-modern monstrosity of some of the modern banking headquarters bordering Gracechurch Street that any attempt to re-envision the neighborhood as it might have looked early in the eighteenth century requires a near-Herculean effort of sympathetic imagination. Gray, again, makes scant reference to the Cornhill house in his surviving correspondence, and at no point does he offer any extended reminiscences connected with his childhood home. Yet is was here, in Cornhill, that he would have spent some of the most formative years of his life. The amount of the policy subsequently paid by the London Assurance in 1748, and the fact that the rebuilding of the site, which began later that same year, cost a further £175 (an outlay of expense which would in turn appear to indicate that the property was at the time of the fire under-insured) suggest that the structure was a handsome one, not at all unlike those buildings that were to escape the 1748 fire and remain standing on the opposite side of Cornhill and along Lombard Street. No. 41 would have been a substantial brick building some four storeys in height. Its ground floor was occupied by a milliner's shop jointly owned and operated by Gray's mother and her sister, Mary Antrobus. Gray's friend and biographer William Mason noted the business vaguely to have been 'a kind of India warehouse'.[24] The term 'warehouse' may in the early eighteenth century already have been perceived by many to be a more dignified way of designating a mere retail 'shop'; signs advertising 'India' or 'Italian' warehouses, supposedly indicating the primary origin of some of the materials or articles of apparel sold in the store, were relatively common in the area. Dorothy and Mary's own sign, affixed to the side of the building above the ground floor and jutting prominently out into the bustle of Cornhill, was perhaps ornamented, like those of more traditional linen-drapers, with a graphic image of an exotic, Indian Princess. The shop run by Gray's aunt and mother most likely offered for sale such stuff as bonnets, laces, ribbons, and gloves; the fashion for silks and fabrics of colourful oriental design would naturally have led a great many customers to their door. Indian calicoes were so popular in England in the early decades of the

---

[24] Mason (1775) 120n.

eighteenth century that pressure from indigenous cloth manufacturing and weaving interests led in time to Acts of Parliament protesting the wearing or selling of calicoes and silks imported from India,
Persia, and China. Dorothy Gray's Cornhill establishment, in response
to such laws, is likely simply to have stocked more traditional English
fabrics and materials such as pulerays, bombazines, satinets, and
coloured crepes.

The ground floor of the Cornhill building would have been occupied
by the retail space itself. The Antrobus sisters together paid Philip Gray
£40 a year for the privilege of renting the downstairs shop. Some
few goods would have been displayed in the commercially valuable
window which faced onto Cornhill. The cellars would also have been
well stocked with the business's merchandise. When Dorothy and
Mary Antrobus first began occupying the Cornhill site in the first decade
of the eighteenth century, they had already assembled a substantial
stock-in-trade of some £240 (Daniel Defoe estimated that the mere
'setting up' of such a retail shop in the City in 1710, involving as it
did a substantial effort to attract customers could easily run upwards
of £300 a year). The downstairs space having thus been devoted to
the operations of Dorothy's retail establishment, the upper floors
consequently housed the living quarters both of the family and the
servants. The latter group would have mixed pretty freely with their
employers. Although the house itself belonged to Gray's father, the
furniture in the home was the property of his mother Dorothy. The
sisters' business was later described as having been a 'tolerable' if not a
spectacular success. The family dwelling probably provided most if not
all of the comforts demanded by an upwardly mobile, bourgeois family
in the period.

*

The poet's father, Philip Gray, was born on 27 July 1676, the fifth son
of Thomas and Alice Gray. Apart from the fact that the couple produced
in the course of their marriage six sons and five daughters (three of the
children died in infancy) very little is known about Gray's paternal
grandparents. Surviving evidence indicates that the poet's nearest ancestors came to the City from Wanstead, and ties to the Essex town remain
acknowledged throughout the poet's own lifetime. 'Whatever Wanstead
may be today', as one local historian observed some years ago, 'it was
once wealthy, and this affluence was partly a reflection of the steady
growth of commerce in the [eighteenth century]'; the prosperity of the
small community in the period was evidenced by the fact that some
eighty per cent of the village's roughly one hundred and twenty house-

holds were 'gentry-owned'.[25] The small estates of the successful City merchants formed a small community focused around the central estate of Wanstead House, the home of the famous merchant banker and head of the East India Company, Sir Josiah Child. Both the elder Thomas and his brother Matthew – Gray's great uncle – were themselves in the service of the East India Company. When Thomas Gray was admitted to the freedom (i.e. membership) of the Company in August 1678, the court minutes noted that Matthew Gray had by that date already 'died in the Company's service in Suratt'. Unlike his brother, Thomas – described in one document simply as a 'London merchant' – appears to have remained in the City throughout his life-long career with the Company. He supplied wines to the organization, and was recognized officially as a citizen and Cooper (a retailer of wines or 'wine-cooper') of London and Wanstead. When he died on 26 June 1696, he was buried in the middle chancel of St. Olave's, Hart Street, London (the same church where the diarist Samuel Pepys often worshiped and one which – remarkably – managed somehow to survive both the Great Fire and, later, the Blitz). The interment of Gray's grandfather in such a conspicuous location gives some indication of his status, at the time of his death, as a wealthy merchant of considerable social standing. On his death, he was to leave an estate of some £10,000. His widow, Alice, who died at the age of 58 on 24 July 1702, and of whom we know very little, was herself subsequently buried at St. Botolph's, Bishopsgate.

Thomas's eldest son was named after his uncle Matthew. Like his father, this Matthew was also a merchant of London and Wanstead. A second surviving son, named for his father, was elected a Factor or commissions merchant at Fort St. George, Madras, in December of 1687. Fort St. George had been established as a Fort and trading post in southern India by the Company in 1639–40, and had by the time of Thomas's death developed into the administrative centre of the region. This younger Thomas died in Madras at the age of twenty-three, on 6 August 1692. He was buried in the Old Cemetery of St. Mary at Fort St. George, where his tomb displays a representation of the armorial bearings of the coat of Lord Gray of Forfarshire, Scotland. On this possible connection to the family of Baron Gray of Gray, in Forfarshire (who later in the eighteenth century was to claim the poet as a relation), Thomas Gray would himself write: 'I know no pretence, that I have, to the honor Lord Gray is pleased to do me: but if his [Lordship] chuses to own me, it certainly is not my business to deny it'. The poet's lifelong acquaintance William Cole recalled that Gray possessed and made use

[25] Winifred Eastment, *Wanstead Through the Ages*. 3rd ed. (Letchworth, Herts: Essex Countryside, 1969) 83.

of a bloodstone seal, which had been passed on to him by his father, and which was engraved with Lord Gray's arms (which were gules, a lion rampant with a bordure, engrailed argent).

The third and youngest surviving son of the elder Thomas Gray was Philip Gray, father to the poet. He was baptized on 27 July 1676, at St. Olave, Hart Street, and was eventually apprenticed to John Chambers, Citizen and Draper, in January 1693. Philip Gray was admitted to the freedom of the Draper's Company in 1701 and soon thereafter became a money scrivener and exchange broker, working probably at the Blackamoor's Head in Abchurch Lane. He was much later, in 1730, to hold office in the Company as Junior Warden, and would serve as Second Master Warden in 1739. The term 'scrivener' in the period was applied not only to one who served as a professional copyist or amanuensis, but to an individual who received money to be placed out at interest, or one who, conversely, supplied cash to those who wanted to borrow money on commission. Despite later evidence of his quick temper and erratic behavior, Philip Gray appears to have been perceived by others for much of his professional career as a reasonably sound and successful financier. His name began appearing regularly in the St. Michael Cornhill Parish Vestry Minutes Book from April, 1704 onward; he was elected to the position of churchwarden in 1715, and became an Upper or Senior churchwarden in April, 1716 – the year of his son Thomas's birth. Even in the months prior to his own death, he was called upon to act as an auditor for church funds. Following Philip Gray's death in 1741, both *The Daily Post* and the *London Evening Post* were to carry notices announcing his status as 'an Exchange Broker of Reputation and Fortune'. He had married the poet's mother, Dorothy, sometime in 1709. Although no evidence regarding the earliest meeting and subsequent courtship of Philip Gray and Dorothy Antrobus survives, it is likely that the earliest relationship between the poet's parents was a professional one, maintaining – as they continued, on some level, to maintain even throughout the later years of their marriage – their respective standings not merely as husband and wife, but as landlord and tenant. Indeed, the parish records of St. Michael's Cornhill would appear to indicate that Philip Gray had been married prior to his union with Dorothy Antrobus. Two infants – Charles (born 9 October 1704) and Sophia (born 30 September 1707) – were recognized in the church's baptismal records as the children 'of Philip Gray and Catherine his wife'. This same Catherine (or Katherine) Gray was herself buried in the Lower Vault of St. Michael's on 8 December 1708. The first of the ten children specifically recorded as born to Philip and Dorothy Gray (a son, James, born in October 1710) – followed Philip's first wife to the grave after having survived just over three weeks. As we shall see, almost all of Thomas Gray's other brothers and sisters – Dorothy (I), Katherine, Philip

(I), Dorothy (II), Philip (II), Anne, Mary, and James – likewise died within only months or even weeks of their birth; only three survived above two years, and only one (the elder Dorothy, born on 8 March 1711 and buried 2 January 1718) lived beyond the age of six.

The poet Thomas Gray had four surviving paternal aunts. The eldest – Mary Gray – was born in London and baptized at St. Olave's in March, 1671. She was twice married. By her first husband, whom we know only by the name of Mr. Jones, she bore a daughter, Anna, who in turn married a Mr. George Williamson and gave birth in 1739 to the 'George Williamson, Esq.' (the poet's second cousin), to whom Gray would leave a legacy of £500 in his will. This George Williamson, continuing the family tradition, held several posts in the East India Company. He appears to have been drowned in a shipwreck on his return voyage to England from Calcutta in about 1771 (the year of Gray's own death). Mary Jones was married a second time to a Mr. Pattenson, who died before 1725, at which time his wife described herself as 'Mary Pattenson, widow'. The Pattensons had one daughter, Alice. This Alice Pattenson eventually, in March 1746, married John Forster, the Governor of Bengal, at Fort William. The post of Governor was even at this time a prestigious one. Bengal had already established itself as a central base for British expansion in India, and the governor general of the region was in the near future to assume the grander title of 'governor general of India', and effectively to become the chief executive of British India. Alice Forster's only child, a daughter recorded to have been given the strikingly odd name of John Anna (a variation perhaps or, rather more likely, a simple mistranscription of 'Johanna' or 'Joanna') was born at Fort William in May 1748, and eventually returned to England to marry Sir Henry Goring in September 1767. Goring eventually became sixth Baronet of Highden, Sussex, and his wife is referred to as 'Anna, Lady Goring, my second cousin by my father's side' in Gray's will. The poet's remaining paternal aunts were Alice Gray (1674–1724), Sarah Gray (1678–1736), and Susannah Gray (noted only to have been under 21 and unmarried at the time of the writing of her father's will in 1691). As we shall see, of these three aunts only Sarah Gray, of London, was to play any significant role in Thomas Gray's life and fortunes.

*

Gray's mother was christened Dorothy Antrobus in August 1685, the fifth of six children born to William and Jane Antrobus (née Goodwin). Her father, William Antrobus, a Citizen and Scrivener of London, was a member of a St. Albans and London branch of a prosperous Cheshire family bearing the same name (the secluded hamlet of Knutsford, in Cheshire, claims some attention as the place 'where the ancestors of the mother of Gray are first heard of'; the members of the Antrobus family were traditionally tanners, skinners, and 'mercers' or wool merchants).[26] Dorothy's mother (née Jane Goodwin) was likewise the daughter of a London scrivener. Her eldest sister, Anne (born 1676), married an attorney named Jonathan Rogers in 1710. Soon after their marriage the couple moved to south Buckinghamshire, where they settled in the village of Britwell, near Burnham. They would later remove to the small house variously known as 'Cant's Hall', 'Cat's Hall', or 'Catshill' (at the time the property passed into the hands of Mrs. Rogers, it was described as 'Goldwin's House and grounds at Cantshill near Burnham', and was thought originally to have been a hunting lodge in what was then Royal Windsor Great Park). It was there that the young Thomas Gray would visit his aunt and Mr Rogers in the summer of 1736, describing his by then gout-ridden uncle (who looked upon Gray's bookish temperament with barely concealed contempt) as 'a great hunter in imagination'. The rural community near Burnham, nestled as it was within the shade of hundreds of acres of old beech pollards and tall grey poplars, seemed an idyllic one. Gray would later describe the area as a miniature paradise. The couple eventually shifted their residence to a two-storey farmhouse known as West End Cottage, at Stoke Poges. The house at Stoke, where Mrs. Anne Rogers eventually died in September 1758, was to prove in time to be an important retreat for the poet.

The second of Dorothy's sisters, Jane, was born in 1681. She married one William Oliffe, a 'gentleman of Norfolk'. Gray did not get along at all well with Mrs. Oliffe in later years, describing her typically in his correspondence as 'the Dragon of Wantley' or, with even fiercer elaboration, as 'an old Haridan, who is the spawn of Cerberus & the dragon of Wantley'. The fact that, despite such animosity, he still continued actively to provide for Mrs. Oliffe's care and maintenance in her old age may perhaps be seen to stand as a testament to his strength of character, or at least to his sense of family responsibility. The fourth Antrobus sister, Mary, remained unmarried. Mary Antrobus was very close both to her sister Dorothy – with whom, as we have already seen, she was a business partner – and to her nephew Thomas. She died and was buried at Stoke in 1749.

Dorothy's two brothers, Robert and William Antrobus, were to play particularly important roles in the poet's life. The elder, unmarried Robert (born 8 July 1679) had graduated Peterhouse in 1701. He was later a Fellow of his Cambridge College, and served for thirty years an Assistant Master at Eton (though the range of instructors at Eton had

---

[26] H. Hulme, 'The Poet Gray and Knutsford: An Unpublished Pedigree', rpt. from *The Knutsford Division Guardian* (7 July 1911) 1.

consisted originally only of a Head Master and 'Usher' or Lower Master, by the end of the seventeenth century the school had recognized the need for an expanded teaching staff; Robert was among the very first, small group of instructors thus to be dignified by the title of 'Assistant'). When Robert died in January 1729, a tablet was erected to his memory in the church at nearby Burnham. Dorothy's younger brother, William (born 6 March 1688), was a Fellow of King's College, Cambridge. He too was for some time an Assistant at Eton, although he was eventually to leave the position for a living as Rector of Everdon in Northamptonshire. In February 1727, William married Elizabeth Nutting, the eldest daughter of Thomas Nutting, an Alderman and established merchant of Cambridge; the couple were to have four children. It would be with the assistance of Dorothy's two brothers that Gray would eventually be placed at Eton in 1725.

*

On both sides of his family, then, Gray came from a solidly middle-class, mercantile background. The male members of his father's family who had not pursued careers as merchants or exchange brokers in the City itself, had established themselves in comparable positions of author-ity in the chief administrative centres of the East India Company. While it was not at all uncommon for even the poorest of London families to retain resident servants as part of their domestic households, Philip Gray's family appears to have maintained an unusually faithful and devoted household staff (and they were well taken care of – several of the elder Thomas Gray's servants were buried in the churchyard of St. Olave's near the family; another was buried at Wanstead). Moreover, the paternal properties in Wanstead and in London seem for the most part – at least into the early years of the eighteenth century – to have been well and easily maintained. On his mother's side, Gray's family was likewise characterized by no small degree of business acumen and pros-perous professional activity. Dorothy's family, like that of her husband, was part of a long and well-established line of London merchants. The impulse that prompted Dorothy Antrobus herself both to open and to manage a retail business with her sister must have been a natural and comfortable one. Dorothy's brothers, though not engaged in trade, were each of them College Fellows in religious orders, and were both employed early in life in eminently respectable positions as school-masters by the most prestigious institution of its kind. Far from coming from the sort of grievously depressed or penurious background that critics have sometimes ascribed to him, Thomas Gray was born into a household that had united two reasonably well-to-do and materially comfortable London families. He was, as the modern critic James Steele put it, 'very much a part of the *rentier* stratum of the capitalist ruling class in England'.[27]

The home of Philip and Dorothy Gray could not have been a happy one, however. Very little is actually known about the poet's childhood in Cornhill. This absence of information – an initial, narrative gap only further underscored by Gray's persistent reticence in later life concerning the details of his early history – is itself something of an indication that all was not well within the household. Children who have enjoyed what might conventionally be described as a 'normal' childhood – by which I mean to designate a childhood at least free from any single terrifying event, or one left unscarred by the residual effects of any longstanding physical or emotional trauma – tend for the most part willingly and easily to recall the events and even the felt emotions of their early lives. Such recollections may admittedly, as Freud reasoned, differ from the conscious memories of adulthood and maturity in their susceptibility to being altered by the later events of one's life. Yet even what individuals think or imagine they remember from their childhoods, Freud further observed, is not a matter of indifference; residual memories can conceal crucial pieces of evidence regarding the most important features of an individual's mental development and disposition. At the same time, however, it is generally beyond dispute that the very notion of childhood development as we tend to envision that process today (and certainly the belief that the events of infancy and childhood are of crucial and defining importance to any human individual's later health and maturity as an adult) had yet to be conceptualized or 'invented' as a social construction in the eighteenth century. Children then, as critics of the origins of modern childhood in eighteenth-century Britain have often observed of family relations in the period, though typically loved and valued by their families, were for the most part typically looked upon as smaller and weaker versions of their adult counterparts.

It remains striking, however, that Gray is unique among the major literary figures of the period (or at least among those about whom we possess an otherwise reasonable amount of biographical information) in having left his earliest years such a complete blank. Jonathan Swift may later in life have characterized at least one childhood incident (in which, while angling as a child, a fish drawn almost to shore and within reach dropped from the end of his line at the last moment) as the prophetic 'type' of all his future disappointments; yet even Swift was capable of recalling, on occasion, some of the happier moments of his boyhood – the 'pleasant side' of his childhood, vague but still cherished memories of 'the delicious holidays, the Saturday afternoon, and the charming

[27]　James Steele, 'Thomas Gray and the Season for Triumph' in Downey and Jones, 98.

custards in a blind alley'.[28] Likewise Samuel Johnson, who passed his earliest years in his parents' morose and generally unhappy Lichfield home, could nevertheless, when pressed, recall some few brighter memories – his father Michael ('with gentle voice') teaching him to swim, for example.[29] Gray alone tells us next to nothing of his early life. In fact, we possess only one family anecdote – possibly true, very possibly not – relating to the poet's earliest years. While yet in swaddling clothes, Gray is said to have suffered from what was then described as 'too great a fullness of blood'. He fell into a 'fit' and would certainly have died, his biographer Mason would later write, 'had not his mother, with a courage remarkable for one of her sex, and withal so very tender a parent, ventured to open a vein with her own hand, which instantly removed the paroxysm'.[30] It remains unclear as to precisely what might have caused such an apoplectic 'paroxysm' in an infant only several months (or even weeks) old. We also possess one chilling and unalterable fact about the household in Cornhill. Thomas was the only one of no less than twelve children born to the family of Philip Gray to survive infancy.

III. A Most Unhappy Case

Childhood in the eighteenth century was a dangerous and uncertain state. Records of infant mortality dating from early in the period indicate that the expected survival rate for newborn children was by twentieth-century standards shockingly low. The prospects of survival for a child born into the often primitive sanitary conditions that prevailed in many areas of the metropolis could be particularly dim. The percentage of individuals who died before reaching the age of fifteen has been estimated by some historians as having been as high as twenty-five or even thirty per cent. Those children who managed somehow to survive the many illnesses that tended to ravage the younger population (diseases such as smallpox, measles, and consumption) might just as soon succumb to any number of lesser ailments, including fevers, intestinal worms, inadequate diet, and a host of other bacterial and viral infections. The chemical or medicinal remedies and treatments for such ailments often proved as dangerous as the afflictions themselves. Child-rearing and home health manuals from the period tended to advocate tightly drawn swaddling clothes designed to receive and retain

[28] Jonathan Swift, *The Correspondence of Jonathan Swift*, ed. Harold Williams, 5 vols (Oxford: Oxford University Press, 1963–65) i.109.
[29] See Walter Jackson Bate, *Samuel Johnson* (London: Chatto & Windus, 1970) 38.
[30] Mason (1775) 2–3.

'evacuations' (the resulting rashes, skin diseases, and infections could themselves be deadly), and squalling infants were not infrequently quieted by doses of spirits or laudanum that would today be considered poisonous. Accidental death or abandonment by parents who were either unprepared or unwilling to take on the responsibilities of rearing children were also possibilities. Abortions were necessarily dangerous and uncertain procedures (common methods for inducing an abortion included inflicting violent and traumatic physical harm upon the body – such as throwing one's self down a flight of stairs – or regularly swallowing the kinds of heavy potions that were beginning to be advertised in some newspapers, purges that promised first to poison and then facilitate the removal of the fetus). Unwanted children were often more easily killed at birth or, as was increasingly the case in the eighteenth century, simply abandoned to the city streets soon after being born. The records of St. Michael's, Cornhill – including as they do such entries as 'A child left in the parish was baptized John [Cornhill]' – attest to the staggering number of infants left to fend for themselves on the parish's streets and doorsteps. In the paternal village of Wanstead, matters were no less grim; the parish records for the Essex town routinely contain items such as: 'George Foundling. A Child that was found upon Mr. Martin's Dunghill. Bap: June the 9th'. The very prospect of being in labour and giving birth, it need hardly be added, was not an experience anticipated with much eagerness by young mothers. Deaths in childbirth were high, and it was not without reason that many women resorted to such superstitious preventatives as the 'celebrated Anodyne Necklace' then being advertised within the pages of weekly London papers like the *Post Boy* and the *London Chronicle*. Such necklaces – supposedly Doctor recommended – promised to alleviate the pain of 'Women in Labour'. The efficacy of such products would no doubt have been questioned by the credulous if only because of their promise similarly and arbitrarily to ease the pains of teething and other, unspecified 'Distempers of the Head'.

The several children born to Dorothy Gray were not unwanted, however, nor, as has sometimes been asserted, did those children necessarily represent the last, enervated branch of a 'weakening stock'; the strength of both Gray's maternal and paternal lineage would in fact seem to indicate otherwise. For Dorothy to have lost all but one of her children to natural causes is not inconceivable, but – given the extraordinary care and devotion subsequently lavished on her fiercely protected fifth child – such a loss may well have been unlikely. We will probably never know exactly what killed Thomas Gray's infant brothers and sisters (it has been suggested that the same sort of apoplectic fit from which his mother rescued Gray claimed the lives of at least some of his less fortunate siblings), but there is reason to suspect that his father, Philip Gray, may indirectly or even directly have been responsible for the loss. To fill out the picture of what the household in Cornhill was like in Gray's childhood we need to look ahead for a moment to 1735. In February of that year, her son having long since been removed to the safety of Eton and, subsequently, Cambridge, Dorothy Gray finally took steps legally to separate herself from her husband. Although filed nearly two decades after Gray's birth, the documents relating to Dorothy's case against her husband bear vivid testimony that the abuse and mistreatment that they chronicle had been taking place since the earliest years of the couple's marriage in 1709. The remorseless pattern of domestic violence would already have been well established by the date of Gray's birth in 1716.

*

Dorothy Gray submitted the details of her case to Dr. John Audley. A contemporary of Dorothy's brother Robert Antrobus at Peterhouse and, like Robert, a Fellow of that College, Audley had been admitted as an Advocate (i.e. a legal counselor or counsel) in 1710. His services were probably suggested to Mrs. Gray by her brother. The case begins by recapitulating the terms by which Philip Gray, before his marriage, had agreed to allow Dorothy and her sister Mary to have the 'sole benefit' of the profits arising from their milliner's business, of which establishment their brother Robert was then a trustee.[31] (Dorothy's undisputed status as one of the owners of her business was quite an exception to the general rule; most female businesswomen in the period, as one recent critic has noted, became owners only because of 'situations in which a widow inherited her husband's business or . . . in which a wife had managed somehow to keep her "separate estate" '.)[32] The document goes on to state that the sisters had by 1735 conducted their business for nearly thirty years with 'tolerable success' (a chronological anecdote that again, incidentally, suggests that Philip Gray's earliest relationship with his wife was a professional – rather than exclusively personal – one; the Antrobus sisters may have been renting the Cornhill shop from Philip even in the earliest years of the new century). Throughout that period, however, Philip Gray, notwithstanding his substantial income as an exchange broker, is noted to have contributed virtually nothing to the support of his wife and children. Dorothy Gray is stated to have clothed not only herself but all of their children, to have supplied 'most of the furniture of his [Philip's] home', to have paid a rent of £40 a year for the use of the retail shop in the Cornhill home and, finally, to have provided 'almost . . . every thing' toward her son

---

[31] The Case submitted to Dr. Audley is reprinted as Appendix A in *CTG* (1195–97).
[32] Elizabeth Kowaleski-Wallace, *Consuming Subjects: Women, Shopping, and Business in the Eighteenth Century* (New York: Columbia University Press, 1997) 114.

Thomas's education both at Eton and Cambridge. 'Notwithstanding which', Audley wrote,

> almost ever since he hath been married, he hath used her in the most inhuman manner, by beating, kicking, punching, and with the most vile and abusive language; that she hath been in the utmost fear and danger of her life, and hath been obliged this last year to quit her bed, and lie with her sister. This she was resolved, if possible, to bear; not to leave her shop of trade for the sake of her son, to be able to assist in the maintenance of him at the University, since his father won't. (*CTG* 1196)

Audley further speculated on the elder Gray's motives for such behavior:

> There is no cause for this usage, unless it be an unhappy jealousy of all mankind in general (her own brother not excepted); but no woman deserved, or hath maintained, a more virtuous character: or it is presumed if he can make her sister leave off trade, he thinks he can then come into his wife's money, but the articles are too secure for his vile purposes.
> He daily threatens he will pursue her with all the vengeance possible, and will ruin himself to undo her, and his only son; in order to which he hath given warning to her sister to quit his shop, where they have carried on their trade so successfully, which will be almost their ruin: but he insists she shall go at Midsummer next; and the said Dorothy, his wife, in necessity must be forced to go along with her, to some other house and shop, to be assisting to her said sister, in the said trade, for her own and son's support. (*CTG* 1196)

Dorothy Gray's immediate purpose in filing such a document was to determine just what legal action her husband could take against her should she choose physically to leave the home in Cornhill and live with her sister. Gray's mother was particularly troubled by the possibility that Philip Gray might have some legal claim to dispose of her stock and profits, and that he might even, in his desire to maintain control over her material estate, 'force her to live with him'. It should be pointed out that divorce was not even available as a realistic option for Dorothy; women could not themselves sue for divorce. Moreover, 'Divorce was possible only by private act of Parliament, but getting such an act passed could be difficult, time consuming, and expensive; this method was therefore reserved only for the very rich and very determined. Only thirteen such divorces were granted between 1700 and 1749.'[33]

---

[33] Kirstin Olsen, *Daily Life in 18th-Century England* (London and Westport, Connecticut: Greenwood Press, 1999) 44.

Dr. Audley posed the 'Question' in the second section of the document. His initial response to Dorothy Gray's case sheds grim light on
the legal rights of married women in the early eighteenth century. Audley
noted that should Dorothy choose to leave her husband's house and live
with her sister, 'her husband may, and probably will call her, by process
in the Ecclesiastical Court, to return home and cohabit with him, which
the court will compel her to do, unless she can shew cause to the contrary'. While there was always the possibility that the court would decree
for a separation if the judge could be convinced that it was impossible
for Dorothy to live in safety with her husband, such a possibility, Audley
warned, was slight, 'sentences of separation, by reason of cruelty only',
he observed, 'being very rarely obtained'. Audley could in fact do little
more than suggest that Dorothy make the best of a bad situation and
'bear what she reasonably can, without giving [her husband] any provo-
cation to use her ill'. Audley finally warned his client that since no power
of making a will had previously been reserved to Mrs. Gray by her
marriage settlement, her stock and profits would necessarily be settled
on her husband, should he outlive his wife, and that, moreover, 'she has
no power to dispose of it by will, or otherwise'.

Dorothy Gray may thus have failed in her original purpose legally to
remove both herself and her estate beyond the grasp of her husband, yet
her case chronicling Philip Gray's life-threatening 'beating, kicking, and
punching' throughout her entire married life paints a vivid and ghastly
picture of an abusive and very possibly alcoholic household. Even if
Philip Gray was not directly responsible for the deaths of his children
through physical abuse or infanticide, the near pathological hatred and
self-destructive behavior described in the case submitted to Dr. Audley
leaves room to consider that his treatment of his wife prior to her giving
birth – the atmosphere of physical abuse, fear, and desperation he seems
consciously to have fostered – would adversely have affected the
outcome of Dorothy's several pregnancies. Philip Gray's beatings may
well have injured Dorothy's children while they were yet within the
womb; we can be nearly certain that he neglected to provide his wife
with adequate pre-natal and postpartum care.

Dorothy used her own resources as best she could, but her husband's
stubborn 'inhumanity' must have made her lying-ins painfully difficult
at best. It will forever remain unclear how exactly it came about that a
woman such as Dorothy Antrobus – the daughter, again, of a respectable
London businessman from a well-established family, and a person, more
to the point, who throughout her life demonstrated herself to be an individual of strong character and intelligence – ever came to marry such an
ill-natured man as Philip Gray in the first place. The very independence
of spirit that she manifested against her husband and his continued
tirades later in life may, when she was yet a young woman, have been

directed rather against some aspect of her own family and up-bringing. Her marriage may even itself have been an act of domestic or personal rebellion; the accommodating imagination of her youth may well have suggested to her otherwise discriminating mind that Philip Gray offered an attractive alternative to some aspect of her own family situation – her own desires may have clouded the perception, in other words, that he was anything other than a sullen and abusive boor. We should not, at the same time, overlook the possibility that Philip Gray may himself have possessed one of those personalities that is almost schizophrenically capable of manifesting a certain, seductive charm until it achieves its immediate goals or desires, at which point its character reveals itself in all the true colours of its egoism and hard-hearted selfishness. The destructive brutality of Dorothy's husband may have been masked in their early courtship under the guise of an intriguing and forceful sexuality – an erotic charisma alluring and compelling even in the seeming simplicity of its strength. The hours after marriage, in any event, had obviously held some dreadfully unwelcome surprises for a woman as honest, hard-working, and deserving as Dorothy Gray would, throughout her life, demonstrate herself to be.

*

By the early 1720s, however, Dorothy needed to think not only of her own welfare, but of that of her small child as well. Thomas was himself probably a thoughtful and sensitive boy, perhaps withdrawn and even slightly dreamy. Needless to say, such a disposition did little to endear him to his father, who, looking at the boy's pale face and into his timid eyes, would have detected in their fearful glimmers of anxiety only a distant and unspoken echo of Dorothy's own reproach. Such a daily affront to his own virility – and Philip Gray must no doubt have regarded this timid child as precisely and primarily such an affront – must only further have stoked the fires of anger and resentment that glowed ominously and at all times on the Grays' domestic hearth. Contemplating the profound and lingering effect Gray's early home life was to have on his later poetry, the modern critic Jean Hagstrum speculated: 'Who can say what he saw within as he dreamed of some kind of union in mind and body that the evidence suggests his nature deeply craved? Did he see his mother? Or his mother and his father (unreal and idealized) together and in love? Or did he see other successful lovers in the serene and perfect joy he never knew?'[34] As David Cecil, again, observed of the effects of Gray's childhood environment: 'precociously

---

[34]   Hagstrum in Downey and Jones, 17.

aware, as he was, of the possibilities of disaster, his free response to experience was chilled and chastened'.[35]

Many of young Thomas's mornings and afternoons would have been spent in the company of his mother and of his aunt Mary in the shop downstairs. Between the day-to-day demands of running the milliner's business, however, and the attention demanded by their some-times capricious retail customers (to say nothing of the distraction of Dorothy's five, subsequent pregnancies), the sisters would often have had no other choice but to leave the child largely to his own devices. The kinds of thefts committed by Daniel Defoe's Moll Flanders in the shops of mercers and apothecaries in the streets and alleys surrounding Cornhill remind us that merchants needed constantly to keep a sharp eye on all their supposed customers, no matter how honest or prosper-ous they appeared to be. As a small boy, Gray most likely found the comparatively vast spaces of his mother's India 'warehouse' – crowded as they were with all manner of invitingly soft and colourful materials – exotic and intriguing, yet at the same time somewhat frightening. The smells of strange dyes and fabrics filled the air, and the fear of being spoken to sharply for handling and perhaps soiling something he had been instructed not to touch in the first place would have led him to keep his hands largely to himself.

Slight and silent, the young Thomas must have preferred whenever possible to stay close by his parent's side. Under his mother's watchful eye he probably first learned to spell his letters and to read through his alphabet. His earliest lessons may have been conducted with the aid of an ABC or hornbook – those small, hand-held and durable wooden battledores on which a thin layer of translucent horn covered and pro-tected a presentation of the alphabet, a syllabary, the ten digits, and the Lord's Prayer. He would have progressed in time to metrical versions of the psalms and to the rather more compelling chapbook romances – slim and comparatively inexpensive pamphlets that reprinted everything from history and religious tracts to popular dramas and children's fables – which had become so popular and so widely available in recent years. The Bible and the Book of Common Prayer were of course considered appropriate material even for the youngest readers. Mrs. Gray herself must in time have grown adept at carrying on several occupations at once – of practically conducting her daily business activities with one part of her mind, while another part continued to trace the intricacies of grammar or spelling along with her son. Turning her attention again to Thomas's lessons after having completed a transaction at the shop's counter, she could soon pick up just where she had left off, or with little effort join him in whatever progress he had made in her absence. Books,

[35] Cecil, 83.

though expensive, seem never to have been considered a luxury by
Dorothy and her family, but rather a necessity, and one senses that Gray's
references later in life to the volumes contained within his own personal
library as his closest 'friends' and 'companions' formed part of an intimate response toward literature and writing which had been suggested
and fostered extremely early in life. Much like Samuel Johnson some
few years earlier, Gray probably soon grew into a child who liked
nothing better than to secret himself in some comfortable corner of his
mother's shop, so as to spend the long afternoons as quietly as possible
reading through whatever volumes were placed at his disposal or, indeed,
whatever books he happened to have discovered for himself. His education at home may have been supplemented by lessons conducted by
the parish clerk at St. Michael's, in those days an apparently likeable
man by the name of Cary Kibble. Such clerks typically took under their
care the parish's many vagabonds and foundlings, but were expected as
well to catechize the local children, and to set a general example for
parishioners in the way of writing, reading, and singing.

Mrs. Gray would not have been slow to recognize her son's precocious and voracious intellect. She no doubt encouraged Thomas in his
reading, and doubtless sought her brothers' professional advise as to just
which books and materials her child should be studying. She may even
have been able, with the aid of such basic grammars provided by Robert
or William, at least to assist him, and perhaps confidently to lead him,
on the road toward an elementary understanding of Latin. Unlike
Johnson, Gray even as a young man was a precise and careful reader –
he no doubt, even as a child, made a point of 'reading books *through*'
(to use the phrase Johnson would himself later in life employ with such
dismissal), and he in all likelihood took to the habit of making slight
notes and comments on his readings as soon as such a notion was even
suggested to him. Bishop Percy tells us that Johnson, when himself a
child, was 'immoderately fond of reading romances of chivalry', and that
he retrospectively attributed to such 'extravagant' fictions 'that unsettled turn of mind which prevented his ever fixing on any profession'.[36]
Gray's childhood reading similarly cultivated a life-long fondness for
such chivalric romances, and he must have made his way through sensational new collections such as the *Arabian Nights' Entertainments*
with genuine delight (the latest volumes of that collection were still
making their way from France to be published in England for the first
time while Gray was yet a young boy). It would be difficult to say if he
ever suspected, like Johnson, that such fictions encouraged a certain
professional indecision later in life, but, as a child, escapist romances –

[36] Boswell, *Life of Johnson*, 36.

the larger and lengthier the better – would always have been welcome treats. From his earliest years Gray appears to have been conditioned to look toward books and literature as providing a safe haven and a peaceful retreat from the pressures of the larger, adult world. Captivated by the exotic adventures of an Aladdin or an Ali Baba, or immersed in the more home-spun histories of Tom Thumb, or even imagining himself as standing by Christian's side and with him battling Apollyon in the Valley of Humiliation, Gray could shut out the angry shouts and quarrels that so often filled the Cornhill home. The sounds, too, of more dreadful physical abuse – fearful cries and plaintive whispers the true meaning of which he dared not even think about nor, at such an age, ever fully understand – could be muffled, if not silenced completely, within the pages of an absorbing and fantastic romance.

Being of such a shy and bookish temperament himself, Gray no doubt tended to look upon the ragged children who seemed to roam the City streets outside the Cornhill shop in wild and predatory packs as little less than alien creatures. Their rough and tumble amusements (and crimes) were for the most part completely foreign to him. The trials and deprivations of the unfortunate young boys and girls who, like Defoe's Colonel Jack, thought that to nestle among the warm ash heaps under the arches of the glass houses in nearby Stepney was to lie 'not only safe, but very comfortably', were of course, to a child of Gray's social standing, completely unknown.[37] Thomas may have watched such children from behind the safety of the shop window, and he might even, on occasion, have ventured in his curiosity into St. Michael's Alley or onto Cornhill itself so as to gain some closer glimpse of their activities, or to listen to their shouts echoing jubilantly and defiantly within the nearby lanes and alleys. He would invariably have been called back within doors by his anxious mother. The City streets, Dorothy Gray knew, were a dangerous place for small children. Only a generation earlier, the three-year-old Alexander Pope – still dressed in his infant 'coats' – had nearly been trampled to death when a wild cow, being driven through the same neighborhood to nearby Smithfield market, had run out of control and plunged into the *cul de sac* of Plough Court. Livestock (some 80,000 heads of cattle and a staggering 610,000 sheep were led to Smithfield every year)[38] were herded, often chaotically, down the City's central thoroughfares. And there were already reasons enough, as Dorothy Gray also knew, to concern herself about young Thomas's health without having to worry about any unruly farm animals he might accidentally encounter in the streets. The children she had conceived and carried to

[37] Daniel Defoe, *Colonel Jack* (Oxford: Oxford University Press, 1970) 16.
[38] Porter, *London: A Social History*, 143.

term subsequent to Thomas's own birth had each followed one another
to the churchyard with dread certainty. One of Gray's infant brothers
– a child christened Philip on 20 July, 1729 – survived for almost
three years. An earlier daughter, Dorothy, likewise lived until January,
1718.

Just how Gray's mother responded to such losses is difficult to say.
Writing about the manner in which poor and middle-class families in
the period remembered and commemorated their infant dead, the social
historian Beatrice Gottlieb has observed:

> Religious beliefs contributed to the tendency to regard babies as without
> individuality. Their deaths could be seen as part of the mysterious
> workings of evil in the world and were sometimes taken to be punish-
> ment for the sins of the parents, helping to displace grief over the death
> of a little person with concern about the state of one's own soul. This
> encouraged a strangely forward-looking attitude, a resolve to go on and
> do better the next time.[39]

There was, in actual fact, nothing all that 'strange' about such an
attitude. As she buried one child after another, Dorothy's sorrowful
despair must nevertheless have given way to a peculiar brand of grim
resignation and determination. In the few quiet minutes she had to
herself, Dorothy may sometimes have observed her only surviving child
unawares, and he no doubt seemed to her in those same moments to be
invested with the lives and the souls of all his less fortunate brothers and
sisters. Their several deaths only increased the value of his own young
life. So many of Dorothy's waking hours must have been spent in
devising ways to protect her child from the harsher realities of the world
– in trying to rescue and to preserve him for the better life she was certain
he deserved. Her conduct suggests that, like so many mothers, she would
gladly herself have borne any of the suffering or affliction that were
destined to pass her son's way. As if things were not already bad enough
in the City, the winter of 1721 had seen the passage of a new Quaran-
tine Act. It was feared that the epidemic of bubonic plague that had
raged in the preceding year throughout the south of France – spreading
from the port city of Marseilles to nearby communities such as Arles
and Toulon – was imminently to arrive in England. The Great Visitation of 1666 being for some few, neighboring Londoners still within
living memory, and the chaos and civil unrest that had followed and
compounded the devastation of the disease at places like Toulon only
the year before being vividly reported in publications such as *Applebee's*

---

[39] Beatrice Gottlieb, *The Family in the Western World: From the Black Death to the
Industrial Age* (Oxford: Oxford University Press, 1993) 134.

Journal, residents of London braced themselves for the worst: a visitation of plague followed by riots and civil disorder and perhaps (who could be sure?) once again a providential judgement of fire. Dorothy Gray looked with concern at her fragile child – only five years old – and wondered once again just what she could do to protect and save him for the hopes she so carefully cultivated in his name, and for the dreams he had perhaps already begun to dream for himself.

It would in fact be a matter of years before she arrived at any certain course of action. By the summer or autumn of 1725 – a full decade before Dorothy Gray was to explore the possibility of a legal separation from her husband – the situation in Cornhill seems already to have become intolerable. Periodic and extended visits to the homes of his maternal uncles and to the household of Jonathan Rogers near Burnham may from time to time have eased the situation for young Thomas, but such brief absences offered no real solution to the problem. Some more permanent arrangement would need to be made. If Dorothy was herself inextricably bound to her husband and to the milliner's shop in Cornhill, Thomas could at least be sent to an environment far removed from his father's tirades and abuses. For such an environment, Dorothy looked to her brothers William and Robert, and found, nestled in the Thames Valley near Windsor, a place of safety for her only surviving child.

CHAPTER TWO

TAUGHT HARMONIES

Eton
1725–1734

I. In Henry's Holy Shade

By the late autumn or early winter of 1725, just before his ninth birthday, Gray had already been permanently removed from his father's home in Cornhill and placed under the supervision of his maternal uncle Robert Antrobus at Eton. Dorothy's brother, who had first entered Eton as a pupil himself in 1692, had by the time of Thomas's enrollment been teaching at the school for nearly twenty-five years. He had at one point, in about 1718, been joined in Windsor by his brother William, who had himself first been admitted to the school as a student in February, 1705, and who had then moved on to graduate from King's College in 1713. Yet the younger Antrobus would within less than a year after his nephew's arrival at the school leave the college in order to marry and take up a clerical living in Northamptonshire. Clearly, nine-year-old Thomas was throughout his earliest time at Eton to be under the very particular care of his uncle Robert.

Robert Antrobus's duties as an Assistant Master at Eton included tutoring the boys in the standard subjects of Greek and Latin. It is likely that he also spent some time instructing his students in those disciplines that were considered less important by the school authorities of the day, such as mathematics and geography. Robert's own personal interests lay in the areas of botany and 'physic', or medicine. He encouraged Thomas also to study natural history and, as Horace Walpole would later comment of the close tutorial relationship between the teacher and his nephew, 'took prodigious pains with him, which answered exceedingly'. 'He particularly', Walpole further recalled of Robert's efforts with Thomas, 'instructed him in the virtues of simples'.[1] Prior to his own death in January 1730, Robert directed his brother William 'to give to my nephew Thomas Gray all such books as relate to the practice of physick, provided he be educated in that profession'. Throughout his life Gray would keep in his library many of his uncle's books of classical authors, including volumes of Euripides, Virgil and Horace; he even

---

[1] See *CTG* 1287; Walpole's *Memoir* of Gray, first printed by Mitford in 1853, is reprinted as Appendix Y in *CTG* (1286–1288).

preserved several original Latin poems subscribed only by the signature 'Antrobus'. Among Gray's oldest and most treasured possessions, on his death, would be volumes such as Eleazar Albin's 1720 *Natural History of English Insects* – a handsome collection of coloured, copper-plate engravings, with the name of 'Robert Antrobus, A. M.' prominently listed under the 'Names of the Subscribers' prefaced to the collection. Although Gray was not, of course, to follow his uncle's particular desires with regards to his professional career, he was nevertheless reputed by Walpole to have developed into 'a considerable botanist at fifteen'. He would much later in life return to the study of natural history as one of his favourite pastimes, busily collecting plants and insects in the Physick Garden in Chelsea or in the botanic garden at Cambridge, peering into his microscope by the light of a candle in his rooms in college, or dutifully recording his notes in his copy of Benjamin White's *Naturalist's Journal*, a notebook especially designed for such observations. Gray's later-life fascination with such matters as the precise patterns and rhythms of the natural world – with the passage of the seasons, for example, or with the subtle bonds of temperament and temporality that bind man to his environment: these were in many ways the direct outgrowth of an interest in the world around him first fostered by the careful observations of his uncle Robert. It has likewise with good reason been speculated that his uncle's interest in botany and in the possibilities of what we would today call herbal medicine encouraged Gray in what was to become a life-long affinity for the sights and sounds of the rural countryside – an affinity nurtured by the long walks first taken in the fields, meadows, and woods in and around Windsor with his favourite uncle.

*

It would be no exaggeration to say that life at Eton was for Gray quite literally a breath of fresh air. Although the distinction between 'town' and 'country' was in eighteenth-century England far less dramatic than it is today, any reasonably intelligent child could not help but have been affected by such a sudden and momentous change in the circumstances of his or her outward environment. The city of London may still have been only a short day's carriage ride away from Eton, but the metropolis and its concerns must very soon have formed, for the new student, a world entirely apart from the realities and the routines of his everyday life. The days near Windsor were filled with the smells not of the city but of the seasons. Nights were quieter, but the evenings, too, were likely to be punctuated by the unfamiliar sounds of the natural world. The creaking boughs and branches of tremendous old trees in the gales of winter, birdsong that filled the pre-dawn darkness even in the winter months, the sight of mist hanging heavy over the nearby fields and river-meadows, or the banks of the Thames lined not with barges and ferries, but with meadowgrass and wild flowers: all these things formed part of a brave new world for young Thomas. His uncle was no doubt well aware that he would need himself to take extra care in order to make the boy feel at home in this comparatively strange environment. The 'prodigious pains' that Walpole later recalled Robert Antrobus as having exerted on his nephew's behalf in academic matters would surely have extended beyond the bounds of the class-room, and into the delicate arena of young Thomas's emotional and psychological health.

Fortunately for his new pupil, Robert Antrobus, much like his sisters, appears by all accounts to have been a kind, self-sacrificing, and gentle individual. Both his comfortable if possibly Spartan academic home and his generous personality could only have been regarded as a welcome alternative to his eight-year-old nephew. Although he may have been upset at the thought of leaving his mother behind in London, Gray found waiting for him at Eton the next best thing to her affection and caresses – the heartfelt protection and guardianship of an uncle who seems happily to have resembled his younger sister in many significant ways. For the first time in his life Thomas could live without the daily unpre-dictability and fear that had so often reigned in the Cornhill household. For the first time in his life, too, he was to have the near countenance of a dignified and personally respectable male relative. His daily life in the classroom would be dominated by more masculine (or at least male) figures. Though the relationship between Gray and his uncle may have taken some time to develop, young Thomas could now at least begin to trust and to confide in an older man – a father-figure if not a father – who obviously cared for him deeply, and who seemed to have his own best interests at heart. One of Gray's early schoolbooks still in the pos-session of the Eton College Library is a copy of the small 'Delphin' edition of Juvenal and Persius, on which is written the poet's name. The volume also carries a plate with the name 'R. A. Worsop, Esq.' engraved on it; beneath the plate are inscribed the words 'To his godson, Thomas Gray, as a token of his regards'. Nothing more is known about this individual, but the likelihood that Gray further enjoyed the protection of a god-father in his earliest days at Eton adds yet another male figure to the group of Antrobus relatives who had together joined forces to shield him from the domestic situation in Cornhill.

*

By the time Gray was first sent to Eton in 1725, the college had already distinguished itself as one of the finest grammar schools in the country. John Macky, a flamboyant government agent whose *Journey Through England* had been published just two years before Gray's name first appears on the college lists, noted that by the 1720s Eton had already achieved the reputation of being 'esteemed the first School in England'.[2] By mid-century, Eton, its preeminence in both social and academic matters assured, could legitimately claim to have overtaken Winchester as the leading school in the land. Many of the young scholars first educated at Eton would, as adults, eventually move into positions of power and influence at other schools, such as Harrow and Rugby. As schoolmasters themselves, they would often take care to spread the particularly 'Etonian' methods of learning and education first instilled in them in the school elsewhere.

In the years surrounding Gray's arrival at the school, Eton had even been improving physically. Admittedly, certain aspects of college life remained bleak. The school's central courtyard had been paved only in 1706–7. The Chapel was cold and, in those days, remarkably unornamented; William Baker's wall paintings – depicting scenes from the New Testament and the lives of the patriarchs, and paid for by Bishop Wayneflete – had been covered from view by seventeenth-century Reformers, and were not to see the light of day until the 1920s. The dining hall, too, was yet to be enlivened by any stained-glass windows or oil portraits; even the original fireplaces had been obscured by the 'restoration' of the structure which had been undertaken in 1721. The Lower School, however, where Gray would have spent his earliest years at Eton, remains today very much as it would have looked in the 1720s. The original Eton schoolroom, Lower School was built by 1500, and has been in continuous use as a classroom ever since. The students of three forms huddled together on graffitied, oak benches in the low-ceilinged chamber, facing each other over angled desks across a bare, central aisle, and separated by a double row of wooden pillars (according to an unsubstantiated school legend, the wood for these pillars had been presented to the school by Queen Elizabeth herself, and had been taken from one of the vessels of the Spanish Armada). The room would have been heated in the early eighteenth century only by a single, central brazier, the heat from which could not have travelled very far from its source. Under the headmastership of John Newborough in the late seventeenth century, the poorly constructed Upper School building originally erected by the Provost Robert Allestree (at his own expense) only a few decades earlier had been pulled down. A new Upper School building, the design of which has been credited by tradition to Christopher Wren, opened its doors

---

[2]   John Macky, *Journey Through England* in *Familiar Letters from a Gentleman Here, to His Friend Abroad*, 2 vols. (London, 1722) 49.

in 1694. The rebuilt structure, which remains standing to this day, again connected the ante-Chapel, to the south, with the tower at the end of the Long Chamber, to the north, thus completing the west side of the quadrangle and presenting a noble and elegant main entrance on the highroad to the central School Yard. At about the same time that Gray first arrived at Eton, the Provost Sidney Godolphin (brother to the Minister) also constructed a library on the south side of the cloister. Godolphin re-roofed and redecorated the college Chapel ('beautifying and enlarging the choir of it', as the public appeal of subscriptions noted, 'so that all the children of the school might appear under one view').[3] He also facilitated the erection of Francis Bird's famous statue of Henry VI that still stands in the centre of the School Yard quadrangle.

Throughout his years at Eton, Gray was to be surrounded by the children of wealthier families and the scions of aristocratic birth who would later in life achieve the highest positions of political power. The future statesman and orator William Pitt, who was to leave for Oxford in 1726, was still a member of the Sixth Form when Gray was enrolled in the school (Pitt would as an adult hold the system of English public schools in great disdain, declaring famously that boys were cowed for life at Eton; his own son William was educated by Pitt himself and by private tutors at home, and was later ridiculed by his political enemies for having been 'taught by his dad on a stool').[4] Two more future Prime Ministers, John Stuart (who had succeeded his father as third Earl of Bute in 1723) and George Grenville, were also at Eton at the same time as Gray. Likewise, the future Lord Chancellors Henry Bathurst and Charles Pratt (later first Baron Camden), Frederick Cornwallis (the future Archbishop of Canterbury), and John Manners (later Marquis of Granby and Commander-in-Chief of British forces against the French) were among Gray's earliest schoolfellows. John Montagu, who was to become fourth Earl of Sandwich and, by mid-century, First Lord of the Treasury and a principal Secretary of State, was likewise a contemporary, though one for whom Gray had no great affection. Gray was much later in life to satirize Montagu as 'sly Jemmy Twitcher' in his poem *The Candidate*. Gray seems in fact with some few important exceptions to have kept his distance from most of the other members of the school and from their activities. Soon after leaving Eton, he would write cryptically to a former schoolmate of 'my Lords * * * and * * *' [referring probably to Lords Halifax and Sandwich], asking 'Do you not remember them dirty boys playing at Cricket?'. Even so, although the

[3]   Christopher Hollis, *Eton* (London: Hollis & Carter, 1960) 122.
[4]   See Derek Jarrett, *Pitt the Younger* (London: Weidenfeld and Nicolson, 1944) 21.

humour and incongruity of watching his former rude and sometimes grubby schoolmates rise to positions of influence and political power would never be lost on Gray, neither he nor his family could have been blind to the fact that his place at Eton gave him an enormous social and intellectual advantage over the sons of other London merchants. The family connections of Eton's other students, much like the physical location of the school itself, within the shadow of Windsor's majestic Round Tower, were themselves a mark of social prestige – an indication of the institution's proximity to power.

The Headmaster in charge of the entire school at the time of Gray's arrival in late 1725 was Dr. Henry Bland. True to his name, Bland proved himself to be a dull if carefully chosen Whig successor to his controversial Tory predecessor, Dr. Snape. Despite a minor student uprising in 1727, Bland managed to increase enrollment and keep the school relatively prosperous. Gray's fellow Etonian William Cole commented that the school 'was never known to be in a more flourishing and thriving condition than under his [Bland's] management'.[5] Under Bland's administration the total number of boys in the school rose to about four hundred (individual classes could number as many as one hundred boys). Bland nevertheless had his critics. The antiquary Thomas Hearne grumbled that while the headmaster was said to be 'an industrious man in the school', he yet lacked the basic ability to express himself 'clearly and intelligently' in Latin.[6]

Bland was succeeded as headmaster in 1728 by his son-in-law, William George. Although George was an able classical scholar, he lacked the administrative skills necessary to run the school efficiently, and was soon known among the boys as 'Dionysus the Tyrant' (after the infamous, fourth-century BC ruler of Syracuse, Dionysus II). If he had been grudgingly critical of George's predecessor, Hearne had some even harsher words for the new headmaster, dismissing him contemptuously as 'a little poor despicable man'. The mid-century Lord Chancellor Camden, Charles Pratt, similarly described George as pedantic and ill-suited to his position:

He undertook the care of that School without parts, of the kind I mean that was necessary to govern it. This brought him under difficulties from which he had not either sense or spirit enough to extricate himself. These plagues and vexations wrought upon his temper and made him sour. His absurdity, the gift of Nature, still remained; and by working upon a mind

---

[5] Hollis, *Eton*, 126.
[6] See Leonard Whibley, 'Thomas Gray at Eton' in *Blackwood's Magazine* (May 1929) ccxxv, 615.

crossed by ill-success, made him not only foolish but proud, illmannerly and brutal.[7]

In 1729, the students at Eton responded to George's ineptitude by staging a disruptive rebellion unprecedented in the college's history. Their rioting left 'the whole government of the school' as the Earl of Bristol described the student revolt to his wife, in a 'state of anarchy'.[8]

The end result of George's tenure as headmaster was a reduction in the number of students from about 380 to just over 200; even by the time of his departure in 1743 enrollment was not to rise above 265. While there is no information as to precisely how Gray himself behaved during the disturbances (as Robert Antrobus's nephew he clearly would not have taken any active part in what was soon being referred to as 'the Schollar's rebellion at Eaton'), the wholesale expulsion of some of the school's rowdier, insolent, or anarchic element was in the long run probably beneficial to his education. Class sizes were reduced to more manageable levels, and the Lower Masters (or Ushers) and Assistants could devote more time to tutoring those individual students who were actually interested in their studies, or interested in the very least – as we might still put it today – in 'making something' of themselves.

The institutional structure of the school and the college curriculum in Gray's day was memorably described by Daniel Defoe in his *Tour Through the Whole Island of Great Britain* (1724–26). 'The school is divided', Defoe discovered on his *Tour*:

> into the upper and lower, and each into three classes. Each school has one master, and each master four assistants, or ushers. None are received into the upper school 'till they can make Latin verse, and have a tolerable knowledge of the Greek. In the lower school, the children are received very young, and are initiated into all school-learning. Besides the seventy scholars upon the foundation, there are always abundance of children, generally speaking, of the best families, and of persons of distinction, who are boarded in the houses of the masters, and within the college.[9]

It was to this second group of students, known as Oppidans (those boys who were not 'on the foundation', i.e. had not been elected to a scholarship) that Gray belonged. Defoe's only significant misapprehension in his description of the school seems to be his assertion that all Oppidans lived either within the school itself or with Masters. Most Oppidans, as

---

[7]   Pratt's remarks are reprinted in Hollis, *Eton*, 129.
[8]   Hollis, *Eton*, 130.
[9]   Daniel Defoe, *A Tour Through the Whole Island of Great Britain*, ed. Pat Rogers (Harmondsworth, 1971) 284–285.

the name itself suggests, lodged within the town (L. *oppidum*) with women who were known as boarding dames. The practice of boarding the boys out with dames (or dominies, as their male counterparts were called) dated from the school's earliest history; many of the boarding dame and dominies of Gray's era were probably relations of the head-master and his assistants, or were otherwise connected in some way with the college staff.

When Gray first entered Eton, the Oppidans, as opposed to Collegers, numbered just over three hundred. Collegers were considered by some to be rougher and less responsive to the threat of discipline than Oppidans. Hoping eventually to benefit from any vacancies that might occur at King's College (the benefactor's Cambridge foundation), members of the former group tended to stay on longer at the school than the Oppidans. The daily life of Oppidans too, however rough or rowdy they might have seemed to outsiders, could also be made tiresome and difficult. As a group, and thanks in part to their longer tenure at the school, the Collegers were in fact usually older and taller than their fee-paying counterparts, and they seem often to have subjected those smaller than themselves to an unpredictable tyranny. Collegers, however, had no relief from the confinement of the school and its concomitant hardships. When Gray's friend Thomas Wharton wrote to the poet in 1761 regarding his young nephew Robert, asking the poet's opinion as to whether the boy should be sent to school as a Colleger or an Oppidan, Gray advised him to send the child to the school as a member of the latter group. 'My notion is', he wrote,

> that your Nephew being an only Son, & rather of a delicate constitution, ought not to be exposed to the hardships of the College. I know, that the expense in that way is much lessen'd; but your Brother has but one Son, & can afford to breed him an Oppidant. I know, that a Colleger is sooner form'd to scuffle in the world, that is, by drubbing & tyranny is made more hardy or more cunning, but these in my eyes are no such desirable acquisitions. (*CTG* 741)

In the early and middle part of the century reasonably well-to-do parents could expect to spend as much as £60 a year on their sons' educations (the novelist Henry Fielding is thought to have cost his father roughly that amount for each year he was an Oppidan at the school). A surviving school bill dating from 1719 for Oppidan William Pitt amounted to £29 0s. 3d. for half a year. The bill includes expenditures for tuition, board, books, and various articles of clothing (Eton boys had not yet adopted their now-famous uniform attire of white collars and short coats, and parents were left to clothe their children as they saw fit). A half-yearly bill dating from 1726 for the child of a less wealthy family, Walter Gough, who boarded in town, amounted to £22 5s. 4d. Of that amount, two guineas were set aside to go to Dr. Bland 'for half-a-year's tutoring'; separate charges were listed for servants, 'fire in his chambers' and candles, as well as a spending allowance of one shilling per week. Masters and instructors typically received separate payment. A fee of £2 2s. each was due to the headmaster and to the lower master on entry, for example, while individual tutors stood to receive as much as £4–5 each half-year. If in his earliest years at Eton Gray was indeed boarding with his uncle (and depending on the remuneration accepted by Robert to house his nephew), Gray's bills may have totaled as little as £15–£20 per term, or £30 or £40 a year.

*

When Gray's name first appears in the School Lists in 1725, he is placed at the lower end of the Second Form – 41st on a list of 44 boys. Beneath him stood the First Form and what was known as the 'Bible Seat', in which the very youngest boys at the college were taught to read. In the lists for November 1728, he is advanced to the Third Form, where he is again posted toward the end of a list that now totals 91 students. In the next year he moved on to the Upper School, and by December 1732 – at fifteen years of age – he had passed through the Fourth Form and the Remove (an interpolated Form, at other schools sometimes called the 'Shell'), and had reached the Fifth Form. He probably passed his last year in the school (1733–34) as a member of the Sixth Form.

The Eton curriculum in Gray's day, again, consisted almost entirely of Greek and Latin. In the Lower School the boys were drilled in Latin Grammar. By the Third Form they were expected to be able to translate, parse, memorize, and compose Latin verse. Early texts would have included William Lily and John Colet's *A Short Introduction to Grammar* (often referred to simply as the *Eton Latin Grammar* and, quite appropriately, the topographically specific source of Shakespeare's parody of 'some questions [of] accidence' in *The Merry Wives of Windsor*). Students also read the Latin Testament, the *Commentaries* of Julius Caesar, and the fables of Phaedrus. The students would then begin studying the fundamentals of Greek, using as their primary text William Camden's famous *Grammar*. In the Upper School emphasis was placed on the translation, memorization, and repetition of both Greek and Latin verse (perhaps amounting to over one hundred lines each week). Gray's own, few surviving efforts from this period demonstrate that the students were also expected to be able to translate Latin into English verse and English, in turn, into Latin. Scholars leaving Eton for Cambridge would be well acquainted with (at least) the selections in the *Poetae Graeci*, Homer, Lucian, Virgil, Ovid, Horace, and Terence. Horace Walpole later in life half-jokingly complained about the manner in which he had been made to learn Latin at Eton, voicing particular resentment that the students were never allowed to 'become acquainted with the names of the commonest things, too undignified to be admitted into verse'.[10] A fellow student and friend of Walpole's, William Cole, observed in much the same manner observed that Eton's pedagogical methods seemed impractically to consist of 'teaching boys to make Latin verses and get <by rote 600> verses of Homer and Virgil even when they have no taste for them'.[11] For all such complaints, the Eton curriculum, with its heavy emphasis on verse and almost complete neglect of the classical prose writers, remained for many years widely influential and, as already noted, served as a model for other English grammar schools. Some geography, mathematics, and algebra were also taught, though not much. Wealthier students were often attended by private tutors, and further instruction in 'Extras' or accomplishments that lay beyond the bounds of the normal school curriculum (such as drawing, dancing, fencing, and boxing) could be had for an additional fee. Gray himself, for example, would appear to have left Eton a fluent reader (if not speaker) of French.

Some aspects of daily life in the public school seem to have changed little since Gray was a student. In addition to having to endure the casual and erratic tyranny of upperclassmen, newly enrolled students at Eton (and we should keep in mind that it was not all that unusual for boys to be admitted to the school at an even younger age than the eight-year-old Thomas) often suffered through the perennial heartache of homesickness. Contact with or packages from parents, family, and friends proved often to be a mixed blessing. The reminder (or in some cases the revelation) that the life one seemed to have left behind at the school gates continued on at a distressingly complacent diurnal pace – that even one's mother, father, sisters, and brothers could and did pursue their own lives separate and apart from one's self – was for many students, to say the least, an unwelcome one. That the world would, perforce, keep on turning was one thing; that one's own parents could even contemplate going about their social and domestic business as usual was quite another. The slightest contact with home could conjure not only absent individuals, but also (and, oddly, often more hauntingly) absent things and places – rooms left untenanted and playthings lying untouched, pets disconsolate and unattended, familiar views and vistas, even, stretching in vain toward a distance with no one to appreciate them or even to take comfort and solace in their familiarity. The fundamental yet at the same

[10]   WC xxviii.160.
[11]   WC ii.214–15.

time profound realization that there exists in this life a seemingly dispassionate synchronicity – that the world outside of one's own perceptions, sensations, and feelings has a relentless life of its own – is itself
one of the minor revelations of the young child at school. The psychic
rite of passage that draws the individual first from the trauma of simply
missing one's home and family, through the sense of betrayal and self-
pity accompanying the realization that life and lives will go on without
him, toward, finally, the maturity of acceptance and the attempt to craft
a life of the self, can be a harrowing journey. Students such as Gray and
Horace Walpole, both of whom had formed close attachments to their
mothers, might also find themselves in the doubly bewildering predicament of both missing their absent parent, while at the same time being
mocked or made fun of by their new schoolmates. Not only were they
made to feel the pain of what must have seemed to be some puzzling
form of rejection by mothers who had, until then, loved them uncondi-
tionally, but the only individuals to whom they could now turn for
support – their new 'friends' and daily companions – would probably
heap ridicule on them for being too closely bound by their parents'
apron-strings. What had till then seemed the healthiest and most natural
of attachments was transformed – within days or even hours, it must
have seemed – into a shameful and embarrassing dependency. The loneliness and sense of loss consequent on this inexplicable transformation
could easily be experienced as a personal trauma approaching the pain
of bereavement.

The comforting presence of Gray's uncle Robert surely helped him
through the emotional darkness of those earliest days and weeks at Eton.
That his friend-to-be Horace Walpole found the transition from home
life to school life to be an unsettling one can be seen in the few letters
to his own mother that survive from the period. Even after he had
spent five years at the school, Walpole would still write to his 'dear
Mama' at the family's London home with the aching affection and
heart-sickness of a new arrival. Lady Walpole, like anxious and over-
protective mothers before and since, would quickly respond in kind.
Having complained of a slight cold and fever shortly after his sixteenth
birthday in September 1733, for instance, young Horace promptly
received what today's boarding-school students would have little trouble
recognizing as an eighteenth-century version of the 'care package' from
home. Responding to Horace's complaints of the 'heats', Lady Walpole
not only quickly dispatched some hand-mixed 'physic' as medicine for
him, but also sent a box containing some new 'breeches' to keep him
warm as the last of the summer weather gave way to the chill nights of
autumn. Having addressed some queries concerning his friend and
cousin Henry Seymour Conway, who was then also at the school,

Walpole feelingly noted that such questions from his mother were almost unnecessary. 'My sentiments always sympathize so exactly with my dear Mama's', he concluded, 'that I don't doubt you can read in your own heart how much I long to be with you'.[12] There is more than a touch of precocious gallantry in Walpole's language here, just as there is a healthy resistance in his next letter home against the maternal insistence that he still – 'since my dear Mama desires it' – take daily doses of his medicine despite the fact that he no longer feels ill. In letters such as these, we see Walpole before our very eyes negotiating the divide between a proper love and respect for his parent, and a desired independence of thought and action – between submission to parental authority on the one hand, and the persistent note of rebellion (however reluctant) sounded in the struggle for self-sufficiency and young adulthood, on the other.

Like Walpole, Gray must only slowly have groped his way down the awkward and often painful road that led through the undergrowth of early adolescence. There were times when, for all his father's threats and violence, and for all his uncle's corresponding, sympathetic support at Eton, he probably missed his home and his mother desperately. The demands of the classroom and the time spent on one's study and school-work of course helped to focus emotional energy and – quite simply – to pass the time. But what of the hours spent outside the classroom? The school's academic year was in Gray's day divided into three 'halves', and punctuated by holidays at Christmas, Easter, and in August. Regular school hours seem to have extended from eight to nine o'clock, from eleven to twelve, from three to four, and from five to six. The Christmas holidays typically began by the end of the second week of December and lasted a month; the Easter holidays might extend the length of a fortnight, from the Monday before Easter Sunday. Out of school, the boys could apparently go to bed at any hour they chose. There were in Gray's years at the school no organized games – no such thing as supervised team sports or intermural competitions of any kind. The boys were thus left to dispose of the substantial amount of free time granted to them pretty much as they pleased (though they were generally forbidden to go on the river). They were given one whole holiday (normally Tuesdays) and as many as two half holidays a week, in addition to Founder's day and other regularly scheduled college breaks. The most popular pastimes appear to have included Cricket, 'Fives', 'Battledores', hop-scotch, hoops, peg-in-the-ring, marbles, puss in the corner, and football or 'Goals'.

Both Gray and his friend Walpole drew attention to themselves for their lack of interest in physical activities. 'Mr. Gray and his friend',

12 WC xxxvi.3–4.

Jacob Bryant would recall of the pair years after having left the school, 'were looked upon as too delicate, upon which account they had few associates and never engaged in any exercise nor partook of any boyish amusement. Hence they seldom were in the fields, at least they only took a distant view of those who pursued their distant diversions'.[13] Walpole would later recall with no small amount of pride that he had never taken part in the cruder physical activities – 'an expedition against bargemen, a match at cricket' – to the detriment of his reading and romantic temperament.[14] 'I can remember with no small satisfaction' he wrote to his former schoolmate Charles Lyttelton not very long after leaving the school, 'that we did not pass our time in gloriously beating great clowns, who would particularly bear children's thumps for the collections [i.e. payment], which I think some of our cotemporaries [sic] were so wise as to make for them afterwards'.[15]

It is all too likely, however, that a substantial number of school boys did indeed spend their free time 'thumping' local labourers and peasants, and wasting long hours in the nearby ale and coffee houses, or at the local pastry-cook's shop. Pony races, cock-fighting, and bull fights were possible entertainments, and even the most ritualized pastimes could quickly transform themselves into remarkably brutal spectacles. A ram hunt, in which a hamstrung ram was ritually beaten to death next to the school in Weston's Yard, was finally deemed so barbarous that it was banned by the school by mid-century. Even casual playfulness was liable to get out of hand. The church yard inscription on one Edward Cochran's grave dated 1730 noted that he was 'accidentally' stabbed by one of his fellows. The Parish Register recorded more simply and bluntly that he was 'murdered by his schoolfellow, Thomas Dalton, with a penknife'.

II. The Quadruple Alliance

What was Thomas Gray like when he was a student at Eton? Whatever letters Gray wrote to his mother (or, for that matter, to his father) from the college were unfortunately burned by Mason shortly after his death. Jacob Bryant, who recorded his personal reminiscences of Gray nearly seventy years after he had himself first entered Eton, provides us with one small but vivid anecdotal picture of the young poet in 1729, dressed

[13]   Jacob Bryant, 'Letter from Jacob Bryant, Containing Particulars of the Poet Gray' in the *Gentleman's Magazine* (February 1846) i.141.
[14]   WC ix.93.
[15]   WC xl.2.

in mourning for his uncle Robert. 'I remember', Bryant wrote of Gray, 'he made an elegant little figure in his sable dress, for he had a very good complexion and fine hair, and appeared to much advantage among the boys who were near him in the school, and who were more rough and rude'.[16]

Bryant's anecdotal recollection of Gray – a memory that provides us with our earliest image of what the poet looked like, physically, as a boy – is almost too neat to be true. Bryant's memory is itself a retrospective 'portrait of the elegist as a young man'. It seems rather too appropriate, for instance, that the child who, as an adult, would write the *Eton Ode* and the *Elegy*, should be glimpsed by history for the first time dressed in the heavy sable of mourning, and that he should likewise be set apart from his schoolfellows by a dreamy delicacy of face and feature that seemed to transcend the coarser realities of the Eton schoolyard. Yet a surviving portrait of Gray, perhaps painted by the well-known artist Arthur Pond (who also painted contemporary celebrities such as Alexander Pope and the celebrated comic actress Peg Woffington) when Gray was perhaps 13 or 14 years old, would seem to confirm much of Bryant's recollection of the young Gray's tidy elegance and gentle dignity. The painting, a full-length portrait that would almost certainly have been commissioned by the poet's mother, shows Gray seated cross-legged next to a table on which are placed a pen and standish, and several books appropriate to the aspiring scholar – volumes written by the famous classicist and patron, William Temple and, even more significantly, the work of John Locke. Locke's *Essay Concerning Human Understanding*, we remember, was to leave its determining mark on almost all of Gray's mature poetry (students entering the English universities were often advised to familiarize themselves with Locke's work by the end of their second year of study; Gray was clearly thought to be well ahead of his contemporaries when it came to an appreciation of the range and extent of 'human understanding'). His left hand rests lightly on one knee; in his right he casually holds another small volume. He is richly dressed in an embossed blue coat with a peach-coloured silk lining, waistcoat, velvet breaches, white silk stockings, and slim, elegant leather slippers. His slender figure is topped by a slightly oversized head, but Pond – if the work is indeed his – seems accurately to have captured the 'fine hair' and 'good complexion' described so many years later by Bryant. Subsequent portraits of Gray reveal the painter adeptly to have copied the poet's general physiognomy. We see here the same soft, expressive eyes, the same long nose and thin but slightly smiling lips – the same air of quiet but not quite arrogant

---

[16]   Bryant, 141.

dignity and superiority – found in later portraits of the poet by John G. Eccardt and Benjamin Wilson.

Although the conventions of children's portraiture in England were to change rather dramatically in the course of the eighteenth century, it was not uncommon for an artist early in the period to attempt to capture the 'moment' of childhood, such as it was, when painting a young subject for his or her parents and relatives. The refined and at times dreamy elegance of artists such as Thomas Gainsborough or Thomas Lawrence lay still in the future, yet young subjects were often presented in portraits cradling a favourite toy in a nursery, or standing among favoured objects of amusement, or perhaps even teaching a pet a new trick. The children depicted in such portraits may, to some extent, still look in the eyes of a modern viewer like stunted or oddly proportioned, miniature adults; yet one of the reasons for having children painted at such an early age was precisely to offer an eighteenth-century version of a photographic 'snapshot' of their youth or pre-adolescence. The clothing in such depictions was frequently the attire of the nursery, and poses and attitudes were often designedly 'artless' and unknowing. The portrait of Gray, however, appears to be of quite another sort, and seems to reflect quite another agenda. Whoever commissioned the portrait seems almost to have been willing its subject into his destiny. Gray is dressed as an adult, and his attributes are those of a learned and academic career. The portrait superimposes over the *tabula rasa* of Gray's budding identity in actual time a visualization of what this young man is capable of (hence the particularly appropriate inclusion in the painting of Locke's volume); it offers a prophecy of the kind of civilized, professional identity that awaits him should he choose to strive towards it. Dorothy Gray was obviously very proud of the young student, and the portrait, which probably first hung in the Cornhill home, served to remind her on a daily basis that her son was now safely removed from a dreadful home environment and fixed already in a protected world, the delicacy and high aspirations of which defied her husband's ever-increasing brutality.

Bryant's reminiscences underscore the observation that Gray and his few select friends clearly saw themselves as distinct and set themselves apart from the more 'rough and rude' Collegers by whom they were surrounded. Writing of Gray and Walpole, Bryant observed, 'some . . . who were severe, treated them as feminine characters, on account of their too great delicacy, and sometimes a too fastidious behaviour'.[17] The time that Gray might have spent in physical activity on the playing fields was spent instead cultivating a friendship with three schoolfellows close to him in age and even closer in temperament. The tightly knit group –

[17]   Bryant, 140.

consisting of Gray, Thomas Ashton, Richard West, and Horace Walpole
– dubbed themselves the Quadruple Alliance; their juvenile friendship
and society was to have consequences reaching far beyond their years
at Eton. The members of the Quadruple Alliance were bound together
by similar characters and interests. All were, if not the best of scholars,
at least academically inclined. They were likewise, with the possible
exception of Ashton, 'delicate' (as Bryant put it) or less physically robust
and athletic than most of their schoolfellows. They shared a penchant
for the romantic and, rather than rough-housing with the other students,
preferred to spend their leisure hours reading (they seem particularly to
have devoured the expansive French romances of the late seventeenth
and early eighteenth centuries), and re-imagining their potentially
mundane surroundings transformed into the landscapes of fantasy and
enchantment. 'Were not the playing fields at Eton' Walpole would ask
a friend not very long after having left the school for Cambridge,

> food for all manner of flights? No old maid's gown, though it had been
> tormented into all the fashions from King James to King George, ever
> underwent so many transformations, as those poor plains have in my
> idea. At first I was contented with tending a visionary flock, and sighing
> some pastoral name to the echo of the cascade under the bridge. How
> happy should I have been to have had a kingdom, only for the pleasure
> of being driven from it, and living disguised in a humble vale! As I got
> further into Virgil and Clelia, I found myself transported from Arcadia
> to the gardens of Italy; and I saw Windsor Castle in no other view than
> the *Capitoli immobile saxum* . . . I can't say that I am sorry I was never
> quite a schoolboy: . . . The beginning of my Roman history was spent in
> the Asylum, or conversing in Egeria's hallowed grove; not in thumping
> and pummeling King Amulius's herdsmen. (*WC* ix.3–4)

The easy elision in Walpole's recollection of classical and Romantic
texts (one 'got into' Virgil's *Aeneid*, it would appear, just as easily and
enjoyably as one 'got into' Madam de Scudéry's *Clelia*) reveals
something of the fluidity with which the members of the Alliance moved
between the assigned and required readings of their education, and
those works which they pursued merely through their love of narrative
excess and penchant for the exotic. The nicknames by which the
members of this select society would even later in life address each
other emphasized their commitment to the liberating alternatives of the
world of the romance and of the pastoral idyll. Ashton, for example,
was 'Almanzor', a name taken from John Dryden's vaguely oriental
The Conquest of Granada. West was naturally 'Favonius' or 'Zephyrus',
a reference to the gentle west wind. Walpole was distinguished among
the friends as 'Celadon', the name of a lovesick shepherd Honoré

d'Urfey's pastoral romance *Astrée*, and subsequently of a virtuous swain in the 'Summer' portion of Thomson's *The Seasons*. Gray himself was dubbed 'Orosmades' – an anglicized version of the wise and beneficent Persian divinity Ormuzd or Ahura mazda, but a name also used in several other popular romance narratives and dramas, most notably Nathaniel Lee's 1677 blank verse tragedy *The Rival Queens*. In the second act of Lee's play, a soothsayer named Aristander tells the character of Alexander the Great of a prophecy received from the Zoroastrian god in 'Orosmades' cave'. Perhaps Gray, while playing with his little band of 'bold adventurers' in the fields near Windsor, had himself descried a particularly sheltered haunt or retreat easily invested with an aura of mystery and magic – an 'Orosmades' cave' of his own – by which he earned the name. Nothing would have been more likely than for this group of friends to have sought out and discovered a secret bower or nook that they could then designate as the topographical centre of their 'little reign' (an avenue of lime trees just beyond the Fellow's Pond and known as 'Poet's Walk' was likewise long connected by tradition with Gray). However Gray came by the name, the designation 'Orosmades' bespoke Gray's own innately gentle and – to his friends, at least – indulgent temperament. As David Cecil wrote, 'Walpole and West, Gray and Ashton saw themselves as Damon and Pythias, Orestes and Pylades, inheritors of the glorious tradition of antique comradeship, united to on another by a refined affinity of soul beyond the reach of commonplace pursuits'.[18]

*

Of the three other members of the Quadruple Alliance at Eton, 'Almanzor' or Thomas Ashton was to play the least prominent role in Gray's subsequent life. Described by Gray just a year after having left the school as a 'long ungainly mortal' (an emphatically physical description reinforced by William Cole's later characterization of him as 'a large raw-boned man'), Ashton – born in 1716 – was slightly older than both Gray and West; Walpole, born in 1717, was the youngest member of the foursome. The son of a Lancaster schoolmaster, Ashton entered Eton some time shortly after Gray. Eliot Warburton would record that Ashton's father 'had for fifty years been usher to a grammar school at Lancaster, with a salary of only 32 l. per annum; but having received a small estate with his wife, he sold it for the purpose of providing his children with an efficient education'.[19] Both Thomas and his younger

---

[18]   Cecil, 92–93.
[19]   Eliot Warburton, *Memoirs of Horace Walpole and His Contemporaries* (London: 1851) i.76.

brother John would be sent to Eton and Cambridge. As a student Ashton appears to have been focused and scholarly, but whatever qualities of personality and imagination he possessed as a young man were unfortunately obscured by his behavior towards both Gray and Walpole later in life. Walpole, who throughout the 1730s and 1740s would use his own position to advance Ashton's career within the church, was finally to wash his hands of the friendship in 1750, at which point he went so far as to forbid Ashton entry into his house. Gray's friendship with Ashton would similarly cool following (and even, one suspects, during) their early years together at Cambridge. Gray was at least capable of corresponding 'civilly' with him concerning practical matters later in life. Ashton, as we shall see, appears to have played an important if not instigating role in the quarrel that was to disrupt the friendship between Gray and Walpole in 1741. As an adult Ashton was to enjoy a considerable income from a number of fellowships and church livings, and became, in Warburton's words, 'one of the most popular of the metropolitan preachers', numbering among his many audiences the governors of Middlesex hospital in St. Anne's, Westminster, participants in the commencement ceremonies at Cambridge, and the members of the House of Commons.[20]

Richard West or 'Favonius' was considered by many to be the most promising poet of all the members of the Quadruple Alliance. While yet a student at Eton, West had been famous, both Gray himself and Jacob Bryant would later recall, for 'versifying' in his sleep ('I remember' Bryant wrote, 'some who were of the same house mentioning that he often composed in his dormant state, and that he wrote down in the morning what he had conceived in the night').[21] The somnolent poet who 'writes' or otherwise devises poetry effortlessly and even without realizing what he is doing was already a familiar figure to many readers of classical verse; it was a trope that would in time become part of the traditions of English poetry as well (the modern reader might recall Pope's protestation in his *Epistle to Dr. Arbuthnot* that even as an infant he 'lisp'd in Numbers, for the Numbers came'). It remains worth keeping in mind, however, that even as a very young man West was considered by many of his peers to have been *poeta nascitur*.

Described by Cole as 'tall and slim, of a pale and meager look of complexion . . . [that] promised not half of what he performed', West remained in precariously ill health throughout much of his short life.[22] He was the only surviving son of Richard West, an eminent London

---

[20]   Warburton, i.77.
[21]   Bryant, 141.
[22]   See *CTG* 28n.

lawyer and playwright who had in May 1725 been appointed Lord
Chancellor of Ireland. His mother, Elizabeth, was the second daughter
of the outspoken Bishop Burnet. West's parents had married in
April 1714. Following the sudden death of the elder Richard West in
December 1726, Elizabeth's conduct came under close public scrutiny.
She was widely suspected to have poisoned her husband, and it was
further rumored that she had been assisted in the project by her
husband's private secretary, John Williams. It was about the time of his
father's death that the young Richard West would first have been sent
to Eton, and the personal and financial shadows that hung over his
arrival and early years at the college must have made his years at the
school even less comfortable than they appear to have been either for
Gray or, certainly, for Walpole. Many years after West's death, Gray
would note that his friend's constant ill heath was exacerbated and even
brought about by 'the fatal discovery which he made of the treachery of
a supposed friend, and the viciousness of a mother whom he tenderly
loved'. 'This man', Gray noted of Williams, 'under the mask of friendship to [West] and his family, intrigued with his mother and robbed him
of his peace of mind, his health, and his life'. Unlike Ashton, whose character would only diminish in the eyes of his schoolfellows, West matured
in the years following his departure from Eton and his separation from
the other members of the Quadruple Alliance into an intelligent, sensitive, and winning if enervated young man. While the more spectacular
and worldly Walpole may have claimed Gray's earliest enthusiasms, the
poet's love and esteem for West was to deepen dramatically over the
years. Some recent scholars, most notably Robert Gleckner, have argued
that Gray's relationship with West, rather than his friendship with
Walpole (a connection the intensity of which Gleckner himself dismisses
only as 'something like "hero worship" on Gray's part'), formed the
central romantic attachment of the poet's life.[23]

Yet Horace Walpole would only naturally have been looked to as
the 'leader' and facilitator of this small band of like-minded friends –
he was the negotiating arbiter of their social and academic 'Alliance'.
The son of the most powerful man in England (Sir Robert Walpole's
reign as Prime Minister had only just begun when his youngest son
was first sent to Eton in 1725), Horace's appeal derived not merely
from his social preeminence. From the earliest age, he seems to have
evinced those qualities of easy charm, delicate grace, and natural self-
confidence that were to remain with him throughout his long life. To be
sure, the young Walpole did not look at all like his father's son. As a
child, he was thought to be weak and generally unhealthy, and he

[23]   Gleckner, 55.

claimed as an old man to have overheard, while still a very young child, darkly whispering adults doubt that he possessed the strength necessary even to survive infancy. Strikingly dissimilar to his father and his older brothers in looks, physique, and temperament, Horace, it would many years later be suspected, was thought by some to have been the illegitimate product of a romantic union between Lady Walpole and Carr, Lord Hervey (brother to Pope's famous 'Sporus'). Although such rumors did not circulate generally in Walpole's own lifetime, and although, as Brian Fothergill reminds us, he bore 'a very marked physical likeness to his half-sister, Lady Mary Churchill, a daughter of the Prime Minister by Maria Skerrett', it was known pretty generally by the time of Horatio's birth in 1717 that neither Catherine Walpole nor her husband any longer claimed any great affection for one another.[24] Maria or 'Moll' Skerrett had already been living openly as Sir Robert's mistress.

Though slightly more active and self-assured than the other members of the Alliance, Walpole was still considered by most of his peers to be, like Gray and West, small, frail, and 'delicate'. 'As a boy, as a youth, and as a man', Eliot Warburton would write in his two-volume *Memoir* of Walpole, 'his character bore but faint traces of masculine impress; owing, no doubt, to that motherly influence to which he often acknowledged his infinite obligations'.[25] Remembered as a youth likewise for his loud and unrestrained laugh, and for his refusal ever to cultivate 'a dignified public presence', Walpole was treated with greater deference than his friends and, aware of the power which attached itself to the simple conditions of his birth, could afford to be a little more stubborn and even insolent with his instructors. 'I remember when I was at Eton', he once wrote, 'and Mr. Bland [Rev. Henry Bland, Walpole's tutor and the son of the headmaster] had set me any extraordinary task, I used sometimes to pique myself on not getting it, because it was not immediately my school business: What, learn more than I am absolutely forced to learn! I felt the weight of learning that, for I was a blockhead, and pushed above my parts'.[26] Walpole, unlike Gray, West, or Ashton, actively cultivated friendships outside the Quadruple Alliance. One such group of friends, similarly dubbed the 'Triumvirate', consisted of Walpole, George Montagu, and Charles Lyttelton (later Bishop of Carlisle). Walpole's other close friends included William Cole, Henry Fiennes Clinton (9th Earl of Lincoln), George Selwyn, and – most significantly – his beloved cousin Henry Seymour Conway. Walpole

---

[24] Brian Fothergill, *The Strawberry Hill Set: Horace Walpole and his Circle* (London: Faber and Faber, 1983) 17.
[25] Warburton quoted in Fothergill, *The Strawberry Hill Set*, 18.
[26] WC xxxvii.161.

would make a point of maintaining close ties to almost all of his Eton acquaintances throughout his later life.

While the powerful combination of Walpole's social position and his confident, dynamic, and outgoing personality may thus have provided a primary focus for the other members of the Quadruple Alliance, we would be wrong to discount in their attractions for one another the fact that at least three of the group's members had come to the school from broken or unhappy home environments. There is little information concerning Ashton's early life, although his later reputation as a cold, dour, and bullying Fellow at Eton (and his seemingly deliberate attempts to make life for his students as miserable as possible), would appear to indicate a similarly unhappy and 'dysfunctional' background in his own childhood. Gray, as we have seen, was the lone, surviving product of a household tyrannized by an abusive husband and father. Walpole was the exceedingly late child – probably accidental, possibly illegitimate – of an equally loveless marriage. West, to add one grim and final turn of the screw, was the neglected son of a couple whose own lives would end shadowed by accusations of adultery and even murder. It is little wonder that three such boys found solace in one another's company. They were each of them juvenile survivors of some form of emotional trauma; they had all passed through childhood experiences which had taken a deep if silent toll on their respective senses of personal worth and self-esteem. They found in each other companions who sought similarly, to some degree, to escape the rhythms, the routines and – not at all surprisingly – the brutality of a harsh, masculine physical world, in favour of the transforming and infinitely transmutable environment of the feminine (at least as such a world might be represented by its manifestation in romance, in poetry, and in the drama). Gray was not attracted to Walpole simply, as earlier accounts of his life have tended to suggest, because the younger boy represented a social and aristocratic ideal; far more significantly, Gray was attracted to Walpole, just as Walpole was attracted to Gray, because each recognized in the other a mirror image of his own self – and of his own psychological history – only slightly altered. Each of the young boys who formed the Quadruple Alliance at Eton were creating a defensive structure – a treaty of like-minded souls who had undergone similarly painful experiences – against an aggressive outside world. The very name of their confederacy managed to evoke the sorts of political allegiances formed among governments represented by Walpole's own father, while at the same time playfully devaluating such treaties and turning the rigorous, impersonal agendas of those confederacies on their heads. The Quadruple Alliance which united Gray, Walpole, West, and Ashton, was emphatically *not* meant to be a hollow, public display – it was emphatically not to be a subtly rhetorical or temporary Machiavellian allegiance; it was, rather, a deeply felt alliance of the personal and of the poetic. In the very codification and naming of their friendship, Gray and his schoolmates deliberately appropriated an articulation from the world which had typically excluded them and, within the mode of an intimate and personal parody, naturalized it and made it their own.

III. The Shower of Language

Even as he escaped with 'Celadon', 'Favonius', and 'Almanzor' into a romantic world of their own devising, 'Orosmades' was encountering for the first time in the Eton classroom those same authors and poetic techniques that would forever place their stamp on the poetry of Thomas Gray. The emphasis resulting from the Etonian methods of pedagogy described briefly above – the concentration in the Eton classroom on memorization, for example, or the priority placed not only on the ability to translate Latin verse into English, but also and just as intuitively to turn English into Latin – were in time to exert a profound effect both on the style and on what might be called the internal or thematic coherence of Gray's poetry.

Writers on Gray have routinely looked to the *Ode on a Distant Prospect of Eton College* to provide first-hand information as to just how Gray felt about the years he spent at the school. The second verse stanza of the poem, in particular, has most often been quoted as straightforward evidence of Gray's attitude with regard to the time passed at Eton:

> Ah, happy hills, ah, pleasing shade,
> Ah, fields beloved in vain,
> Where once my careless childhood strayed,
> A stranger yet to pain!
> I feel the glades, that from ye blow,
> A momentary bliss bestow,
> As waving fresh their gladsome wing,
> My weary soul they seem to soothe,
> And, redolent of joy and youth,
> To breathe a second spring. (*PTG* 57)

'When he came to write the *Ode on a Distant Prospect of Eton College*', one modern biographer of Gray has written, 'it was through no haze of retrospective sentiment that he viewed those idyllic years. Even while they were passing he seems to have known instinctively that they were the golden period of his life; and afterwards their mere recollection could

refresh and console him'.[27] Another chronicler of Gray's life concludes
his account of the poet's years at Eton by quoting some lines from the
same verse stanza and observing simply that at Eton, 'he had been
happy'.[28]

Yet the *Eton Ode*, as critics like Gleckner have rightly made a point
of emphasizing, is no simple, autobiographical document. At the very
least, the historical Thomas Gray who 'strayed' in Eton's fields from
1725 to 1734 could never accurately have been described, even at that
time, as a 'stranger yet to pain'. When Gray came to write the *Eton Ode*
in the summer of 1742, the pressures and anxieties that would prompt
him to posit his earliest childhood years at Eton as a prelapsarian idyll
were necessarily far different from those feelings that may have characterized his actual time at the school. In the year previous to writing the
poem, as we shall see, Gray was to experience such traumatic events as
the lingering death of his father, and the sudden and largely unexpected
death of his dear friend West. He would also by that point in time have
lost his cherished friendship with Horace Walpole (apparently for good),
and would likewise have witnessed the fall of Walpole's father, Sir
Robert, from political power. All these events inform and influence the
Eton Ode, a poem that – far from being written in the frank and spontaneous language of autobiographical reminiscence – is highly artificial
and (as always with Gray's poetry) densely allusive. The *Eton Ode* is a
re-visioning – a reinterpretation, a poetic palimpsest – in which a
fictional, Etonian past is used as a foil against the overwhelming
cares and concerns of adulthood. The *Ode* is neither realistic, nor is it
accurately memorial. It is, rather, quite literally *nostalgic*, insofar as its
subject longs not only for the past, but for an absent home (the Greek
verb νοστέω or *nostéo* means 'to return' or 'go back to' one's own home
or country) that is now posited as having once existed *in* the past. Just
as the archetypal wanderer of epic poetry (and we might think here not
only of the Mediterranean heroes of classical mythology, but also of the
Wanderers and the Seafarers of the native Anglo-Saxon lyric tradition)
is tossed about on the sea of experience and constantly turned aside from
his tribal or domestic goal, so too the speaker in the *Eton Ode* seeks
some respite from the cares and afflictions of the world by looking once
again to return to a home now absent and unattainable – to a necessarily retrospective paradise forever lost to him. Gray even as a child
knew well enough that life within the college was less often one of 'gay
hope' and light-heartedness than, as he would later point out in the letter
to Wharton quoted earlier, one of 'drubbing and tyranny'.

[27] Ketton-Cremer, 8.
[28] Sells, 7.

Gray's meticulously constructed mystification and mythologization of an Eton youth untouched by the cares and trials of adulthood in the first half of the *Eton Ode* may well succeed as an evocation of a (supposedly) lovingly remembered and even idyllic childhood; Gray's poem as a whole, however, seeks to capture the relentless and inevitable human movement towards darkness, night, decay, and death – much the same movement simultaneously captured and (through the powers of poetry) resisted in the late *Elegy*. The daily sunshine of the breast and the languid movement of youth that is conveyed through the poem's early imagery of calm and gentle stasis, as the critic Pat Rogers has pointed out, gives way in time to the quick and erratic actions of maturity: snatching, seizing, tearing, gnawing.[29] The movement of the poem is a movement from languid happiness to tragic action, and the catalyst for such a change is the very *fact* of masculine maturity itself. The enemies that wait in prey for the children on the playing fields of Eton are enemies more insidious and more inevitable than any others precisely because they emerge from within; they are evils inherent even in the moments of 'fearful joy' which are snatched, retrospectively, out of the jaws of time and approaching maturity.

Rather than looking to the *Eton Ode* to provide any historically accurate account of the poet's years at the school, we stand to gain a better understanding of precisely how Gray responded to his environment in Windsor if we turn instead to those few pieces of his writing which themselves actually survive from the period. The college curriculum instilled in Gray certain ways of thinking about writing and poetry that were to influence his work for the rest of his life. If Gray failed to respond to or unconsciously repressed the stimuli of Cornhill and the city that might later have provided him with a rich and varied source of visual imagery for his mature poetry, the classical literature he first encountered as a young boy in the Eton classroom served as the formal, thematic, and stylistic models for nearly all his later work. Gray's reading outside the classroom provided him with a wealth of escapist narrative, and with a dramatic idiom that would vividly make itself felt in his letters to his friends. His reading while in the classroom worked more fundamentally to structure his attitude – his stance, perhaps, or what might even be described as the climate within which his inner spirit lived – in relation to the world at large, and to provide him with instructive models for imitation. The verses written by Gray while yet a student at Eton are admittedly school exercises which have survived to some degree only by

[29] Pat Rogers, *The Augustan Vision* (London: Methuen, 1974) 137.

chance, but even these short fragments evince certain themes, concerns, and methods of composition that were to resurface in Gray's poetry throughout his entire life.

*

Only four examples of Gray's Latin poetry and one English translation (from the first century Roman poet, Statius) dating from his time at Eton are still in existence. The first of the Latin pieces is in actual fact no more than a second-hand fragment recalled in later years by Jacob Bryant and preserved in Norton Nicholls's *Reminiscences* of Gray. Having been asked by Nicholls what sort of scholar Gray had been while a young student at Eton, Bryant, who in the College Lists was once listed as the next boy to Gray, recalled simply that he was 'a very good one'. Bryant added, however, that he could still remember part of an exercise of Gray's on the subject of 'the freezing & thawing of words', which he supposed had been based on a passage from Addison's popular periodical, *The Spectator*. Bryant then quoted Gray's lines from memory:

> . . . pluviaeque loquaces
> Descendere iugis, et garrulus ingruit imber. (*PTG* 285)

[. . . and the babbling rains came down from the hills, and the shower of language fell heavily.]

These lines, 'composed' by Gray probably while he was in the Fifth Form at Eton, were in reality based not, as Bryant later recalled, on a passage from *The Spectator*, but found their source rather on a memorable number of that periodical's predecessor, *The Tatler*. In *Tatler* Number 254 (an issue first printed on 23 November 1710) Richard Steele had offered his readers a passage from the improbable travels of Sir John Mandeville. In the excerpt Mandeville describes how, stranded on one occasion in the frigid latitudes of 'Nova Zembla' (the Arctic Ocean), he and his crew were perplexed to discover that their words appeared literally to freeze in the air before they could even reach the individual to whom they were spoken. Entire, articulated sentences hung like lines of stiff and frozen washing in the cold. When, upon a turning of the wind, the air began to thaw and the temperature began to rise, these supernaturally pendant syllables, words, and sentences tumbled from the air and crashed noisily to the ground. 'Our cabin', Steele reports Mandeville as having written, 'was immediately filled with a dry clattering sound, which I afterwards found to be the crackling of consonants that broke above our heads, and were often mixed with a gentle hissing, which I imputed to the letter s, that occurs so frequently in the English tongue'.[30]

The simple fact that Mandeville's fantastic account of the freezing and thawing of language should have provided the subject for this – Gray's earliest remembered school exercise and the earliest fragment of his poetry – is in its own small way pleasantly appropriate and even, should we chose to treat it as such, prophetic. The slight fragment stands as a suitable epigraph to Gray's entire poetic career. Throughout his life as a poet, Gray would typically take the language of classical antiquity – the language of poets such as Virgil, Ovid, and Horace – and breathe new life into that language by encoding it and rewriting it into his own work. The 'frozen' language of the classics would itself be 'thawed' and used to new effect in Gray's poetry. It is similarly appropriate that there is a pseudo-Virgilian allusiveness about even these slight and memorially reconstructed lines; Gray may have been recalling in the phrase 'garrulus ingruit imber', a phrase from *Aeneid* XII.284 ('ferreus ingruit imber') in the fragment's second line.

Like many English poets writing in the eighteenth century, Gray routinely enriched his own verse through classical reference and imitation. As the critic Eric Rothstein has observed, there were at least three common attitudes among poets of the period regarding such purposeful imitation and use of the past.[31] A poet might, to begin with, choose to refer to the classical text purely as a neutral model. Most of his (male) readers could be counted on to be intimately familiar with the work of authors such as Martial, Virgil, Ovid, Horace, and Juvenal. Consequently, when the modern poet chose to write a piece that imitated or reflected the work of those authors, the members of his audience would have known exactly what *kind* of poem they were about to read. The eighteenth-century reader who held in his hands a copy of James Thomson's *The Seasons*, for example, would have been aware that he was embarking upon a poem that consciously and conspicuously modeled itself on Virgil's *Georgics*. While the modern poet may not have possessed the stylistic resources (or the sheer, native talent) necessary fully to capture or to translate his classical model, the *substance* of that model could, nevertheless, designedly be reflected in his conscious and often precise 're-presentation'. In fact, the relationship between Virgil's original and Thomson's immensely popular imitation (which began

---

[30] *Tatler* No. 254 (23 November 1710) in *The Tatler*, ed. Donald F. Bond, 3 vols. (Oxford: Clarendon Press, 1987) iii.290.

[31] I rely in the discussion that follows on some of the distinctions outlined by Eric Rothstein in his excellent survey of poetic reference and allusion in the period, 'The Uses of the Past' in *Restoration and Eighteenth-Century Poetry, 1660–1780* (London, 1981) 84–118.

appearing in 1726) can serve us briefly here as a useful and necessary example of just how the interpretive dynamics of such a process of neutral reference or recollection generally worked. If we fail to grasp the centrality of this mode of reference throughout the period in which Gray was writing his poetry, we risk profoundly misunderstanding his work. Thomson's *The Seasons* was being well received by readers in precisely those years (1726–30) when Gray himself was studying the art and techniques of classical poetry at Eton. Gray much later in life confessed to Nicholls that he considered Thomson to have possessed a talent 'beyond all other poets' in describing 'the various appearances of nature'. The genuine delight that *The Seasons* takes in the reassuring and recurring patterns of the natural world likewise makes it a particularly appropriate text to examine as we prepare to turn our attention to Gray's own mature poetry – a poetry that will itself help to redefine the relationship between the lyric voice and external nature in the latter half of the eighteenth century. Finally, Thomson was no less influenced than Gray was himself to be by the epistemology of John Locke; both men were to be continually fascinated in their poetic careers by Locke's presentation of (in Thomson's words) 'the mind, / The varied scene of quick-compounded thought, / And where the mixing passions endless shift.'[32]

Virgil's original poem opens with a dedication to the great Roman patron of poetry, Gaius Cilnius Maecenas; each of the *Georgics* four, short books deal with such seemingly straightforward matters as planting and husbandry. The first book of Virgil's poem tells how fields are ploughed. The second methodically outlines the proper manner of planting and tending the soil. Virgil's third book tells the reader how best to manage cattle, and then describes the effects of a devastating cattle-plague. The fourth and final book of the *Georgics*, which includes a moving retelling of the story of Orpheus and Eurydice, describes the proper methods of bee-keeping among the Romans. The patient and loving surface of Virgil's seemingly straightforward and uncompromisingly didactic agricultural poem, however, masks deeply felt personal, political, and even religious messages.

Throughout the four books of the *Georgics*, Virgil emphasizes the notion that there exists between man and nature an intrinsic covenant of what might be called ministering care – a covenant that inescapably binds mankind to what Milton would in *Paradise Lost* describe as the 'pleasant labour' of agricultural pursuits. Man finds himself in a divinely ordained and appointed position to monitor, tend, and facilitate the

---

[32] James Thomson, 'Autumn' (ll. 1362–64), *The Seasons and The Castle of Indolence*, ed. James Sambrook (Oxford: Clarendon Press, 1972;1984) 125.

progress of the natural world. Such a concern in the *Georgics* in some respects reiterates the message of the Hebrew Genesis, which also and emphatically stresses man's 'dominion' over the natural world.[33] The rural industries of the farmer, the herder, and the beekeeper are all part of a divine scheme that looks to balance the (at times unpredictable) forces of the natural world with the reassuringly orderly processes of husbandry. Moreover, in this perception of the balance and order of nature as it is looked after and governed by its caretakers, the poet can recognize and articulate in microcosm the position of man in the world at large. The natural world – of which man necessarily forms a part – is left to the particular care of mankind, but man is himself subsumed within an order comprehended and governed by a presiding deity. This god can be propitiated by proper observances of piety and prayer. Concealed (but only barely) within this larger message is a political sub-text which incidentally acknowledges the need for a strong central and stable political authority as well. The hive of the bees itself becomes, in Virgil's words, 'the perfect, model state'; the natural world everywhere provides models of and images for the way in which man's own social world ought 'naturally' to be structured. Virgil, who had himself lived through the chaos of civil war, praises – with careful and important qualifications – the achievements of peace under the emperor Caesar Augustus. The past may have seen a Golden Age, but the will of the divine 'Father' has of necessity ordained that mankind must now work for a living. The 'arts of husbandry', Virgil tells his readers in his first book, have themselves been established 'to sharpen human wits'. Thus Virgil's poem, which at first presents itself almost as a kind of practical, agricultural guide – a manual for husbandry and bee-keeping – resolves itself at length into a poem of epic proportions, or, at the very least, a poem of epic concerns. In dealing with such subjects as the proper treatment of the natural world and the proper balance that ought to exist between man and nature, the poem turns perforce to the proper relations that ought to exist between men within a political society, and, finally, to the proper relationship that ought to exist between a man and his god. Virgil's *Georgics*, again, is a poem that deals at once with the personal, the political, and the divine.

Let us return now to the eighteenth-century reader who holds in his hands and is about to enjoy Thomson's *The Seasons*. Almost from the moment he first picked up Thomson's volume, the reader would have

---

[33] For the text of the *Georgics* see *Virgil: Eclogues, Georgics, Aeneid I–VI* with an English translation by H. Rushton Fairclough, revised by G. P. Gould (London and Cambridge, Massachusetts: Harvard University Press, 1999); see also Smith Palmer Bovie's *Virgil's Georgics: A Modern Verse Translation* (Chicago and London: University of Chicago Press, 1956).

recognized that the modern poet was placing himself in a declared line
of succession to his Roman original. In the opening inscription to
'Spring', Thomson even makes the connection between the two works
explicit:

> Ye fostering breezes, blow;
> Ye softening dews, ye tender showers, descend;
> And temper all, thou world-reviving sun,
> Into the perfect year. Nor, ye who live
> In luxury and ease, in pomp and pride,
> Think these lost themes unworthy of your ear:
> Such themes as these the rural Maro sung
> To wide-imperial Rome, in the full height
> Of elegance and taste, by Greece refined.[34]

That which had once formed the stuff of poetry for Virgil ('rural Maro')
and his audience in 'wide-imperial Rome', Thomson reminds his readers,
should not for one moment be thought material unworthy of or inappropriate to an eighteenth-century 'Augustan' audience.

As Thomson's poem unfolds (and the final text of *The Seasons* is by
no accident divided into four books) the reader is led through a natural
history of the vernal year. Thomson's 'Spring', which opens the completed poem, celebrates the forces of love, reproduction, and desire in
the natural world. 'Summer' follows a day of hay-making and sheep-
shearing in the simple yet 'solid grandeur' and boundless meridian
splendor of the British Isles at mid-summer; this second book also retells,
in proper Ovidian fashion, two etiological myths rooted in the local
landscape. 'Autumn' details the activities of the harvest and viticulture,
and praises the simple pleasures of the rural life. 'Winter', finally, con-
fronts the harsher side – 'sullen and sad' – of the natural world, yet ends
with a vision of the rebirth of the 'new-creating world' and a justification
of the 'great eternal scheme' of things.

At each stage of the poem – and as he rewrote *The Seasons* over the
years Thomson took pains to make such connections even clearer and
more obvious to his readers – the ties that bind *The Seasons* to its classical, poetic progenitor are ever more pronounced. Like Virgil, Thomson
looked to the labours of the rural community and to the annual rituals
of an agricultural life to provide the framework for his poetry. Like
Virgil, too, Thomson found in the simple science of husbandry and in
the accumulated wisdom of the farmer and the ploughman a reflection
of man's understanding of and contract with the divinely ordered natural

---

[34] Thomson, 'Spring' (ll. 49–57) in *The Seasons*, 4.

world. For Virgil, the balance and order of the simplest of rural tasks reflected the larger harmony of the Roman Empire at work. For Thomson, the same clarity and simplicity of order and purpose in the world of pastoral England likewise bodied forth and reflected the greater glory of the British Empire, also hard at work. For both poets, the comprehensive order and purpose of the world is best captured and reflected in the diurnal order of the countryside and its rustic tasks. By connecting his poem to the world of Augustan Rome, in general, and to Virgil, in particular, Thomson both enriched the message of his poetry and forged a direct link between British Imperial power and the glory of the Roman Empire itself.

The reader who brought his knowledge of its Virgilian model to bear on Thomson's *The Seasons* was engaged in what, for a great many readers in the eighteenth century, at least, was one of the fundamental pleasures of reading verse in the first place. Much of the fun in one's encounters with poetry lay precisely in playing this game of connecting the historic and poetic 'dots', as it were. Much of the reader's enjoyment, in other words, lay in a readily passive acquiescence to the active role of intellectual complicity. In fact, in so pointedly modeling his work on Virgil's *Georgics*, Thomson was playing according to the generally accepted rules of poetic composition early in the eighteenth century; the informed reader would have a very good idea about what his poet was up to well before he had even begun reading the poem itself, much less before he had finished it.

Innumerable poems written in the eighteenth century made use of this first sort of neutral classical reference. By so economically setting up and defining what some modern critics might call their reader's 'horizon of expectations' – by using an instantly recognizable and respected form of literary–cultural shorthand – a poet could easily establish the formal, stylistic, or thematic boundaries within which he or she was working. In many instances, however, the dialogue between the two works was even simpler than that which Thomson so explicitly set up between himself and Virgil. A specific linguistic echo or even a larger generic reference might be brought into play simply to alert the reader that the dialogue was there in the first place – to let the reader know that there existed between himself and the poet a shared body of knowledge which, if necessary, *could* be brought into play. The 'rules' here were extremely flexible. Alexander Pope, for example, included in his 1717 volume of collected *Works* an heroic epistle written in imitation of both the style and the content of Ovid's *Heroides*. In the classical original, the Roman poet had written a series of amatory poems in the form of epistles, most of which had supposedly been written by the legendary heroines of antiquity to their husbands and lovers; hence Ovid includes letters directed from Dido to Aeneas,

Penelope to Odysseus, Leander to Hero, Paris to Helen, and so on. Imitating the *Heroides* in the eighteenth century, Pope chose as his correspondent not one of the heroines of classical Greece or Rome, however, but rather the tragic figure of Eloise. Most of Pope's readers would at least have been familiar with the famous romance between Eloise and the great twelfth-century scholar and theologian Abelard, an illicit liaison that resulted in Eloise's eventual confinement in a convent and in Abelard's physical disfigurement (to say nothing of his professional downfall and the disgrace of his academic career). Pope's eighteenth-century reader, then, would have found it necessary to balance his awareness of Pope's classical model, on the one hand, with his knowledge – such as it was – of the historical circumstances the poet was dramatizing in the letter. In a case such as this, it would soon become clear that Pope would not be asking his readers to make any kind of precise correlation between his classical models and the contemporary poem. Readers are not asked to compare his work with Ovid's on any line-by-line basis, nor even are they meant to attempt any synoptic reading of *Eloisa* with the Roman originals on which it is based; it is enough that the reader be familiar with the simple fact that this is an amatory epistle written in imitation of a classical model which dealt typically with similar materials.

Pope's purpose in writing *Eloisa to Abelard* – a work that by all accounts sits at best uncomfortably with his other writing – seems on at least one level to have been to alert his readers to the simple fact that he was writing a certain *kind* of poem. Having demonstrated in his earliest works (poems such as the *Pastorals* and *Windsor Forest*) the ability to write in the pastoral or bucolic mode, and having followed those early published works with a series of elegies, mock-heroics, and translations of Homer, Pope appears to have looked over the body of work and noted that one of the required modes or genres in which he had not yet written was that of the heroic epistle. In order to be a proper poet, even in the eighteenth century, it was recommended that one still follow the arc or professional, generic path of the discipline precisely as that path had been laid out by the great Roman poets such as Virgil, Ovid, and Horace. Each poetic 'kind' – the pastoral, the elegy, the ode, the epistle, and, finally (the greatest and most respected of all), the epic – needed somehow to be represented in the body of a poet's work. In writing *Eloisa to Abelard*, Pope was in some ways filling in what he would otherwise have perceived to have been a gap in his poetic *curriculum vitae*. Having written an heroic epistle in the manner of Ovid and having then submitted that poem to the public, his credentials to be considered a true poetic heir to the Greek and Roman tradition were that much closer to being fulfilled – the Virgilian arc of his poetic career, in other words, was closer to being completed.

Twentieth-century critics such as Rothstein have described this second type of classical imitation in eighteenth-century poetry as 'normative', in the sense that the Greek or Latin original is invoked most prominently 'as a norm of art or as a bearer of values'.[35] Pope, for example, has recalled Ovid to his readers for this first reason – 'as a norm of art' – and the classical original by association lends prestige to his own work. When the classic work was invoked for the second of these two purposes – as 'a bearer of values' – the resulting eighteenth-century poetic product was likely to be a satire (Pope's reworking of the tropes of Homer's *Iliad* in his several versions of *The Rape of the Lock* can stand as a good example of this sort of relationship) in which the standards and cultural values of the original work were held up and contrasted to those of the (seemingly degenerate) modern world.

One final way of making use of the classics in one's own writing was to invoke the original for its accepted artistic and aesthetic value, but then subtly to rework its central message in some way. Perhaps the best example of this type of use of the past (a use which, as Rothstein points out, is confined largely to the first half of the eighteenth-century) would be Samuel Johnson's *The Vanity of Human Wishes*, in which Juvenal's tenth satire is tempered with a Christian conclusion – a conclusion the essence of which had quite simply been unavailable to its original Roman author. Rather than ending his satire, as Juvenal had done, on a note of profound pessimism and despair, or suggesting that the only hope for a man confronting the rising tide of moral chaos and disorder in the world was to live the life of simple virtue and resist the temptation to transform chance and 'fortune' into our earthly guides and goddesses, Johnson instead offered his readers the stoic consolations of Christianity. A 'humble confidence' in the divine plan and a modest Christian devotion, Johnson intimates in his own work, are the only possible and proper responses to the inequities of fortune and the world. In such a case, again, the classic model is respectfully invoked so that its substance can be corrected and adapted to the moral needs of modern society. The fact that the reader would himself have been able to recall the original ending of Johnson's Juvenalian model would only have added more force and vigor to the newer version. The original has not been replaced, but simply and effectively enhanced.

*

Like most eighteenth-century poets, Gray even as a young boy routinely turned to the Greek and Roman classics for his own poetic

---

[35] Rothstein, 95.

models. Much has been written regarding the allusive quality of
Gray's verse and his problematic relationship with the burden of the
literary past. In the composition of some of the most universally evo-
cative and seemingly 'transcendent' or 'timeless' verse ever to be written
in the English language – verse that seems to draw its primary strength
from the very beating heart of a sensitive poetic persona – Gray
managed, paradoxically, to create some of the most elaborate imitations
and parodies ever to be crafted in the English literary tradition. The
seemingly simple images of Gray's poetry involve not only some of
the most familiar *topoi* of Western literature (the restful calm of a
pastoral environment or rural churchyard, for example, or the supposedly pre-lapsarian innocence of childhood), but invoke and rely
upon the linguistic specificities of literally hundreds if not thousands
of earlier poems.

In the course of completing what now stands as the authoritative scholarly edition of Gray's poetry, Roger Lonsdale was compelled
closely to confront the problem of precisely how meaningful the
echoes of Gray's literary allusions are actually meant to be to a
complete understanding of his writing.[36] Lonsdale concluded both in
that edition and elsewhere that the allusions in Gray's poetry need
not necessarily be traced back to and contextualized within their
original sources. As is the case with the work of many poets in the
period, the meaning of Gray's poetry is informed but not fundamentally determined by his textual references, imitations, echoes, and
parodies. Lonsdale incidentally observed that the issue of precisely what
constituted literary imitation as opposed to, say, plagiarism was an issue
that only itself emerged in the 1740s and 1750s; a growing awareness
of the possible boundaries or limits of one's textual indebtedness may
have been responsible for Gray's apparent withdrawal from 'creative'
work and publication as he grew older. As an editor, Lonsdale seemed
finally to settle on the side of those who read the textual references in
Gray's poetry as examples only of the poet's 'compulsive acquisitiveness'
and not necessarily as significant or purposeful allusions. Bruce Redford,
though drawing a further and important distinction between the
allusive power of Gray's letter-writing as opposed to the references
and borrowings which make themselves heard in his verse, has convincingly argued in support of such a conclusion, commenting that 'the
multiplicity of potential sources and the thorough blending of echoes

---

[36] See Lonsdale, *PTG*, passim; also Lonsdale, 'Gray and Allusion: The Poet as Debtor',
in *Studies in the Eighteenth Century, IV*, eds. R. F. Brissenden and J. C. Eade. Canberra:
Australian National University Press, 1979, 31–55; Redford, *The Converse of the Pen*,
97–98.

[in Gray's verse] muffle the precise import of a given borrowing'. Attempts to argue that allusions in Gray's poetry are 'specific and meaningful', Redford rightly contends, '[must] somehow come to terms with the embarrassment of choice and the distorting resonance of the echo chamber'.[37]

Gray would certainly have been aware of the fact that there were precedents for such a manner of reference and allusion. We need now to take one moment to look at the most significant of those precedents. One of the poets whose work Gray probably first encountered in the classroom at Eton was a writer of the late Roman Empire whose work remains largely unfamiliar to most modern readers, even to those who have studied or read what is commonly thought to be a respectable amount of Latin in school. Decimus Magnus Ausonius (AD 310–95) was a grammarian and a teacher of rhetoric. Of aristocratic descent, Ausonius spent much of his life in or around Burdigula, or what is now Bordeaux, in southwestern Gaul. He was educated at Tolosa (modern Toulouse) and for thirty years served as a teacher of grammar and rhetoric. Rather late in his professional career he was summoned to the imperial court, then at Trier, where he became the tutor of Gratian, the six-year-old son of the Emperor Valentinian. While at court Ausonius held several high offices and eventually, from 379, served as consul; though it had by that time lost much of its practical political importance, the office was still regarded as a post of considerable honour. The consulate seems in fact to have been something of an institutional reward from Gratian for having already served as a Praetorian Prefect or governor of, respectively, Gaul, Italy, Illyria, and Africa. Ausonius' verses, which have traditionally been regarded more highly for their technical expertise than for any particularly poetic vividness or inspiration, seem largely to have been the product of his retirement following the assassination of Gratian in 383. After his student was murdered, Ausonius returned to Burdigula, where he lived on his estates until his death in AD 393 or 394.

Ausonius' poetic work was, in certain curious respects, peculiarly suited to an eighteenth-century audience in general, and even more precisely suited to a temperament such as Thomas Gray's, in particular. Much like many English authors in the extended 'Augustan' era in England, Ausonius seems similarly to have felt that there was no subject either too great or too small that could not serve as the suitable material for *some* sort of poetry. He delighted, like many if not all eighteenth-century English poets, at least as much in *bravura* displays of metrical innovation and mastery as in the representation of deeply felt

---

[37] Redford, 98.

and expressed emotion. Ausonius was consequently regarded by some readers as more of a craftsman or a technician, even, than a poet. In one of his most highly regarded works – the aptly titled *Ephemeris* – the reader accompanies Ausonius through the commonplace occurrences of a single day in the poet's life. Ausonius includes snatches of his conversations with his many servants, cooks, and secretaries. Other poems similarly follow the author as he deals with personal matters concerning his estate and consulship. Ausonius' catalogue poems (such as the *Ordo urbium nobilium* or 'List of Noteworthy Cities' and the *De Nominibus septem dierum* or 'Names of the days of the Week') are, in fact, not at all unlike those verses and exercises which the boys at Eton were themselves required to produce for their schoolmasters. Other works are straightforward bits of virtuosity, technical and generic *tours de force* – what we might today regard as 'novelty' poems, meant primarily to impress us with the writer's wit and skill. Some of these poems end every line in a monosyllable, for example, while others are innovative macaronics combining Greek and Latin. The general effect of many of these works – particularly those which read like excerpts from Ausonius' versified diary – resembles nothing less than reading a poem by a fourth-century, stylistic predecessor of the American poet Frank O'Hara. Like O'Hara, however, Ausonius did not always deal in the trivial, and even when he did, he could almost magically infuse into the seemingly random or meaningless circumstances of daily life a profound and far-reaching significance.

One of Ausonius' best and lengthiest poems, the *Mosella*, describes a trip to and along the Moselle river, with careful and still-entertaining descriptions of the water itself, the many fish to be glimpsed in the stream, and the vineyards and villas one passes while making one's way down the river and its 'azure tributaries' (Pope's influential *Windsor Forest*, incidentally, includes several passages which explicitly echo the *Mosella*; Sir John Denham's *Cooper's Hill* [1642] and John Gay's *Rural Sports* [1713] likewise display an easy familiarity with Ausonius' work). In his poem, Ausonius departs from Vingo (Bingen) and follows the path of the river to Augusta Trevirorum (Trier). His descriptions of the natural world in his native Gaul and of the familiar rhythms of a provincial, middle-class life are genuinely felt and gently humorous. There is every reason to believe that they would have impressed a reader such as Gray deeply. Apart from a similar attention to the natural world around him, Gray seems to have shared with Ausonius a comparable affection for the fleeting 'ordinariness' of daily life. Ausonius, as his modern editor R. P. H. Green has observed, was 'a bookish writer' – one whose work, moreover, 'rarely disguises the fact' of his literariness; he was also 'generally a very polished writer, not easily satisfied by his first thoughts . . . The arrangement of words within the [poetic] line [was] a matter to which he devoted great attention'. As Green further notes of the Latin poet:

> It is true that he makes not fewer than six references to his consulship, but in general he does not seem to hanker after praise or immortality .... The largest of his curricula vitae ends on a self-deprecating note; the *Ephemeris* gives the impression of somebody more comfortable in a *popina* than in a *palatium*. In the *Parentalia* he appears as the modest provincial surveying his humble origins and almost surprised by his access to power; in the *Professores* he is not ashamed to recall even the humblest and most obscure of his colleagues. Nor is there a note of apology, except perhaps in the ḤEREDIOLUM and EPICEDION *IN PATREM*, when one detects an eagerness to reintigrate himself into provincial society after mixing successfully with the great, and to show himself ... rich in virtue if not in possessions.[38]

It is startling just how easily (specific details aside) one might mistake the essence of such descriptions of Ausonius' career as a poet for one of Gray's own hundreds of years later. Yet for both writers, as we shall see, such classical allusion served not only as a simple technique of diversionary and 'external' ornamentation, but helped to instill form and structure within the often idiosyncratic vision of the poet itself. Green unreservedly describes Ausonius as 'not only the most brilliant and prolific writer of his age, but one of the most versatile and skillful writers in the history of Latin literature'.

Like Ausonius, Gray has on occasion been dismissed by critics as a trifler – a dilettante, a poetaster, a 'versifier' – rather than a *true* poet. The genial affection of both poets for the natural world militated, in the manner of a vague, pantheistic rebellion, against the orthodoxies of the day, and both found in the language of their classical models (though for Ausonius there could hardly have been the necessary distance to look upon those models as anything other than contemporaries only slightly removed in time from himself) their own means of expressing their ideas. Of even greater significance is that Gray almost certainly, in the classroom at Eton, first learned from Ausonius the techniques of the *cento*. A cento is a form of poetic composition in which individual passages from some great and respected poet of the past are excerpted and stitched together to form a new piece of poetry (the term, which derives ultimately from the Greek verb which literally means 'to plant slips' or 'cuttings' of trees, came in time to connote a 'patchwork' quilt or garment). The most common source of material for centos was the work

---

[38] R. P. H. Green, ed. *The Works of Ausonius* (Oxford, 1991) xvii.

of the most respected poets – Homer and Virgil, in Greek and Latin respectively. Ausonius was the most celebrated writer of centos in late antiquity; he typically used the material of the older, more venerable poets to new and unexpected effect. One of the best descriptions of the kind is that offered by Ausonius himself in the dedicatory epistle (to one 'Paulus') that prefaces his own nuptial cento. He writes:

> Et si pateris, ut doceam docendus ipse, cento quid sit, absolvam. variis de locis sensibusque diversis quaedam carminis structura solidatur, in unum versum ut coeant aut caesi duo aut unus et sequens <medius> cum medio. nam duos iunctim locare ineptum est, et tres una serie merea nugae. (Ausonius 372)

> [If you will allow me, who is in need of instruction myself, to instruct you, I'll try to tell you what a cento is. It is a poem neatly constructed out of a variety of passages and diverse meanings, in such a way so that either two half lines are joined together to form one single line, or one line and the following half of the next line. To place two entire lines side by side is poorly done, and three in a row is downright disgraceful].

After explaining some particular metrical matters in greater detail, Ausonius proceeds aptly to compare the form of the cento to a kind of geometrical puzzle:

> Hoc ergo centonis opusculum ut ille ludus tractatur, pari modo sensus diversi ut congruant, adoptiva quae sunt, ut cognata videantur, aliena ne interluceant: arcessita ne vim redarguant, densa ne supra modum protuberent, hiulca ne pateant. (Auxonius 374)

> [And so, this little work, the cento, is handled in much the same way as this puzzle, so as to bring together different meanings, to make pieces which are in fact arbitrarily connected seem to fit in naturally with one another, to let foreign elements let no crack of light slip between them, to prevent the far-fetched from proclaiming the metaphysical force which yokes them together, the densely packed from bursting, the closely knit from gaping.]

Ausonius himself dismisses such a poem as a work 'solae memoriae negotium sparsa colligere et intergrare lacerata, quod ridere magis quam laudare possis' – that is to say, 'the sort of task fit only for the memory, which has to gather up scattered tags and fit the mangled bits together into a whole, and as such more likely to provoke laughter than praise'.

While such a poetic technique might indeed, for the modern reader, immediately recall the kinds of absurdities produced by the character in Dickens's *Nicholas Nickleby* who had 'proved, that by altering the received modes of punctuation, any one of Shakespeare's plays could be made quite different, and the sense completely changed', the effect of classic centos was not always exclusively or inevitably comic. The oldest extant cento, *Medea*, written by Hosidius Geta in the second century AD, is in fact a tragedy. The best-known, self-proclaimed cento in the English tradition is probably the *Cicero princeps* (1608), which is a serious treatise on government. Surviving Greek centos include the restructurings of Trygaeus of portions of the *Iliad* and the *Odyssey*, and the *Homerokentrones* of the Byzantine period.

The Ausonian cento encountered by Gray would have been the *cento nuptialis* or 'wedding cento', a work commissioned by the Emperor Valentinian and created entirely out of tags or textual snippets culled from Virgil. After a brief preface, Ausonius' cento begins by describing the marriage feast, and the vision of the bride and the bridegroom as they step forward for the ceremony. A short passage demonstrates just how Ausonius' 'patchwork' composition is sewn together. Describing the bride as the 'lawful charge' of Venus, for example, he writes:

> qualisque videri
> caelicolis et quanta solet Venus aurea contra,
> talis erat species, talem se laeta ferebat
> ad soceros solioque alte subnixa residit. (Ausonius 380)

[Such as Golden Venus is apt to appear before the heavenly gods in stature and in beauty, so seemed she, and in such a way the joyful maid drew close to the parents of the bridegroom, and sat upon a lofty throne.]

This deceptively simple and straightforwardly fluid passage has been artfully constructed from six separate bits and pieces of Virgil. All of those pieces, in this particular instance, have been drawn from the *Aeneid*. Rather than coming from any single book or selection, however, they have been gathered from four separate passages, ranging from Books I to X. The first tag, for example – 'qualisque . . . solet' is drawn from *Aeneid* ii. 591–92: the short second bit – the three words 'Venus aurea contra' – comes from x.16. Yoked together in this 'metaphysical' fashion the two combine to create a new meaning. The reader is not asked to trace the allusions back to their sites in the original text; even if the reader did make such an effort, the rewards would be virtually nonexistent. The referential contexts of the cento are not meant to be traced and analyzed; the recombined tags and the new meaning they present to the reader are meant to stand on their own (sometimes deliberately dubious) merit.

The nuptial cento of Ausonius moves on to describe the offering of the marriage gifts and the joyful epithalamium addressed by the assembled company to the new couple. Having ushered the newlyweds into the bedchamber, Ausonius pauses and warns his reader that his allusive technique will now permit him to disclose as he might not otherwise have done 'the secrets of the bedchamber and couch'. He justifies his presentation of such 'immodest' material by protesting (more or less with writers before and since) that 'everybody does it'. The greatest writers of the past – Plato, Cicero, and even Virgil himself – permitted themselves to indulge in a bit of 'lofty obscenity' once in a while. The technique of allusion here allows Ausonius to distance himself from his own work, by naively protesting that it is made of the 'stuff' of other writers anyway. He writes:

> et si quid in nostro ioco aliquorum hominum severitas vestita condemnat, de Vergilio arcessitum sciat. igitur cui hic ludus noster non placet, ne legerit, aut cum legerit, obliviscatur, aut non oblitus ignoscat. (Ausonius 392)

> [And if the prim propriety of some people happens to find fault with anything in my playful little piece, let them know that it is taken from Virgil. So anyone who shakes his head at this farce of mine should simply not read it, or, if he has read it, he should forget about it; and if he can't do that, then at least let him forgive it.]

Ausonius' allusive–parodic technique thus allows the author to distance himself from his own poetic constructions, to deny responsibility for his poem's meaning and even to shift the burden of composition, such as it is, onto the shoulders of the very individual whose work he has 'plundered' – Virgil himself. The cento might particularly have attracted the attention of schoolboys for precisely this manner in which it took Virgilian phrases and, wrenching them from their original contexts, placed them in linguistic constructions which gave them new and sometimes giddily obscene meanings. Like schoolboys before and since, even the supposedly privileged and proper youth of eighteenth-century Eton were invariably titillated by the scurrilous – by the 'fearful joy' inherent in almost any examination of that which remained officially forbidden and out-of-bounds. The techniques of the cento as a referential poetic form unlocked the possibilities of language to describe even these most proscribed if most obsessive of schoolboy topics: sex and sexuality.

Gray certainly read Ausonius. He probably first encountered the work of the Roman poet while he was yet a student at Eton, and we now know for certain that Gray would have been thoroughly familiar with his Latin predecessor by the time he first left Cambridge as an undergraduate. A hefty edition of Ausonius' collected *Works* was among the small selection of volumes that Sir Robert Walpole permitted his son Horace to borrow from his own private library at Houghton and carry with him to his rooms in King's College; the same edition highlighted the parodic techniques of the cento by noting the original sources of Ausonius' fragments and half-lines in the margin of the *Cento nuptialis*. Gray later carefully numbered among his own possessions a copy of Ausonius' complete works (throughout his life the poet maintained catalogues of his library, in most instances patiently entering into various folio notebooks or among the pages of his Commonplace Book the author's name, work, edition, and date of publication; the item detailing his Ausonius, for example, is entered in one such list: 'Ausonius. Tolli (Folli Amst, Blacu. 1670)'. The recombinative techniques of the classical cento to which Ausonius thus exposed Gray left him with a potent and highly versatile model of literary reference and allusion while still a schoolboy. Gray encountered a poetic technique through which it was possible obliquely to express one's own sentiments and observations in the language of the most respected and unassailable of classical authors. Of no small significance, again, was the fact that this new, encoded and referential language could easily and without claiming absolute responsibility re-present and manifest the otherwise off-limit terrain of human sexual experience. Gray was exposed to a form of classical reference that was on at least one level – to return for one moment to the reader about to embark for the first time on Thomson's *The Seasons* – 'neutral'. He does not absolutely *need* to be aware of the classical, textual point of origin of the work he is now holding in his hands, but it helps a great deal if he does. The source or target text of the imitation is chosen essentially for its value as a familiar point of reference. While there was often some humour inherent in the sheer disjunction of meaning that resulted when Virgilian phrases were taken from their original contexts and placed, paratactically, in centos, by and against one another, the main intent of such a compositional method was not disrespectful nor was it even necessarily satiric. It was parodic in the most literal sense of that word, insofar as the new constructions were *para odos* – comprehensive 'beside songs' – songs and poems that gained at least part of their meaning by taking a side-long glance at or towards another and often better-known work. Allusions or excerpts were not laboriously meant to be traced back to their source text for their full gloss and meaning, if only because such sources were quite simply not where their meanings resided.

References in general and centos more particularly provided a shared vocabulary of classical allusion – a semi-secret language – among an

educated (and largely male) audience, in and through which it was possible indirectly to communicate new and potentially dangerous ideas.
The knowledge of Greek and Roman classics itself functioned as a kind
of living language; imitations, parodies, echoes, and allusions were made
not so much to add precise weight or meaning and significance to a contemporary product, but to provide a means of oblique articulation, and
to add what might best be described as a semi-classical 'aura' to any
given work. One might even interpret Gray's life-long fascination with
the techniques of the cento as a practical, literary manifestation of the
faith he invested in Locke's philosophy, and the manner in which,
according to that philosophy, external objects were impressed upon the
mind, and so transformed into Ideas. According to Locke's philosophy,
the mind is stocked with simple ideas by sensation – by the natural
working of the senses; it then acquires 'new' ideas by reflecting on its
own activities relating to the ideas sensation has provided (in the words
of Locke's versifier, Richard Blackmore, 'The Mind proceeds, and to
Reflection goes, / Perceives she does Perceive, and knows she Knows')[39].
The processes of the cento, in other words, can in some respects be
thought of as the literary–textual equivalent of the similarly acquisitive,
recombinative workings of the human mind.

In his own attempt to describe the peculiar texture, effect, and 'atmosphere' of Gray's allusive language, Bruce Redford turned to an entirely
different poetic tradition in his attempt to describe for the modern reader
a model for such poetic borrowings. A painstaking reader both of Gray's
poetry and of his correspondence, Redford argued persuasively that
Gray's 'foremost aesthetic aim' in much of his writing – the 'rigorous dis-
tillation of thought and feeling' to which he attained – necessarily entailed
the practice of textual allusion. Redford found only in the poetic technique of the Japanese *honkadori* a model for such borrowing. *Honkadori*
involves a borrowing not only of the raw 'material' – the vocabulary, language, phrasing – of an older poem or poems, but a borrowing too of
'something of the situation, the tone, the meaning' of the original as well.[40]
The technique aims not at a specific allusiveness, but a general and indirect conjuring of what might most accurately be described as poetic
atmosphere. Redford's understanding of the nature of Gray's allusive
practice was keenly perceptive. Only on rare occasions would Gray's
encoded references either in his poetry or his correspondence be 'specific
and meaningful'. Safety (emotional and personal safety, at least) lay rather
in a discrete indirection – in what other critics have called Gray's 'evasion-
by-reticence'. Critics such as Redford need not, however, have travelled

---

[39]   Richard Blackmore, *Creation: A Philosophical Poem in Seven Books* (vii.253–54),
quoted in MacLean, *John Locke and English Literature in the Eighteenth Century*, 61.
[40]   Redford, *The Converse of the Pen*, 97–98.

quite so far afield as Asia to find a model for such compression and echoing richness of texture in Gray's poetry. The ancient techniques of the cento in the classical western tradition had already been encountered by Gray at Eton and at Cambridge even as a very young man.

IV. Knowledge of Himself

A Latin translation or (rather more accurately) paraphrase of the Bible's Eighty-Fourth psalm is the earliest complete poem written by Gray to have survived. The translation is not itself a densely allusive work, but it too anticipates Gray's later poetry in several significant respects. The stanzas were transcribed and preserved by Gray's nineteenth-century editor John Mitford with the observation that the ode was 'written in Mr Grays Hand: but evidently when young, the hand being unformed, & like a Schoolboys, tho' very plain & careful'. Mitford added: 'The Leaf on which it is written, apparently torn from a Copy-book. Some of the expressions resemble those in the Gr. Chartreuse Ode.' This last reference is to a Latin poem that Gray was to write many years later while completing the Grand Tour of Europe with Horace Walpole; Mitford was right to suggest that certain turns of phrase and attitudes of thought would be re-used and recycled from a work even as early as this in Gray's later poetry. Gray's mind, when it came to his poetry, at least, was meticulous and economical, not to say obsessive. Language and ideas once used could and indeed *should* be used over and again if they correctly expressed or suitably embodied a certain concept. Certainly the ideas expressed in this psalm would have been recognized even by a very young Thomas Gray as close to timeless.

The work in question is one of the seventy-three biblical songs traditionally assigned by many readers to King David himself, though the psalm is one of only ten lyrics included in the collection preceded by ascription to 'the sons of Korah'. Portions of the psalm are of course used in public worship to this day. The poem's message is a simple one: worldly fame and glory should be rejected by the godly in favour of spiritual well-being. The speaker is a pilgrim who has journeyed to God's temple; his song expresses thanks and relief at having finally been allowed to enter the precincts of God's presence. Gray's admittedly formal, schoolboy Latin manages nevertheless to capture something of the spiritual beauty and depth – something of the 'living joy' – of his original:

> Oh! Tecta, mentis dulcis amor meae!
> Oh! Summa Sancti religio loci!
>   Quae me laborantem perurit
>   Sacra fames, et amoenus ardor?

Praeceps volentem quo rapit impetus!
Ad limen altum tendo avidas manus,
　　Dum lingua frustratur precantem,
　　　　Cor tacitum mihi clamat intus.

　　. . .

Bis terque felix qui melius Deo
Templum sub imo pectore consecrat;
　　Huic vivida affulget voluptas
　　　　Et liquidi sine nube Soles. (*PTG* 285–86)

[O dwellings, the dear love of my soul! O supreme sanctity of
this holy place! What is this sacred hunger, this kindly flame that
burns me in my toils? Where does this headlong impulse take
me, willing as I am? I stretch out eager hands to the threshold
high above. While my tongue makes me falter as I pray, my silent
heart shouts within me. . . . Twice, three times happy he who sets
up a better temple to God deep in his heart. A living joy shall
shine on him, and clear suns without a cloud.]

Even as a child Gray seems intuitively to have understood the psalm's
peculiar veneration of physical *place* – its devotion to the Holy City and
the blessing it bestows on those who move within the temple – and
perhaps even already to have appreciated something of the true value of
spiritual as opposed to temporal glory. The 'pride of tyrants' and the 'pleasure of kingship' are here rejected in favour of the 'lasting riches' that
are seen to constitute an individual's spiritual peace of mind. Both the
topographical focus and thematic thrust of the psalm will resurface in
Gray's mature poetry. Eugene McCarthy has rightly commented that
'given what we know of [Gray's] unfortunate home life', the desire
expressed in the poem for a stable domestic existence was very possibly
appealing to the poet; John Sparrow likewise observed that 'Gray takes
the Psalmist's idea of the good man who, making a virtue of necessity,
turns his adversity to gain (a theme he [was to treat] somewhat differently
in his own *Ode to Adversity* in 1742), and transmutes it – or, rather,
substitutes for it his own reflections on the same theme'.[41] One of the
central poetic messages that emerges from any reading of the psalms, too,
is the rather straightforward notion that good lyric poetry is the result of
intense emotional experience – that only by passing through both suffering and joy, both trial and triumph, can one produce genuinely felt and
truly lived paeans of praise. It is important for readers of Gray's poetry
to remember that for all his recourse to the techniques of allusion and
intertextual reference, Gray will also carry with him throughout his career

---

[41]　Eugene B. McCarthy, *Thomas Gray*, 21; John Sparrow, 'Gray's "Spring of Tears"',
Review of English Studies 14:53 (1963) 60.

as a writer this notion that lived experience informs the most memorable poetry – that intensely personal and even idiosyncratic emotions can be crafted within the crucible of poetic form to produce an artefact which can speak to many. It is striking that the one Latin translation of Gray's from the Bible to have survived is a poem from a collection that is itself valued for the timeless universality of its messages. Although rooted to some degree in the specific cultic and historical circumstances of Exilic and post-Exilic history, the psalms reflect upon the joys inherent in God's providential design in a manner which continues clearly to remain relevant to the modern reader. Much of Gray's best verse will similarly aim to translate the stuff of individual suffering and experience into the seemingly universal language of lyric poetry.

*

The second of Gray's surviving poems to be written while he was yet a student at Eton is a Latin translation of an anonymous English lyric beginning 'Away: Let Nought to Love Displeasing'. The original work, which boasts of having been a translation 'from the Ancient British', was first printed in David Lewis's *Miscellaneous Poems by Several Hands* in 1726. John Gilbert Cooper was to include the work in his 1755 *Letters Concerning Taste*, and for many years the work was mistakenly attributed to Cooper himself (though he never made any pretense of claiming the ode as his own). Gray's translation is preserved in a holograph manuscript, on which the poet's original pencil has been traced over by the pen of his editor John Mitford. Two of Gray's twentieth-century editors have observed that the hand 'seems definitely to be Gray's, although somewhat sprawling and ill-formed as compared with his mature hand'.[42] Before turning to Gray's Latin version of the ode, it is best to read the original English poem in its entirety:

I

Away: let nought to Love displeasing,
My *Winefreda*, move your Care;
Let nought delay the Heav'nly Blessing,
Nor squeamish Pride, nor gloomy Fear.

II

What tho' no Grants of Royal Donors
With pompous Titles grace our Blood?
We'll shine in more substantial Honours,
And, to be Noble, we'll be Good.

[42] H. W. Starr and J. R. Hendrickson, eds., *The Complete Poems of Thomas Gray* (Oxford: Oxford University Press, 1966) 250.

III

Our Name, while Virtue thus we tender,
　　Will sweetly sound where-e'er 'tis spoke:
And all the Great ones, They shall wonder,
　　How they respect such little Folk.

IV

What tho', from Fortune's lavish Bounty,
　　No mighty Treasures we possess?
We'll find, without our Pittance, Plenty,
　　And be content without Excess.

V

Still shall each kind returning Season
　　Sufficient for our Wishes give:
For we will live a Life of Reason,
　　And that's the only Life to live.

VI

Through Youth and Age, in Love excelling,
　　We'll Hand in Hand together tread:
Sweet-smiling Peace shall crown our Dwelling,
　　And Babes, sweet-smiling Babes, our Bed.

VII

How should I love the pretty Creatures,
　　While round my Knees they fondly clung,
To see them look their Mother's Features,
　　To hear them lisp their Mother's Tongue.

VIII

And, when with Envy Time transported
　　Shall think to rob us of our Joys:
You'll, in your Girls, again be courted,
　　And I'll go wooing in my Boys. (*PTG* 287–88)

Readers already familiar with Gray's mature poetry will again be impressed by the manner in which even this slight ode anticipates both the thematic concerns and, indeed, the very imagery of works such as the *Elegy* and the *Eton Ode*. We are confronted with a love poem – a seduction poem, in fact – which, oddly and rather uncharacteristically for the genre, plays on the very possibility of procreation to accomplish its purpose. Like many *carpe diem* poems, the work first posits a genuine and passionate valuation of the moment – of the here and now – as an effective albeit temporary means of defying envious Time. Although the couple in the poem are of humble birth and possess no 'pompous Titles', their innate virtue and goodness remain so strong, the speaker suggests, that even 'all the Great ones' of the nobility will stoop to respect and to venerate them. They will live the humble life of reason and such a life, as the wooer succinctly puts it, is 'the only Life to live'. The writer proposes finally to outrun the theft of Time and his deserts of vast eternity not by engaging in the rough strife characteristic of the archetypal, Marvellian seducer, but rather by reproducing the simple joy of his own youthful love in his 'sweet-smiling Babes'. The couple's own courtship, in other words, will be reproduced and replicated in the romances and courtships of their children. Rather than being reduced and diminished to a solipsistic singularity in death, the pair shall – on the contrary – find Time itself to be their reluctant ally in multiplying and forever increasing with each returning season their simple but yet substantially 'noble' passion.

Gray's Latin translation of the ode faithfully reproduces the sentiments of the original. Effecting only the most minor changes in substance (the rather unwieldy 'Winefreda' of the original, for example, is transformed into a suitably generic 'Delia') Gray maintains the rhetorical focus of the poem on the dual points of his English model, i.e. on the notion that the innate worth of the lovers is an easy match for the prideful pomp of any who would criticize their union and, consequently, on the belief that such worth will find itself replicated in succeeding generations. Gray's Latin translation concludes:

> Nostros interae ornabit pax alma Penates,
> iucundum pueri, pignora cara, torum.
> Oh quanta aspicerem lepidam dulcedine gentem
> luderat ad tpatrium dum pia turba genu
> Maternos vultu ridenti effingere vultus,
> Balbo maternos ore referre sonos.
> Iamque senescentes cum nos inviderit aetas
> nostraque se credet surripuisse bona,
> In vestris tu rursus amabere pulchra puellis,
> rursus ego in pueris, Delia, amabo meis. (*PTG* 289–90)

[Meanwhile, kindly Peace will adorn our house, and sons, dear pledges, our happy bed. O with what rapture would I look on the charming creatures while, a loving band, they play at their father's knee, displaying their mother's looks in their own smiling faces and echoing their mother's accents in their stammering voices. And when at last, as we grow old, age blights us and believed it has snatched away our joys, then you will be loved again, beautiful as you are, in your daughters and I, Delia, will love again in my sons.]

Readers familiar with the *Eton Ode* will note that the entity that would work to destroy or to diminish the lover's relationship in the English original is transformed in Gray's translation into a more emphatically abstract personification; 'all the great Ones' becomes, in Gray's version, simply 'superbia' or 'Pride'. Similarly, the forces that will preserve and protect their union are now rather more solidly evoked as allegorical presences – 'natura' and 'pax', 'Nature' and 'Peace'.

Gray was not, of course, alone among the Augustan poets in his penchant for referring to human and even cosmic powers and emotions as personifications. The eighteenth-century turn of mind that fully appreciated the genuine depth of powerful feeling which animates what we today read only as a rather debased and wooden poetic shorthand seems, rather puzzlingly, no longer to be accessible to modern readers. Gray's ability fully to conjure the potent significance of allegorical personification as an effective means of communicating to his readers the awesome power of the natural world and the terrific force of human emotions was to be more fully realized in the closing stanzas of the *Eton Ode*. In that later poem, as we shall see, the misfortunes that gather to destroy the little victims on the playing fields at Eton are so far from being rhetorical commonplaces as to be genuinely appalling and awe-inspiring entities. Already in this translation, however, we see Gray adapting the expression of an earlier poetic document to a peculiarly eighteenth-century turn of mind.

One image from this early poem that will reappear more famously in a later work is of course that of the 'loving band' of children who crowd and stammer at their father's knee. The *Elegy* will memorably picture a group of children rushing to embrace their father, who has just returned from his long day's labour in the surrounding fields. Those children will similarly climb onto their father's knees, 'the envied kiss to share', while their mother sits nearby 'plying her evening care'. This comfortable and physically reassuring picture of domestic contentment and security – a picture of a family gathered at the end of the day around a comfortable fireside and a snug hearth – deeply impressed Gray. Gray found in this highly visual and tactile image of familial love, unity, and warmth a poignant crystallization of what remained for him an impossible domestic ideal. He saw in the scene an evocation of love as a reassuring and comforting *physical* act. Within and upon the knees of their father the children in both poems are touched, cherished, caressed, and protected by their parents in a manner that Gray himself may only rarely have experienced. The emphasis that the poem places on the simple value of children – on their importance in the greater scheme of perpetual and self-perpetuating nature – is in itself striking. Although it is perhaps too much to suggest that Gray, writing and translating this lyric as a pre-pubescent child, naively assumed that he would himself, as an adult, marry and have children of his own, it is noteworthy that the 'answer', as it were, to the challenge posed by devouring Time is in this early work an obvious one: a willing and cheerful desire for procreation. Death will be defeated in and through time not by one's self, but by one's children, and by one's children's children. A Thomas Gray only slightly older and wiser perhaps already realized with some regret that such an answer was for him, at least, in actual practice to offer no workable solution to the challenges posed by time, death, and remembrance.

*

The last of Gray's Latin poems to survive from his days at Eton is at once (at a full seventy-three lines) the lengthiest and the most impressive of his juvenilia. The poem is preserved in the first volume of Gray's Commonplace Book, where it is noted marginally to have been written initially as a 'Play-Exercise at Eton'. The index to the same volume gives the lines the title 'Knowledge of Himself, Latin Verses at Eton'. An exercise that had been turned in or 'sent-up for Play' at the school was one that was particularly honored by being made the occasion of a school holiday. If a sufficiently competent set of verses was sent up to the Provost 'for play' on any normal Thursday at Eton, the students might be granted a half-holiday on the basis of their merit (regular exercises were simply 'sent-up for good'). Masters were known on occasion to correct or 'embellish' student verses themselves. Whether or not Gray's lines effected their purpose of an early release from the tedium of the classroom (and whether they, too, were later doctored by the Head Master) is not known for certain, but one might hazard a guess from their unusually careful preservation by the writer, if not from the elegantly referential fluidity of the Latin itself, that the effort was, practically speaking, a successful one.

Gray's lines had been heavily influenced by the first book of Alexander Pope's *Essay on Man*, which was published in February, 1733; their ultimate source was once again the empiricism of John Locke. The lines were thus written sometime between that February and the September of the following year, when Gray was to leave Eton for Cambridge. The Latin verses, composed when he was seventeen or even eighteen years old, represent in some respects the end-result of Gray's elementary classical education. As might be expected from an individual of Gray's growing abilities and inclinations as a writer, the poem is allusively well-crafted and rather more than competent in its emulation of both classical and contemporary models. The degree to which the work anticipates the thematic concerns of the poet's later writing is once again impressive.

Gray prefaces his lines with a brief quotation from Persius' *Satire* III (71–73):

                              – quem te Deus esse
                    Iussit et humana qua parte locatus es in re
                    Disce – (*PTG* 290)

          [Learn what God has commanded you to be, and in what station
          you are placed in human affairs]

The Roman satirist's admonition to rest content within the cosmic
scheme of things will reappear in many forms throughout Gray's work,
not least of which will be the exhortation of the *Elegy* to its readers that
they each attempt to pursue the 'noiseless tenor of their way' in
serenity and silence. The classical lines stand as a suitable epigraph to
verses that repeatedly stress the wisdom of temperance, humility, and
the *via media* – 'the middle way'. It is in fact perfectly reasonable to
regard the school exercise not so much as an original composition, but
rather as a Latin summation of the first book of Pope's *Essay* – a simultaneous précis and translation of the older poet's own vindication of the
ways of God to man (and like that same poem, of course, a dramatiza-
tion of some of the most significant elements of Locke's *Essay*). Gray
would continue to admire and in many ways to imitate Pope's work
throughout his career as a poet, and he seems at some point in his life
even to have been privileged enough to meet him. Two years after Pope's
death in 1744, Gray would write in defense of his predecessor, that 'it
is natural to wish the finest writer, one of them, we ever had should be
an honest Man. . . . It is not from what he told me about himself that I
thought well of him, but from a Humanity and Goodness of Heart, ay,
& Greatness of Mind, that runs thro his private Correspondence'.
    The first epistle of Pope's *Essay on Man* had succinctly set out Locke's
implicit belief in the divinely ordered patterns of Creation. The busy
'scene of man' may appear to be a 'mighty Maze' to the earth-bound
observer, yet it is nevertheless a maze that has been constructed according to a careful and lovingly detailed plan. Mankind is itself only a small
(if essential) link in a Great Chain of Being that stretches with vast
immensity from the Godhead itself, through each and every being in
created nature, to the lowest of forms of existence, even to this abyss of
nothingness. By virtue of his Reason, Man is 'little less than Angel' –
little less, that is, than the spiritual beings who stand immediately above
him on this great chain of nature and the cosmos. Since all the beings
in the created universe influence and affect each other, it is important
that each and every creature fulfill its role in the grand scheme of things.
A sin against the laws of Order, as Pope points out, is tantamount to a
sin against the 'Eternal Cause' itself. Pride and a concomitant egocen-
trism seem to be mankind's particular weakness, having been the immediate causes of its momentous fall from prelapsarian felicity. Since man

can himself perceive only a tiny portion of created reality, he has no perspective from which to discern or to judge the divine perfection of the
universe. What blinkered man sees as flaws in himself and in the world
may work actually and finally to make the universe a more perfect entity.
Man's fundamental 'flaw', then, is his belief in moral and epistemological self-sufficiency, his presumptuous and impious supposition that the
universe has been created to be perceived and evaluated from his own
necessarily and inescapably anthropocentric perspective. Pope concludes
the epistle with an exhortation to man to recognize his own manifest
limitations. Happiness on this earth rests not in trying vainly to
understand or to conceptualize an incomprehensible God, but to trust
serenely in the fate that awaits us. Man should look forward to the
eternal promise of future blessings, rather than present ease. The
poem's final, emphatic assertion that regardless of pride and 'in erring
Reason's spight, / One truth is clear: "Whatever is, is Right"' is not a
complacent justification of the status quo either in nature or in human
society, but a profession of profound and oddly reverential ontological
agnosticism.

Almost all of Pope's major points in the epistle are recapitulated in
Gray's Latin school exercise. Gray first follows Pope's lead in offering
his readers a description of man's place within the order of creation, and
of his accompanying misapprehension that the universe has been created
solely to be appreciated from his partial and diminutive perspective:

> Pendet homo incertus gemini ad confinia mundi
> Cui parti accedat dubius; consurgere stellis
> An socius velit, an terris ingloria moles
> Reptare, ac muto se cum grege credere campis:
> Inseruisse choro divum hic se iactat, et audet
> Telluremque vocare suam, fluctusque polumque,
> Et quodcunque videt, proprios assumit in usus.
> 'Me propter iam vere expergefacta virescit
> 'Natura in flores, herbisque illudit, amatque
> 'Pingere telluris gremium, mihi vinae foetu
> 'Purporeo turget, dulcqie rubescit honore;
> 'Me rosa, me propter liquidos exhalat odores;
> 'Luna mihi pallet. mihi Olympum Phoebus inaurat,
> 'Sidere mi lucent, volvunturque aequora ponti.'
>   Sic secum insistit, tantumque haec astra decores
> Aestimat esse suae sedis, convexaque caeli
> Ingentes scenas, vastique aulaea theatri. (PTG 290–92)

[Man is suspended in doubt on the borders of two worlds, not
knowing to which side he should tend: whether he should wish to

rise to join the stars, or, an ignoble hulk, to crawl over the earth
and trust himself to the fields with the dumb flock. He boasts that
he has taken his place in the chorus of the gods and dares to call
the earth, the waters and the sky his own, possessing for himself
whatever he sees. 'It is on my account that in the spring renewed
nature blossoms into flower, lavishes her plants and loves to colour
the lap of earth: for me the vine swells with its purple fruit, and
grows red with its sweet adornment. It is on my account, mine
alone, that the rose breathes out her pure scents: for me the moon
shines pale, and for me Phoebus gilds Olympus: for me the stars
shine and the waters of the sea role in.'

So he persuades himself and imagines these stars to be simply
the ornament of his dwelling and the vaults of heaven a vast
stage, and the curtains of an immense theatre.]

Like Pope, Gray mocks the egocentric arrogance of tiny and
hubristic man. While certain elements of Gray's language and phraseology in this passage will resurface to different effect in his *Sonnet* on
the death of Richard West, the earlier poem's fundamental point that
mankind is mistaken in its partial and self-partial valuation of its allot-
ted place in the universe – its fundamentally Augustan vision of a human
race blindly trapped on the isthmus of a middle state – more thoroughly
informs works such as the *Eton Ode* and the *Elegy*. Gray's verses follow
Pope's *Essay* in stressing the limitations of man's knowledge as he makes
his feeble way across 'the remote and lonely regions of the world'. And
again like Pope, Gray observes that the seeming limitations of man as a
species really mark the necessary boundaries of his physical and sensual
experience. The decorum of a wise and knowing nature has delimited
the possible extent of man's responses to the world around him. Pope
in his *Essay* had memorably paraphrased Locke in asking:

> Why has not Man a microscopic eye?
> For this plain reason, Man is not a Fly:
> Say what the use, were finer optics giv'n.
> T'inspect a Mite, not comprehend the Heav'n?
> Or Touch, if tremblingly alive all o'er,
> To smart, and agonize at ev'ry pore?
> Or quick Effluvia darting thro' the brain,
> Dye of a Rose, in Aromatic pain?[43]

Pope's lines reflect a characteristically eighteenth-century fascination
with the very idea of the human nervous system, a physiological concept

[43] Alexander Pope, *The Poems of Alexander Pope*, ed. John Butt (Bungay, Suffolk 1963)
511 (ll. 193–200).

now so commonplace that it is difficult to recapture just how startling and intriguing it must have been to realize that one's own body was a dazzlingly complex network of receptors and transmitters – a true 'system' linking the brain with the spinal cord, nerve endings, ganglia, and the sensory organs themselves – that received and interpreted the stimuli of the outside world. To Pope's generation the concept was a comparatively novel one and consequently opened all sorts of doors to new and revised notions of man's capacity for 'fellow-feeling', 'sensitivity' and – as the literature of the second half of the eighteenth century would so abundantly demonstrate – 'sensibility'. The lines of Gray's Latin exercise explicitly echo Pope's own fascination with such ground-breaking scientific knowledge; they similarly stress the belief that the more mankind comes to learn about himself and the world, the more he will begin to perceive the divine plan – and by implication the divine creator – that has both ordered and set the divine machine in motion:

'Quid mihi non tactus eadem exquisita facultas,
'Taurorumve tori solidi, pennaeve volucrum.'
    Pertaesos sortis doceant responsa silere.
Si tanto valeas contendere acumine visus,
Et graciles penetrare atomos; non aethera possis
Suspicere, aut lati spatium comprendere ponti.
Vis si adsit maior naris; quam, vane, doleres,
Extinctus fragranti aura, dulcique veneno!
Si tactus, tremat hoc corpus, solidoque dolore
Ardeat in membris, nervoque laboret in omni. (*PTG* 291–93)

['Why have I not the same delicate sense of touch <as a spider> or the powerful frame of bulls or the wings of birds?' May these answers teach those who are dissatisfied with their lot to be silent. If you were able to compete with such a sharpness of vision, and make out the minute atoms, you would not be able to look up at the sky or take in the extent of the broad sea. And if you were to have a more acute power of smell, what pain you would feel, foolish man, dying of a fragrant breeze, a sweet poison! If a more sensible touch, the body would tremble and burn in all its limbs with unrelieved pain, and suffer in every nerve.]

Human attributes, Gray stresses, are commensurate with human needs. Again, like Pope, the young poet underscores the simple notion that Providence is good and wise not only in what it bestows, but likewise in what it withholds from mankind. The minute gradations of the universe – the 'dread Order' of its articulated categories, as well as the limitations therein – are the products of a caring and beneficent deity.

Gray's lines conclude with a return to the substance of the admonition first given voice in the poem's epigraph:

> Nubila seu tentes, vetitumque per aera surgas,
> Sive rudes poscas sylvas, et lustra ferarum;
> Falleris; in medio solium Sapientia fixit.
> Desine sectari maiora, minorave sorte,
> Quam Deus, et rerum attribiut natura creatix. (*PTG* 291–93)

> [If you aim for the clouds or try to soar through the forbidden air,
> or if you demand untrodden forests and the lairs of beasts, you
> will be wrong. Wisdom has set up her throne in the middle way.
> Cease from trying to pursue a lot greater or lesser than that which
> God and Nature, the mother of all things, has bestowed.]

Gray's self-styled 'knowledge of himself', then, is even at this early age an understanding and an intuition that acknowledges the incomprehensible order of creation, and looks preemptively to circumscribe and to confine the boundaries of personal as well as social endeavor. Many years before writing the *Elegy*, Gray sought spiritual consolation in the fact that 'whatever is' – however wrong it may appear – 'is right'. 'Natura creatix' – maternal nature – keeps an ever-watchful eye on the affairs of this world, and ensures that her beleaguered children at least fulfill the roles for which they are destined.

The image of the nurturing, protective mother in the poem's final line is a telling one, and effects a slight but intriguing link to one last, undated fragment that may likewise have been a product of Gray's earliest years at Eton. The fragment is an English verse translation of a short passage from the ninth book of Statius' *Thebiad*. Gray seems always to have enjoyed translating Statius. He would return to the *Thebiad* again and again while at university – commenting in one letter to West, typically, that he had recently been misspending his days 'playing with Statius', when he should have been devoting himself to his studies. The sixteen-line fragment he translated as a very young man is a brief and self-contained description of the warrior Crenaeus, a child of the woodland deity Faunus and the nymph Ismenis, the female personification of a stream of the same name. In the course of the expedition against Thebes, Crenaeus finds himself fending off his attackers within the very waters that gave him birth. 'In this clear wave', Gray translates,

> he first beheld the day;
> On the green bank first taught his steps to stray,
> To skim the parent flood and on the margin play:
> Fear he disdains and scorns the power of fate,

Secure within his mother's watery state.
The youth exulting stems the bloody tide,
Visits each bank and stalks with martial pride,
While old Ismenus' gently-rolling wave
Delights the favourite youth within its flood to lave.
Whether the youth obliquely steers his course
Or cuts the downward stream with equal force,
The indulgent river strives his steps to aid. (*PTG* 277)

One need not be a committed or rigorous Freudian to make much of Gray's imaginative participation in the pseudo-natal chaos of blood and water in this passage. Perhaps we are meant on some level to read Crenaeus' violent exaltation within his mother's 'watery state' as a reflection of the still unresolved conflicts and tensions of the writer's Oedipal stage, the stage at which a child works through the foundation of his mature relationship with his parents. Gray's Crenaeus demonstrates a fraught combination of attraction and rebellion – of simultaneous desire and repulsion – to his liquid, incarnadine mother. Might the passage then be the work of a child who is drawn to his own mother but, because of the threat of violent retribution from his father, was repelled and threatened by her as well? Are the lines, more specifically, a reenactment of the writer's own possibly masochistic relationship to his father? The hero of the passage, at least, seems to crave the sexual possession of his mother against both his own better instinct of self-preservation, as well as against the established order of things – 'Fear he disdains and scorns the power of fate'. Gray's attraction to the passage in this translation (which was preserved by Walpole only with the observation that it was written by the poet 'when he was very young') may be a result of his own continuing identification in the universal psychological conflict with his female parent. Readers reluctant to entertain such hypotheses will at least note that in both the early Latin exercise as well as in this short fragment from Statius, the poet focuses on the figure of an indulgent and protective mother.

*

Slowly and imperceptibly, Gray's earliest days and weeks at Eton had soon turned into months and even years. Readers of eighteenth-century poetry tend often and rather statically to picture the Gray who 'strayed' in the school's fields and courtyards as a very young child. He is at most a timid and studious teenager preoccupied with his work, or looking forward to the time spent with his closest friends in the mutual fantasies of their romantic and classically fueled imaginations. Such images are to some very real extent the legacy of the *Eton Ode* itself. Gray's years at the school in reality, of course, covered a long and incalculably significant period of childhood and adolescent experience. Having first entered the school when he was a boy only nine years old, Gray was leaving Eton in 1734 a reasonably confident and suitably learned young adult of eighteen.

Much later in life Horace Walpole, looking back upon his friend's mature and outwardly serious demeanor even as a child, would observe curiously that Gray 'never was a boy'.[44] To the extent that Gray *was* 'a boy' while at Eton, however, that boy had now given way to the man. Gray's later comments on and references to the school suggest that he had been only intermittently happy there. He valued the closest of the friendships he had formed while yet a student at the college and, although it may have taken some time for him to realize it, he would likewise come to value the habits of learning that the school had instilled in him. In the course of time the prospect of Eton College would memorably inspire his nostalgic recollection of prelapsarian innocence and 'careless' childhood, but it is important for us once again to remember that the Eton of Gray's famous *Ode* is a consolatory fiction to be read only through the eyes of an adult. The college of Gray's poem is, at the very least, as we shall see, an Eton viewed explicitly at a *distance* both in time as well as in place.

As Gray prepared to leave the school for university in the spring and summer of 1734, he more than likely looked around and assessed his physical surroundings with the simultaneously self-deprecating and self-important affection so often assumed by schoolboys towards the academic environments within which so much of personal significance has been passed or endured. Gray was now officially an 'old boy'. As such, he could participate in the knowing and sometimes secretive camaraderie peculiar to his school and to his class. He would forever share with his Eton classmates a complex bond of experience – a bond comprised in part by the idiosyncratic twist that same schooling had imparted to certain forms of knowledge and language, and further reinforced by a great many shared memories. Perhaps the *Eton Ode* does, finally, contain a germ of strictly autobiographical truth. Perhaps before leaving Eton for Cambridge that year, Gray did indeed trace his way one final time down the familiar stairwells and through the cloisters and court-yards. He would have passed among the shaded hedgerows spotted with spring's campion or the pale yellow of the primrose. Crossing the fields spotted with constellations of flowers and alive with the sounds of birds, he might naturally have headed in the direction of his uncle's house in nearby Burnham. From such a point he could have looked back upon the college, as Eton's spires and pinnacles trembled with the growing

---

[44] Bryant, 141.

heat of the season in the valley's middle distance. Resting his arms on a wooden stile, Gray would have been able to gaze thoughtfully at the school. There he had lived for nearly ten full years. There he had experienced loss in the death of a close relative – his uncle Robert – as well as the birth of new friendships and affections. There he had come to know and to love Horace Walpole and Richard West and, to a lesser degree, Thomas Ashton. Long having echoed with the sounds of his own sighs and of his own laughter, the school's buildings sat now in the quiet of the summer months, waiting indulgently for the rare calm to be shattered by the nervous clamor of new arrivals and the reappearance – both reluctant yet at the same time oddly excited – of returning students. Carrying with him his learning, his friendships, and the unmistakable combination of apprehension and confidence so characteristic of a young man just setting out on the road of life – one for whom, as the novelist Evelyn Waugh would put it, 'the whole business of living is itself a source of excitement' – Gray was more than ready to leave Eton. It was time now, after all, to see what the new world of Cambridge had to offer.

CHAPTER THREE

SARAG, THE DEAD CITY

Cambridge
1734–1738

I. Terra Incognita

Gray was admitted as a pensioner to Peterhouse, Cambridge, on 4 July 1734; he was nearly eighteen years old. Although Etonians more often went up to King's College, Gray attended Peterhouse because his uncle Robert had been a Fellow there. The fact that another Eton Fellow, Thomas Richardson, had lately been Master at Peterhouse created a further connection to the college. Gray came into residence on 9 October and was just over one week later – on 17 October – elected to a Bible Clerkship or Cosin scholarship of £10 a year. The scholarship had been established by the school's former master Bishop Cosin in 1669 and had for over two generations now been bringing to the college a series of promising young freshmen. The future physician, free-thinker, and poet, Sir Samuel Garth (M.D., 1690) – author of the popular burlesque, *The Dispensary* – had first come up to Peterhouse as a Cosin Scholar in 1676. Likewise, Shallet Turner, a future Regius Professor of Modern History at the university, was a Cosin Scholar of 1710. The Cosin connection, in particular, as historians of the college have observed, had drawn to Peterhouse as Fellow-Commoners a steady 'stream of representatives of the best blood of Northumbria: Liddells and Forsters, Conyers and Lambtons, Blacketts and Reeds', and in their wake followed others – often scholars and pensioners like Gray – such as William Browne, Clement Wearge, Thomas Heyrick (grand-nephew to the poet Robert), Richard Chenevix, and Bernard Hale.[1]

The Cosin scholarship required that Gray study music under the College organist, and that he regularly participate in the chanting and singing in the Chapel choir. He was likewise on the dinner hour of each Sunday and feast day required to produce to the Master and Senior Dean fair copies of Greek and Latin verses written on a subject drawn from the Gospel for that day. The scholarship also stipulated some regulations regarding dress and general appearance. Cosin scholars were forbidden to wear 'perukes' or wigs, to wear their hair long (it was not to touch their shoulders) or to use hair powder. They were

---

[1] Thomas Alfred Walker, *Peterhouse* (Cambridge: W. Heffer and Sons, 1906; 1935) 87.

required also to wear a 'meet' or wide-sleeved gown and squared cap. Toward the end of his third term at Peterhouse, Gray was to exchange his Bible clerkship for a Hale scholarship (established by the mid-seventeenth-century Master Bernard Hale), the stipulations of which were similar to Bishop Cosin's foundation, and the financial remuneration of which was slightly higher. Gray seems again to have been indebted to a fellow Etonian, in this instance the Master's grandchild, William Hale – for the opportunity to take advantage of this second scholarship. He was to remain a Hale scholar until he went down for the first time in 1738.

*

Eighteenth-century Cambridge has long had a reputation for having been the ideal refuge for the indolent, the lazy, and the lascivious. The traditional picture of life at both sister universities in the Georgian era – a picture drawn primarily from novels and collections of scurrilous undergraduate verses – invariably features port-soaked dons and wildly inebriated undergraduates involved in every possible activity other than study and scholarship. Recollections (often reprinted) by authors and university graduates such as Edward Gibbon and James Woodforde, when taken with the illustrations of graphic satirists such as Robert Cruickshank and Thomas Rowlandson, have only helped to reinscribe this image in the popular imagination.

In reality, the situation was probably far less scandalous – and far less entertaining. True, Cambridge in the eighteenth century could hardly be described as a bustling centre of intellectual activity. Having played a relatively prominent role in the political struggles of the mid-seventeenth century, the university settled down for an extended period of quiet inactivity following the Hanoverian succession of 1688. The Chancellorship of the Duke of Newcastle from 1748 to 1768 would by mid-century again involve the university to some degree in national affairs, but life in general centered far less on that elusive and ill-defined entity of the 'university' than it did on the daily practicalities of college life. As is still very much the case to this day, Fellows and undergraduates alike considered their primary allegiance lay not so much to 'Cambridge', but rather more practically to 'Kings' or 'Trinity' or 'Peterhouse'. And although the activities of some few arrogant and well-healed sons of wealthy families could cause the townspeople to regret that their market town had ever been chosen as the site of England's second university, most undergraduates, hoping only to take orders and to secure a living, were far too poor to engage in the stereotypical bacchanalian routs. Dons, too, though more comfortably established with satisfactory stipends (ranging from about £60 to £100 per year) could hardly be numbered among the wealthy. Heads of Houses who, unlike mere Fellows, were often permitted to marry, might likewise look forward to earning, at most, £120 a year. Some professorships in the eighteenth century, including the chairs of chemistry and botany, entailed no stipend at all, a situation that was compensated only incidentally by the fact that the statutory duties of other chairs were so ill-defined as to permit those who held them from rarely, if ever, having to offer any public lectures. Some of the more recently established professorships, on the other hand, were well compensated. The chair of Modern History, founded in 1724 and eventually to play a significant role in Gray's own life, carried an annual stipend amounting to roughly £400 and entailed only a small amount of actual work. The scholar who held one such position when Gray first came up to Cambridge, the above-mentioned Shallet Turner, though at first a promising scholar, consequently earned himself a reputation (acquired is perhaps a better word) for doing 'absolutely nothing' for twenty-seven years.

It must be remembered, too, that eighteenth-century Cambridge was by any stretch of the imagination still a small, provincial, East Anglian town with a tiny permanent population. The entire university boasted a mere four hundred undergraduates, and as many Fellows. Most colleges sent to London for a remarkable number of their basic provisions, including wine, plates, furniture, candles, and delicacies such as oranges and oysters. A daily post with London was not yet established, and the first direct mail coach to the capital would not take effect until much later in the century, by which time the 60-mile journey could still take well over seven hours. Contact between London and Oxford, by comparison, was far more efficient, so that Cambridge, effectively out of the way of the ever more sophisticated routes of communication between the city and the increasingly important industrial centres in the midlands and the north, can to some degree be excused for resolving itself into a slightly self-satisfied indolence. Readers familiar with Cambridge in the late twentieth century would almost certainly have had trouble even recognizing precisely where they were. Providing it was daylight – and providing they had not been so badly bruised and muddied when crossing the bogs of Foulmoor fields to the south as to have given up the pretense of paying any significant amount of attention to their physical surroundings – eighteenth-century travellers from London might, if they were lucky, first catch a glimpse of the roof of King's College Chapel in the distance. A row of alms houses lined the road into town and then, almost before they knew it, travellers were deposited among the colleges themselves. Searching for the Cam and the magnificent 'Backs', they would find only a slow moving and weedy stream meandering between the often undistinguished college buildings and the rural fields and meadows to the west. Many of the landmarks which the modern visitor thinks of as defining Cambridge – the Bridge of Sighs and New Court at St. John's, the screen of King's College, the Fitzwilliam Museum – had yet to be built when Gray first arrived in 1734.

*

Peterhouse was the oldest college at Cambridge, having been founded by Hugh de Balsham, Bishop of Ely, toward the end of the thirteenth century. The grounds of the college, particularly when compared with those of its grander neighbors down river such as Trinity and Kings, remain to this day remarkably small. In Gray's day the school consisted of only one court. The poet early in his residence unflatteringly described the complex as 'a thing like two Presbyterian Meeting-houses with the backside of a little Church between them'. The College is far from undistinguished, however. The Hall buildings, which are still in use, date from the college's earliest history, and Peterhouse boasts both an impressive eighteenth-century library and a seventeenth-century chapel, the latter designed and built by Matthew Wren (uncle to Sir Christopher Wren), who was Master of the College from 1626 to 1634.

Peterhouse also boasted a long tradition of religious and political activity. In the fifteenth century some of its most prominent members supported the Lancastrians against the Yorkists in the War of the Roses. In the seventeenth century Petreans were well-known for their sympathies for the Stuarts. Throughout the Civil Wars the college had a reputation for being fiercely anti-Puritan. By the time Gray arrived, the struggles of the nation played a less prominent role in the daily life of the institution, and the course of college life had long settled into a slower, less contentious, and rather more predictable routine. Morning prayer would typically be read in the college chapel at six o'clock in the summer, and at seven o'clock in the winter; evening prayer was read at 6 p.m. Dinner was the main meal of the day, and might be served on pewter trenchers some time between midday and two o'clock, and was often comprised of a single serving of meat, with bread and butter. Students wanting anything in the way of vegetables had to order 'sizes', or, in other words, had to pay extra for them. Main courses were likely to consist of such wide-ranging fare as gruel, mutton, sweetbreads, minced pie, wild fowl, turkey, and rabbit, or fish caught in the local rivers and streams. Only rarely (on feast days or other holidays, perhaps) would members of the college encounter anything as exotic as 'hott salmon' (or 'samand') with lobster sauce, or, for their desert, 'strawberryes'. The lighter, eight-o'clock supper – often consisting of gruel, bread and butter, and perhaps eggs – was likely to be more meager than dinner, although many Fellows would take advantage of the fact that this meal could easily be taken in one's own rooms, and so order something a little more special from the kitchen. The college gates were generally closed at around ten o'clock each evening, and by eleven o'clock the keys were brought to the Master or Dean. Anyone wishing to gain admission to the college after this nightly ritual had been completed would be required to have the porter send his name to – and no doubt, often, awaken – either of those college officials. Members returning to their colleges after the gates had been shut could likewise expect to pay gate-money for the simple privilege of being able to gain access to their rooms.

*

Arriving in this new environment, having spent nearly nine years at Eton surrounded by the close-knit friendships of the Quadruple Alliance, Gray, not surprisingly, was lonely. Ashton had come up to King's a few weeks earlier in September, but Gray still sorely missed both West (who would be heading not to Cambridge but to Christ Church, Oxford) and – more significantly – Walpole, who was not to arrive in Cambridge until the middle of March, 1735.

Gray's earliest letters from Cambridge bear ample testimony to his affection for his closest friends. Yet his obvious sense of isolation – his fear that this new distance between them would work to impair their intimacy – was even at the time nicely balanced in the correspondence by a painfully crafted persona of self-sufficiency and maturity. Gray in many ways seized the upper hand of his situation with regard to Walpole by presenting himself, perhaps for the first time in the chronicle of their personal histories, as the one who was in a position to educate, to inform, to be in some control of their relationship. His very first letter to Walpole from university, written at the end of October, began by informing his friend of everything from the basic geography of the town to some of the particulars of college life. Gray's pages were amusingly written at one and the same time entirely from the perspective of one who has long observed the workings of academic and social life at Cambridge, while professing the bemused ignorance and curiosity of an alien on foreign soil. 'What to say to say about this Terra Incognita', Gray at first confessed to Walpole, 'I don't know;'

> First then it is a great old Town, shaped like a Spider, with a nasty lump in the middle of it, & half a dozen scrambling long legs: it has 14 Parishes, 12 Colledges, & 4 Halls, these Halls only entertain Students, who after a term of years, are elected into the Colledges: there are 5 ranks in the University, subordinate to the Vice-chancellour, who is chose annually: these are [Masters, Fellows, Fellow-Commoners, Pensione]rs, & Sizars; the Masters of Colledges are twelve grey-hair'd Gentlefolks, who are all mad with Pride: the Fellows are sleepy, drunken, dull, illiterate Things:

the Fellow-Com: are imitatours of the Fellows, or else Beaux, or else
nothing: the Pension: grave, formal Sots, who would be thought old; or
else drink Ale, & sing Songs against the Excise. The Sizars are Graziers
Eldest Sons, who come to get good Learning, that they may all be
Archbishops of Canterbury. (*CTG* 3)

Gray's characterization of the college Fellows here as 'sleepy, drunken,
dull, illiterate Things' has on occasion been quoted out of context as
the summary judgement of a lifelong Cambridge man on his neighbors,
colleagues, and contemporaries; it is of course worth reminding
ourselves that when he wrote this letter, Gray had been at Peterhouse
for just three weeks. His comments are emphatically the first impressions of a very young man, not the considered opinions of a comfortably tenured don, much less the final judgement of a well-known poet
on his less famous or less distinguished academic peers. Gray was not
even, at this early stage, beyond getting some of his facts muddled. The
distinctions his letter draws between Colleges and Halls were in fact
nonexistent; there were no technical differences between the two, and
Gray would in time himself, later in life, date his letters from 'Pembroke
College' or 'Pembroke Hall' as the fancy took him. Likewise the
unflattering affectation and snobbery of the last line (Gray, the son of
a London milliner and a scrivener, however respectable, ought perhaps
already to have learned better than to sneer at the aspirations of
'Grazier's sons') is forgivable only when we remember that he was
himself very much out of his depth in this new environment. His early
childhood in London had prepared him for far more noise and bustle
than Cambridge generally had to offer, but running into strangers in the
streets and bumping into unfamiliar faces in the college passageways and
at the stair heads – even listening to the shouts and laughter echoing
through the courtyards as nearby coffee houses (there was one just opposite neighboring Pembroke College) spilled their revelry into the late
Cambridge evenings – had a way of reminding Gray just how alone he
was in his new surroundings.

Never to grow into an imposing physical figure, Gray felt in these
early days at Cambridge particularly small and vulnerable. Ashton,
flaunting the distinctive and rather fabulous attire of a King's College
man, was a welcome visitor to Gray's rooms at Peterhouse, and he
offered to introduce Gray into the company of the other old Etonians
who now kept a juvenile 'Club of Wits' at the Mitre tavern. Never having
had much to say to his former schoolfellows when their company had
been forced upon him at Eton, Gray had even less inclination to spend
his time among them now that he was free to do as he chose. He ventured once or twice into the taverns, where the company assembled in
small and smoky hired rooms at about seven in the evening, remaining

there for parties that lasted well into the small hours of the morning. Such gatherings were for Gray at best uncongenial and at worst positively intolerable. In one game attempt to convey to Walpole some more vivid idea of what such festivities were like, Gray asked his friend to picture him perched precariously on a stool in a tavern surrounded by hogsheads of liquor and large quantities of tobacco ('there is not a soul in our College' he wrote with some disgust, '. . . who does not smoke or chew'). There he rubbed elbows with thirty young men who were 'infinitely below the meanest People you could ever form an idea of; toasting bawdy healths and deafened with unmeaning Roar'. His clothes already reeking from the smoke and his head spinning and ringing – if not from drink, then at least from the surrounding chaos and noise – Walpole was further to imagine Gray as having been squeezed on one side by a fat, maudlin drunk whose meandering stories were interrupted only by moral digressions 'upon God knows what!'. On his other hand sat an equally repulsive young fop who affected the idiom of an experienced London rake. However welcome any relief from the over-familiar sot to his right might have been, Gray soon found that this only slightly more presentable alternative seemed capable of offering to the assembled company no observations that had not already been encountered in the pages of *The Spectator*. His neighbor's entire conversation consisted of warmed-over Addison and Steele, writers whose work – at the distance of some two decades – was no doubt all very well, but tediously familiar. Pretending to a knowledge of the contemporary London theatre and social scene that could only have irked a born Londoner to his very bones, the fop ventured out on his own only to criticize the popular actors and performances in the metropolis. One new actor – a 'Mr. Stevens' – was compared unfavorably to the veteran Shakespearean James Quin; Gray observed quietly to himself that a remarkably similar opinion of the new arrival had been voiced less than two weeks before in the *Grub-street Journal*. The opera, in turn, was disparaged because it was patently incomprehensible. This popular sentiment proved too much for the assembled company to resist seconding, and prompted still another individual to opine that these new-fangled Italian imports would eventually prove 'the ruin of the nation'. No 'honest' people frequent the opera, a fourth observed loudly, a view which, he claimed, was irrefutably supported by the fact that those who did attend such performances were so ashamed of their behavior that they did so only in masques and disguises. Gray, forgetting for a moment where he was, reasoned that he could not possibly be the only individual present to find a provincial inebriate who did not know the difference between a masque and an opera ridiculous, and laughed out loud at the blunder. His outraged bark of ridicule, however, was taken as a sign rather of approval and applause and – in all likelihood having been roughly patted on the back for his sound and patriotic judgement – he found himself comfortably counted as a fellow-member of the company as the conversation tottered imperceptibly on to other topics. By that point in the evening, Gray could only look wearily around him with more bemusement than hostility, and console himself in the midst of the noise and disturbance with the thought that his rescue from such company by the arrival of Walpole could not be accomplished too soon.

Gray's sense of physical insecurity was given voice in other early letters to Walpole. In one passage, excusing and defending himself from not taking up Ashton's invitations to go out and socialize more frequently, Gray jokingly protested that his own accommodations were themselves so cavernous that he had no need of such superfluous entertainment; he was already sufficiently at a loss as it was in attempting merely to navigate his own lodgings. 'I am got into a room; such a hugeous one', he wrote,

> that little i is quite lost in it; so [that] when I get up in the morning, I begin to travel [tow]ards the middle of it with might & main, & with much ado about noon bate at a great Table, which stands half-way it: so then, by that time (having pursued my journey full speed); that I arrive at the door, it is so dark & late, & I am so tired, that I am obliged to turn back again: so that about midnight I get to the bedside: then thinks you, I suppose, he goes to sleep: hold you a bit; in this Country it is so far from that, that we go to bed to wake, & rise to sleep: in short, those that go along the street, do nothing but walk in their sleep. (*CTG* 5)

The fact that Gray's room was located on the ground floor of the quadrangle, on the north side of what is today the First Court, probably did little to improve his sense of security and repose. The steps of every passer-by slapped loudly into his own large chamber, and Gray was no doubt often awakened by the conversations which echoed erratically in the stone courtyard, or by the unpredictable noises resulting from the simple, daily business of college life. Gray's sense of diminution was compounded by the very real necessity of keeping a close eye on his financial comings and goings. A sound and responsible domestic economy had always been something of a fact of life in the Cornhill household, and Gray was painfully aware that any extra spending money he might have at his disposal came always out of his mother's own hard-earned store; Philip Gray continued even at this late date to resist bearing any of the financial responsibility for his son's education.

Life in Cambridge appeared forever to be throwing some new expense in Gray's way. Even the simplest of necessities – many of which, again, had to be transported to the town by wagon or by river carriage – seemed to cost far more than they did in London. Gray was consequently frugal to the point of parsimony. The college bills from his earliest years at Peterhouse, at least, show a scrupulous modesty with regard to dietary indulgence. Although his name first appears in the College Books of Account on 28 June, 1734, Gray was careful to incur no extra expenses whatever in his earliest weeks at Peterhouse, and though his name is written regularly at the bottom of the list throughout the summer months, his additions were few and infrequent; for 1734–35, his entire charge for 'Sizings' – the extra dishes that could be ordered from the college kitchens to supplement the regular meal or 'Commons' – amounted to little more than a few shillings. Gray, in other words, ate what was served him and asked for little from the college Cook in the way of sauces and relish to 'mend' his dinner. Likewise neither the college Butler, who was contracted to brew strong ale and small beer for the Fellows, nor the Junior Bursar, who in turn managed the bake house, had particular cause to value Gray's custom. The local merchants, mercers, and drapers advertising fine gentlemen's wear similarly may have attracted the notice of other new arrivals out to make a fine show in their colleges, but held few attractions for Gray. Whatever money he did have at his disposal was better spent on books in shops such as Crow's bookstore in Cambridge or later, perhaps, at Elizabeth Rogers's establishment in Bury, or, even better yet, set aside and saved to pay for plays, operas, and other entertainments when he returned to London. Part of Gray's early economy in matters of dining and dress can of course be chalked up to simple youth and inexperience. As the wider world slowly opened itself to him and enticingly introduced him to what commonly pass for the finer things in life, Gray was never one to be behindhand in cultivating expensive and suitably refined and fashionable tastes. The dilettante in him could respond relatively quickly to changes and fluctuations in the dictates of the *beau monde*. It takes some time for an eighteen-year-old boy who has spent the better part of his young life in a Spartan school environment – even an eighteen-year-old boy who is the child of shrewd London merchants – to realize that a modest, if suitable, remuneration can in most cases purchase a marked improvement in one's situation and circumstances.

*

For all such practical financial worries, however, the main source of anxiety for 'little i', as Gray genially referred to himself in the early letter to his friend, was clearly Walpole's own continued absence from the university. In his letters to Walpole, Gray began to assume a variety of outrageous poses and personalities, and cultivated in his prose a technique of literary ventriloquism that rarely found him maintaining for any significant stretch of time a single, epistolary voice. At the same time, as critics such as Raymond Bentman have observed of the degree of personal intimacy betrayed by the letters, 'the language used in these letters is unlike the language used by most contemporary writers in the letters that they wrote to other men, even to men with whom they were intimate friends'.[2] In one early letter, Gray pretended to regard Walpole as his 'Nuss at London' and addressed himself to his 'Honner'd Nurse' in the letter. 'This comes to let you know', he wrote,

> that I am in good health; but that I should not have been so, if it had not been for your kind promise of coming to tend me yourself, & see the effect of your own Prescription: and I should desire of you, so please you, as how that, you would be so good as to be so kind, as to do me the favour of bringing down with you a quantity of it, prepared as your Grandmothers Aunt, poor Mrs. Hawthorn (God rest her soul, for she was as well a natured, a good Gentlewoman, as ever broke bread, or trod upon Shoe-leather; though I say it, that should not say it; for she was related to me, and marry! not a jot the worse, I trow) used to make it. (CTG 5–6)

Gray subscribed the letter, 'your ever-dutifull & most obedient & most affectionate, loving God-daughter . . . Orosmades'. Quite apart from Gray's own self-consciously, high-spirited mockery of unnecessary formality in passages such as this ('so please you . . . you would be so good as to be so kind, as to do me the favour', etc.), and apart even from the very status the eccentric fiction of the letter granted to Walpole as Gray's nurturing and patently maternal God-parent, the letter stands out for its almost instinctive use of parody and burlesque as deflective and self-defensive literary tools. Gray appears seamlessly to incorporate into his own prose fragments and half-sentences from not one but two Shakespeare plays. His description of Mrs. Hawthorne as 'as well natured, a good Gentlewoman, as ever broke bread, or trod upon Shoe-leather' links surreptitious quotations from both *The Merry Wives of Windsor* ('an honest maid as ever broke bread') and *Julius Caesar* ('As proper man as ever trod upon neat's leather'). The same paragraph later includes oblique references to the language of *Romeo and Juliet*, as well as two distinct echoes of William Wycherley's *The Plain Dealer*.

Gray in fact seems typically in these early letters to speak in voices other than his own. Or perhaps it would be more accurate to observe that Gray's own language – in his letters if not in his conversation – was

---

[2] Bentman, Raymond, 'Thomas Gray and the Poetry of Hopeless Love' in *Journal of the History of Sexuality*, 3 (1992) 204–05.

itself a complex compound or amalgam of all he has yet met on the page and in the classroom. The very process of writing triggered in Gray a mechanism that conjured in his mind familiar sayings, phrases, or amplifications which were then passed on to his own correspondent. An isolated phrase or even a single word was enough to signify to his thought an entire, recollected passage. So, for example, as he began with his pen to write 'as well natured', his head appears already to have resonated with familiar Shakespearean echoes and near-literary relatives beginning 'as proper' or 'as honest'. Such a trait of recollection was not, of course, peculiar to Gray alone. Eric Rothstein has commented that when it came to classical allusions, at least, 'for most people the great quantities of Latin devoured in school lingered in the memory like the picked carcass of a holiday goose; the shape was there, and scraps of meat, but with most of the nourishment already assimilated and the taste a recollection'.[3] For writers such as Gray, however, the recollections could be particularly strong, and the metaphor held true not only for the Greek and Latin he had learned at Eton, but for his other, wide-ranging reading as well. It was a trait that had been reinforced by his close, continued contact with a small tightly knit group of friends – friends who themselves not only called one another by familiar nicknames, but who had together memorized certain passages from poetry and plays that they had then endowed with a special and peculiar significance that was now second-nature to them. Smiles of complicity and surreptitious winks signaling a secret, valued understanding would have passed between the four members of the Quadruple Alliance when any individual who was not a member of their little coterie unknowingly made a reference to their arcane and idiosyncratic language. Similarly, their own identities only just being formed, they delighted in their almost schizophrenic ability fluidly to slide in and out of other personalities. The classical notion of decorum or propriety that they had imbibed at Eton – the notion that language ought itself to be the suitable dress or garment of one's thoughts – served practically and unintentionally to provide them with an outrageous wardrobe of styles and identities. Their transformations and disguises could be accomplished with remarkable economy. One or two words would have been enough to set the entire labyrinthine process of playful recollection in motion.

Some modern readers might better understand such a mechanism if they take a moment to reflect upon the manner in which, when hearing the words 'Our Father', they almost instinctively call up to their conscious memory the entire Lord's Prayer. The Old Testament's apodictic

---

[3] Rothstein, 87.

injunction 'Thou shalt not . . .' – the antiquated formality of its second-person pronoun further highlighting its status as 'text' – might similarly conjure for many the entire decalogue. Most readers of Shakespeare, likewise, upon spotting a line beginning 'To be or not to be . . .' can at least make some headway towards completing the famous soliloquy (albeit often in fragmented fits and starts) and, indeed, are on some level compelled to do so. The reaction is a kind of extended metaleptic impulse which is at one and the same time close to automatic and unthinking – a knee-jerk reaction of the mind, so to speak – yet it is also potentially productive of the most profound and far-reaching connections in thought and language; a staggering range of literary reference – the reading and acquired knowledge of an entire lifetime – lies open and immediately accessible at one's mental finger tips. In this last sense, such a reaction constitutes a technique of epistemic shorthand that renders its practitioners capable of an extraordinary density of substance as well as style. This is not to suggest that we should ever lose sight of the fact that Gray's parodies are very often deliberately light-hearted and, quite frankly, funny. His natural instinct for mimicry, combined with the practices of literary recollection and recombination inherent in forms such as the cento that he had learned from authors like Ausonius at Eton, had worked already to furnish him with a manner of direct and indirect reference which, as we shall see, could be put to a dazzlingly wide variety of uses.

In Gray's early correspondence the chameleon conceit of always speaking in voices and literary languages other than his own and of subsuming his own person in a multiplicity of more dramatically highlighted personalities is more often than not used to deliberate comic effect. The anxieties lurking just beneath these boyish absurdities, however, are only barely concealed. As the biographer Peter Levi has written of the similar, early parodies of the eccentric Victorian poet Edward Lear, 'his despair underlay [such] performances', just as clearly as 'his gaiety riotously invaded them'.[4] By affecting the language of Shakespeare, Milton, Dryden, and Wycherley – to name only a few – Gray pointedly avoided having to speak in his own tongue. He consequently drew the attention of the modern reader, at least, to the loneliness, insecurity, and self-doubt lurking all too close to the surface of the trembling and fearfully *in*substantial identity of 'little i'. We see in Gray's early epistolary parodies a manner of deflection and distancing – of apotropaic defense – that will in time develop into a defining feature of his mature poetry as well.

Gray's early letters from Cambridge also began to reveal the potential extent of his wildly fanciful imagination. He was capable not only

---

[4] Peter Levi, *Edward Lear* (London: Macmillan, 1995) 14.

of assuming the garb of another's language, but of fully re-imagining himself from within the identities of others and of picturing himself in dramatic situations that entailed an ability to convey an idiosyncratic sense of perception which was nothing less than Dickensian in its precise attention to (often macabre and sometimes bawdy) comic detail. Addressing Walpole in one letter as his 'Dear Dimidium animae meae' or the 'dear man who is half of [his] very soul' (a tag itself characteristically lifted with Ausonian second-nature from Horace's *Odes*), Gray suggested that since the infrequency of his friend's correspondence obviously led him to assume that Walpole supposed him to have died, the one recent letter he finally had received from London found him not in his room but, appropriately enough, in the charnel house of nearby St. Peter's church. Cambridge itself, in the same letter, has been mysteriously transformed to 'Sarag' – an apparent reference to 'Saraka', a dead city in the Arabian desert. 'As you take a great deal of pleasure in concluding that I am dead', he wrote,

> & resolve not to let me live any longer; methinks you ought to be good to my Ashes, & give 'em leave to rest in peace: but instead of that, whereas I ought to be divested of all human Passions, & forget the Pleasures of your World; you must needs be diverting me, so that I made every nail in my Coffin start with laughing: it happen'd, that on the 26th Instant at twelve of the clock at midnight, being a hard frost; I had wrapt myself up in my Shroud very snugg & warm; when in comes your Letter, which (as I told you before) made me stretch my Skeleton-jaws in such a horse-laugh, that all the dead pop'd up their heads & stared: but to see the frowzy Countenances of the Creatures especially one old Lady-Carcase, that made most hideous Grimaces, & would needs tell me, that I was a very uncivil Person to disturb a Woman of her Quality, that did me the honour to lie so near me: & truly she had not been in such a Surprise, this threescore & ten Year, come next March: beside her Commode was discomposed, & in her hurry she had lost her Wedding Ring, which she was buried in; nay, she said, she believed she should fall in fits, & certainly, that would be her Death . . . 'i'gad: I told her Ladyship the more she stirred, the more she'd stink, & that to my knowledge, tho' she put a good face upon the matter, she was not sound; so she lay'd her down very quietly, and crept under her Winding-Sheet for Fear of Spirits. (*CTG* 11–12)

While emphatically juvenile both in its gleeful delight in the grotesque and in its desire to upset the often reticent formalities of conventional adult behaviour (mature individuals tend not, in their correspondence, to joke about death and corpses), the sense of humour here is nevertheless rather black and even morbid. Gray seems to evince a fascination – or at least a thoroughly imagined curiosity – with the disintegrating processes of human decay and decomposition which, in less forcefully light-hearted moments, might well inform some of the trepidation concerning man's eternal fate which eventually forms the background of poems such as the *Elegy* and, to a lesser degree, the *Eton Ode*. The man who was once heralded by critics as having been the melancholy 'psychopomp' of an entire generation of poets – the mournful and morose headmaster of the so-called Graveyard School – was heretically capable as a young man of presenting human carcasses in antic postures, arguing and bantering with one another in the clammy air of the charnel house like Punch and Judy in a squalid London street-fair. Gray jokes that only Walpole's arrival in Cambridge can 'reanimate' his corpse, since his friend's expansive soul is fortunately 'large enough to serve for the both of us'. If Gray's earlier letter to his 'Nuss at London' found him ventriloquising in the voice of a dependent child calling for maternal care and sustenance, this slightly later missive, written in the chill of December, when the nights closed in early and his own large room seemed even more blank and dreary than usual, finds Gray even further reduced to an effigy in need of a ventriloquist himself. His own soul has been paralyzed and left dumb by abandonment. Like the 'old Lady-Carcase' next to him whose rattling and immanent disintegration so offends his nostrils, Gray's own frailly articulated, skeletal limbs in the letter threaten to fall apart completely. Without the company of his friend to motivate and breath life into him – without Walpole to complete him, that is – Gray suggests that he might just as well be dead.

*

The letter from the charnel house was not the only occasion on which Gray wrote to Walpole in a voice from beyond the grave. Earlier that same month, he had responded to a 'diverting' letter from Walpole written in verse by likewise assuming the 'Poetical Strain', and pretending to write in the person of the recently deceased author and critic John Dennis. The resulting lines constitute Gray's earliest original extant verse in English. Dennis (who died on 6 January 1734) had himself attended both Caius College and Trinity Hall, Cambridge (where he later became a Fellow) following his early education at Harrow. A critic devoted to neo-classical dramatic theory who in the course of his career tried his hand at several tragedies including *Orpheus and Eurydice* (1707), *Appius and Virginia* (1709), as well as his own version of Shakespeare's *Corialanus*, Dennis unwisely attracted the attention of Alexander Pope, who from about 1711 onwards set about caricaturizing him as a blind and unthinking arch-classicist. Pope's characterization was largely unjust. Dennis, in no less than thirty critical works, for the most part more than ably championed the views of ancients such as Aristotle and Longinus. His championship of the observations of the latter was, in fact, to some degree substantially ahead of its time. His admiration of geniuses nearer his own day such as Milton and Dryden was likewise genuine and profound. However, he proved himself distressingly incapable of applying the theoretical principles of his classical models in his own dramatic work. One is almost compelled to admit that Pope had found a suitable target for his satiric animosity in anyone who could produce a couplet that reads, 'All around Venereal Turtles / Cooing, Billing, on the Myrtles', as Dennis had so famously done in his predictably ill-fated tragedy, *Rinaldo and Armida* (1699). Pope, in any event, found in Dennis an early model for the various incarnations of literary hacks and dunces – the Ogilbys and Wards, Eusdens and Blackmores, Theobalds and Cibbers – who he would in time set up as the antitheses of true literary endeavor. Gray, who was at an age when anything from the pen of the popular Pope invariably attracted his attention and admiration (he would in just two months' time be 'charmed' by the brand-new *Epistle to Arbuthnot*), was thus repeating in his attitude toward Dennis the received opinions of the master. As Roger Lonsdale has pointed out, the figure of Dennis as the appropriate voice for Gray's letter to Walpole seems to have been suggested by the fact that the last work published by the critic before his death had been a translation of Thomas Burnet's Latin *Treatise Concerning the State of Departed Souls*. Once Gray conceived the fiction of having visited the Devil tavern in Fleet Street when he was last in London (the same inn is mentioned several times in Pope's poetry), it may only have seemed natural that, searching in his modesty for someone to undertake the writing of a complimentary epistolary verse to return to Walpole's letter in kind, he turn to the appropriately spectral and conveniently penurious Dennis. The hack Dennis of Gray's creation, 'being tip'd with a Tester' or bribed with sixpence, instantly dashes off an account of life in the underworld.

Just as Dennis's own plays were criticized by Pope for their bathetic reduction of sound classical principles to a debased contemporary idiom, so too the 'Elysian Scene' from which he has been summoned is not recognizably the underworld both Gray and Walpole had so often visited in their own readings of classical literature, but rather a suitably fashionable resort for the departed of all ages past, a confused and hurly-burly 'underworld-turned-upside down'. The transformation from life into death, the speaker complains, is a confusing and unsettling one. Having been divested of his corporeal identity, Dennis needed some time to acclimatize himself to his new surroundings:

That little, naked, melancholy thing,
My soul, when first she tried her flight to wing,
Began with speed new regions to explore,
And blundered through a narrow postern door.
First most devoutly having said its prayers,
It tumbled down a thousand pair of stairs,
Through entries long, through cellars vast and deep,
Where ghostly rats their habitations keep,
Where spiders spred their webs and owlish goblins sleep.
After so many chances had befell,
It came into a mead of Asphodel:
Betwixt the confines of the light and dark
It lies, of 'Lysium the St. James's Park.
Here spirit-beaux flutter along the Mall,
And shadows in disguise skate o'er the iced Canal;
Here groves embowered and more sequestered shades,
Frequented by the ghosts of ancient maids,
Are seen to rise. The melancholy scene,
With gloomy haunts and twilight walks between,
Conceals the wayward band: here spend their time
Greensickness girls that died in youthful prime,
Virgins forlorn, all dressed in willow-green-i,
With Queen Elizabeth and Nicolini.
   More to reveal, or many words to use,
Would tire alike your patience and my muse.
Believe that never was so faithful found
Queen Proserpine to Pluto under ground,
Or Cleopatra to her Marc Antony
As Orozmades to his Celadony. (*PTG* 14–16)

Gray's own, proper voice – both in the evocation of the soul as a 'little naked, melancholy thing', as well as in the equally naked and straight-forward protestation of affection and continuing fidelity in the final lines quoted here – seems rather more in evidence than is usually the case in his early correspondence; that this voice managed to poke through the elaborate fiction of the letter at all is itself worthy of note. Dennis's trans-lation of Burnet's *Treatise* on the soul had suggested to Gray's mind an entire tradition of 'dialogues of the dead' that stretched through French writers of the seventeenth and early eighteenth centuries such as Fontenelle and Fénelon, all the way back to the Greek writer Lucian, who, in devising his own satiric take on the conventions of the Platonic dialogue in the second century A.D., had invented the form. Gray seems particularly to be recalling the Englishman Thomas Browne's 1702 attempt at the genre, a collection of *Letters from the Dead to the Living* that had included items such as 'A Letter of News from Mr. *Joseph*

Haines of Merry Memory, to his Friends at *Will's* Coffee-House in *Covent Garden'*. Gray's editors have been correct to point out that more serious and devout 'correspondence' from the denizens on the 'other side' – volumes such as Elizabeth Rowe's popular *Freindship in Death, in Twenty Letters from the Dead to the Living* – seem likewise to have occurred to his memory as being ripe for parodic deflation and burlesque. The elaborate flow of recollection and reference here helps to give the modern reader some idea as to just how Gray's encyclopedic memory (a memory that was only to grow more capacious with time) actually worked. Just as a single word or phrase could spark a chain of verbal or thematic references in Gray's mind, so too a single text inevitably conjured an entire tradition. Even as a writer only seventeen years old, Gray was already extraordinarily responsive to any twitch upon the thread of literary reference; even as a young man the web of intertextuality for him stretched far into the classical past and deep into the increasingly bewildering maze of contemporary literary production as well. Volumes did not sit alone and silent on his shelf but – as he was soon to put it in a letter offering his own personal version of the 'battle of the books' – constituted an extensive, on-going conversation of ideas both strange and related – a 'great hubbub of Tongues'. Hence, the verse-letter supposedly from John Dennis is an extraordinarily complex pastiche of genres as well as a cento-like reference to texts which the (supposedly) hack-writer himself would probably never have had the wherewithal to plunder. The fact that Gray's 'own' voice seems, again, to persist among this welter of literary reference and allusion offers some indication of how lonely and isolated he was feeling. Both the 'Lines Spoken By the Ghost of John Dennis at the Devil Tavern' (as this fragment was designated when it finally appeared in print in 1915) and the letter from the charnel house of St. Peter's church are early, mock elegies for a Thomas Gray who feels that he has been left by his friend for dead.

There is every indication that Walpole responded to the parody of Gray's earliest letters from Cambridge in kind. The singular epistle of Walpole's written to his friend that survives from only a little later in this period covering their early years at Cambridge, at least, is undertaken 'in the style of Addison's *Travels'*. Walpole was no less able a literary ventriloquist than Gray. Walpole's habit later in life of addressing various categories of letters (e.g., political, social, literary) to a carefully selected group of recipients when crafting the body of his own voluminous correspondence was to some degree an extension of the early abilities of the members of the Quadruple Alliance to slide in and out of different styles with ease. Speaking or writing were themselves to be regarded as acts of assumption and disguise, games of playful deceit wherein the participants knowingly masqueraded their native identities within multiple layers of referential generic and linguistic subterfuge.

And just as the habits of childhood would resurface in Gray's poetry as deflective techniques of echo and allusion, so too would they make themselves known in Walpole's mature correspondence in his development of a wide and varied body of epistolary voices – a fragmented coterie of many 'Horace Walpole's', no one of whom speaks quite the same language as the other.

In the 'Lines' from the Devil Tavern, Gray pointedly compares his relationship to Walpole both to that which existed between the god of the underworld, Pluto, and his queen, Proserpine, as well as to the notorious and illicit liaison of Marc Antony and Cleopatra. What is the reader to make of such comparisons? That Gray felt for Walpole an attraction recognizably to be classified as romantic love is not to be doubted. Moreover, unlike many other boys in similar circumstances – boys who had only recently left the sheltered environments of their schools (where such relationships were permitted and in some ways even encouraged) and submitted themselves to the glares and examination of the larger and rather less protected worlds of their university colleges – Gray appears never even to have considered redefining his relationship to his beloved. He seems to have been mercifully free (at least in his actual language and behaviour with reference to Walpole himself) of the self-directed anger, recrimination, and guilt that could and no doubt often did accompany the remove from a school such as Eton to a university such as Cambridge. His long letters to Walpole express not so much the delicate shades of feelings of a heart-felt passion slowly recognizing the boundaries of its own, appropriate limitations, but are painted – and continue to be painted – rather in bold and unapologetic colours. The truth of his own affections did not yet appear to daunt him in any significant way. No storms of self-loathing brewed in the obscurities of his being needed to be expelled or dispersed. It seemed to Gray in these early days at Cambridge that he loved Walpole – was infatuated with Walpole, felt more for Walpole – more even than he loved his own mother. The maternal attachment was of course secure and unalterable; Dorothy Gray had already stood by her son in bad times and had protected him, and there was no doubt in his mind that she would continue to do so in the future. Yet, however secure in himself Gray felt with regards to his relationship with Walpole, the distance now established between the two friends always threatened vaguely to weaken the bond between them. Hence Gray never fails to remind Walpole that without him he is like a child without his nurse; a body without its soul; a queen, even, without her king. Gray is startlingly unselfconscious in most often assuming the feminine role in the relationship. The psycho-sexual nature of his attraction to Walpole lies not so much beneath the surface of their connection to one another, as it sparkles with the dazzling and reflective play of a gilding and welcome light upon its waters. Any role Gray can assume to highlight his eagerly submissive posture to Walpole's recognizably greater authority is gratefully accepted. The Proserpine he plays to Walpole's Pluto is one paradoxically trapped in the underworld of Cambridge without his or her proper king and master. 'Orozmades' would just as willingly submit himself to the sting of the asp for the sake of his 'Celadony', as Cleopatra did for the sake of her honour when she believed Marc Antony to have been lost to her.

Gray's verse love-letter to Walpole closes with a postscript offering a briskly anecdotal account of the hurly-burly saturnalia one might expect to find in the 'new Regions' of Dennis's underworld:

> P. S. Lucrece for half a crown will show you fun,
> But Mrs. Oldfield is become a nun.
> Nobles and cits, Prince Pluto and his spouse,
> Flock to the ghost of Covent-Garden House:
> Plays, which were hissed above, below revive,
> When dead applauded that were damned alive.
> The people, as in life, still keep their passions,
> But differ something from the world in fashions.
> Queen Artemisia breakfasts on bohea,
> And Alexander wears a ramilie. (*PTG* 16–17)

Even the smallest details in this scene of concise, Hadean carnivalesque can be read as carrying some larger significance. Queen Artemisia, the wife and sister of Mausolus, who in antiquity was said daily to have mixed the ashes of her departed husband with her own drink as a sign of her grief and loss, has in the afterlife forsaken the proper mourning of the sublunary world in favour of more fashionable beverages. Not so, Walpole is meant to understand, has Gray forsaken him. Even the great Macedonian general Alexander seems to neglect his cherished companion Hephaestion in pursuing the fashionable dictates of the Stygian *ton*. Sexual roles in the underworld, too, 'differ something' from the world above. The virtuous Lucrece has become a common prostitute, while actresses of easy virtue such as Anne Oldfield have retreated into celibacy. Gray alone, the letter looks to alert Walpole, remains constant and unchanged in his love and affection.

*

Walpole's repeated delays were nevertheless maddening for Gray. His friend's imminent arrival at King's was forever being announced only to be postponed. There were several false alarms concerning his appearance in town which set Gray's heart on edge. Once he had decided to spend the Christmas vacation in Cambridge rather than return to

Cornhill (where his mother's situation was fast approaching its climax in her attempt to seek legal redress), Gray had little to do other than study in his rooms and obsess about his family and his friend. The combination of his concern for his mother's continued abuse and his anxiety regarding Walpole's prolonged absence must have left his nerves raw. Reported 'Walpole-sightings' could lead to absolute breakdowns. Wandering along King's Parade towards Trumpington street from St. Mary's church on a Tuesday afternoon before Christmas, Gray was casually informed by a passing acquaintance that Walpole had only that moment arrived in town and had already sent his servant to Peterhouse to enquire after his friend. Gray, 'throwing off all the prudery and reserve of a Cambridge student', ran the rest of the way to his college, only to be informed as he reached the porter's lodge – gasping for breath and probably clasping one hand to his side to assuage the pain of such unusual exertion – that it was not Walpole himself who has arrived, but only one of his servants. Gray's spirits were crushed, but even the sight of one of Walpole's retainers, himself cutting a fine figure in a fancy laced hat and scarlet stockings, was better than nothing at all. 'I was ready to eat him', Gray confessed to Walpole with greedy abandon, 'for having your livery on'.

On another occasion Walpole sent word to Gray that he was to hasten to Ashton's rooms over at King's, where the two could await his arrival and greet him together. Walpole never showed up. In his next letter to London, Gray's understandable pique was held in check only by his manifest disappointment. For all Walpole seemed to care, he pouted, he and Ashton might be waiting at King's still! Gray suggested facetiously that Walpole's conception of time is much different from his own, and that perhaps if he continued patiently to wait with Ashton in Cambridge 'there may be some small probability of your being just a-going to think of setting out' from London the following year, and arriving the year after that. He would still be waiting to meet him, Gray assured him, 'but in the mean time', he wrote,

> I would advise with you how Almanzor & I shall pass the time; wither you think it best for us to double ourselves up nicely in the corner of some old Draw, that at your arrival we may come out spick & span new in all our pleats; but perhaps by that time we may grow out of fashion, or moth-eaten; or to compose ourselves with a good dose of Laudanum for a year or two, & so dream of you. (CTG 26–27)

And so, over and again, it went. 'Thou hast been for this past month, like the auctioneer's mallet', he wrote in February, 1735, 'just a-coming! just a-coming! and pray what has next Thursday in it, more than last Wednesday, to make me expect you with any tolerable Certainty? when these two eyes behold thee, I question, whether I shall believe them'.

When Walpole finally arrived at Cambridge in the middle of March, Gray probably did have a hard time believing his eyes. He must have had an even more difficult time containing his enthusiasm and relief. Gray envied Ashton his proximity to their mutual friend, but took some small solace in the fact that as time went by it seemed that 'Almanzor' was not looking entirely to monopolize Walpole. Unlike Gray, Ashton was to begin forming a wider circle of acquaintances both within his college and among the university at large. He would keep a sharp eye out to remain intimate with Walpole; he already realized that the connection could prove to be a very advantageous one socially and professionally, and must have worked to give Walpole the impression that his time was completely at his friend's disposal. But, son of Sir Robert or not, there were other influential people to meet while at Cambridge as well. It was unwise, Ashton felt, to have only one iron in the fire that fed the ambitions of his career.

Gray, on the other hand, seems never seriously to have considered such ulterior motives in his attachment to his friend. His devotion to Walpole was complete and wholehearted. He looked not for a court appointment or a government sinecure, but for the honest return of his infatuation. And that, Walpole – insofar as he was then capable – gave him. The subtle distinctions in class and social standing that were ignored if only because they had not yet been fully comprehended when the friends had been at Eton, however, began now to exert some slight pressure on their behaviour toward one another. Walpole's standing as a Fellow-Commoner at the university entailed not only a distinction in academic dress (the silk gowns of Fellow-Commoners were trimmed with ornamental gold or silver lace, and their velvet caps were likewise graced with a gold or silver tassel) and higher academic fees, but fine discriminations in certain privileges as well. The very designation 'Fellow-Commoner' was derived from the right such students enjoyed of being able to dine at the Fellows table in their respective colleges. They sat removed from the other students, and there they enjoyed better food and, often, wine with their meals. One suspects, too, that this 'higher grade' of undergraduate sometimes indulged in the sort of behaviour that would not have been tolerated from the same college's less fortunate scholars. Not long after Walpole and Gray were themselves students at Cambridge, Samuel Johnson, in one of his *Idler* essays, would represent the plight of one university undergraduate who was kept awake at night by 'a young fellow-commoner, being very noisy over [his] head'.[5] Gray himself, as we

---

[5] Samuel Johnson, 'Idler' No. 38 (Saturday 2 December 1758) in *The Idler and the Adventurer*, ed. Walter Jackson Bate, John M. Bullitt, and L. F. Powell (New Haven and London: Yale University Press, 1963) 103.

shall see, in time ran into some trouble with the Fellow-Commoners – the 'Bucks' – at his own college. The fact that the term 'fellow-commoner' came by the end of the century to be the commonly accepted nickname for an empty bottle of wine likewise speaks well neither for the drinking habits of the class of students as a whole, nor for their general reputation when it came to intellect and study; a decanted bottle of liquor earned the designation 'fellow-commoner', as contemporary dictionaries of slang observed, for not being considered 'over full', just as such students were not themselves in general considered to be 'over full' of learning.

Walpole bore the brunt of bridging any such gaps in the newly articulated social hierarchy that existed between the Cantabrigian members of the former Quadruple Alliance. And he appears to have done so with admirable grace and tact. Whether Walpole was the natural son of his father or not, the society by which he had been surrounded ever since his infancy had already imparted to his manners, bearing, and demeanor a perception regarding social niceties and a subtle understanding of what was 'due' to various people in general that had become second-nature to him. It is significant that he made a point of maintaining contact with West – the son of the former Lord Chancellor of Ireland, remember – at a time when Gray, as we shall see, was neglecting him. Likewise, West had been invited to spend time at Sir Robert's hunting-lodge in Richmond Park, where he actually met and dined with the Prime Minister, while Walpole's other friends, Gray included, were tendered no such invitation. Social decorum could not, it seems, be ignored entirely, even when it came to affairs of the heart.

Still and all, Walpole's very real affection for each and every one of his friends tended for the most part to guide his behaviour well. He was very much aware that his status distinguished him from Gray, Ashton, and West. He knew that his movements and activities might be reported in the newspapers like those of a celebrity and that his travel plans (both real and imaginary) were to be considered as the common property of the social pages, but he tried as much as he could to make such differences work in the larger interests of his friendship. He was as generous as possible both of his time and of his comparative material wealth as was possible. Not very long after his arrival in Cambridge he wrote to West that things had pretty much settled down into a comfortable routine. Taking care first to compliment West on a verse letter he received from Oxford earlier that month, Walpole suggested that since he could not respond in kind, and since West had in any event said in verse 'all that [he] intended to have said in far inferior prose', they might do well to establish some other theme in their correspondence. 'But why mayn't we hold a classical correspondence?', Walpole asked,

I can never forget the many agreeable hours we have passed in reading Horace and Virgil; and I think they are topics which will never grow stale. Let us extend the Roman Empire, and cultivate two barbarous towns o'errun with rusticity and mathematics. The creatures are so used to a circle, that they plod on in the same round, with their whole view confined to a *punctum, cujus nullus est pars*. . . . Orosmades and Almanzor are just the same; that is, I am almost the only person they are acquainted with, and consequently the only person acquainted with their excellencies. Plato improves every day; so does my friendship with him. These three divide my whole time – though I will believe you will guess there is no quadruple alliance; that was a happiness I only enjoyed when you was at Eton. (*WC* xiii–xiv.94)

The identity of 'Plato' – like that of other Etonians referred to in some of these early letters only cryptically as 'Tydeus' and 'Malepert' – has never satisfactorily been made. The nickname may well have belonged to William Cole who, though slightly older than Gray, Walpole, and West, had been a casual friend to all three at the school, or it may have referred to Walpole's tutor, John Whalley. It would be very like Walpole gently to remind West that he had more than one friend who was thinking about him in Cambridgeshire, just as it is like him to recall their time spent reading together and to emphasize that, despite the distance between them, there is no one who is capable of taking West's place in the 'alliance' of their friendship. Walpole's letter might even have served to remind Gray himself (it is likely that they would have spoken freely between themselves of their correspondence to and from their other friends) that there was now someone in Oxford who was feeling far more lonely and isolated than he had been in the earliest months at his own university. With Walpole safely by his side in Cambridge, Gray could finally settle into a routine himself, and turn a necessary attention to his other friends, to his family, and to his studies.

II. Profits and Amusements

For a student who had found the emphasis on the imaginative literature of the Greek and Latin tradition at Eton so congenial to his own tastes – for one who had even, by the time he arrived at university, grown into an adept writer of Latin poetry himself – the academic curriculum at Cambridge came as something of an unwelcome surprise. No more were the 'agreeable hours' of study to be passed reading Horace and Virgil. Gone too were the lazy afternoons devoted to his favourites among the Greeks: Homer, Sophocles, Euripides, and Plutarch. Time had to be carefully carved out of Gray's daily schedule even to read more popular authors – French and Italian writers such as Dante, Ariosto, Racine, and La Fontaine, or English poets like Milton, Waller, Prior, and Pope. The course of study at the university insisted that one's afternoons be spent rather in the considerably drier company of Aristotelian metaphysicians. All the members of the now-fragmented Quadruple Alliance, as West would write of his own inability to spend a desired amount of time among his favourite classical writers, were 'unwillingly obliged to follow . . . less agreeable engagements'.

Gray at first tried his best to maintain an interest in his work. Such study at least served to keep him busy while his residency requirements, if nothing else, kept him waiting in Cambridge for Walpole. In addition to his responsibilities as a Cosin scholar, and apart from college tutorials, there were lectures and disputations to be attended, assigned texts to be read, rhetorical exercises to be written, and lengthy passages of Latin to be committed to memory. Preparing a weekly essay on an assigned text or philosophical proposition, perhaps reading that essay aloud and then defending it against the criticisms of a tutor or of another student, meant spending much of one's time in study. One needed likewise always to look beyond such weekly tutorials or supervisions to the assessment of examinations. For all the apparent lack of attention paid to providing its students with suitable tuition and instruction, the university tended to regard such exams themselves rather seriously. Candidates looked not merely to pass these tests and so earn their degrees, but were aware as they sat their exams that their results would be graded and ranked. The top candidates in the exams in mathematics and philosophy were qualified as honours candidates under the heading 'First Tripos'; the next level of students earned the designation 'Second Tripos'. The names of these candidates would then be printed on one side of a sheet of paper circulated at the university 'Congregation' or Commencement, on the verso of which appeared the 'Tripos verses' – a set of Latin verses, usually humorous or satiric – that were read by a specially selected Bachelor of Arts. This oratorically privileged student traditionally sat upon a three-legged stool, hence the designation 'Tripos'.

A proper mastery of the sciences in the early eighteenth century required that Gray and his fellow students demonstrate their competence in the areas of metaphysics, physics, mathematics, and, to a slightly lesser degree, cosmography. Despite his weary protestations to the contrary, Gray was not, of course, entirely without an interest in the first and most important of these provinces. His secondary-school training had provided him with a sufficiently solid foundation in Latin, Greek, and logic to make the task of learning itself a relatively easy one. Indeed, compared to some of his contemporaries who appear to have been sent on to Cambridge having mastered only a few shreds of Latin and hardly any Greek to speak of, Gray's path should have been comparatively smooth. Moreover, his own early Latin poetry, as we have seen, already demonstrates a developed interest in the order and structure of the universe, in being *qua* being – an interest, that is, in metaphysics. Metaphysics studied this question of being itself, comprehending its transcendental attributes (i.e. 'the Good'), and its principles (potency, act, and the four causes: efficient, final, material, and formal). The science of metaphysics, as historians of the scholastic curriculum at Cambridge have summarized, asked students to consider the divisions of being according to the ten *Catagoriae* of Aristotle, starting from the Prime Cause or Mover, God Himself.

Such consideration of the ultimate principles and causes of things was not incidental to Gray's interests. The lines of Latin poetry based largely on Pope's *Essay on Man* and on the empirical philosophy of John Locke that he had written while yet a student at Eton had addressed precisely such 'metaphysical' questions and concerns. And that, in some ways, was precisely the problem for Gray. Metaphysics, as it was taught and considered at the university, lacked poetry; physics and mathematics, it need hardly be added, were positively prosaic. Gray consequently resented the hours spent in study, and begrudged the time he devoted to his course work as being stolen from that which might better have been set aside for his own leisure reading. 'I have endured lectures daily and hourly since I came last', he would eventually write to West,

supported by the hopes of being shortly at full liberty to give myself up to my friends and classical companions, who, poor souls! though I see them fallen into great contempt with most people here, yet I cannot help sticking to them, and out of a spirit of obstinacy (I think) love them the better for it; and indeed, what can I do else? Must I plunge into metaphysics? Alas, I cannot see in the dark; nature has not furnished me with the optics of a cat. Must I pore upon mathematics? Alas, I cannot see in too much light; I am no eagle. It is very possible that two and two make four, but I would not give four farthings to demonstrate this ever so clearly; and if these be the profits of life, give me the amusements of it. The people I behold all around me, it seems, know all this and more, and yet I do not know one of them who inspires me with any ambition of being like him. Surely it was of this place, now Cambridge, but formerly known by the name of Babylon, that the prophet spoke when he said, 'the wild beasts of the desert shall dwell there, and their houses shall be full of doleful creatures, and owls shall build there, and satyrs shall dance there; their forts and towers shall be a den for ever, a joy of wild asses; there shall the great owl make her nest, and lay and hatch and gather under her shadow; it shall be a court of dragons; the screech owl also shall rest there, and find for herself a place for rest'. You see here is a pretty collection of desolate animals, which is verified in this town to a tittle'. (*CTG* 56)

Gray's fast and furious references in this letter to the book of Isaiah – from which there are no less than five distinct 'quotations', ranging from Chapters 13 to 34 – transparently encode within his denunciation of the university curriculum the promise of his eventual redemption and restoration from his own Cantabrigian exile. Much as the biblical prophet had foretold the downfall of the oppressors of Israel and the eventual and assured salvation of the suffering servants of God, so too Gray's fidelity to his 'classical companions' will in the fullness of time be rewarded in the new heaven and new earth of his own personal, post-Exilic history – a history which he here prophesies as gloriously succeeding his career at Peterhouse.

In the meantime, however, he would simply have to make do as best he could. Hours would just have to be stolen from his studies to make room for Horace and Virgil, and, no doubt, they were. Gray, like university undergraduates to this very day, took care always to maintain the fiction among his friends and colleagues that he did little or no work. Getting caught with one's nose in a textbook, let alone pretending that such reading was anything less than completely odious, was a social *faux pas* of the gravest kind. 'Take my word & experience upon it', Gray wrote with the constitutionally uncongenial assumptions of a cultivated and affected indifference to West, 'doing nothing is a most amusing business'.

When he was not banging his head against Aristotle, Gray could probably be found rereading his Virgil and his Ovid or (a favourite pastime of his early months and years at Cambridge) translating passages of Propertius and, particularly, Statius for his own amusement – tasks that would doubtlessly have been considered just as much 'work' by many of his Cambridge colleagues as their assigned studies. Along with the various books on metaphysics and mathematics he was purchasing in Cambridge and London bookstores at about this time, he continued to pick up the odd volume of poetry, history, and philosophy. Nor, as we have already seen, had the romantic imagination that had helped him to pass so much of his time at Eton with his friends in such a fanciful and expansive fantasy-land of an Arcadia *redux* abandoned him entirely. One early letter to Walpole from university found Gray interpreting the spectacle of Plough-Monday celebrations at Cambridge as if they were vivid *tableau vivant* interpretations of the romance *Amadis de Gaule*. New romances, such as Crébillon fils' *L'Écumoire, ou Tanzai at Néadarné*, and collections of *Arabian Nights*-inspired narratives like Ambrose Philips's translation of François

Petis de la Croix's *Persian Tales*, were also being bought and devoured in these years.

Not content to read some of his favourite 'modern' continental authors only in translation, Gray soon joined both Walpole and William Cole in taking lessons in Italian from one Hieronomo Bartolommeo Piazza, an apostate Italian priest then living in Cambridge. Ashton refers slightingly and dismissively to Piazza as 'Walpole's Italian', but his seeming disdain may well be a mark of his own abstention and subsequent exclusion from the little band of newly designated *amici*. One can easily picture Gray, Walpole, and Cole playfully trying out their new phrases and vocabulary on one another, supplementing their words with the kinds of exaggerated, over-expansive gestures and emphasis they may well have regarded as indigenous to the language and, in so doing, irritating their increasingly serious and career-minded friend, who of course had no use for such nonsense. Gray soon wrote to West that he was progressing very well in his new language. 'I learn Italian like any dragon', he in time confessed to West, 'and in two months am got through the 16th book of Tasso, whom I hold in great admiration'. It is characteristic of Gray at this stage in his life (and so like many students at the same age who approach Gray's learning and ability) to make a point of noting his own peculiar 'admiration' for authors whose works possess a weight of cultural seniority that in turn makes such idiosyncratic and slightly condescending protestations of worth at best thoughtlessly charming, and at worst positively precious. It would be a surprisingly long time before Gray stopped almost instinctively echoing aesthetic and literary opinions that were fashionable and culturally correct. The development of his own taste and the careful and meticulously informed formulation of his own opinions in literature and art would come later. As Gray settled into the routine of his Cambridge days and nights, his letters bristled with the 'Have you reads?', the 'Have your heard ofs?', and the 'Have you seens?' of a clever and vitally intelligent young man who was for the first time in his life truly drinking deeply from the Pierian spring.

*

These days may similarly have planted the seeds of understanding that would in time grow and blossom into other, more personal kinds of revelation as well. Walpole was now a fixture in Gray's life. Gray's every movement revolved around those of his friend. The two were very close to inseparable, and the porters and servants at King's College must soon have grown used to the sight of the little Petrean – no longer a freshman but perhaps still 'waddling' as he scurried to keep up with his companions – passing among the courtyards to Walpole's rooms.

Together they tackled the indomitable Cambridge curriculum, a challenge that soon proved even more insurmountable for Walpole than it was for Gray. A mere two weeks after he had begun his mathematics lectures with the blind Nicholas Sanderson, then Lucasian Professor of Mathematics at the university, Walpole was informed that his attempts at the discipline, however valiant and well-intentioned, were hopeless. Mortified and positively tearful at this assessment of his abilities, Walpole quickly hired a fellow of Clare College – Luke Trevigar – as his private instructor. Trevigar tutored him in the subject every day for a year, but Sanderson's perception of his student's abilities proved genuinely prophetic; try as he might, Walpole never *would* learn mathematics. Meanwhile he diligently went to lectures in civil law under Francis Dickins, and likewise attended the young Dr. William Battie's lectures on anatomy. His own supervisor for the better part of his time at King's was John Whalley. Whalley's tutelage, however, was probably of little practical value to Walpole. 'Excessive Drinking, high and luxurious Eating, and other riotous Behaviour was the daily and Common Way of Life with Mr. Whalley', William Cole would later write; Whalley would eventually, Cole added unpleasantly, die 'as sleek and fat as any mole'.[6] Walpole's first assigned tutor – his father's former chaplain, James Anstey – died while incarcerated for insanity not long after his association with young Horace.

While Walpole thus seemed at least to attempt seriously to devote himself to his studies, he could not but have been very much aware of the fact that whether he eventually read for a degree or not would make little difference with regard to his career and, indeed, with regard to his life generally (he in fact took his name off the college books at the beginning of Michaelmas term 1738, without taking a degree). Even while he remained at Cambridge, Walpole was appointed by his father first to a post in the Customs House worth almost £800 a year, and then to a place as Usher of the Exchequer, the remuneration of which was even more substantial. Needless to say, Gray had in these first years at university the promise of no such sinecures and (unlike Ashton) appears never seriously to have considered parlaying the influence of his best friend into a career in government or the clergy. The fact that Walpole may have shared with Gray the kinds of begging letters he received even from the likes of the famous Cambridge theologian Dr. Conyers Middleton (who in one such letter suggested that Walpole inform his father that he had himself a dependent client 'who, in the decline of life, would be proud to receive from him, what he never received, or asked before from any minister, some mark of public favour,

[6] William Cole, *A Journal of my Journey to Paris in the year 1765*, ed. F. G. Stokes (London, 1931) 75.

proper to his character and his profession') can only have served to put Gray on his guard against ever sounding like such a 'client' himself. Walpole's social status, Gray must have vowed at the time, would never impair their friendship or otherwise compromise their affection for one another.

And yet, the differences in station between the two men existed and simply could not be ignored. Whereas Walpole routinely broke the drudgery of his Cambridge academic schedule by spending the vacations in London and indulging in the manifold pleasure of the metropolitan social scene, Gray – for his entire first year at university – dared not even risk a visit to his father's Cornhill home. When he finally did return to spend the Christmas vacation of 1735–36 in the city, he was painfully aware of the fact that, for all his detailed accounts of play-going and opera-watching, he couldn't pretend to emulate Walpole's own social schedule. 'I don't', he wrote with a knowing modesty, 'succeed to your diversions in town, I believe'. Likewise when Walpole visited his father at Houghton, and spent the summer surrounded by the stunning and now materially palpable achievement of his father's career as Prime Minister, Gray could only watch from a distance:

> I sympathize with you in the Sufferings, which you foresee are coming upon you; we are both at present, I imagine, in no very agreeable situation; for my own part I am under the misfortune of having nothing to do, but it is a misfortune, which, thank my Stars, I can pretty well bear; You are in a Confusion of Wine & Bawdy & Hunting & Tobacco; & heaven be praised, you too can pretty well bear it; while our evils are no more, I believe we sha'nt much repine. (*CTG* 45–46)

Gray's attempt at an easy and obvious comparison here – his attempt to describe his own situation as in any way similar to that of his friend – is a painful one. Cut off now from his own father (emotionally if not physically) by his mother's recent attempt at a legal separation, Gray could not but have envied Walpole the opportunity of growing closer to and appreciating the achievements of Sir Robert. Horace Walpole had nothing of which to be ashamed, nothing to hide – or so, at least, his socially confident pose seemed to indicate. If Horace's mother and Sir Robert had not, ultimately, been a happy couple themselves, there was perhaps some small solace to be taken in the fact (by Gray, at least) that their separation had at least been regarded as productive of polite and eminently civilized domestic disagreement – the stuff of court gossip and the social pages – and not of bruises, blood, and battery. While Walpole could begin to understand the struggle and achievement of his father's political career and look proudly on the unarguably 'splendid' results of his worldly success at Houghton, Gray could only watch as his own father, cowed finally by his mother and his aunts, retreated even further in shame from the active society of those London merchants who had once been his colleagues. Walpole's family fortune and reputation seemed only to increase, while Gray's own seemed only, irretrievably, to diminish.

Such a perception may ultimately have played some small role in Gray's growing realization throughout his early career at Cambridge that although his friendship with Walpole was the relationship he most valued, and that although he felt secure in the knowledge that his love for Horace could withstand whatever stress their differences in social standing placed upon it, there were connections also to be maintained and cultivated to those who were in many ways clearly nearer to him both in heart and in spirit, even though he might not wish fully, at the time, to recognize the true extent of such proximity of soul. In his earliest days at Cambridge, Gray's neglect of West did him little credit. Long letters from his friend lay neglected on Gray's table at Peterhouse even as he skipped dinners to take 'a better opportunity of writing' to Walpole. He might from time to time glance guiltily in the candlelight at the pages of West's aching correspondence, but his pen went on busily writing to Walpole, for whom he claimed to be 'starved'. By the time he had arrived at Christ Church, Oxford, in the summer of 1735, West was genuinely pained by his friend's neglect. The contrast between the snug, central Schoolyard at Eton and the immense, impersonal expanse of Tom Quad, moreover, was too great to be ignored. If Gray had at first felt lonely and morosely out of his element at tiny Peterhouse, West at Oxford was positively sick with nervous anxiety and depression. Regular migraine headaches confined him to the darkness of his rooms, and his studies – which, thanks to his low spirits and constant illness, could be pursued only sporadically and with indifference – were a little less than a 'bondage'. His new 'discipline', he soon confessed, was neither metaphysical nor mathematical, but personal; being 'the most irregular thing alive at college', he admitted that all of his time and effort seemed to be spent merely in maintaining his own health. His pain was compounded by Gray's neglect. 'You use me very cruelly', he wrote from the depths of his first Michaelmas term,

You have sent me but one letter since I have been at Oxford, and that too agreeable not to make me sensible how great my loss is in not having more. Next to seeing you is the pleasure of seeing your handwriting; next to hearing you is the pleasure of hearing from you. Really and sincerely I wonder at you, that you thought it not worth while to answer my last letter. I hope this will have better success in behalf of your quondam school-fellow; . . . Consider me very seriously here in a strange country, inhabited by things that call themselves Doctors and Masters of Arts; a

country flowing with syllogisms and ale, where Horace and Virgil are
equally unknown; consider me, I say, in this melancholy light, and then
think if something be not due to [me]. (*CTG* 33–34)

The complaints of Gray's self-deprecatingly styled 'quondam school-
fellow' here could not help but strike at his conscience. West was
offering an assessment of his situation which was, after all, nearly a
precise copy of that which Gray had himself sent off to Walpole soon
after his own arrival in Cambridge. Both felt lost, both felt surrounded
by 'foreign' strangers and abandoned by the individuals who had
helped to infuse their lives with a daily meaning. And while Gray at least
had been able to take solace, however qualified, in the presence of
Ashton, and while he had been able similarly to look forward to the
arrival (however delayed) of Walpole, West had nothing to console him.
The gray November evenings closing in around him held no promise of
delivery, and he heard in the monotony of the neighboring bells only
a presage of his own thudding pain in the dreary perseverance of
an enforced and unwelcome routine. The tolling of Great Tom – the
magnificent, six-ton bell of Christ Church's Tom Tower the deep voice
of which signaled the college curfew each night with its traditional 101
rings – echoed the throbbing of his head, and reminded him that the
gates leading to the outside world on St. Aldate's had once again been
shut for the evening.

Despite such pleading from his friend, Gray was a long time in
responding to West's letters. Protesting first, in December of the same
year, that he would soon no doubt be seeing West in person during the
vacation in London, Gray then backed off from the excuse that he had
been too busy to write, and took up the equally unacceptable pose that
he had nothing to write *about*. Even as he addressed himself to West,
however, his better impulses appear to have overpowered him. After a
brief spasm of self-pity, his confession of neglect gains the voice of
genuine honesty. 'I do not wonder in the least at your frequent blaming
my indolence', he began with an affected attempt at an apology,

it ought rather to be called ingratitude, and I am obliged to your goodness for softening so harsh an appellation. When you have seen one of
my days, you have seen a whole year of my life; they go round and round
like the blind horse in the mill, only he has the satisfaction of fancying
he makes progress, and gets some new ground; my eyes are open enough
to see the same dull prospect, and to know that having made four-and-
twenty steps more, I shall be just where I was. . . . However, as the most
undeserving people in the world must sure have the vanity to wish somebody had a regard for them, so I need not wonder at my own, in being
pleased that you care about me. You need not doubt, therefore, of having

a first row in the front box of my little heart, and I believe you are not in danger of being crouded there; it is asking you to an old play, indeed, but you will be candid enough to excuse the whole piece for the sake of a few tolerable lines. (*CTG* 34–35)

Gray may have begun writing the theatrical conceit that carries the last lines here as a quaint and even jaunty rhetorical flourish with which elegantly to end his letter, but the distance of time has not impaired the fact that as his pen passed over the paper, he must have felt a real rush of affection for West. He perhaps thought shamefacedly of the weekly correspondence he had carried on with Walpole when he had first arrived at Cambridge, and of the countless hours the two had now spent in the company of familiar faces like those of Ashton and Cole, while poor West sat friendless and alone in Oxford. They passed and repassed in and out of one another's colleges to share their tea and suppers with one another; West could look for no such reciprocation. While the air in their now-comfortable rooms at Cambridge had hung heavy with the pleasant warmth of coffee and conversation, Gray realized as he thought more and more of his 'quondam school-fellow', and while the fire dancing on their hearths had cast its shadows both on their moments of quiet discussion and comraderie as well as on their sometimes boyish instances of playful horse-play and genial, self-dramatizing foolishness, the quiet solitude of West's suite at Christ Church similarly reflected his own morbid state of mind. Gray must have folded his letter rather guiltily, sealed it, and placed it to one side to be sent off the following morning. In any event, he may very well have thought, leaning back in his chair and staring into the fire, things will be different in future. The Christmas holidays were at hand, and with them an entire range of activities – new plays, new operas, new music – in addition to those lively diversions that the season regularly had to offer. West could no doubt comfortably be included in at least some of the seasonal outings; with the demands on Walpole's time being what they were, Gray's attention toward the one friend would not even have to be charged against his affection to the other. With Ashton on the scene as well, Gray may finally have reasoned as he shrugged off the gloom into which the writing of the letter would have thrust him, the Quadruple Alliance itself could even, for some few weeks at least, be entirely restored.

David Cecil observed that if Walpole provided a link between Gray and 'the outer world', it was West who remained 'the companion of his inner life'.[7] Yet for all of Gray's good intentions, his gradual realization that the ties of temperament and intellect which bound him to West were

---

[7] Cecil, 103.

of stronger stuff than the bonds of sheer affection or even infatuation that linked him to Walpole, developed at a painfully slow pace. Two short weeks after he had protested his deep friendship for West, and had assured him that they would soon see enough of one another in the city, Gray wrote to Walpole describing his busy social schedule while in London. He had been to see Dryden's *King Arthur* at Goodman's Fields, and was considering heading over to the King's Theatre in Haymarket to attend a performance of the opera *Artaxerses*. The sets, costumes, and 'machinery' of the productions were carefully critiqued, and the performers and their respective reputations were minutely examined, but for all his effort cleverly to describe the 'Beauties' both of the actors and their plays, Gray made no mention of having made any contact with West, much less of having included him in any of his outings. Seemingly concerned more with impressing Walpole with his own involvement in the world of contemporary fashion, Gray again allowed himself to neglect West. The two may well, in the end, have seen one another in London. West would certainly have gone so far as to insist on such a reunion. But by now Gray's repeated excuses and half-hearted attention were themselves beginning to grow dispiriting (nearly a year later West would again complain of having seen only a 'slight shadow' of Gray when the latter visited town). West would gladly have turned to other companions but, again, he had none. Moreover, he seemed increasingly to lack not only the time, but also the health and the energy to cultivate new acquaintances. The poem West eventually sent to Gray and addressed (*Ad Amicos*) to all three of his former Eton schoolfellows and offers a summation of his feelings as he continued in his 'exile' at Oxford:

> Yes, happy youths, on Camus' sedgy side,
> You feel each joy that friendship can divide;
> Each realm of science and of art explore,
> And with the ancient blend the modern lore.
> Studious alone to learn whate'er may tend
> To raise the genius or the heart to mend;
> Now pleas'd along the cloyster'd walk you rove,
> And trace the verdant mazes of the grove,
> Where social oft, and oft alone, ye chuse
> To catch the zephyr and to court the muse. (*CTG* 61–62)

These verses, based largely on one of Tibullus' elegies, made a profound impression on Gray. He eventually copied the lines into his own Commonplace Book, making some few changes in West's Latin original. Many years later, Walpole would suggest that Gray publish some of West's work along with his own. The poet (who at that point had almost certainly not even finished, let alone published, *The Elegy*) protested that even when taken together their ' "Joynt-Stock" would hardly compose a small volume'. Lines such as these verses *Ad Amicos*, however, at least suggest the possibility that Gray – always very wary (and with good reason) of being perceived as being too heavily indebted to the works of others poets – may never seriously have considered presenting his own writing to the public in such close proximity to the work of friends to whom he was so clearly indebted.

From about the spring of 1736 onward, Gray began with a growing sense of maturity and responsibility to write to West with greater regularity. Walpole's own correct and thoughtful conduct toward their friend may have provided something of a model for Gray's behaviour. In May of that year, Walpole surprised West with a visit to Christ Church. Gray pictured West's initial confusion and then his characteristically ecstatic elation when he realized that the magnificent coach and six that had just pulled to a stop at the college gates was about to deliver to him not one but three visitors; Walpole had been accompanied on his journey by his tutor, John Whalley, and his close King's College friend, John Dodd (the two men shared the same birthday, a circumstance to attract Walpole's interest and affection if ever there was one). Walpole – 'so very gay, high spirited, and *allegro*' – brought Oxford momentarily to life for West. Even after his departure, the effects of his visit lingered. Once he had returned to Cambridge, Walpole sent West a short panegyric that he had composed to the rival university town which, as West describes it, animated the very Cotswold stone of its buildings. 'The royal statue in the dome of Queen's College', West wrote in thanks, 'has been thrice seen publicly to dance a courant, and last night all the great heads round the [Sheldonian] Theatre shouted for joy, to the great astonishment of all that were present'. The same letter closes with a request that Walpole 'remember [him] to Gray', and asks plaintively, 'and where is Ashton?'[8]

*

West, who at least appears capable of taking Ashton's disappearance in stride, may have been troubled by the fact that Gray – who had that very month confessed that 'all the employment of [his] hours may be best explained by negatives' – did not bother to accompany Walpole on the journey to see him in Oxford. Gray by this point in 1736, however, had reasons that were more than sufficient to excuse or to explain his behaviour. For once it was his family, and not his friends, who demanded

---

[8] WC xiii. 99–100.

the greater share of his attention. Dr. Audley's opinion concerning his
mother had been given to Dorothy Gray on 9 February. While Audley
himself quite clearly sympathized with Mrs. Gray, he stressed the fact
that there were few means of legal redress available to her in such a
situation. The best she could do, Audley essentially advised her, was to
lie low and take care not to provoke her husband to 'use her ill'. If Philip
Gray's violent behavior did, indeed, finally force her out of her own
home, such a circumstance might – but only might – be turned to her
advantage. If her husband himself went to law against their marriage,
Dorothy's subsequent status as a defendant rather than a plaintiff in such
a case could possibly work in her favour, insofar as the court would
probably consider her evidence of abuse in a less prejudicial light if her
husband himself 'proceeded to extremities'.

Like many brave women before and since, Dorothy Gray found it necessary to take matters into her own hands. If things were going to change
in her Cornhill home, then it was she – not Doctor Audley, not Doctors
Commons, and certainly not her husband – who would have to change
them. If this meant standing up to Philip Gray and defying him with a
strength and a sense of purpose she had never quite summoned before,
so be it. As she allowed the weight of Audley's considered opinion to
make some impression on her mind, we can only hope that she was filled
with a new resolve. Crossing the cold and quiet courtyards and passing
the old red brick houses on her way back toward the bustling activity
of Ludgate Hill and St Paul's, she must have come to some sort of decision. Audley's only practical advice had been to suggest that she ask that
'some common friend' intervene and act as a bridge between herself and
her husband. But to whom could she turn? The people who she naturally trusted most – her brothers and sisters – were the very same
individuals who most violently provoked her husband's increasingly
irrational anger and jealousy. Philip Gray had already attempted to drive
her closest sister and business partner, Mary, from her very home, and
Dorothy did not wish any longer to risk the possibility that her husband's
physical violence might extend itself to the other members of her family.
Thomas had now reached an age when it was no longer necessary
for her physically to shield him from his father's wrath, but he had for
years been too much himself a party of the conflict ever to effect any
resolution. He could now enter and leave the house in safety, but the
situation within the home was of too longstanding a nature for Gray,
acting alone, or even with his mother's explicit support, to alter. Besides,
Dorothy must have reasoned, he had already suffered and endured
enough. The burden of changing her own married life was not one for
her child to bear. Even by the time she had travelled the half mile
between St. Paul's churchyard and St. Michael's Alley, Dorothy Gray
may have made up her mind. She would at least confront her husband

with the possibility of initiating proceedings that could lead to a legal separation. If the law would not readily stand by her side in such a case, its processes would at least buy her some time in the matter; there was no need to let her husband know that she was aware of the fact that she was, from the beginning of such a course of action, operating at a disadvantage. Only if such a threat proved entirely ineffectual would she consider retreating to the safety of her family connections. For the time being at least, she was resolved to fight and to stand her ground in Cornhill.

As is often the case in such situations, Philip Gray, when finally confronted with the potentially nasty legal mess he had made of his domestic situation, and when faced with his wife's determination not to be bullied into submission without first putting up a fierce fight, collapsed and all but disappeared into the insecurity that must have prompted such abusive behaviour in the first place. Given the fact that no legal proceedings were initiated, it is difficult even to begin to reconstruct Philip's state of mind at this point. The trail of documentary evidence pretty much ends the moment Dorothy Gray stepped out of Dr. Audley's office and into the courtyards of Doctors Commons. It is also difficult to account for the fact that Dorothy's husband appears so quickly to have capitulated to his wife's demands for fair and civil treatment – demands that must surely have been made to no avail in the very recent past. From this point, we hear nothing of any profound domestic upset in the Gray household; at the very least the situation seems not to have grown any worse for Dorothy.

But let us look a bit more closely at the circumstances surrounding the crisis. Philip Gray was now approaching sixty; his wife was past fifty. They had been married for some twenty-five years. It is perhaps too much to hope that they were able finally to sit down and talk to one another – to reevaluate their relationship now that their only child was well established at university and they themselves faced the prospect of having to spend their final years in one another's company – but such a hope is at least not beyond the bounds of the possible. Faced with the combination of Dorothy's ultimatum, young Thomas's ever-growing independence, and the increasingly shaky state of his own business affairs (a financial situation concerning which he took care to keep both his wife and his son in the dark), Philip Gray may have been forced to examine his life, and to address his manifold failures as a husband, a father, and a provider. Philip Gray had been brought up to realize that his wife and perhaps his son and many of his relatives felt that the world would be a better place – would at the very least be no worse off – without him. If, as indeed seems to have been the case, he began to leave his wife to herself (neglect would by this stage have been counted as a comparative blessing) one of his more concrete responses to such a realization, as we shall see, was to turn to his own family and to the roots of the Grays' family history in Wanstead, to provide some kind of validation for his very being. A failure as a husband and a father, Philip sought solace and safety within the group. He looked to escape from a troubled sense of his own personal identity by immersing himself in (and trying literally to reconstruct the family fortunes and reputations of) the past. Consequently Cornhill, London, and (we can assume) Dorothy and Thomas were, he may inevitably have convinced himself, simply no longer all that important to him.

One very strong reason for speculating that this was indeed the case is the fact that in the very same week that Dorothy Gray informed her husband of the circumstances surrounding her recent consulta-tion with Dr. Audley and the resolutions she had made as a result of their meeting, Philip Gray also received the unexpected news of his sister Sarah's death. Sarah Gray's passing on 12 February was not in itself what shocked Gray most; only two years younger than her brother, she was almost sixty when she died. He would have been stunned rather by the unexpected terms of her will. The unmarried Sarah Gray had passed over her only surviving brother to leave her entire inheri-tance to her nephew Thomas. The property was by no means insub-stantial. In addition to an unrecorded amount of 'ready money, goods, chattels, . . . [and] effects', his aunt bequeathed to Thomas 'all my mes-suages, tenements, and houses upon London Bridge or elsewhere'.[9] 'Mes-suages', in the sense that the word is used here, probably meant land which had been purchased and approved for the building of residential dwellings – in other words, prime commercial real estate in a city that was already experiencing an unprecedented boom in growth. The houses on London Bridge (which was soon to be stripped of such structures) were probably not in very good repair, but the will's tantalizingly unspecific language ('and elsewhere') suggests that the properties of which Gray was suddenly an owner may have been numerous if not palatial. Gray, in any event, seems quickly and efficiently to have sold the properties and directed the money into other investments. He proved the will, of which he had been named executor, on 16 February, and spent the better part of the next three weeks in London settling his aunt's affairs.

The experience seems to have conferred upon Gray an unexpected dignity. As he found himself capably and efficiently managing the legal and practical details of these sales and exchanges, he discovered for the first time within himself a new sense of confidence and perhaps self-sufficiency. With only his mother by his side, Gray saw his way through the financial maze of the court system and dealt with attorneys and

---

[9] See *CTG* 1307.

agents like one who had long had experience in such affairs. Indeed, considering Dorothy's recent experiences in Doctors Commons, the two must have made a formidable pair. Philip Gray, still reeling from his wife's own newfound strength of will, could only watch dumbfounded as his former victims supported one another in their determined steps towards independence. The money he must have been counting on in time to prop up his own faltering business schemes had found an unexpected recipient, and it was by now clear that not a penny of it would be headed in his direction. Defied by his wife, snubbed even in death by his sister, and apparently ignored or – at best – pitied by his son, Philip Gray's personal reign of terror in Cornhill was fast approaching its end. Sic semper tyrannis.

III. Like Adam in Paradise

Gray now had an income of his own. He could take comfort in the fact that not only was he from this point on in his life to be entirely beyond the domineering control of his father, but also that his mother, who had for so many years worked hard to protect him and to see that he had the advantages of education and up-bringing which she felt he deserved, could herself begin to ease up a bit. They were neither of them rich, but a substantial emotional as well as financial burden had been lifted from their shoulders. Gray probably felt that his situation was now somehow more respectable, more 'fitting', and even – though he might never consciously have admitted it to himself – finally free of some slight and lingering shame. Eager to appear at ease among his friends and college acquaintances, he no longer laboured under the knowledge that his university lifestyle, as modest as it was, was in reality supported by his mother's daily hard work as a craftswoman and retail merchant. He was still the son of London merchants, but he was now the son of London merchants who was himself a man of some small 'property'. No longer would he have to count every penny. No longer would the expenses that friends such as Walpole (as sensitive and tactful as he tried always to be) gave no indication of ever noticing, be for Gray a bar or a barrier. Having any money at his disposal would in fact take some getting used to. The economic habits even of the youngest lifetime are deeply impressed and hardly shaken off. There was to be no running out and buying clothes and books, no sudden transformation of the modestly if tastefully dressed young scholar into the fully fitted-out peacock of contemporary fashion. But subtle changes could be made, minor improvements in lifestyle with which one soon and imperceptibly grew comfortable. One small but significant indication of the change in Gray's economic fortunes can be read in the account books at Peterhouse. In the year following his aunt's legacy, his 'sizings' for each academic quarter exceeded his commons. His mother could at least rest assured that Gray was now eating better.

Some of Gray's critics have traced in his correspondence from this point onward in his life a dramatic shift in tone and attitude. A new note of confidence and self-assurance, some have argued, is sounded in his epistolary dialogues not only with Walpole, but with West as well. There is some small truth in this. From the early spring of 1736, Gray was, in the back of his mind, constantly considering and reconsidering just what changes his aunt's money could make with regard to his plans for a career. Until that point, he had necessarily acquiesced to the apparent decision of both his parents that he take up the profession of the Law. On 22 November 1735, well into his second year at Cambridge, he had been admitted as his father's heir to the Inner Temple. Plans were clearly being laid for him to become a lawyer. However much he was committed to such a course of action on paper, however, Gray was already admitting to himself that he was personally disinclined to embark upon such a career. Having as yet reached no final decision in the matter, he realized that he might now have more to say with reference to such affairs than had previously been the case. The note of self-assurance some hear in his letters would seem to owe a great deal to this simple realization that his life was – more than it had ever been before – his own to live. From this point on the choices and decisions would likewise be his own to make. It would be wrong to suggest, however, the such clear-eyed sobriety of spirit and purpose effected any truly profound changes in Gray's epistolary voice. The letters to Walpole and West still echo with the ventriloquistic babble of voices which had characterized his earliest surviving correspondence and, if anything, they indulge even more confidently and whole-heartedly in poetic play and reference. Far from forsaking his love for and by-now almost instinctual inclinations towards parodic play and allusion, Gray, as we shall see, was to begin more carefully to tame them into art.

Gray felt that the stress and activity of the spring had earned him something in the way of real holiday. He left Cambridge almost immediately after term had ended (left so quickly, in fact, that Walpole uncharacteristically remained behind at King's without him) and for the first time in his life he may have returned to his Cornhill home without experiencing a general sinking feeling of depression or fighting against a ball of nervous anxiety in the pit of his stomach. He headed immediately for the opera, where he attended the final performance of Handel's new work *Atalanta*. The piece had only the preceding month made its premiere in London, on the occasion of a state visit of the court to the Haymarket theatre. The royal visit celebrated the forthcoming marriage of Frederick, Prince of Wales to Princess Augusta of Saxe-Gotha. On the night Gray attended the performance, the Queen was also a member of the audience. A letter dashed off to Walpole a few days after the event found Gray dropping the names of leading singers and fashionable sopranos (e.g., 'Conti I like excessively in everything'). As we have already mentioned, Gray, when still a young man, was apt to be a follower and not a leader (and certainly not a renegade) in matters of taste and fashion. If the society in which Walpole moved had decreed something – a play, an actor, a musician, an opera, a singer, an artist – to be of value, we are almost certain soon to find Gray cultivating an interest in that 'something' as well. Of course, there is nothing necessarily bad or wrong in such a response. Quite the contrary. The 'fashionable' model which Gray had set up for himself in actual fact effected a nice balance with what might be described as his more learned, bookish, or classical side. He had introduced a fine array of 'moderns' to compliment an impressive and otherwise weighty assembly of ancients. His own true taste in all aesthetic matters would make itself known in time.

Even at twenty years of age, however, Gray was not content simply to follow in the footsteps of the crowd. If the London opera-going public declared that the performances of a Conti or a Strada were vigorously to be applauded, then we might very well expect to count Gray among those doing the applauding. But how many members of the *beau monde* made a point within days or even hours of the performance of rushing an order for the entire musical score of Handel's work? How many planned to value it not merely for the moment, but to study it and spend time with it for months and perhaps years to come? Gray, at least, did. Moreover, he was certainly not blind to the fact that whatever the societal honour the occasion of the royal nuptials had glancingly bestowed on the performance of Handel's opera, the composer himself was no longer at the height of his popularity in England (he was already, in fact, turning away from opera to concentrate more on the oratorios of his later career). The main point is that Gray seems already to have been allowing his real inclinations – his genuine likes and dislikes – to temper and to influence his developing taste in matters cultural and artistic. The members of the fashionable world may in many cases still have been the ones clearing the central path, but Gray was already capable of initiating diversions and striking out in idiosyncratic directions of his own.

Atalanta pretty much marked the end of the London season; it had not, as it so happened, been a particularly exciting one. Operas and plays, as Gray put it, had been 'beat off the stage' by the new competition of the entertainments provided in Jonathan Tyers's revived 'Spring Garden'. Spring Garden – or Vauxhall, as it came more commonly to be known – had been reopened two years earlier with great public fanfare and was now beginning truly to find its audience. Not having yet journeyed across the river to experience the delights of the gardens for himself, Gray pretended to withhold any judgement on their charms even as he disparaged the possibility of their appeal and underestimated the longevity of their attractions for the public ('as the beauty of the place, when lighted up' he notes, 'and a little musick are the only diversions of it, I don't suppose it will be any long time in vogue'). The dust that settled heavily on the streets of the City and Whitehall that summer was momentarily disturbed by the attempt of a nonjuring clergyman to blow up some judges and counselors of the Court of Chancery who were then in session in Westminster Hall, but the torpor and heat of the long vacation soon reasserted itself. By the beginning of August, Gray was more than ready to take advantage of his uncle Jonathan Rogers's invitation to spend the rest of the summer with him and his wife – Gray's maternal aunt, Anne Antrobus – at their home near Burnham in Berkshire.

*

We have already, when discussing Gray's family connections in the first chapter, had reason briefly to mention Gray's extended visit to Burnham in August and September of 1736. The home in which he stayed had originally been the property of his uncle Robert – the same Robert who had been Gray's friend, tutor, and *de facto* foster-father at Eton. Upon Robert Antrobus's death in 1730, the small house and grounds had passed into the hands of his sister Anne. She and her husband had lived at the Burnham property since Gray was fourteen years old. The house was therefore, for Gray, a place with a past, a home that was filled with memories of his uncle and, by a natural extension, with those of his own days at Eton. Readers who would argue that the *Eton Ode* is an autobiographically based and wistfully retrospective account of the poet's actual days at the school should once again take note that although Thomas was now for almost two months within easy walking distance of Eton, not once did he set foot in that direction. Walpole confided to West that he found Gray's studied avoidance of their old haunts rather puzzling. 'Gray is at Burnham' Walpole wrote from Cambridge, where he was still engaged in his hopeless struggle against mathematics, 'and, what is surprising, has not been at Eton. Could you live so near it without seeing it? That dear scene of our quadruple alliance would furnish me with the most agreeable recollections. 'Tis the head of our genealogical table, that is since sprouted out into the two branches of Oxford and Cambridge'.[10] West's terse and

[10]   WC. xiii.107–08.

rather tight-lipped echo of Walpole's query in the postscript of his own next letter to Cambridge – 'Gray at Burnham, and not see Eton?' – suggests that, unlike Walpole, he could well see why Gray might choose not to revisit their old school. Not just yet, at least. We are once again struck with the fact that for all the supposed equality of the Quadruple Alliance – for all of Walpole's suggestion that it created between them ties which were nothing less than familial – its members had each had very different experiences at Eton. Walpole did not yet understand that Gray and West's years at the school had been less enjoyable – less productive of entirely 'agreeable recollections' – than his own. Gray was only that very summer beginning to adjust to the new balance of power in the Cornhill home; he had not yet experienced the necessary distance both in time and place likewise to reinvest 'Etonian ground' with new meaning. Years later Eton would come to mean something very different to him that it did that summer. He would be able to use both the pain and the pleasure of those years to reinvent his past and redefine his future. For the time being, however, he had enough on his mind. His destined date with the several shades of darkness which lurked in the shadow of Henry's statue over two miles to the south-east would have to keep.

Gray devoted himself instead to the shady pleasures of the country-side. His aunt's home, already cramped to begin with, was so crowded with his uncle's hunting dogs – their curled and drowsing forms occupied every chair and settle – that Gray was forced to stand at the mantle-piece even when writing letters. Once an active hunter (Gray draws him in a note to Walpole as the kind of character who would not be at all out of place in the company of a later generation's Mr. Facey Romford), Gray's uncle Rogers was now laid up with gout. Though unable to follow them on the chase, Rogers's dogs were still kept about him, Gray wrote, 'to regale his Ears & Nose with their comfortable Noise and Stink'. Rogers could not understand why his nephew preferred only to walk in the nearby lanes and fields when he could be riding, nor why he bothered himself with reading when he could be hunting (William Cole later claimed that he once heard Gray 'say he was never across a horse's back in his life' – an almost impossible accomplishment for an eighteenth-century gentleman).[11] Like many dense people who have never been crossed in their own confirmed habits, Rogers was incapable of perceiving that his pleasures were not necessarily the pleasures of others – that just because reading was for him a chore and smacked somewhat of work (he was, after all, a lawyer), did not necessarily mean that everybody else considered it to be a burden, and not a pleasure, as

---

[11] Cole, 'Miscellaneous Extracts', c.

well. That his nephew not only did not enjoy hunting, but did not ride a horse at all was simply inconceivable.

Rogers's disposition, confined as both he and it were to a chair and cushioned footstool in the family manse, could easily be avoided. Passing down just a half-mile's length of green lane over-arched with the thick and luxuriant growth of the high summer's leafy trees, Gray arrived at East Burnham Common, which adjoined the forest of Burnham Beeches. Following a generous country breakfast each day, he could then choose the author with whom he was to spend the long summer morning or afternoon (it would more often than not be Virgil) and, his aunt busy with the household chores and his uncle perhaps temporarily distracted by the cacophonous baying and yapping of his erstwhile pack, he could slip out the door and head for his green retreat. Nearly a generation later, Cole, who was then living as a vicar in the neighbourhood, would describe the lane down which Gray travelled each day of the summer as 'very romantic' and the scenery in general as 'remarkably diversified for that county'.[12] He observed too that its paths and by-ways were shaded by 'some of the largest beeches [he] ever saw'. Even today the area is home to a stunning array of old beech pollards, ash trees, oaks, and tall grey poplars, and at dusk many of the common woodland bird species can be seen flying their regular routes among the nearby bog and heath. Gray himself was struck both by the area's diversity and by the delicious circumstance of his seeming to be the only one within miles to appreciate it. The forest, he wrote, was 'all [his] own' or, at least,

> as good as so, for I spy no human thing in it but myself; it is a little Chaos of Mountains & Precipices; Mountains it is true, that don't ascend much above the Clouds, nor are the Declivities quite so amazing, as Dover-Cliff: but just such hills as people, who love their Necks as well as I do, may venture to climb, & Crags, that give the eye as much pleasure, as if they were more dangerous: both Vale & Hill is cover'd over with the most venerable Beeches, & other very reverend Vegetables, that like most ancient People, are always dreaming out their old Stories to the Winds

> > And, as they bow their hoary Tops, relate
> > In murm'ring Sounds the dark Decrees of Fate;
> > While Visions, as Poetic eyes avow,
> > Cling to each Leaf, & swarm on ev'ry Bough:

> At the foot of one of these squats me I; il Penseroso, and there grow to the Trunk for a whole morning,

---

[12]   Cole, MS. notes, quoted in *CTG* 47.

> – the tim'rous Hare, & sportive Squirrel
> Gambol around me –

like Adam in Paradise, but commonly without an Eve, & besides I think
he did not use to read Virgil, as I usually do there: in this situation I often
converse with my Horace aloud too, that is, talk to you. (*CTG* 47–48)

If the referential echoes that crowd into Gray's original lines here
are to serve as any indication, he seems to have been busy reading
Virgil that very morning. The image of poetic 'visions' clinging to the
leaves, boughs, and 'hoary tops' of the majestic beech trees is a directly
imitative and parodic quotation of some lines from Book VI of the
master's *Aeneid* (283–85), in which Virgil describes the entrance to the
underworld:

> In medio ramos annosaque bracchia pandit
> Ulmus opaca, ingens, quam sedem Somnia volgo
> vana tenere ferunt, foliisque sub omnibus haerent

> [In the midst an elm, shadowy and vast, spreads her boughs and
> aged arms, the home which, men say, false Dreams hold here and
> there, clinging under every leaf.]

There are more than enough echoes of other poets in Gray's apparently impromptu verses (he recollects, among others, both Dryden and
Pope as well as Milton) at least to qualify any particularly close textual
and thematic comparison between his own description and Virgil's
original. It is striking, however, that immediately prior to Virgil's account
of the false dreams that cling to the branches of this tree in the very
courtyard of Dis, the poet had been describing the other miseries that
cluster about the entrance to the underworld. Among these are to be
counted (in English) 'Grief and avenging Care', 'pale Disease', 'sad Age',
'Dread', and 'the Hunger that compels men to commit crime', 'sordid
Want', 'Toil', and 'raging Discord': all can be discerned within the gloom
by a terrified and understandably fearful Aeneas. Such a list, it need
hardly be pointed out to those familiar with Gray's own work – such a
litany of horrors – might very well be mistaken by the modern reader
as having been drawn from the poet's *Eton Ode*. The dangers and curses
that Virgil places at the very jaws of hell are almost word for word the
murderous 'ministers of human fate' who will likewise crouch in the
vales of adulthood, waiting for their moment and opportunity in time
to ambush the blissfully ignorant schoolchildren at Eton. Is Gray making
a pointed connection between the actual, physical world around Eton –
the happy hills and pleasing shades of Burnham Beeches, Windsor, and

the lanes that led eastward towards the familiar courtyards – and the forest of souls which linger mournfully on the shores of Virgil's underworld? Are the groves, lawns, and meads of his old school themselves the deceptively 'innocent' gates to Hell – or at least the hell-on-earth of adulthood – itself? We will have an opportunity to look more closely at such questions (and some other possible references) when we turn our attention specifically to the composition of the Eton ode. Gray was, again, not quite prepared to sort out in his own mind just how he felt about Eton and its experiences at this point in life. Like his classical model, who, before presenting his hero's journey into Hades, wonders aloud to his readers whether it is wise ever to undertake such an exploration – whether it is 'right to tell what [he has] heard', whether it is 'fitting [to] describe the deep world sunk in darkness', Gray similarly doubted the advisability of such a 'journey' himself. The possibility that he was not only feeling, as he wrote to Walpole, 'like Adam in paradise', but perhaps also like Aeneas on the verge of Hades is a telling one. Whatever Gray's precise state of mind, we can at least be sure that, as usual, his writing benefitted simultaneously from the environment of his reading at least as much as the environment of his physical surroundings – from a combination both of the Virgilian trees he envisioned in his mind's eye, and of the trunks of the actual trees he saw arching in the forest towards heaven. In writing even the slightest fragments of poetry Gray, typically, is responding just as much to the word, as to the world.

However we wish to characterize the nature of the elaborate games of literary reference and cross-reference which Gray played within his own mind on the summer mornings, such games need not necessarily have come to an end as the days drew to their close. Having spent the warm and lazy afternoons tracing the verities of the heart along the pages of familiar classics (the wonderful conflation of 'his' Horace with Quintus Horatius Flaccus of classical antiquity in the passage quoted above speaks volumes for the ease with which his own life moved in and among his reading), Gray managed to spend many of his evenings in literary company as well. The dramatist Thomas Southerne, then seventy-seven years old, was staying at the house of a neighbor only a little way off. Southerne, who was known as the 'Nestor' of English poets, was by this late point in his life something of a living legend. Although Gray noted that the dramatist had by then 'wholly lost his Memory' (William Broome commented in a letter to Alexander Pope some ten years earlier that Southern's bays were even then 'withered with extreme age'), it was something even to be in the company of the man who had brought Oroonoko and Isabella (in *The Fatal Marriage*) to life on the stage. Here, Gray must have thought as he looked across the comfort of his aunt's parlor, was someone who had been a friend of Dryden himself. One might almost suspect that there was something peculiar to the salubrious air of the forests around Windsor which particularly attracted the aging dramatists of the Restoration, and somehow preserved them for the further edification of their poetic heirs. Living in roughly the same neighbourhood just a generation earlier, Alexander Pope had cultivated the acquaintance of William Wycherley as one who could effect for the younger poet 'imaginative contact with the literary lions of the past age'.[13] Southerne's extreme old age prohibited much in the way of anecdotal reminiscence, but for someone possessing Gray's active and animating imagination, the mere presence of this author whose works he had read with as much passion and enthusiasm as he had any classical text brought with it the faded and lingering glamour of an earlier literary era. He could imagine late nights spent in conversation with the likes of Dryden or Wycherley by the fire in Will's coffee house, or relive in his own memory Southerne's powerfully pathetic retellings of Aphra Behn's moving and heroic stories. Over his tea in the summer evenings, he built a slender bridge of the mind that further connected him to the world of the theatre and its passions, in which he already took an active role.

While at Burnham Gray also spent some time with another friend of Walpole's, Richard Owen Cambridge. Cambridge is one of those elusive figures (one of the breed of multi-faceted 'men of letters' that seems to have been peculiar to the eighteenth century) who for the modern reader exist largely on the margins of English literary history. Such figures are liable always to turn up at unexpected times in unexpected places – spending the weekend at the country home of some prominent politician or writer since characterized as especially gifted precisely in gathering company on such weekends, for example, or dining with a coterie of wits on a night memorialized by some particularly splendid conversation and repartee. Cambridge, who would in time as Walpole's near-neighbor in Twickenham be dubbed 'the everything', was himself to achieve the most fame in his own lifetime as a host to the literary and political elite of his day. As an adult he would count among his friends and acquaintances not only Walpole and Gray, but also Soame Jennings, William Pitt, Henry Fox, and Lord Chesterfield. His mock-heroic poem *The Scribleriad* (1751), like its inspiration, Pope's *Dunciad*, would satirize false learning and pedantry, appropriating as its hero the figure of Martinus Scriblerus.

Gray was pleased in the August of 1736 to encounter Cambridge – whom he too may have known casually or at least by name while both had been students at Eton – if only because such a meeting allowed him

[13] Mack, *Alexander Pope: A Life*, 96.

the opportunity of conversing with someone roughly his own age about his favourite subject. Cambridge, as Gray characterized him, was also a fan of Horace Walpole's; indeed, so great an ally was he that he had worked his entire family around to supporting the political fortunes of his friend's father. 'Your name, I assure you', Gray wrote to Walpole describing his summer parish companion, 'has been propagated in these countries by a Convert of your, one Cambridge: he has brought over his whole family to you: they were before pretty good Whigs, but now they are absolute Walpolians'. For Gray, Walpole's cherished friendship is tantamount to a religion to which one wins 'converts'. One 'went over' to the Walpolians much in the same way an apostate of the Church of England might 'go over' to Rome. Gray further informed Walpole that the already fabled magnificence of his father's mansion at Houghton is the stuff of all the local gossip, that there is hardly anybody 'but knows exactly the Dimensions of the hall & Saloon' of Sir Robert's home. Whatever slight resentment is betrayed in Gray's account of this local gossip (it was both soothing and exasperating to his own ego to hear the material wealth of his best-friend's family so much talked about), Gray began quietly to look forward to his return to Cambridge and to the contentment he could take in being included in the most intimate company of a friend whom others knew and spoke of almost exclusively by reputation.

Before returning to Cambridge that autumn, Gray passed a few more weeks with his parents in London. Life in the Cornhill house must have seemed surprisingly bearable since his father's recent humbling. Although a slight summer cold kept him at home for much of the time, Gray did manage to attend a memorable performance of *The Way of the World* at Covent Garden at the beginning of October. Following the presentation of Congreve's comedy, an entertainment was presented in which the machinery designed to hold a flying 'car' above the stage broke – the strings holding the back of the car snapped first, throwing the weight of the occupants onto the remaining front cables, which likewise soon gave way – and the actors were flung to the boards below. The accident seems to have been a particularly gruesome one (the pregnant actress Elizabeth Buchanan, immediately breaking her thigh and knee, died in childbed soon after the incident), and the house was filled with the noise of chaos. As is often the case when such an accident occurs in the middle of a theatrical performance – particularly a comic one – the audience was at first oblivious to the fact that anything was out of the ordinary. Only the confusion and the unmistakably real cries of pain that followed the incident alerted them to the gravity of the situation. For Gray the accident seems to have brought home just how tenuous the theatrical illusion really was. Being laid up in one's bed with a fever was not so bad when one considered that even a visit to the playhouse could bring him within such grim proximity of a far less desirable fate. Chalking up his own disinclination to attend any more plays to 'a sort of Surfeit of [the theatrical manager] Mr Rich & his Cleverness', Gray kept to his bed in the now more comfortably designated 'Cornhill-shire' until it was time to return to university.

One letter from Gray to his college tutor, George Birkett, survives from these last weeks in London. Both the letter and the reply it prompted are of some minor interest in being the only items of correspondence between Gray and his supervisor to have survived. Writing on 8 October and noting that he would be staying in Cornhill for a further two weeks before returning to Cambridge, Gray requested that his accounts be posted to him in London. 'I'll beg you to give yourself the trouble of writing out my Bills, & sending 'em', he asked Birkett, who as Tutor would be personally responsible for collecting from his students any College charges,

> that I may put myself out of your Debt, as soon as I come down: if Piazza should come to You, you'll be so good as to satisfie him; I protest, I forget what I owe him, but he is honest enough to tell you right: my Father & Mother desire me to send their compliments, & beg you'd believe me,
>
> Sr
> your most obedt humble Servt
> T: Gray. (*CTG* 52–53)

Critics have on occasion taken Gray to task for what they have interpreted as a somewhat peremptory tone of voice – an 'offhand', 'jaunty', or even 'unseemly' manner – in this note. Most of Gray's twentieth-century biographers have characterized the letter as 'offensive' or even 'annoying'. One can only suspect that such a response was prompted at least in part by their own condescending attitudes towards students in general, or by a correspondingly inflated sense of their own importance as teachers or educators themselves. The letter has far more significant things to tell us about what was going on in Gray's life. It is far more interesting to observe, for example, that Gray refers casually to both his mother *and* his father in the note as a unit acting in harmony with one another and, moreover – if his inclusion of their compliments to Birkett represents anything more than the most artificial of rhetorical formalities – he for the first time ever suggests that his father is now taking a personal interest in the progress of his education. While there may be a touch of xenophobia in the implication that one needs to keep a sharp eye on the billing accounts of Italian tutors in general, Gray's tone is far from arrogant. In any event, he knew the character of the individual with whom he was dealing better than we do. It would appear that – far from being arrogant – he demonstrates in his casual manner a forbearance of which many of us would be incapable. For not only does a draft of Birkett's reply to Gray survive, but the sheet on which it is written contains an even earlier draft of the same letter. It is clear both from the substance and from the style of this first attempt that Birkett was drunk when he wrote it. The first draft – scored, smudged, and scratched through – begins:

> Sr
> As you shall stay only a fortnigh [sic] in Town your Bills shall be with you as inclosed. Wt you ow Piazzo I hope may be easily discharged. What I wish you is without Tyrants in ye . . . or Rebulicans [sic] your
>   But pretty Mr Gray [altered from Day]
>   I miss spled [sic] . . .
> I wd doe any service for yr Uncle Antrobus tho'. (*CTG* 53–54)

The draft of Birkett's reply finally sent to Gray was only slightly more coherent; the tutor may well have been forced to put the matter aside until morning. There is no trace in his final letter, at least, either to the intriguing political convictions hinted at in the reference to 'Tyrants' and 'Republicans', or to the lachrymose testament of affections to Robert Antrobus the mere recollection of his nephew seems to have inspired. 'Not all dons', wrote one biographer defending Birkett, 'would have been so forbearing towards a conceited undergraduate'.[14] Nor, we should add, might all such 'conceited' undergraduates have been so conscientious about paying their bills to tutors who seem for large portions of the day or evening to have been incapable even of calculating them.

IV. The Physic of the Mind

Gray returned to Cambridge toward the middle of October. He had managed to arrange a meeting with West just prior to leaving London, but their dinner together had not gone well. 'We both fancied at first', Gray wrote soon after the event to Walpole, 'we had a great many things to say to one another; but when it came to the push, I found, I had forgot all I intended to say, & he stood upon Punctilio's and would not speak first, & so we parted'. It would probably be a mistake – particularly in light of the unbroken line of interest and affection that is reflected in their subsequent correspondence with one another – to make too much of the awkwardness and reticence which characterized

[14] Ketton-Cremer, *Thomas Gray*, 20.

this hastily arranged supper. It is more than likely that West was typically not feeling very well. The prospect of returning to Oxford did little
for his spirits, and Gray's delay in seeing him until the last possible
moment (they met the night before he left town for Cambridge) would
have depressed him even further. Gray, as usual, was full of Walpole and
the fact that three members of the old alliance would soon be reunited.
William Cole – another former Etonian, it should be remembered – was
playing a greater role in their lives at university as well, and Gray probably chattered on a bit too much about what a wonderful time they
would all be having together before even noticing West's silence. His
own cheery anticipation – the anticipation of a student now boastfully
familiar with Cambridge ways and habits – must have stood in sharp
contrast to West's dread of returning to his own 'dismal land of
bondage'. West was probably guilty not so much of 'standing upon Punctilio's', as Gray suggests, but rather of feeling neglected and too easily
forgotten or dismissed by his old friends. In his renewed attempts to
craft a social self that could survive in the rarer air breathed by Walpole
and his peers, Gray seems still to have refused to realize just how much
he really had in common with West, and just how similar the two were
in temperament.

Gray's situation at university had in fact changed to the point where
he and West appeared no longer even to be heading in the same professional direction. By the end of Michaelmas term 1736, Gray had clearly
decided that he would not be taking a degree (he had been toying with
the idea before he returned to Cambridge that autumn; it would not be
required for him to hold a degree even if he chose to continue in pursuing a career as a lawyer). In practical terms, this meant that he no
longer had to endure tutorials, lectures, disputations – all of which he
now blithely dismissed as 'college impertinencies' – and that he would
not have to sit for any examinations. It meant that mornings would no
longer have to be spent easing the venerable Dr. Birkett through the after-
effects of a night of indulging too heavily in the college port, afternoons
were now free to be devoted rather to his 'classical companions' (the
door was emphatically shut to the likes of Ward's *Algebra*, Wingate's
Arithmetick, and Watt's *Logick*), and evenings were blissfully liberated
from a bondage to metaphysics into the hands of Walpole and his other
friends. West wrote from Oxford congratulating him on his decision,
and commented that the time his friend could now spend cultivating
poetry would serve them both well in the fast-approaching months
when they would together engage in 'the disgusting sober follies of the
common law'. West understandably envied Gray his newfound freedom
(both academic and financial) and sought some reassurance that the
plans which they had together laid for their respective futures in the
Inner Temple were not entirely to be abandoned.

Gray, meanwhile, reveled in his freedom. It was at about this time that he wrote to West of learning Italian 'like any dragon', and perhaps followed up a translation from Book VI of Statius' *Thebiad* that he had already sent to Oxford, by now passing on to his friend English versions of passages from both Tasso's *Gerusalemme Liberata* and Dante's *Inferno*. Such a progression, he at least wrote West, was a logical one. 'Nothing can be easier than [learning the Italian] language', he opined, 'to any one who knows Latin and French already' (Gray's own ability in reading French was by now fluent enough for him to be racing through the original works of writers such as Boileau, Racine, La Bruyère, Montesquieu, La Rochefoucauld, and Madame de Sévigné). All of Gray's Italian translations that survive from these early years at Cambridge are competent pieces which perhaps most clearly demonstrate just how much at home their writer felt within the language of other poets. Working through the words of another was already, for Gray, a confirmed habit of mind – a manner of self-expression that conveniently avoided having to direct too much attention to the self – a form of articulation which 'common-sensically' and 'naturally' placed the immediate speaker in the textual background. The conceit of inhabiting the poetic skin of another writer was one that suited Gray perfectly, and he seems clearly to have enjoyed the sensations of privileged and vicarious creativity such ventriloquism encouraged.

*

The section from Statius that Gray had sent West in the spring of 1736 had been a translation he claimed to have undertaken not because he 'liked that part of the Poem', but simply to show his friend, as he put it, 'how I misspend my days'. Gray, we should remember, had already undertaken translations from Statius while he was yet a student at Eton. Statius' epic tells the story of the legendary expedition of the 'Seven against Thebes', the mission of seven great heroes of antiquity – Adrastus, Polynices, Tydeus, Amphiaraus, Hippomedon, Capaneus, and Parthenopaeus – to restore Polynices to the throne usurped by his brother, Eteocles. The passage sent to West recounts the funeral games for the child Opheltes, the son of Lycurgus, King of Thrace, and contains some nice descriptive poetry. Describing the performance of Hippomedon, Gray writes:

> Artful and strong he poised the well-known weight,
> By Phlegyas warned and fired by Mnestheus' fate,
> That to avoid and this to emulate.
> His vigorous arm he tried before he flung,

Braced all his nerves and every sinew strung;
Then, with a tempest's whirl and wary eye,
Pursued his cast, and hurled his orb on high;
The orb on high tenacious of its course,
True to the mighty arm that gave it force,
Far overleaps all bounds and joys to see
Its ancient lord secure of victory.
The theatre's green height and woody wall
Tremble ere it precipitates its fall;
The ponderous mass sinks in the cleaving ground,
While vales and woods and echoing hills rebound.
As when from Aetna's smoking summit broke,
The eyeless Cyclops heaved the craggy rock:
Where ocean frets beneath the dashing oar,
And parting surges round the vessel roar,
'Twas there he aimed the meditated harm,
And scarce Ulysses scaped his giant arm.
A tiger's pride the victor bore away,
With native spots and artful labour gay:
A shining border round the margin rolled,
And calmed the terrors of his claws in gold. (*PTG* 19)

It may be of some significance that at about the same time his mother's case was being presented to Dr. Audley, Gray was drawn to a poem which itself told the story of a struggle for power between the members of a single family (it is likewise interesting to note that the narrative of the Thebes saga as told by Statius leads immediately to the attempts of Antigone to bury the past, and to that same heroine's uncompromising insistence on the precedence of the laws of the gods above the regulations of men). Mason was content to comment that Gray had attempted in the passage to imitate 'Dryden's spirited manner'; Robert Gleckner has more recently drawn attention to Miltonic echoes in Gray's versions of Statius.[15] More concretely, as Eugene McCarthy has observed, the passage is noteworthy for the translator's attempt 'to create not what we might have assumed would be lyric expression but rather a dramatic scene chiefly by means of diction'.[16]

The passage that Gray chose to translate and to preserve from Tasso's epic is one in which readers are offered a privileged glimpse of creation-in-progress. Gray drew his selection from Canto XIV of *Gerusalemme Liberata*, in which two of the Christian warriors (Charles and Ubald) from the camp of Godfrey of Bouillon, which is then

---

[15] Mason (1775) i.9n; Gleckner, *Gray Agonistes*, 102–03.
[16] McCarthy, *Thomas Gray: The Progress of a Poet*, 32.

besieging Jerusalem, have embarked upon a search for the epic's renegade romantic hero, Rinaldo. Having followed the instructions of the
sage Peter the Hermit, the pair have pursued the road to Ascalon, and
have met with a mysterious old man walking upon the surface of a river.
This strange apparition – who will eventually reveal to the two heroes
the circumstances of Rinaldo's imprisonment in the enchanted Palace of
Armida on the Peak of Teneriffe – first leads them to his habitation under
the river bed. Gray's translation reads:

> The flood on either hand its billows rears,
> And in the midst a spacious arch appears.
> Their hands he seized and down the steep he led,
> Beneath the obedient river's inmost bed.
> The watery glimmerings of a fainter day
> Discovered half, and half concealed, their way,
> As when athwart the dusky woods by night
> The uncertain crescent gleams a sickly light.
> Through subterraneous passages they went,
> Earth's inmost cells and caves of deep descent.
> Of many a flood they viewed the secret source,
> The birth of rivers, rising to their course;
> . . .
> Further they pass, where ripening minerals flow,
> And embryon metals undigested glow;
> Sulferous veins and living silver shine,
> Which soon the parent sun's warm powers refine,
> In one rich mass unite the precious store,
> The parts combine and harden into ore. (*PTG* 22)

One might imagine that the translator, much like the world exposed
to Tasso's warriors here, is himself in some ways 'discovered half, and half
concealed'. He acts as the facilitator rather than the originator of language – the literary mid-wife to a creative mind that has already born a
poetic image fully conceived and created. The poetic Idea may in some
respects be inseparable from the poetic Form, but the translator negoti-
ates the gap that is perforce to be bridged in the attempt to link one language to another. He is the lapidary craftsman who witnesses the creation
of 'ripening minerals' and 'embryon metals', and polishes them to the surfaces of another world. Given the larger implications of the role played
by the poet-translator in Gray's rendition of Tasso here, it is almost anti-
climactic to observe that the image of the incipient gem resting unnoticed
and as yet unappreciated in the 'dark unfathomed caves of ocean' is one
to which Gray will of course return more famously in the *Elegy*.

*

If we choose to read the selection from Tasso as containing within its narrative and its imagery some as yet dimly perceived truths about the processes of poetry that may have rendered it more intriguing or relevant to Gray at this particular moment in his life, the passage he translated from Dante's *Inferno* at about the same time may likewise have something significant to tell us about Gray's state of mind in the winter of 1736/37. Dante was eventually to be counted as one of Gray's favourite authors; some critics have gone so far as to say that Gray would as an adult scholar be more intimately acquainted than any other Englishman of the period with Dante's poetry. We should remember that reading Dante in the eighteenth century usually meant reading Dante in his original Italian; a complete English translation of the *Divina Commedia*, at least, would not appear until 1802. Throughout his life, Gray would be particularly drawn to the story of Count Ugolino, recounted in Canto XXXIII of the *Inferno*. A chance remark of his friend-to-be Norton Nicholls, in 1762, for example, that he had in fact been reading Dante was what prompted Gray's immediate interest in him. Hearing Nicholls's comment on the author, Gray spun around with the immediate and vibrant display of interest so peculiar to someone who has just heard one of their own private obsessions mentioned in open conversation, querying eagerly 'Sir, do *you* read Dante?'. Nicholls's reply in the affirmative proved to be the foundation of their subsequent friendship. On that occasion, Gray immediately suggested to Nicholls that he turn to the episode of Count Ugolino. Nicholls promptly read it 'the next morning', and was soon concurring with his newfound companion that it was 'one of the finest Things I had ever read in [his] Life'. Such a reaction is not all that surprising. The story of Ugolino – the longest narrative episode related within the first book of the *Commedia* – is often cited with the story of Paolo and Francesca, in Canto V, and with the stunning account offered by Ulysses of his final voyage which occupies much of Canto XXVI, as one of the highpoints of Dante's epic work. Taken together, the three stories represent, as Dante's twentieth-century translator John D. Sinclair has observed, 'the greatest examples of dramatic imagination in the whole poem'.[17] Yet while Francesca's recollection of a tragic passion fueled by tales of fiction and romance recounted early in the poem has gone on to capture the imaginations of many modern readers, and while poems such as Tennyson's *Ulysses* have furthered Dante's image of the classical hero as a transgressor who cannot resist the hubristic impulse that keeps him always travelling with a 'hungry heart', Ugolino, though equally memorable within the *Inferno*, has not proven to be so prolific a figure. That such is the case is

[17] John D. Sinclair, trans. Dante, *The Divine Comedy 1: Inferno* (New York: Oxford University Press, 1979) 415.

understandable. Dante's extraordinarily powerful tale is also an extraordinarily gruesome and discomfiting one. Ugolino's story is the concluding instalment in a trilogy of instructive narratives that present to readers of the *Inferno* indelible images of great love, great daring, and – finally – great hatred.

The close of Canto XXXII had left Dante observing two figures frozen together in the cold blood that forms the ice of the 'river' Cocytus in such a manner so that 'l'un capo all'altro era cappello: / e come 'l pan per fame si manduca, / cosi 'l sovran li denti all'altro pose / là 've l cerval s'aggiugne con la nuca' ('the head of the one formed a sort of hood for the other, and, as bread is devoured by those who are famished, the one on top dug his teeth into the other at that point where the brain is joined to the nape of the neck'). The opening of the next Canto explains this cliff-hanging scene of necrophilic cannibalism by informing the reader that these two figures had once, in the world above, been the enemies Count Ugolino delle Gherardesca, the leader of the Guelph government at Pisa, and Archbishop Ruggieri, the head of the Pisan Ghibellines. In 1289 the historical Ugolino, having first betrayed his own family to Ruggieri, was in turn betrayed by the Archbishop, who threw the Count into prison along with two of his sons and two grandsons. All five starved to death. Even an Italy already inured to such horrors was shocked by the betrayal and by the barbarity of its punishment. In Dante's retelling, Ugolino's various offspring have been transformed (for a more uniform, dramatic effect) into his four sons, all of them young children. The grim despair of his description is indeed one of the greatest narrative moments in a great poem. Gray translates part of Ugolino's speech to Dante:

> 'The morn had scarce commenced when I awoke:
> My children (they were with me) sleep as yet
> Gave not to know their sum of misery,
> But yet in low and uncompleted sounds
> I heard 'em wail for bread. Oh! thou art cruel,
> Or thou dost mourn to think what my poor heart
> Foresaw, foreknew: . . .
>   But oh! when I beheld
> My sons, and in four faces saw my own
> Despair reflected, either hand I gnawed
> For anguish, which they construed hunger. Straight
> Arising all they cried, 'Far less shall be
> Our sufferings, sir, if you resume your gift;
> These miserable limbs with flesh you clothed;
> Take back what once was yours.' I swallowed down

My struggling sorrow, nor to heighten theirs,
That day and yet another, mute we sat
And motionless. O earth, could'st thou not gape
Quick to devour me? Yet a fourth day came,
When Gaddo, at my feet outstretched, imploring
In vain my help, expired; ere the sixth morn
Had dawned, my other three before my eyes
Died one by one. I saw 'em fall; I heard
Their doleful cries. For three days more I groped
About among their cold remains (for then
Hunger had reft my eyesight), often calling
On their dear names, that heard me now no more;
The fourth, what sorrow could not, famine did.' (PTG 24–25)

The reader is all the while compelled reluctantly to keep in mind that even as Ugolino is telling Dante his horrific tale, he is himself visibly anxious to get back to his own 'hellish feast' – the 'teschio misero' or 'wretched skull' – of his enemy Ruggieri. While engaged in the task of translating Dante some hundred years after Gray, the American poet Henry Wadsworth Longfellow would be inspired to write a series of original sonnets, in one of which he asks the Florentine master both out of horror and respect 'from what agonies of heart and brain, / What exultations trampling on despair, / . . . / What passionate outcry of a soul in pain, / Uprose this poem of the earth and air[?]'[18] We might similarly ask Gray why he should have been so drawn throughout his life to this particular passage in Dante's 'medieval miracle of song'. What 'passionate outcry of a soul in pain' does the translation itself represent?

If the answer – given what we know about Gray's family and domestic life – by now presents itself as a somewhat obvious one, it would none the less appear to be true. It is possible that in rereading, translating, and preserving this image of a father who is eternally punished for the betrayal of his own family, Gray was inflicting within his own mind a suitable vengeance on the emotional cannibalism in which he felt his own father had participated. Working within the framework of language provided by Dante's epic, the young poet Thomas was able to take imaginative revenge on Philip Gray. The poem even worked to cast Ugolino's children (or grandchildren, as the case may be) in the role of self-sacrificing martyrs to their father's greed, victims who – even in death – would ease their own father/murderer's pain. Thus, in translating Dante's

---

[18] Henry Wadsworth Longfellow, 'On Translating the Divina Commedia' (ii.9–14) in *Selected Poems*, ed. Anthony Thwaite (London: J. M. Dent, 1993) 319.

verse, Gray could simultaneously punish his father, while at the same
time paradoxically consoling himself with a reassuring image of filial
selflessness and piety (the children's naive offering of their own bodies to
preserve their father, as Dante's English translator Robert Pinsky has
emphasized, is meant to recall for his readers not only Christ's offer
of his 'flesh' to his disciples in John 6, but other Biblical and Classical
narratives – e.g., the story of Abraham and Isaac, the Theban story of
Oedipus and his father – as well).[19] Dante, again, was to remain with
Gray for the rest of his life. It is no accident that the *Elegy* itself begins
with a half-suppressed translation of a line from the *Puragatorio*, and
that later in life Gray was still capable of spontaneously quoting a line
from his favourite Italian author in a letter to a friend.

It is likely that the episode of Ugolino – an episode that places such
memorable emphasis on the undeserved suffering of children at the
hands of a selfish and untrustworthy parent – and his place in that
deepest ring of hell which provided an appropriate punishment for the
cold-blooded sin of betrayal, also stayed with Gray forever. The opening
lines of his translation describing the Pisan traitor begin:

> From his dire food the grisly felon raised
> His gore-dyed lips, which on the clottered locks
> Of the half-devoured head he wiped, and thus
> Began: . . . (*PTG* 24)

The manuscript of Gray's translation has unfortunately disappeared
since the passage was first published in its entirety in 1884 by Edmund
Gosse. John Mitford's transcription of the lines, however, recorded a
small number of variants – a few changes that Gray perhaps never
quite decided upon in his draft. The noun 'felon' in the first line had
apparently been pencilled in substantially enough for it to be considered
(quite literally) Gray's final word. He had been seeking a proper equivalent for Dante's Italian, and had apparently been undecided as to
precisely which English word best conveyed the ramifications of the original's 'peccator' – its sense of 'sinner', 'transgressor', 'wrong-doer',
'felon', and 'criminal'. It is well worth noting that Gray had, in his first
draft, translated the word simply as 'father'.

*

A third translation from Italian that appears to date from this period
in Gray's life is a rendition of a Petrarchan sonnet (Book I, sonnet 170)

---

[19]   Robert Pinsky, trans. *The Inferno of Dante* (London: J. M. Dent, 1996) 424.

into Latin. Unlike Tasso and Dante, Petrarch would seem in general to
have made no very great *emotional* impression on Gray as a writer.
Although both West and his later friend Norton Nicholls mention
Petrarch with approval in letters to Gray (West commends Petrarch's
verse as 'sometimes very tender and natural', while Nicholls refers casually to the Italian's wonderful account of his ascent of Mount Ventoux),
the poet himself refers only once in his surviving correspondence to
the writer, and in that single case writes rather of the larger virtues of
a biography of Petrarch, a work that should be read primarily not so
much for the information it provides concerning the author himself, but
because it 'takes in much of the history of those obscure times, & the
characters of many remarkable persons'. Nicholls nevertheless testified
in his *Reminiscences* that Gray was 'a decided, and zealous admirer'
of Petrarch, and like any voracious and well-guided reader, Gray read
through a great many of the works of the popular Italian poet, concentrating probably on the 366 poems of the *Rime sparse* or *Canzoniere*
written in praise of the beloved lady Laura.

It is some indication as to just how habitually acquisitive Gray's
mind was by now that even the work of a writer with whom he makes
no profound emotional connection – a writer who intrigues him on
a much less visceral level than, say, Dante or even Tasso – is nevertheless quickly absorbed by his own poetic intelligence. Perhaps Gray
found Petrarch's brand of peculiar self-absorption uncongenial (he
was far less interested in all that was connoted by Petrarch's 'Laura'
than he was by the dazzling spiritual perfection of Dante's 'Beatrice').
And although he may have shared with Petrarch a deep-rooted love
and respect for classical literature (both writers devoted much of their
lives to the study of their Roman predecessors and both would in time
amass famously impressive, personal libraries) Gray emphatically did
not share Petrarch's inclination for rigorous and prolonged 'psychoanalytic self-examination' – what one modern translator has nicely
characterized as 'Petrarch's love of Petrarch' – nor did he have any real
sympathy with the Italian's genuine and truly insatiable desire for
worldly fame and glory.[20] The profound narcissism, and perhaps even
the attempt at transparent psychoanalytic honesty, of Petrarch's
analyses of his own emotion and passion in the *rime* were ultimately
alien to Gray's temperament.

The Latin translation of sonnet 170 betrays something of the distance
– the lack of a truly vibrant sense of *simpatia* – between the two writers.
That Gray even chose to render Petrarch's original into Latin rather than
English may itself hint at something. Latin was for Gray as truly close to

[20] Mark Musa, trans. and ed. *Petrarch: Selections from the Canzoniere and Other
Writings* (Oxford: Oxford University Press, 1985) xiv.

a second tongue as any modern language – it would certainly always be easier for him to write and even to think in Latin than in French or Italian. Yet might not Gray's decision in this particular instance to translate the sonnet into Latin, rather than English, indicate that he felt somehow distant or disconnected from its emotions and concerns? Might not such a move suggest that the translation was undertaken more in the way of an academic exercise in competence and ability than (as was certainly the case with the Ugolino episode from the *Inferno*) a genuinely felt piece of *poetry*? Gray's version is by no means false or unfeeling, yet it does lack the energy of realized vision that so clearly motivates his translations of Dante and, to a slightly lesser degree, Tasso. Gray's muted resistance to his author's situation is perhaps reflected in the confusion of the Petrarchan persona himself in the poem's opening lines:

> Uror, io! veros at nemo credidit ignes:
>   quin credunt omnes; dura sed illa negat.
> Illa negat, soli volumnus cui posse probare:
>   quin videt, et visos improba dissimulat. (*PTG* 309)

[Alas, I am on fire: but no one believed that the fires are real: or, rather, they all believe – it is just she, hard as she is, that denies it. She denies it, whom alone I long to convince. In fact, she sees them, and, wicked woman, pretends that she had not.]

The lover in the sonnet seems uncertain as how properly to give voice to his love – unsure of just how he can overcome his beloved's studied indifference to an otherwise recognized and even renowned passion. Petrarch, as usual, finds substantial consolation in the fact that even if the worldly Laura never deigns to recognize his devotion, his love will survive in the eternal life destined for his poetry:

> nos duo, cumque erimus parvus uetrque cinis,
> Iamque faces, eheu! oculorum, et frigida lingua
>   hae sine luce iacent, immemor illa loqui:
> Infelix Musa aeternos spirabit amores,
>   ardebitque urna multa favilla mea. (*PTG* 309)

[Even when we two will each be no more than a handful of ashes, then, alas, the flames of my eyes will lie deprived of light, and my cold tongue forget how to speak: but the ill-starred Muse will breathe out eternal love and many a spark will glow in my urn.]

Gray will return to this same image of the 'wonted fires' that continue to live in the 'ashes' and 'urns' of those long since dead at line 92 of the *Elegy*. He would also acknowledge another passage from that later poem (an image of the merits and frailties which repose in 'trembling hope' in the bosom of God) likewise to be at least partially Petrarchan in origin – an echo of the 'paventosa speme' or 'fearful hope' of Sonnet 115. It was by now second-nature for Gray to echo an author such as Petrarch in cento-like cuttings and fragments. Petrarch's larger interests and concerns as a writer, however – his otherwise influential obsession with self-examination, idealized feminine beauty, and the adulation of posterity – Gray did not, at least at this point in his career as a poet, find all that compelling.

*

It has already been noted that one of Gray's responsibilities first as a Cosin scholar and then, subsequently, as a Hale scholar at Peterhouse, entailed the writing of certain verses in Greek and Latin on Sundays, feast days, and holidays. The anniversaries of Guy Fawkes's failed attempt to blow up Parliament in 1605, of the execution of Charles I in 1649, of Charles II's birthday, and of his Restoration to the English throne in 1660, were all occasions that called for such commemorative and celebratory exercises. At worst, such metrical testaments of patriotic memory could be unimaginative and predictably workman-like. At best – and one might include here John Milton's *In Quintum Novembris*, written by the poet when he was a seventeen-year-old undergraduate at Christ's College – they provided a kind of proleptic glimpse of what a great poet could accomplish in the way of 'occasional' poetry when faced with the most pedestrian – or at least the most publicly political – of occasions. 'Some glimmerings of interest can always be found by lively minds' as A. N. Wilson has written of Milton's collegiate verse, '. . . even in academic exercises'.[21]

The several such exercises that survive from Gray's years at Cambridge all testify to his own particularly gracious and smiling brand of poetic ingenuity. In one short Latin poem, written to celebrate the twenty-ninth day of May – the precise date of Charles II's return to London in 1660 – Gray playfully places words of praise for the oak tree that once sheltered 'the hope of the [English] throne' quite literally within its branches in the mouth of the 'patria cara', the 'beloved fatherland', itself:

> Sacra Iovi Latio quondam, nunc sacra Britanno.
> Olim factus honus, illi velasse capillos,
> Qui leto civem abripuit, salvumque reduxit;
> Iam potes ipsa tribus populis praestare salutem. (*PTG* 297)

---

[21]   A. N. Wilson, *The Life of John Milton* (Oxford: Oxford University Press, 1983) 22.

[Once you were sacred to Jove in Latium and now you will be sacred in Britain. Of old the honor was conferred of crowning [with oak] the head of a man who rescued a fellow-citizen from death and brought him back in safety; now you yourself can claim to have been the salvation of three peoples.]

Having the soil of the kingdom itself rather complacently congratulate a tree (of its own growth, no less) on a job well done in such a manner as this begins to balance the propriety and seriousness of purpose demanded by such occasions with a subtle sense of the humour of the absurd. The short poem of Gray's that commemorates the discovery of Guy Fawkes's plot similarly pushes the limits of a micro-genre which, by the mid 1730s, must have seemed maddeningly limited and played out (even a frustrated Milton, writing over a hundred years earlier, seems desperately to have tried out various ideas in short Latin epigrams before settling on the narrative treated at greater length in his longer poem for the celebrations).

Gray begins his thirty-four-line exercise by asking to whom the prize for outstanding wickedness should be awarded. Who, in the entire history of the world, he queries, has been the most notorious tyrant, the most cunning and inventive traitor? Turning his back on the impressive contestants who present themselves for such a dubious honour within the annals of classical antiquity – theatrically spurning even the murderous credentials of Nero, Domitian, and the Sicilian tyrant Phalaris – Gray affects a mock-patriotism in conditionally awarding such a distinction to his own countryman, Guy Fawkes. After all, if Fawkes had succeeded in his original design, as Gray observes, he would not only have created a veritable hell on earth, but would himself have perished in the event. Such solitary self-sacrifice – such abnegation in the service of his larger cause – would surely have won him the 'praemia palmae', would it not? Yet Fawkes's plot, as we all know, was thwarted:

> effulget subito lux aurea caeli,
> (aspice) rimanti dum domus atra patet;
> Reclusamque vides fraudem, letique labores,
> antraque miraris sulphure foeta suo:
> Quod si venturi haec armamentaria fati
> panderat haud sacri gratia dia poli;
> Iure scelus se iactaret, procerumque ruina
> tantum una gentem perdomuisse manu. (*PTG* 298–99)

[Behold, suddenly the golden light of Heaven shines forth until the black vault lies open to the searcher. And you may see the plot revealed and the works of death, and marvel at the caverns filled with their own sulphur. But if the blessed grace of the sacred Heaven had not revealed this armoury of coming doom, then he could rightly boast of his wickedness and that single-handed, by the destruction of its leaders, he had overwhelmed such a nation.]

Of all the battles contesting the rival claims of the ancients and the moderns in the literature of the eighteenth century, these lines that retrospectively and almost proudly pretend to award the worldwide palm of wickedness in an 'evenly balanced' dispute to the Jesuit adventurer Guy Fawkes is surely one of the most bizarre.

Walpole appears consistently to have dismissed school exercises such as these as unworthy even of the name of poetry. Writing to West only a few months after his arrival in Cambridge in 1735, he had complained: 'We have not the least poetry stirring here; for I can't call verses on the 5th of November and 30th of January by that name, more than four lines on a chapter in the New Testament is an epigram'.[22] Lengthier efforts in a similar vein may also have earned Walpole's undeserved disdain, but even he – along with both Gray and West – submitted original verses to collections published early in 1736 to celebrate the upcoming marriage of the Prince of Wales. Gray's otherwise untitled 'Hymeneal' – while it lacks the more obvious and broadly elaborate humour of his shorter efforts – is easily the most successful of the friends' several contributions. Having first considered pitying the prince for being in a position that prohibits him from experiencing the 'sweet flame' of romantic love, the persona of Gray's poem decides that it is rather only the 'harsh beginnings' and the early trials of romantic affection to which royal couples are strangers. Their exalted status, he reasons, generally paves the way for an easy and untroubled courtship. The public nature of their connection may delay any actual contact between the prince and his partner, but such a delay will only increase the ardour of their wedding night. Gray ends the poem with a neat passage which compares Frederick to the sculptor Pygmalion of Greek legend:

> Sculptile sicut ebur, faciemque arsisse venustam
> Pygmaliona canunt: ante hanc suspiria ducit,
> Alloquiturque amens, flammamque et vulnera narrat;
> Implorata Venus iussit cum vivere signum,
> Femineam inspirans animam; quae guadia surgunt,
> Audiit ur primae nascentia murmura linguae,
> Luctari in vitam, et paulatim volvere ocellos
> Sedulus, aspexitque nova splendescere flamma:
> Corripit amplexu vivam, iamque oscula iungit

---

[22] WC xiii.94.

Acria confestim, recipitque rapitque; prioris
Immemor ardoris, Nymphaeque oblitus eburneae. (*PTG* 295)

[So, the poets tell, did Pygmalion burn for the lovely form of the
sculptured ivory. Before it he breathed sighs and addressed it
wildly, telling of his burning passion and the wounds of love. But
when Venus at his entreaty ordered the statue to live, imbuing it
with a woman's soul, what joys surged up as he heard the nascent
sounds of her first utterances and eagerly watched her struggle
to life and little by little roll her eyes and grow bright with a new
radiance. He seizes the living creature in his embrace and at once
presses his burning lips to hers, giving and taking kisses, oblivious of his former love and forgetful of the ivory nymph.]

The comparison ends the poem on an elegantly Ovidian note. Much
as the cold ivory of Pygmalion's marble statue was miraculously
transformed and ensouled by Venus into the lovely Galatea, so will
Frederick's insubstantial (because as yet unseen) Princess Augusta likewise soon cease to be a mere idea whose reality waits to be transported
from across the English channel, into a living creature to be embraced
and covered with burning kisses. Such a compliment hearkens back to
the conceit with which the poem opened. The prince and princess, far
from being unfeeling strangers to the 'flamma dulci' of Venus themselves,
are at heart creatures of flesh and blood much like everybody else. Gray,
like the eternal Goddess of Love herself, works to make that which now
appears distant or inaccessible seem instead to be palpable and 'real'.
Both breathe life into situations which otherwise seem static, distant, or
immobile. It has often been pointed out that most of the metamorphoses
in Ovid's collection are changes downward – changes, as Northrop Frye
once noted, 'from some kind of person or human being into a natural
object, a tree, a bird, or a star'.[23] Gray focuses instead on one of Ovid's
rare, ennobling changes 'upward', Galatea's transformation from the
cold ivory of marble into a human being. In just such a manner does
Gray himself, emulating the classical poet/maker, do his best to breath
the gentle, mythical breath of life into an otherwise cold and impersonal
public occasion.

    Yet there is, as usual, an undertone of humour in the poem as well.
William Mason was harshly critical of the 'Hymeneal'. 'Adulatory verse
of this kind', he wrote shortly after the poet's death, 'are usually buried,
as they ought to be, in the trash with which they are surrounded. Every
person, who feels himself a poet, ought to be above prostituting his

[23] Northrop Frye, *Northrop Frye on Shakespeare* (New Haven and London: Yale
University Press, 1986) 170.

powers on such occasions, and extreme youth (as was the case with Mr. Gray) is the only thing that can apologize for having done it'.[24] Apart from doing an undeserved and rather vicious disservice to the tempered and stately Latin of Gray's prothalamion, Mason very badly misses the point here; Gosse was right to observe that had he 'glanced through the lines again, of which he must have been speaking from memory, Mason would have seen that they contain no more fulsome compliments than were absolutely needful on the occasion'. 'The young poet', Gosse added, 'is not thinking at all about their royal highnesses, but a great deal about his own fine language, and is very innocent of anything like adulation.'[25] Gray's poem, published in the very officially titled *Gratulatio Academiae Cantabridgiensis Auspicatissimus Frederici Walliae Principis & Augustae Principissae Saxo-Gothae Nuptias Celebrantis*, may have been written partly out of a sense of collegiate obligation, but it was nevertheless undertaken partly, too, out of a simple sense of fun. Gray's experience as a student of Ausonius must certainly have recalled that poet's own *cento nuptialis* to his mind (Gosse was acute enough to note that one fine passage of the poem was 'almost a cento from Ovid').[26] Accepting the structure of compliment noted above may be one way of reading the poem, but it is of course by no means the only way. The writing of the Hymeneal formed part of a larger group effort on behalf of Gray and his friends. The poems written by both Walpole and Ashton were printed alongside Gray's in the same Cambridge volume, and West also wrote a Latin original for the Oxford version of the *Gratulatio*. Gray's friend-to-be, Thomas Wharton, wrote a poem for the Cambridge selection in Greek. Ashton tellingly commented in a letter to West that he thought Gray's effort seemed 'to touch upon the manner of Claudian', a reference to that poet's many official works in praise of the Roman emperor Honorius, and more particularly, to the politically motivated *Epithalamium* in which Claudian celebrated Honorius' marriage to Maria, daughter of 'Stilicho the Vandal'.[27] Honorius was an emperor of the western Roman Empire who died at the age of 39 in AD 423. He had succeeded his father Theodosius, a ruler who had earned himself the sobriquet 'the Great', and whose reign had been marked by several significant campaigns and military victories against the encroaching barbarians. Honorius, by contrast, was perceived to be weak, inefficient, inactive, and generally unsuited to his public position. He displayed no real interest in the declining fortunes of the fast splintering empire, and

---

[24] Mason, 10n.
[25] Gosse, 11–12.
[26] Ibid, 12.
[27] *Correspondence of Gray, Walpole, West, and Ashton*, ed. Paget Toynbee, 2 vols. (Oxford, 1915) i.68.

he turned the reigns of government over to his ministers and generals. In so deliberately affecting 'the manner of Claudian' (and even the plodding and generally unimaginative Ashton was alive to the reference) Gray may very well have intended his readers to make some kind of comparison between Honorius and the equally indolent Prince of Wales. It had certainly not taken long for most Englishmen to realize that Frederick, who had arrived in England in 1728, was a decidedly shallow-minded 'puppy' and – rather like Honorius so many years before him – a pawn rather than a player. The prince's relationship with his parents was notoriously dismal, and both Robert Walpole and the opposition politicians had soon found themselves looking to secure his otherwise erratic and questionable loyalty. He was certainly no Pygmalion – a creative sculptor neither of his own nor his country's destiny.

Such a comparison is perhaps the source of the humour, then, which lies at the heart of Gray's poem. The comic circumstances surrounding the prince's marriage on 27 April 1736, would certainly have done justice to the irony of Gray's poetic vision of the prince as a gifted, discriminating, and talented craftsman. Throughout the wedding supper on the night of the ceremony, Frederick conspicuously and winkingly consumed large quantities of jelly (thought to be an aphrodisiac), and made a point of sharing his vulgar anticipation of the pleasures of the wedding bed with the servants. Bundled off for the night after being ceremoniously dressed by his father in a nightshirt and absurdly tall nightcap, Frederick looked a lot less like a creating artist than he did a regal dunce. The wedding night was presided over not by Hymen or Venus, as Gray's poem had, with mock solemnity, suggested it would be, but by a king and a queen anxious to get their awkward and 'good-for-nothing' son off their hands.

*

If Gray intended his lines allusively to suggest a less than reverential or even less than respectful portrait of their subject, most contemporary readers appear to have been no more alive to the poem's ironic subtext than Mason was in 1775. The Hymeneal attracted general admiration, and its young author achieved something of a reputation as writer of Latin verses. The undertone of humour did not, however, pass entirely without appreciation. Sometime towards the end of Michaelmas term, 1736, Gray was officially asked to write the Tripos verses for the upcoming university Congregation. The verses would be distributed with the Second Tripos list issued by the moderators on the Thursday following mid-Lent Sunday, which in 1737 fell on 24 March. The prescribed topic for Gray was 'Luna habitabilis' or the notion that 'the moon is habitable'. Another set of Tripos verses that survives from the same year, written by Jacob Bryant, who was then a freshman at King's, undertook to expound on the similar proposition, 'planetae sunt habitabiles'. Such fanciful topics were generally the norm for the Tripos exercises, part of the very purpose of which was to provide a bit of comic relief amidst all the solemnity and ceremony of the university Congregation. Gray, who was understandably proud of the distinction that had been conferred upon him in having been asked to write the verse in the first place, worked hard on his ninety-five-line effort. The project came to him just as he was lamenting the status of Cambridge as a modern-day Babylon to West. At least now there was something 'official' to be undertaken which could at the same time be instilled with some real interest and scholarly ingenuity.

Gray's finished project resembles his other Latin verses in its characteristic mixture of allusion and originality, of decorum and irreverence. Gray once again imitated his predecessor Claudian, if not this time in subject, than at least in his elegant and highly self-conscious manipulation of the Latin language. His poem begins with an invocation to the muse Urania. Gray asks the youngest of the daughters of Mnemosyne to accompany him into the open sky and explain the stars and their 'numbers' to him. The muse smilingly replies to his request by observing that it is no longer necessary for him to possess wings in order to undertake such stellar exploration, and promptly places him in front of a telescope that is at that very moment focused on the moon. Gray's view then easily travels across vast distances to study the caves, hills, woods, and mountains of the lunar region. He professes not to be surprised at the fact that the moon boasts its own, indigenous population:

> Et dubitas tantum certis cultoribus orbem
> Destitui? exercent agros, sua moenia condunt
> Hi quoque, vel Martem invadunt, curantque triomphos
> Victores: sunt hic sua praemia laudi;
> His metus, atque amor, et mentem mortalia tangunt. (*PTG* 301–02)

> [And can you believe that a sphere such as this lacks some kind of inhabitants? These too work their own fields, and found their own cities; and perhaps they go to war, and the victors celebrate triumphs; for here too renown has its own rewards. Fear and love and mortal feelings touch their hearts.]

Earthlings marvel at the sight of the moon and mythologize its nightly display of beauty, but the inhabitants of the moon are no less enamoured of their view of 'the greater sphere of Earth'. They watch in fascination as the land masses of France, Germany, and Italy are gradually exposed to their scrutiny in the course of a long summer evening. Tiny England, though a mere spot on this great golden ball, shines more brightly than any other region. It is the 'lovely light' – the 'gleaming dot' – on which all the nobles of the moon wish to bestow their own name. Gray ends his poem with a vision that outdoes even the conclusion of Pope's *Windsor Forest*, and extends England's imperial glory to the *ultima thule* of conceivable mercantile expansion in the eighteenth century:

> Foedera mox icta, et gemini commercia mundi,
> Agminaque assueto glomerata sub aethere cerno.
> Anglia, quae pelagi iamdudum torquet habenas,
> Exercetque frequens ventos, atque imperat undae;
> Aeris attollet fasces, vetersque triumphos
> Huc etiam feret, et victis dominabitur auris. (*PTG* 301–03)

> [Soon I see treaties made and traffic between the two worlds, and troops of men gathered under a sky with which they have grown familiar. England, which for so long has held sway over the sea and so often set the winds to work and ruled the waves, will assume the symbols of power in the sky, will bring her wonted triumphs even here and have dominion over the conquered air.]

Readers in the late twentieth century who have long grown familiar with actual images of the fragile blue and white eggshell of our planet home as viewed from the distant surface of the moon – its seas, clouds, and continents an oasis of swirling colour set in the darkness of deeper space – no doubt underestimate just what an imaginative leap it would have been for Gray, writing in the early eighteenth century, even to conceive of presenting earth from such an eccentric perspective. Works such as Bernard de Fontenelle's 1686 *Entretiens sur la pluralité des mondes* (or 'treatise on the plurality of worlds') may to some degree have encouraged the earliest speculation that the moon and other planets were themselves inhabited, but few ever attempted to imagine what kind of impression the earth and its own inhabitants would make on visitors from any other, distant world. It is difficult to imagine a modern poem in which a scientific or technological advance is so enthusiastically and even lovingly embraced, as the telescope is here (one is always surprised to be reminded that Urania's 'art' of astronomy is akin to those of Calliope, Erato, Terpsichore, and the other 'sisters of the sacred well'). The poem captures a delicate moment when art and science could be seen as moving forward together and in harmony, each in some way advancing the claims of the other.

Gray perhaps intended his readers to hear some slight echo of Milton's description of the Tuscan artist Galileo (who views the mountains of the moon through his 'Optic Glass' in Book I of *Paradise Lost*), but his sight was probably more firmly fixed on another epic, Ludovico Ariosto's *Orlando Furioso*. In canto 34 of Ariosto's sprawling comedy, the English paladin Astolfo travels to the moon to recover the lost wits of his cousin Orlando, who has gone completely mad upon learning of his beloved Angelica's marriage to a young African soldier named Medor. Astolfo travels in appropriately lofty company, his guide to the moon being none other than St. John the Evangelist himself. Ariosto's depiction of the allegorical lunar landscape is one of the most wonderfully entertaining and parodic moments in all epic poetry, and it clearly made a memorable impression on Gray. We notice on a closer reading of Gray's own poem that he has basically ignored the topic set for him by the moderators – that the moon is habitable – for one that more readily reflects the images he has only recently culled from his Italian model: that the moon is inhabited. West, to whom a copy of Gray's poem was quickly sent by Walpole, caught several allusions in Gray's verses to Virgil and Horace, but having been making his own way through Italian at Gray's instigation, likewise realized that any poem on the moon and its inhabitant would naturally have to refer to Ariosto. We see in 'Luna Habitabiles' the twin halves of Gray's literary background – the classical and the romantic, the ancient and the modern – momentarily joining forces. The poem can even stand as something of a testament to Gray's inclusive and various reading, a poetic emblem of how his early years at Cambridge had been spent. Within the confines of an officially sanctioned and dictated structure, Gray carved out a world of his own creation, a world in which a private, referential language was masked by the public and respectable rhetoric of praise.

*

The moderator who almost certainly asked Gray to write the Tripos verses was Reverend James Brown. Brown would in later years become one of Gray's closest friends within the university. Although slightly older than the poet (he had already been ordained and been made a Fellow of his college when Gray was still a first year student), Brown shared with Gray a common background. Both were Londoners and, perhaps more importantly, both were the children of London professionals, of London merchants. They were also strikingly similar in stature and temperament. Brown, like Gray, was short, neat, and precise in his habits. He had first come up as a Sizer to Pembroke College from Christ's Hospital in 1726. The connections between Pembroke and Peterhouse, situated as they were just across the street from one another, had traditionally been strong, and had been made even stronger in recent years by the fact that the current Master at Peterhouse, Walpole's John Whalley, was himself an old Pembroke man.

The precise circumstances under which Brown and Gray first met one another are not known. Perhaps a chance encounter in Trumpington Street revealed in its responses, gestures, and topics of conversation a depth of mutual interest that both were eager to cultivate and pursue. Or perhaps the frequent comings and goings between the colleges served to introduce the two to one another on a slightly more professional footing. Once having made each others acquaintance, however, Gray and Brown became fast friends. Brown at first cultivated Gray's acquaintance as a kind of mentor, but the younger man's obvious talents and abilities soon led him to think of Gray more as an equal and a friend. Still a relatively young man himself, Brown found the Petrean's qualities more congenial than those of his fellow dons at Pembroke.

At about the same time he met Brown, Gray also made two other friends at Cambridge – friends who were likewise to stand by him for the rest of his life. The first, John Clerke, was the son of a Kentish churchman. He had entered the university as a Pensioner at St. Catherine's in the spring of 1734. By the end of that same year he had transferred to Peterhouse. Like Gray, Clerke was first a Cosin and then a Hale scholar. He would receive his BA in 1738, his MD in 1753, and was for many years a practicing physician at Epsom, in Surrey.

Gray's other friend, Thomas Wharton, had been admitted as a Pensioner to Pembroke in 1734. Just as Gray had come up to Peterhouse thanks largely to the hereditary connection between his college and his uncle, so too Wharton had gone on to Pembroke because both his uncle and his great-grandfather had been members of the college. Wharton came from a rather illustrious line of Durham citizens and physicians. His father Robert, who had served as the Mayor of Durham, was the son of Dr. Thomas Wharton (1652–1714), who was himself the son of the Dr. Thomas Wharton who had served as Censor for the Royal College of Physicians, and who had counted among his friends both Izaak Walton and Elias Ashmole. Young Thomas Wharton was a genial and sensitive companion, a man who even as an undergraduate seems to have evinced those traits of loyalty and reliability that would in time bring Gray to count him among his very dearest friends.

In the meantime, Gray's other, older friends still demanded much of his attention. Ashton left Cambridge in 1737 and, thanks largely to Walpole's influence, was soon installed as tutor to Lord Plymouth (a rambunctious young boy to whom Gray refers in his letters to Walpole as Ashton's 'Lordling') and as such was comfortably settled in the house of Mrs. Anne Lewis (wife of Thomas Lewis of Harpton Court, Radnor) in fashionable Hanover Square. Ashton would soon take orders, and his sights were set on a prosperous career within the Church. West had continued at Oxford in dangerously low spirits. His brief meetings with Gray during the vacations only underscored how dreary and monotonous his lonely months at university had really become. Writing to Gray at the end of Michaelmas Term 1737, he once again complained of his friend's neglect:

> Receiving no Answer to my last letter, which I writ a month ago, I must own I am a little uneasy. The slight shadow of you which I had in town, had only served to endear you to me the more. The moments I past with you made a strong impression upon me. I singled you out for a friend, and I would have you know me to be yours, if you deem me worthy. – Alas, Gray, you cannot imagine how miserably my time passes away. My health and nerves and spirits are, thank my stars, the very worst, I think, in Oxford. Four-and-twenty hours of pure unalloy'd health together, are as unknown to me as the 400,000 characters in the Chinese vocabulary. One of my complaints has of late been so over-civil as to visit me regularly once a month – jam certus conviva. This is a painful nervous headache, which perhaps you have sometimes heard me speak of before. Give me leave to say, I find no physic comparable to your letters. If, as it is said in Ecclisiasticus, 'Friendship be the physic of the mind', prescribe to me, dear Gray, as often and as much as you think proper, I shall be a most obedient patient. (*CTG* 70)

Gray promptly responded to West's request with a lengthy 'prescription' in Latin, recommending 'risus, festivitas, & facetitae' ('laughter, pleasure, and wit'), for which the despondent Oxonian was truly grateful. By the beginning of 1738, the end of West's career at Christ Church was at last within sight. 'Wish me joy of leaving my college', he wrote to Gray early in the year, 'and leave yours as fast as you can'. By early spring, West was already settling into his chambers at the Inner Temple and eagerly looking forward to being joined there by Gray, who in turn seems to have been determined to put off beginning his legal studies for as long as possible. Although he no longer had any academic commitments to his college, Gray remained in Cambridge for much of the summer of 1738. In June he sent an original sapphic ode to West, in which he humorously suggested that he would be content to remain in the university town forever, rather than join his friend in 'the barbarous dwelling where unquiet fright forever reigns'. The ode, written 'Ad C: Favonium Aristium', toys with the notion that his legal studies will never be compelling enough to tear Gray away from the attention he has lately been bestowing on the favourable muses:

> Et, pedes quo me rapiunt, in omni
> Colle Parnassum videor videre
> Fertilem silvae, gelidamque in omni
>   Fonte Aganippen.

Risit et Ver me, facilesque Nymphae
Nare captantem, nec ineleganti,
Mane quicquid de violis eundo
              Surripit aura:

Me reclinatum teneram per herbam:
Qua leves cursus aqua cunque ducit,
Et moras dulci strepitu lapillo
              Nectit in omni.

Hae novo nostrum fere pectus anno
Simplices curae tenuere, caelum
Quamdiu sudum explicuit Favoni
              Purior hora:

Otia et campos nec adhuc relinquo,
Nec magis Phoebo Clytie fidelis:
(Ingruant venti licet, et senescat
              Mollior aestas). (*PTG* 306–07)

[And, wherever my feet bear me, I seem to see Parnsassus, richly
wooded, in every hill, and cool Aganippe in every fountain. The
spring smiles on me, and the kindly Nymphs, as I catch with no
undiscriminating nostrils whatever the morning breeze steals
from the violets as it passes; and lie back on the soft grass, wherever the stream makes its rippling way, and dallies at every pebble
with a pleasing murmur. These innocent cares absorbed my heart
at about the time when the year was new, as long as the fresher
season of Favonius provided clear skies; nor do I yet renounce
idleness and the fields, no is Clytie more faithful to Phoebus (even
if the winds are rising and the balmier summer grows old.)]

*

When the time came for Gray finally to depart from Cambridge, he
was surprised at how reluctant he was to leave the place. The town he
had first described to Walpole as a nasty lump of spider inhabited by
drunks and illiterates could not have changed all that much in only four
years, but Gray himself, within that same period of time, had changed
a great deal. He was, at the very least, no longer a stranger in a strange
land. He had made new friends both at Peterhouse and at Pembroke
College, and by the summer of 1738 he wound his way through every
street and alley of the university town with the knowing confidence of
the born native. Its local customs and rituals had long grown familiar
to him, and at least part of the summer months had been idled away
simply in enjoying spectacles like Midsummer or 'Pot' Fair – an annual
fair for the sale of horses, cattle and pottery – and the larger Stourbridge

Fair, a three-week long extravagance of ancient standing less than two miles from Cambridge itself. Gray claimed not to have revised his first impressions of the town all that radically, but rather simply to have grown comfortable in his surroundings. 'Tis true Cambridge is very ugly', he wrote to Walpole shortly before leaving, 'she is very dirty & very dull, but I'm like a cabbage, when I'm stuck, I love to grow: you should pull me up sooner, than anyone, but I shall ne'er be the better for transplanting.'

The Peterhouse books show that Gray left college sometime in the middle of September, probably on the 16th or 17th of the month. For several days prior to his departure, he was at his wits' end, as the normal placidity of his surroundings was thrown into an unaccustomed chaos of noise and commotion. Books were carefully loaded into wooden boxes, bedsteads dragged across the floor to be disassembled for the wagon journey back to Cornhill, and other pieces of furniture secured and made ready for the trip as well. Tutors and other members of the college, startled by all the activity, would have poked their heads in his doorway and peered curiously into his windows, but probably offered little in the way of any practical help. The thin layer of dust that was everywhere disturbed and stirred up as possessions were packed into crates in the course of the afternoons, in the evenings hung heavy in the air, and made Gray more aware that the whole process of moving, once begun, could not be accomplished too soon. By 18 September, Gray was back in Cornhill. Almost immediately upon his arrival at his father's house, he wrote to Walpole, eager to know when and where the two could meet up and discuss how they were going to spend their time in London. He had little idea just how profoundly Walpole's own plans for the immediate future were soon to shape and forever to change his own.

Walpole had left Cambridge sometime towards the end of 1738. His name was removed from the college books at the beginning of Michaelmas term, and his last payments to King's were entered for the Long Vacation term of that same year. He left the college 'in form', as he put it in his *Short Notes of My Life*, without taking a degree in 1739. As surprising as it may now seem to those familiar with Walpole's subsequent history and activities, he too, like Gray and West, was prepared at least in theory to embark on a legal career. His name was entered in Lincoln's Inn in 1731 – four years before Gray had been admitted to the Inner Temple. Neither his erratic and generally undistinguished performance at university, nor the fact that he already held several government posts that had been at his father's disposal (including a lucrative one as Usher of the Exchequer, a place worth almost £1,000 a year, as well as 'two other little patent places', worth united about £300 a year) effected any change in these well-laid family plans. Even as he prepared to leave

Cambridge, however, Walpole's state of mind was so uncertain as to attract the serious attention of his friends and relatives. At the beginning of 1738 his uncle Horatio – Sir Robert Walpole's younger brother and his nephew's namesake – had noted that Horace had lately been 'a good deal out of order', adding, 'he has his choice to take a turn abroad and stay some time at The Hague, or to study and stick to the Common Law. He has not yet decided his opinion'.[28]

Walpole had reason enough to be 'out of order'. The last year had been a disastrous one for him personally. In the summer of 1737 his mother had died following a short illness. Walpole was devastated by her loss. His sorrow was complicated by the fact that neither his brothers, his cousins, nor even his father seemed to have taken the slightest notice of her passing. Sir Robert displayed his apparent indifference by marrying his long-standing mistress, Maria Skerrett, a mere six months after his wife's death. But that union too was to prove ill-fated. The second Lady Walpole died in childbirth only three months after her marriage. Walpole was left both to console his father at Downing Street, while at the same time dealing as best he could with his own grief. At home he tended to be morose and uncommunicative, and when abroad his social posture was recognizably forced and strained. He did not look forward to his legal studies, nor could he muster any real enthusiasm for the fact that his father had already arranged that he should take a place in Parliament – as representative of the Cornish borough of 'Kellington' or Callington – at the earliest opportunity. Life without his mother lacked order, meaning, and consolation. The prospect of having to remain physically in London, where he was constantly being surrounded and haunted by her memory, was unbearable.

It is possible that Sir Robert, recognizing and even sympathizing with his son's depression and uncharacteristic lack of spirits, was the first to suggest that he undertake to travel a bit further abroad than The Hague, a city which – then as now – conjures few visions of continental gaiety and *joie de vivre*. Why not really travel abroad, and spend some time in France? Perhaps even journey as far as Italy? Such a trip would do more to advance and to enrich his social, cultural, and political education than a lifetime spent in the fenlands of Cambridgeshire. One can picture the younger Walpole's face slowly becoming enlivened and then animated at the possibilities. Why not, he asked himself, make the Grand Tour in real style? He was, after all, the son of the first minister of England, and if the aristocracy and the Whig gentry now saw fit to send their own sons abroad to add a necessary polish and sophistication to their

[28] *H. M. C. Buckinghamshire MSS.*, 10 (Horatio Walpole to Robert Trevor, January 3/14, 1737/38); reprinted in Ketton-Cremer, *Horace Walpole*, 32.

otherwise home-spun acquirements, why should not he also undertake such a protracted odyssey? There was much still to be learned about architecture, painting, sculpture, music, the theatre – and who could better appreciate such things than himself? Moreover, as Walpole well knew, there would be much more freedom abroad to give some scope to his otherwise suppressed emotional and sexual self; when individuals like Horace went abroad, as G. S. Rousseau has pointed out, 'they were searching, like their heterosexual counterparts, for eros *and* antiquity'.[29] If London had become burdensome, what better solution than simply to leave it behind? His legal studies could wait. The very thought of Lincoln's Inn momentarily put a damper on Walpole's newly kindled enthusiasm. What would be the fun of the Grand Tour if it was to be spent merely in the company of one's servants? Every night he attended the theatre or the opera – every time he visited a museum or a gallery – he would be thinking of Gray and West, picturing them confined to their cramped and dusty chambers, insensibly falling asleep while huddled over impenetrable mountains of legal documents. While he was making his way light-heartedly from the Tuileries to the Louvre, his friends would be treading the same old path between the Inns of Court and Westminster Hall. Sensing his son's indecision, Sir Robert perhaps suggested that one or both of these friends could likewise spare themselves from the law for a few months or even longer and undertake the tour with him? The addition of one more traveller would not add all that much in the way of expenses. That young Mr. West he had met at Richmond Lodge just last August – the son of the poor Lord Chancellor of Ireland – surely he would be a suitable companion, though physically rather too frail to endure the rigours which such an extended overland journey would entail. What about his other friend, Gray? What was his family? Could he, perhaps, be spared?

And so, perhaps, the conversation went. It was soon settled that Walpole was to travel to Paris, and that Gray was to accompany him. Walpole would pay for the better part of Gray's share of the costs, but such an arrangement was in no way to affect relations between them. They were to be treated as equals. Sir Robert could now concentrate on his increasingly embattled political position with some confidence that at least one department of his life was in order. By the time he returned from the continent, his son would almost certainly have shaken off the depression consequent upon his mother's death. Horace, meanwhile, could hardly wait to tell Gray the good news. Just how Gray received such a welcome reprieve from the law books can only be imagined. He was probably stunned, rather shocked, and, when the idea had time to

---

[29] Rousseau, *Perilous Enlightenment*, 175 (italics mine).

sink in, certainly delighted. The Cornhill household may have had some lingering reservations about the monetary arrangements – they were proud enough to wonder if it was really proper for their son's friend to bear the financial burden of the entire trip – but any time they tried to put any objections into words the overwhelming fact of their son's situation would gradually have represented itself in all its seductive grandeur. To think that their child should be chosen to accompany the son of Sir Robert Walpole on the Grand Tour, and chosen not as a paid companion or an escort, but as a beloved friend. It was all too much to be believed. Just prior to his departure, Horace even went so far as to draw up a will bequeathing to Gray everything of which he might die possessed.

Whatever qualms his parents (and particularly, of course, his mother) may have been experiencing about the trip, Gray himself would almost certainly have had none. It was quickly decided that they should set out as soon as possible in the spring. This meant a departure, if they were lucky and if the weather cooperated, sometime in March or early April at the latest. The winter of 1738 may well have been one of the happiest of Gray's life. He and Walpole would have met whenever possible to discuss their plans and to decide on just which sights they would see. The scope of the Grand Tour in the early eighteenth century extended to include Paris and the principle Italian cities – Rome, Venice, Florence, and Naples. Tourism even within France and Italy had not yet developed into the tidy industry it was to become later in the century. The twentieth-century critic Clark S. Northup has reminded readers that not very many literary men in eighteenth-century England travelled very far abroad, and almost none were to pursue their journeys to the south of Europe. The dangerous conditions of the Alpine pass had forced John Locke to turn back from his proposed journey to Rome in 1678. Although Addison's experience in Italy, having been recounted in his *Remarks on Several Parts of Italy* (1705) was generally well-known, his partner in *The Spectator*, Richard Steele, had never even made it as far as the Channel. Nor, for that matter, were authors as celebrated as Alexander Pope or – later in the century – Samuel Richardson ever to undertake any extended travel outside of England. Samuel Johnson made it to Paris for two months in 1775, but plans for an even lengthier excursion with his friends the Thrales to the Italian peninsula had to be abandoned following the death of that couple's nine-year-old son, Henry. The magistrate and novelist Henry Fielding travelled as far as Lisbon, of course, though only in the final months of his life.

Many of the conveniences which travellers in the 1760s or 1770s were already beginning to take for granted had in 1739 not even been conceived of or yet invented. Arrangements often had to be made well in advance of one's arrival and with painstaking care. Reliable guidebooks and phrase books were hard to come by. Gray and his mother made a point of gathering together informative volumes to be left at home in Cornhill, so that Dorothy could track her son's progress. Maps, too, would have to be found so that she could trace his path through France. Fiercely proud of her son's social and academic accomplishments, she naturally wanted as much as possible to share this adventure with him. Mother and son together poured over all the 'travel' books they could lay their hands on; these volumes may have included works such as François Maximilian Misson's *Nouveau Voyage d'Italie, fait en l'année 1688*, Bishop Gilbert Burnet's *Travels*, and George Sandys's popular travel account. Gray's own feeling would have been hard to put into words. On the one hand he could hardly wait to leave, and yet, on the other, the anticipation was delicious enough for him to want to prolong it and savor it, slowly, for itself.

Toward the end of March the winter finally broke, and the weather favoured the friends' immediate departure for France. Long and tearful goodbyes were probably taken in the Cornhill home, and fervent promises were made to write on both sides. Even Gray's father – now bowed into a state of uneasy submission by the formidable combination of his wife's continued defiance, his son's independence, and frequent, crippling attacks of gout – seems to have watched young Thomas's departure with some regret, and asked to be remembered in his letters home. Many years later, after Gray's death, Walpole was to look back across the gulf of time and recall with an odd mixture of vivid memory and retrospective foreboding the very first days and hours of their trip. 'We had not got to Calais', he wrote, 'before Gray was dissatisfied, for I was a boy, and he, though infinitely more a man, was not enough so to make allowances'.[30] ('I have known a hundred instances of men setting out in couples', the poet Byron would write many years later, and with reference to his own split while travelling with John Hobhouse in 1810, 'but not one of a similar return'.)[31] As the coach carrying Gray and Walpole rumbled heavily over the Southwark stones towards Kent and Dover, however, minor differences and disagreements were not yet taken as the harbingers of any more serious divisions to come. The two young men were off to begin the adventure of a lifetime. The course was set, their journey was finally begun, and the world was all before them.

[30] WC xxviii.114.
[31] *The Works of Lord Byron: Letters and Journals*, ed. Rowland E. Prothero, 6 vols. (London: John Murray, 1898–1901) i.286.

CHAPTER FOUR

CREATION'S HEIRS

The Grand Tour
1739–1741

I. Enfin Donc Me Voici À Paris

Walpole and Gray crossed the Channel at Dover on Easter Sunday, 29 March 1739. The sails of their packet-boat were filled by a brisk gale which carried them to Calais in just five hours. The crisp weather of the crossing cheered and excited most of the passengers; the pitch and roll of the small boat made Gray extremely sick from the moment the boat left the English port. By the time they came into Calais harbor and prepared to disembark for the smaller vessel which was to ferry them to shore a heavy snow had begun to fall. The clean and glistening mantle which the snowstorm laid down upon the roofs and spires of the town only rendered the foreign port more captivating to the newly arrived travellers.

The Calais that greeted Gray and Walpole, after all, was not yet the bomb-scarred and war-weary veteran through which today's visitors to the continent are processed and funneled with bureaucratic inefficiency towards Paris and beyond. Here was a strange and ancient city – a wealthy capital of the lace industry, a smart and turreted gateway to a thousand eagerly anticipated wonders – which even in the growing darkness of the approaching evening excited in the young men that unique sensation of being for the first time in one's life in a foreign land. The *frisson* of strangeness transformed everything they saw into novelty. If things were not necessarily managed better in France, they were at least, one could not help but observe, managed differently. As their coach bounced and rumbled through the unfamiliar streets of the town towards their inn, the two travellers looked eagerly about them. The houses they passed, the road itself, the way the people dressed, the churches and seemingly innumerable convents and chapels of the various religious orders: how different it all was from England! The journey that truly began on that snowy evening in March would extend to include a great many sights and experiences, but nothing, Walpole would later recall, could ever match the simple joy of Calais – the surprise of being for the first time in France.

Walpole and Gray awoke on Easter Monday to attend a high Mass at the great church of Calais, the Eglise Nôtre Dame. They spent the rest of the morning visiting the Convent of the Capuchins and the nuns of St. Dominic. They were surprised at the latter convent to encounter an English nun by the name of Mrs. Davis, with whom they soon entered into conversation. Gray took the first opportunity of preserving a souvenir of his journey for his mother, and sent by return of the same packet on which they had just arrived a letter case embroidered by the Englishwoman. There was little time to be spent exploring Calais, however. The two men were determined to stop and see a number of sights as they passed their way along the post-route towards Paris, and it was still snowing heavily. In the afternoon they took a postchaise for the eighteen-mile journey to Boulogne. Gray found even the chaise itself to be 'a strange sort of conveyance', quite unlike the kind they were used to in England. The weather, to their surprise, proved no problem for the travellers. The roads were uncommonly smooth, and the horses, through not very graceful, managed well enough at the easy speed of about six miles an hour. That same evening found them passing through the gates of Boulogne ('a large, old, fortified town'), and on the following day they made the considerably longer journey towards Abbeville, which lay a further fifty-one English miles to the southwest. Both Gray and Walpole remained enthusiastic about their progress and wide-eyed at the fine, unfamiliar countryside through which they were being driven. Even at this early stage in their travels they began, too, to encounter some of the less pleasant 'surprises' involved in such an undertaking. Lunching in Montreuil on the way to Abbeville, the pair dined ('much to our hearts' content' as Gray wrote to his mother) on 'stinking mutton cutlets, addle eggs, and ditch water'. Rendering the meal even less digestible for the travellers was the appearance of the hostess and innkeeper in an unfamiliar and shapeless sack dress of coarse linsey-woolsey. Abbeville itself proved more hospitable, however, and the tourists spent a morning examining the chapels in two of the city's seventeen convents. Both Gray and Walpole were fascinated by the strange Catholic institutions of the French. Even the crucifixes or small shrines erected to the Virgin Mary on the rural hillocks and in the fields were thought curiosities worthy of comment.

Amiens, the chief city of the province of Picardy, was the first large cathedral town visited by the travellers. Here Gray, much like almost every other visitor before or since, was close to overwhelmed by the tremendous Gothic cathedral, the largest church in France. He and Walpole spent some time exploring the separate chapels of the Jesuits and the Urseline Nuns, and marveled at the gold shrine on the high alter preserving the relics of St. Firmin. For Gray, the Cathedral at Amiens – the exterior of which is beset with thousands of small statues and beautiful painted windows – conjured a vision of just what Canterbury Cathedral must have looked like in the years before the Reformation.

Characteristically, when Gray looked at the world around him, he saw at the same time in his mind's eye the world as it once existed in the past. He possessed the double-vision of a trained and by now intuitive classicist. The two stayed overnight at Amiens, where they dined on suitably exotic paté de perdrix. The next morning they moved on towards Paris, passing through the park at Chantilly to catch a glimpse of the palace of the Duke of Bourbon, breaking down briefly near Luzarches, and making one final stop before reaching the capital to see the relics and royal monuments at Saint-Denis. They were fortunate to have for their guide at Saint-Denis a Benedictine monk who had served as a soldier prior to taking orders. They enjoyed his idiosyncratic and irreverent tour through the abbey's collection of treasures, where they seem to have been most impressed not by the royal tombs, but by a vase of solid onyx some two thousand years old, on which were represented the mysteries of Bacchus.

Late that Saturday afternoon they piled back into their coach, and by the early evening were winding their way through the outskirts of Paris. The extended labyrinth of the city streets was bewildering even to these experienced Londoners, and the two peered out the windows of the chaise hoping to get some clearer idea of just where they were headed. When the postchaise finally came to a halt outside the Hôtel de Luxembourg in the Rue des Petits Augustins and the doors were opened, they found themselves being warmly greeted by Walpole's cousins Lord Francis Seymour Conway and Henry Seymour Conway, both of whom had been among their schoolfellows at Eton; with them was their friend Lord Holdernesse. Together the three men made sure that the new arrivals were comfortably settled, and gave them a taste of the Paris fashion by eating supper in the early hours of the morning and staying till two o'clock. 'Here nobody sleeps', Gray drily observed to West soon afterward of Paris, 'it is not the way'.

The dizzy excitement of their first evening in the French capital was as nothing compared with the social whirl of the next few weeks. Walpole's social connections opened the doors of the English community in Paris to the travellers, and the two men were soon inundated with introductions and invitations. On the evening following their arrival they dined with Lord Holdernesse, where they met the Abbé Prévost d'Exiles, best known to later generations as the author of *Manon Lescaut*. They then went to see a spectacle representing the myth of Pandora in the Grande Salle des Machines in the Palais des Tuileries, where Gray conceded the theatre to be 'one of the finest . . . in the world', but found the piece itself to be 'an absurd design' (both Walpole and Gray – no strangers to the fashions of the London stage – would nevertheless be frankly baffled by some of the elaborately artificial conventions of the French theatre and opera). The following night they dined at the residence of James Waldegrave, who had been serving as the English Ambassador in Paris for nearly ten years. Within less than a week they had attended a number of operas, tragedies, comedies, and ballets. Their days were spent in a flurry of sightseeing, and Gray soon claimed that there were few churches or palaces containing anything worth seeing that could possibly have escaped their attention. Henry Conway, whom Gray only half-jokingly accused of having succumbed to the local fashion by not displaying any curiosity with regard to his surroundings, usually accompanied them on these outings; the three men fell into a pattern of exploring the city together by day, dining sumptuously in the evening, and moving on to the theatres until the early hours of the morning. They soon visited a Parisian tailor to exchange their unfashionable English clothing for something more *à la mode*, and emerged – at least according to Gray's amusing account of the visit – transformed into creatures of high Parisian fashion. Gray's hair was curled and worn, as was then the fashion, *a la negligée*, and secured in front and back by a large solitaire or black silk neck-tie. His waistcoat and breeches were tightened 'so strait, (one) can neither breath, nor walk', and his coat was widened and stiffened with buckram. The ruffles of his sleeves were extended to the ends of his fingers, and the entire outfit was bedecked with an abundance of silk and fringe. Completing the outfit was a tremendous muff into which he was told to thrust both his arms, thereby rendering him completely incapable of movement. Following his own outfitting in Paris, Gray must have looked something like the elaborately-dressed French refugees depicted in Hogarth's 1738 engraving 'Noon' (from his 'Four Times of the Day' series). Students in the later years of Gray's life would recall that the poet continued to wear a muff when he returned to Cambridge. The cost of such clothes in France would have been considerable. As one historian of the Grand Tour, Tony Black, has calculated: 'The accounts of Sir John Swinburne on his 1749–51 trip to France give some indication of the cost of clothes: 48 livres for a laced hat and a feather bought at Lille, 216 for a waistcoat of rich Lyon stuff, 84 for six pairs of worked ruffles, 1,367 for "my Taylor's bill", etc.'[1]

Despite such inconveniences, the strangeness of it all remained exhilarating. The typical English visitor's list of sights in Paris would have included the Louvre, the Tuileries, the Luxembourg, the factories which produced luxury goods (such as the Gobelins tapestry works), and churches such as Nôtre Dame and St. Suplice. Gray's letters home are crammed with hyperbole. The view from the Pont Neuf along the Seine could only be described as 'the charming'st Sight imaginable'. The

[1] Tony Black, *The British Abroad: The Grand Tour in the Eighteenth Century* (Stroud: Sutton Publishing, 1992) 100.

buildings that lined the river near the Île de la Cité were likewise not to be outdone, and were therefore 'as handsome . . . as any in the world'. 'I could entertain myself this month', Gray wrote to West a week after his arrival in Paris, 'merely with the common streets and the people in them'.

The slight differences of custom and manner that had so captivated both Gray and Walpole when they had first landed at Calais continued to intrigue and delight them. The number of people and coaches in the streets, the amount of make-up used by Parisian women, the fashions and the hectic decorum of the social scene – all these things fascinated the travellers. Their one complaint was that for all of their own socializing and activity, they seemed to be meeting remarkably few Frenchmen. One obvious obstacle was the language. Both Gray and Walpole realized that their own command of French – of the spoken French idiom, at least – was imperfect, and in their fairer moments confessed that they could hardly complain of not being introduced into the higher levels of French society when anyone with whom they conversed would have to spend half their time correcting 'a stranger's blunders'. Another problem was that the primary entertainment at all the best French houses was gambling and card playing ('a professed Gamester being the most advantageous Character a Man can have at Paris'), and neither Gray nor Walpole had the inclination or the experience for such pursuits. Working against them too was the simple fact that English society in Paris tended to be very closed. Members of the English community were all well-acquainted with one another within their own circle, but they rarely strayed outside that circle and tended, as Gray quickly observed, to 'herd much together'.

Toward the middle of May the trio of travellers set their sights beyond the capital and ventured twice within the course of one week to the spectacular royal residence at Versailles. Gray's easy dismissal of the great front of the palace, which he compared with Timon's Villa described in Pope's fourth Moral Essay ('What a huge heap of littleness') is rather more understandable in light of the fact that by mid-century the palace already presented a weather-stained and slightly haphazard look from the front. Like many visitors to Versailles, Gray and his companions were far more impressed by the 250 acres of grounds and gardens, designed by the French landscape architect Le Nôtre, which seemed to stretch forever beyond the tremendous fountains behind the palace. Even here, however, the monotony of the endless walks and the elaborately overdone emblems and statuary excited contempt rather than admiration. 'Everything you behold', Gray complained in a letter to West, 'savours too much of art; all is forced; all is constrained about you'. The Grand Trianon, at least, built by Mansart in 1687, was generously declared an exception to this general rule. On their second visit to the palace the travellers attended a High Mass which included a ceremony of the installation of nine 'Knights of the Holy Ghost'. King Louis XV, Queen Maria, and the Dauphin were in attendance; both Gray and Walpole were again intrigued by the heavy formality and trappings of the Catholic ceremonies involving great crowds of Cardinals, impressive music, and clouds of incense.

Back in Paris, the travellers returned to their hectic social schedule and continued to attend the theatre as much as possible. Gray was particularly impressed by productions of Racine's *Britannicus* and of his *Phèdre*. He also enjoyed the unusual experience of watching a performance of one drama – Henry Brooke's *Gustavus Vasa* – the production of which had been prohibited in England under Robert Walpole's Licensing Act of 1737. Gray and Walpole took care to include their friends back in England as much as possible in their entertainments, and together prepared for West a small package containing copies of the plays they had seen, as well as the latest Parisian 'best-sellers', including Crébillon's *Lettres* and Bougeant's popular *Amusement Philosophique sur le Langage des Bêtes*.

By the end of May, it was clear that the time had come to move on. After some hesitation and indecision on the part of Walpole which Gray (not surprisingly) appears to have found exasperating, they decided to leave Paris for a smaller, more provincial French town. Perhaps recalling the fond memories of their brief visit to Amiens in the very first week of their tour, and probably at the immediate suggestion of Lord Conway, they quickly settled on the cathedral town of Reims. There, free from the distractions of the capital and the social customs that had denied them entrance to the *salons* of Paris, they would settle for some one or two months and devote themselves to perfecting their knowledge of the language. Lord Conway had by now returned to London, but Henry Seymour Conway – who was always Walpole's favorite of the two cousins – was more than willing to accompany them.

It is difficult to say how Gray felt about leaving Paris for Reims. Already in his letters home one gets a sense that the differences in temperament between him and Walpole were starting to cause some slight friction between them. Gray's penchant for rigorous and almost scholarly sight-seeing had already begun to set itself apart from Walpole's more intense interest in socializing and entertainment, although at this early stage the two were still more than willing to take part in each other's pleasures. In a letter written to Ashton just prior to leaving Paris, Gray candidly confessed that his 'conversations' with Walpole consisted less of language than of 'looks & signs', and conceded that any accurate representation of their substance would be better rendered in drawings rather than words; Conway's presence, Gray further observed, at least helped to make them 'a little more verbose'. Such comments in themselves, however, are not necessarily negative. The members of the Quadruple Alliance had now known one another for over ten years; it was only natural, as we have already mentioned, that the intimacy of their friendship should have resulted in a private 'language' of glances, gestures, and innuendo far more powerful than that of ordinary conversation. Yet in another letter to West, Gray clearly complained of some aspects of Walpole's behavior at this point in their journey. The letter unfortunately does not survive; it was probably destroyed by Mason while he was completing his *Memoirs of Gray* in 1773. At that time, Mason, wondering whether to include the piece in his *Memoirs*, showed the letter to Walpole, who observed rather sadly, 'You see how easily I had disgusted him; but my faults were very trifling, and I can bear their being known, and forgive his displeasure'.[2] The 'fault' in question was probably little more than the sort of youthful indecision or impetuosity about which Gray had already grumbled to Ashton; we would no doubt be mistaken to overemphasize the degree to which they were aggravating each other's nerves. The best of friends, when travelling together for an extended period of time, experience trifling quarrels and disagreements. Moreover, as Walpole was paying for almost all of Gray's expenses, it was only natural – whatever the pretense of fraternal equality – that he subtly exercise a greater say in determining the course of their affairs. The interlude in Reims would prove in some ways a necessary respite from the disorienting bustle and activity of the previous two months.

*

Notwithstanding their favourable impression of Amiens and the advantage of Lord Conway's connections in the city, Reims was a decidedly odd place for the visitors to have chosen to settle. As Gray soon wrote to his mother, there was little in the town apart from the ancient Gothic Cathedral Nôtre Dame to attract a stranger's curiosity. The streets of the city were drab and melancholy, the houses were old, and already in June the heat was stifling. The surrounding countryside – distressingly proximate to the city's walls – was flat, unvaried, and covered with vines. The only sound to be heard throughout the long, hot afternoons of the early summer was the continual croaking of frogs in the great moat which bordered the town's extensive ramparts.

The social life in Reims, as in Paris, seemed to consist of long sessions of card playing and gambling, varied only by extended walks undertaken

---

[2] WC xxviii.95.

in small groups of three or four individuals. Although the food was deemed better even than that of the capital city, and although there was no shortage of fine local Champagne, there were seldom any formal dinners or suppers. Gray supposed that the lack of any extended contact with the Parisians had served to render the local inhabitants more formal and reserved in their habits. They were not, however, entirely incapable of spontaneity. One evening early in their stay, Gray and Walpole found themselves in a company of some eighteen people 'of the best fashion here' who had assembled in one of the gardens in town to walk and spend the evening. 'One of the ladies', Gray wrote,

bethought herself of asking, Why should not we sup here? Immediately the cloth was laid by the side of a fountain under the trees, and a very elegant supper served up; after which another said, Come, let us sing; and directly began herself: From singing we insensibly fell to dancing, and singing in a round; when somebody mentioned the violins, and immediately a company of them were ordered: Minuets were begun in the open air, and then came country-dances, which held till four o'Clock next morning; at which hour the gayest lady there proposed, that such as were weary should get into their coaches, and the rest of them should dance before them with the music in the van; and in this manner we paraded through all the principle streets in the city, and waked every body in it. (CTG 113–14)

Walpole quickly proposed that such lively entertainments should become regular occurrences among the party at Reims. The local women, however, displayed a decided lack of interest in such schemes. Any such plans were soon dropped and, while Walpole and Gray again took up their dictionaries, the group insensibly returned to their round of 'dull cards, and usual formalities'. Gray himself continued to lament the slowness and sterility of the town, and began to look forward with eager anticipation to their removal to Dijon.

Yet the journey southward to Burgundy was soon to be post-poned. In mid-July Walpole received word that George Selwyn and George Montagu, both of whom had been friends of his since his days at Eton, were prepared to join the travellers at Reims. The day on which they were to have started on their first leg of their southern tour (9 September) found Gray and Walpole still waiting in Champagne; Gray now began to worry that by the time they got around to beginning their journey southward, the best part of the summer would have passed, and they would have nothing to look forward to but dirty, impassable roads and fallen leaves. Selwyn and Montagu finally arrived in Reims toward the end of the first week of August. They stayed just over one month. Gray had little enough to say about their visit. He was close to neither of them and was doubtless more than a little jealous of the time and trouble Walpole was prepared to take for the sake of their comfort and convenience. An aggrieved tone crept into at least one of his letters to Ashton (who had recently been ill) when he wrote, 'I make everything that does not depend on me, so indifferent to me, that if (the end of our expedition) be to go to the Cape of good Hope I care not'. Gray of course cared a great deal where he was headed, and we hear in this letter the faint stirrings of resentment against Walpole's absolute control of the purse-strings in the journey. After a painfully dull four weeks (in which he took a selfish satisfaction only in watching the visitors grow 'pretty heartily tired' of Reims within a very short period of time), Selwyn and Montagu were packed off back to England, and Gray and Walpole, with Henry Conway still in tow, finally began their journey south.

The road to Dijon lay through some of the loveliest and most fertile country in France. The three companions travelled in three short days through the small towns of Verzenay, Sillery, Châlons-sur-Marne, Vitry-le-François, Saint-Dizier, Joinville, Vignory, Langres, and Thil, before entering Burgundy by way of a noble avenue of lime trees. On the evening of 9 September, just as the sun was setting, they entered Dijon. For all of Gray's worries, the weather had remained mild, and the journey was a glorious adventure. While some towns, such as Saint-Dizier, were old or rendered unattractive by sprawling suburbs, the better part of their way wound itself along the banks of the Marne, and from their carriage they could see woods and vineyards on either side, and occasionally even glimpse the ruins of a castle perched on the top of a distant hill. Dijon they found a surprisingly small but beautiful city. Within days they visited the Palais des Ducs or 'Palace of the States' – the sometime residence of the Duke of Burgundy – and explored the abbey of the Carthusians which lay just outside the town. Immediately they regretted ever having spent so much time at Reims, and lamented that while the society of Dijon was much more lively and prosperous than that which they had found in Champagne, there was little point in being introduced into it for such a short stay.

Within only a matter of days, the trio moved on toward Lyon. Again the weather proved fine, and again their journey – the road now winding its way through Nuits, Beaune, Châlons-sur-Saône, Mâcon, and Ville-franche-sur-Saône – carried them through some increasingly spectacular scenery. Lyon itself did not impress Gray; he was at first inclined to grant that the city was a lively one, but was soon describing it in his letters as one of the most dismal places they had yet visited. The streets were too narrow and nasty, he complained, the buildings were too high, and the inhabitants themselves 'too much given up to commerce, to think of their own, much less a stranger's diversions'. The countryside surrounding this second city of France, however, was another matter altogether. Not only did the mountains – 'bespeckled with houses, gardens, and plantations of the rich Bourgeois' – offer impressive views of the city, the rich plains of the Lyonnais, and the Alps beyond, but here Gray's knowledge of classical history began to impart to his sightseeing an added excitement (even at Lyon he had begun to note such details as the fact that 'Hannibal is supposed to have passed the Rhone hereabouts', or, of a local temple, 'Drusus is said to have consecrated it').[3] The climb up Mount Fourvière found Gray examining the ruins of the palaces of Augustus and Severus; little of the structures remained, but for the first time in his life he was truly coming into contact with the ancient world, the writings and philosophies of which had dominated his imagination since his earliest days at Eton. In the south of France he was tempted to forsake abbeys and nunneries for a closer examination of the remnants of empire, and spent the sunny autumn afternoons wandering among the remains of the theatres, baths, and aqueducts of the Romans.

Walpole received little mention in Gray's surviving letters either to his mother or – more significantly – to West from this stage in their travels. While there is no indication of any profound disagreements between the two, it is again possible that Gray's patient examination of antiquities was already at odds with Walpole's own desires for a more active social schedule. There was certainly little enough for Walpole to do in Lyon. They had no acquaintances in the town and, despite its large size, Lyon that September was host only to a tiny handful of English travellers (no more than thirty, Gray estimated) most of whom were only passing through on their way to Italy and the South. The time had now come, too, for Henry Conway to depart for Geneva, where he planned to spend the winter. Desiring perhaps to extend Conway's companionship on the tour, Walpole immediately proposed that they accompany him on his journey. The plan met little resistance from Gray, particularly as they proposed to travel to Geneva by way of the longest route and stop near Les Échelles to visit the monastery of the Grande Chartreuse.

At the very end of September, then, the three began their journey eastward. The roads were difficult and the travelling was slower than they had expected, but by the early afternoon of the second day they had arrived at Les Échelles. There they left their coach to pursue the six-mile journey up the mountainside to the monastery on horseback. The road lay in many places no more than six feet across, and this first encounter with the landscape of the sublime clearly fascinated the travellers. On one side of them rose the mountain itself, its peaks obscured by the dense

---

[3] 'Gray's Notes on Travel', from the collection of John Morris in the Eton College Library, included in Duncan C. Tovey, *Gray and His Friends: Letters and Relics* (Cambridge: Cambridge University Press, 1890) 211.

growth of pine trees that clung to its rocky slopes and formed a thick canopy over their heads; on the other the road fell sharply away towards the torrential river below. Across the precipice towered the crags and cliffs of the surrounding mountains, spotted here and there with cascades and waterfalls that hurled themselves into the vale. The scene was, Gray wrote to his mother, 'the most solemn, the most romantic, and the most astonishing . . . I ever beheld'. Walpole, too, was impressed. Addressing his next letter to West from 'a Hamlet among the mountains of Savoy', he wrote similarly: 'Precipices, mountains, torrents, wolves, rumblings, Salvator Rosa – the pomp of our park and the meekness of palace! Here we are, the lonely lords of glorious desolate prospects. . . . Yesterday I was a shepherd of Dauphiné; today an Alpine savage; tomorrow a Carthusian monk; and Friday a Swiss Calvinist'.[4] The changing scenery seems only naturally to have encouraged Walpole in his propensity for role playing and histrionic disguise.

     Already having felt the pains of their journey to have been rewarded, the travellers reached the summit to spend two hours exploring the monastery itself. They were greeted by the two fathers who together shared the task of escorting visitors within the community; all other members of the Grande Chartreuse were bound by a vow of silence. Served a simple lunch of dried fish, eggs, butter, and fruits, both Gray and Walpole were impressed by the simplicity and decency of the order. The community appeared to them a self-sufficient little city, one made only the more dramatic for its remarkable situation. Although pressed by the guest-masters to spend the night or even several days among the brethren, the three travellers protested the necessity of continuing on their journey. As the evening clouds began to form along the mountain's side, they began their descent to Les Échelles. Again the remarkable sounds – the tremendous shattering of the rocks slipping from great heights to the river below, the rumblings of the mountain thunderstorms seeming to echo and respond to one another across the narrow valley – and the awe-inspiring views of their passage had a profound effect on both Walpole and Gray. Walpole wrote to West that he felt the scene taxed their own powers of description, and that as they 'rode back through this charming picture, [they] wished for a painter, wished to be poets!'[5] Gray himself, in a letter written some time later to West, frankly confessed that he thought art of any kind incapable of capturing and conveying the immensity of such a scene. While for Walpole the scene – for all its romantic power and sublimity – could still be described as 'charming', for Gray the journey amounted to little less than a religious

---

[4]   WC xiii.181.
[5]   WC xiii.182.

and aesthetic epiphany. 'Not a precipice, not a torrent, not a cliff', he wrote to West, 'but is pregnant with religion and poetry, There are certain scenes that would awe an atheist into belief, without the help of other argument'. As the critic William Ruddick has recently observed of Gray's travel writing, the poet was adept in the 'vividly descriptive' style characteristic of earlier 'voyage writers' on the continent. Yet unlike writers such as Addison (who seems never to have gone out of his way to describe the natural landscape, and who hurries over the sublimity of the Alpine scenery rather than describing it in any detail) Gray was no less capable of offering his reader descriptions which are 'still precisely visualized, but also explanatory of the emotional, psychological, and even spiritual stimuli which novel aesthetic experiences derived from a direct contact with natural forces could bring him'[6].

The rest of their journey through Dauphiné and Savoy was anti-climactic. Passing through Chambéry and stopping briefly at Aix and Annecy, they arrived within three days at Geneva, where they saw Conway comfortably settled in his quarters. Geneva they found an attractive and populous city – 'small, neat, and prettily built' – the obvious prosperity of which set it in stark contrast to the extreme poverty and 'nastiness' of the dominions of the King of Sardinia, which lay just across the river Arne. They spent several days at Geneva, sailing on the magnificent lake and stopping at some of the many little 'houses of pleasure' which dotted its shores. The interlude was an enjoyable one, but it was soon time for them to be returning to Lyon and its environs, where they now planned to spend the winter. Gray appears to have considered the departure of Conway from their entourage no great loss to their enterprise; he may even have been a bit jealous of the obvious affection and intimacy which existed between the two cousins. Nevertheless the journey back to Lyon – this time via a different route, crossing the Rhône at Seyssel and taking them through the mountains of Bugey – he confessed in a letter to his mother to be a 'solitary' one. Left to themselves for the first time since their arrival in Paris several months earlier, Gray and Walpole each felt the burden of the other's sole companionship weighing somewhat too heavily on their minds throughout the five-day journey back to Lyon (neither really had anything to say of the trip at all). Thus far their travels had been enlivened by the exuberance of other companions – the Conways, Lord Holdernesse, George Selwyn and George Montagu – all of whom were friends primarily not of Gray but of Walpole. The two men now faced each other in the carriage wondering just how their relationship was going to fare in the uncertain, winter months ahead.

---

[6]   Ruddick, 'Gray's Travel Writing' in Hutchings and Ruddick, 127–28.

Fortunately for both Walpole and Gray, their friendship was not yet
to be put to any great test. A reprieve of sorts soon arrived at Lyon in
the form of a letter from Walpole's father, encouraging his son to continue his travels southward into Italy. Walpole quickly jumped at the
scheme of heading to Italy. Gray, if anything, was even more excited by
this unexpected and unlooked for opportunity of seeing 'the place in the
world that best deserves it'. The timing of the suggestion was also propitious, at least for the travellers themselves. The eighty-eight year old
Pope Clement XII lay at the point of death in Rome, and Gray anticipated that they would soon have the chance to be present when the
Conclave elected a new Pope, an occasion on which 'Rome will be in
all its glory'. They lost no time in preparing for the eight-day journey
from Lyon which would take them over the Alps to Turin. Additional
muffs, fur boots, masks of beaver, and bear skins were all quickly assembled to protect the travellers against the cold. Already the weather had
turned chilly and winter had begun in the south of France, and Gray
rightly anticipated that they could expect a harsh and bitter crossing
this late in the year before reaching the winter sunshine of Italy. On 31
October they at last left the crowded city of Lyon behind them, and
began their journey towards the 'much finer country' which lay beyond
the imposing wall of mountains to the south.

II. Falling Flump into Italy

The first three days of their progress toward Italy lay along much the
same route that they had taken when travelling to Geneva. Only on the
morning of the fourth day did they veer southward and begin passing,
as Gray put it, 'rather among than upon the Alps'. For the next two days
of their journey they clung to the valley road that wound itself along
the side of the river Arc, the torrent of which worked itself a passage
among the tremendous mounds of stone and rock which had tumbled
from the mountain tops. The crossing proved a tedious one, the winter
– already well advanced in such terrain – having stripped the moun-
tainsides of much of their verdant beauty to reveal only the native 'sav-
ageness and horror of the place'. Still, although the weather was often
foggy, there were an abundance of cascades (Gray counted thirteen in
a single day, the least of which, he claimed, was over one hundred
feet in height) and he could always turn to his copy of Livy, which he
carried with him in the chaise, to provide an apt description of the
natural wonders he was witnessing for the first time. On the sixth day
the chaise began finally to ascend the mountains. The road was very
much like that which had so impressed the travellers on their ascent
to the Grande Chartreuse – the one side falling off into a deep ravine,

the other a sharply angled wood thick with pine trees. Again the path seemed to extend little more than six feet from side to side. The day was unusually bright with sunshine and Walpole had by late morning taken advantage of the opportunity to set his small black spaniel 'Tory' – a gift given to him by Lord Conway before leaving Paris – to exercise himself beside the chaise and run before the horses as they made their way up the mountain. The party was progressing easily enough when a large wolf suddenly leapt from the woods, seized the dog in its mouth, and bounded again through the pines and up the side of the hill. So quick was the attack that the servants had not even had the time to draw their pistols or to do anything to save the dog. 'What the extraordinary part is', Walpole wrote to West, 'that it was but two o'clock, and broad sunshine. It was shocking to see anything one loved run away with to so horrid a death'.[7] The incident fresh in their minds, Gray and Walpole settled back uneasily among the cushions and blankets of the coach, reflecting that had the smaller animal not been present, the wolf might just as easily have attacked one of the horses, dragging the chaise and everything in it off the narrow road, to tumble down the precipice which fell fifty fathoms perpendicular just outside the window.

By the evening of the seventh day the travellers had arrived at Lanslebourg-Mont-Cenis, the town that lay at the northeast foot of the Mont Cenis pass. Here, their chaise was disassembled in order to be carried, along with their luggage, by mules over the mountain. The travellers themselves were bundled into their furs and placed on padded chairs without legs (uncomfortably resembling biers), to which were attached two long poles. Eight men – four assigned to each chair – then began swiftly to carry them the six miles to the top of the mountain. Gray, who later dismissed the inhabitants of the area as deformed 'Alpine monsters' who were 'in all respects, below humanity', did not have a comfortable journey. The descent on the far side of the mountain was accomplished with terrifying swiftness, and the surrounding ice, snow, and fog-enshrouded scenery was impossible to describe ('though we heard many strange descriptions of the scene, none of them at all came up to it'). The two parties jostled against one another on the steep and rocky mountain paths. At one point Gray's bearers, skirting along a crag 'where there was scarce room for a cloven foot', rushed him breathlessly past Walpole's group, leaving him to anticipate that he might at any moment be flung into the fog, never to be seen again. After travelling over ten miles across the top of the mountain in an astounding five hours, the two were bought to rest at the tiny village of La Ferrière, in Piedmont, still wrapt in the alpine clouds, but intrigued

[7] WC xiii.190.

already to hear the language of the new country being spoken about them. After passing through the Pas de Suse and staying overnight in the small town of Bussoleno, they found themselves approaching Turin by a handsome, straight avenue nine miles long. All in all their Alpine crossing was to remain one of the highlights of their tour, though not one that either of them had any great care to repeat in the near future. 'Mont Cenis, I confess', Gray wrote from the safety of Turin to West, 'carries the permission mountains have of being frightful rather too far; and its horrors were accompanied by too much danger to give one time to reflect upon their beauties'. Walpole wrote more plainly, 'Such uncouth rocks and such uncomely inhabitants! my dear West, I hope I shall never see them again!'[8]

Following what Gray was soon calling their 'eight days journey through Greenland', the travellers at first welcomed the simple uniformity of Turin, a city they found to be of a surprisingly clean and regular design. They had arrived at the wrong time of year, however. The operas, balls, and masquerades that together constituted the highlight of the city's social calendar took place only during the Carnival, which lasted from Christmas to Lent. The court of the King of Sardinia had taken itself to its country palace at 'La Venerie', and the only amusements in town were card games, puppet shows, and 'execrable' Italian comedies. Rather than repeat what they now felt to be the mistake of their extended stay at Reims and spend any more time in the city than was necessary in order to recover from the fatigues of their crossing, the two hurried on through the small cities of Moncalieri, Asti, Alessàndria, and Novi towards Genoa.

Here was change indeed from their recent surroundings. Both Walpole and Gray confessed themselves so enamoured of the city's situation that they feared meeting anything further in their travels to match it. A cluster of palaces, churches, fountains, and vine-covered terraces filled with orange and cypress trees seemed to jostle one another picturesquely around the busy harbor basin, while the waters of the Mediterranean – which they were of course seeing for the first time – stretched into the distance beyond. The town itself was perched along the sides of the semi-circular bay like a stately ancient theatre, its white marble and sun-drenched stucco forming a perfect contrast to the bright blue of the sea and the toy-like colours of the many ships bobbing in its waters. So striking was this first coup d'oeil that Gray and Walpole quickly busied themselves in renouncing all that was French and embracing everything Italian. If anywhere in their travels one finds the two recapturing the sheer exuberance of experiencing the foreign for the first time, it is naturally enough here in Genoa, where the seductive powers of the

---

[8]   WC xiii.189.

Mediterranean and of Italy first truly made themselves felt. A new amity is infused even into their correspondence. One senses that Gray was again actively and enthusiastically enjoying the time spent with Walpole; there is a much greater sense of each of the travellers participating in their journey as members of a happy and equal *couple*.

On the morning after their arrival in Genoa they attended a festival service at the church of the Madonna delle Vigne ('I forgot to tell you', Gray jokingly confided to West, 'that we have been sometime converts to the holy Catholic Church'), where they observed the arrival of the Doge Constantino Balbi, richly arrayed in a cap and robes of crimson damask. The Doge's approach was celebrated by a concert featuring the voices of two eunuchs. For two hours Gray and Walpole sat contentedly in the church, deeply inhaling the heavy incense and listening to the intoxicating music, its unfamiliar melodies and delivery made only more appealing by comparison to the 'cracked voices' of the French opera to which they had now grown so familiar. The rest of the afternoon was spent marvelling over the rich marble of the church of the Annonciata and the Palazzo Doria, and simply admiring the harbor view from the terraces and balustrades of the city. 'We are fallen in love with the Mediterranean sea', wrote Gray to West affecting with mock solemnity the affectations of the experienced traveller, 'and hold your lakes and your rivers in vast contempt'. He even began his letter to West with four lines of Latin that celebrated and commemorated his safe passage through the mountains and final arrival in the milder south:

> Horridos tractus, Boreaeque linquens
> Regna Taurini fera, molliorem
> Advehor brumam, Genuaeque amantes
> Litora soles. (*PTG* 309–10)

[Leaving behind the rugged passes and wild realms of the Taurine Boreas, I am conveyed towards a milder winter and the suns which love the shores of Genoa.]

The 'suns' that embraced 'the shores of Genoa', as Gray pictures them here, could hardly have found a more grateful recipient of their warmth.

*

Unfortunately, Gray's stay in Genoa was to be too short. The end of the year was fast approaching, and the glories of Florence and, of course, Rome still lay ahead of them. Within days they were again on the road, now headed by way of Piacenza, Parma, Reggio, and Modena for Bologna

and thence towards Florence. The journey began well, and they wound
their way among pleasant, country roads, the hillsides beyond studded
with the massive unhewn chunks of the green, black, and white marble
that so distinguished the region. Intending originally to make a stay
of several days at Piacenza, they were so unimpressed by the 'frippery'
of its appearance that they decided to stop there only to eat (dining on
crow's gizzards seasoned with mustard and sugar), and headed quickly
on towards Parma. Yet both Parma and Modena too – though resting
within 'the happy country where huge cheeses grow' – proved to be smoky
brick cities that had little attraction for the pair. Only at Modena,
in fact, where they spent a day and a half examining the art collection
of the local duke did they finally make a stop of any real significance.
Gray's imagination throughout the journey from Genoa was captivated
most not by the towns and cities through which they passed, but by
the fact that the countryside through which they were travelling had
once witnessed the events of classical history about which he had been
reading all his life. Piacenza, Parma, and Reggio may have been dis-
appointing, but just beyond the chaise lay the vast plains of Lombardy,
'where Scipio incamped, after Hannibal had crossed the Po'. And it
was still, Gray observed with delight, 'as Livy has described it'. Piacenza
to his mind was not so much the smoky modern city in which they
had dined, but still, in his journal, the 'Placentia' of the Roman world.
As the two friends travelled across the level plains, Gray reconstructed
in his imagination the vast aqueducts – now only ruinous masses of
brick – which had once carried water to these ancient centres. For the
second time in his correspondence to West, Gray included a fragment
of his own Latin composition in order better to capture the resonance
of the scene for his friend. 'We passed the famous plains', Gray began
in English,

> Qua Tribiae glaucus salices intersecat unda,
>   arvaque Romanis nobilitata malis.
> Visus adhuc amnis veteri de clade rubere,
>   et suspirantes ducere maestus aquas;
> Maurorumque ala, et nigrae increbescere turmae,
>   et pulsa Ausonidum ripa sonare fuga. (*PTG* 310)

> [. . . where the stream of Trebia cuts through the grey-green
> willows and fields made famous by Roman woes. The current,
> even now, seems to run red from the ancient slaughter, and to
> bear down in grief its sighing waters; the Moorish cavalry, the
> dark-skinned battalions, to prevail, and the trampled bank to
> resound with the flight of the sons of Ausonia.]

One senses that Gray was genuinely excited by what he was seeing here. His verses are significant not only because they give a sense of the degree to which Gray felt his history books finally coming to life for him in Italy, but also because they contain certain notions about landscapes and *places* that will make themselves more forcefully felt in his later poetry. They were to some degree very straightforward and commonly held ideas; places can be transformed by the history and by the emotions enacted within them. Such transformations occur not so much because of any alteration in the physicality or situation of the space itself, but rather because subsequent visitors will bring *to* those places a knowledge of what has passed therein – a kind of historical variation on 'the genius of the place'. Here, where the river Trebia meets the Po, the Carthaginian general Hannibal had been defeated by the Romans in 218 BC. For the visitor aware of this ancient history, the seemingly placid stream, guarded by fertile fields and grey-green willow trees, is metamorphosed into a living symbol of sorrow and loss; its waters seemed still to run red with the blood of ancient slaughter, its banks seemed even at this distance in time to resound with the hoofbeats of the 'departure of the sons of Ausonia'. The frame of mind of the observer within the place observed bestowed meaning on the environment.

The final stretch of their journey towards Bologna, undertaken on broad roads through the rich country of Lombardy, carried them through beautiful countryside. Gray lamented that they were not seeing it in its 'proper' season, although even in these early months of winter the vast plantations of mulberry, elm, and olive trees that stretched as far as the eye could see on either side of the road were richly entangled in a grotesquerie of vines, and the hedgerows between them neatly cut. The city of Bologna proved yet another disappointment ('at least as bad [in] appearance as Parma'), and after twelve days of frantic sight-seeing – 'churches, palaces, and pictures from morning to night' – the pair were back in their carriage, travelling over the misty Appenines on their way to Florence. To the two travellers – now veterans, after all, of an Alpine crossing – the journey was an unimpressive one (the Appenines were deemed 'not so horrid as the Alps, though pretty near as high'). On the afternoon of 16 December, they found themselves descending the mountains. Directly ahead of them, rising dimly through the winter mists that shrouded the olive and lemon trees of the Tuscan plain, rose the domes and towers of Florence, where they now planned to spend the Christmas holidays.

Waiting to greet them at the city gates was one of Horace Mann's servants. The son of a prosperous London merchant, Mann had in 1737 been appointed as the assistant or *chargé d'affaires* to the absentee British minister at the court of Tuscany. He was soon – in 1740 – to be appointed minister himself, a post he would hold for over forty-five years, until his death in 1786. Mann was a distant relation of Walpole's, and he owed his present position to the influence of Sir Robert. His duties as an assistant minister to the crown included – most intriguingly – spying on the exiled Stuarts and their supporters throughout Italy (James Edward Stuart, 'the Old Pretender', had been recognized by some European powers as the legitimate King James III of England; he and his two sons Charles Edward and Henry Benedict were then residing in Florence). He was also responsible for keeping an eye on the English travellers who happened to be passing through Tuscany. Although fifteen years older than the two new arrivals, the diffident Mann was well suited in temperament to both Walpole and Gray; while the former may have had the better claim on his attentions, he seems graciously to have treated them both with equal affection and respect. Gray immediately described him to his mother as 'the best and most obliging person in the world'. For Walpole, this initial meeting in the Tuscan twilight was to have consequences that would stretch far beyond the months of the Grand Tour. Although the two men were never actually to see one another again following Walpole's return to England the following year, Walpole and Mann began a correspondence anatomizing English and European fashion and affairs that continued, uninterrupted, for well over forty years. For the time being all three got on remarkably well together; Gray and Walpole could have asked for no more genial or obliging a host for their stay in Florence. G. S. Rousseau, who has argued at length that Walpole's Grand Tour had in fact 'evolved to a great extent out of his homoerotic needs' – had evolved, in other words, out of his desire to participate in a homosocial environment which would not merely countenance but advance such bonding – rightly notes that both he and Gray discovered in the figure of the English envoy in Florence a 'symbolic father . . . whose brilliant powers of organization gave further approbation to [their] homoerotic activities'.[9]

Gray was quick to dismiss the general situation and beauty of the Tuscan capital as inferior to that of Genoa, but there was no denying that the cultural wealth of the city was overwhelming. Although Walpole would have to wait for the fast-approaching season of Carnival to pursue the livelier pastimes of Balls, Masquerades, Operas, and Illuminations, Gray's mornings and afternoons were spent in perfect contentment, slowly examining the treasures of the Pitti Palace and the Uffizi. The last gallery alone, Gray commented, provided 'amusement for months'. He patiently catalogued the paintings, statues, medals, and precious jewels he encountered, often venturing comments and judgements on their quality that are seldom at odds with the established taste of the

[9]   Rousseau, 181.

day. Like many of his peers, Gray tended to value the achievement of seventeenth-century artists such as Carlo Maratti, Salvator Rosa, and Guido Reni, at the expense of the masters of the *quattrocento* (e.g. Raphael, Veronese, Titian), whose work has been rated more highly by later generations. The central figure of Andrea del Sarto's 'Assumption of the Virgin' in the Pitti, for example, was dismissed by Gray as looking 'like a dirty ordinary Girl', while the same figure in a painting by Maratti was described as possessing 'a most aweful beauty'.[10] Stepping from the dust and silence of the great galleries into the busy streets of Florence, Gray found still more splendours to which he might devote his attention. 'You can hardly place yourself any where', he wrote his mother, 'without having some fine (palace or church) in view, or at least some statue or fountain, magnificently adorned'.

Walpole, meanwhile, thanks to the attentions of Mann, was busy being introduced into the highest social circles (both homosexual and heterosexual) of this famously aristocratic city. He dutifully patrolled the galleries with Gray, but within a month's time confessed himself to West as being tired with such sightseeing. He grew blasé, and admitted that although he had for years anticipated the pleasure of passing even a single afternoon among the glories of the Uffizi, he now took the collection for granted. 'I walk into it now', he wrote of the gallery to West, 'with as little emotion as I should into St. Paul's'.[11] While we would no doubt be wrong to read into such comments as these any profound dissatisfaction on the part of Walpole with the manner in which their tour was progressing (travellers who have spent far less time abroad than Walpole will honestly admit to a similar feeling of cultural or aesthetic fatigue after encountering so many cathedrals and museums within so short a period of time), we do see in such observations the beginnings of the more profound rift which was eventually to split the two travellers apart. It was at this very point in the tour that Walpole surprised himself by observing, as we have already mentioned, that the simple *difference* of Calais from England was by far the most shocking and delightful thing he had yet experienced in his travels. Having journeyed together now for nine months, the two were indeed more aware of the disparity in their interests. While Gray spent his afternoons and, one gathers from some of his letters, many of his evenings 'making catalogues' and keeping track of all he has seen, Walpole ached for more active and probably more sexually charged entertainment. Gray may have professed to his mother that it was 'impossible to want entertainment' in a city so plentifully supplied with history and culture, but the lively and elegant son of the Prime Minister of England, not all that

[10]   See Tovey, *Gray and His Friends*, 221.
[11]   WC xiii.199.

surprisingly, thought otherwise. Walpole soon wrote to West: 'I know not what volumes I may send you from Rome; from Florence I have little inclination to send you any. I see several things that please me calmly, but *à force d'en avoir vu* I have left off screaming, Lord! this! and Lord! that!'.[12]

Horace Mann was the perfect person to remedy such a situation. Following Walpole's arrival in Florence, Mann had immediately introduced both him and Gray into the society of the Prince de Craon. Craon, a nobleman of Lorraine, was then serving as regent in Florence for Francis, Duke of Lorraine, who had himself, upon the death of the last Medicean Grand Duke Giovanni Gastone, exchanged his own duchy in France for the hand of the Austrian Empress Maria Theresa and the throne of Tuscany. There is perhaps some slight resentment in Gray's comment to West that Craon and his Princess (the former mistress of Leopold, Duke of Lorraine, by whom she had no less than twenty children) were 'extremely civil to the name of Walpole', but invitations were quickly extended to both of the young men – not Walpole alone – to visit the couple whenever they pleased. Mann also introduced them to the influential Countess Suarez, who had been a favourite of Gastone's, and the one, Gray wrote, 'that gives the first movement to every gay thing that is going forward here'. Walpole was presented on his own to the Electress Palatine Dowager – Anna Maria Luisa, the last remnant of the House of Medici. She was, Gray wrote his mother,

> a stately old lady, that never goes out but to church, and then she has guards, and eight horses to her coach. She received him with much ceremony, standing under a huge black canopy, and, after a few minutes talking, she assured him of her good will, and dismissed him: She never sees any body but thus in form; and so she passes her life, poor woman! (*CTG* 136)

Gray seems rather too eager in this account to dismiss Walpole's visit. 'Poor woman', perhaps; but also 'poor Walpole', he affects to say to his mother, having to spend his time in such tedious social formalities with such unpleasant eccentrics. Far better to spend one's time quietly and pleasantly employed with museums and catalogues – with what Walpole would soon be calling his piles of 'charts and pyramids'.

The Christmas season (and his own birthday) passed without much comment from Gray. When Carnival did finally get underway in the early months of 1740, he significantly had nearly nothing to say about the festivities. Walpole, on the other hand, could not get enough of the

[12] WC xiii.199.

excitement. He had finally succeeded, thanks to Mann, in being introduced not merely into the English society of a city, but in holding a prestigious place among the indigenous social hierarchy as well. Walpole's mornings were crowded with meetings in the shops and at the coffee houses; his evenings were spent at operas and balls. 'The end of Carnival is frantic, Bacchanalian', he exclaimed to West joyfully. 'All the morn one makes parties in mask to the shops and coffeehouses, and all the evening to operas and balls. *Then I have danced, good gods, how I have danced!*'[13] Gray, all the while, grumbled only half-jokingly to Wharton that having observed the true manners of the inhabitants of Florence during Carnival, he could now deliver 'a learned Dissertation on the true Situation of Gomorrah'.

There is a curious gap in Gray's letters home at this point of his travels. Until this stage of his journey almost all of his letters had been written to his mother or to West. He generally made a point of keeping them both up to date with regards to the details of his itinerary. Yet just as Walpole would later in life designate various correspondents as the recipients of various *types* of letters, Gray too discriminated in his on-going travelogue as to precisely what information was imparted to whom. To his mother Gray wrote rather straightforward accounts of his progress and passage through France and Italy. This is not to say that his letters to her lack intimacy and humour. They are candid enough (the account of the evening dinner party and dancing till the early hours of the morning at Reims, it may be remembered, was included in a letter to Dorothy Gray), and the poet's affection for his mother is evident throughout. Even when glorying in the sunny Italian winter he does not forget that back in England she is suffering through frosts and snows, and probably experiencing some uncomfortable shortness of breath as she trudged up and down the stairs of the chilly Cornhill home. He even feels free to tease her as he might tease his friends. Writing from Bologna and anticipating his imminent arrival in Florence, Gray bemoaned his ignorance of news from England, noting that all their letters had for some time been forwarded to their final destination in Tuscany. 'If I do not find four or five from you alone', he chided playfully, 'I shall wonder'. For her own part Mrs. Gray, as might be expected, comes off well in the correspondence. Her son does not talk down to her, and he seems to take for granted on her part a wide knowledge of European history and politics. He supposes at one point that she will naturally be consulting George Sandy's 1615 travel account when corroborating the details of his own itinerary (it will be remembered that he supplied her with a number of books and maps before leaving London), and when he refers casually to 'the famous gallery' in

---

[13] WC xiii.201.

Florence, he knows that she will immediately understand him to be speaking of the Uffizi.

The letters that passed between Gray and West are naturally still filled with the shared humour of a schoolboys' correspondence, yet both writers had grown considerably more mature even since their university days. West could still sound forlorn ('here I am doomed to fix' he had written to Gray from the Inner Temple towards the end of September, 'while you are fluttering from city to city, and enjoying all the pleasure which a gay climate can afford'), but a new note of seriousness and introspection seems to have entered his voice. Spending a joyless season at Tunbridge for the sake of his mother's health, West – to the detriment of his own frail constitution – had become a man of responsibilities. While protesting that it was beyond his power to envy Gray's good fortune, the stark contrast between West's situation and Gray's own must have been painfully obvious to them both. To his credit, Gray tried as much as possible to raise West's spirits. He typically included references to authors and subjects which he knew West would recognize and enjoy and, as we have already seen, enclosed particularly to his friend both the fragment ('Horridos Tractus') and the elegiac verses in Latin that he had composed.

As his friendship with Walpole began less successfully to bear the strain of their long companionship with one another, Gray appears to have sought to strengthen his ties to other friends and correspondents back home through his letter writing. In March 1740, just as Walpole was beginning to complain in his letters to Ashton of Gray's seemingly endless capacity for sightseeing and cataloguing, Gray and West exchanged a series of letters which Mason, having judged them 'too bizarre for the public', subsequently destroyed. We know little of what the letters (Gray's were written in Italian) actually contained, but it is likely that they revealed a growing intimacy between the two authors which Walpole, even later in life, was disinclined fully to acknowledge. As his relationship with Walpole began to be transformed, Gray probably sought to distance himself from a potentially hurtful situation through his by-now habitual techniques of deflection and parody. The missing letters were themselves perhaps mock-imitations of the correspondence of romantic travel writers, or maybe even centos or pastiches of a silly Italian correspondence; it is possible that, sensible of the growing and inevitable rift with Walpole, Gray burrowed deeper into the allusive languages he shared more fully with West in order to protect himself. He certainly began to include more Latin verse in his correspondence to his friend, and West responded in kind. One senses that Gray felt that if Walpole could not appreciate the impulse of his scholarly admiration for the past, then he could readily turn to someone who could.

At about the same time that Gray was writing these letters to West, he also sat down to write to his Cambridge acquaintance Thomas Wharton. Gray's letter to Wharton is most striking because it contains an extended burlesque of contemporary travel accounts, pretending to include a proposal for printing by subscription 'The Travels of T: G: Gent:'. That Gray had read and enjoyed such accounts before undertaking his own tour we know through his earlier correspondence; such travel literature formed a ready part of his parodic vocabulary. The earliest surviving letter from Walpole to Gray is written 'in the style of Addison's *Travels*'; it contains marginal notes to its source text, and faithfully imitates in the style of Addison's *Remarks on Several Parts of Italy* that same author's stately and somewhat pedantic progress through Europe. Later in life Gray would make a habit of reading as much ancient travel literature as he could, devouring volumes of such authors as Strabo, Ptolemy, Xenophon, Herodotus, and Diodorus Siculus. He would later make his way through Simon Ockley's 1706 *Introductio ad linguae orientales* and George Sale's 'Preliminary Discourse' to his translation of the *Koran*. The last hundred pages of the first volume of his Commonplace Book are crammed with notes on various accounts of travel to the near east. Accounts of travel to the orient – through Egypt, the Holy Land, and the Levant – would always fascinate him. That Gray should display an easy familiarity with the kinds of popular travel adventures retailed to an audience back home is thus not at all surprising; just why he should choose to parody the kind of travel writing most familiar both to himself and to Walpole at this particular point in their journey is another question. The tone of the letter to Wharton is quietly affectionate. 'My Dear, dear Wharton, ' he begins, only to stop and note parenthetically, '(Which is a dear more than I give any body else)'. But Gray also feels free to write to Wharton in a broadly humorous style – and to use a coarser vocabulary – which would be out of place in letters to his mother or even to West. He asks Wharton, for instance, to send him not only 'News' and 'Politics', but also 'Bawdy'. It is here, in the parodic précis of his travels, that he talks of falling 'flump' into Italy, and of how he 'grows as fat as a Hog' on the local sausages. It is here, too, that he has the comic audacity to dismiss the Venus de Medici as 'much inferiour' to the statue of King Charles which had long stood at the site of Charing Cross. And although he may have spoken of the Alpine natives as harsh and uncouth in his other letters, it is only to Wharton that he writes, 'they are always in a Sweat, & never speak, but they fart' (adding that they 'think him very odd for not doing so too'). In short, the parodic style in this instance allowed Gray a freedom of expression that he might not otherwise have obtained, and let him speak openly and with good humour about some elements of his tour to which he might not otherwise have been able to give adequate voice. It is both an attempt to draw himself closer to Walpole (one senses that Walpole's own letter to Gray in the same style from Cambridge remained clearly in his mind here) while at the same time constructing a defense against his recent criticisms. 'Look!', Gray seems to be saying: 'I don't need you to make fun of me and mock me. I am quite capable of poking fun at myself.' The fact that Gray writes in a style burlesquing widely popular travel writers such as Addison might further signal to his reader that all such writers have their own petty faults and obsessions, and that travelling in and of itself can for that matter be a pretty absurd occupation anyway.

III. The Cloak of Friendship

On 6 February 1740, Pope Clement XII – 'at last', as Gray wrote somewhat uncharitably to his mother – died. Toward the middle of March, Walpole and Gray prepared to head for Rome. Gray was genuinely excited about the prospect of witnessing the Conclave and (he hoped) the installation of a newly elected pontiff at St. Peter's. Although by the time the young men set out for Rome the Conclave had already been sitting for several weeks, the French Cardinals had, by the middle of March, only just arrived, and the German ones were still expected. The election of the new Pope was a process fraught with arcane ritual and complexity, and the Vatican had already on this occasion not fallen short of delivering drama. Cardinal Pietro Ottoboni, it was rumoured in Florence, had dropped dead of an apoplexy in the chamber. Several other octogenarian prelates were rumoured to be lingering on the verge of death. Still, the Conclave was not expected to reach any decision regarding their new temporal and spiritual leader until after Easter. Although considerably less interested in the proceedings than Gray, Walpole too was by now ready to leave Florence, at least for a little while. Carnival had been succeeded by Lent, the seasonal diversions of which were not quite so appealing as those of its predecessor. As even Gray wrote, the unappealing outline of their day consisted of 'a sermon in the morning, full of hell and the devil; a dinner at noon, full of fish and meager diet; and, in the evening, what is called a Conversazione, a sort of assembly at the principal people's houses, full of I cannot tell what'.

They planned to make the journey to Rome in four days. They stopped for one day at Siena, where Gray was impressed by the 'gothic niceness and delicacy' of the great cathedral, and where an afternoon was spent exploring the collections of paintings and statuary shown to them in some of the private homes into which they were introduced. They then passed southward through a landscape which seemed at one moment to consist of well-cultivated little mountains rich with vine-covered olive and elm trees, but at the next transformed itself into a panorama of black and barren hills 'that seem never to have been capable of culture, and are as ugly as useless'. As they prepared to ascend Mount Radicófani, one of their horses slipped and their chaise caused a minor traffic jam. A coach that had been at that point descending the mountain was obliged to stop for them. Peering from its window was a comic-looking figure in a red cloak and handkerchief whom Gray – on the basis of appearance and the sound of a high-pitched voice – judged at first to be a fat, old woman. No sooner had the figure stepped from the chaise, however, than the travellers recognized Francesco Bernardi, better known in London by the name of 'Senesino'. The famous soprano was one of the Italian singers who had been first brought to London by Handel; he had sung on many occasions in the capital in the preceding twenty years. Senesino, as his name implied, was from Siena, and was then making a return journey home after an engagement in Naples.

Gray and Walpole lodged for the night at the highest point of the mountain, where a former hunting lodge had recently been transformed into an inn. The accommodations were grim. Since it was the eve of a holy day the lodge served no meat, and they were offered for their supper only eggs ('your cat' Gray wrote his mother in disgust, '. . . sups much better than we did'). The cavernous rooms of the lodge had haphazardly been converted to their present purpose, and the cold mountain wind whipped through the thin shell of the walls, chilling the travellers to the bone. In a vain attempt to achieve some rest, Walpole and Gray stopped up the windows of their chamber with their quilts, and lay for the night shivering in their clothes on the comfortless straw beds. 'Such', Gray wrote with stoic resignation, 'are the conveniences in a road, that is, as it were, the great thoroughfare of the world'. The next day's journey brought them down the mountain and finally to Viterbo, which they were surprised to find a lively town, its buildings boasting glass windows – 'which is not very usual here' – and its streets terminating usually in small plazas with handsome fountains. They still complained about the food ('we had the pleasure of breaking our fast on the leg of an old hare and some broiled crows'), but Viterbo had other gifts to offer; it was from here that Gray – from across the plains and at a distance of some thirty miles – first glimpsed the cupola of St. Peter's shimmering in the distance of an Italian spring.

As they journeyed towards Rome the excitement of the two young men began to mount. Making their progress along old Roman roads that had borne the weight of centuries of armies, pilgrims, and travellers, they watched as the landscape around them seemed to spring to life with history and meaning. On one side of the chaise lay ruined towers and fortresses; on the other, sepulchres and monuments. As they drew closer to the city along the Via Flaminia, the neighbourhoods seemed filled with magnificent villas and gardens abundant with flowers and produce. Finally crossing the Tiber itself, their carriage rumbled over the ancient stones through the Porta del Popolo. Before them, guarding the entrance to the Via del Corso, sat the twin churches of Santa Maria dei Miracoli and Santa Maria di Montesanto. 'As high as my expectation was raised', Gray wrote to his mother soon after his arrival, 'I confess, the magnificence of this city infinitely surpasses it'.

In fact, it was all a bit overwhelming. Even Gray had to pause for a moment and collect his breath before attempting to confront the city's riches. He and Walpole decided first to take a slight, transient view of some of the city's most remarkable sights. Accordingly, on the day after their arrival – the afternoon of 26 March – they made their way to the Vatican City, where Gray confessed himself 'struck dumb with wonder'. His wish to experience some of the excitement of the Conclave was immediately granted with a glimpse of the Cardinal d'Auvergne, who had only just arrived from France. Gray watched as the Cardinal, at age sixty-nine one of the younger members of the Conclave, quickly paid his devotions at the high altar of St. Peter's before being ushered in to his immured colleagues. The solemnity and mystery of the proceedings were fascinating, and Gray felt himself to be a privileged observer even as he watched the huge doors swing open on their hinges, only to catch the most fleeting glimpse of the Cardinal being greeted by his peers. This feeling of being within close proximity to the grand affairs of history was to be a sensation he would experience several times during his stay in Rome. Only a few days following his first visit in the Vatican, Gray watched from a distance as the young Pretender and his brother, Henry Benedict Stuart, amused themselves shooting in the gardens of the Villa Borgese, and – imagining his own letter to his mother to be passing under the eyes of the Stuart spies in Rome – saw his own travels inextricably becoming part of the great and clandestine world of foreign intrigue and diplomacy. His letters home began now to be filled with glancing references to world affairs (he mentions several times the recent victory of English forces against the Spaniards at 'Porto Bello'), a similar indication that his travels were indeed widening his view of the world.

For a time Gray and Walpole seemed once again to be getting along perfectly well together. They addressed joint letters both to West and to Ashton, and were drawn closer to one another by the simple experience of seeing much of the substance of their earliest schooldays so vividly close at hand. This was a knowledge they shared with one another, and while Walpole professed himself to have been irritated by Gray's more systematic and scholarly attention to artefacts and museums, each of the travellers could speak the language of antiquity with fluency, though perhaps with different accents (it was Walpole, after all, who commented casually to Gray that 'our memories see more than our eyes in this country'). In his notes on Rome, Gray catalogued more than two hundred and fifty paintings, and forty pieces of sculpture, and made a careful commentary on all of them. His remarks were conventional. 'In judging a picture', as Clark Northup has commented of the poet 'he was likely to note the propriety of the subject and treatment, the correctness of the drawing, characteristics of the painter, and state of preservation'.[14] The rituals of the Catholic church still fascinated the travellers, and together they made a memorable visit to St. Peter's by night, where they watched in horror as some dozen penitents – stripped to the waist – publicly scourged themselves throughout a ceremony in which such sacred relics as St. Veronica's handkerchief, the head of the spear that was supposed to have wounded Christ, and a relic of the true cross were exposed to public view. The basilica had lost none of its power to impress Gray, who found the spectacle of its illumination to rendered it even more imposing than before. Both men were likewise clearly awe-struck by the cosmopolitan quality of the city, a quality that was heightened by the presence of so many foreign cardinals and dignitaries. 'Nations', Walpole wrote to West succinctly, 'swarm here'. The very cosmos seemed to be responding to the events of the Conclave, and even the unseasonably cool and rainy weather of the spring season, Walpole was clearly delighted to retail to correspondents back home, was believed by the common people to have been occasioned by the agitation of the Pope's soul, 'which cannot find Rest'.[15]

Excursions were duly made to the house and gardens of the Duke of Modena at Tivoli – where the intricate system of fountains failed to impress Gray ('half the river Teverone', he wrote in exaggeration, 'pisses into two thousand several chamber-pots') – as well as to Frascati and Palestrina. They sat contentedly as their carriage rumbled over the ancient pavement of the Via Praenestina and watched the aqueducts of Rome stretch into the distance. They travelled along the Appian Way to Albano, where they visited the ruins of Pompey's villa. The trip occasioned a wonderfully spirited letter from Gray to West, in which the former pretended to recount having partaken in just the kind of 'admirable meal' that might have taken place there among the ancient Romans. 'We had the dugs of a pregnant sow' he wrote,

---

[14] Clark S. Northup, 'Addison and Gray as Travellers' in *Studies in Language and Literature* (New York: Henry Holt and Co., 1910) 435.
[15] WC xiii.217.

a peacock, a dish of thrushes, a noble scarus just fresh from the Tyrrhene, and some conchylia of the Lake with garum sauce. . . . We drank half a dozen cyathi a-piece of ancient Alban to Pholoë's health; and, after bathing and playing an hour at ball, we mounted our essedum again, and proceeded up the mount to the temple. (*CTG* 159–60)

Precise (and precisely correct) in its details, Gray's otherwise fanciful account of his own 'Banquet of Trimalchio' once again suggests the sophisticated degree to which thoroughly educated travellers on the continent were capable of bringing the world of antiquity to life before their eyes.

Toward the end of May the weather finally changed, and the two travellers were soon captivated by the fragrant beauty of the Roman spring. Following his visit to Frascati and Tivoli, Gray had sent to West a thirty-six-line poem in Latin entitled 'Ad C. Favonium Zephyrinum', which toyed with the resonance of West's old Eton college nick-name and celebrated the coming of Zephyrius or the west wind. Gray could now write to West describing the very real luxuriance of the view that lay just beyond the windows of his room. Orange flowers scented the night air, and the splash of distant fountains echoed languidly through the moonlit streets; the cypress and pine trees that covered the Quirinal behind the quiet convent of St. Isadore across the way swayed gently in the warm breeze. Gray – his days filled with sightseeing and his evenings spent compiling his notes and observations or contentedly watching Walpole negotiate the 'secular grande monde' of the city – was as happy in Rome as he had yet been anywhere in his travels.

The papal conclave continued to meet without yet having been guided to any decision. By the beginning of June, Walpole, who was growing a bit tired of Roman society and for whom the excitement of the Vatican meeting had perhaps grown cold, decided that he and Gray should make the short journey south to Naples. The trip took them through some of the most beautiful countryside they had yet encountered on their tour, and Gray was once again impressed by the incomparable layering of history and meaning in the landscape. Each day found them amid sights and places that were not only beguiling in their current beauty, but that were also 'famous for these three thousand years past'. Their road lay through Velletri, Cisterna, Terracina, Cápua, Aversa, and thence to Naples. The fertile farmland south of Rome was covered in the growth of late spring and early summer. Groves of elm and olive trees were festooned with tangles of vines which seemed to leap from one row of trees to the next, while myrtles grew rich in the hedge rows which stood between the blossoming alleys of orange and fig trees. Gray was impressed by the size and activity of Naples, and charmed by its inhabitants' more relaxed way of life. 'The common sort are a jolly lively kind of animals', Gray wrote,

> more industrious than Italians usually are; they work till evening; then take their lute or guitar (for they all play) and walk about the city, or upon the sea-shore with it, to enjoy the fresco. One sees their little brown children jumping about stark-naked, and the bigger ones dancing with castanets, while others play on the cymbal to them. (*CTG* 163)

The common people were not the only ones to gain the attention of the travellers. They happened to have arrived in Naples just in time to witness the procession and mass celebrating the feast of Corpus Christi. Charles, King of the Two Sicilies, walked in the parade while his queen, Maria Amelia of Saxony, watched from a nearby balcony. The royal couple stood in stark contrast to the native inhabitants. 'They are as ugly a little pair as one can see', Gray wrote, 'she a pale girl, marked with the small-pox; and he a brown boy with a thin face, a huge nose, and ungain as possible'. Gray and Walpole also spent several days exploring the sights around the bay. They were most fascinated by the on-going excavations at Herculaneum, the roman town that had been obliterated by the eruption of Mount Vesuvius in AD 79. From where they stood at the base of the great volcano itself, they watched anxiously as a thin trail of smoke wound slowly skyward from the mouth of the gigantic crater; Vesuvius' last eruption had occurred only four years earlier.

Having spent just more than week in Naples, the two returned to a Rome that had made little progress in their absence. The Conclave appeared, if anything, to be manifesting an even greater state of uncertainty than it had been when Gray and Walpole left. There were reports of intractable divisions, and there were even rumours of fist-fights having broken out among the cardinals, two more of whom had died within the last ten days. There now appeared to be little hope of seeing a new pontiff chosen before the end of September. The inertia of the Conclave, the prospect of spending another two months or more amid the city's wearying formal assemblies, and the threat of the '*mal'aria*' finally decided Walpole; the travellers would leave Rome and return to spend the rest of the summer in Florence. While Gray confessed in a letter home that there could never be an end to the amount of sightseeing one could undertake in Rome, he went along with Walpole's decision uncomplainingly. The ceremonies that would greet the new pope he now dismissed as little more than a 'great show' – and one which, moreover, could prove of only moderate interest. His earlier stay in Florence had been productive and enjoyable enough, and the prospect of spending the next two months there before

heading northward towards either Venice or Milan was a reasonably
pleasurable one.

*

Walpole and Gray returned to Tuscany on 8 July, and at first found
Florence to be in many ways even more appealing then when they had
left it just a few months earlier. The weather had of course grown
warmer here as well; the sky was now clear and serene, the air now temperate. Soon the people of Florence would be spending their evenings
entirely out of doors – on the bridges and along the river – listening to
music, eating iced fruits, and even dining in the open air by the light of
the moon. Windows could be left open in the evenings, and one only
had to wear the slightest of cotton gowns to sleep comfortably throughout the soft summer nights. Walpole and Gray now stayed at the Casa
Ambrogi on the Via di Bardi, a house provided by Horace Mann where,
leaning from the building's northern windows, one could dip a line into
the water and catch fish from the Arno itself. Mann, now the official
British minister in Florence, had taken up residence in the elegant Casa
Manetti on the Via Santo Spirito, located in what was known as the
Oltarno or the 'Arno di là ('that side of the Arno' – its south bank – as
opposed to the Arno di quà – '*this* side of the Arno', its northern bank).
Mann's grand palazzi, which is still standing today, loomed over the
narrow street and looked north toward the river.
     They had no sooner returned to Florence, however, before Gray began
to miss the more learned and scholarly diversions of Rome. Florence, he
wrote to West, was 'an excellent place to employ all one's animal sensations in, but utterly contrary to one's rational powers'. He continued:

> I have struck a medal upon myself: the device is thus O, and the
> motto *Nihilissimo*, which I take in the most concise manner to contain
> a full account of my person, sentiments, occupations, and late glorious
> successes. If you choose to be annihilated too, you cannot do better
> than undertake this journey. Here you shall get up at twelve o'clock,
> breakfast till three, dine till five, sleep till six, drink cooling liquors till
> eight, go to the bridge till ten, sup till two, and so sleep till twelve again.
> (*CTG* 172)

As the summer wore on Gray seemed to grow ever more restless.
Towards the end of August a pope – Benedict XIV – was finally elected.
Yet although they were now within a four-day journey of Rome, the
combination of the heat and the threat of contagion from the 'infectious
air' to the south kept them firmly in Florence. If they had had any need
to confirm their fears regarding the reality of malaria in Rome, Gray and

Walpole could watch while native travellers from the south stumbled into the city, exhausted and delirious, only to be carried to the nearby hospitals where they soon died from the disease. The pair did attempt a brief and rather uneventful journey westward, to Bologna, where they stayed for one week. Walpole was happy enough in Florence, and that, for the time being, would have to suit his fellow traveller as well.

Gray attempted to pass the time as productively as possible in reading his guide-books and volumes of history, by copying out for his own use collections of manuscript music, and – as usual – by writing to his family and to West in London. (A manuscript catalogue of his own library, which Gray began maintaining at about the time he first went up to Cambridge, indicates that he purchased more than fifty books while in Italy, many of them 'profusely illustrated with fine engravings'.) Having recently received an account from West detailing the latter's removal from his lodgings in the Inner Temple and his disinclination to continue studying the law, Gray had responded with a lengthy and patient letter encouraging his friend to persist in his efforts, while at the same time emphasizing that whichever course he chose, he could remain certain of his friend's affection. Gray also sent to West sixty-one lines of a Latin poem in imitation of Virgil which he had begun earlier that summer. The fragment described 'the Gaurus', or Monte Barbaro – a mountain that stands between Cumae and Naples – and Monte Nuovo, a peak that had risen from the Lucrine Lake during a volcanic eruption in 1538. His recent visit to Herculaneum still fresh in his mind, Gray set out to describe the devastation of such a cataclysm. He concluded the piece:

> Montis adhuc facies manet hirta atque aspera saxis
> Sed furor extinctus iamdudum, et flamma quievit,
> Quae nascenti aderat; seu forte bituminis atri
> Defluxere olim rivi, atque effeta lacuna
> Pabula sufficere ardori, viresque recusat:
> Sive in visceribus meditans incendia iam nunc,
> Horrendum! arcanis glomerat genti esse futurae
> Exitio, sparsos tacitusque recolligit ignes.
>   Raro per clivos haud secius ordine vidi
> Canescentum oleam. Longum post tempus amiciti
> Vite virent tumuli, patriamque revisere gaudens
> Bacchus in assuetis tenerum caput exerit arvis
> Vix tandem, infidoque audet se credere caelo. (*PTG* 313–14)

[Even now, the appearance of the mountain remains bristling and rough with rocks; but the violence has long since been stilled, and the flames which assisted at its birth have died away. It may be that the streams of black bitumen ran dry long ago, and the spent crater refuses fuel and strength to feed the fires; or even now (appalling thought!) it is brooding, hoarding flames in its secret depths for the destruction of some future race, and is amassing its scattered fires. Nevertheless, I have seen the hoary olive tree in a thin line across the slopes; after a long time the vine-clad hillocks grow green; and Bacchus, glad to revisit his old home, is raising his delicate head once more, though with difficulty, in the accustomed fields, and dares to entrust himself to that treacherous sky.]

Gray at times manages in these lines not only accurately and appropriately to imitate his Virgilian models, but also to capture and vividly to convey his own impressions of the returning Italian spring and summer. The vines and olive trees he describes as once again covering the fields are a poetic hybrid of those immortalized in classical poetry and those he himself had seen on his journey south to Naples. Travelling through a landscape that seemed to resonate so profoundly with the literature of classical antiquity, Gray was attempting in his own manner to grant some sort of permanence to his *own* impressions of Italy.

The beginning of October seemed at first to promise some substantial improvement in their social calendar. The arrival of 'a great Milanese Lady' a few weeks earlier had occasioned a continuous round of balls and entertainments in which even Gray participated with delight. News of the wit, intelligence, and good humour of the new pope provided everyone with a font of gossip and anecdote, and we can picture Gray at many of the evening gatherings spending less time on the dance floor than sitting, as he once described himself to have done when in Rome, chatting and watching contentedly from a corner, regaling himself 'with iced fruits, and other pleasant rinfrecatives'. Mann had also introduced Walpole and Gray to some new acquaintances, John Chute and his cousin Francis Whithed. Chute, who was as old as Mann, was the last descendant in the male line of Chaloner Chute, who had been Speaker of the House of Commons two generations earlier. He was a strange and affected man (a straightforward homosexual in an age little given to toleration of such behaviour) who, thanks to recurring attacks of gout, subsisted largely on a diet of milk and turnips. His amateur enthusiasms were to be well matched by Walpole's own antiquarian fancies later in life, and the two got along well together. At the time he and his silent, younger cousin had simply been wandering around Europe and had decided to spend several months in Florence.

At about this time Walpole seems publicly to have become the *cicisbeo* of a beautiful young Florentine woman by the name of Elisabetta Capponi, the wife of one Marchese Grifoni. The practice of *cicisbeatura* in eighteenth-century Italy, by which a young man openly and respectably served as a kind of *cavalier servente* and public escort to a married woman, seems rather strange to modern custom, and there is reason enough to believe that some of Walpole's own contemporaries were slightly baffled by the liberties allowed this chosen 'servant' (the *cicisbeo*, as Byron was eventually to put in Canto IX of his *Don Juan*, was even to him the 'strange thing that some Women set a value on, / Which hovers oft about some married beauties')[16]. Although the conventions of custom originally suggested that the chosen follower provided an escort for the married woman and nothing more, Walpole was generally supposed by some to have served as the mistress of Elisabetta Capponni – at least both his English and Florentine acquaintances took this to be the case. The rules of the *cicisbeatura* themselves made certain that the veneer of respectable public behaviour was at all times maintained. In actual practice, the activities of the *cicisbeo* might extend from platonic admiration to outright adultery. (Walpole's cousin bluntly described the 'scene of cicisbeship' as one 'of intrigue and lewdness beyond anything, in all kinds of people of all orders, ages, and conditions and in all ways'.)[17] Walpole and his partner appeared publicly with the blessing of Elisabetta's husband, who may very well himself, and in turn, have been the *cicisbeo* of another woman. Walpole, who was never in his long life to evince anything remotely resembling an explicitly sexual attraction for the opposite sex, and who clearly reserved his greatest affections for men rather than women, was nevertheless gamely open to assuming the socially popular role of a romantic gallant. The entire arrangement no doubt appealed less to his heart than to his histrionic need for self-dramatization. Walpole was acting a part, and a popular part at that. It was all just another aspect of the grand social game. He was to have no deep or long-standing attachment to Elisabetta. Soon after his departure from Florence he wrote to Mann about his *cisisbea* with an indifference approaching scorn. Gray – whether out of tact, jealousy, or bemused humour – makes no reference whatsoever to Walpole's Elisabetta in his surviving correspondence.

The early promise of October had been dampened in time by news of the death of the Emperor Charles VI, in Vienna, on the twentieth of that month. The subjects of his son-in-law, Francis II of Lorraine, Grand Duke of Tuscany, were accordingly thrown into an extended period of mourning. Balls, masquerades, and public gatherings and celebrations were prohibited and, as the grey autumn drew on into the prospect of an even grayer winter, it appeared that the populace would even be forced to forego the festivities of the yearly Carnival. The Emperor's obsequies were not to be celebrated publicly until the 16th of January,

---

[16] Byron, *Don Juan*, Canto IX. 51.3–4.
[17] WC xxxvii.323.

a delay which made for a particularly dreary Christmas season. Toward the beginning of January, Gray, whose letters home at this time were filled only with news of common occurrences and gossip, had sincerely begun to think Florence 'one of the dullest cities in Italy'. To make matters worse, the Arno had lately flooded and the entire population – now not only deprived of amusement but also threatened with contagion and disease – was in a rebellious mood. In an effort to divert his subjects, the Duke's Government took recourse in an ancient ceremony. A few miles from the city of Florence, in the Church of Santa Maria dell'Impruneta, on the San Miniato side of the Arno, there stood a famous statue of the Madonna which was long believed to be capable of working miracles. At times of real civic distress, the statue was removed from the Church and carried with great ceremony into the city (readers of George Eliot's *Romola* will recall the novelist's elaborate recreation of just such a ceremony as it might have been witnessed in the late fifteenth century). The so-called statue, in reality a bas-relief sculpture of the 'pitying mother', was housed within an elaborate tabernacle and covered in seven veils. Legend held that the image had been discovered hundreds of years earlier buried in the fertile soil of L'Impruneta, uttering a cry of pain when the spade of a farmer struck it by accident. Toward the end of December a great and solemn procession accordingly escorted the statue into Florence, where it was to be placed in the Duomo. The ceremonies were conducted at dusk. From where Gray watched the slow-moving crowds took almost three hours to pass by. Individuals who were supposed to have been possessed by demons were brought before the image to be exorcized, and mobs of people swarmed each day before the alter of the vast church to pay their devotions to the icon. After two weeks had passed the statue of the Virgin was returned to its permanent home, again accompanied by the Council of Regency, the Senate, the nobility, and representatives of all the religious orders, on foot and bare-headed. The exit of the icon – conducted in the full darkness of the evening – was an even more impressive sight, and Gray again watched from a window as the torches of thousands and thousands of devout Florentines passed slowly below.

Such solemn diversions notwithstanding, Gray remained bored and anxious to move on. He spent some of the cold afternoons working on a 'Metaphysical' poem in Latin hexameters ('to increase the absurdity', he joked) based on the philosophy of John Locke that he called *De Principiis Cogitandi* ('The Principles of Thinking'). The undertaking may seem at first to have been an odd one with which to engage himself, considering his situation and recent experiences, but Gray was once again – as in his Latin poem on Monte Nuovo – attempting to codify his own experiences within a classical mode. His impulse now was to set his own reading of Locke's *Essay Concerning Human Understanding* to verse in much the same way Lucretius had made use of the Dogmas of Epicurus in his *De Rerum Natura*. Gray was once again being inspired by his classical models to create a similarly intellectually rigorous poetry for his own day. The work – which was to consist of four books – was wildly ambitious, and Gray was to spend hours working on it in Florence. He continued to work on the poem even following his return to England later in the year, and not until the beginning of 1744 was it clear that he had finally abandoned the project altogether. Its central concerns, however, were to resurface in almost all of Gray's later poetry, both in Latin and in English.

Although Gray had written home of the possibility of leaving Florence even before the end of January, the travellers lingered at Casa Ambrogi well into April. On about the 24th of the month they finally set out for Règgio, stopping once again on their way at Bologna. They were accompanied now by Chute and Whithed, as well as by a young man named Francesco Suarez, the son of a Florentine *grande dame*, who had become an acquaintance of Walpole's. Their return visit to Bologna was made expressly to hear a performance by the singer Caterina Visconti. Règgio, which had held few charms for them on their original journey south the previous year, was now more promisingly hosting a fair which was to consist of 'nothing but masquing, gaming, and singing'. The plan was then to head on to Venice (to see the wedding of the 78-year-old Doge Luigi Pisani) and thence a swift progress towards the northeast – not staying above two weeks at any one place – stopping at Verona, Milan, Marseilles, Lyon, and finally Paris. Writing a last letter to West three days prior to his departure from Florence, Gray included some Latin verses bidding farewell to the hills of Fiesole and the valley of the Arno. The short piece concludes:

> Non ego vos posthac Arni de valle videbo
> Porticibus circum, et candenti cincta corona
> Villarum longe nitido consurgere dorso,
> Antiquamve aedem, et veteres praeferre cupressus
> Mirabor, tectisque super pendentia tecta. (*PTG* 315)

[Henceforward I shall see no more of the valley of the Arno, rising up far away, with your gleaming ridge encircled all about with porticoes and a shining crown of villas; no more shall I gaze in wonder at the ancient church and the aged cypresses before it, and the roofs overhanging roofs.]

For all the tedium and unexpected solemnity of the time spent in Tuscany, then, Gray could still muster a genuinely felt goodbye to the cypress-shaded churches and red-tiled roofs that stretched across the

Arno from the windows of Mann's guest house. Even more tellingly, Gray took the opportunity to include in the same letter a verbal self-portrait, detailing the ways in which he felt he had changed within the past two years. Perhaps the prospect even of beginning the long journey home prompted Gray already to anticipate seeing West again and to prepare him for the meeting. Gray wrote:

> As I am recommending myself to your love, methinks I ought to send you my picture (for I am no more what I was, some circumstances excepted, which I hope I need not particularize to you); you must add, then, to your former idea, two years of age, reasonable quantity of dullness, a great deal of silence, and something that rather resembles, than is, thinking; a confused notion of many fine and strange things that have swum before my eyes for some time, I want a love for general society, indeed an inability to it. On the good side you may add a sensibility for what others feel, and indulgence for their faults or weaknesses, a love of truth, and detestation of every thing else. Then you are to deduct a little impertinence, a little laughter, a great deal of pride, and some spirits. These are all the alterations I know of, you perhaps may find more. (CTG 181–82)

The description is a surprisingly candid one. It is not overly self-flattering, and certain details of Gray's account of himself – particularly the notion that he had yet to assimilate the many and varied experiences of his tour into any coherent vision of the past or, indeed, of his own personality, as well as the self-confessed tendency towards silence and solitariness – tend to be borne out by the bulk of his travel correspondence. The assertion that he now possessed a sensitivity to the feelings of others, while at the same time detesting their 'faults and weaknesses' came at a significant moment in his journey with Walpole, as did the profession of maintaining a 'great deal' of pride. (David Cecil observed that Gray was 'comically wrong' in thinking that he had learned somehow in the course of his travels to be more indulgent of the weaknesses of others.)[18] Gray and Walpole had no sooner arrived at Règgio before the tensions which had been building between them for the past two years broke out into an open and ugly quarrel.

IV. The Cares of Men

Passing through Règgio over two years earlier, on their way from Genoa to Bologna in December of 1739, Gray and Walpole had not even both-

---

[18]   Cecil, 127.

ered to take the time to stop their carriage and view the town itself. Whether on this more leisurely return visit even Gray would have had the necessary imagination effectively to reconstruct the *Regium Lepidi* of the Romans, or whether he would have recollected that Règgio was the birthplace of one of his favourite Italian poets – Lodovico Ariosto – is difficult to say. The modern city of Règgio, as Walpole was eventually to write in a letter to West, seemed at best to be 'a dirty little place'. The attractions of the annual fair being held in the town in the fullness of spring, however, managed to transform even this comparatively unattractive agricultural and manufacturing centre into a popular social resort. All the nobility of Lombardy flocked to the small town for the festivities, and the crowded streets echoed with the distinctive, broken dialects of Genoa, Milan, Bolgona, and Venice. Five nights of the week were spent pursuing the now-familiar round of morning visits and promenades, afternoon riding and shopping (often in the company of the ducal family), and evenings at the opera and the *ridotto*. Weekends were set aside for balls and masquerades at locations such as the spectacular Palazzo ducale di Rivalta, a villa that Walpole and Gray would by now have had little trouble recognizing as having been built on the model of Versailles. 'In short', Walpole commented succinctly to West, 'one diverts oneself'.[19]

Yet something was about to set the travellers' well-laid plans terribly awry. The company (Walpole and Gray were now, it should be remembered, not only joined at Règgio by Chute and Whithed, but accompanied on their journey by the shadowy figure of Francesco Suarez as well) arrived at Règgio on the 5th of May. Less than three days later Gray, Chute, and Whithed had hastily left the town to arrive at Venice, perhaps by way of Bologna and Ferrara, by the 11th. Walpole remained behind at Règgio, where within weeks he fell ill with a quinsy – a painful inflammation of the throat and tonsils – and nearly died.

The quarrel between Gray and Walpole must have been quite a furious one – it was, after all, a dispute which came close to severing their close friendship almost permanently. Had it been left to Gray alone, the two might well have passed the rest of their lives without ever speaking to one other. What, precisely, did they quarrel about? In 1772, shortly after Gray's death, William Mason tactfully appealed to Walpole for his own version of the dispute to be included in his narrative of the poet's life. Mason's readers would need some account, however brief and succinct, which might explain the circumstance of Gray's abrupt return to England, as well as to account for the ensuing silence between him and Walpole which was to last nearly five years. Walpole responded to Mason's request by enclosing a brief passage suitable for inclusion in

---

[19] WC xiii.242.

Mason's volume. He elaborated at greater length in a private letter addressed to the author. 'I am conscious that in the beginning of the differences between Gray and me', he wrote to Mason,

> the fault was mine. I was too young, too fond of my own diversions, nay, I do not doubt, too much intoxicated by indulgence, vanity, and the insolence of my situation, as a prime minister's son, not to have been inattentive and insensible to the feelings of one I thought below me; of one . . . whom presumption and folly perhaps made me deem not my superior *then* in parts, though I have sense felt my infinite inferiority to him. I treated him insolently: he loved me, and I did not think he did. I reproached him with the difference between us, when he acted from conviction of knowing he was my superior; I often disregarded his wishes of seeing places, which I would not quit my amusements to visit, though I offered to send him to them without me. Forgive me, if I say that his temper was not conciliating; at the same time that I will confess to you that he acted a more friendly part, had I had the sense to take advantage of it; he freely told me of my faults. I declared I did not desire to hear them, nor would correct them. You will not wonder that the dignity of his spirit, and the obstinate carelessness of mine, the breach must have grown wider, till we became incompatible. (WC xxviii.68–69)

It has often been remarked that Walpole seems even in this more thorough and thoughtful account of the disagreement written to Mason diplomatically to avoid making any direct mention of the specific circumstances that brought about the friends' final quarrel in Règgio. Some have suggested that Walpole actually took the trouble secretly to open one of Gray's letters to West or Ashton because he suspected that his companion had been making unflattering or critical remarks about him in his correspondence, and that his actions and his suspicions were somehow discovered by an outraged and resentful Gray. Such a scenario (which was given a general currency by John Mitford in his multi-volume edition of Gray's works in the mid-nineteenth century) is unlikely at best. However much 'insolence' and 'vanity' Walpole admits to having possessed as a young man, such sneaking and frankly deceitful behaviour would have been for him very much out of character. Walpole may have been an intriguer and a gossip, but he was not fundamentally dishonest. Far more likely is the possibility that a criticism of Walpole's behaviour that Gray had indeed made privately in a letter to Ashton was in turn related back to Walpole in a missive written by Ashton himself. Some few years later – immediately after his reconciliation with Walpole in 1745 – Gray was to write to Wharton that when he visited Walpole at his home in Arlington Street, he found Ashton to be

a member of the company assembled to dine there that evening. Gray
would confess himself on the occasion to be rather amused by the formality of Ashton's behaviour, particularly because 'he I found was to be
angry about the Letter I had wrote him'. The 'letter' referred to on that
occasion was almost certainly one written by Gray from abroad, which
contained the criticisms of Walpole's behaviour which Ashton (perhaps)
then passed on to Walpole himself.

Gray's own account of the quarrel, eventually included in Norton
Nicholls' *Reminiscences*, does not contradict speculation that his own
negative remarks and observations on Walpole's haughty and sometimes
condescending demeanor throughout their travels together were indiscreetly and obviously without Gray's knowledge returned to the ear of
the Prime Minister's son. 'When I once endeavored to learn from him
the cause of his difference with, & separation from Walpole', Nicholls
would write,

> he said 'Walpole was son of the first minister, & you may easily conceive
> that on this account he might assume an air of superiority' (I will not
> answer for the *exact expression*, but it was to this effect) 'or do or say
> something which perhaps I did not bear as well as I ought.' This was all
> I ever heard from him on the subject, but it is instead of a volume to
> those who know the independent, & lofty spirit of Gray. – Without con-
> sidering the particular cause of difference mentioned above I agree with
> Mr. Mason who once said to me that it was more surprising that two
> persons of characters so opposite to each other should ever have agreed
> than that they should finally have separated. (*CTG* 1299)

A further reference to the quarrel made incidently by Gray in a letter to
Chute in October, 1746, implies that Chute himself thought Gray to be
the injured party in the dispute, and appears likewise to suggest that
Chute – even at that distance in time – disapproved of his friend's acceptance of an apology from Walpole, and that he was not particularly
happy to hear of the their long deferred reconciliation.

Writing from Florence some two weeks after the actual dispute, on
23 May, Mann had referred to a letter of Gray's in his attempt to reconcile the two friends. Mustering all his talents as a diplomat and professional go-between, Mann did his best to bring Walpole and Gray back
into harmony with one another. He had clearly received a full account
of their disagreements from Walpole; he perhaps solicited a corroborating and slightly more detached and rather less passionate version of
events from Chute and Whithed as well. Confined to his bed with a fever
and a debilitatingly painful attack of the piles, Mann had been mulling
over the affair throughout his convalescence, and his letter is unchurac-
teristically agitated and nervous:

From an horrid uneasiness I find and in justice to Gray (from whom I have received no letter or wrote to, though I designed to have done it last Saturday but was prevented by my fever) I cannot help adding two or three lines to assure you that in the late affair except writing that letter he was not so much to blame as on the sight of it you might imagine. I take the greatest part of the fault on myself and am convinced of his regard for you; nay I have been witness to his uneasiness and tears when he suspected you had less confidence in him than his inward and real friendship for you made him think you deserved. This I think myself bound in justice to tell you, as I believed him sincere. As to the oddness of his behaviour with C—— and the particulars you mentioned and Bologna, they indeed surprised me much, and would almost induce me to give another turn to the whole. Adieu my dear Sir, I can say no more, but that I heartily wish you could forget all that has passed. (WC xvii.50)

Mann's remarks clearly support the general assumption that the quarrel hinged on a letter written by Gray himself. His comments likewise support the notion that he himself, at least, thought that an immediate reconciliation between the two was not entirely out of the question. In his next letter, written on 30 May, Mann's anxiety regarding Walpole's own health does not prevent him from making another plea on Gray's behalf. 'It gives me too much uneasiness', he concludes his letter,

to think of the late affair and the despair [Gray] is in; therefore I will not enter into any detail. I do beseech you only that you will reflect on what I wrote in my last and former letter about it. I can only say that you have it in your power to do a most generous action, to forget and forgive. I would ask it on my knees if I was with you. (WC xvii.54)

Mann's consternation and distress lie very close to the surface here. His own health has clearly been troubled by the quarrel, and he twice risks offending Walpole and passing beyond the bounds of a proper decorum when he suggests that it lay within the latter's power to mend any damage done with a timely and gracious apology.

Yet a great many questions still remain unanswered. What are we to make, for example, of Mann's plea to Walpole to lay 'the greatest part of the fault' for the incident on his own head? Such a desire hints at a scenario wherein Gray, having written some scathing criticisms of Walpole to Ashton back in England, repeated those criticisms to Mann himself, or perhaps showed him the letter containing such criticisms. Even more intriguing, however, is Mann's cryptic reference in his first letter to the 'oddness' of Gray's 'behaviour with C——' and the 'particulars' mentioned by Walpole concerning the time spent by the travellers in Bologna. Walpole later crossed out the entire sentence containing this reference with dark ink, although its substance can still be deciphered beneath his over-hasty if heavy scrawl. There is some slight possibility that 'C——' is merely Mann's own shorthand for Chute. Such casual abbreviations are common throughout Mann's correspondence and – indeed (for what it's worth) – common throughout the familiar letters of all those involved in the affair. Yet 'C——' might just as likely stand for 'Cecco', the nickname of Walpole's Florentine companion, Francesco Suarez. What might have passed between Suarez and Gray so that the latter's behaviour should subsequently be deemed decidedly 'odd' by Mann? Too little is known about Suarez for us to hazard any substantial conjectures about his role in the quarrel, but there is certainly the possibility that Gray, at least, found his presence in their company irksome. Let us try for one moment to reconstruct the days in Règgio from Gray's own point of view. His very real love for his closest friend had been tried to the breaking point within the past several months, and he was doubtlessly frightened by his own realization of the perception later given voice in Nicholls's account of the dispute – by the perception, that is, that he and Walpole, now that they were growing in different directions and were no longer bound each to the other by the simple affections of the Eton schoolyard or even by the shared memories of their less emotionally fraught days and Cambridge, really had very little in common with one another after all. A future without Walpole – and, retrospectively, a past largely wasted in attempts to gain and to secure his papilionaceous regard – gaped both before and behind Gray, and left him alone and confused. The months and years of their time together on the continent had shown Gray all too clearly that their relationship, when they returned to England, was due to undergo some changes. Gray suspected that his own love of study and the quiet of scholarly pursuits would only grow stronger as the years drew on. Walpole's penchant for the social whirl of balls, masquerades, and operas could likewise be expected to intensify as he assumed more responsibility and authority within his father's government. Was their friendship, then, necessarily and perforce to come to an end? Had all of Gray's time and love been wasted? Gray's letter to West of 21 April reveals that he was in a highly sensitive state of mind as he prepared to leave Florence for the first leg of the extended, return journey home. He was prepared to reassess both his own character as well as the characters of those with whom he travelled.

For all the attention paid to the quarrel between Walpole and Gray, few commentators have remarked upon the simple fact that the dispute took place within days of the travellers' first, homeward steps towards England. That homeward journey had effectively begun the moment they set out from Florence at the end of April. Gray's anxieties concerning the future of his relationship with Walpole, while they still need not have been dealt with or openly acknowledged for a good many weeks to come, may well then have risen before him in his mind's eye as a vast and impassable barrier – a barrier that made the necessary ease of their day-to-day contact – the necessary smooth and well-oiled social mechanisms that in other situations pass for simple good manners and forbearance – seem to him a pretense he could no longer maintain, a role he could no longer play. Gray, it must be said, was, indeed, jealous of Walpole's attentions. Yet without the perception of any genuine threat to their intimacy, it is unlikely that his jealousy would have made itself known with such bitter force. The two young men had for several months been prepared to act out their dramatic break-up – to fill out with a solicitous audience the histrionic performance of a dispute that in truth amounted to little less then a lover's quarrel; into this volatile situation stepped the figure of 'Cecco' Suarez. Walpole may well have been ready by this point to use Suarez – or anyone else for that matter – as a foil to Gray. Yet the real enemy to the stability of their relationship and the continuance of their friendship, as Gray probable realized for himself, was the simple perception that their journey *together* was soon to come to its inevitable end. Once the note of that perception was struck for Gray – once he felt the sense of an ending beginning to reveal itself to him in Florence – he knew that he had on some level lost a battle he had long been waging for the sovereignty of his own mental and emotional soul. In losing Walpole, he felt that he had lost his very sense of identity, and that the greater world itself was suddenly transformed into a violent and brutal chaos of indifference. Venice, that magical city which Byron would describe as 'bright' and 'free' and 'inviolate' seemed for Gray even in the midst of a Mediterranean spring, with its fresh breezes sweeping in from the Adriatic, to be little more than a tomb.

*

In Règgio, at least, there was activity. Walpole's illness was perceived to be serious. By the time his old school friend Lord Lincoln (accompanied by his tutor Joseph Spence) arrived from Florence to see him, Walpole was, in Lincoln's own words, 'swelled to such a degree as I never saw anyone in my life'.[20] Spence had the good sense immediately to send for a respectable local physician, and wrote to Mann asking him to dispatch his own friend Dr. Cocchi from Florence with all possible speed. 'You see what luck one has sometimes in going out of one's way',

---

[20]   Quoted in Ketton-Cremer, *Horace Walpole*, 57.

Spence wrote to his charge's mother soon after the episode, 'if Lord Lincoln had not wandered to Règgio, Mr Walpole (who is one of the best natured and most sensible young gentlemen that England offers) would in all probability have been now under the cold earth'.[21]

Mann, still in Florence, was initially frightened 'a great deal' by the news of Walpole's illness, and was a bundle of nervous energy until the return of a messenger from Cocchi and the arrival of a short letter from Spence assuring him that Walpole was now on the road to recovery. On 30 May he wrote to Walpole of his worry:

> I had everything prepared to set out in case the notices I had received of you had made it necessary; nay not-withstanding your great amendment I was a long while determining whether I should not still do it, but on reflecting that I must have represented you very ill (in England) to be an excuse for my quitting this state, I thought it was not fair to give them that alarm, to gratify my inclination to see you. I here receive other letters by a *pedone* [i.e. a foot-soldier]; I read Dr. Cocchi's first as I charged him to be particular and conceal nothing. He has confirmed the good news Mr Spence wrote. I am sorry to find Cocchi has quitted you so soon or before the swelling in your parotides as he calls them (which I find are commonly called the almonds of the ears) was down, but he assures me you will soon be quite well and that you had no fever. (WC xvii.51–52)

Still, he wrote, he was worried about Gray; it was in this letter of 30 May that he continued to wring his hands over 'the late affair and the despair Gray is in', and ended by begging Walpole 'to forget and forgive' everything.

Walpole apparently did write to Gray very soon after his recovery, suggesting at least that he cool down and return to Règgio, and that the two make some attempt to patch up their differences there. Gray, who continued to be profoundly alienated from the considerable charms of the Venetian republic, and whose own state of nervous anxiety led him now to clutch at any possibility of a reconciliation with his friend, promptly returned to Règgio as requested. His pride, however, pushed such a reconciliation just beyond his grasp. No first-person account of that meeting between Gray and Walpole in the first week of June survives, but we can begin to piece the scene together from one of Mann's subsequent letters to Walpole in which he refers to the interview. 'I conclude you are [at] Venice', Mann wrote from Florence on 10 June,

---

[21] Spence to his mother, 29 May, 1741; quoted in Ketton-Cremer, *Walpole*, 57.

and that you received my last letter of the 3d instant. . . . Two days after the departure of that letter I received yours of the 2d and to my great surprise read the account therein of the interview, which I fear has destroyed all the hopes of a reconciliation with which I flattered myself, for the reasons I mentioned at large in a former letter. I must own I wished it extremely, and should have been happy to have been the means of bringing it about. I was astonished to see the terms and the reproaches, and much more that he could withstand your entreaties to return with you to England. I am highly sensible my dear Sir this was done at my request and heartily thank you for this proof of your goodness. I cannot help repeating again how sorry I am that it had no effect but I will not dwell on so disagreeable a subject or trouble you any more on this affair. (WC xvii.58–59)

The matter, it seems, was to be considered as closed. Gray returned immediately to Venice. Walpole followed him there, arriving on 9 June and staying with Chute and Whithed in a residence on the Grand Canal. Exactly where Gray himself spent these awkward few weeks in Venice is not known, and no letters written by him survive from this unsettled period. In all likelihood his time was largely unoccupied. It must be remembered, after all, that he had until now been entirely dependent upon Walpole for almost all his financial needs. It had even been necessary for him to borrow ten *zecchini* (about £5) from Chute in order to defer the immediate expenses of his brief, return journey to Règgio. He wrote to his parents in early June asking them to send him letters of credit – documents that essentially authorized local bankers to advance money to the bearer on demand. Before those letters arrived, however, he was compelled to survive as best he could. Mann (at Walpole's own request, it should be noted) had arranged with Joseph Smith, the British Consul at Venice and a fellow collector of antiquities and curiosities, to advance Gray an additional 40 *zecchini* (roughly £20). Mann took great care to keep Gray in the dark regarding the source of this advance, not to mention the fact that the gesture had apparently been prompted by Walpole's own concern in the first place. 'This affair', he wrote to Walpole, 'is delicate, as I am unwilling to let Gray think he is obliged to me and yet I have wholly concealed it from his because you insisted upon it.' 'I do not wish him to return it', he continued, 'yet I am ignorant what he designs to do when he receives his credit from England.'[22] Although he described Gray as being 'wholly destitute' of any financial resources, Mann was similarly aware of the fact that Gray's pride – his 'great delicacy' – was liable to render any overt attempt to assist him rather touch-and-go. The subtle ramifications of every possible

[22]   WC xvii.82

encounter with or even reference to Walpole on the part of Gray himself likewise made Mann desperately anxious. 'Tell me', he wrote to Walpole despairingly from Florence, 'what I shall do.'[23]

Walpole, behind the scenes, managed to arrange everything. Money was temporarily and discretely provided for Gray, and his letters of credit finally arrived in Venice sometime in the middle of July. Towards the end of that month, Gray left Venice, heading via Padua, Verona, and Milan to Turin, where he arrived on 15 August. Taking the place of the several servants and the elaborate equipage of the earlier stages of his journey with Walpole was, for much of the time, a single *laquais du voyage* – a paid foreign servant. More often than not, Gray's eyes rested unseeing upon the by now familiar landscape which blurred across his vision beyond the carriage windows. He seemed to have lost all interest in the larger world; he felt worn out by the sheer movement and business of it all. As unlikely as it sounds – as unlikely as Gray, knowing the intimate details of Cornhill household as well as he did, himself felt such an impulse to be – he wanted simply to go home. The political situation – the consequences of which Walpole himself would have been well aware – also underscored the wisdom of a swift journey home. Walpole was to hasten back to Dover before being faced with the possibility of having Spanish forces (which were soon to invade Italy) cut him off from a return to England. The War of the Austrian Succession was to have a profound and far-reaching effect on travel on the continent. As Jeremy Black has observed, not only did the war disrupt all routes of communication and supply, but the random seizure of horses further harmed the postal system, and travellers of all nations 'could be ill-used whatever their legal status'.[24]

He had yet one more visit to undertake, however. On 16 August, Gray once again found himself passing across the Alps, and among the mountains of Dauphiné and Savoy. On what may have been a sudden impulse, he decided to revisit the Grande Chartreuse. The realization that it had been nearly two years since he and Walpole had visited the monastery together – nearly two years since their exclamations of delight and surprise had prompted them both, in Walpole's words, to 'wish themselves poets' – was almost too much for Gray to bear. He was sensitive enough by nature not to want to aggravate any of the more pleasant memories of the earlier days of his journey with Walpole, yet the immensity of his surroundings led him on this one occasion to brush aside his trepidation. He was in the midst of a painful, confusing, and unlooked-for period of transition, and he was yet unwilling to confront the ruin of his past relationship. The calm of the monastic environment, situated

---

23   Ibid.
24   Black, *The British Abroad: The Grand Tour in the Eighteenth Century*, 162.

as it was within such an awe-inspiring physical landscape, drew him onward. He needed once more briefly to inhale the placid grandeur of the place before finally undertaking the final stages of his journey homeward. He needed, amidst all his disorientation, the breathing place of stillness.

On this second visit Gray stayed with the monks for at least two and perhaps as many as three days. In an album kept by the monastery to record the thoughts and impressions of guests and travellers, he took the time to write a short Latin poem, which has since come to be known simply, by virtue of its arrangement in four-line stanzas of strophes, as the 'Alcaic Ode'. The lines contain some of the most affecting verse Gray was ever to write in that language:

> O Tu, severi religio loci,
> Quocumque gaudes nomine (non leve
>   Nativa nam certe fluenta
>   Numen habet, veteresque silvas;
>
> Praesentoriem et conspicimus Deum
> Per invias rupes, fera per iuga,
>   Clivosque praeruptos, sonantes
>   Inter aquas, nemorumque noctem;
>
> Quam si repostus sub trabe citrea
> Fulgeret auro, et Phidiaca manu)
>   Salve vocanti rite, fesso et
>   Da placidam iuveni quietem.
>
> Quod si invidensis sedibus, et frui
> Fortuna sacra lege silentii
>   Vetat volentem, me resorbens
>   In medios violenta fluctus:
>
> Saltem remoto des, Pater, angulo
> Horas senectae ducere liberas;
>   Tutumque vulgari tumultu
>   Surripias, hominumque curis. (*PTG* 317–18)

[O Thou, divine spirit of this forbidding place, by whatever title pleases thee (for certainly no mean power rules over these native streams and ancient forests; and we perceive God closer to us among pathless rocks, wild ridges, and precipitous ravines, and in the thundering of the waters and the darkness of the woods, than if, kept under a roof of citrus-wood, He glowed with gold even from the hand of Phidias): Hail! And if I invoke Thee rightly, grant a calm repose to this weary youth.

But if Fortune forbids me, in spite of my wish, to enjoy this enviable dwelling and the sacred rule of silence, sucking me back violently into the midst of the waves, then at least grant, Father, that I may pass the untroubled hours of old age in some secluded corner; and bear me off unharmed from the tumult of the crowd and the cares of men.]

The original draft of Gray's poem (inscribed by the writer himself in the monastery's album-book) was destroyed during the French Revolution, when foundations such as the Grande Chartreuse were pillaged and often looted. Fortunately, Gray copied the Ode into his own Commonplace Book as well, in which it is dated simply, 'August, 1741'.

For Gray, the magnificent scenery surrounding the monastery once again provoked a gesture of poetic genuflection before a deity which, until it is encountered among the 'thundering of waters' and the 'darkness of the woods', one tends to take for granted. Gray realized that the time he will be allowed to spend in the silence of repose is short. 'Fortuna' or Fortune herself (alternately Destiny, Fate, or the Ways of the World) will 'suck him back violently' into the overwhelming waves of activity that constitute the span of a man's natural life. The most that one can hope for, the poet concludes, is to pass one's old age in 'some secluded corner', a place reserved from 'the tumult of the crowd' and 'the cares of men'. Gray appears almost to have been incapable of writing a completed poem that did not deliberately set out to recall or to anticipate his other works. Perhaps more than any other English writer of the period, he is one whose writing can be said truly and without affectation to form an *oeuvre* – a coherent body of work every echo of which seeks its response in a referentially similar moment elsewhere in the poet's work. A single pebble dropped in the receptive pool of Gray's sensibility, its ripples cross and recross one another like tiny waves on the surface of an otherwise untroubled, yet still deep, body of water.

The 'Alcaic Ode', at the same time that it so clearly anticipates the desired withdrawal from humanity given full voice in the *Elegy* – at the same time that it similarly prefigures the freedom and seclusion fleetingly granted to a careless youth in the *Eton Ode* – reaches back as well to Gray's earlier Latin poems, to the paraphrase of the eighty-fourth Psalm, and to the play-exercise he had written while yet in school at Eton. As is usual in the case of Gray's work, a seemingly simple reference can prompt remarkably complicated patterns of resonance. At the beginning of the poem's third verse stanza, for example, Gray concludes the parenthetical phrase begun as early as the poem's second line – a phrase that attempts to describe the apparent manifestation of divine power within both humble and exalted settings. God is 'closer' to us in nature, the poet suggests, than if kept and worshipped under *sub trabe citrea*, i.e. under a roof of simple citrus wood, even, the poet adds, *fulgeret auro, et Phidiaca manu* – even, that is, if such a roof is gilded with gold even from the hand of Phidias. The greatest of Athenian artists, in other words, would have been incapable of crafting an image of the divine spirit that could begin to match or compete with the image God Himself bodies forth in the most awe-inspiring scenes of nature. Gray's poem on the one hand, then, undermines or at least questions the power of the artist in the face of nature; no 'civilized' artisan can adequately represent the face of the divine spirit better than such a 'forbidding place' itself.

The poem's very reference to Phidias, however, suggests that the lines contain some even more intensely personal resonances than those which rest merely on the surface of work. The narrative of the famous Athenian sculptor Phidias is largely one that details the fated relationship between an artist-creator and his highly placed and politically influential close friend, the statesman Pericles. It is a narrative the classical sources of which – Pausanius, Strabo, Quintillian, and Plutarch – Gray would himself have known well. Having once been an intimate of the great Pericles, and having created the gold and ivory statue of Athena that stood in the Parthenon, Phidias was eventually imprisoned and, some say, poisoned by his former friend and patron. The precise reasons for the falling-out between the politician and his favourite were obscure. Plutarch, in Dryden's translation, contended that Phidias,

> being admitted to friendship with Pericles and a great favourite of his, had many enemies upon this account, who envied and maligned him; who also, to make trial in a case of his, what kind of judges the commons would prove, should there be occasion to bring Pericles before them. . . . But the reputation of his works was what brought envy upon Phidias, especially that where he represents the fight of the Amazons upon the goddess's shield, he had introduced a likeness of himself as a bald old man holding up a great stone with both hands, and had put in a very fine representation of Pericles fighting with an Amazon. And the position of the hand which holds out the spear in front of the face, was ingeniously contrived to conceal in some degree the likeness, which meantime showed itself on either side.[25]

As he wrote the 'Alcaic Ode', Gray may well in the back of his mind have been considering the classical narrative as something of an ana-

---

[25] Plutarch, 'Pericles' in *The Lives of the Noble Grecians and Romans*, trans. John Dryden (New York: 1992) I, 227.

logue to his own situation. Rather like Phidias, he saw himself as an artist and a creator who had been mis-used and eventually discarded by the great. Like Phidias, who after his trial in Athens was banished to Elis, where he began planning his colossal image of Jupiter Olympius – a work destined to outshine even the Athena of the acropolis – he was condemned now to live in exile. Like Phidias too, however, he was determined on one level that those who had maligned or discarded him had heard the least neither of him nor his work.

Gray's 'Alcaic Ode' at least gives adequate voice to the subject that now motivated his every move – whatever the reasons for the rift between him and his friend consolation was for the time being to be found only in the extremes of complete and utter seclusion or in rapid and busying flight. Shortly before leaving Florence, on 21 April, Gray had sent to West a Latin imitation of some verses by an Italian poet – Giuseppe Maria Buondelmonte – whom he and Walpole had met several months earlier. Walpole had dismissed Buondelmonte as 'a low mimic' who 'talks irreligion with English boys, sentiments with my sister, and bad French with anyone who will hear him.' Gray took the time, however, to translate into Latin a 'little saying' of the Italian's:

> Lusit amicitiae interdum velatus amictu,
>   et bene composita veste fefellit Amor.
> Mox irae assumpsit cultus, faciemque minantem,
>   inque odium versus, versus et in lacrimas:
> Ludentem fuge, nec lacrimanti, aut crede furenti:
>   idem est dissimili semper in ore Deus. (*PTG* 316)

[Sometimes love jested, concealed in the cloak of friendship, and disguised himself in seemly attire. Next, he assumed the mask of anger and a threatening visage; turned now to hate and now again to tears. Flee him when he sports, nor trust him whether he weeps or rages. For all his different faces, he is always the same god.]

The mercurial god of love represented in this light translation, and the 'divine spirit' so reverentially evoked in the 'Alcaic Ode', are of course radically different entities. One is to be found within the 'cloak of friendship'; the other is confronted only among the pathless rocks and ravines of the natural world. One is flippant and changeable; the other, eternal and immutable. It clearly seemed to Gray, as he travelled north from Dauphiné to Paris, that a choice would have to be made between the two, and that such a choice was – to his manner of thinking at least – an easy one to make. He would flee the busy world. But he needed first to return home, where he could try to figure out how best to flee the world, while still faced with the disagreeable necessity of having to make one's way in it. He needed to return home to London, to his parents, to West, and to the familiar environments of his thoughts. At the beginning of September 1741, Gray landed in England, and returned to London after an absence of almost two and a half years.

PART TWO

PART TWO

CHAPTER FIVE

THE LIQUID NOON

London, Stoke, and the Death of Richard West
1741–1742

I. Prima Genas

A grey September evening in London – gloomy, close, and stale. As Gray sat in the window of Dick's Coffee House and looked out upon the steady stream of carriages and foot passengers who were wearily making their way through Temple Bar from the City, he felt uncomfortably like a stranger in his own land. The incessant rain fell in slanting lines against the narrow houses that lined Fleet Street, forcing the pedestrians – men of business being spattered by the mud and dirt spun from the wheels of the passing coaches, servants half hidden from view by wet and oily coverings – more determinedly to bend their heads to the pavement, and to move with even greater hurry into the Strand and on to the West End. The elaborate statues of James I and Anne of Denmark dripped forlornly in their niches on the Fleet Street side of the famous gateway; Charles I and Charles II seemed fixedly to stare and shiver at the back of St. Clement Danes on the other.

The weather's inclemency seemed only to reflect and to exacerbate the already foul mood of the people in general. Gray had returned to an angry country. Despite the Prime Minister's practical peace policy and his continued opposition to any involvement in armed, continental conflicts, the British had gradually been drawn into an Anglo-Spanish trade dispute (the so-called 'War of Jenkin's Ear') which had then mushroomed into the full-scale War of the Austrian Succession. The War, which pitted the alliance of England, Hanover, Austria, and Holland against the combined forces of France, Spain, Prussia, and Bavaria, was nominally being fought by the British to prevent the attempts of Frederick the Great of Prussia to obstruct the Pragmatic Sanction. The Sanction had been a provision of the Treaty of Vienna signed by the European states in 1731; its intent was to guarantee the secession of the Emperor Charles VI's Hapsburg territories to his only daughter, Maria Theresa. The ensuing conflict, which was in reality fueled less by strategic than economic aims, formed part of the larger struggle between France and England for commercial supremacy on the continent and elsewhere. As such, the quarrel was a prelude of sorts to the genuine world war in which the two powers were to engage later in the century.

Having initially supported the conflict with Spain with a wild enthusiasm, the British public found their early fascination with the war had quickly grown sour. What had at first been regarded merely as 'a buccaneering adventure', as the historian Paul Langford has observed, had been transformed with startling and unexpected suddenness into 'a deadly war for survival'.[1] The early success of Admiral Edward Vernon's naval forces at Puerto Bello (a success commemorated to this day in the very name of London's famous Portobello Road) had by April given way to a disastrous British defeat – an engagement in which both Vernon and the commander of the land forces, General John Wentworth, had participated – at Cartagena, in Colombia. The defeat put an abrupt and ignominious end to the wildest British dreams of commandeering the fabled treasures of Spanish America. Both support for the war as well as confidence in the government's prosecution of it ebbed with startling swiftness to debilitating new lows. Much of the blame was laid on the doorstep of the Prime Minister himself. 'Everybody', Gray observed as he looked around him rather nervously in the coffee house that drear September evening, 'is extreme angry with all that has been, or shall be done'. 'Even a Victory at this time', he added cynically, and with what may have been a grudging loyalty to Walpole's father (and perhaps a slap at the perceived infidelity of his fellow countrymen), 'would be looked upon as a wicked attempt to please the nation'.

To be restored to an England in the midst of such a crisis of national confidence was for Gray, of course, only the tip of an even larger and more intensely personal iceberg of troubles and anxieties. His anticipated return journey to London – a journey that was to have been undertaken in leisurely stages and in the company of a beloved friend – had instead been accomplished in a bewildering and emotionally draining matter of weeks. Sitting in the coffee house and staring into the pall of rain, Gray tried vainly to reconstruct how his own glorious adventure had come to such an unforeseen and disastrous end. As if sartorially to underscore the parallel between the country's disillusionment and the gloomy despondency of his own dashed hopes and spirits, Gray had discovered, much to his chagrin, that he had returned to a city wherein the prevailing spirit of fashion dictated that everybody dress 'with a Seafaring air, as if they were just come back from Cartagena'. Samuel Johnson, who throughout his life contemplated a journey to the Mediterranean himself, would once comment in a conversation with Boswell and General Paoli that 'a man who has not been in Italy, is always conscious of his inferiority, for his not having seen what it is expected a man should see'.[2] Gray now *had* been to Italy, and he had in fact witnessed

---

[1]   Paul Langford, *A Polite and Commercial People: England 1727–1783* (Oxford: Oxford University Press, 1989) 53.
[2]   Boswell, *Life of Johnson*, 742.

on his privileged journey more than most travellers to the continent might ever reasonably hope to see. Having experienced for himself those European scenes which had witnessed what were commonly regarded as the greatest achievements of western civilization, he felt that he should have been able, as Henry James would put it in the mid-nineteenth century, always to carry with him a little *reflet* of splendour. However, any sense of superiority or attainment Gray attempted outwardly to cultivate as a consequence of his travels – any little *reflet* – seemed doomed to be ridiculed at every possible opportunity by his fellow Londoners. Even the simple activity of walking the city streets had become for him a dangerously uncertain undertaking. Merely striding down the Strand towards Dick's, he had been pointed to by the boys who roamed the city's streets, many of whom now loudly jeered and hooted at the outlandishly foreign style of his dress. His (formerly) chic continental bag wig – so much the *ton* in Paris – was much too full for London tastes. The frills and ruffles of his shirt were likewise too deep and involved, too showy and effeminate in their intricate splendour. The sword that he affected to wear at his side may itself have been an accessory appropriate to a gentleman of the period, but Gray's own blade was derided for being far too long and unwieldy. Unfamiliar faces turned to stare at him from among the crowds in the street, their looks credulous and grossly condescending, and their behaviour at times even violent. 'Look in their face', Gray shuddered to his correspondents, 'they knock you down. 'Speak to them', he added,' they bite off your head'.

*

The letters from Chute and Mann that Gray found waiting for him at the coffee house – fat, folded packets covered with the wonderfully tell-tale seals and nearly indecipherable scrawls of foreign origin – at least had the effect of producing a momentary break in the clouds. Shaking off his dripping outer coat, raising a dish of steaming coffee to his lips, and spreading the pages out on the table in front of him, Gray would have been momentarily transported back into the sunny company of his friends. He already missed their conversation and their emotional support terribly. Only days after his return to London, Gray had hurried to pay a visit to Mann's twin brother, Galfridus, who was then living in the Strand, a short distance from his own parent's Cornhill home. The call had proven to be an experience not entirely unalloyed in its pleasure. 'Gal', as Mann's brother was more familiarly known among his friends, not surprisingly bore a remarkable resemblance to his twin. The uncanny *frisson* of simultaneous familiarity and strangeness which seemed already to have characterized Gray's every waking moment since his return to English soil had perhaps only then hit him with its full force. Mann himself seemed to be standing before him in London; only this was not quite the Mann whom Gray had known in Florence. Only on closer inspection did this near double of his friend strike him as just a little heavier and fuller about the face than the Horace he had not so very long ago left behind in Italy. Was he wrong in supposing, too, that Galfridus seemed likewise a little less lively and jovial than his brother – less socially easy and adept, less smooth and facilitating? His friend, in any event, had most certainly not been married to the dour and ill-tempered woman who sat alternately convalescing and glaring at them in the corner. Once again Gray had probably needed to shut his eyes and shake his head slightly before he could convince himself that he was even awake. Galfridus Mann was certainly the closest thing possible to those friends he had only weeks before left behind in Italy, and any connection that kept the reality of their presence alive and firmly in his mind's eye was to be seized upon. The reasonably amenable 'Gal' and his rather less charming partner (Walpole in his own letters refers to her as nothing less than a 'little white fiend') could serve for the time being as a bridge whereby Gray might construct for his life a tenuous continuity. They helped at least to form some kind of actual, physical link with a past which was paradoxically both achingly close in time, but now maddeningly distant and removed from him physically.

The letters themselves, of course, formed another such link. Like so much correspondence written to companions from whom one has only just separated – like so many letters sent and received while the glow of recent, shared experiences is still vividly fresh in the mind – Gray's earliest missives to Chute and Mann sought touchingly to perpetuate a diurnal intimacy doomed in time, and by the very fact of their distance from one another, to fade. 'Now I have been at home', he wrote to Chute,

> & seen how things go there, would I were with you again, that the Remainder of my Dream might at least be agreeable. As it is, my prospect can not well be more unpleasing: but why do I trouble your Goodnature with such considerations? Be assured, that when I am happy (if that can ever be) your Esteem will greatly add to that happiness, & when most the contrary, will always alleviate, what I suffer. Many, many thanks for your kindness; for your travels, for your News, for all the trouble I have given, & must give you. Omit nothing, when you write, for things that were quite indifferent to me at Florence, at this distance become interesting. (CTG 187)

Gray seems already to have realized that it was the smallest, most ephemeral details – the otherwise imperceptible minutiae of one's life abroad – which were missed first and most when no longer present to one's daily sensations. 'Distance' alone could highlight the significance of such casual, daily interaction.

A great many other matters to which he had previously been 'indifferent' would now need likewise to acquire an interest of their own. Gray had never really looked much beyond his return to London. His professional 'prospects', as he wrote Chute, were indeed 'unpleasing' at best. Possessed still of his modest income, he was nevertheless faced now with the question of deciding just what he would do for a living. How and where, Gray needed to ask himself, was he to spend his time? Gray's mother may still have hoped that he would pursue the path of the legal career she had long ago sketched out for him in her own mind. Yet now that he had returned to England, Gray seemed inclined to do little either to foster or to discourage such hopes. If his father had gone so far as to hire or to purchase rooms for him in the Inner Temple, as was later assumed by Mason, there is no indication that any such rooms were ever occupied. (Members of the Inn often sub-let their Chambers to those intending to follow the profession of law, so there still exists a slight possibility that Gray, whose own name is not to be found among the records of those who purchased a set of Chambers, might nevertheless have taken up residence upon his return to London. The fact that some of Gray's mail from overseas appears to have been directed to Dick's Coffee House, rather than delivered to his Cornhill home, might support such a conjecture.) The question again arises as to whether or not Gray had ever even faintly hoped that his connection with Walpole eventually would lead him, as it had led the more worldly and calculating Ashton, to some sort of court appointment. As we have already seen, the genuinely impassioned nature of Gray's relationship with Walpole, taken together with his own substantial sense of pride and even diffidence, renders such a possibility highly unlikely. The subject of Walpole, however, was now for Gray a forbidden one. A terse postscript apparently written in response to Chute's own queries and contained at the end of the letter quoted above, noted succinctly and with a transparent attempt at dispassionate calm that 'Nobody' was 'come from Paris yet'. Gray had been so devastated by the loss of his best friend's love and companionship that he could not even bring himself to write Walpole's name.

It was hard, at the time, to tell just how long such a state of affairs would or could last – certainly many months, possibly even years. However much he may eventually have acknowledged himself to have been at least partially responsible for their break-up (and we should bear in mind that there is no firm indication that he ever really did admit himself to any blame or shortcoming in the affair) in the months just after the quarrel with Walpole Gray seemed to take a great deal of comfort in portraying himself as the innocent and unreservedly injured party. He had done nothing wrong, the very tenor of his letters to his friends in Italy argues; how could an individual who was so clearly attentive to his chosen correspondents and companions of the heart – someone who was so playful in style, so cultivated in attitude, so thoughtful in affection, so solicitous in attention – ever have done anything so wrong? It was all 'nobody's' fault. 'Nobody', who was not to be mentioned. 'Nobody', to whom Gray now denied his very name.

Banished from his lips and from his pen, Walpole nevertheless must have continued to wreak havoc in Gray's mind. Each waking morning may very well have renewed the circumstances of the quarrel and refreshed the memory of his own loneliness. Gray must often have played and replayed the anguished and angry conversations which had passed between them in his head, and he seems to have turned only to his books for escape. Even to think of Walpole made him uneasy, and a host of subsidiary horrors made him both anxious and afraid. The likelihood of their meeting one another on the street or at the theatre was too great entirely to be ignored or overlooked. How, in such circumstances, would he conduct himself? How should he act? What could he say? Could he even trust himself to retain his own self-control? Gray's pride may have been so far injured that he possibly never worked his way through such questions. Perhaps the pain of losing Walpole, and the abrupt and unlooked-for manner of losing him, just began slowly to go away. Perhaps he found himself falling asleep one evening, only to awake with the sad, sudden shock of realization that he had – for the first time – not consciously thought of his friend at all that day. If Gray had been as intuitive an imitator of Petrarch as he was of Dante, we might have a better sense of the answers to questions such as these. A too rigorous examination of his own feelings was not, unfortunately, something Gray's favourites literary models had necessarily encouraged. The period of intensely personal self-examination was yet to come. In the autumn of 1741, Gray half-heartedly turned his back on the possibilities of a life he had only begun to live, and slowly, reluctantly, began patiently to brick up the disappointed chambers of his heart.

*

Gray's depression lasted for many months. Walpole, who had stopped to spend a final few days in Paris before returning home, had landed at Dover on 12 September. He completed the journey to London only two days after Gray himself. Walpole's spirits formed a sharp contrast to those of his former travelling companion, whom he made no effort to contact. His cousin Henry Conway had written to Gray shortly after the two friends' last, angry meeting in Venice. Conway's letter does not survive, but sometime in September, Walpole wrote to his cousin himself, thanking him for his attention to Gray and for his general assistance and support throughout such a personal 'crisis'. 'Before I thank you for myself', Walpole commented, 'I must thank you for that excessive good nature you showed in writing to poor Gray. I am less impatient to see you, as I find you are not the least altered, but have the same tender friendly temper you always had.'[3] Walpole's confident and self-assured voice in the letter his striking: 'Poor Gray' was never reduced or relegated in his eyes to the status of a 'nobody'. Walpole appears at the distance of only a few weeks time to have been much less deeply hurt by their quarrel. The wounds for him appear, in fact, already to have begun to heal. One might have expected this to have been the case. Walpole was both by nature and by habit far more resilient than Gray. He had always been the less dependent and the less obviously needy of the two friends. He possessed the confidence and the emotional wherewithal easily to strike out on his own. Unlike Gray, who was clearly reluctant to envision a future in which his longtime companion did not play a central and determining role, Walpole tried and apparently succeeded in soon putting the quarrel and its ramifications behind him. In so doing he was not being deliberately hard-hearted, nor, even, was he being determinedly 'forgetful'. There was simply little else, he seems to have felt, that he *could* do in such a situation. Like many individuals otherwise nostalgic in their impulses and their aesthetics, when it came to matters of his personal life, Walpole had very little trouble turning his back on the past – on what was done and beyond recall – and addressing the present moment.

And there was indeed much for Walpole, at present, to address. For all of Gray's anxieties about actually encountering Walpole socially or by accident, the Londons to which they respectively returned might just as well have been entirely different cities. While still abroad, Walpole had been returned to Parliament by the pocket borough of Callington in Cornwall. Although the House was not scheduled to meet again until 1 December, there was much to be done before then in preparing to defend his father's increasingly besieged government. In February 1741 motions had been brought forward in both Houses which requested that the King dismiss Sir Robert from his presence and councils forever. A grimly detailed survey of Robert Walpole's career had been presented in the Commons, in which his enemies charged him with various degrees of corruption, incompetence, and criminal mismanagement. The loyalty of his sometime allies – Newcastle and Hardwicke among them – was now proving uncertain. Sir Robert had been able to recover from the February assault, making an impressive speech in his own defense which prompted the Commons to defeat the motion against him by a tally which matched 290 votes in Walpole's favor to only 106 against. He had won this round, but the end of his career as influential first

---

[3] WC xxxvii.109.

minister to the King appeared to be in sight. Without neglecting the necessary duties of a rising young minister who was only expected to lead
a lively social life – being seen at the popular balls and attending the
latest Italian operas – Walpole set his sights firmly on assisting his father
in his struggle against the government opposition in whatever manner
he could. The recent fight for his political life had taken its toll on Sir
Robert's health and spirits. In addition to being generally dispirited,
Walpole's father succumbed soon after his son's arrival home to a cold
and fever that left him bodily weakened. The *London Evening Post* even
reported that he was 'so very bad, . . . that there was no hopes for him'.[4]
His son stayed close by his side at Downing Street, and was soon able
to write to Mann in Italy that the prime minister was recovering.

Gray's own father had also been taken ill. Repeated attacks of gout
had by the autumn of 1741 left Philip Gray close to crippled in Cornhill.
The end stages of the gout, rarely seen today, could be excruciatingly
painful. The large joints of the foot, leg, and other extremities would
usually be infected and swollen with pain, the inflamed areas red and hot
to the touch. The accumulation of uric acid in the body led finally to the
infection and failure of the kidneys. On 7 November both the *Daily Post*
and the *London Evening Post* (for the 5–7 November) carried the
announcement that Philip Gray, 'an Exchange Broker of Reputation and
Fortune', had died in Cornhill. Since no letters to or from Gray survive
from that period, it is difficult to reconstruct precisely how he and his
mother responded to his father's death. There can be little doubt,
however, that Philip Gray's passing came as a relief to them both. The
elder Gray's tyrannical hold over his family had been weakened and
finally broken by their continued defiance of his spectral authority; the
legacy of his abusive behaviour, however, was a powerful one, and such
legacies cast long shadows. Philip Gray had in recent years become less
of an actual threat to his wife and child, but his diminished stature did
little to rehabilitate his domestic status. A bully whose bluff has been
called is a pitiable figure, and just as Philip Gray's domestic mask of
casual arrogance had been stripped from his face, so too his boastful
power had deflated as swiftly as any punctured balloon. Dorothy and
Thomas had bravely moved on with their lives and had left Philip to look
after his own affairs as best he could or cared to. Their independent
behaviour may finally have demonstrated to him that they could get along
without him better, even, than they could get along with him.

Philip Gray seems to have responded to the awful fact of his irrele-
vance, as so many of his kindred spirits have before and since, by attending not to the more practical aspects of his business affairs, but rather
in fostering the most desperate and visionary of his schemes. Dorothy

---

[4]   *London Evening Post*, No. 2170, 6–8 October 1741; quoted in WC xvii.165.

and Thomas's declaration of domestic independence (for their behavior in recent years had amounted to precisely such an ultimatum) had left Philip Gray frighteningly alone in the world. For someone who had treated his own immediate family so badly, he seems to have taken a great deal of pride in the accomplishments of his own pedigree – in his status as a respected London merchant descended from an established family of citizens. Having thoroughly alienated his wife and child, to say nothing of his younger sister and his surviving nieces, Philip Gray turned his fuddled thoughts melancholically to the past, and to his family roots in Wanstead. Only there, he must have thought, did he stand any chance of regaining the respect and the attention he felt he deserved. In Wanstead, at least, he could extract himself from the negligible mess into which his practical business affairs had dwindled, and show his upstart wife and son just what they had lost when they turned their backs on a man such as Philip Gray.

Such, at least, must have been his thoughts in the months before he died his slow and painful death. When Dorothy and Thomas finally disentangled Philip Gray's financial affairs, they discovered that his imaginative investment in his family's past – his last, desperate attempt at some kind of self-justification for his very existence – had cost them both dearly. All too familiar with Philip's increasingly sloppy business habits, they had expected to find little in the way of any real income. The two were nevertheless stunned to discover just how much money Philip had been pouring into the building of a large country mansion in Wanstead. That he had been engaged in such an ambitious undertaking at all seems to have come as a complete surprise to them. An unexpected portion of the capital or savings they might have expected to realize from Philip's death had long since been sunk into the construction of this fanciful 'estate'. The building was a clear attempt on Philip's part to claim some kind of real and demonstrable value for himself. The news of such a costly investment took his family by surprise, but both Dorothy and Thomas had long ago learned that Philip Gray was to be counted on for little or nothing. They salvaged what they could. It was decided that the Essex property, at least, could be let to a tenant (the house was eventually purchased by Alderman Ball – a former Lord Mayor – who still owned the property in 1776; it was later sold at £2,000 less than its original cost of construction). The home and retail property in Cornhill were secure, so there was no question of them having immediately to leave the place they had for better or worse come to think of as home. When all was said and done, they may even have made their way back from the lawyer's chambers and breathed a long sigh of relief that they were really no worse off than before; the depth of Philip Gray's vindictiveness threatened at times to render the distance across the grave a negligible one. Both mother and son probably began at once to wonder if it were financially prudent for them to remain in London at all. Their incomes were by no means great (though some have estimated that the elder Gray had left his survivors no less than £10,000, thus guaranteeing a yearly income of as much as £1,000), but they could get by comfortably enough in some more retired spot. The Cornhill house, in any event, held too many memories – too many ghosts – nor was it the kind of place easily to be exorcized.

*

The fact of Philip Gray's death took time to work itself into the fabric of their lives. As the winter of 1741 passed slowly into the spring of 1742, both mother and son saw fit to rest and regroup before preparing themselves to meet the challenges of what would for both amount to entirely new lives. From Gray's point of view, the parameters of his life had changed a bit too suddenly. He seemed truly to have left an entire world behind him – to have been plucked from his own developing experience and dropped into that of someone else. Cornhill was blessedly no longer what it once was, but he had neither the energy nor the inclination to take it over for himself, or to create it anew. Cambridge, likewise, was no longer an obvious place of refuge. The quarrel with Walpole had transformed even the world of Peterhouse, Pembroke, and Kings into a landscape of painful memory. His father was dead, Walpole was as good as dead, and so too – Gray may have convinced himself in his darker moments – was he.

Gray buried himself in those winter months with attending to and attempting as best he could to tie up his father's business affairs. He also tried as much as possible to see to his mother's health and comfort. There could now be no question of his taking up or continuing residence in the Temple. He seems to have felt that his proper place, for the time being at least, was by his mother's side. His social life – so recently a whirl of operas, balls, and masquerades – was now limited to visits to West and perhaps to the Inns of Court. One strongly suspects that it was at about this time that Gray began finally to realize just how much West meant – or *should* have meant – to him. Having himself passed through the anger, the mortification, and the sense of loss consequent upon the break-up with Walpole, Gray seems in the breathing space that followed his father's death seriously to have re-evaluated the several relationships of his life. For all the emotion he had invested in his connections with Walpole, he may reluctantly have begun acknowledging in his more rigorously honest moments that their friendship had always been an unequal one – that their quarrel was more than a momentary flare up on either side, and that he and Walpole had to some degree grown temperamentally unsuited to one another. Walpole's easy charm had for years operated as a kind of enchantment upon Gray. Everything in his life had been coloured by his infatuation with his great friend. Now, left finally to himself, he realized with regret that he had neglected – and had at times neglected shamefully – other friends who had equal or even better claims on his love and attention.

Foremost among these friends, of course, was West. Since leaving Oxford, West had devoted his days and nights wearily to the study of the law. Letters from his friends abroad had afforded him a mixed and often melancholy consolation. Gray and Walpole's enthusiastic accounts of their continental socializing had served only to underscore the continued isolation and drudgery of West's own daily existence. All through his miserable years at Oxford, West had held before him the prospect of finally spending time with his friends in London. To have been left behind and separated from them once again, however graciously he had dealt with their immediate departure, must have been felt in time as a great injustice.

West's health was now worse than ever; his family situation, likewise, seems further to have deteriorated. By the early spring of 1742, West appears no longer to have felt comfortable spending time with his mother and sister at Epsom, and his relationship with his surviving parent seems to have been severely strained. We again remind ourselves that many years after West's death, Gray would observed to Norton Nicholl that his friend's illness had been exacerbated by 'the fatal discovery which he made of the treachery of a supposed friend, and the viciousness of a mother whom he tenderly loved'. 'This man', Gray continued, 'under the mask of friendship to him and his family, intrigued with his mother, and robbed him of his peace of mind, his health, and his life.' Nicholls noted that even as Gray spoke of West's unhappiness in later life he looked profoundly disturbed and 'seemed to feel the affect of a recent loss'. The 'supposed friend' mentioned cryptically by Gray in his recollection was no doubt John Williams – formerly secretary to West's father – who would in time marry Elizabeth West. West must have been aware of the possibility that the two had planned his father's murder years earlier. In the years following her husband's death, Elizabeth West's mind was slowly poisoned against her son by Williams. A weak-minded woman clearly given to prioritizing her own comfort and happiness above those of her own children, she seems to have cared little for the fate of her son. It is striking, however, that no one – not even West himself – seems to have noticed how serious the young man's illness had become in recent months. Tuberculosis of the lungs (and it seems clear that this is the 'consumption' that attacked West's health) was by no stretch of the imagination a silent or unobtrusive killer. The cold and dreary winter of 1741–42 may well have aggravated West's condition, though it would appear from his complaints of weakness, fatigue, and general lassitude throughout much of his time at university that he had been exposed to the disease some years before, and that it had taken its usual course in incubating slowly before undertaking entirely to consume him. He was now feverish and unable to sleep for tossing and coughing in bed the entire night. Sometime toward the middle of March the smoke and the fog that dampened the claustrophobic London air became too much for him, and he decided that if he were to recover his 'spirits' at all, it would be necessary for him to leave the city and spend some time in the countryside. He removed himself to the house of one David Mitchell, at Popes, near Hatfield in Hertfordshire. In so doing, he defied the contemporary medical treatment of tuberculosis which misguidedly favoured a vegetable diet and convalescence within tightly close environments.

West's spring move to Popes may well have extended his life. The old town of Hatfield, with its half-timbered houses, was in the early and mid-eighteenth century still nestled in a green and pleasant stretch of country, and the area around the town savoured in its local history of a bluff and hearty 'England' which might in certain circumstance do much to restore one's spirits. The grounds and gardens of Hatfield house lay close by, and at the end of the gentle slope of the town's main street the Eight Bells Inn stood (and still stands today), where Dick Turpin is said to have jumped from an upper-storey window onto the back of his faithful steed 'Black Bess' in order to escape from the Bow Street runners who were at that very moment entering the inn to apprehend him. It was in such country that West was able finally and with good reason to forget about his legal studies, and devote himself to what he hoped would be his own recovery.

*

Throughout the winter of 1741, Gray spent as much time as possible with West. When West finally left the city for Popes, he did so with the understanding that the two would continue to share with one another their thoughts and opinions concerning their reading and, indeed, their own essays at literary endeavor. As ill as he was, West could not help but regard his convalescent retreat to Hertfordshire as having provided him with a welcome sabbatical from his regular studies. He was free to read what he pleased, and that was in itself an unaccustomed luxury. He accordingly drew a comfortable armchair close to the fireside and sat 'purring' over the several volumes which were now conveniently placed on his lap or within easy reach on the floor beside him. He had begun Tacitus, he wrote to Gray towards the end of March, but was finding the Roman historian dull. Would the *Annals* become more interesting, he asked his friend? West wondered too what Gray himself thought of the 'new' Dunciad (the fourth Book of Pope's much revised and rewritten poem had been published that month).

The intense burst of correspondence between West and Gray which followed the former's settling into his retreat at Popes in the spring of 1742 provides the best evidence we have as to just how intimate the two young men had become in the course of the preceding winter. The anxiety and sense of neglect that had so often sounded in West's early letters from Oxford is gone, replaced instead by a certain seriousness of purpose, and by an unstated confidence that his thoughts and opinions are being listened to carefully – by a quiet perception that his inner, emotional life is in a similar manner now regarded as a matter of real consequence. Gray also writes in these letters with a new voice. The obvious and elaborate burlesques of his earlier correspondence with Walpole were now superseded by an epistolary style which was more unobtrusively allusive than it had been in the past, and by a voice even (and rather remarkably for Gray) at times utterly straightforward in its seeming honesty, and in its genuine concern for West's health.

Much of their correspondence was devoted to matters of literary taste and style. Since the earliest days of their friendship at Eton, the two seem to have felt most comfortable when sharing with one another their thoughts and opinions about their reading. Gray responded to West's concerns about Tacitus by pressing him to continue reading the *Annals*, and by asking him to imagine, if certain subjects could be tedious when treated by an author with such a generally engaging style as Tacitus himself, just how insupportable they would have been in the hands of any other historian. The new *Dunciad* Gray admitted to be 'greatly admired' in town, and certain passages were distinguished by the poet as constituting verse 'as fine as anything [Pope] had written'. However, Gray finally judged the book only to be good in parts, and dismissed some sections as not only 'ill-expressed', but 'hardly intelligible'. He informed West, in turn, that he had been supplementing his own regimen of the classics (he had that month not only been dipping into Anacreaon, Theocritus, Pliny, and Plutarch, but making his way with greater diligence through Thucydides' *History of the Peloponnesian War*) by reading Henry Fielding's new novel, *Joseph Andrews*. Fielding's plot was criticized as hackneyed and ill-laid but, Gray allowed, 'the characters have a great deal of nature, which always pleases even in her lowest shapes'. Weighty moral treatises and other such 'grave discourses upon the mind' may well have their place, Gray confided to West, but should one really desire to learn about the passions and the inclinations of the human heart, one could do far worse than rely on novels and romances for one's education. 'Now', he even confessed, 'as the paradisiacal pleasures of the Mahometans consist in playing upon the flute and lying with Houris, be mine to read eternal new romances of Marivaux and

Crébillon'. Gray meant in such a comment specifically to contrast several supposedly 'light' and inconsequential works such as Pierre Carlet de Chamblain de Marivaux's *La Vie de Marienne* and Claude-Propser Jolyot de Crébillon's *Égarements du coeur et de l'espirit*, with the dry and dusty heaviness of essays such as Frances Hutcheson's 1728 *On the Nature and Conduct of the Passions and Affections with Illustrations on the Moral Sense*. The notion that a comfortable terrestrial paradise might be created merely by supplying readers with an unending source of new French romances, however, hearkens back to the young men's days as Eton schoolchildren, when writers who anticipated the work of Crébillon and Marivaux had provided a generous landscape of escape from the pressures and the rigours of their daily life both in and out of the classroom. Gray seems subconsciously to be asking West to remember, for the benefit of his own current health, the best of their earliest days together – the days when, in fact, it had not been all that difficult actually to put their voracious reading to practical use in the interests of their own mental, physical, and spiritual health.

The most important portion of the spring exchange between the two friends on literary matters for modern readers, however, followed upon Gray's decision on 1 April to send West 'a long speech of Agrippina', a speech that he then asked his friend to critique and even to 'retrench'. This 'long speech' already had something of a history. It will be remembered that one of the plays that Gray had attended soon after his arrival in Paris in the spring of 1739 had been a production of Racine's *Brittanicus*. Gray had enjoyed the play immensely and, according to several other friends throughout his life, continued always to profess a profound admiration for the work. It seems likely that very soon after his return to England, he decided to try his own hand at a dramatic tragedy following Racine's model. The character of Agrippina plays a significant role in Racine's own *Brittanicus*, and Gray's rereading of Tacitus provided him with a reliable historical source to match the dramaturgy of his French model (Racine's play had itself been based on material from the *Annals*, a circumstance that the young poet must have regarded as a happy coincidence, uniting as it did two of his most passionate enthusiasms – theatre and ancient history – in one single and innovative dramatic spectacle).

However, Gray seems to have found the necessary work of the tragic dramatist rather slower going than he had at first anticipated. Like so many of his other pieces, *Agrippina, A Tragedy*, would be toyed with and added to for many years before being set aside and abandoned altogether. Gray's executor William Mason, hoping to demonstrate that 'the action itself was possest of sufficient unity' for a successful drama, later reconstructed the anticipated plot and under-plot of the drama from 'two detached papers' that he discovered among Gray's notes and journals after the poet's death. According to Mason's conflation of Gray's notes, the play was to have focused primarily on the imperious Agrippina's tortured relationship with her son, the Roman emperor Nero – a struggle for power that resulted in the emperor's first attempt on his mother's life in AD 59, and eventually in her subsequent murder at the hands of his henchmen. The anticipated sub-plot of Gray's drama, as outlined by Mason, followed Nero's relationship with Poppaea Sabina – an ambitious woman whose own thirst for power contributed to Agrippina's fate and lead also to the banishment of her former lover, Otho. The early portion of the play that Gray sent to West in the spring of 1742 was a 100-line speech spoken by Agrippina to her confidante Aceronia; the speech would have stood very close to the opening of the drama.

The fragment finds Agrippina defying Nero, whom she dismisses as a 'silken son of dalliance, nursed in ease / And pleasure's flowering lap', and threatening cynically even to invoke the name of liberty ('a senseless word, a vain tradition') to challenge the emperor's authority. If she is to be stripped of the power and influence still left to her, Agrippina warns, she shall drag Nero himself with her in her downfall and, as she puts it, 'sink the traitor in his mother's ruin'. The entire speech is undertaken in the deliberately artificial and antiquated high style of heroic drama. Rejecting Aceronia's plea for her to recall the conditions under which she first resigned her political power to her son, for example, Agrippina responds:

> Thus ever grave and undisturbed reflection
> Pours its cool dictates in the madding ear
> Of rage, and thinks to quench the fire it feels not.
> Sayest thou I must be cautious, must be silent,
> And tremble at the phantom I have raised?
> Carry to him thy timid counsels. He
> Perchance may heed 'em: tell him too, that one
> Who had such liberal power to give, may still
> With equal power resume that gift, and raise
> A tempest that shall shake her own creation
> To its original atoms – tell me! say
> This mighty emperor, this dreadful hero,
> Has he beheld the glittering front of war?
> Knows his soft ear the trumpet's thrilling voice,
> And outcry of battle? (PTG 36)

Such deliberately overwrought dramatic language recalls, as several critics have observed over the years, the diction of tragedies such as Samuel Johnson's 1736 *Irene* and James Thomson's *Sophonisba* (1730).

We cannot ignore the possibility that in writing about a troubled relationship between a mother and son, Gray was in some way displacing and working his way through some of the more predictable tensions that had arisen between his own mother and himself in the wake of Philip Gray's death. There may well have been some vexed question that arose in connection with the elder Gray's property and estate – questions that created an unavoidable friction even between two individuals who were as close to one another as Dorothy Gray and her son. Gray was for the first time in his life assuming a real, personal authority in financial affairs, and he was perhaps beginning himself to assert the authority of the 'parent' in domestic and professional matters. *Agrippina*, however, is so clearly an attempt to emulate Racine's artistic achievement and is itself such a consciously crafted artefact, that any attempts to pursue a rigorously autobiographical reading of the drama are almost certainly misguided. Gray in his more wistful moments that winter may have considered the possibility of a career as a dramatist. Indeed, his early association with Thomas Southerne at Stoke Poges may even have encouraged such aspirations.

West's response to Gray's work quickly and rather uncharitably threw some cold, critical water on any such hopes. His objections to Agrippina's speech focused not, as Gray appears to have anticipated, on its (alterable) length, but rather on its style, which, West complained 'appears to me too antiquated'. Racine did not himself, when writing in French, affect the sixteenth-century idiom of Ronsard, so why is it that Gray should try to write like Shakespeare? Racine's language, West contended,

> is the language of the times, and that of the purest sort; so that his French is reckoned a standard. I will not decide what style is fit for our English stage; but I should rather choose one that bordered upon Cato than upon Shakespear [sic]. One may imitate (if one can) Shakespear's manner, his surprizing strokes of true nature, his expressive force in painting characters, and all his other beauties: preserving at the same time our own language. Were Shakespeare alive now, he would write in a different style from what he did. These are my sentiments upon these matters: Perhaps I am wrong, for I am neither a Tarpa, nor am I quite an Aristarchus. You see I write freely both of you and Shakespear; but it is as good as writing not freely, where you know it is acceptable. (*CTG* 190)

Gray was not offended by West's criticisms. He knew already that his Agrippina was decidedly a little long-winded (Mason so far objected to the dramatic practicality of such a lengthy speech as to divide it between two separate characters when he transcribed the work following Gray's death). Gray had even joked to West when first sending him the fragment that were he ever to finish the drama, it would in all likelihood resemble nothing so much as the twenty-five act tragedy Nathaniel Lee was said to have written while incarcerated in London's Bedlam insane asylum in the late 1680s. Gray seems in fact to have been genuinely grateful to West for his honesty. He did not, however, entirely agree with his friend's observations concerning poetic diction and the vocabulary of the drama. He replied,

> As to the matter of stile I have this to say: The language of the age is never the language of poetry; except among the French, whose verse, where the thought or image does not support it, differs in nothing from prose. Our poetry, on the contrary, has a language peculiar to itself; to which almost every one, that has written, has added something by enriching it with foreign idioms and derivatives: Nay sometimes words of their own composition or invention. Shakespear and Milton have been great creators this way; and no one more licentious than Pope or Dryden, who perpetually borrow expressions from the former. (*CTG* 192)

Gray then quotes eight lines from the opening scene of Shakespeare's *Richard III*, with the caveat that 'the affectation of imitating Shakespeare may doubtless be carried too far'.

Much has been made of Gray's so-called 'manifesto' regarding poetic diction in this letter to West, but he was really saying nothing new. Nor, certainly, would he ever have claimed for his remarks the status of novelty. In advancing the notion that the affectation of a deliberately antiquated style and the systematic use of archaism was the surest way to distinguish the language of poetry from the language of prose, Gray was very much one with his age. The notion that poets needed to cultivate an elaborate syntax, an ornamental vocabulary, and an etymologically precise use of language peculiar to themselves was a prevalent one throughout the Augustan era. Gray would in time, as the critic Richard Terry has pointed out, attempt to take the 'autonomy' of poetic language one step further in a passage included in his Commonplace Book later in life, when he concludes 'that poets should shoulder the principal arms of reinvigorating the language of good usage, for [in Gray's words] "to Poetry Languages owe their first formation, elegance & purity" '.[5] In the spring of 1742, however, Gray and West were casually exchanging what really amounted to little more than commonplaces of early Augustan discourse concerning prosody and rhetorical decorum. It is perhaps of more importance to Gray's inclination and career as a poet, for example, to note that his letters to West reveal that he was already – even as he produced his first extended and original compositions in

[5] Richard Terry, 'Gray and Poetic Diction' in Hutchings and Ruddick, 80.

English – in the habit of slowly and constantly rewriting his verses. 'I am a sort of spider', he confided to West, 'and have little else to do but spin [my words] over again, or creep to some other place and spin it there'. The simple fact, too, that Gray is now comfortable composing his lines in English rather than Latin is itself worthy of note; West's own effort and support encouraged him in this.

Gray soon followed Agrippina's speech with a translation of one of Propertius' *Elegies*. West's criticisms of his dramatic efforts seem to have hit home. 'As to Agrippina', he wrote at the end of April, 'I begin to be of your opinion, & find myself (as women are of their children) less enamored of my productions the older they grow. She is laid up to sleep till next Summer; so bid her goodnight'. West's own translations of Tacitus (he had included a 'bold' rendition of a speech of Germanicus in his last letter) prompted Gray to respond in kind. He had been trying his best that month to translate Thucydides' notoriously difficult and complex Greek into the English tongue ('which is too difficult, & daily grows more and more enervating'), but had soon given up on the attempt, as he found it tended only to produce 'mere Nonsense'. He chose instead to send West an English version of Propertius' *Elegy* II.i, a work which the Roman writer had dedicated to the patron Maecenas. Gray's Commonplace Book reveals that he had already, while still at Cambridge in December 1738, tried his hand at another of Propertius' *Elegies* (III.iv), but had left that work – fifty-eight lines of rhyming couplets – unfinished. *Elegy* II.i, however, is a complete and elegant translation that met with West's considered approval.

Propertius was an author whose work in many ways suited Gray's temperament. The five-year infatuation with the beloved 'Canthi' documented and dramatized in Propertius' most famous poems inspired a state of amorous melancholy often punctuated by serious and extended (not to say sombre) meditations on the transience of human life and passion. Propertius was generally acknowledged to have been one of the masters of the Latin elegy, along with writers such as Gaius Cornelius Gallus, Albius Tibullus, and other poets under the patronage of Marcus Valerius Messalla. Many of the earliest latin elegies (our English word is derived from the Greek ἔλεγος or *elegos*, meaning 'song of mourning') were written as general lamentations and meditations on the transience and insubstantiality of human existence. They were composed in a specific distich (couplets consisting of one hexameter followed by a pentameter line) which was thought to suit the poetic 'kind'. The poet had usually been led to contemplate 'the tragic aspect of life' through the ingratitude or casual neglect of his mistress (e.g. 'Canthi', 'Lycoris', 'Delia'). The elegiac form was thus not necessarily and perforce linked to the subject of death and lament for the dead; nevertheless, in the course of time, an important thematic connection arose between the subjects of love and death – a connection that led to a scenario in which a poet, slighted by his beloved object and the 'tyrant' Cupid, turned his thoughts instead to his own imminent passing, and the desire to be remembered by posterity as a sincere and faithful lover.

Such a scenario is very much in evidence in the elegy that Gray chose now to translate into English. The poet opens by protesting that whatever the activity his Canthi chooses to undertake, it is sure to provide him with matter enough for his poetic praise. A lover's book can be filled with those observations that might otherwise pass unnoticed or unremarked, 'And many a copious narrative you'll see,/ Big with important nothing's history'. Were he to write an epic poem, he suggests, its subject would be chosen not from any established list of poetic 'matters' (no 'tale of Thebes or Ilium there should be'), but would be written rather with the sanction of the god of love; it would detail the 'milder warfare' of the heart – it would concern itself, in other words, with the 'war' between the sexes or a war of eros. The poet ends his work with a prayer that he may never fall the victim to his lover's scorn:

> The power of herbs can other harms remove,
> And find a cure for every ill but love.
> . . .
> For ills unseen what remedy is found,
> Or who can probe the undiscovered wound?
> The bed avails not or the leech's care,
> Nor changing skies can hurt nor sultry air.
> 'Tis hard the elusive symptoms to explore:
> Today the lover walks, tomorrow is no more;
> A train of mourning friends attend his pall,
> And wonder at the sudden funeral.
> When then my fates that breath they gave shall claim,
> When the short marble but preserves a name,
> A little verse, my all that shall remain,
> Thy passing courser's slackened speed retain
> (Thou envied honour of thy poet's days,
> Of all our youth the ambition and the praise!):
> Then to my quiet urn awhile draw near,
> And say, while o'er the place you drop a tear,
> Love and the fair were of his life the pride;
> He lived while she was kind, and, when she frowned,
>   he died. (PTG 46–47)

The sentiments expressed here are conventional enough, and readers familiar with the later *Elegy* cannot help but notice that Propertius' lyric seems to have placed in the poet's mind the seeds of certain imagery that will reappear more fully grown in Gray's later poetry. The sudden disappearance of the ailing lover from his accustomed haunts, the train of mourning friends who follow the modest pall to its final resting place, the 'short marble', 'little verse' and 'quiet urn' that alone commemorate and memorialize his self-consciously diminutive existence: each of these will be reimagined in greater detail and with careful elaboration within the churchyard of St. Giles at Stoke Poges.

*

West welcomed the distraction of Gray's verses. April had come and gone and it was now nearly the second week of May, yet still the weather in rural Hertfordshire remained cold and damp. Although West had looked forward to being able to read in his country solitude, he had likewise anticipated being able to breath the fresh, invigorating spring air of the rural lanes and by-ways, and to watch the skies turn clear and the meadows grow green and rich with blossoms in the warmth of a restorative sun. May too was now passing, however, and here he was still confined to his armchair by the fireside, the heavy cough in his lungs growing worse, not better, and the chill air – if anything – seeming to grow even colder in the damp of his country retreat. Each time the weather appeared finally to be breaking, a sudden blast of cold winter storms would sweep in from the north and once again cast a gray pall across the disappointed landscape. West consoled himself as best he could, sending Gray a 'little Ode' that gamely attempted to 'invoke the tardy May'. In the Ode, West nicely combined an elegant compliment to his friend with an invocation of the season that anticipates in its use of personification some of Gray's own poetry:

> Dear Gray, that always in my heart
> Possessest far the better part,
> What mean these sudden blasts that rise
> And drive the Zephyrs from the skies?
> O join with mine thy tuneful lay,
> And invocate the tardy May,
> Come, fairest Nymph, resume thy reign!
> Bring all the Graces in thy train!
> With balmy breath, and flowery tread,
> Rise from thy soft ambrosial bed;
> Where, in elysian slumber bound,
> Embow'ring myrtles veil thee round.
> . . .
> Come then, with Pleasure at thy side,
> Diffuse thy vernal spirit wide;
> Create, where'er thou turn'st thy eye,
> Peace, Plenty, Love, and Harmony;

Till ev'ry being share its part,
And Heav'n and Earth be glad at heart. (*CTG* 201)

Gray, too, had been feeling the depressive drag of the extended winter and the wet English spring. His translations of Propertius and Thucydides and his other classical readings had left him at times feeling that he did nothing but converse with the dead. 'They are my old friends', he observed of his classical companions to West, 'and almost make me long to be with them'. Gray seemed increasingly and instinctively to turn to his 'old friends' the classics as he felt his 'old friends' from Eton slowly and each in their separate ways growing distant from him. Since he had left London for Popes, West had tried his best to convince his friend (and perhaps also to convince himself) that his move to the country was only a temporary measure. If he could but make it through the winter, he told Gray – if he could only rid himself of the terrible cough which 'shook' and 'tore' his body for half an hour at a time – he could return to London, and maybe then they could finally pursue their long-deferred plans for living and studying together.

Gray eagerly drank in his friend's reassurances. 'I trust to the country', he had written to West soon after the latter's initial arrival in Hertfordshire, 'and that easy indolence you say you enjoy there, to restore you your health and spirits and doubt not but, when the sun grows warm enough to tempt you from your fireside, you will (like all other things) be the better for his influence'. Not long afterward he again protested his confidence in the imminence of his friend's speedy recovery. 'These wicked remains of your illness', he wrote at the beginning of the second week of April, 'will sure give way to warm weather and gentle exercise; which I hope you will not omit as the season advances. Whatever low spirits or indolence, the effect of them, may advise to the contrary, I pray you add five steps daily to your walk for my sake; by the help of which, in a month's time, I propose to set you on horseback'. And yet again, toward the end of April, Gray suggested that the length of West's own letters was itself 'a kind of Symptom' of the recovery of his friend's physical health, and claimed to flatter himself that West's bodily strength was returning in proportion. 'Pray do not forget', he reminds West, 'to mention the Progress you make continually'.

Gray was probably not, however, completely blind to the extreme seriousness of his friend's condition. The very injunction quoted above barely conceals the anxiety that lurked beneath the pretense of West's supposedly continual 'Progress'. The state of West's health, though generally poor, had never interrupted his life so completely as his consumption did now, and even individuals younger than Gray – who had so recently felt the touch of death in his own life, in witnessing the slow and painful death of his father – might recognize the curious psychic *frisson* that can often herald the approaching end of a loved one. Gray seems in fact to have anticipated his friend's death with increasing distress, and in his final letters to West confessed that he was himself feeling in lower spirits than usual. His habitual depression now widened at times into a black abyss of complete and unutterable despair. 'Mine, you are to know,' he wrote in one memorably specific description of his state of mind,

> is a white Melancholy, or rather Leucocholy for the most part; which though it seldom laughs or dances, nor ever amounts to what one calls Joy or Pleasure, yet is a good easy sort of state, and ça ne laisse que de s'amuser. The only fault of it is insipidity; which is apt now and then to give a sort of Ennui, which makes one form certain little wishes that signify nothing. But there is another sort, black indeed, which I have now and then felt, that has somewhat in it like Tertullian's rule of faith, Credo quia impossibile est; for it believes, nay, is sure of every thing that is unlikely, so it be but frightful; and, on the other hand, excludes and shuts its eyes to the most possible hopes, and every thing that is pleasurable; from this the Lord deliver us! for none but he and sunshiny weather can do it. (CTG 209)

Gray inadvertently admitted that he has recently been in the grip of precisely this darker melancholy when he wrote to West that he would very soon be leaving to spend a few weeks in the country at Stoke, in hopes of enjoying 'the kind of weather' conducive to the recovery of his spirits.

Gray left London for Stoke at the end of May. Shortly afterwards, he sent to West the beginning of an heroic epistle written in Latin. The imaginary *Sophonisba Massinissae Epistola* is at first glance one of the most curious and arcane of Gray's literary productions. The poem, as Gray pointed out to West, is based in part on incidents drawn from Books 29 and 30 of Livy's history of Rome. A second source was the Alexandrian Appian's narrative history of the Punic Wars. Every schoolboy would have been familiar with the circumstances surrounding Sophonisba's suicide and her history had several times been adapted for the English stage. John Marston had written a *Sophonisba* in 1606, Nathaniel Lee's *Sophonisba; or, Hannibal's Overthrow* had been produced in 1675 and, more recently, Thomson's *Sophonisba* had given the world the unforgettable (and often parodied) dramatic line: 'Oh! Sophonisba, Sophonisba, Oh!'.

Briefly stated, Sophonisba was the daughter of the Carthaginian general Hasdrubal. She was the wife of Syphax, a king of Numidia who was at the time of their marriage an ally of the Romans. Sophonisba's influence eventually prompted her husband to forsake his alliance with Rome in the course of the second Punic War. He was captured by his rival, Masinissa, a Numidian prince who soon found himself falling in love with his captive's bride. Masinissa consequently took Sophonisba

for himself. Fearing that Sophonisba's considerable charms and persua-
sive rhetoric could lead Rome to lose the allegiance of Masinissa just as
easily as it had lost that of Syphax, the consul Scipio Africanus claimed
Sophonisba as a captive of war and demanded that she be sent to Rome.
Anticipating the qualms of a later and similarly seductive captive of the
Romans who was equally loath to have her personal tragedy played by
'quick comedians' on the Roman stage, Sophonisba avoided captivity by
swallowing the poison surreptitiously sent to her by Masinissa, who had
wished to spare her the trauma of such a public disgrace.

Gray's Latin elegiacs are written as if in a letter to Masinissa from
Sophonisba. We are meant to believe that the writer has only moments
before received the poison from one of Massina's messengers. The epistle
begins with fierce anger. Rather than thanking Masinissa for the bowl
of poison he has sent her, Sophonisba taxes her husband with his treachery to 'the Carthaginian gods'. Reminding Masinissa of her own grand
heritage as one of the daughters of Elissa (the legendary daughter of the
Tyrian king Matgenos), she stresses that she delays swallowing the fatal
poison only because she does not want to appear as if she overvalued
Masinissa's love, or that she has been intimidated by her political
enemies. She then recalls the circumstances of their first meeting; Gray's
Sophonisba retreats from the realm of the public to recount the circumstances of that encounter in close and personal detail:

> Prima genas tenui signat vix flore iuventas,
>   et dextrae soli credimus esse virum.
> Dum faciles gradiens oculos per singula iactas,
>   (seu rexit casus lumina, sive Venus)
> In me (vel certe visum est) conversa morari
>   sensi; virgineus perculit ora pudor.
> Nescio quid vultum molle spirare tuendo,
>   credideramque tuos lentius ire pedes.
> Quaerebam, iuxta aequalis quae dignior esset,
>   quae poterat visus detinuisse tuos:
> Nulla fuit circum aequalis si dignior esset,
>   asseruitque decus conscia forma suum.
> Pompae finis erat. Toto vix nocte quievi:
>   sin premat invitae lumina victa sopor,
> Somnus habet pompas, eademque recursat imago;
>   atque iterum hesterno munere victor ades. (PTG 320–21)

[First manhood has hardly set its mark on your cheeks with its
fine bloom and it is only by the deeds of your hand that we
believe you a man. As you walked along, and you cast casual
glances at every object (whether change directed your gaze, or
Venus), and I felt your eyes linger as they turned on me (or so,
at least, it seemed); and maiden shame suffused my face, I felt

sure that your expression softened a little as you gazed and that
your feet went forward more slowly. I looked to see whether
there was any one of my companions around me who could have
been more worthy and conscious beauty claimed the honour for
itself. The procession came to an end. All night I hardly rested;
or, if drowsiness overcame me and closed my eyes against my
will, then sleep held its own procession and the same image
recurred; and once more you, the conqueror, were there, as in
the spectacle of the previous day.]

Gray's epistle is obviously a work written within the tradition established by Ovid's *Heroides*, and certain phrases in the dramatic mono-
logue seem to recall several of Ovid's other works (lines 19–20 echo the
Latin poet's *Fasti*, for example, while other passages suggest that their
author had only recently been rereading both the *Amores* and the
Tristia). Yet the fifty-two-line work is one of the most original – that is
to say, one of the less clearly derivative and allusive – of Gray's Latin
poems. The recollection of Sophonisba's romantic first glimpse of her
captor-to-be is fully imagined and remarkably clear in its perceptive, psychological detail; her recollection of the lingering power of Masinissa's
glance possesses the force of a sudden divine clearance of haze – of a
new clarity of vision.

   Why did Gray choose to write this epistle and send it to West at this
particular time? There is a possibility that he had recently been reading
Thomson's popular version of the tragedy as he moved forward with his
own dramatic version of *Agrippina* (the two works evince certain peculiar similarities in language and style) and Thomson's work might easily
be read as having provided a suitable model for Gray's own drama. The
historical circumstances of Gray's heroine, however, suggest several
intriguing parallels to the poet's own situation in the spring of 1742. He
may even have seen, in Sophonisba's tragedy, some foreshadowing of the
emotional trauma that was about to devastate his own life, and he may
likewise have tried to mitigate that trauma by picturing and ennobling
himself as a second, though admittedly more modest, 'Sophonisba'.
Much like the classical heroine to whose feelings he chose now to give
voice, Gray himself had been forced by circumstances largely beyond his
own control to relinquish any claims he may have had on the first patron
of his heart – in his case Horace Walpole. Likewise, the passage quoted
above, in which the maidenly Sophonisba recognizes for the first time the
depth of her attraction to another of her captors, might well have been
suggested to Gray's unconscious mind by his own growing realization
of the mutual ties of affection that now bound him more closely to
West. The latter part of the poem offers an accurate portrait of an individual struck for the first time with the recurring sensations dependent

upon the growing realization of romantic obsession. The better part of
Sophonisba's epistle to Masinissa is in fact a confession of true and ardent
passion. It is also an angry letter of farewell. Sophonisba realizes that
despite her reluctance to concede any victory to 'arrogant, haughty
Rome', she will soon have to swallow the poison that has been sent
to her, or endure further mockeries at the hands of a cruel mob as she
is made the central focus of a triumphal procession. The more precise
parallels to Gray's own situation here, of course, fall to one side, but
readers could do a much greater disservice to the letter than to read
Gray's assumption of Sophonisba's position and all that such an identification implies – his assumption, that is, of her suicidal role, and the
contribution of that same suicide to Masinissa's continued prosperity –
as a kind of wish-fulfillment on the part of the poet. In taking her own
life, Sophonisba allows Masinissa to live. Gray seems to be saying that
were it possible, he would do as much for West. He has only begun to
realize the true state of his affections for his long neglected friend, and,
even as he does so, he is aware of West's increasingly tenuous hold on
life. The *Sophonisba Masinissae Epistola* is in some respects Gray's
fearful, anticipatory, and coded letter of farewell to his second love – the
same second love he was to lose within the course of less than a year.

II. Empty Words and Silent Ashes

One hopes that in the days and weeks that followed Gray's writing of
the heroic epistle, the poet drew some obscure comfort and perhaps even
some strength from the simple fact that he had committed to writing in
the classical language they had both understood so well – and with an
ingenuity and a genius peculiar to them both – a message of love and
affection for West. After so many dull and dreary months of rain, the
weather had finally taken a turn for the better; the warmth of an
extended summer seemed instantly to have touched the countryside.
Gray now spent the mornings and the afternoons much as he had on his
previous, extended visit to his aunt and uncle in the later of summer of
1736. He was probably joined at the Rogers' home by his mother and
his aunt Mary. The two women, together with their elder sister Anne,
created a close and comfortable household. The easy companionship of
the genial sorority promised a welcome sense of domestic order in Gray's
life. The three sisters may already have begun contemplating the possibility that they might soon live together permanently. Having nursed
Philip Gray through the final months of his own illness, Dorothy (and
perhaps her sister Mary as well) surely recognized in the complaints and
in the increasing disabilities of their brother-in-law Jonathan the symptoms of one who was himself not very long for this world. The three

sisters were very soon to be faced with the possibility of forming a complete society of their own. Men in general had done remarkably little to enhance the quality of their lives; the sisters began now to contemplate the scheme of their own existence together as the reward of retirement following a near-lifetime of trial and tribulation. With only Thomas to 'look after' – and they knew in their hearts that he shared their sensibilities and was in his own ways more Antrobus than Gray – their modest desires might finally rest fulfilled and largely contented.

Such a plan would eventually meet with Gray's own support and approval. There were worse things to endure in this world than the fussing care of a loving mother, or the constant solicitation of her equally loving and doting sisters. Life at Stoke Poges looked soon to be as comforting and sedate as Gray could possibly desire. The indigenous delights of an English spring had lost nothing in now being compared to the rather more spectacular glories of their several counterparts on the Continent and along the Mediterranean. Like Robert Browning just over one hundred years later, Gray in the spring and early summer of 1742 felt an intense connection with the peculiarly English behaviour of a peculiarly English spring – the buttercups, the blossoming hedges, and the thick, luxurious shade of the English oak. Following a sound night's sleep and a leisurely breakfast, he once again traced the lanes and hedges of the Buckinghamshire countryside until, volume in hand, he settled on a suitable place to resume his conversations with the literary past. Some afternoons found him basking in the sunlight beside a slow-moving stream, its rushes gently swaying in a mild wind. On other occasions he sought the thicker canopy of a glade of beech trees and, letting his book fall to his side, lay on his back in the blue-green shades of the foliage and lost himself in merely listening to the sounds of the season – the passing of herds in the midday heat, the quiet buzz and flutterings of bees, butterflies and other insects in the heavy, post-meridian air. The church-yard of St. Giles, too – the rays of the late afternoon sun falling aslant its ancient graves and crumbling pavements – invited retreat and meditation, and Gray would often have turned his footsteps in the direction of the tombstones on those warm and quiet afternoons.

Sometime toward the very beginning of June, the clear weather having finally settled over southern England like an enchantment auguring nothing but fine health and recovery, Gray was prompted by West's own poetic 'invocation' of the spring to write his own poem of praise to the season. The result was a five-stanza poem that he called 'Noon-tide, an Ode'. The work would later be generally retitled as the *Ode on the Spring*. The poem powerfully and paradoxically combines Gray's growing preoccupation with the state of West's health and his strong forebodings of his friend's imminent death, on the one hand, with the wishful optimism of a young man who cannot yet bring himself to believe the truth of his own intimations of mortality, on the other. It seemed on some level impossible to Gray – as well as inescapably *wrong* – that sickness and death could ever find a hold in such a landscape, a landscape teeming with renewed life, and with the verdant promise of the perennially renewing 'untaught harmonies' of nature. The first of Gray's mature English poems, the *Ode on the Spring* anticipates his later works stylistically, both in its use of the kind of poetic diction he had so readily defended as the proper language of poetry in his recent letter to West, and in its thorough-going reliance on allusion and textual reference. The *Ode* is also, of course, thematically of a piece with Gray's more famous poems. The scene of nature, even in the first glow of its rich and vernal beauties, is the very same scene that prompts the poet's meditation on mortality, and the seemingly inevitable passing of all natural and – more particularly – of all human things.

*

The *Ode* opens with a vision of spring which – in its references to the nightingale or 'Attic warbler', to the goddess Venus and her attendant hours, and to the personification of the winds themselves as 'cool zephyrs' – explicitly connects the countryside around Stoke with the ancient landscapes of classical mythology. As in poems such as Pope's *Windsor Forest*, the fields and hedgerows of a tame and rural England are effectively endowed with the richness of a pseudo-Ovidian past:

> Lo! where the rosy-bosomed Hours,
> Fair Venus' train, appear,
> Disclose the long-expecting flowers,
> And wake the purple year!
> The Attic warbler pours her throat,
> Responsive to the cuckoo's note,
> The untaught harmony of spring:
> While whispering pleasure as they fly,
> Cool zephyrs through the clear blue sky
> Their gathered fragrance fling. (*PTG* 48–49)

The range of cento-like references and quotations in these opening lines alone is staggering. Lucretius, Horace, Anacreaon, Virgil, Ovid, Propertius, Milton, Dryden, Pope, Thomson, and Matthew Green: all are among the poets whose descriptive language is conjured in this opening verse stanza. We remind ourselves that the effect of such textual reference, as critics such as Roger Lonsdale and Bruce Redford have pointed out, is an overall and pervasive richness of allusion, rather than an echo or recollection of any particular model. Gray effectively enriches and historicizes his own language by fortifying it with the elusive and allusive weight of a diffuse and historically wide-ranging literary past. We are meant to hear the sound or echo of no one poet or poem in particular, but rather – like a multitude of church bells, all tolling to call one to religious observance, all subtly overlapping and imitating one another in the repetition and close harmony of their scales – the polyphony of linguistic allusion reinscribes an ever-widening variety of voices within a fundamental singularity of poetic purpose. We are *meant* to remind ourselves, in other words, that the poet is operating here within a great and grand tradition.

It is important to remember likewise that this poetic tradition is pointedly one with which we are already supposed to be familiar. The poem's second stanza further describes the rural scene and suggests that both the poet and his muse have already diligently drawn a moral lesson from their own observations:

> Where'er the oak's thick branches stretch
> A broader browner shade;
> Where'er the rude and moss-grown beech
> O'er-canopies the glade,
> Beside some water's rushy brink
> With me the Muse shall sit, and think
> (At ease reclined in rustic state)
> How vain the ardour of the crowd,
> How low, how little are the proud,
> How indigent the great! (*PTG* 50–51)

The reader is intended to find the 'moral' articulated in the last three lines here an obvious and even a somewhat hackneyed one. The 'littleness' of pride and the 'indigence' of the activities of 'the Great' when viewed from the distance of a rural retreat conducive rather to the priorities of the *vita contemplativa* is a *topos* few if any readers of classical poetry would fail immediately to recognize. It is more than likely, too, that there is a touch of delicate humour in Gray's stanza, particularly in his representation of such a relaxed and companionable Muse. The description of the poet himself reclining beside a quiet stream within the shade of a tree to avoid the midday heat is of course a familiar one (readers of Horace, Virgil, and Lucretius would instantly recognize the posture as a poetic commonplace); the poetic Muse herself, however, is far more often evoked within the same body of literature as a powerful and even an awful figure – a deity demanding reverence, supplication, and respect. In the opening lines of his *Theogony*, for example, Hesiod records how the Muse found him shepherding his lambs on holy Helicon only to chastise him for the 'lies' contained within his verses; the same Muse then imparted the voice of true poetry to him with terrible authority. The Muses of epic poets – the presiding deities of Homer, Virgil, and Milton, at least – are likewise respectfully invoked to govern, bless, monitor, and properly enthuse the work of the inspired singer. Only Gray's Muse so much forsakes her dignity as to lay beside her chosen poet on the ground – 'at ease reclined in rustic state'. She offers her thoughtful inspiration from a decidedly terrestrial point of view. Gray thus seems anxious not only to underscore the familiarity of his moral, but even to parody – or at the very least to domesticate and consciously to toy with – the very notion that his own verse is in any way inspired or *vatic*.

The third and fourth stanzas further Gray's description of the general stillness of the atmosphere in the midday heat. Once again a commonplace moral is extracted from the observation: the lives of men, like those of insects, are pitiably short and certain only in their destined and unavoidable end:

> Still is the toiling hand of Care;
> The panting herds repose.
> Yet hark, how through the peopled air
> The busy murmur glows!
> The insect youth are on the wing,
> Eager to taste the honeyed spring,
> And float amid the liquid noon:
> Some lightly o'er the current skim,
> Some show their gaily-gilded trim
> Quick-glancing to the sun.
>
> To Contemplation's sober eye
> Such is the race of man:
> And they that creep, and they that fly,
> Shall end where they began.
> Alike the busy and the gay
> But flutter through life's little day,
> In fortune's varying colours dressed:
> Brushed by the hand of rough Mischance,
> Or chilled by age, their airy dance
> They leave, in dust to rest. (*PTG* 51–53)

Gray acknowledged several years after writing these lines that the comparison between mankind and the 'insect youth' who eagerly people the air in this description was 'manifestly stolen' from a poem by Matthew Green first printed in 1732 and entitled 'In the Grotto' – 'not' he hastened to add, 'that I knew it at the time'. Gray claimed (not unreasonably) to have read Green's poem years before, to have thoroughly appreciated the aptness of the parallel and, in so doing, to have absorbed the image so much into his own memory and imagination gradually to have forgotten its original source. Gray's own poem persists in pursuing the literary comparison between the life of man and the ephemeral existence of insects to its grim and logical end (one suspects that Gray may also have had several other works, such as Bernard de Mandeville's *Fable of the Bees*, in mind when he wrote his own poem as well). Green's own verses had finally moralized:

> From Maggot-Youth thro' Change of State
> They feel like us the Turns of Fate;
> Some born to creep have lived to fly,
> And changed Earth's Cells for Dwellings high:
> And some, that did their six Wings keep,
> Before they died, been forced to creep.
> They Politicks, like our, profess;
> The greater prey upon the less.
> Some strain on Foot huge loads to bring,
> Some toil incessant on the Wing:
> Nor from their vigorous schemes desist
> Till Death; & then are never mist.
> Some frolick, toil, marry, increase,
> Are sick & well, have War & Peace,
> And broke with Age in half a Day
> Yield to Successors, & away.[6]

Gray chooses characteristically to undercut the earnestness and morbid sincerity of Green's lines with his own, more gentle-handed humour. Having drawn the most obvious lesson from the scene before him, the 'poor moralist' of Gray's poem is turned upon by the very insects whose lives he has so summarily and complacently dismissed. The fifth stanza of Gray's poem in fact turns all that has preceded it playfully on its head:

> Methinks I hear in accents low
> The sportive kind reply:
> Poor moralist! and what art thou?
> A solitary fly!
> Thy joys no glittering female meets,
> No hive hast thou of hoarded sweets,
> No painted plumage to display:
> On hasty wings thy youth is flown;
> Thy sun is set, thy spring is gone ————
> We frolic, while 'tis May. (*PTG* 53)

---

[6]   Reprinted in Lonsdale, *PTG* 52.

Although we may at first be tempted to dismiss the Horatian theme encapsulated here as yet another literary commonplace, it is only on a closer reading that we realize that the *Ode* does not technically belong within the established traditions of the *carpe diem* poem at all – there are for the poet, at least, no more *diei* left to be seized. 'Thy sun is set, thy spring is gone': the very opportunity to live has already and irrevocably been missed; the sensual pleasures of this world – the several consolations of companionship, wealth, and security – have passed away as surely and as certainly as the irretrievable hours of one's own youth. For all of Gray's literary playfulness throughout the poem, then, thematically and fundamentally it is his pessimism and not his hope that prevails. The light-hearted tone of these lines conceals a sympathetic anxiety concerning the state of West's health; the *Ode* at the same time, however, articulates a genuine apprehension regarding the possibilities of his own future – an apprehension strikingly similar to the anxiety indirectly given voice within his most recent translations.

Gray was nevertheless rather pleased with himself in having been able to respond to West's own 'Ode' on the spring with such a casually undertaken yet carefully crafted piece as his own. 'Noontide' stood as a kind of 'answering poem' to West's own work, and Gray was more than happy with the result. He may even have been surprised to find that in writing in English he need lose none of the richness he had so long cultivated in his Latin compositions. The words, phrases, and conceits of the classics (both ancient and modern) were now so inseparably a part of himself that they seemed to rise to his pen and to his lips unbidden and unawares.

*

On about 3 June, then, Gray included his *Ode* in a letter to West, and waited at Stoke with perhaps slightly more anticipation than usual for his friend's response. He was rather nonplussed when, just a few day's later, the same packet was returned to him unopened. There was no cover to inform him of the reason for the letter's return, nor was there any written indication at all as to why the pages – Gray checked again to see that they had been properly addressed to West at Popes – had not been delivered and received as usual. Gray did not himself know the Mitchells, but they would by now surely have recognized his name and perhaps even his handwriting from his frequent correspondence as being a close friend of West's. Had his friend's health taken a turn for the worse? The fine June weather continued, but Gray's peace of mind was now troubled. He spent the mornings and the evenings as usual in the company of his mother and his aunts, and in the afternoons he still walked among the nearby fields with a chosen volume in his hands, but he must now have found his attention frequently wandering and imperfect. His eyes were now more often than not fixed with mock study on his book, and the words on the page swam before his vision. He is likely to have found himself reading the same passages twice over with an intense focus on many things, but with still no better understanding of the meaning of the words themselves. His thoughts returned constantly to his friend. His correspondence with West had within the past few months, he gradually became convinced, been so frequent and so regular that the return of his most recent could not but be interpreted so as to herald something amiss. Try as he might to deny the possibility of there being anything terribly wrong all day, as darkness fell his thoughts must again have turned to West, and again his darkest suspicions would have chilled his heart. So real was his dread – so uncomfortable was his anxiety – that he could not even pick up his pen again to write to West, and thus risk the chance of having yet another letter to his friend returned to Stoke unopened.

By the beginning of the third week of June, Gray was waiting for the blow to fall – and fall it did, in the most disconcerting manner possible. Turning by chance through the June number of the *London Magazine* – perhaps sitting in the parlour at Stoke one morning – Gray found his attention momentarily arrested by some verses which interrupted the otherwise prosaic columns of the newspaper. He must have read their title once, caught his breath, and immediately felt a sensation of nausea spiral through his head and chest. The lines were titled only 'On the Death of Richard West, Esq.'. Gray would have blinked, read the title again, and stared hard at West's name, unable and unwilling to believe his eyes. Unlike the texts which had within the past two weeks insisted on eluding his concentrated attention and sliding from his consciousness, the letters which formed West's name must have held themselves on the page with remorseless fixity and cauterized themselves into Gray's heart. He glanced quickly through the verses themselves, searching more for any clues they might offer as to who had written them than paying any real attention to their specific meaning. The lines Gray read were as follows:

> While surfeited with Life each hoary knave
> Grows, here, immortal, & eludes the Grave,
> Thy virtues immaturely met their Fate,
> Cramp'd in the Limits of too short a Date.
> Thy Mind not exercised so oft in vain,
> In Health was gentle, and composed in Pain:
> Successive Tryal still refined thy Soul,
> And plastic Patience perfected the Whole.

A friendly Aspect, not informed by art;
An Eye, that looked the Meaning of thy Heart;
A Tongue with simple Truth & Freedom fraught,
The Faithful Index of thy honest Thought.
Thy pen disdain'd to seek the servile Ways
Of partial Censure, and more partial Praise:
Thro' every Tongue it flow'd in nervous Ease,
With sense to polish & with Wit to please.
No lurking Venom from thy pencil fell;
Thine was the kindest Satyre, liveing well:
The Vain, the Loose, the Base, might blush to see
In what Thou wert, what they themselves should be.
Let me not charge on Providence a Crime,
Who snatch'd thee blooming to a better clime,
To raise those Virtues to a higher Sphere:
Virtues which only could have starved thee here.[7]

The wave of disbelief that swept through Gray's frame must have left little room for any conscious thought. As he tried slowly to recover his reason, he reread the verses, and thought he recognized in elements of the personal details included in the poem's language the touch of someone who had known West well. He just as quickly suspected Thomas Ashton to have been the author of the newspaper elegy.

Gray's insight was correct. Ashton had been living that spring with Walpole at Downing Street, where he was officially serving in his capacity as 'Chaplain to the Right Honorable Earl of Orford' (Sir Robert Walpole had immediately been created Earl of Orford following his resignation from Parliament several months earlier). Ashton had already begun to enjoy some success, too, as preacher in the Chapel Royal at Somerset House; he had only two weeks earlier been appointed as rector of Aldington, in north Lancashire, a Crown living he had obtained thanks to Walpole's influence with Henry Pelham. Ashton almost certainly learned of West's death through his constant contact with Walpole. Walpole had as recently as May been in touch with West himself; the Mitchells, upon the death of their houseguest, must have felt compelled to notify only those friends of West who were of such exalted social standing. Gray immediately sat down to write to Ashton, soliciting in his letter any further information that the latter might be able to provide concerning their friend's final days and hours. His letter was an angry one, and his anger appeared ready to overflow and direct itself toward anyone or anything outside his small and self-selected circle of friends and family. Gray confessed to Ashton that he had already

---

[7]   Reprinted in Duncan C. Tovey, *Gray and His Friends* (Cambridge, 1890) 171–72.

supposed West to be dead. He was still shocked by the manner in which he had received the news and justifiably outraged by the Mitchells' insensitivity. His letter was written and sent on 17 June:

> This melancholy day is the first that I have had any notice of my Loss in poor West, and that only by so unexpected a Means as some Verses published in a Newspaper (they are fine & true & I believe may be your own). I had indeed some reason to suspect it some days since from receiving a letter of my own to him sent back unopen'd. The stupid People had put it no Cover, nor thought it worth while to write one Line to inform me of the reason, tho' by knowing how to direct, they must imagine I was his friend. I am a fool indeed to be surprizd [sic] at meeting with Brutishness or want of Thought among Mankind; what I would desire is, that you would have the goodness to tell me, what you know of his death, more particularly as soon as you have any Leisure . . . (*CTG* 213–14)

'I have no one to enquire of', Gray pointedly reminded Ashton in a postscript, 'but yourself'.

Whatever information Ashton was able to pass on to Gray concerning the precise circumstances of West's death – if indeed he took the time to answer Gray's letter in any great detail – has not survived. West had already been buried with very little ceremony at Hatfield. His friends were left carelessly and rather heartlessly to mourn his loss however they saw fit. Ashton's lines attempt to commemorate West both by suggesting, familiarly, that his life was itself his finest and most inimitable piece of 'poetry' ('Thine was the kindest Satyre, liveing well'), and by concluding with a consolation which had likewise already become a commonplace in elegiac narrative – that is, by suggesting that his life had only been 'snatched' by Providence to be raised to a higher sphere – a 'better clime' more appropriate to its delicate, ethereal beauty. Gray's protestations of the truths they contain notwithstanding, Ashton's stanzas are predictable and perfunctory. Ashton had never really shared the literary abilities or even the literary interests of West and Gray, and one suspects that his ostentatious show of mourning on this occasion was motivated at least as much by a desire to bolster his growing reputation as a popular public figure (even Walpole joked that he was beginning to become 'mad' with his own 'fame'), as it was by any genuine sense of loss.

Gray, on the other hand, was very close to being in a genuine state of shock. Before leaving Stoke at the end of June, he tried to put his own feelings into words – words written not for the public consumption of the newspapers or even of his friends, but rather for himself and, one cannot help but feel, for West. In the first impulse of his grief he characteristically turned not to his native tongue, but to Latin. West's passing that spring was too recent an event fully to be digested and made sense of, and Gray searched for some way to connect his friend's suffering and death to all that had gone before. Since his return from Europe he had toyed from time to time with the idea of completing the epic 'meta-physical' poem he had first begun in Florence two years earlier. *De Prin-cipiis Cogitandi* was a work that Gray had shared with West, having sent him the first fifty-three lines from Italy in April, 1741. He may have felt that in resuming work on the poem, he was in some way perpetu-ating contact with West himself. The overtly epistemological concerns that had only sluggishly motivated the poem throughout its first two hundred and seven lines were now, however, abruptly abandoned. The beginning of a new 'book' in the work openly laments the loss of the individual who had provided both the 'inspiration' and the 'course' of such an ambitious poetic work; the lines are impressive in their noble simplicity and well worth quoting in full:

Hactenus haud segnis Naturae arcana retexi
Musarum interpres, primusque Britanna per arva
Romano liquidum deduxi flumine rivum.
    Cum Tu opere in medio, spes tanti et causa laboris,
Linquis, et aeternam fati te condis in umbram!
Vidi egomet duro graviter concussa dolore
Pectora, in alterius non unquam lenta dolorem;
Et languere oculus vidi et pallescere amantem
Vultum, quo nunquam Pietas nisi rar, Fidesque,
Altus amor Veri, et purum spirabat Honestum.
Visa tamen tardi demum inclementia morbi
Cessare est, reducemque iterum roseo ore Salutem
Credulus heu longos, ut quondam, fallere soles:
Heu spes nequicquam dulces, atque irrita vota!
Heu maestos soles, sine te quos ducere flendo
Per desideria, et questus iam cogor inanes!
    At Tu, sancta anima, et nostri non indiga luctus,
Stellanti templo, sincerique aetheris igne,
Unde orta es, fruere; atque oh si secura, nec ultra
Mortalis, notos olim miserata labores
Respectes, tenuesque vacet cognoscere curas;
Humanam si forte alta de sede procellam
Contemplere, metus stimulosque cupidinis acres,
Guadiaque et gemitus, parvoque in corde tumultum
Irarum ingentem, et saevos sub pectore fluctus:
Respice, et has lacrimas, memori quas ictus amore
Fundo; quod possum, iuxta lugere sepulcrum
Dum iuvat, et mutae vana haec iactare favillae. (*PTG* 328; 332)

[So far had I, interpreter of the Muses, assiduously uncovered the secrets of Nature and first led a lucid stream from the Roman river through British fields. But now you, the inspiration and the cause of so great a task, have deserted me in the midst of it and have hidden yourself in the eternal shadow of Death! I myself watched your breast cruelly racked by bitter suffering, a breast never slow to respond to another's pain; I watched your eyes grow dull and your loving face grow pale, a face in which only the exalted affection, and loyalty, and deep love of truth, and unsullied integrity were expressed. At last the harshness of your lingering sickness seemed to be abating, and I hoped for the return of Health, with rosy cheeks, and you yourself with it, my dear Favonius! Foolishly trusting, alas, that we might spend the long sunny days as before. Alas, the hopes, sweet but vain, and the ineffectual prayers! Alas, the sunny days, now spent in mourning, which I am forced to pass without you, in weeping because you are not there, and in vain complaints.

But you, blessed spirit, who do not need my grief, rejoice in the starry circuit of the heavens and the fire of the pure ether whence you sprang. But, if, released from cares as you are, but not beyond mortal concerns, you look back with pity on once-familiar toils and are free to perceive our trivial anxieties; if, by chance, you look down from your lofty seat on the storm of human passion, the fears, the fierce promptings of desire, the joys and sorrows and the tumult of rage so huge in our tiny hearts, the furious surges of the breast; then look back on these tears, also, which, stricken with love, I pour out in memory to you; this is all I can do, while my only wish is to mourn at your tomb and address these empty words to your silent ashes.]

Gray's lines appear to betray a slightly unorthodox anxiety concerning the immortality of the individual, human soul; the second verse paragraph, at least, might be interpreted as questioning the belief that a man's individuality – his personality and its thoughts, values, and concerns – extends beyond this corporeal world and into the eternal universe. The poet seems to be even more deeply troubled, however, by the possibility that having ascended into the 'starry circuit of the heavens' and the 'fire of the pure ether', West's 'blessed spirit' will no longer concern itself with the friends he has left behind. He is worried that his own friend, like Chaucer's Troilus in his famous palinode, looking down upon the earth from the height of Heaven, will only 'laugh right at the wo / of them that wepten for his death so forte'. The dead are simply and obviously beyond the cares of this world.

Yet, like the later *Elegy*, this fragment of *De Principiis Cogitandi* also offers some fundamental speculation – a speculation approaching theological inquiry – regarding the manner in which individual souls are *affected* by death. The only option open to the mourner left on earth is to shed fruitless tears and pour out 'empty words' to a cold and silent tomb. But is anybody, anywhere, really listening? Who exactly benefits from such tears? The 'blessed spirit' of the departed manifestly does not 'need' the grief of the human mourner, who now confesses in the dark light of mortality that his own fears and desires, his own joys and sorrows, are in any case of very little consequence in the grander scheme of things.

The fragment of 'Liber Secundus' which Gray added to *De Principiis Cogitandi* in June, 1742 – a fragment that clearly stands on its own as an elegantly crafted and profoundly felt elegy for his friend – is only the first of no less than four poems that owe their existence to the specific circumstances of West's passing. In the months immediately following the event of West's death, Gray worked his way through his anger and his grief, as might by now naturally be expected, by attempting to come to terms with his loss in writing. As the first of several such responses, the Latin poem is arguably the most intensely visceral – the most emotionally devastated and traumatized – of Gray's poems commemorating West's death. Yet it is also the least sophisticated, at least in terms of the final answer it offers to the questions posed for so comparatively young a man by the very problem of mortality itself. 'Gray's completed poems', as the critic Marshall Brown has written, 'typically come two or three to a type'.[8] The elegy contained within the fragment of *De Principiis Cogitandi*, Book II is a 'type' of poem in a more literal sense as well, insofar as it is an imperfect anticipation and patterning forth of things yet to come. The impact of West's death in the summer of 1742 would in many ways remain fresh to Gray throughout his life; Nicholls's recollections remind us that he was never fully to accept nor ever entirely to be reconciled with the fact of his friend's loss. As the summer matured, however, he would find himself able to address both his friend's death and the nature of his own enduring grief in a series of poems that sought with increasing sophistication to make sense of the seemingly paradoxical, emotional spectacle of a stricken and barren grief surrounded by a thriving, joyful, and apparently indifferent universe.

*

Gray returned to London toward the end of June. The simple change of place, he felt, would do him some good. In London he would at least be able personally to undertake any inquiries he still had into the circumstances surrounding West's final days. For once, too, the very bustle of the city might perhaps work to provide something of a diversion. The hours and days seemed that summer to pass more swiftly when tolled by the many, clamorous Cornhill church bells than they did when

---

[8]   Brown, *Preromanticism*, 11.

counted by the ringing of the tower of St. Giles, in the summer's heavy stasis at Stoke. The season to which he had looked forward with such anticipation seemed, in any event, long ago to have lost its power to charm or to beguile him. There were also several practical matters to which he needed to attend. While at home he again consulted with his mother concerning their joint financial fortune. The full impact the folly of Philip Gray's Essex mansion was to have on their lives may only now have begun to sink in. Some serious retrenchments would have to be made, and Gray finally acknowledged openly (to his continental correspondents, at least) that even if he had no intention of ever seriously entering the legal profession, he would once again at least have to make a show to his mother, his aunts, and to his London acquaintances, of preparing to embark upon the course of study leading to a law degree. Time had done little to allay Gray's dread of the sort of life he would necessarily lead while preparing for such a career in the London law courts – the very sight of the Temple and of the other haunts of the city attorneys must have reminded him of West's own drudgery and the toll it had taken on his health. One other option, however, yet remained open to him. Unlike the barristers and sergeants who pled their cases in the common-law and equity courts, such as the King's Bench, the Court of Common Pleas, and the Chancery (and who in fact held no degree, as such, but were simply 'called to the bar' after a sufficient period of time was deemed to have passed since they first began their training as barristers) those advocates entitled to appear before the admiralty and ecclesiastical or Church courts were required to have received a Doctor's degree in civil law from either Oxford or Cambridge. Instead of taking an unwholesome and fusty lodging in the Inner Temple and eating his terms 'in hall' in the city, then, Gray could return to the familiar ground of Cambridge, where he could at least advance the pretense of reading for a Bachelor of Civil Law in comparative peace and comfort. Combining as it did the appearance of diligence and an eminently practical attention to the self-sacrificing demands of economy within the various possibilities inherent in a necessarily self-motivated and self-disciplined plan of study for a due amount of time to be spent in continuing to explore his own chosen course of both modern and classical reading, such a plan suited Gray perfectly. If circumstances dictated that he absolutely had no other choice but eventually to become a lawyer, he could at least become a lawyer the Cambridge way.

Sometime in mid-July, Gray wrote to his friends Chute and Mann in Italy. Mann had recently received his formal appointment to the Grand Duchy of Florence – 'veramente un Ministrone, & King of the Mediterranean', Gray declared exultantly – and the two friends had in their joint letters to Gray gamely kept up the pretense of including him as best they might in all the lively pastimes that still flourished in and around the

Casa Manetti (and now, too, at Chute's own recently engaged lodgings at the Casa Ambrosio). In a letter to Mann written late in June, Horace Walpole had already informed the minister of West's death ('a friend of mine', Walpole had reminded Mann, 'whom you have heard me often mention'), and had even included in his packet a copy of Ashton's commemorative verses.[9] West's passing is not mentioned in Gray's own letter to the pair. Gray seems grateful for the opportunity once again humourously to lament his own absence from Italy ('Do the Frogs of Arno sing as sweetly, as they did in my Days? do you sup al fresco?'), and at least to pretend that his own summer had been so busy that he had not had time – or even that he had been too bored – to take part in any of the more fashionable diversions of the season. Responding to a query from Chute about Ranelagh Gardens, the new London pleasure-grounds that had been opened to the public for the first time on 24 May of that same year, Gray wrote derisively,

> I have never been at Ranelagh Gardens since they were open'd (for what does it signify to me?) but they do not succeed. People see it once or twice & so they go to Vaux-hall. well, but it is not a very great Design, very new, finely lighted? well, yes, aye, very fine truly; & so they yawn and go to Vaux-hall. & then it's too hot, & then it's too cold, & here's a Wind, & there's a Damp; & so the Women go to Bed, & Men to a Bawdy-House. you are to take Notice, that in our Country Delicacy & Indelicacy amount to much the same thing, the first will not be pleased with any Thing, & the other cannot: however to do us Justice, I think, we are a reasonable, but by no means a pleasurable People, & to mend us we must have a Dash of the French, & Italian. yet I don't know how, Traveling does not produce its right Effect – I find, I am talking; but You are to attribute it to my haveing at last found a Pen, that writes. (*CTG* 214–15)

The simple movement of Gray's thoughts in this passage is in many ways more intriguing than the precise details of what he has to say (his judgement on Ranelagh's comparative 'failure' as a fashionable London amusement, it need hardly be observed, was premature). 'Haveing at last found a Pen': Gray writes through his own grief. The disjointed syntax and hesitancy toward the end of the paragraph quoted above find the writer surprised at the self-dictating current and fluency of his own words and sentiments. The passage likewise finds Gray rather tellingly questioning the efficacy of the manner in which he has spent his own, recent past. 'Traveling does not produce its right Effect' is a harsh judgement to be pronounced by one who only months ago returned home

---

[9] WC xvii.470.

after two and a half years spent living abroad. Gray appears on some level morosely to feel that his time has been misspent, and to suggest that at least some of that time – the months that he had passed quarrelling with Walpole – might have been spent rather among friends and family who seem now to have loved him more deeply and sincerely than an individual such as Walpole ever could.

Gray's thoughts having briefly been turned towards the subject of writing, however, his mind led him naturally to the subject of books. The better part of the letter addressed specifically to Mann concerned the substantial cargo of volumes he had assembled at his friend's request and was now shipping (via Mann's brother Gal) to Florence. Most of the books were histories and sixteenth- and seventeenth-century state papers that were of little interest to Gray himself (of a seven-volume Folio selection of Lord Burlington's papers he quipped, 'it would be hard to assemble a pocket-volume worth having'). He was only slightly more enthusiastic about some anti-Catholic propaganda about which he suggests Mann, living in Italy, ought to be aware, as well as about the shipment's 'lighter' content of plays, and Crébillon's *Le Sopha*. Marivaux's *La Vie de Marianne* had been thrown in for good measure for Chute. Gray seemed by the end of the letter to have written himself into a better mood. 'If you can bully the Pope out of the Apollo Belvedere', he concluded, referring to the famous marble torso in the possession of the Vatican, 'well & good. I'm not against it'. Parliament had been prorogued only days before, he noted in a post-script, having intimated that he was himself headed back to Stoke Poges 'for one easy fortnight' before moving back to Cambridge and recommencing his legal studies 'in earnest'.

III. Homeward Returning

It was difficult for Gray to return to Stoke Poges that August. The heavy heat of summer now blanketed the valley in its stillness, and the languor of a satisfied fullness hung like a vast curtain over the rich and ripening fields, shading the hazy purple mass of the woods beyond. The general activity of the world appeared in the country to have been thrown into a genial and pleasantly fecund mode of slow motion. All was hushed and drowsy; the very tolling of the neighbouring church bell at St. Giles seemed, by the time it sounded in the ears of the residents at West End House only several fields away, rather to have taken its time in ambling among the lanes and hedgerows, before reluctantly recalling its task of alerting its listeners to the negligible passing of the hours of the day, or lazily calling them to an evening service.

Apart from the fact that the green of the trees was of a deeper and dustier hue, however, or that the hedgerows were fuller and the 'tribute' of the nearby fields higher and nearer to harvest than when he had left only a month before, little at Stoke had changed for Gray himself. Pushing open the door of what must have long been designated his own little room in his aunt's cottage, he seemed ever so slightly to have stepped backward in time. The grief over his friend's death that he thought he had begun to put behind him while in London returned once more, in these surroundings, with a force undiluted in its strength and in its concomitant, debilitating sense of isolation. Gray discovered that his own deepest feelings lay trapped and fixed within the remorseless amber of the circumstantial dispositions of this world, and he sensed probably from the moment of his return to Stoke that if he was ever effectively to move on with his life – that if his resolution to return to Cambridge, even if it were only to resume his own studies and at least establish a pattern for the coming days and nights, was to be at all fulfilled – the next two weeks would have to see some kind of mental and emotional breakthrough. Something – somewhere and somehow – would have to give.

Sitting down once again to the books and to the bundles of papers which he had left neatly piled on the surface of his desk and had catalogued so carefully within its drawers, Gray turned for what must have seemed the hundredth time to those copies of the letters that has passed between himself and West while both had been at university. Passing his fingers lightly over the surface of the paper, the months and years may have seemed to fall away, and he once again appeared, if only momentarily, to make some slight contact with his friend. One set of sheets in particular stood out and seemed now to solicit Gray's particular attention. They formed the letter that West had originally written from Christ Church and sent to Gray at Peterhouse on 4 July, 1737. West had confessed himself in those pages recently to have been 'very ill' and, indeed, felt himself at the time of writing, 'still hardly recovered'. He had typically amused himself at one point in his illness in attempting a loose translation or imitation of Tibullus' *Elegies* III.v – a work that he expected Gray readily to recall from their days together at Eton. To the sentiments of Tibullus' elegy, West had for good measure added those expressed by Alexander Pope on his own poor health in a letter to Richard Steele originally written in July, 1712, and eventually printed by Steele as *Guardian* No. 132 in 1713. In that epistle Pope had predicted: 'The morning after my *Exit*, the Sun will rise as bright as ever, the Flowers smell as sweet, the Plants spring as green, the World will proceed in its old Course, People will laugh as heartily, and Marry as fast as they were used to do'.[10] West, it will be remembered, had entitled his own version of Tibullus' lament 'Ad Amicos', and he

---

[10]   *The Guardian*, edited with an introduction by John Calhoun Stephens (Lexington, KY: University Press of Kentucky, 1982) 441.

appropriately sent it to his friends at Cambridge protesting that he did
so 'not to divert them, for it cannot, but merely to show them how
sincere I was when sick'. One passage in particular called attention to
itself now as particularly meaningful to Gray. Having first lamented his
own separation from his friends, West had rhetorically asked the 'Stern
Powers of Fate' just what sins or injustices he had committed so to have
had his health taken from him in such an untimely manner; sickness had
so beaten him down, he confessed, that his own shade would pass
'willing' into the 'Stygian deserts' of death. 'But why repine', he asked
in conclusion:

> does life deserve my sigh?
> Few will lament my loss whene'er I die.
> For those the wretches I despise or hate,
> I neither envy nor regard their fate.
> For me, whene'er all-conquering Death shall spread
> His wings around my unrepining head,
> I care not; though this face be seen no more,
> The world will pass as chearful as before,
> Bright as before the day-star will appear,
> The fields as verdant, and the skies as clear;
> Nor storms nor comets will my doom declare,
> Nor signs on earth, nor portents in the air;
> Unknown and silent will depart my breath,
> Nor Nature e'er take notice of my death.
> Yet some there are (ere spent my vital days)
> Within whose breasts my tomb I wish to raise.
> Lov'd in my life, lamented in my end,
> Their praise would crown me as their precepts mend:
> To them may these fond lines my name endear,
> Not from the Poet but the Friend sincere. (CTG 63–64)

Roger Lonsdale was undoubtedly correct in assuming that Gray had
these lines particularly in mind when he wrote his own *Sonnet* on the
death of Richard West in August, 1742; the poem is the first of the
further three elegiac poems in English Gray wrote that summer to commemorate his friend's passing, and to explore the implications of West's
fate for himself. 'West's prediction', Lonsdale has written, 'that nature
would be indifferent to his death and his hope that some friend would
nevertheless remember him may well have influenced the content and
tone of Gray's (sonnet), which describes the indifference of nature to his
own grief.'[11] Gray's sonnet (which was not published in the poet's own

---

[11] Lonsdale in *PTG* 65.

lifetime, but was simply transcribed into his Commonplace Book where it is dated 'at Stoke, Aug: 1742') subsequently attracted attention most for its supposedly deliberate use of an elaborate and highly artificial poetic diction. Indeed, it is largely because of the attention and criticisms of later writers such as Wordsworth and Hopkins, that Gray's poem remains to this day, after those of Shakespeare, Milton and Keats, one of the best-known sonnets in the English tradition:

> In vain to me the smiling mornings shine,
> And reddening Phoebus lifts his golden fire:
> The birds in vain their amorous descant join,
> Or cheerful fields resume their green attire:
> These ears, alas! for other notes repine,
> A different object do these eyes require.
> My lonely anguish melts no heart but mine;
> And in my mind the imperfect joys expire.
> Yet morning smiles the busy race to cheer,
> And new-born pleasure brings to happier men:
> The fields to all their wonted tribute bear;
> To warm their little loves the birds complain.
> I fruitless mourn to him that cannot hear,
> And weep the more because I weep in vain. (PTG 67–68)

Critical discussion of Gray's lines for a great many years concentrated almost exclusively on the debate initiated by Wordsworth's criticism that the language of the sonnet was excessively artificial. The very 'artifice' of Gray's lines was thought by some to be an indication that the work itself was not a deeply or even genuinely *felt* poem, but rather a simple rhetorical gesture – an exercise in, rather than a display of, grief. One might very well argue, however, that the *Sonnet* on the Death of Richard West, far from having been written *invita Minerva*, was at once the loneliest and the most emotionally *fraught* of the three English poems written that summer. In the fragment of 'Liber Secundus' of *De Principiis Cogitandi*, Gray appeared to question the motivations and the efficacy of human grief itself, and to have concluded (if only temporarily) that the 'sunny days, spent now in mourning' were days effectively wasted. Gray's grief, however sincere, could never hope to evoke any response from West's own silent ashes; his words were 'empty' of power, his tears were shed in vain, just as his prayers seemed to have been offered up to the deaf ears of an unlistening God. The *Sonnet* once again and in a similar manner forcefully evokes and laments this sense of impotence in the face of the greater forces of the living universe. The entire world is in fact alive with a meaning which can possess no meaning for the poet himself. Not only is the natural world indifferent to the grief

experienced by Gray following West's passing, but the writer, too, is conversely and equally unmoved by the spectacle of life in nature. Life and
Death – the binary opposites that might normally be expected to find
their meaning *only* as they stand in relation to one another – in the
Sonnet effectively cancel one another out; the result is a grim stasis of
'nihilissimo', a state of self-perpetuated and self-perpetuating non-being.

The referential details of Gray's poem have been discussed at great
length by critics over the years, and the neat manner in which the poem,
anticipating the *Elegy*, in some ways rhetorically doubles back upon
itself (the spectacle of Gray's 'vanity' in mourning the death of West
comes to stand as an emblem of the vanity of all human attempts at
mourning, thus seeming to call into question the validity and value of
the poem itself) has been justly appreciated. One of Gray's earlier biographers, R. W. Ketton-Cremer, suggested that poem was most legitimately to be read as the last of the three poems Gray completed that
summer. Having first attempted in the *Ode to Adversity* and the *Eton
Ode* to 'relate his private sorrow to wider philosophical issues', Ketton-
Cremer wrote, 'suddenly, as so often happens after bereavement, the
sense of utter loss returned, as stark and hopeless on the day when he
first learned of West's death'.[12]

There is no solid textual evidence, however, to privilege such a scenario in the face of other speculations. Speaking more specifically in
terms of the circumstances of Gray's life and state of mind that summer,
the *Sonnet* would appear more logically to have been among the *first*
responses to West's death, rather than among the last. There is, in other
words, no reason to believe that the *Sonnet* is to be read as evidence of
emotional back-sliding on Gray's part. The poem's sense of helplessness
and voicelessness in the face of loss is of a piece with the uncertainty
and the hesitancy expressed in *De Principiis Cogitandi*. The poem might
just as easily embody the initial shock and trauma of bereavement, rather
than a considered or cynical response to that grief. It was natural for
Gray to move through his grief by means of his pen; the *Sonnet* looks
to have been a confession of sorts that in the first glare of such grief one
is at once both naturally and paradoxically inconsolatory. Gray's pen
can still only, at this early stage of his grief and transition, state the emotionally obvious.

*

In the what might then have been the second of the three poems he
wrote in the summer of 1742, Gray grappled with his own attempts to
provide some kind of answer to such inconsolation. The *Ode to Adver-*

---

[12] Ketton-Cremer, 64.

sity is perhaps the least emotionally successful of the three English poems written to commemorate West's death, if only because it is the most pious and traditional – and, consequently, given the continued and unremitting intensity of Gray's own feelings for his friend, the most forced or emotionally strained. Its reassurances, however boldly stated, ring false. The work might even be described as tentative. A synoptic viewing of the *Adversity Ode* alongside the *Sonnet* and the *Eton Ode* reveals Gray to have been groping, in all three works, towards some sort of explanation – some sort of ontological *apologia* – for West's death. Like the *Sonnet*, the text of the *Ode to Adversity* was carefully copied by Gray into his Commonplace Book and similarly dated 'at Stoke, Aug. 1742'; unlike the *Sonnet* (a work which Gray dismissed in his only recorded, critical judgement on the piece to have been 'bad'), the *Ode to Adversity* was perceived by the poet himself to be a competent enough effort to be published in his own lifetime. The work was eventually included in the 1753 edition of Gray's *Six Poems* illustrated by Bentley; it was reprinted just two years later in the fourth volume of Dodsley's popular *Collection of Poems*. In his modern edition of Gray's poems, Roger Lonsdale justified his decision to place the *Ode to Adversity* after both the *Sonnet* and the *Eton Ode* with the observation that the poem 'appears to have been intended as to some extent a reply to' the latter work. Lonsdale observed:

> To assume that *Adversity* was written first . . . entails a strained reading of the *Eton Ode*, which can hardly be shown to embody the attitudes adopted in *Adversity*. It is more natural to read *Adversity* as a mature and positive confrontation of the evils of adult life that he described with such unrelieved gloom in the *Eton Ode*. If the conclusion of the earlier poem is that man is doomed to suffer, the mottoes from Aeschylus which Gray adopted for *Adversity* emphasize that suffering may lead to wisdom and various social virtues. In particular, adversity can lead to a deeper understanding of the suffering of others. The characteristic sense of alienation in Gray's poetry is here, intellectually at least, overcome by a willed self-dedication to that benevolence which his age accepted as the root of all virtue. The resolution undoubtedly represents an advance in Gray's thinking from the *Eton Ode*. The change of heart remains only an abstract proposition, but the stern discipline, both spiritual and technical, which it involves demands respect.[13]

Yet might not this supposedly 'mature and positive confrontation of the evils of adult life' just as readily be shown to have been a step on the way to the *Eton Ode* – an attempt (not wholly successful) to seek consolation and reassurance in those classical and spiritual sources from

[13] Lonsdale, *PTG*, 69.

which such consolation and reassurance were traditionally *expected* to have been found? The simple fact that the *Eton Ode* would in time achieve greater fame and currency among English readers – and the fact too that it is on many levels a more satisfyingly complete poetic work – might argue that readers instinctively have responded to the quintessential human resolution of that poem in favour of the pious and familiar consolations of philosophy to which Gray had given voice in *Adversity*. The simple fact, in other words, that readers are more likely this day to encounter and to enjoy the *Eton Ode* rather that the *Ode to Adversity* suggests that it is on some level the work which was derived more 'truly' from the poet's own feelings on the occasion of West's lost – that it is a more honest work, insofar as it accepts rather than forcefully suppresses the agnostic impulse that haunts all three works. It was only natural that Gray should look first to his classical and spiritual education to help him through such a crisis; yet as so many of those who have passed through such a crisis will recognize, it is precisely in the midst of such trauma that a strictly doctrinal reassurance has a way of demonstrating its own insufficiency – of falling short of the mark. We need perhaps to step back for one moment and ask ourselves just what Gray was attempting to do with the form and purpose of the elegiac impulse which these three poems – four, if we include the Latin fragment of *De Principiis Cogitandi* – illustrate in such dramatically different ways.

All elegies within the English tradition seek on some level not only to commemorate and to memorialize the dead, but look as well to offer some explanation for the awful and grimly irresistible *fact* of death. They enable us to undertake what Freud so accurately described as the consuming *work* of mourning. Many, like Thomas Nashe's famous 'Litany in the Time of Plague' (1600), take the form of public prayers and supplications:

> Adieu, farewell, earth's bliss,
> This world uncertain is:
> Fond are life's lustful joys,
> Death proves them all but toys,
> None from his darts can fly,
> I am sick, I must die.
>   Lord, have mercy on us!
>
> Rich men, trust not in wealth,
> Gold cannot buy you health,
> Physic himself must fade.
> All things to end are made,
> The plague full swift goes by,

I am sick, I must die.
   Lord, have mercy on us!

Beauty is but a flower
Which wrinkles will devour,
Brightness falls from the air,
Queens have died young and fair,
Dust hath closed Helen's eye.
I am sick, I must die.
   Lord, have mercy on us![14]

The formula of response in the last two lines of Nashe's verse stanzas is repeated throughout his poem, and this repetition itself helps to bring a semblance of order, comfort, and resolution to the reader. The 'Litany' stresses both the finality and the universality of death – even the legendary beauty of Helen of Troy, the poet reminds us, has long since been reduced to a tracery of dust and ashes. The acceptance of one's own death – of one's inevitable mortality – is translated through the hypnotic repetition of elegiac, poetic form into an enabling gesture of inclusion. The 'lustful joys' of this world are indeed transitory, we find ourselves admitting almost with a sense of relief and release. All material things will pass into worthlessness, and the vain arts of 'physic' are themselves ephemeral. The imperative of death demands that we look beyond an uncertain world to welcome the destiny ordained by a merciful God. In this we are allowed no other choice: now we live, and now our life is done.

Yet not all elegists can attain to Nashe's impassioned if formally constrained plea for resignation and acceptance. In their implied mimicry of the rituals, gestures, and emotions which constitute the passage through mourning, elegies, for all their fundamental singularity of purpose, mirror the myriad processes and memorial reasoning of individual grief. Some rest in stunned disbelief and defy consolation. The mind simply blinks at the horrible and terrifying glare. Others begin to struggle through the inchoate and incipient steps of loss. Some few (Ben Jonson's slightly baffled poem commemorating Shakespeare, for example, or John Dryden's 1684 'To the Memory of Mr. Oldham') are oddly self-promotional, and appear to seek with an unseemly egoism to perpetuate worldly rivalries beyond the grave. Some resist mourning and rage against the atavistic and democratic injustice of death itself or – and one immediately thinks here of *carpe diem* poems such as Andrew Marvell's celebrated 'To His Coy Mistress', as well as the work of other so-called Cavalier Poets such as Thomas Carew and Robert Herrick –

[14]   See *The Works of Thomas Nashe*, ed. Ronald B. McKerrow, 5 vols. (London: Sidgwick and Jackson, 1910) iii.282–84.

defy the finality of its eternal disaster, flaunting a bold and libidinous defiance in the very teeth of devouring Time. Still others attempt to create consolatory fictions which suggest that death is, to use Donne's vocabulary, simply a 'translation' into a different form of existence – that death and terminal disease can themselves be 'overlived'. It is once again the seventeenth-century poet Ben Jonson, in his delicate epitaph for Salomon Pavy, a child actor and member of the Children of Queen Elizabeth's Chapel who died in 1602 at the age of thirteen, who provides us with a fine example of such a fiction. According to the self-styled 'little story' that Jonson fashions in his elegy for the boy, Pavy was such a talented young actor on the stage and impersonated old men so convincingly and so well, that he fooled even the Parcae, who accordingly took him for an old man in earnest and promptly gathered him to the heavens. The Fates soon recognized their error, but having by then made the child's acquaintance (and having found him 'much too good for earth') they vowed to keep him for themselves. Jonson's verse – the conceit of which is at once elegantly turned and elaborately artificial – is a poetic gem that powerfully combines a certain philosophic resignation in the face of death with the bravery of artistic defiance. Such elegiac narratives in fact often work to form a kind of talismanic defense against mortality, and are best understood if read as the poetic counterparts to the stories contained in collections such as Boccaccio's *Decameron*, stories and acts of articulation which in their very utterance serve to ward off or in some way to deny the *gavòcciolo* of a deadly plague.

Some of the most powerful modern elegies are consumed with anger, yet still recall in their own way Donne's memorable characterization of a Death (in his Holy Sonnet X) which is itself the slave to a greater Fate – a Death that is itself paradoxically condemned to 'die' in the light of our redemption. Hence a poem such as Thom Gunn's 1992 'The Reassurance', which seeks to commemorate a friend who has died before his time:

> About ten days or so
> After we saw you dead
> You came back in a dream.
> I'm all right now you said.
>
> And it *was* you, although
> You were fleshed out again:
> You hugged us all round then,
> And gave your welcoming beam.
>
> How like you to be kind,
> Seeking to reassure.

And, yes, how like my mind
To make itself secure.[15]

Gunn's lines gently and self-deprecatingly capture the human desire – the human *need*, even – to believe that individuality will not be erased in the seemingly merciless obliteration of death. We seek not only reassurance, but also remembrance. We ask both for the sustenance of faith and for some confirmation that we will yet live in the memory-possessed breasts of those we leave behind: that though the person of a man may go, the best part of him stays, and stays forever.

Thomas Gray knew all these things. Each of the three English poems written in the summer of 1742 hesitantly stand at what might be described as a fixed point on the narrative/fictional line of elegiac consolation – each of them attempts to deal with West's death and with Gray's own loneliness using a slightly different strategy, and each arrives at a slightly different conclusion. The *Sonnet* on the death of Richard West, I have suggested, is the earliest of the three poems in terms of the maturity of its emotional response to West's death, and – given its thematic links to Book II of *De Principiis Cogitandi* – it may well have been the first of the poems to have been written. If we accept the suggestion that Gray, after enduring and giving voice to the initial shock of his loss, might naturally then turn to the more supposedly unshakable and unassailable theological and philosophical explanations for human suffering, either the *Ode to Adversity* or the *Eton Ode* might logically stand as the work he next attempted. If we choose to give precedence to the former, however, we establish a line of thought which argues that Gray, although he attempted not only to accept but himself to articulate a resolved, stoic reaction to West's death, was himself emotionally unconvinced of the efficacy of such a grandly and uncompromisingly authoritative response to the fact of human suffering.

The *Ode to Adversity* memorably opens with an epigraph drawn from Aeschylus' *Agamemnon* (ll.176–77) which, in English, reads: 'Zeus, who leads mortals to understanding, has decreed that wisdom can come only through suffering'. Such an epigraph (Gray had alternately toyed with the idea of prefixing to the work a different yet thematically synonymous passage from the same author's *Eumenides* l. 523 – 'It profits one through sorrow to gain wisdom') economically encapsulates, as Lonsdale has suggested, the entire meaning of the work that follows. What Gray in fact does in the *Ode to Adversity* is essentially to parse out a fictional, elegiac narrative from the personifications first given voice by the classical writer. The opening stanzas of Gray's poem invoke the dread goddess, Adversity, and remind the reader of her occupational history:

---

[15]   Thom Gunn, *Collected Poems* (New York, 1994) 471.

Daughter of Jove, relentless power,
Thou tamer of the human breast,
Whose iron scourge and torturing hour,
The bad affright, afflict the best!
Bound in thy adamantine chain
The proud are taught to taste of pain,
And purple tyrants vainly groan
With pangs unfelt before, unpitied and alone.

When first thy Sire to send on earth
Virtue, his darling child, designed,
To thee he gave the heavenly birth,
And bade to form her infant mind.
Stern rugged nurse! thy rigid lore
With patience many a year she bore:
What sorrow was, thou bad'st her know,
And from her she learned to melt at others' woe. (*PTG* 70–71)

Having thus tutored Virtue in the school of human suffering to respond to the 'woes' of others, Adversity herself is then respectfully addressed by the poet, who recapitulates her lessons in temperamental decorum and the solemn worth of the truer and more hard won of human values:

Scared at thy frown terrific, fly
Self-pleasing Folly's idle brood,
Wild Laughter, Noise, and thoughtless Joy,
And leave us leisure to be good.
Light they disperse, and with them go
The summer friend, the flattering foe;
By vain Prosperity received,
To her they vow their truth and are again believed.

Wisdom in sable garb arrayed,
Immersed in rapturous thought profound,
And Melancholy, silent maid
With leaden eyes that loves the ground,
Still on thy solemn steps attend:
Warm Charity, the general friend,
With Justice, to herself severe,
And Pity, dropping soft the sadly-pleasing tear. (*PTG* 71–72)

Only on a second or third reading does one begin to notice that the 'silent maid', Melancholy, is herself distinctly out of place among the stanzas' other personifications, each of which represents, if not an established virtue (as in the case of Wisdom, Charity, and Justice), then at least selfless or generous emotion, such as Pity. Gray seems here to be moving towards a notion that will be more fully and directly articulated in the *Eton Ode*: the idea that the wisdom consequent on human suffering is a painful knowledge, one that may indeed be earned only at the necessary cost of Noise and Folly – themselves no great losses – but which also strips the initiate of laughter, 'thoughtless Joy', and Prosperity. The poem's closing stanzas follow through on this incipient anxiety that the cost of such an understanding is, for many human beings, simply too great or painful a price to pay:

> Oh, gently on thy suppliant's head,
> Dread goddess, lay thy chastening hand!
> Not in thy Gorgon terrors clad,
> Nor circled with the vengeful band
> (As by the impious thou art seen)
> With thundering voice and threatening mien,
> With screaming Horror's funeral cry,
> Despair and fell Disease and ghastly Poverty.
>
> Thy form benign, oh Goddess, wear,
> Thy milder influence impart,
> Thy philosophic train be there
> To soften, not to wound my heart.
> The generous spark extinct revive,
> Teach me to love and to forgive,
> Exact my own defects to scan,
> What others are to feel, and know myself a man. (*PTG* 72–74)

If we need to be educated to virtue through adversity, Gray seems to be saying in these lines, at least permit that virtue in future to be the product of introspection and 'philosophy' – at least allow the Adversity to be abstract or theoretical in contemplation – rather than the result of cruel and wounding experience.

A great many readers have heard in Gray's concern with 'forgiveness' and the notion of an enlightened self-perception in this last stanza specific references to the as yet unresolved quarrel with Walpole. If such is in fact the case, they stand alone as Gray's only hint of public admission that he was at least partly to blame for the rift. More to our purpose in establishing a possible chronology for the three poems, these last stanzas again appear to give first voice to concepts and imagery – the grim quartet of Horror, Despair, Disease, and Poverty – which are developed at greater length and in more explicit detail in the *Eton Ode*. The poem ends in a supplication on the part of the poet that his education in manhood at the hands of Adversity be a gentle one. Gray is ready to learn – if learn he must – yet he understandably questions the pedagogical methods of a Gorgon. The poem strikes one as the response of an individual who, having recently passed through so much tribulation, asks now for a moment of clarity, if not entire justification. The articulation of the poem's slight narrative and personification, and a simultaneous dissatisfaction with the ease with which one was supposed to recognize the chastening virtues pursuant on the stern glare of adversity, may well have prompted Gray to attempt one final formulation of his still unrelieved sense of mental agony. Gray had moved beyond shock and inconsolable disbelief to humbled acceptance and an imploring resolve, yet his heart was still too full to resist the impulse to rage just one more time against the dying of the light.

*

The *Ode on a Distant Prospect of Eton College* is justifiably considered by many to stand among Gray's greatest achievements as a poet. Dated in Gray's Commonplace Book, like the other early elegies, as having been written at Stoke in August 1742, the work is in that volume entitled 'Ode, on a distant Prospect of Windsor, & the adjacent Country'. The lines were eventually to be published under their revised title as a folio pamphlet by Dodsley in May 1747, and the ode stands as the first of Gray's English poems to appear in print (Dodsley likewise included the work in the second volume of his *Collection* in 1748). Gray shared the work with Walpole soon after their reconciliation, and it was Walpole who arranged matters with Dodsley and facilitated the work's publication. Soon after the ode appeared in print, Gray wrote to Walpole describing its reception in Cambridge. 'I promise you', he insisted,

> few take to it here at all, which is a good sign (for I never knew anything liked here, that ever proved to be so any where else,) it is said to be mine, but I strenuously deny it, and so do all that are in the secret, so that nobody knows what to think; a few only of King's College gave me the lie, but I hope to demolish them; for if *I* don't know, who should? (*CTG* 283)

If the fundamental thrust of the *Adversity Ode* is admitted to have been well captured in the Aeschylean motto prefaced to that work, the bleak essence of the *Eton Ode* is likewise well distilled in an epigraph drawn from Menander (an epigraph not included in printed editions of the poem, however, until 1768) which announces a sentiment similar to that which had introduced the earlier poem: 'I am a man, and that in itself is a sufficient reason for being unhappy.' Unlike the speaker in the *Adversity Ode*, the voice articulating the *Eton Ode* does not necessarily ask to be spared the harsher realities of human existence; pain, disease, suffering and death, that voice acknowledges, are among the unavoidable conditions of human experience and man will not – cannot – be shielded from them. The poet's Lockian commentary focuses, rather, on the simple fact that such dread knowledge is kept hidden from men while they are yet young. Youth is blessed with a conditional ignorance that is 'blissful' if only in the time which it grants the young to enjoy pleasures which age and greater understanding will systematically deny them. Like the *Adversity Ode*, the *Eton Ode* is to some degree a poem about what might be called the pedagogy of human experience; the worldly, experiential knowledge that lies in wait and stands sentinel 'all around' the Eton youth is a knowledge to which they will, rather paradoxically, *not* be introduced while yet at school. Indeed, if they knew just what terrors and tortures lay beyond the school's courtyards and playing fields, most of the young men would, quite sensibly, choose never to leave – choose never to grow up at all.

The *Eton Ode*, as we have already observed, is a poem that could only have been written at a considered distance from Gray's own experiences as a schoolboy. We have seen that Gray did not share Walpole's easy and casually nostalgic affection for Eton; the view of the 'antique towers' that crown the fields inspired in his breast no instant recollection of days passed thoughtlessly or carelessly. Time and recent experience, however, had taught Gray that life at the school had been a comparative paradise. The circumstances of the quarrel with Walpole, the passing of West, the upheaval in Gray's life caused by the death of Philip Gray and the domestic arrangements that needed to be made in the wake of that death: all these things now combined together in Gray's mind, prompting him to undertake a retrospective view of the past. 'In this state of mind', Roger Lonsdale has noted, 'Gray could easily idealize his schooldays and the poem is built on a stark contrast between the joys of childhood and the evils that maturity will bring.' 'Eton', as Lonsdale further observed, 'acquires a prelapsarian innocence, which is enforced by the echoes of Milton's description of Eden and other accounts of man in the Golden Age, before the onset of evil passions, by Pope and Thomson.'[16] Like Milton's Eden, Gray's paradise too is beset on all sides by a savage wilderness through which one will be able to carve a profitable path only with the assistance of divine guidance. In Book VIII of Milton's epic, Raphael attempts to teach a prelapsarian Adam that there are certain restraints that he must learn to impose on his own desire for knowledge; the archangel suggests to the human that there are certain kinds of knowledge to which mankind must simply not aspire, declaring memorably:

---

[16] Lonsdale, *PTG*, 55.

> Heav'n is for thee too high
> To know what passes there; be lowly wise:
> Think only what concerns thee and thy being;
> Dream not of other Worlds.[17]

Gray's poem, by contrast, focuses on the type of knowledge that
mature men would only too willingly, were they given the chance, choose
to avoid – a knowledge not, as Adam would have it, 'at large of things
remote', but of 'that which lies before us in daily life'. Such knowledge
may on some level constitute the proper sphere of human endeavour yet,
Gray's lines remind us, the understanding attendant on such perception
is at best a melancholy burden; we grow in time and through experience
only to disillusionment and disenchantment. The most striking passage
of Gray's poem conjures all the demons of maturity that lie in wait
for the Eton youth, and it does so in the particular light of discrepant
awareness; the plagues of mortality are all the more horrific for the poet
(and for the reader) in being unperceived by the 'bold adventurers'
who snatch a 'fearful joy' even from the taste of their inconsequential
transgressions:

> Alas, regardless of their doom,
> The little victims play!
> No sense have they of ills to come,
> No care beyond today:
> Yet see how all around 'em wait
> The ministers of human fate,
> And black Misfortune's baleful train!
> Ah, show them where in ambush stand
> To seize their prey the murtherous band!
> Ah, tell them, they are men!
>
> These shall the fury Passion tear,
> The vultures of the mind,
> Disdainful Anger, pallid Fear,
> And Shame that skulks behind;
> Or pining Love shall waste their youth,
> Or Jealousy with rankling tooth,
> That inly gnaws the secret heart,
> And Envy wan, and faded Care,
> Grim-visaged comfortless Despair,
> And Sorrow's piercing dart.
>
> Ambition this shall tempt to rise,
> Then whirl the wretch from high,

---

[17] John Milton, *Paradise Lost*, viii.172–75.

To bitter Scorn a sacrifice,
And grinning Infamy.
The stings of Falsehood those shall try,
And hard Unkindness' altered eye,
That mocks the tear it forced to flow;
And keen Remorse with blood defiled,
And moody Madness laughing wild
Amid severest woe.

   Lo, in the vale of years beneath
A grisly troop are seen,
The painful family of Death,
More hideous than their Queen:
This racks the joints, this fires the veins,
That every labouring sinew strains,
Those in the deeper vitals rage:
Lo, Poverty, to fill the band,
That numbs the soul with icy hand,
And slow-consuming Age. (*PTG* 59–63)

The horrors that constitute Gray's catalogue of the 'ministers of human fate' in these lines are, again, horrors with which any reader of Virgil's *Aeneid* would have been familiar. The hero of Virgil's work is greeted before the entrance to the underworld by many of same or similar figures – Grief, Care, Disease, Age, Dread, Hunger, etc. Gray appears deliberately to have sought to underscore the connection between the gates of Hades and the gates that led to the school-yard presided over by the 'holy shade' of Henry VI; both lead, in and through time, to inescapable horrors. The lines contain some other significant recollections as well. In the first book of his *De Principiis Cogitandi*, we remember, Gray had attempted to put into verse the philosophy of Locke's *Essay Concerning Human Understanding*. He wrote in the opening lines of that work:

Unde Animus scire incipiat:
. . .
   Ratio unde rudi sub pectore tardum
Augeat imperium; et primum mortalibus aegris
Ira, Dolor, Metus, et Curae nascantur inanes,
Hinc canere aggredior. (*PTG* 322; 328–29)

[From what origin minds begin to have knowledge: . . . whence Reason spreads its gradual mastery in the savage heart; and whence anger, grief, fear, and insubstantial cares are first born to wretched mortals; it is of these matters that I begin my song]

The same passions, of course – Anger, Grief, Fear, and Care – reappear among others in the *Eton Ode*. As Kenneth MacLean observed: 'In writing this ode Gray must have recalled the philosophy of the earlier *De Principiis Cogitandi*, and the ignorance of children he names must resemble that very ignorance in which Locke believed men to be born.'[18]

Gray ends his own poem with a rhetorical gesture which seeks at least temporarily to shield the young from such dread knowledge:

> Yet ah! why should they know their fate?
> Since sorrow never comes too late,
> And happiness too swiftly flies.
> Thought would destroy their paradise.
> No more; where ignorance is bliss,
> 'Tis folly to be wise. (*PTG* 63)

Unlike Gray's other poems commemorating West's death, the *Eton Ode* questions what must be called the simple value of the cares and emotional traumas that follow in the wake of adulthood. In the *Sonnet* Gray essentially confessed himself to have been too shaken by West's death to make any sense of it. In the *Adversity Ode*, the poet moved on to the next stage of mourning, the stage in which he pretended to have extracted a coherent moral lesson from the greater chaos of his emotions; the impulse to do so was not insincere, though the quiet resolution of purpose expressed in that poem's final lines may have been premature. In the *Eton Ode*, Gray admits to himself that the loss has simply been too large for him to comprehend and certainly to accept in strictly rational terms, and states in the strong and uncompromising imagery of its personifications that he still resists that knowledge which maturity has thrust upon him.

Like many of Gray's poems, the *Eton Ode* betrays a dual fascination with the role of Fate or destiny in human affairs, and with the role assigned to Time in bringing that destiny to fruition. Were it possible – the distant prospect of Eton suggests to Gray's mind – the poet would himself willingly transform the inspired 'second spring' of his memories into a permanent state of a restored and 'foolish' childhood. In the *Elegy* Gray will travel into the future to envision what people will think and say of him after his own death; in the *Eton Ode*, he travelled into the past to recapture, for one brief moment, the fleeting joy he now recognizes as having formed a part even of his own, troubled childhood.

As Gray prepared finally to move through the trauma of the last year to begin an entirely new stage of his life, he sought momentarily to revisit his own past. He seemed briefly, in the August of 1742, to be right where he had started from. He was uncertain if he possessed the necessary strength and energy to carry on. The poems he wrote that month them-

---

[18] Kenneth MacLean, *John Locke and English Literature of the Eighteenth Century*, 36.

selves stand as a testimony that for all his seemingly crippling sense of self-doubt Gray possessed a strength of inner reserve the power of which he may himself, at the time, have been unaware. The simple fact that he was able to wring a moment of great creative endeavour from the whole tortuous process of personal transition – the simple fact that the summer of 1742 was easily *the* most active and productive period of Gray's life as a poet – indicates that he was on some level able to turn the entire, complicated process of transition to his own psychic benefit. The apparently solid and unquestionable realities of Gray's old world had faded and finally disappeared before his very eyes. His sense of disenchantment – with his friends, with the world, and even with himself – was profound. Yet before he could grow, and before he could move on to the next stage of his own life, he needed first to pause and to reflect on the past. He needed to confront the connections between that old world and the new one which, he knew, he would soon need to forge for himself. Gray was far too intelligent simply to confess himself disillusioned with life, yet then seek to reenact those same relationships and circumstances which had led to that sense of disillusionment in the first place. He felt the need genuinely to move forward and to grow; and for perhaps the first time in his life, he would learn genuinely and slowly to accept the fact that in order to grow, he needed to accept loss as a natural and catalytic part of the process of growth itself. The events of the last year closed an entire chapter of Gray's life. They also pointed the way in which he might carefully begin to open a new one.

CHAPTER SIX

A MILDER WARFARE

Return to Cambridge
1742–1749

I. Together Again

The autumn of 1742 witnessed some important changes in the disposition and the circumstances of Gray's immediate as well as his extended family. Toward the end of October the poet's uncle, Jonathan Rogers, died at Stoke. Rogers's widow, Anne, appears to have felt that after over thirty long years of marriage, she had earned the right to spend her remaining days precisely as she saw fit. She decided almost immediately to invite her two sisters to live with her permanently in Buckinghamshire. Dorothy Gray and Mary Antrobus promptly joined Anne Rogers at West End House by the end of the year.

Though obviously willing to pass their own remaining years together and in the quiet company of their widowed sister, both Dorothy and Mary must have yielded to Anne's eager invitation to join her at the familiar, rural retreat at Stoke with some small degree of hesitation; there must, on their side, at least, have been some instinctive reluctance to leave off the activity of their busy London 'warehouse' altogether. Both sisters were successful business women by birth, by temperament and inclination, and by long experience. They naturally felt at home and comfortable not only in the otherwise masculine world of the City itself, but more particularly behind the windows and busying about the stock and the counters of the shop they had for so long called their own. Retirement from one's long-established profession is rarely an easy transition to make. Such an abrupt (and so often palpably funereal) withdrawal from one's chosen, professional career and officially public role in life is often rendered only more painful by the marked and sudden absence of the very same behaviour – the same courtesy, respect, deference, authority, and sense of social position – which had worked over time to render that public existence personally rewarding and valuable. For the Antrobus sisters, the decision finally to surrender the accomplishment of such hard-earned acumen could not have been an easy one to make. In the case of Dorothy and Mary, however, the arguments seemed inevitably to run in their sister's favour. The less Dorothy was reminded of Philip Gray the better. Leaving the Cornhill home – leaving behind its domestic history – must have been far less traumatic for her than leaving the space of the retail store itself; the ground floor shop at No. 41 Cornhill was a space by now intimately familiar in its fittings, in the marks of its own history, and even in the inevitably idiosyncratic sights, smells, and sounds that had grown both to define and to measure the course of its daily activity. Still, the valuable Cornhill property was soon and easily let to a younger merchant, and the sisters' ground-floor 'India warehouse' was quickly outfitted for its newest tenant as a milliner's shop. The three sisters, meanwhile, were soon settling down to begin what appears for each of them, in and over time, to have succeeded most as one of the happier and more quietly productive periods of their often worried personal lives.

Earlier that same year, the sisters had suffered another, unanticipated loss in the death of their only surviving brother, William Antrobus, at his parsonage at Everdon in Northamptonshire. William left behind him a widow – Elizabeth Antrobus, née Nutting – and four children (one son, Robert, and three daughters: Mary or 'Molly', Dorothy, and Elizabeth). This widow Antrobus decided to leave Northamptonshire and to return with her young family to Cambridge, where her own father, the once prosperous merchant and Alderman Thomas Nutting, had twice served as mayor, and where he still lived himself. Alderman Nutting was in a few years' time to accept the position of Postmaster of Cambridge, an office he would eventually resign in favour of his daughter Elizabeth. For Elizabeth Antrobus the return to Cambridge, in other words, was a return home. The immediate consequence of all this family reshuffling for Gray, in any event, was the establishment of a small, female-dominated household within Cambridge itself, a household to which he would in time turn for such support – advise regarding such then indisputably feminine niceties of home furnishing and domestic economy – as he felt such relatives might appropriately offer. Although he appears never in his life to have felt any profound, emotional attachment to most of his Cambridge relations (in his will he even mistakenly refers to one of his own first cousins as 'my second Cousin by my Mother's side'), the very proximity of the Nutting household prompted Gray to acknowledge some responsibility for its welfare. Over the years he did develop a great deal of affection for his cousin Molly (*for you*', he would confess to her tellingly in one letter, '*are like none of the Family!*'). The cluster of female relations now gathered in Cambridge replicated or at least mimicked in its own small way, for Gray, his more deeply felt attachments to the trio of women recently established at West End House. The warmth of his love both for his mother and his aunts prompted him eventually to think of West End House at Stoke Poges as an ever-welcoming refuge and even, in time, as a second home.

*

Gray's own proper home – he had returned to Peterhouse College as a Fellow–Commoner by the middle of October – was at once both familiar and yet at the same time decidedly new to him. Since he had not taken a degree when he had first left Cambridge in 1738, Gray returned to the University that autumn still technically an undergraduate. His status as a Fellow–Commoner, however – a position he seems to have been granted with consideration to his age, his previous residence in college, and his comparatively worldly 'experience' both as a traveller and as a scholar – exempted him from the disciplinary rules imposed on undergraduates in general. The rank of Fellow–Commoner likewise entitled him to such privileges as associating socially with the other College Fellows (of whom there were then at Peterhouse only fourteen, with an additional eight adjuncts or bye-Fellows) in the College Combination Room and parlor. Gray also now enjoyed the privilege of dining at the Fellow's table in Hall.

The Master of Peterhouse in 1742 was Walpole's old supervisor, the supposedly dissipated Dr. John Whalley. Whalley had been appointed to the Mastership of the college in 1733. He had subsequently, earlier in the same year which saw Gray's own return to Peterhouse, been offered the Regius Professor of Divinity. His tenure as Master had proven thus far to be at worst unproductive, and at best unexacting; the Fellows and students of the college, at any rate, were far from being goaded into achieving any high academic honours that might reflect on or in any way redound to the credit of their institution. Gray had never felt any great personal affection for Whalley, and his relations with the Master were within a very short time to be strained to an unpleasant degree. Gray realized very soon after his initial return to Peterhouse that if he intended to make any progress whatsoever in his supposed vocation of the Law, he would be left to make that progress entirely on his own.

Rather surprisingly, Gray began his new career at the college with what might well be described as a self-conscious display of academic, institutionally sanctioned diligence. He made a point of attending the lectures then being offered by the Regius Professor of Law, Dr. Francis Dickins, and his lecture notes – still in existence – show that he followed the subject with a precise and (when given the inclination) characteristically careful attention. A little over one year after his return to Cambridge, Gray qualified for the degree of Bachelor of Civil Law. He was entered on the University Books as LL.B. designate on 16 December 1743, and became full LL.B. in 1744. The same Thomas Gray who would later in life protest to Wharton his utter helplessness in 'matters of law', confessed himself at the time to be amused at the easy success of his efforts, and at the incongruity of his supposed achievement. 'I am got half way to the Top of Jurisprudence', he wrote with feigned surprise to Wharton soon after taking his degree, '& bid as fair as another

Body to open a case of Impotency with all Decency and Circumspec-
tion'. Gray's Bachelor's degree placed him at the half-way point in his
journey toward his Doctorate. His point in joking with Wharton about
a 'case of Impotency' rests on the understanding that such a case would
be tried within the Ecclesiastical Courts, where precisely such a Doctor's
degree as Gray looked now to possess was a necessary requirement for
practice. As events turned out, Gray never would finish his course and
take his Doctor's degree. His efforts in 1742–43 appear nevertheless
to indicate that at the time, at least, he still entertained, as he would put
it in a letter to James Beattie many years later, 'some thoughts on the
profession'.

Perhaps it was the simple change of direction – the sense of the
absolute necessity of carving out some sort of place for himself – that
prompted Gray to conform and to work so patiently in those early
months at Cambridge. Few distractions could have presented themselves
to his attention. Very shortly after his arrival at Peterhouse he was
assigned an enviable set of rooms on the second floor of James Burrough's brand-new Fellows' Building. The structure, which completed
the northernmost portion of the college's frontage onto Trumpington
Street and sat parallel to the elegant, seventeenth-century college chapel
(in the centre of an open side of the main court) had taken just five years
to build, and formed a welcome addition to the college accommodations. Although dismissed by some as 'dull' or architecturally unadven-
turous, Burrough's building more often strikes the eyes of modern
visitors to the college as graciously proportioned and in almost every
way appropriate to its site. Gray's new rooms looked northward across
the pinnacled roof-top of King's College Chapel and above the medieval
structures and graveyard of the lovely Church known officially as St.
Mary the Less, but known to everyone in Cambridge simply as 'Little
St. Mary's'. Turning eastward, his eyes rested on the perfectly proportioned cupola of Christopher Wren's 'new' chapel (consecrated in 1665)
for Pembroke College. To the south Trumpington Street stretched into
open country. Gray's fear of fire – a legacy at least in part of his
earliest days as a child in London, but a paranoia sorely to be exacerbated by his emotional condition in the years to come – prompted him
eventually to have an iron bar affixed just outside the window by means
of two brackets, from which, if necessary, he could suspend a rope in
case of emergency, and so descend to the street (the bars remain attached
to the structure to this day). This primitive fire-escape – an unadvisedly
public pronouncement of Gray's private phobia to the undergraduate
population of the University – would, as we shall see, play a small but
important role in the poet's eventual defection from Peterhouse for
Pembroke in 1756.

*

It was probably soon after his return to Cambridge in October 1742 that Gray wrote the fragment of the *Hymn to Ignorance*. The lines survive only from a copy transcribed at a slightly later date into his Commonplace Book. The unfinished *Hymn* was first printed by Mason in his 1775 edition of Gray's *Poems*, in which the editor observed of the work: 'It seems to have been intended as a Hymn or Address to Ignorance; and I presume, had he proceeded with it, would have contained much good Satire upon false Science and scholastic Pedantry.' The affectionate, burlesque verses bear the obvious influence of Pope's recently revised *Dunciad* (1742); they envision a Cambridge that is manifestly *not* the retreat of Science and Learning, but rather the exclusive demesne of the mock-goddess Ignorance. Indeed, the same personification of Ignorance who will be banished with great ceremony in the opening lines of Gray's 1769 *Ode for Music*, written to celebrate the installation of the Duke of Grafton as Chancellor of the University, is in these earlier lines revered with supposed solemnity as the local deity – as the presiding 'genius of the place'. Gray's *Ignorance* fragment amusingly anticipates the physical and inspirational structures later to be described in the opening lines of the *Ode for Music*, complete with melancholic bowers, Gothic turrets and cloisters, and a lone and reverential Cantabrigian. The substance of the opening lines of the later *Ode* ('Hence, avaunt, 'tis Holy ground . . .') is even foreshadowed in the suitably Miltonic opening to the earlier fragment:

> Hail, horrors, hail! ye ever-gloomy bowers,
> Ye gothic fanes and antiquated towers,
> Where rushy Camus' slowly-winding flood
> Perpetual draws his humid train of mud:
> Glad I revisit thy neglected reign;
> Oh, take me to thy peaceful shade again.
>   But chiefly thee, whose influenced breathed from high
> Augments the native darkness of the sky;
> Ah, Ignorance! soft salutory power!
> Prostrate with filial reverence I adore.
> Thrice hath Hyperion rolled his annual race,
> Since weeping I forsook thy fond embrace.
> Oh say, successful dost thou still oppose
> Thy leaden aegis 'gainst our ancient foes?
> Still stretch, tenacious of thy right divine,
> The massy sceptre o'er thy slumbering line?
> And dews Lethean through the land dispense
> To steep in slumbers each benighted sense?
> If any spark of wit's delusive ray
> Break out, and flash a momentary day,

With damp, cold touch forbid it to aspire,
And huddle up in fogs the dangerous fire. (*PTG* 75–76)

Gray is having great fun in these lines toying with the (seriously) skeptical notion that 'Wit' or Reason was, as the Earl of Rochester had put it in his own Hobbesian *Satire Against Mankind* over a generation earlier, 'an *ignis fatuus* of the mind' – an intellectual chimera which served its purpose only when leading men toward the pathless and dangerous wandering ways of Error. The tutelary goddess Ignorance – armed with her leaden shield and Lethean dews – is quick only in her ability quite literally to dampen any enthusiasm for learning. Gray must have had a very strong sense of the torpor – 'that ineffable Octogrammaton . . . the Power of LAZINESS' – which was only too likely to descend upon those among the academic community who rested unaware of or defenseless against its slow-chapt power. Many years earlier, in 1678, the Oxford antiquarian Anthony Wood had noticed that his own university town could easily appear to an outsider to be inhabited almost exclusively by scholars suffering from colds and running noses. The air that one breathed in Cambridge, Gray obviously felt, was no more salubrious than that which cloaked her sister university in the languid and inescapable fogs of lassitude. Laziness was herself, he would write in a letter to Wharton in 1744, the university's 'sovereign Lady & Mistress, the President of Presidents, & Head of Heads'.

The 'fragment' of the anti-Lockian *Hymn to Ignorance* is of course perfect in its own imperfection, paradoxically complete in its very incompletion. The sense of sloth and self-indulgence invoked in the poem's opening lines has worked its soporific magic well. The author of the *Hymn* appears himself to have fallen victim to the indigenous dangers of the academic environment within which he has been writing and to have succumbed to the very particular 'blessings' that he has foolishly gone out of his way to solicit. For all its self-directed humour, however, the *Hymn to Ignorance* gives voice to certain ideas concerning the need for isolation and retreat that we have already seen expressed with far greater seriousness in works such as the *Alcaic Ode*; the notions expressed in the course of the poem that the fire of Wit – however and whenever kindled – is a potentially 'dangerous' one, will similarly reappear in the *Elegy*. Moreover, the desire expressed by the speaker of the *Hymn* to be drawn within the 'peaceful shade' of the domain of Ignorance rephrases the essential and deeply felt prayer of the *Eton Ode* – the desire to be spared knowledge when such knowledge leads only to misery and maturity – only slightly. Gray could joke about his return to the sluggish environment of the college all he wished, but the *Hymn to Ignorance*, at the same time that it pokes fun at academic disciplines and obsessions, inescapably echoes the poet's more genuinely impassioned, poetic pleas that he be granted a momentary respite from his already difficult and painful education in the ways of the world.

Gray was pleasantly surprised by the warmth with which the simple fact of his return to Peterhouse was greeted by the friends who themselves, unlike either Walpole or himself, had not yet had the opportunity (or perhaps even the inclination) to leave the university. Foremost among his old Cambridge acquaintances still in residence were James Brown and Thomas Wharton, both of whom remained Fellows of Pembroke Hall. The small and short-sighted Brown was in several years' time to be created President (i.e. Vice-Master) of Pembroke; Wharton, who had been granted his M.A. in 1741, and who would be made M.D. just over ten years later, was to remain in residence at the college until October, 1746, when he would be compelled to vacate his Fellowship shortly before his marriage to Margaret Wilkinson, of Durham, in 1747. Another friend still at Pembroke was William Trollope, under whose sponsorship Gray was permitted the privilege of borrowing books from the library of the neighbouring college. Trollope, who had been granted his B.A. when Gray was only ten years old, was now practically an invalid. He would eventually go out of residence in 1746. Despite the barriers of Trollope's age and physical condition, both Gray and Wharton appear in the early 1740s genuinely to have enjoyed the older man's company, and often to have conversed with him on terms of the greatest intimacy. At Peterhouse itself was John Clerke, an old and reliable contemporary of Gray's own who had only just received his M.A., and who would, like Wharton, be granted his M.D. in 1753. A young Petrean by the name of Henry Tuthill was also drawn to Gray's attention at about this time, perhaps by Wharton, as an attractive and promising undergraduate worthy of the poet's time and affection; Tuthill would graduate B.A. from Peterhouse shortly after Gray's arrival, in 1743.

One last acquaintance dating from this period, Dr. Conyers Middleton, was to Gray's society neither entirely familiar nor entirely unknown. Gray had almost certainly encountered the controversial deist personally at some point during his earlier residence at Cambridge; at the very least he had known of Middleton by reputation for years. Middleton was now comfortably ensconced as chief Librarian of the University. His recently published Life of Cicero (1741) had brought him a certain degree both of fame and of fortune; he continued throughout the coming decade to write on Roman history and to keep his hand in on the latest theological controversies. Middleton had married no fewer than three times, and he and his series of wives (Gray judged Middleton's third bride with the eye of an amateur as 'really a pretty kind of

Woman both in Figure and Manner') opened the doors of their house on King's Parade to provide what Gray would later describe as 'the only easy Place one could find to converse in Cambridge'. Although Gray confessed on at least one occasion that he didn't approve of 'the Spirit of [Middleton's] books', and although he had reason, too, to question the depth of the sincerity of Middleton's supposed religious convictions, he found the Doctor's easy brand of conviviality much in accordance with his own social temper. Having admitted candidly and without rancour that Middleton's theological positions were for him still open to question, Gray assumed that the status of the Librarian as a truly 'good writer' – one whose work was to be treated seriously – was itself a fact beyond dispute.

*

When the trail of Gray's correspondence resumes toward the end of 1743 (no letters to or from the poet survive from the roughly one-and-a-half-year period immediately following West's death in the summer of 1742), we find him dashing off a gossipy letter to Wharton, who was then at Durham. Having recently taken his own Bachelor's degree, Gray filled his letter with speculation regarding the respective, professional careers both of himself and of his friend. Pretending still to regard the law as 'a Profession perhaps the noblest in the World', he advised Wharton with mock solemnity to establish his own medical practice in London. Were he to do so, Gray reasoned, 'I may reasonably expect in a much shorter Time to see you in your three-corner'd Villa, doing the honours of a well-furnish'd Table with as much Dignity, as rich a Mein, & as capacious a Belly as Dr. Mead' – Dr. Richard Mead being the most celebrated physician of the day.

Gray's few surviving letters from this period (all of them to Wharton) pursue an easy, bantering style of inclusion which dwelled with as much gossipy comfort on individuals as it did on literary matters. In the spring of 1744, Gray informed Wharton that both he and the elderly Trollope had embarked on a course of tar-water (the medicinal drinking of tar-water, which could be purchased at any apothecary's shop, had become something of a fad following its advocation in George Berkeley's *Siris* in 1744). Other University gossip was jumbled together with comments and recommendations concerning recent reading. Gray must have shared some of his work on *De Principiis Cogitandi* with Wharton, since he responded flippantly to the latter's enquiry concerning his progress on that same poem, commenting, 'Master Tommy Lucretius (since you are so good as to enquire after the Child) is but a puleing Chitt yet, not a bit grown to speak off, I believe, poor Thing! it has got the Worms, that will carry it off at last'. Although he may have maintained the pretense of continuing work on *De Principiis Cogitandi*, Gray revealed in such supposedly light-hearted comments that the poem had been as good as buried following the death of West the previous year. The larger concerns of the poem, however, would continue to inform Gray's poetry in the years to come.

The time had finally come, Gray must have felt, to bury some other matters as well. Toward the end of 1745, Gray and Walpole – at the latter's instigation – saw fit to put an end to their long, mutual silence, and were reconciled to one another in London. Sir Robert Walpole had died at his home on Arlington Street at the age of sixty-nine in March of that same year. Although leaving his three sons a considerable portion of debts, Lord Orford had seen to it that the financial futures of his children were reasonably secure. The lease on the Arlington Street property, along with an increasingly impressive share of the income derived from his place as Collector of the Customs, saw his youngest son comfortably settled for life. Horace would be free to cultivate his various talents as a letter-writer, a social historian, and a social butterfly as he alone saw fit. Walpole did not look to remain for very long at Arlington Street, however. The house possessed few happy memories for him, and the spectre of having witnessed his father's final nights passed within that same residence in a haze of pain and frustration haunted its rooms like a ghost. Walpole had already begun looking for a small home just outside London where he would be free to pursue his social and aesthetic interests with greater freedom, and with his own, highly idiosyncratic brand of idle diligence.

Late in 1745 Walpole was approached by a certain 'Mrs. Kerr', an individual about whom we unfortunately know nothing, other than the fact that she professed herself to be 'a Lady who wished well to both parties', who then facilitated the reconciliation between Gray and himself. This Mrs. Kerr clearly persuaded Gray to come up to town specifically with an eye towards once again meeting and spending time with his old friend; she appears not to have been present at their reunion, however, nor indeed, is any reference ever again made to anyone by that name by either Walpole or Gray.

We know from Gray's detailed letters on the subject, however, just what took place when the two men once again found themselves in each other's company. On the evening of 8 November 1745, Gray stepped from a hackney coach in front of the Walpoles' Arlington Street residence; within minutes he was being warmly greeted inside by Walpole, who, approaching him with little pretense of formality and even less self-consciousness concerning the circumstances of their last parting, familiarly embraced him and kissed him, in the European manner, warmly on both cheeks. The record of the reconciliation that followed was included by Gray in a letter he eventually sent to Wharton. That first evening on which, with a great deal of trembling anticipation and restrained dignity, Gray visited Walpole, he was himself, he later confessed, 'something abash'd' at Walpole's own sense of 'Confidence'. His friend's manner, Gray wrote with some stiffness and even with some resentment to Wharton, possessed 'all the Ease of one, who receives an Acquaintance just come out of the Country'. Something more than a casual disagreement or confrontation of wills, one again senses across the years, was being patched over here, and Gray felt that Walpole's 'Ease' was inappropriate, unsuitable, and on a personal level, offensive. Walpole, the poet continued in the account sent to Wharton, 'squatted me into a Fanteuil, begun to talk of the Town & this & that & t'other, & continued with little Interruption for three Hours, when I took my Leave very indifferently pleased, but treated with wondrous Good-breeding'. Gray must nevertheless have been aware that Walpole's garrulous brand of familiar hospitality was only the flip side of his own decorous pose of slightly offended reticence; each of the two men unavoidably dealt with the stress of their reunion in their own way. If Gray had expected to hear any explicit apology or confession fall from Walpole's lips that night, he was disappointed. Both Walpole's 'Good-breeding' as well as Gray's own poise of 'indifference' rendered the explicit details of their past history a forbidden subject; each of them effectively glossed over the more precise circumstances of their quarrel in Italy with a conversational polish – the lacquer of polite, social interaction – which hardened too quickly and shone too brightly ever easily, afterwards, to be broken.

On the very next evening (a Saturday night) Gray returned to Arlington Street as Walpole's dinner guest. On the occasion of their second meeting, Walpole took the precaution of inviting their old friend Thomas Ashton to be a member of the company as well. Walpole may have intended Ashton to serve as a buffer between himself and Gray. It would have been to his mind entirely appropriate that the individual whose epistolary indiscretion appears itself to have played an important if not initiating role in the quarrel between the two friends also be present at their reunion. For his own part, Gray appears to have had little contact with Ashton following West's death over three years earlier. The temporary renewal of their old relationship (Gray must have felt with a profound significance the fact that the gathering of the three men at Arlington Street that night was now the closest they would ever come to a reunion of the old, Etonian 'Quadruple Alliance') struck Gray as both melancholy and farcical. He later wrote to Wharton that he was inwardly 'tickled' at Ashton's 'Formalities'. Ashton, who grew more brittle with age, appears on the occasion to have been excessively stiff and cold towards his old school-friend. Gray finally broke through Ashton's exterior; 'he I found', Gray recounted, 'was to be angry about the Letter I wrote him'. In all likelihood, his former friend probably felt that a letter of Gray's addressed explicitly to him – a letter in which the writer was critical of Walpole's behaviour (and Walpole was already, we must remember, Ashton's own, powerful patron) had placed Ashton himself in compromising positions both personally and professionally. Having pinned all his worldly hopes to the coat tails of Walpole's own foreseeable political and social success, Ashton may have been embarrassed by the fact that the letter in question would appear to have indicated his own agreement with Gray's criticisms; even more mortifying would have been the bald and simple fact that he had been caught in the act of criticizing or in some way deprecating his patron's conduct. Ashton and Gray executed an elaborate conversational dance that evening, and seem to have spoken openly and set aside their wariness with regards to one another only in the physical tumult of their shared cab ride home. 'In going home together', Gray recalled,

> our Hackney-Coach jumbled us into a Sort of Reconciliation: he hammer'd out somewhat like an Excuse; & I received it very readily, because I cared not two pence, whither it were true or not. So we grew the best Acquaintance imaginable, & I set with him on Sunday some Hours alone, when he inform'd me of abundance of Anecdotes much to my Satisfaction, & in short open'd (I really believe) his Heart to me with that Sincerity, that I found I had still less Reason to have a good Opinion of him, than (if possible) I ever had before. (*CTG* 226–27)

Gray's dismissal of Ashton's character in this passage amounts to more than a casual epistolary aside. Whatever sentiments or 'Anecdotes' Ashton chose to pass on to Gray the next afternoon, and whatever aspects of Ashton's personality those sentiments further revealed to him, Gray was sincere in his judgement that his poor opinion of his one-time friend had been entirely justified. Ashton was in the end nothing more, as Gray would soon put it, than 'an ungrateful toady'.

Walpole, however, was another matter altogether; the manner in which the poet finally wrote of their rapprochement is peculiarly telling. When Gray reported the details of the reconciliation between himself and Walpole to Wharton, he began his letter: 'you may be curious to know what has past. I wrote a Note the Night I came, & immediately received a very civil Answer. I went the following evening to see *the Party* (as Mrs. Foible says) was something abash'd at his Confidence . . .'. Gray, as we have seen from the passage already quoted above, was indeed, in actual fact, 'something abash'd' by the ease with which Walpole managed the occasion. Like so many of Gray's literary allusions both in his correspondence and in his poetry, the casual reference encoded here to William Congreve's 1700 masterpiece *The Way of the*

World (in which the character of 'Mrs. Foible' is the servant of the embittered and vengeful Lady Wishfort) is a cutting we trace back to its original source and context at our own interpretive peril. Gray's oblique if
literally underscored reference to Walpole himself as '*the Party*' – a
reference that allows him to conjure the dominating social presence of
his friend without yet naming him – may to some degree be read only
as a logical and psychologically plausible extension of Gray's inability,
in the earliest of his letters to Mann and Chute following his return to
England, to bring himself even to write Walpole's name on paper. Still,
it seems on this occasion no mere accident of textual reference that the
source of the cipher Gray has chosen to use was a drama that had itself
handled questions concerning romantic love and masculine friendship
with a complicated and profound – and arguably a profoundly nasty
and bitter – scepticism. *The Way of the World* cynically complicates the
relationships between its central characters (Congreve's last drama is
among the first English plays pointedly to describe its characters, in the
dramatis personae prefaced to the work, almost exclusively in terms of
the romantic and sexual relation within which they stand towards one
another) to a point at which, by the time the curtain falls on the drama,
nothing – no friendship, no marriage, no illicit sexual encounter – is
what it appears initially to have been on the lapidary surface of its dialogue; even the casual conversation between nominal 'friends', such as
that between Mirabell and Fainall which opens the drama, we realize
only in retrospect to have been loaded with a double (and often a dangerous) significance. The reference to the complicated and frequently
malicious dance of relationships in Congreve's drama, in any event,
appears somehow to have helped Gray himself likewise to view the reconciliation with Walpole (and, by extension, the rather less emotionally
fraught reunion with Ashton) as an elaborate drama, a clever piece of
stage management. Hence his own reference to being inwardly 'tickled'
at the spectacle. Each of the participants in this little bit of play-acting
was ready to avoid topics of genuine, emotional and romantic volatility
– each was ready to maintain a policy of strict silence on the subject of
their own individual and personal 'agendas' – for the sake of a seeming
amicability.

On the morning of Monday, 11 November, Gray breakfasted alone
with Walpole. It was at that breakfast, he wrote Wharton, that the two
men finally 'had all the Eclaircissement I ever expected, & I left him far
better satisfied than I had hitherto. When I return [i.e. to London], I
shall see him again'. 'Such', he concludes casually, 'is the Epitome of my
four Days.' Although it would be nice to possess the details of precisely
what passed over the breakfast table that morning, it is likely, given the
private and by that point intimate circumstances of the week-end reconciliation, that specific apologies were in very short supply.

Gray's personal sense of satisfaction in once again being on good terms with his former best friend was consequently complicated by a sense of the anti-climactic. Some few of his comments relating to Walpole that followed hard upon the heels of their initial reconciliation that November continue to betray a wounded impatience with Walpole's apparent flippancy. Gray felt that his old companion had too swiftly resumed a light-hearted posture; though he no doubt persisted in taking offense at the easy familiarity of Walpole's outward manner, he would just as soon have been offended by any seeming reticence or coyness – by the sense of an unspoken offense which yet lingered in the air between them. It was hard, in fact, for Gray himself to envision just what was supposed to happen now. If things were not to be re-established just as they had been before, did that then mean that the easy manner now assumed by Walpole was meant to serve as a genially apotropaic shield against the possibility of any genuine intimacy between the two men? Was Walpole being deliberately casual in his desire actually to ward off any attempt on Gray's part to talk seriously about the relationship between them or, for that matter, about their interdependent friendships with West? Or with Ashton? We know only that Gray was at times rather taken aback by the casual and unbroken ease of Walpole's behaviour. The past seemed almost magically (and this is a trait already noticed in his behaviour) to carry little weight with Walpole; while Gray now read the present only through the veil of the past, Walpole attempted to live *in* the present moment as much as possible, unburdened by the weight of his own personal history. The following summer – by which time Gray and Walpole had already seen a 'good deal' of one another and had resumed a casual correspondence – Gray once again grumbled to Wharton that his old friend was 'mighty free, & even friendly . . . more than one could expect'. More too, Gray managed to insinuate in his own reticence, that one could desire.

Sometime toward the end of September, John Chute and Francis Whithed returned to England. Displaying an appropriate sense of delicacy, neither man, visiting Walpole in London, was the first to mention Gray by name. Once apprized of the recent reconciliation, however, both were cautiously happy for Gray. Gray responded to a letter from Chute with the clearest statement he was ever to make regarding the several motives surrounding his resumption of contact with Walpole. 'I find Mr. Walpole then made some Mention of me to you,' he wrote on 12 October 1746,

> yes, we are together again. It is about a Year, I believe, since he wrote to me to offer it, & there has been (particularly of late) in Appearance the same Kindness & Confidence almost as of old. what were his Motives I can not guess: what were mine, you will imagine, & perhaps blame me.

however as yet I neither repent, nor rejoice overmuch: but am pleased. (CTG 248)

Gray's remarks in this letter indicate that he feared that Chute himself would not personally have approved of his reconciliation with Walpole. Gray may at some point in the crisis have confessed the depth of his affection for Walpole to Chute. He obviously regretted the appearance of weakness on his own part which he felt Chute would carry away from news of any reunion between the two men. How otherwise might one interpret his anxiety that Chute might 'blame' him for such a reunion?. Equally important in Gray's recounting, however, is the concluding state-ment that he neither regrets the rapprochement nor is too sanguine regarding its prospects for continued success. He was content in himself, for the time being, to sit back and allow the vexed but persistent rela-tionship with Walpole to take whatever course it would.

II. Heedless Hearts and Lawful Prizes

Gray passed much of the late summer and early autumn of 1746 at Stoke Poges. Toward the end of July he spent a few days undertaking a brief 'Excursion' to places of local attraction reasonably close to the city – Hampton Court, Richmond, Greenwich – before staying another two weeks in London. Although the London season had recently ended, there was much to keep a young man occupied in town that particular August. Evenings might be spent (as Gray sometimes spent his own) at the plea-sure gardens of Ranelagh and Vauxhall; mornings could be whiled away in the company of friends, as Gray now passed his mornings comfort-ably enough at Walpole's Arlington street home. The main attraction of London that summer, however, was the short but spectacular trial of the rebel Lords in Westminster Hall, which began on 28 July and ended on 1 August.

The battle of Culloden in April of 1746 appeared finally to have put an end to the ambitions of 'Bonnie Prince Charlie' and his Jacobite army to overthrow the Hanoverian dynasty and re-establish his father's claim to the throne in England. The Duke of Cumberland's artillery had destroyed the rebel army on the moors near Inverness, and Charles Edward himself only narrowly escaped to the safety of the continent; many of his supporters were not so fortunate. In the summer of 1746, three of those individuals who had fought with the Pretender's forces against their anointed monarch – William Boyd, fourth Earl of Kil-marnock, Arthur Elphinstone, sixth Lord Balmerino, and George Mackenzie, third Earl of Cromarty – stood trial for their lives in West-minster Hall. The charge was high treason. The pomp and ceremony of such a trial would alone have guaranteed some degree of popular interest in its proceedings. The fact that two at least of the three individuals facing execution were themselves rather dashing and good-looking men only added to the aura of sentimental Jacobitism that seemed to hover around them in the great hall. The cast of supporting characters too, including the distraught and impassioned Lady Cromarty and her children, was exceptionally colourful. And while London crowds may have grown used to treating the hanging of criminals on Tyburn as a commonplace event, the prospect of multiple beheadings on Tower Hill was compellingly gothic in the barbaric connections it seemed to forge to the nation's past.

Individuals such as Walpole, of course, had a genuine and compelling interest in the outcome of events. When the rebellion of 'Forty-five' had been at its height (just prior to Walpole's own reconciliation with Gray), he had written to Montagu: 'Now comes the Pretender's boy, and promises all my comfortable apartments in the Exchequer and Custom House to some forlorn Irish peer, who chooses to remove his pride and poverty out of some large unfurnished gallery at St. Germain's. Why really Mr. Montagu, this is not pleasant!'[1] Not pleasant, indeed, had the rebellion succeeded and had Walpole been forced into exile thanks to his father's political success. Walpole eventually included a memorably detailed and sweeping account of the trial in his letters to Horace Mann ('a coronation', he wrote to Mann with undisguised glee of the trial on 1 August, 'is a puppet show, and all the splendour of it, idle; but this sight at once feasted one's eyes and engaged all one's passions').[2] Gray, writing to Wharton at Cambridge, though still clearly moved by the spectacle, was far less passionate in his own retelling. 'Kilmarnoch', he wrote in a letter just a week after the trial itself had ended,

> spoke in Mitigation of his Crime near half an Hour with a decent Courage, & in a strong, but pathetic, Voice. his Figure would prejudice people in his Favour being tall & genteel: he is upwards of 40, but to the Eye not above 35 Years of Age. What he said appears to less Advantage, when read. Cromartie (who is about the same Age a Man of lower Stature, but much like a Gentleman) was sinking into the Earth, with Grief & Dejection. with Eyes cast down & a Voice so low, that no one heard a Syllable, that did not sit close to the Bar, he made a short Speech to raise Compassion. It is now, I see, printed; & is reckon'd extremely fine. I believe, you will think it touching & well-expressed: if there be any Meanness in it, it is lost in that Sorrow he gives us for so numerous & helpless a Family. (CTG 234)

---

[1] WC ix.24.
[2] WC xix.280.

The third defendant excited less compassion on Gray's part, yet even his actions and comments proved too morbidly interesting entirely to be passed over:

> as to Balmerino he never had any Hopes from the Beginning: he is an old soldier-like Man of a vulgar Manner & Aspect, speaks the broadest Scotch, & shews an Intrepidity, that some ascribe to real Courage, & some to Brandy. You have heard perhaps, that the first Day (while the Peers were adjourned to consider his Plea, & he left alone for an Hour & half in the Bar) he diverted himself with an Ax, that stood by him, played with its Tassels & tryed the edge with his Finger: & some Lord, as he passed by him, saying he was surprised to hear him alledge anything so frivolous, & that could not possibly so him the least Service: he answer'd, that as there were so many Ladies present, he thought it would be uncivil to give them no Amusement. (CTG 234–35)

Gray would not be the first observer to apply to a criminal trial the histrionic criteria of the drama. The intricate connections established by writers such as John Gay, Henry Fielding, and George Lillo (who wrote the enormously successful tragedy *The London Merchant* in 1731) between the stage of politics and the politics of the stage – between the human tragedies enacted daily in the Old Bailey and those enacted with rather more ceremony in Westminster – had already encouraged such a fashionable London 'audience' for the proceedings. The trial of the rebel Lords in Westminster Hall was treated by those who attended it as a grand and moving theatrical spectacle, the combination of high tragedy, domestic drama, and momentous, national history within which was close to unprecedented.

The executions on Tower Hill later that same month (Balmerino and Kilmarnock were beheaded at the Tower on 18 August; Cromarty, also originally sentenced to death, was reprieved and eventually received a conditional pardon, in 1749) formed a gory coda to the drama of the trial itself. Gray and Walpole soon returned to the more routine concerns of their own daily lives. Walpole, Gray reported to Wharton on 10 August, was then actively searching for a small house 'somewhere about Windsor', on which property he could obtain a short-term lease of some three or four months. By the second week of August, he had settled on renting the furnished home of one Mr. Jordan which he described to Mann as being 'within the precincts of the Castle at Windsor'. Gray, meanwhile, had left London for Stoke soon after the trial was over. No sooner had he been reconciled to his old school friends, it seems, than he once again found himself in something of an embarrassing position with regards to some gossip concerning Ashton that he had passed on to his Cambridge acquaintances. Ashton had recently confided in Gray his plans to marry as soon as possible. He even told Gray the 'profound secret' of an engagement he had apparently only just broken off with a young woman who 'had 12000 [£ in] her own Hands'. Gray indiscreetly passed this information on to his old Cambridge acquaintance, Richard Stonhewer, who told it to schoolfriend from Eton, who – completing the circle – promptly passed it on to Ashton himself. 'Whereby', Gray confessed jokingly to Wharton, 'I incurr'd a Scolding; so pray don't let me fall under [a] second, & lose all my Hopes of riseing in the Church'. Of rather more significance, Gray also commented in an aside to Wharton in the same letter that 'the Muse, I doubt, is gone, & has left me in far worse Company; if she returns, you will hear of her'.

A letter written almost exactly one month later finds Gray again referring to 'a few Autumnal Verses' that had providing his 'Entertainments dureing the Fall of the Leaf'. The two references are among the most significant clues we possess that Gray had already begun work on the actual composition of the *Elegy* at least as early as the late summer and early autumn of 1746.

*

In the several months that had passed since their initial reconciliation, Gray had begun cautiously to share some of his poetry with Walpole. Walpole's little house at Windsor was within easy distance of Stoke, and for a period beginning in the late summer of 1746, the two friends saw one another on a casual basis at least once a week. Walpole was at the time engaged in a number of literary 'projects'. Gray amused himself with the picture of his friend 'in his rural capacity, snug in his tub on Windsor-hill, and brooding over folios of his own creation'. Gray claimed to regard his friend's writings as his own 'god-children'. In November 1746, Walpole had written a timely epilogue for a production of *Tamerlane* then being staged at Covent Garden. He had also, by that date, at least begun to contemplate writing his *Memoirs*, a work (less a personal memoir than a record of parliamentary proceedings) which he had already begun planning several years earlier. However great his own ambitions as a writer, Walpole may well have realized that the accomplishment of his own public literary productions was destined in time to be overshadowed by that of his friend – and he must be given credit for the honesty of his perception. It was probably Walpole who first suggested that West's literary remains, when combined with Gray's own poetry, would be substantial enough to constitute a small, publishable volume. It was probably Walpole, in other words, who set before Gray's eyes the possibility of seeing his lyrics appear in print in the first place.

Throughout the winter of 1746–47, the two young men frankly discussed the possible publication of such a volume. Gray had shared his *Ode On a Distant Prospect of Eton College* with Walpole some time before the middle of October 1746, by which date he had also passed on to his friend the *Ode on the Spring* – the same poem he had originally sent to West before the latter's death in the spring of 1742. 'All it pretends with you is', he wrote to Walpole, 'that it is mine, & that you never saw it before, & that it is not so long as t'other'. In January 1747, Gray likewise passed on to Walpole 'the remainder of Agrippina' – the same 'tragic torrent' to which West, he now jested, had put an end when he first saw it 'breaking in upon him' nearly five years earlier. Walpole himself seems freely to have shared Gray's manuscripts with his other friends and acquaintances. In February 1747, Gray was surprised and actually distressed to hear some gossip being passed around among his own University colleagues that he was at work on a tragic drama – to be named *Agrippina*. 'I hope in God', he wrote quickly to Walpole, 'that you have not mention'd, or shew'd to anybody that scene (for trusting in it's Badness, I forgot to caution you concerning it)'. Gray, far from anxious to see his own work in print, seems genuinely to have sought to advance West's claims to reputation and respect at least as much his own. Apart from what he might have considered his own indebtedness to West, Gray's only real worry with regards to the project of a dual-authored volume published with Walpole's assistance, it would seem, was the fear that such a collection – even when the work of both men was brought together – would prove too insubstantial to enjoy any real success or, indeed, to merit any real critical attention. 'I much fear that our Joynt-Stock', he wrote in a memorable letter to Walpole early in 1747,

> would hardly compose a small Volume: what I have, is less considerable than you would imagine; & of that little we should not be willing to publish all. there is an Epistle, ad Amicos (that is, to us all at Cambridge) in English, of above fourscore Lines: the Thoughts are taken from Tibullus, & from a Letter of Mr. Pope's in Prose. (*CTG* 266)

Gray goes on in his letter to offer a short inventory of West's other poetic writings in his possession; the list details some eleven fragments and finished pieces in all. He then speculates of West's literary remains:

> This is all I can any where find. You, I imagine, may have a good deal more. I should not care, how unwise the ordinary Sort of Readers might think my Affection for him provided those few, that ever loved any Body, or judged of any thing rightly, might from such little Remains be moved to consider, what he would have been; & to wish, that Heaven had

granted him a longer Life, & a Mind more at Ease. I can't help fancying, that if you could find out Mrs West, & ask her for his Papers of that
kind (Ashton might do it in your Name) she would be ready enough to
part with them, & we might find something more: at least it would be
worth while to try. (*CTG* 266–67)

Walpole's apparently disinterested desire to see something of his
friends' writings in print prompted Gray himself once again to pay close
attention to 'matters poetical' and to comment more extensively than
he might otherwise have done on current and popular authors. The
literary criticism that Gray would more naturally have shared with West
he now passed on to Walpole. Although Gray nowhere in his correspondence makes any explicit reference to the death of Alexander Pope
in May 1744, he was no doubt very much aware of the fact that the
passing of a poet whose style and whose political concerns had dominated an entire generation of readers had left a vacancy in the world of
English letters that no one, as of yet, had displayed any signs of filling.
A possible reference to Pope in the same letter to Walpole of February,
1747, may have been a way for Gray to make clearer to his friend his
own perception of the fact that the world of poetry – and indeed, the
world of 'literature' in general – was even then in the midst of a period
of profound change. He wrote:

> Literature (to take it in its most comprehensive Sense, & include every
> Thing, that requires Invention, or Judgement, or barely Application &
> Industry) seems indeed drawing apace to its Dissolution; & remarkably
> since the Beginning of the War. I should be glad to know why, if any one
> will tell me. for I believe there may be natural Reasons discoverable
> enough without haveing Recourse to St. John, or St. Alexander's Reve-
> lations. (*CTG* 265)

Gray moves on in the letter to comment on Joseph Spence's recently published *Polymetis: or an Enquiry concerning the Agreement between the
works of the Roman Poets and the Remains of the Antient Artists*, a
work some portion of which he had already read in manuscript. Of the
several, recently published poets whose work Gray read and appreciated
at around this time, Joseph Warton and William Collins were singled
out for particular comment. Each, he wrote 'is the half of a considerable Man, & one the Counter-Part of the other'. Warton, Gray judged,
had a 'good Ear' and expressed himself well, but possessed little skill at
'Invention' – his work was, in other words, familiar and for the most
part unoriginal. Collins, on the other hand, though possessing a 'bad
Ear', nevertheless displayed a fine sense of fancy and cleverly drew much
of his imagery and language from classical sources. 'They both deserve

to last some Years', he ended, 'but will not'. However much one may choose to agree or disagree with Gray's criticisms of the work of the two poets, he was of course only partly correct in his assessment of their 'lasting' with the reading public for any length of time; for a great many years in the late nineteenth and twentieth centuries, Collins's odes were to appear as companions to Gray's own poetry in small volumes devoted to the work of both men.

*

The combination of Walpole's continued encouragement, the competitive stimulus of the work of slightly younger poets such as Warton and Collins, the sense that – for better or worse – a new 'era' in English literature was waiting to begin and, finally, the increasing awareness that the time of his own life was swiftly passing by ('I was 30 Year old yesterday', he wrote apprehensively in a holiday letter to Thomas Wharton at the end of 1746, 'what is it o'clock by you?'): each of these facts contributed to Gray's need to feel that he, too, was entering a busy and productive period of his own life. It may have been in these months that Gray decided in the haziest of fashions to risk a 'career' as a poet and scholar, rather than seriously to pursue his education in the law any further. He was at the very least setting about entering the world again – laying aside a young man's unanswerable grievances to assume the inescapably heavy burdens of responsibility that came with maturity.

Such burdens, however, need not always be carried wearily upon one's back; from time to time they could momentarily be set aside – and it was in such a moment of rest that Gray undertook the remarkably uncharacteristic gesture of writing, at Walpole's request, a poem fit to order. Not very long after Walpole had moved into his new home at Windsor, it happened that one of the two 'handsome' cats that he had left behind at Arlington Street – the exotically named 'Selima', the designation itself drawn from her owner's lifelong fascination with pseudo-oriental fictions and French romances, as well as from his own, recent rereading of Rowe's *Tamerlane* – lost her footing as she perched on the edge of an elegant china basin. Selima had been in the habit of peering intently at the goldfish that swam within the confines of the cistern. On this occasion she tumbled into the bowl and, unable to crawl free of the basin's slippery sides (and no doubt surrounded by several suitably astonished goldfish) was heard from no more. Walpole was genuinely if only briefly upset by Selima's drowning (one recalls his equally emotional – and equally short-lived – response to the sudden loss of his spaniel when crossing the Alps years several earlier) and soon wrote to Gray requesting that he write an epitaph for the pet. Gray replied at once, joking in a letter of 22 February 1747, that he could hardly begin mourning Walpole's loss properly, when he had for some time now been unable to distinguish just which of Walpole's cats had been called Selima in the first place – if, indeed, that was the correct name at all. 'As one ought to be particularly careful to avoid blunders in a compliment of condolence', he wrote,

> it would be a sensible satisfaction to me (before I testify my sorrow, and the sincere part I take in your misfortune) to know for certain who it is I lament. I knew Zara and Selima, (Selima, was it? or Fatima) or rather I knew them both together; for I cannot justly say which was which. Then as to your handsome Cat, the name you distinguish her by, I am no less at a loss, as well knowing one's handsome cat is always the cat one likes best; or, if one be alive and the other dead, it is usually the latter that is the handsomest. Besides, if the point was never so clear, I hope you do not think me so ill-bred or so imprudent as to forfeit all my interest in the survivor: Oh no! I would rather seem to mistake, and imagine to be sure it must be the tabby one that had met with this sad accident. Till this affair is a little better determined, you will excuse me if I do not begin to cry: 'Tempus inane peto, requiem, spatiumque doloris.' (CTG 271)

Gray was certain that Walpole would recognize the source of this last line – a slight adaptation of Virgil's *Aenead* iv.433 ('I plead for empty time, for peace and a respite from my sorrow'). The fact that Gray, in this first letter to Walpole following the latter's domestic, feline tragedy, ventured to compare his own 'sorrow' at Selima's death to that of Dido's frenzied madness when confronted with the fact of her lover's departure from Carthage, may well have served as some slight indication – as a literary–referential warning shot across the supposedly solemn bow of Walpole's feelings, as it were – that although Gray may have been in the mood to honour his friend's request for an epitaph, he would set about doing so in his own way, in the mimickery of loss.

On 1 March, having ascertained that it was indeed Selima and not Zara who had fallen so indecorously to her watery death, Gray sent to Walpole the poem subsequently published as an *Ode on the Death of a Favourite Cat, Drowned in a Tub of Gold-Fishes*. The poem, rather improbably, has since become one of the best-known short poems in the English language. Much of the work's original popularity can be ascribed to the simple fact that most eighteenth- and nineteenth-century readers – possessing no real familiarity with the sense of humour often betrayed by Gray in his private correspondence and in his occasional lyrics – found the short, mock-heroic epitaph compellingly at odds both in tone and in treatment with poems such as the *Eton Ode*, and the (by then

1. The Parish Church of St. Giles, Stoke Poges, as it looks today. The tomb of Thomas Gray is located under the east window of the Hastings Chapel – the red brick portion of the church which in the photo is on the left, closest to the pathway through the church-yard itself.

2. The Royal Exchange, Cornhill, designed by Edward Jerman; opened in 1669 and destroyed by fire in 1838.

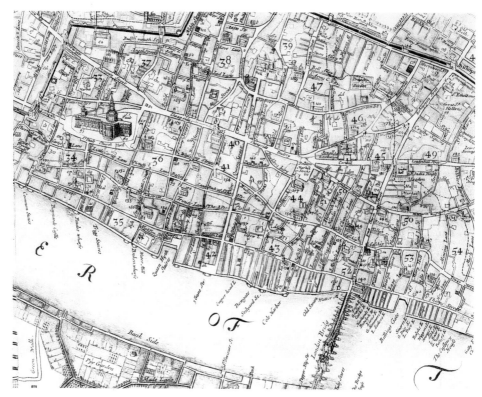

3. Detail from A. Lea and Richard Glynne's 1716 map of London, Westminster and Southwark, showing the Cornhill and the Royal Exchange. The house in which Gray was born stood on the corner of St. Michael's Alley and Cornhill itself, directly across the alley from St. Michael's Church.

4. Cornhill Parish Register, with the entry detailing the christening of Thomas Gray on 26 December 1716.

5. Thomas Gray, in a painting variously attributed to Arthur Pond and Jonathan Richardson the Elder. The image would appear to have been painted when the sitter was an adolescent or very young teenager (c. 1729–32), and still a student at Eton. Two volumes on the table on which Gray rests his right arm are labelled 'Locke' and 'Temple'.

6. A view of Eton College as it appeared in the late seventeenth century.

7. The Right Honble. Sr. Robert Walpole, by G. Bockman after T. Gibson.

8. Horace Walpole, aged 10 (1727–28) by William Hogarth.

9. Peterhouse College, Cambridge, showing the seventeenth-century chapel (1628–32) in the centre of the main court.

10. King's College, Cambridge, showing the great fifteenth-century chapel.

Cathedral of Amiens, ~ Shrine of S.t Firmin, of massy Gold ~ rich painted windows.

Abbey, & Cathedral of S.t Dennis ~ Monuments of the Kings of France ~ Lewis 12 Francis 1.st, Henry 2.d, Catharine of Medicis, particularly fine; some good Bas-reliefs. rich mosaic windows ~ the Treasury ~ inestimable antique Vase of oriental Onyx with admirable Sculptures representing the mysteries of Bacchus. ~ Crown of Char=lemagne; Rubies, Emeralds & Sapphires of vast bigness ~ Coronation robes & other Regalia:

Paris.

The Palais Royal, built by Card: Richelieu, inhabited at present by the Duke of Orleans ~ a noble collection of near 500 Pictures of great masters ~ the S.t John Baptist of Raphael ~ Naked Venus, wringing her hair, by Guido ~ the Leda & Danae of Correggio ~ a whole room of the finest Paul Veronese ~ the 7 Sacra=ments of Poussin ~ small copies in Bronze of the Toro, Lyon & Howe, &c: ~ the new Gallery, design'd by Mansart, & richly adorn'd with sculpture, gilding, & furnit=ure of fine embroidery; painted by Coypel with stories from th' Eneid. ~ The Walks belonging to the Palace.

2. The Palace Luxembourg. built by Mary of Medicis; at present the residence of the 2.d Queen Dowager of Spain ~ the Gallery so well known, of Rubens.

3. The Invalides ~ the Church, beautiful disposition of the Chapels, & Dome; Altar imitated from S.t Peter's at Rome.

4. The Val de Grace. ~ fine Chappel, beautiful Statues of the Virgin & Joseph by Anguier.

5. The Hotel de Toulouse. ~ the grand Gallery, rich gilding, embroidery, & Glasses, on each side 5 Capital pictures ~ the Rape of Helen, by Guido. the Sabine Wives separating the two armies, by Guercino. a Divorce, by P: di Cortona. ~

6. Cathedral of Notre Dame ~ Statues of the Virgin with the dead Christ, & those of Louis the 13.th, & 14.th, by the 2 Coutoux, & Coysevox.

7. Church of the Carmelites. ~ a fine Annunciation, of Guido ~ a Magdalen, of Le Brun. Statue of Card:l Berulle, by Sarazin.

8. The English Benedictins. Body of K: James 2.d, deposed here.

11. Gray's travel notes on Amiens and Paris, from his Unpublished Autograph Notes, currently in the Eton College Library.

12. 'English Milordi' or 'Four Learned Milordi', a caricature by Sir Joshua Reynolds (1751); the image is a burlesque of English travellers on the Continent based on Raphael's *School of Athens*.

13. *Entrance to the Valley of the Grande Chartreuse* by John Robert Cozens.

14. Portrait of Horace Walpole (c. 1741) by Rosalba Giovanni Carriera.
The portrait currently hangs at Houghton in Norfolk.

15. Portrait of John Chute by Johan Heinrich Müntz. Chute and his young cousin, Francis Whithed, were introduced to Gray and Walpole in Florence by Horace Mann.

16. View of the Vyne, the Hampshire property eventually inherited by
John Chute.

17. Portrait of Thomas Gray by John Giles Eccardt. This portrait and those of Walpole and Bentley (nos. 18–19) were originally hung in Walpole's Strawberry Hill home.

18. Portrait of Horace Walpole by John Giles Eccardt.

19. Portrait of Richard Bentley by John Giles Eccardt.

20. View of Strawberry Hill, the small Twickenham property purchased by Walpole in the spring of 1747, which he transformed over the years into a Gothic fantasy.

21. Horace Walpole in his library at Strawberry Hill, from a water-colour by J. H. Müntz.

22. The Manor House, Stoke Poges, as it looks today.

23. Miss Henrietta Jane Speed, afterwards Comtesse de Viry, by Peter Falconet. The painting shows Miss Speed as she looked many years after her earliest acquiantance with Gray in 1751.

J. Reynolds pinx.ᵗ   J. McArdell fecit 1757

Horace Walpole

Youngest Son of S.ʳ Rob.ᵗ Walpole Earl of Orford.

24. Portrait of Horace Walpole by Sir Joshua Reynolds.

J. Reynolds pinx.   *Thomas Ashton D.D.*   *J. M. Ardell fecit.*

Collegii Etonensis, prope Windesoram Socius ;
Ecclesiæ Sancti Botolphi ad portam Episcopalem,
extra Muros, Londini Rector.

25. Portrait of Thomas Ashton by Sir Joshua Reynolds.

26. Detail of a portrait of William Mason by Sir Joshua Reynolds.

27. Portrait of Richard Stonhewer by Sir Joshua Reynolds, painted after Gray's death (in 1775) for the Duke of Grafton.

28. Portrait of Christopher Smart (artist unknown).

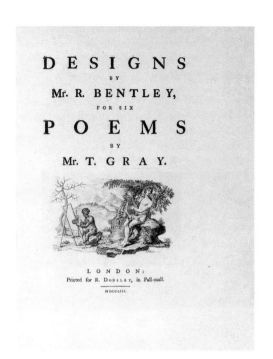

29. Richard Bentley, Frontispiece, *Designs*.

30. Richard Bentley, Tailpiece, 'Eton Ode', *Designs*.

31. Richard Bentley, Frontispiece, 'Elegy', *Designs*.

A LONG STORY.

32. Richard Bentley, Tailpiece, 'A Long Story', Designs.

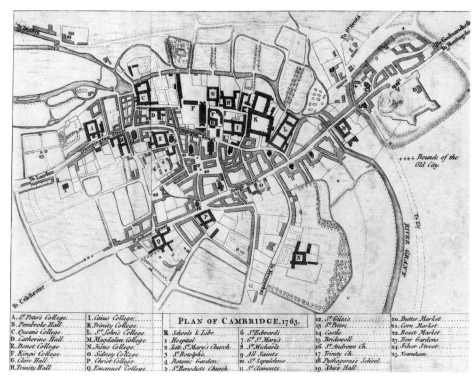

		PLAN OF CAMBRIDGE, 1763.			
A. St Peter's College.	I. Caius College.			12. St Giles's.	20. Butter Market.
B. Pembroke Hall.	K. Trinity College.			13. St Peters.	21. Corn Market.
C. Queen's College.	L. St John's College.	R. Schools & Libr.	6. St Edwards.	14. Castle.	22. Beast Market.
D. Catherine Hall.	M. Magdalen College.	1. Hospital.	7. Gt St Mary's.	15. Bridewell.	23. New Gardens.
E. Benet College.	N. Jesus College.	2. Litt. St Marys Church.	8. St Michaels.	16. St Andrews Ch.	24. Silver Street.
F. King's College.	O. Sidney College.	3. St Botolphs.	9. All Saints.	17. Trinity Ch.	25. Newnham.
G. Clare Hall.	P. Christ College.	4. Botanic Garden.	10. St Sepulchres.	18. Pythagoras's School.	
H. Trinity Hall.	Q. Emanuel College.	5. St Benedicts Church.	11. St Clements.	19. Shire Hall.	

33. Plan of Cambridge, c. 1763, from *Cantabrigia Depicta, A Concise and Accurate Description of the University and Town of Cambridge.*

34. Caricature of the Rev. Henry Etough, from an engraving by I. Parke of a drawing by William Mason.

35. Portrait of Dr. Roger Long, Master of Pembroke College, by Benjamin Wilson. The portrait was painted toward the end of the Master's long life, when he was nearly ninety years old.

36. Portrait of John Lyon, Ninth Earl of Strathmore (1762). Artist unknown.

37. Gray's rooms at Pembroke College, from an engraving by W. B. Cook, after a drawing by J. M. Ince.

38. Pencil sketch of Gray (early 1760s) apparently by Francis Mapletoft.
39. Silhouette (or 'shade') of Gray by Francis Mapletoft, Fellow Pembroke
College, made sometime between 1761 and 1764.

40. Silhouette of Gray, seated, cut by Mrs. Wray, wife of the antiquary Daniel
Wray, 1762.
41. Silhouette of William Mason, copying the *Venus de Medici*, by Francis
Mapletoft.

42. Thomas Gray, from a painting by Benjamin Wilson.

43. John Montagu, Fourth Earl of Sandwich.

44. Portrait of Henry, Lord Holland, by William Hogarth.

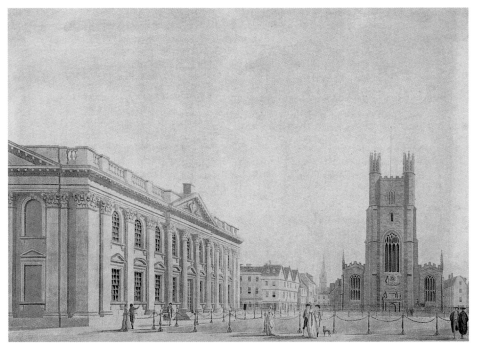

45. The South Front of the Senate House, Cambridge, and the West End of St. Mary's Church, Cambridge by Thomas Malton Jr. (1748–1804).

46. Charles Victor de Bonstetten as Hamlet. Artist unknown.

47. Gray's outline notes for his projected History of English poetry, from a manuscript.

48. Frontispiece to William Mason's edition of Gray's *Works*.

49. Gray's Tomb at Stoke Poges by Hendrik de Cort.

widely known) *Elegy*. Yet there were some significant points of contact, as well as difference, between the three works. All three poems treated the subjects of death, loss, and mourning; all three pretended to ask profound questions about just what constitutes the *value* of a lived existence – where is one to locate worth in life? What is the spiritual or metaphysical reality that lies hidden beneath external appearances? Yet what were readers to make of the humourous articulation of these questions in the *Ode*? Was Gray making light in his humorous, lyric epitaph of some of the very same subjects and concerns with which he had dealt more solemnly in the *Eton Ode*, and that would later motivate his popular and (seemingly) sincere meditation on mortality? Walpole, for one, did not read the poem in this light, and modern readers appear to have had less of a problem than many of their predecessors in accepting the *Ode*'s unapologetically witty attempt to handle serious matters lightly. Gray's poem gently and effectively places the loss of Selima, when viewed even from a sympathetic human point of view, in its proper perspective.

In Gray's hands, the death of Selima appears first to have been transformed from a minor domestic tragedy into a grand, admonitory parable on the nature of human – and particularly of feminine – desire and ambition. Selima's death, the reader is made to understand in no uncertain terms, is meant to stand as an emblem for the reward invariably reserved for female covetousness and desire. Like many of Gray's other poems, then, the *Ode* is consumed by the notion that only by keeping one's desires and expectations securely in check – only by putting a restraint upon seeming *need* – does one pass unmolested or unharmed through this world. To give free reign to one's own personal desires is, in the language of the poem itself, 'presumption'. As in several of Gray's other works, 'malignant' Fate is always sitting and waiting somewhere nearby to cut the thread of life, and so put a swift end to any unreasonable expectations fostered by her fond charges. The poem's final verse stanza is among Gray's best known pieces of poetry. Its final line helped popularize – although it did not originate – the familiar proverb warning against the deception of appearances. Having told the story of Selima's death with mock-heroic solemnity, the poet draws an explicit and uncompromising moral from his own tale:

> From hence, ye beauties, undeceived,
> Know, one false step is ne'er retrieved,
>   And be with caution bold.
> Not all that tempts your wandering eyes
> And heedless hearts is lawful prize;
>   Nor all that glisters gold. (*PTG* 84–85)

Many modern readers take offense at what they interpret to be the underlying (and surprisingly gratuitous) misogyny of the poem – a misogyny that is at best casual and representative of the larger views of society at the time with regards to the proper sphere of woman's activity, and at worst (at least to followers of Gray's life) the spitefully catty and unintentionally venomous product of an embittered and perhaps increasingly lonely homosexual man. Yet the poem needs carefully to be placed within the even more precise personal contexts that produced it. Gray's reconciliation to Walpole was an event yet near enough to him both in time and in emotional volatility for the poet still to feel the need to seek some way of asserting his mastery over the situation. The activity of these early, middle years was already providing Gray with the kinds of mental diversions and stimulations that would help him finally to move through the sense of chaos and loss which had followed the spring and summer of 1742. If the elegiac impulse of those poems Gray wrote in August, 1742 had allowed him to sort through his emotions by means of several different narrative–poetic responses to such loss, the comic *Ode* written at Walpole's request gave him a similar opportunity to treat some of the same subjects handled in those earlier poems – death, loss, transience, deception – in a considerably more light-hearted, though still therapeutic, manner. Gray's *Ode* on the accidental death of Selima is very much of a piece with his more serious work; as a poet he sought always to bracket questions concerning the ultimate designs of Fate and Destiny within the familiar comfort of a quiet and consolatory allusion. Confronted with questions concerning the unfathomable, guiding forces of human life and of the universe in general, Gray sought temporary refuge in the simple, articulated structures of poetic form, and in the power of referential fragments that could, at the very least, remind us that man had been asking these same questions since he first began to articulate his thoughts at all.

*

Walpole, again, was pleased with Gray's poem, and seems gracefully to have accepted it in the spirit with which it had been offered. He even went so far as to have the six lines of the first stanza inscribed on a commemorative plaque that he then affixed to a pedestal, on which he placed the China vase in which the unfortunate Selima had drowned. For many years the blue and white cistern was to stand in a place of ceremonial importance in the cloister near the entrance of Walpole's Strawberry Hill home. Gray sent another copy of the poem to Wharton, who had recently returned home in order to be closer to his family, and who was himself now contemplating marriage to one Margaret Wilkinson, of Durham (the two were eventually married in April, 1747).

He joked with Wharton that the poem's superficial warning against female avarice was particularly appropriate to his friend's own situation, and suggested that the work was 'of a proper Size & Subject for a Gentleman in your Condition to peruse'. He called the poem on this occasion, an ode 'On a favourite Cat, call'd Selima, that fell into a China Tub with Gold-Fishes in it & was drown'd'. Gray himself appears content to have written the poem primarily for the private amusement of these two friends and their chosen acquaintances. Walpole, however, had by now begun to contemplate other plans for his friend's work.

On 30 May 1747, Robert Dodsley published Gray's *Eton Ode* as an anonymous folio pamphlet, priced 6d. It was the first of Gray's poems to appear in print. We have already seen that Gray was pleased to maintain his anonymity in the face of speculation by his Cambridge colleagues that the work was in fact his own. Gray's work was not to enjoy such complete and unquestioned anonymity for very long, however. The January of the following year saw the publication of Dodsley's three-volume *Collection of Poems*. The *Collection*'s first volume contained fugitive pieces by authors including Samuel Johnson, Matthew Green, William Shenstone, John Dyer, and William Collins. Dodsley's third volume included three poems by Walpole (published anonymously) and West's 'Monody on the Death of Queen Caroline', a piece originally composed in 1737, and described in the *Collection* as having been written 'By Richard West, Esq.; Son to the Chancellor of Ireland, and Grandson to Bishop Burnet'. Thus comfortably sandwiched between his two closest childhood friends, Gray was represented in the collection by three poems – the *Eton Ode*, the *Ode on the Spring*, and the *Ode on the Death of a Favourite Cat*. His name was nowhere mentioned with connection to any of these poems, though he may well have suspected that he was not for very long successfully to deny attribution of the works. His initial response to the collection, however, was quietly contended in his own representation, and genuinely stimulated by the variety and achievement represented in the three small volumes (although he was distressed by the rather poor quality – 'whited-brown paper, and distorted figures, like an old ballad' – of the publication itself). He wrote to Walpole shortly after the collection appeared; his friend had obviously solicited his opinion on this new crop of probable contenders for England's laurels. 'I am obliged to you for Mr. Dodsley's book', Gray wrote in thanks,

> and, having pretty well looked it over, will (as you desire) tell you my opinion of it. He might, methinks, have spared the Graces in his frontispiece, if he chose to be economical, and dressed his authors in a little more decent raiment – . . . I am ashamed to see myself; but the company keeps me in countenance. . . . (*CTG* 294–95)

Gray then offered some of his own criticisms on and opinions of selected poets included in the volume. Thomas Tickell's *The Prospect of Peace*, which opened the collection and which had first been published in 1712, he dismissed as weakened by 'a great poverty as sense, and a string of transitions that hardly become a school-boy'. Matthew Green, who had died in 1737 and to whom, it should be remembered, Gray confessed himself indebted for the 'thought' of his *Ode on the Spring*, was congratulated on his natural talent with a glancing reference to England's greatest playwright himself ('even his wood-notes' Gray wrote in compliment of Green, 'often break out into strains of real poetry and music'). Both Samuel Johnson's *London* and his *Prologue Spoken by Mr. Garrick at the Opening of the Theatre Royal, Drury Lane* were singled out for praise, as were John Dyer's *Grongar Hill* and *The Ruins of Rome*. Censure was as freely poured on the offerings of William King, Abel Evans, Edward Rolle, Thomas Seward, and on the historically significant parodies by Isaac Hawkins Browne reproduced in the collection's second volume. Gray could not, of course, omit reference in his letter to Walpole's own poems. He revealingly placed himself as standing in relation to his more worldly and successful friend in much the same manner that the learned playwright Ben Jonson once stood in relation to Shakespeare (having referred earlier in the same letter to Matthew Green's 'wood-notes', Jonson's criticisms of Shakespeare seem to have continued revolving slowly in Gray's mind). Of Walpole's satire – *An Epistle from Florence to T. A. Esq., Tutor to the Earl of P . . .* – Gray wrote:

> You know I was of the publishing side, and thought your reasons against it none; for though, as Mr. Chute said extremely well, the *still small voice* of Poetry was not made to be heard in a crowd; yet Satire will be heard, for all the audience are by nature her friends; especially when she appears in the spirit of Dryden, with his strength, and often with his versification; such as you have caught in those lines on the royal unction, on the papal dominion, and convents of both sexes, on Henry VIII. and Charles II. for these are to me the shining parts of your Epistle. There are many lines I could wish corrected, and some blotted out, but beauties enough to atone for a thousand worse faults than these. (*CTG* 296–97)

Gray then reports to Walpole on the general reception of the Dodsley's *Collection* among his Cambridge acquaintances:

> As to what one says, since it came out; our people (you must know) are slow of judgement; they wait till some bold body saves them the trouble, and then follow his opinion; or stay till they hear what is said in town, that is at some bishop's table, or some coffee-house about the Temple. What they are determined, I will tell you faithfully their verdict. (*CTG* 297)

Before closing his letter, however, Gray refers casually to the work of one 'Mr. Mason', also included in Dodsley's anthology. This Mr. Mason, Gray confides to Walpole, was himself 'a new acquaintance' of the poet's, 'whose Musaeus [a monody on the death of Pope included in the collection] too seems to carry with it the promise of at least something good to come'. The reference is among Gray's first to William Mason – a gentleman whom he was soon to count among his closest confidants, and whom he familiarly and affectionately dubbed 'Scroddles' or 'Skroddles'. In order properly to introduce Mason into the narrative of Gray's life – and in order likewise to give an account of Gray's other new friends and acquaintances dating from these early years as a college fellow – we need briefly to return to Cambridge and resume the narrative of Gray's personal life in the university town where we last left off, sometime in the autumn of 1746.

III. Friends and Fiends

Gray seems genuinely to have looked forward to his return to Cambridge at the beginning of Michaelmas term, 1746. 'My time lies heavy on my hands', he had written from Stoke on 11 September, '& I want to be home again'. When Gray spoke of home now, strikingly, he spoke neither of London nor of Stoke, but rather of Cambridge itself; a period of genuine resettlement had begun in earnest. Thinking of Cambridge as his proper 'home' prompted Gray to begin taking a more active part in college and university affairs. For one thing, he had begun cautiously to enlarge his circle of friends and acquaintances. The time he had recently spent with Chute and Whithed both at the latter's home in Fareham and in London itself (Whithed had taken lodgings in New Bond Street) – and, of course, the time spent with Walpole, as well – reminded him that he had for some time now left unsatisfied a real taste for the company of like-minded, witty individuals. The two weeks Gray spent 'flaunting about at publick Places of all kinds with my two Italianized friends' had left him in an unusually social and convivial mood. 'The World itself' he had continued in a letter to Wharton written after the period that he would later call 'my Dissipation de quinze jours',

> has some Attraction in it to a Solitary of six Years standing; & agreeable well-meaning People of Sense (thank Heaven there are so few of them) are my peculiar Magnet. It is no Wonder then, if I felt some Reluctance at parting with them so soon; or if my Spirits, when I return'd back to my Cell, should sink for a time, not indeed to Storm & Tempest, but a good deal below Changeable. (CTG 255)

Gray continued in this unusually confessional manner:

> It is a foolish Thing, that one can't only not live as one pleases, but where
> & with whom one pleases, without Money. Swift somewhere says, that
> Money is Liberty; & I fear money is Friendship too & Society, & almost
> every external Blessing. it is a great tho' ill-natured, Comfort to see most
> of those, who have it in Plenty, without Pleasure, without Liberty, &
> without Friends. (*CTG* 255)

Once again at Cambridge Gray opened himself to the possibility of
meeting new people – and he soon found himself successful.

Foremost among Gray's new acquaintances was William Mason
himself. Gray would in time grow to trust Mason completely. He eventually chose Mason to serve as his 'official' biographer, and asked him
to act as his literary executor. Mason was first introduced to Gray sometime in 1747 (Gray still, in the earliest months of 1748, refers to him in
a letter to Walpole as 'a new acquaintance of mine'). Some seven years
younger than Gray, Mason had been admitted to St. John's College in
1742 and had graduated B.A. in 1745–46. He came to the Cambridge
originally from Hull, where his father was a clergyman. Gray, who seems
first to have discovered his future friend through the perusal of what
Mason himself later in life dismissed as 'some very juvenile imitations
of Milton's juvenile poems', was to play a significant role in Mason's
subsequent nomination to a Fellowship in Pembroke College and was
to take an active interest in his highly successful ecclesiastical career. 'He
has much Fancy', Gray wrote of Mason not very long after having met
him, 'little Judgement, and a good deal of Modesty. I like him for a good
and well-meaning Creature; but then he is really *in Simplicity a Child*,
and loves everybody he meets with'. Gray continued to be charmed –
and in time even to be a little worried – by Mason's seemingly straightforward personality. In August 1749, he wrote to Wharton that Mason
'grows apace into my good Graces, as I know him more':

> he is very ingenious with great Good-Nature and Simplicity. a little vain,
> but in so harmless and comical a Way, that it does not offend one at all;
> a little ambitious, but withall so ignorant in the World & its Ways, that
> this does not hurt him in one's Opinion. so sincere and so undisguised,
> that no Mind with a Spark of Generosity would ever think of hurting
> him, he lies so open to Injury. but so indolent, that if he can not over-
> come this Habit, all his good Qualities will signify nothing at all. (*CTG*
> 323)

Gray rediscovered another lifelong friend at about this same time in
the figure of Richard Stonhewer. He first met Stonhewer when the latter

was still a precocious undergraduate at Trinity College. He had first come up to Cambridge as a Pensioner in 1745 from Durham, where his father served as rector of the parish of Houghton-le-Spring. He was eventually, in 1753, to become a Fellow of Peterhouse. Gray on at least one occasion chose to call him his 'best friend'. Stonhewer was also an intimate friend to Mason, who upon his own death turned over Gray's manuscripts and books to his care. William Cole would write of Stonhewer: 'he was one of the prettiest Figures of a Man I ever saw, & was as pretty a scholar'.[3]

Among Gray's other Cambridge acquaintances dating from around this period, three individuals need particularly to be distinguished from among the rest. The first was Nicholas Bonfoy, a young man whom Gray and Walpole had originally encountered in Paris in 1739 and whom they subsequently met again at Florence. Bonfoy – a Pembroke man – was just a few years older than Gray, and the two shared a similar temperament. Quite apart from their common experiences as travellers on the continent, both men cultivated their close connection to university society; both had laid the ground for legal careers before the opportunity to pursue less rigorous 'professional' courses presented themselves. Following his adventures from the Grand Tour, Bonfoy had returned to his family home at Abbot's Ripton, near Huntingdon (some twenty miles from Cambridge), where he lived with his mother and enjoyed the privileges attendant upon being the local squire. He was later in life (in 1762) to become Serjeant-at-Arms in the House of Commons. Gray and James Brown would within the coming years often visit Bonfoy at Abbot's Ripton, and he came within time to know both Bonfoy and his mother quite well. On the latter's death many years later (in 1763) Gray was to write to Wharton that 'Mrs. Bonfoy (who taught me to pray) is dead'. Although the purport of Gray's aside has often been misinterpreted, nothing could have been to him more natural than the company of such an older, maternal figure. The company of his mother and his aunts had served to make Gray his most comfortable among such elderly females. Gray was at ease and at home among both the genial Bonfoy and his equally sociable mother.

The second acquaintance whose company Gray found to be particularly amusing was that of the recently elected Master of Magdalene College, Thomas Chapman. Chapman had come up to Cambridge as a Scholar at Christ's College in 1734, and became a Fellow of the same college in 1741. He was best known outside the small Cambridge academic community itself as the author of an *Essay on the Roman Senate*. Although Gray's other friends appeared to find little of value in Chapman's company (William Cole thought him pompous and 'over-

---

[3] William Cole, quoted in *CTG* 238.

bearing'), Gray himself was amused at the manner in which Chapman fulfilled his role as Master with 'a great Deal of comic Dignity'. He possessed no great respect for Chapman as a scholar, yet Gray nevertheless followed his career as Master and clearly spent time with him on relatively easy terms.

The third individual with whom Gray also appears to have spent time possessed a lively personality that formed an odd and striking contrast to Chapman's pompous conformity; the fact that the two men were often to be found in one another's company only further highlighted the obvious differences in their personal appearance and demeanour. Henry Coventry was a young and highly energetic Fellow of Magdalene College who had taken his B.A. in 1729 and his M.A. four years later. Coventry was of striking personal appearance, and he accented the birthright of his physiognomy by a wildly ornate style of dress. For all his sartorial flamboyancy, Coventry conducted himself with suitable decorum and dignity. 'He used to dress remarkably gay', Cole (himself betraying the slightest uneasiness) wrote of Coventry, 'with much gold lace, and a most prominent Roman nose . . .'. He was nevertheless, Cole hastened to add, 'much of a gentleman'.[4] Gray himself found Coventry's peculiar combination of sophistication and naiveté to be a breath of fresh air. 'He is', he wrote succinctly of Coventry to Wharton, 'the best Sort of Man in this Place'.

'This place' – Cambridge in general and the small, twin communities of Peterhouse and Pembroke Colleges in particular – had been uncharacteristically rife with internecine intrigue, gossip, and out-and-out scandal of late. Most of the rivalries and cabals produced nothing of any more consequence than similar academic wrangling before or since. Several such 'incidents', however, appear to have excited Gray's particular interest, insofar as they touched the lives of individuals with whom, for better or for worse, he had begun to grow close. The first was a matter of simple and slightly sexually charged scandal. Just prior to the holidays in December 1746, a young man recently matriculated as an undergraduate at Pembroke by the name of John Blake Delaval only barely escaped being caught in the act of secreting a female visitor in his rooms (women were permitted to visit members of the college only under circumstances of tightly controlled decorum and even supervision). Delaval was the second son of Francis Blake Delaval, an influential Northumberland magnate whose good graces and favourable opinion the master of Pembroke, Dr. Roger Long, had no desire to forego. The case against Delaval, however, was black. As Gray reported to Wharton in a letter of 27 December, the young man had boldly paraded his female companion – 'a certain Gentlewoman properly call'd

---

[4]   William Cole, quoted in *CTG* 276.

Nell Burnet' – disguised as a 'Captain Hargraves' in an officer's habit throughout the town. The couple visited college chapels and libraries like any other tourists to the university, and made visits to Delaval's acquaintances 'in the Face of Day'. Forced by the outright audacity of Delaval's behaviour to take action, Long actually raided the student's room and searched about its furnishings even as the woman herself hid locked in a nearby cupboard, awaiting from Delaval the signal that she should escape the room from one of its windows. Gray had great fun picturing Long to Wharton as indecorously 'Feeling and Snuffleing about the Bed' in his search for the young lady. Even though Long failed in his search to produce either a captain or a gentlewoman ('had he but caught her', Gray reports Long as having boasted coarsely, 'he would soon have known, whether it was a Man, or a Woman'), Delaval was asked by the Master to 'cut out his Name' from the college books and so terminate his residency. Lying in bed that night, Long may well have passed through waking nightmares regarding the consequences of having thus alienated or offended – possibly without reason or defense – an important family such as the Delavals. The following morning he immediately sent a message to Dr. Whalley across the street at Peterhouse to the effect that he 'never knew any Hurt' of Delaval, and asked that the student be admitted without question to the rival college. Whalley, with an eye to the future, was very much in favour of gaining such a potentially influential pupil and, Gray believed, 'would have directly admitted him here', had not the application been blocked by another Fellow of Peterhouse, Dr. Charles Stuart. Long himself then called two meetings with the purpose of reversing his own earlier decision and readmitting Delaval to Pembroke, but everyone, Gray wrote, 'was inexorable, and so he has lost his Pupil'. Long, incidentally, had only within recent weeks asserted the right to call Delaval 'his' Pupil; for the better part of his short career at the college, Delaval's private tutor had been an erratic and intemperate – and unquestionably gifted – young Fellow by the name of Christopher Smart.

Smart was not the kind of individual entirely to endear himself to a customarily neat and fastidious sort of person such as Thomas Gray. He had been admitted to Pembroke as Sizar in 1739 and had distinguished himself as the Craven University Scholar for Classics in 1742. He was granted his B.A. in 1743–44, and made a Fellow of the College just one year later. Smart was without question a gifted Latinist (he was asked to write the Tripos verses on three separate occasions), but the signs and portents of his later-life struggle with alcoholism, insolvency, and madness were evident even in his earliest years at the University. He was constantly in debt, and his seemingly constitutional inability properly to manage the small allowance of £40 yearly granted to him first by the Duchess of Cleveland (and subsequently, following her death in 1742, by her husband the Duke) led him to great mental anguish. His constant drinking only further exacerbated his fragile state of mind so that, as Gray wrote, 'he must necessarily be abimé'. Gray, like so many of Smart's other Cambridge acquaintances, appears to have been torn between a desire on the one hand to assist this talented young man in whatever way he could, and a reluctance, on the other, to lift a finger in the aid of someone whose behaviour was so frequently juvenile and inconsiderate as to be a constant source of comment within the University. Gray nevertheless saw precisely where Smart's eccentric behaviour would eventually lead. 'His debts daily increase (you remember the State they were in, when you left us)', Gray told Wharton,

> Addison [Smart's former tutor], I know, wrote smartly to him last Week; but it has had no Effect, that signifies. only I observe he takes Hartshorn from Morning to Night lately: in the mean time he is amuseing himself with a Comedy of his own Writing, which he makes all the Boys of his Acquaintance act, & intends to borrow the Zodiak Room, & have it performed publickly. our Friend Lawman, the mad Attorney, is his Copyist; & truly the Author himself is to the full as mad as he. his Piece (he says) is inimitable, true Sterling Wit, & humour by God; & he can't hear the Prologue without being ready to die with Laughter. he acts five Parts himself, & is only sorry, he can't do all the rest. he has also advertised a Collection of Odes; & for his Vanity & Faculty of Lyeing, they are come to their full Maturity. All this, you see, must come to a Jayl, or Bedlam, & that without any help, almost without Pity. (*CTG* 274–75)

Gray's assessment here that Smart's troubles had grown to their 'full maturity' was, of course, mistaken; far darker days for Smart still lay ahead. The play on which he had been working so enthusiastically – *A Trip to Cambridge, or, the Grateful Fair* – was staged the following year in Pembroke College Hall. Gray's new friend Stonhewer served as prompter on the occasion, and other Cambridge worthies – among them John Randall, organist at Pembroke and a Professor of Music, and Richard Forester, also a Pembroke Fellow – gamely joined the undergraduate cast, undertaking roles as actors and musicians. Smart was eventually to pass out of residence in 1749. He necessarily vacated his college Fellowship completely following the revelation of his clandestine marriage to the step-daughter of the well-known London bookseller John Newbery some four years later. To his credit, Gray appears anxious to have kept some track of Smart's circumstances throughout the years and, as we shall see, appears likewise to have made some attempt to rescue him from financial insolvency following his eventual incarceration. Despite what he on one occasion described as Smart's 'Lies, Impertinence, and Ingratitude', Gray did what he could to ensure the continuance of the young man's stipend and when, many years later, Smart announced his intention of offering to the public his *Translation of the Psalms of David*, Gray generously put his name down for not one, but two copies of the work.

College Fellows such as Smart may alternately have amused and annoyed Gray to little real effect. The university environment, then as now, tended to provide a convenient refuge for a great many individuals whose behaviour would otherwise have been deemed far too eccentric or irrational to be tolerated by the busy world at large, and Gray (no stranger himself to the strains and pressures accompanying social conformity) rather prided the Cambridge community on the colourful plumage of its own peculiar and indigenous breeds of *avis rarae*. An individual openly hostile to Gray's interests and wishes in any position of real power, however – and such a one was Dr. Roger Long of Pembroke – was another matter altogether, and a cause for real concern.

Long had first entered Pembroke as an undergraduate prior to the end of the last century – in March 1698. He had been elected a Fellow as long ago as 1703. Having left Pembroke for a brief period of time to serve as private tutor to Sir Wolston Dixie, at Emmanual College, Long returned to the college only a few years later and had remained there ever since. On 12 October 1733 he had been elected Master of Pembroke, and in November of the same year was distinguished even further by his elevation to Vice-Chancellor of the University. In 1750 he was appointed as the first occupant of the newly established Lowdean chair of astronomy and geometry. Long is reported to have been a scholarly man whose delicate health led him to lead an abstemious lifestyle. Like many men of his status and temperament, he appears to have had few if any very close friends. His primary interests were academic and professional, and he was fiercely tenacious of the power and privileges traditionally adhering to his several academic positions. His battles with the other college Fellows – battles in which he rarely if ever wavered or conceded a point – were notoriously unpleasant and unproductive; he was a Tory among Whigs, and his bluff, Norfolk character was likely, on occasion, to grate against the sensibilities of some of the institution's more delicate, academic elite. Long was not, however, without his own (to modern eyes, at least) rather admirable and even daring eccentricities. In 1765, he had built in one of Pembroke's courts a primitive sort of planetarium. The hollow sphere – into which as many as thirty spectators could be squeezed at one time – was a full eighteen feet in diameter, and represented on its inner surface the movements of the various planets and other celestial bodies. Long's revolving planetarium, which remained in the college's possession well into the nineteenth century, must have looked wildly futuristic, resting as it did so incongruously in

the midst of Cambridge's otherwise gothic and neo-classical surroundings. The planetarium was only one of a number of unfamiliar-looking
scientific models, instruments, and machines which, by the end of his
life, the Master had crowded not only into his own rooms, but into the
courts and gardens of the college as well.

Because so many of his friends and acquaintances were now in residence across the street at Pembroke, Gray took at least as much
interest in the affairs of that college as he did in those of his own. Long,
who seemed always to be setting up some obstacle before the wishes of
his friends within the college, he regarded as something of an enemy. In
1746, Long blocked the election of Gray's new friend Henry Tuthill to
a college Fellowship, despite the fact that the Fellows themselves had
voted unanimously in Tuthill's favour. Tuthill, who had taken his B.A.
from Peterhouse in 1743, had three years later migrated to Pembroke at
Wharton's suggestion. Wharton assured Tuthill that the existing Fellows
supported his nomination, but had clearly not anticipated the degree to
which the Master's veto of 'Ego non consentio' scrawled at the bottom
of the page of the College Register could, according to current College
statute, apparently stand uncontested. Gray eventually advised Tuthill
to 'give up his Pretensions with a good Grace', but Long's unreasonable
intractability had caused him a great deal of trouble and annoyance. In
November 1747 Long once again thwarted Gray's own particular wishes
when he similarly vetoed the election of another of the poet's close
friends – William Mason, then a scholar at St. John's – to a vacant
Fellowship. As had been the case with Tuthill, the college Fellows once
again voted unanimously in favour of the designated candidate (Mason's
nomination had in fact been advanced by Gray himself), and once again
Long withheld his approval and consent, this time at least giving a supposed reason for his veto ('Ego non consentio ut extraneus eligatur
socius cum domesticos habeamus idoneos dignos qui in ordinem
sociorum cooptentur'). Mason was rather more determined than Tuthill
to pursue the matter to the bitter end (Gray described him to Wharton
with no small degree of admiration as 'fixed & obstinate as a little
Rock') and the protracted dispute which consequently arose between the
Master and the Fellows would not be settled until March 1749, by which
date it had been referred to the Court of the King's Bench.

There was little peace to be had at Gray's own college as well. The
poet was, if anything, on even worse terms with the master of Peterhouse, John Whalley, than he was with the implacable and often casually designated 'Roger' across the way. In the same letter of February
1748 in which he thanked Walpole for having sent Dodsley's *Collection*
to him at Cambridge, Gray also included a post-script mentioning a
bizarre predicament, prompted by a comment of Whalley's, into which
Gray had managed to involve himself. Gray wrote to Walpole,

If You chance to see a Letter of mine in any body's hand, this is the History of it. Dr. Whalley, who has hated me ever that Affair of Mr. Turner, thought fit to intimate to a large Table full of People, that I was a Kind of Atheist. I wrote to him partly to laugh at, & partly to reprove him for his Malice; & (as what he said was publick) I shew'd my Letter to several of those, who had heard him; & threaten'd (not in earnest, you may imagine) to have it hawk'd about Streets. They took me literally, & by Way of Anticipation of my Letter has been consign'd to one Etoffe (a Fiend of a Parson, that you know) to shew about here, & carry to Town, if any one will read it. He makes Criticisms on it, & has found out a false Spelling, I'm told. (*CTG* 302–03)

In a letter to Wharton written shortly afterwards, Gray further elaborated on the dilemma to which his misguided attempt at self-justification had eventually led. 'My Letter was by no means intended as a Composition', he complained, '& only design'd to be shew'd to some, who were Witnesses to the Impertinence, that gave Occasion for it . . .'.

Walpole knew only too well the 'Fiend of a Parson' to whom Gray referred. The Revd. Henry Etough (or Etoffe), who then resided not very far from Cambridge, at his rectory at Therfield in Hertfordshire, owed his living at least in part to the favour of Walpole's own father. Since the elder Walpole's death, Etough had curried favour with Sir Robert's brother, Horace Walpole of Wolverton, and had sought to maintain his social position primarily by (as one of his critics was to put it) 'the intimate knowledge he had obtained of the private and domestic history of all the great families in the kingdom'.[5] He was by almost all accounts a repellant, meddlesome, and malicious trouble-maker. William Cole was on several occasions compelled to record his disgust with Etough, whom he, like Gray, thought to be 'a pimping, tale-bearing dissenting teacher, who by adulation and flattery, and an everlasting fund of news and scandal, made himself agreeable to many of prime fortune, particularly Sir Robert Walpole'. 'He used to be much at Cambridge', Cole also wrote, '. . . and was a busy, impertinent, meddler in everyone's affairs'. One writer in the *Gentleman's Magazine* went even further, describing Etough as possessing a particularly loathsome aspect, and alleging that his head was 'so hot and reeking that when he entered a room he often hung up his wig on a peg and sat bare-headed'.

It was apparently Gray himself who first bestowed upon Etough the sobriquet of 'Tophet', a *nom de nique* in the truest sense of that term ('Tophet', an phonetic anagram of 'Etough', is mentioned both by Bunyan and Milton as a location near Jerusalem also proximate to the very gates of Hell). Some time shortly after the above-mentioned

---

[5] See *PTG*, 100.

incident, Gray and Mason met together and decided to have a further, private bit of fun at Etough's expense. Mason, for his part, drew a particularly unflattering and bestial caricature of Etough, and Gray composed a suitably bitter epigram to be inscribed beneath the drawing:

> Such Tophet was; so looked the grinning fiend
> Whom many a frighted prelate called his friend;
> I saw them bow and, while they wished him dead,
> With servile simper nod the mitred head.
> Our Mother-Church with half-averted sight
> Blushed as she blessed her grisly proselyte:
> Hosannahs rung through Hell's tremendous borders,
> And Satan's self had thoughts of taking orders. (*PTG* 102–03)

Although a number of critics have pointed out that Gray was most annoyed and resentful at Etough's continued interference in University affairs, the epigram focuses rather on the religious hypocrisy both of the 'fiend' Etough, and of the Established Church itself. Gray's keenest outrage is reserved for the sheer indecorousness of Etough's presence – and of his comparative success – within both the community of scholarship and the community of believers. Cambridge may jokingly have been regarded by the poet as a suitable refuge for the indolent and even the ignorant, but the intrusion of near-demonic malignity on such soil was a cause for genuine concern. Much the same sort of outrage that motivates Gray's eight-line satire on Etough – 'Tophet' would resurface years later when the poet would compose a similarly bitter and vituperative short poem on the activities of Lord Sandwich, entitled 'The Candidate'. Gray seems to have been content, on this occasion at least, slowly to allow the corrosive nature of his illustrated satire to accomplish his revenge (the lines were not printed until after Gray's death, in October 1785; a Michael Tyson created an etching based in Mason's original drawing in 1769). The poet's own attention was, at any rate, soon demanded elsewhere; there occurred at about this time an event that necessarily turned Gray's mind from the internal, academic disputes at Cambridge once again to London, and to – of all places – his own childhood home.

IV. Fiercer Flames

On 25 March, 1748, just two months after the publication of Dodsley's *Collection*, an event that had haunted Gray's dreams ever since he was a young child first growing up in Cornhill in the earliest decades of the century came finally to pass. At about one o'clock in the morning of that

Friday, a fire broke out in the home of a barber and wig-maker by the name of Mr. Eldridge in Exchange Alley. Eldridge's home and business were quickly consumed by the blaze; both he and his wife, as well as their two daughters, were lucky to have escaped from the building with their lives. Another gentleman who lodged with the family – a Mr. Cook – was killed when he tried to avoid the flames by throwing himself from an upper-storey window. The fire spread quickly through the circuitous turnings of Exchange Alley, and within hours the blaze had thrown its deadly arms into the nearby streets, lanes, and passageways of Birchin Lane, Castle Court, and reached as far to the east as St. Michael's Alley. By the time the sun had risen on the morning of Saturday, 26 March, a large area of the City had been burnt to the ground, and no fewer than six people had lost their lives. The homes and businesses on the southern, Lombard Street side of the fire had been spared, but those on its northern perimeter of Cornhill Street itself had been lost to the flames.

Among those structures consumed by the blaze was the house in which Gray had been born. The premises were at the time being let to one Mrs. Sarrazine, who owned and operated the milliner's shop in the same retail space that had once served as the 'India warehouse' of Gray's aunt and mother. Mrs. Sarrazine, whose business stood just within the northeastern-most extent of the fire (the flames had only just singed the structures on the eastern side of St. Michael's Alley), may have been alerted to the danger in enough time to carry some of her own stock and personal effects to the safety of the streets, but the building itself was a total loss. Within three weeks of the blaze, a payment of £485 was made to Dorothy Gray by the London Assurance Company – whose own nearby offices had likewise been burnt to the ground – on a £500 policy. The three percent reduction on the policy was probably accepted by Gray and his mother in the interest of a swift and undisputed settlement to the claim. Gray himself estimated that the rebuilding of the property would cost roughly £650, and he soon found it necessary to turn both to family and friends for financial assistance. Mrs. Rogers offered to advance him a substantial £100 toward the costs of rebuilding of the property. He likewise hoped at first that his aunt Mrs. Oliffe, herself increasingly incapacitated by illness and old-age, might be counted on to provide another £50 in assistance. Gray eventually accepted a further 20 guineas from Wharton, who alone among his acquaintances offered to place his own, modest financial resources at his friend's disposal the moment he heard of the loss. Gray professed himself to Wharton privately amused at the more impractical offers of assistance that the crisis had prompted on the part of his other friends – friends whose privileged and apparent, profoundly unworldly existence rendered them somewhat immune to the often brutal demands impendent upon real financial exigency. 'Do not imagine', he wrote in a letter of thanks to Wharton not long after the fire,

> I am at all less sensible to your Kindness, which (to say the Truth) is of a Sort, that however obvious & natural it may seem, has never once occur'd to any of my good Friends in Town, where I have been these seven Weeks. Their Methods of Consolation were indeed very extraordinary: they were all so sorry for my Loss, that I could not chuse but laugh. one offer'd me Opera-Tickets, insisted upon carrying me to the Grand-Masquerade, desired me to sit for my Picture. others asked me to their Concerts, or Dinners & Suppers at their Houses; or hoped, I would drink Chocolate with them, while I stayed in Town. all my Gratitude (or if you please, my Revenge) was to accept of every Thing they offer'd me: if it had been but a Shilling, I would have taken it. thank Heaven I was in good Spirits; else I could not have done it. I profited all I was able of their Civilities, & am returned into the Country loaded with their Bontés & Politeses, but richer still in my own Reflexions, which I owe in great Measure to them too. (CTG 303–04)

For all Gray's protestation of being 'in good Spirits' here, the Cornhill fire and its devastation troubled him deeply. The necessity of having to rely upon his aged, female relatives for financial assistance in rebuilding the property only added to the ignominy of his burden. Ever since he could remember, Gray had suffered to an unnatural degree from a fear of fire. There was, as far as we can tell, no actual, historical incident which grounded this fear – no particular childhood confrontation that might obviously have resulted in the acute pyrophobia which consequently manifested itself throughout his adult life. A healthy caution and a constant vigilance with regard to the dangers of fire formed a necessary part of any householder's – and particularly of any city-dwelling householder's – mental constitution in the eighteenth century. Flammable building materials in older structures, and the constant use of open flames by home owners and businesses alike for heating, cooking, lighting, and even the disposal of rubbish formed a volatile combination. The close proximity of city buildings and the presence in many neighborhoods of dwellings that did not conform to the building standards and safety codes such as those instituted in the City following the Great Fire of 1666 rendered the danger of another such cataclysmic conflagration a very real and dreaded possibility. The fact that even a relatively new quarter of the city such as Cornhill – one whose structures had been built specifically with an eye towards averting precisely such a disaster – could succumb so quickly to the detestation of the flames seemed only to underscore the pathetic inadequacy of man's attempts to frustrate such a powerful force of nature. The buildings and neighbourhoods in which Gray had spent so much of his life – the crowded precincts of Cornhill, the many ancient and highly flammable structures both at Eton and at Cambridge – may well have aggravated his innate fear of fire. The often neat and precise habits of his life further distanced him from the chaos represented by the flames. Fire was in many ways a symbol for Gray of everything against which his entire life's philosophy, as expressed in his poetry, sought to protect him: disorder, impermanence, obliteration, frantic and chaotic *action*, and an ultimate lack of emotional – perhaps even sexual and erotic – control. Fire stood in his own mind for worldly engagement of the worst possible kind, frustrating his own domestic, familial, and fraternal goals of order, symmetry, remembrance, and quiet memorialization. The sight of the burnt-out buildings and the heaps of darkened ash piled high in the very streets where the shops and taverns of his earliest childhood had once stood must have sent a chill through his heart. Once again something that had appeared to be so permanent and solid had been swept away in the blink of an eye.

*

One of the friends whose impractical offers of assistance Gray professed to Wharton to have found so amusing – the friend who appears to have felt that attendance at the opera and five-guinea tickets to a fashionable Haymarket masquerade would help to dispel any of the worry and anxiety that followed hard upon such an affair – was of course none other than Walpole himself. The 'picture' for which Gray sat at his friend's request has since the poet's death become the most popular and memorable portrait of the poet. The painting was the work of the well-known German artist John Giles Eccardt. Eccardt based the pose and attitude of the portrait on a picture of a musician by the Dutch artist Van Dyke that he had seen on display in the collection of the Duke of Grafton. While some have dismissed the conceit of Eccardt's painting as 'fanciful', there is no reason to suggest that it is not – for all the idealized artificiality of its subject's pose and dress – a reasonably accurate representation of the way Gray really looked. The poet is represented in the half-length portrait in a standing position. His attitude is confident and relaxed. His left hand rests languidly on a support just above the level of his waist; his right hand – in which is held a copy of the *Eton Ode* – crosses his left near the wrist. Dressed in an elegantly loose-fitting jacket of rich material in the style of the previous century over a white shirt, the collars of which open softly at the neck, Gray directs his gaze to the viewer's left. His light, shoulder-length hair, brushed back from the forehead, tumbles in still-tidy curls on either side of his pale and full, smooth-skinned face (as in the childhood portrait of the poet that once hung in the Cornhill home, Gray here also evinces 'fine hair' and a 'good complexion'). His features are classically symmetrical, with large, liquid eyes, gracefully arched eyebrows, perfectly proportioned nose, and a fashionably thin and faintly smiling mouth. The designed effect of the whole is to produce a portrait which signals very clearly to the viewer its subject's status as a poet whose sympathetic sensibility leads him to look beyond the immediate cares of the world; Eccardt's Gray seems to fix his eyes smilingly on the past, even as he quite literally hands on the substance of that past – in the shape of his own suitably nostalgic writing – on to the future. The poet of this flattering and friendly portrait is paradoxically one to whom poetry comes easily – a poet confident in the value of his work, and one who carries the potentially weighty burden of his own God-given talent with a natural ease and grace.

Eccardt's portrait of Gray was only one of several such paintings that Walpole had commissioned in mid-century to grace the walls of his new home at Strawberry Hill in Twickenham. Walpole had purchased a seven-year lease on the property – a patch of what originally amounted to nothing more than 'a little farm' some fifty years old plumped in the middle of five acres of land set on the rise of 'Chopp'd Straw Hill' on the banks of the Thames across from Richmond Park – in the spring of 1747. He was eventually able to purchase the property outright, by an Act of Parliament. In the years to come Walpole effected a miraculous metamorphosis in the undistinguished and largely unpromising, three-storey dwelling, transforming its precincts in time into one of the greatest architectural follies ever to be constructed in England. In so doing, he almost single-handedly transformed cultural and aesthetic history, changing the epithet 'Gothic' from a term of scorn and derision into one connoting a recombinative style of architecture and decoration characterized by a light-hearted and fanciful sense of nostalgia and happily 'medieval' play. Strawberry Hill was to be calculatedly 'over-the-top' in every way, from the ornate Library and medieval Refectory or Great Parlour, to the Little Venetian Parlour, the China Closet, and the so-called 'Beauty Room' – a ground floor bedroom decorated with portraits of English queens, kings, and several of the more favoured mistresses of those same monarchs.

The portrait of Gray was eventually hung in the upstairs, Blue Bed-chamber, where the image of the poet was among familiar company; a portrait of Walpole himself (also in the style of Van Dyke), as well as representations of Henry Seymour Conway and his family (after Watteau), were placed near to Gray's own. A portrait of Ashton from Walpole's own brush was eventually hung in Walpole's bedroom, though this formerly intimate friend was to have few occasions to visit his friend and patron's new residence in the years to come. The final breach in the friendship between Walpole and Ashton, which was to occur in 1750, was preceded by a bitter quarrel shortly after the former had first settled at Strawberry Hill. On this latter occasion, Gray drew tellingly upon the hard-learned knowledge borne of his own experiences quarreling with his friend, and wrote to Walpole suggesting that the two men simply sit down in private and work through their differences as honestly as they could. 'For it is a tenet with me . . .', he added knowingly, 'that if ever two people, who love one another, come to breaking, it is for want of a timely eclaircissement, a full and precise one, without witnesses or mediators, and without reserving any one disagreeable circumstance for the mind to brood upon in silence'. Gray looked back, then, with regret on the manner in which he had handled his own 'break up' with Walpole, and he mourned the several years' active friendship which he had consequently forfeited in the pride attendant upon his own rigorous and uncompromising sense of personal injury. His advice to Walpole indicates that he had learned the hard-taught lessons of reconciliation, forgiveness, and straightforward honesty well. Ashton's abrasive and by now blatantly greedy personality was ill-suited to the necessary give-and-take of such friendships, however, and from this point on he was to make only rare and largely inconsequential appearances in the lives of both men.

*

Toward the end of August 1747, Gray had twice written to Walpole, accepting his friend's invitation to visit his new home. 'You must inform me what Place on the Windsor Road is nearest Twickenham', he wrote, 'for I am no Geographer: there I will be at the appointed Day, & from thence you must fetch me'. (If Gray's casual pretense here to such local, navigational ignorance was at all true, one is almost compelled to speculate, the quarrel between him and Walpole while on the Grand Tour might well have been the result of such a bemused and cultivated indifference on the part of either man to the practicalities of geography, and of one's own place within the space of the physical world.) Gray visited Strawberry Hill for about a week in September of that year; he would again stay at Twickenham in 1748. He enjoyed the playfulness with which Walpole himself approached Strawberry Hill as a kind of artistic and cultural 'project', and throughout the remainder of his life professed an interest in his friend's on-going and increasingly elaborate additions to the property. Yet Gray was never to be included as a member of Walpole's exclusive, self-designated 'Committee of Taste' (a select trio comprised only of Walpole himself and of his two friends Richard Bentley and John Chute), which over the years pretended to advise the owner of Strawberry Hill on the aesthetic desirability of the various Gothic and pseudo-classical additions to the house and its grounds. Gray passed the time easily enough in the company of Walpole's 'Italianized friend', Chute (though the two were to have a falling-out later in life), and he remained on similarly easy if not intimate terms with Bentley – a remarkably talented young artist (and the son of the famous Cambridge scholar of the same name) whose skill in graphic design was soon to have consequences for Gray's own poetry. He had increasingly little patience, however, with another of Strawberry Hill's more frequent guests, the gossipy George Montagu. Although he yet retained some fond memories of the time he had spent with Montagu and his companion George Selwyn at Reims nearly a decade earlier, Gray appears by now to have found Montagu's particular brand of charm and easy indolence – so suited and so similar to Walpole's own taste and temperament – more often than not something of an annoyance. Conversely and for his own part, Montagu himself considered Gray to be a socially inept (and socially out-of-place) pedant. Montagu evidently shared his opinions on the subject with Walpole himself, who, following one simultaneous visit of both men to Twickenham in 1748, told him that he shared his opinion of Gray's discomfiting demeanour as a conversationalist. 'I agree with you most absolutely in your opinion about Gray', a seemingly candid Walpole confessed in September of that year,

> he is the worst company in the world – from a melancholy turn, from living reclusively, and from a little too much dignity, he never converses easily – all his words are measured, and chosen, and formed into sentences; his writings are admirable; he himself is not agreeable. (WC ix.76)

Walpole's comments have been misinterpreted by some critics as constituting a final, harsh, and irrevocable judgement on the behaviour and social *persona* of his lifelong friend. One must always keep in mind, however, not only that Walpole was careful in his letters to Montagu to cultivate a consciously easy-going and worldly epistolary voice (the young and often blasé 'peer-about-town'), but that he was likewise commenting very particularly here on Gray's inability to participate in precisely the kind of elegant, esoteric, and socially allusive conversation that came so easily to Walpole himself, and to the select group of friends with which he had chosen to surround himself as an adult. Gray, in sharp contrast to these more recent acquaintances of Walpole, must unavoidably have seemed bookish and scholarly; those social skills polished by frequent interaction with the fashionable world necessarily grew rusty in the rarified air of Cambridge. Walpole may (unfortunately and rather to his own discredit) have felt the need publicly to apologize for the shortcomings of his childhood friend – to confess that Gray's presence among an otherwise socially fluid and aristocratic company was inevitably awkward and 'not agreeable' – but in his less self-conscious moments he would no doubt have been ready, for the sake of that same friendship, to forgive a far greater multitude of less venial sins.

*

The necessity of attending to the several financial matters relating to the rebuilding of the Cornhill property found Gray spending rather more time than he had anticipated in London throughout the late spring and summer of 1748. A scheduled visit to Wharton, who was now permanently settled with his wife and newborn daughter near Durham, would simply have to be put off until the next year. As it was, Gray tried to spend as little time in the city itself as possible. His mother and his aunts sought the comfort and reassurance of his presence at Stoke. Dorothy Gray and Mary Antrobus, we remember, had only recently left the Cornhill shop for Stoke, and they no doubt felt deeply the physical loss of the shop within which they had spent so much of their daily lives. Gray, too, seemed to deal with the pressures of the situation – settling the insurance claims, handling the many practical decisions that needed to be made with reference to the new structure and its potential tenants – in the comparative quiet of the nearby country. Walpole and his many acquaintances were now within easy distance of Windsor, and the thought that he could always call upon his friend should he need to do so may also have been something of a comfort to him. The last thing he wanted to do was spend time in Cornhill itself, where the noise, the clamour, and the chaos of such a massive reconstruction project must have begun almost immediately. Once again, as in the earliest years of Gray's own childhood, the city of London found itself dealing with the consequences of the ruin and transforming change wrought by fire. This time, the poet must have consoled himself in Stoke, it could do so without him.

Gray's professed regret at not being able to visit Wharton was genuine. Increasingly throughout these years, Wharton began in many ways to take the place of West, at least when it came to the flow and direction of Gray's own correspondence. The reading and the literary opinions he would in other circumstances have shared with West, Gray now passed on primarily to Wharton. Walpole too, it must be admitted, invited more than his fair share of such information from Gray, who now assumed his place among the former's correspondents as a chosen and authoritative voice on literature, poetry, publication, and academic affairs. Yet the self-consciousness that often clouds Gray's latter-day letters to his one-time confidant is rather less in evidence in the letters to Wharton; Gray is manifestly more at ease in his letters to Durham than he is in those directed to Arlington Street or Strawberry Hill.

In his letters to Wharton in the late summer of 1748, Gray eagerly shared his responses to a number of authors, both ancient and modern. In much the same way he had once encouraged West to persevere in his reading of Tacitus, for example, he now exhorted Wharton similarly to be patient with the historical writings of Diodorus Siculus – 'there are Things in him very curious', Gray reminded his friend, 'got out of better Authors now lost'. Confessing his own readings to have been 'cruelly interrupted' by the recent events in London, Gray nevertheless passed on to Wharton his enthusiastic approval of a new comedy recently imported from Paris, Jean Baptiste Louis de Gresset's *Le Méchant* ('one of the very best Drama's I ever met with' and even more glowingly, in a later letter, 'the best Comedy I ever read'). The same author's *Epitre à ma Soeur* – a work that William Mason later heard Gray admit to have been a source for his own, fragmentary ode *On the Pleasure Arising from Vicissitude* – is recommended to Wharton's attention, as is James Thomson's lively and characteristically eighteenth-century imitation of Spenser, *The Castle of Indolence*. Wharton, who had in his own letters directed the poet's attention to one of Mason's own odes, 'To a Water Nymph', included in Dodsley's *Collection*, is gently reminded by Gray that its author has since become a favourite acquaintance of his. 'He has much fancy', Gray wrote of Mason, 'little Judgement, & a good deal of Modesty'. I take him for a good & well-meaning Creature; but then he is really *in Simplicity a Child*, & loves everybody he meets with'. Gray elsewhere asked Wharton to keep an eye on his 'young Friend' Stonhewer, who had been spending much of the long, summer vacation with his family close to Wharton's own residence at Durham.

Gray closed his letter to Wharton of 19 August 1748, with what he described as 'the Beginning of a Sort of Essay' – the first fifty-seven lines of the fragmentary, philosophic poem that has since come to be called *The Alliance of Education and Government*. This work – in which Gray set out to demonstrate the notion that those two, eponymous forces 'must necessarily concur to produce great & useful Men' – was, much like the similarly, conceptually ambitious (not to say practically impossible) *De Principiis Cogitandi*, destined never to be completed. The transcription of the poem eventually included in Gray's Commonplace Book extended the work by a mere fifty lines. Wharton had clearly encouraged Gray, at some point in the late summer or early autumn of 1748, to continue working on what Mason in time dubbed the poet's 'Ethical Essay'. Gray further shared the work only with Stonhewer, whose youthful enthusiasm had also at some point flattered Gray into further efforts on the poem.

The epigraph prefixed to this fragment is drawn from the pastoral *Idylls* of Theocritus, in which the Greek poet seems to exhort both writer and reader at once: 'Begin, my friend, for surely you shall not be permitted to carry your song with you to Hades – the place which obliterates all things from your mind'. The poem itself opens by drawing a familiar connection between the climate and soil of a nation, on the one hand, and the peculiar gifts and abilities – the native and indigenous 'genius' – of its inhabitants, on the other. Just as the variously distributed circumstances of nature can affect the character of a population, so too does 'Instruction', Gray suggests, possess the power similarly to shape and to transform the national temperament. The easy and temperate climate of the southern, Mediterranean nations, Gray was largely one with his era in believing, tended to incline those people towards 'contemplation and pleasure'. Such epicurean and meditative qualities could, if given too free a reign, lead in time to the systemic corruption and emasculation of a country. The decline and fall of the Roman Empire was largely the history of precisely such a process of 'effeminate' decay. The moral arc of its self-fuelled destruction was meant to serve as a caution and as an exemplary warning to modern European powers such as France and England (it comes as no surprise that later in the century the historian Edward Gibbon lamented the fact that Gray had never finished the poem, the surviving portion of which he regarded as an 'exquisite specimen' of his genius).[6] The Northern races, by contrast, were characterized rather by a natural resilience to 'hardship', a proclivity for swift and decisive action, a near-irresistible bellicosity of temperament, and an inclination towards armed conflict. Education alone, to Gray's mind, could serve to balance these inherent and inescapable characteristics, cancelling out or at least tempering and softening the negative effects of each, and, in turn, highlighting their more positive features.

In a number of papers brought together by Mason shortly after the poet's death, Gray stated the larger intention of his poem outright – an intention the existing, decasyllabic couplets of the work set forth rather more obscurely. 'It is the proper work of education and government united', he wrote, 'to redress the faults that arise from the soil and air', or, even more specifically: 'The principal drift of education should be to make men *think* in the northern climates, and *act* in the Southern.'

Having first begun to suggest the differences of geographic temperament which work to separate mankind and to distinguish various races one from the other, Gray moves on in the second stanza of the existing poem to pursue the notion that an underlying sense of fraternity and fellow-feeling – a universal urge towards freedom and 'happiness' – nevertheless motivates the spirit of all nations. His lines seem deliberately to recall earlier efforts by James Thomson and Sir Richard

---

[6] Edward Gibbon, *The History of the Decline and Fall of the Roman Empire*, ed. J. B. Bury (New York: F. Defou and Co., 1906–07) iii.372.

Blackmore (particularly the latter's *The Nature of Man* [1711]), at the same time that they anticipate, both in style and in substance, the topographical poems of writers only slightly later in the century, most notably Samuel Johnson's *The Vanity of Human Wishes* (1749), and Oliver Goldsmith's *The Traveller* (1764):

> This spacious animated scene survey
> From where the rolling orb, that gives the day,
> His sable sons with nearer course surrounds,
> To either pole and life's remotest bounds.
> How rude so e'er the exterior form we find,
> Howe'er opinion tinge the varied mind,
> Alike to all the kind impartial heaven
> The sparks of truth and happiness had given:
> With sense to feel, with memory to retain,
> They follow pleasure and they fly from pain;
> Their judgement mends the plan their fancy draws,
> The event presages and explores the cause.
> The soft returns of gratitude they know,
> By fraud elude, by force repel the foe;
> While mutual wishes, mutual woes, endear
> The social smile and sympathetic tear. (*PTG* 93–95)

Why then, Gray asks, do physical conditions seem so often to mar and to pervert the essential, social compatibility of mankind? Why is it that the 'sparks of truth' are among some people blown into the vigorous flames of liberty and prosperity, while among others they are dampened into the ashes of tyranny and enslavement? 'Why does Asia', the poet wonders,

> dread a monarch's nod,
> While European freedom still withstands
> The encroaching tide, that drowns her lessening lands,
> And sees far off with an indignant groan
> Her native plains and empires once her own?
> Can opener skies and suns of fiercer flame
> O'erpower the fire that animates our frame,
> As lamps, that shed at even cheerful ray,
> Fade and expire beneath the eye of day? (*PTG* 97)

Only the force of Reason, the poet quietly responds to such questions, can teach mankind to transcend and to overcome the several circumstances of its myriad birth; though 'various tracts' may necessarily enforce a 'various toil', the light of Reason uniquely possesses the power to 'raise the mortal to a height divine'.

Gray's verses unfortunately break off before he has had the opportunity to pursue this line of thought much further. The notes and papers
brought together by Mason after the poet's death indicate that he may
eventually have included in his discussion of the virtues and civilizing
powers of such an education in 'reason' a digression on the virtues of
fame and remembrance. The forces of a rational education might permit
a people to achieve the inherent extent of their national and communal
potential, but a sustained and continuing fame could alone hope to pass
the legacy of that achievement on to later generations. Without fame –
without the desire to be remembered and memorialized for the life-
lessons learned both as individuals and as part of the larger community
of mankind – the achievements of the past are in time lost and effectu-
ally rendered meaningless; hence the suitability of the poem's classical
epigraph, an epigraph to which the substance of the existing poem is
only vaguely connected, if at all. 'One principal characteristic of vice in
the present age', Gray wrote in the maxims assembled by Mason after
his death, 'is the contempt of fame'. He elsewhere elaborated:

> Many are the uses of good fame to a generous mind: it extends our exis-
> tence and example into future ages; continues and propagates virtue,
> which otherwise would be as short-lived as our frame; and prevents the
> prevalence of vice in a generation more corrupt than our own. It is impos-
> sible to conquer that natural desire we have of being remembered; even
> criminal ambition and avarice, the most selfish of all passions, would
> wish to leave a name behind them.[7]

Gray's final thought here – the notion that even those individuals characterized by 'criminal ambition and avarice' seek to be remembered from
beyond the grave – may well have been prompted at least in part by his
lifelong reading of Dante. 'In the *Inferno*', as one modern critic has
observed, 'the prime urge of the dead is to ensure that they are still
remembered on earth because without reputation, whether good or bad,
what does life on earth mean?'[8]

Had Gray been moved to complete *The Alliance of Education and
Government*, he would almost certainly have undertaken a further
exploration of the complicated relationship between individual achievement and worldly fame, between national or civic virtue and the instructive and at times treacherous pedagogy of renown. As it was, Gray seems
very soon after sending the poem to Wharton to have put this second
of his lengthy and ambitious didactic poems to one side. When, many
years later, Norton Nicholls asked him why he had failed to complete

---

[7] Quoted in Lonsdale, *PTG* 91.
[8] Leo Braudy, *The Frenzy of Renown* (Oxford: Oxford University Press, 1986) 234.

this 'beautiful fragment', Gray replied simply that 'he could not'. Pressed
further, Nicholls recalled, Gray more patiently explained,

> that he had been used to write only Lyric poetry in which the poems being
> short, he had accustomed himself, & was able to polish every part; that
> this having become habit, he could not write otherwise; & that the labour
> of this method in a long poem would be intolerable; besides which the
> poem would lose its effect for want of Chiaro-Oscuro; for that to produce
> effect it was absolutely necessary to have weak parts. – He instanced in
> Homer, & particularly in Milton, who he said in parts of his poem rolls
> on in sounding words that have but little meaning. (CTG 1291)

For all the possible injustice to Milton's *Paradise Lost* implied by his
comments to Nicholls here, Gray's admission of his own inclination
towards the peculiar, stylistic intensity of the lyric mode – and, indeed,
his realistic assessment of his own strengths as a precise and advisedly
cautious, poetic craftsman – is strikingly candid. An alternative suggestion, first advanced by Mason, that Gray abandoned his 'epic' project
after having discovered himself to have been pre-empted by the ideas
expressed in Montesquieu's *L'Esprit des Lois* (published in Geneva in
November, 1749) may likewise contain some small grain of truth; Gray
wrote admiringly of Montesquieu's volumes, which he described as 'generally admirable' and 'very lively and concise', only months after sending
the first fifty-seven lines of his own poem to Wharton. Yet his confession to Nicholls later in life that his reasons for abandoning the project
were more formal and stylistic than they were substantive would seem
to be confirmed by the fact that – far from resigning his interest in the
questions of fame, renown, memory, and the indigenous characteristics
of the national genius – Gray was shortly to return to those same questions within the more congenial literary mode of the personal lyric. The
interest expressed early on in *The Alliance of Education and Government* in the determining features of place and topography both in individual as well as national destiny were very soon to be raised yet again
in the poem that would itself carry Gray's own name, writing, and reputation far beyond the limits of his natural life, and into the future of the
English language itself.

CHAPTER SEVEN

THE PATH OF GLORY

The Elegy Written in a Country Church-yard
1749–1752

I. Going Forward

Gray spent the late winter and early spring of 1749 quietly in Cambridge. Having for the immediate future resigned the fate of his 'Ethical Essay' into the trusted, metaphorical hands of Wharton's judgement and criticism, he once again found the time to focus his attention more closely on College and University affairs. The on-going dispute between the Master and the Fellows of Pembroke College was only then drawing to a close. Matters had come to a head some time toward the end of February. By 9 March, Gray was able to write to Wharton, triumphantly announcing the achievement of what he facetiously and with a glancing reference to the recently concluded Peace of Aix-la-Chappelle between the English, Dutch, and French, had dubbed 'the Peace of Pembroke'. As had much earlier in his life been the case with the playful naming of the Quadruple Alliance at Eton, Gray's appropriation of the specific language and designations used properly to describe larger political affairs in Europe was employed at least in part in an attempt to extend a greater meaning and importance to the events of his own small world. He was at the same time, however, very much aware of the genial mockery and self-deprecation also implied by such potentially pompous parodic christenings. Gray's *modus operandi*, in his personal life as in his poetry, seems constantly to have been fuelled by the impulse of parodic deflection.

The highly partisan Gray had every reason to be pleased and even light-hearted with regards to the result of the internecine conflict. Both of the candidates to whom the poet had extended his warm support (William Mason and Henry Tuthill) were among those who, in the event, had eventually been elected to college Fellowships. The Master, to whom Gray referred now with casual irreverence in his letter to Wharton as 'Prince Roger, surnamed the Long, Lord of the Great Zodiack, the glass Uranium, & the Chariot that goes without horses', had agreed to their election only after being convinced that the intervention of a designated 'Visitor' external to the college would favour the cause of his opponents. Having finally despaired of finding an outside arbitrator who was 'to his Mind', Long had abruptly conceded defeat. The end of the affair itself

– the struggle for college authority had by then dragged on for more than two years – was consequently a bit anti-climactic. 'All was over', Gray wrote to Wharton with a sigh of triumph and relief, 'in a few Minutes'.

One might suppose that the uncharacteristically busy activity of the previous year would have left Gray content enough in passing the spring of 1749 in the quiet solitude of his college. And there were, indeed, times when the familiar, diurnal routine of life at Cambridge suited him perfectly. His days in residence were typically spent reading in his own rooms (he persisted in his early habit of borrowing books from the Pembroke library, just across the street, in preference to the smaller collection then housed at Peterhouse itself) and in taking patient, careful notes on his increasingly wide-ranging studies. Like so many readers who would, in any other circumstance, protest an honest veneration for the simple property of the written word, Gray very frequently became so immersed in the text in front of him that he absent-mindedly scribbled his own thoughts and reactions in the margins of the volume. He was often 'guilty' of writing both in his own books, as well as in those he borrowed from others.

Gray was nothing, however, if not systematic in his larger and more long-standing strategies for effective note-taking (and, unlike Samuel Johnson, he rarely if ever returned borrowed books to their proper owners in such a state as to render them fitter to – as Gray would later put it in one of his own *jeu d'esprit* – 'bottom tarts and cheesecakes nice', than be returned to their rightful place on the bookshelf). The Commonplace Book Gray had first begun compiling in a hefty folio of some four hundred and sixty pages purchased while he was yet an undergraduate would swell in time almost completely to fill three such volumes – a total of over thirteen hundred pages. Smaller notebooks were likewise crammed with extracts from and précis of the work of individual authors. Gray also made use of a number of pocket–diaries, diaries in which he habitually recorded everything from his notes on his close observation of natural history (e.g. weather conditions, the budding of various plants and flowers, the appearance of noteworthy birds and other fauna), to jottings in Latin on the state of his own health and, in his later years, the symptoms of the gout, financial expenses and notations of receipts, and even, finally, reminders of the dates of his various extended absences from Cambridge. Still other notebooks and detached sheets and scraps of papers from a slightly later period in life were to serve the poet as impromptu travel–diaries.

Beginning in about 1747, Gray devoted the better part of his scholarly attention revisiting those classical authors whom he had so much enjoyed first as a precocious student at Eton, and away from whom he later, as an undergraduate, lamented having to spend so much time. In

March of that year, he had written to Wharton not only of having recently reread the tragedies of Aeschylus, but of undertaking also to make his way well into the second-century historian Pausanias (whose easy and often refreshingly incredulous personality informs his casual guide book to Greece, in English called simply the 'Description of Hellas'). Gray was also moving 'all thro' the surviving volumes of the anecdotal and informative *Deipnosophistae* ('Connoisseurs at Dinner') of the second-century grammarian Athenaeus, nearly thirteen of the fifteen original volumes of which survive. 'I am now in Pindar & Lysias', he continued, 'for I take Verse and Prose together, like bread & Cheese'. Gray's casually humorous metaphor only barely conceals a telling and essential truth, however. Such reading had by now become little less than sustenance for the poet, and the time spent in the reassuringly familiar company of one author seemed comfortably and invariably to lead him on to another. Gray's earlier biographer Ketton-Cremer was absolutely correct in observing that by this point in his life, Gray had moved well beyond a simple or an isolated interest in classical 'history' or 'philosophy', to an ambitious desire comprehensively to view the whole of the ancient world, ranging from the most profound sublimities of its thought and writing to, conversely, 'the smallest details of domestic life'.[1] Needless to say, he read all these works in their original Greek. As time passed, there seemed to be nothing that lay beyond the wide-ranging and what we would today characterize as aggressively interdisciplinary provenance of Gray's sites as a cultural historian.

By the spring of 1747, he and some few, select colleagues had made significant progress in assembling an ambitious, synoptic chronology of ancient Greek history and culture; Gray had written to Wharton, proudly describing an early version of this 'great Chronological Table' which had been laid out 'with our own hands' at the very end of December, 1746. The table, he joked, was

> the Wonder & Amazement of [the Master] Mr. Brown; not so much for Publick Events, tho' these too have a Column assign'd them, but rather in a literary Way, to compare the Times of all great Men, their Writeings & Transactions. it begins at the 30th Olympiad, & is already brought down to the 113th; that is, 332 Years, our only Modern Assistants are [Sir John] Marsham, [Henry] Dodwell, & [Richard] Bentley. (*CTG* 259–60)

For all of Gray's seeming modesty to Wharton, this was impressive company in which to spend one's afternoons and evenings; their joint Chronology must have been a suitably impressive document. Each page

---

[1] Ketton-Cremer, 93.

had first been carefully ruled to accommodate nine, clearly distinct columns. Each column was then devoted to a particular facet of Greek life. The first detailed the Olympiads, by which four-year periods the exact time of other important events in ancient Greek history had been fixed and measured. The second traced the rule of the three *archons* and the later *thesmothetai* (the six additional *archons* or magistrates appointed specifically as codifiers of written law). A third column kept track of important public and cultural affairs. The remaining six sections of the Chronology were equally divided between scrupulously thorough notations of the work of, respectively, the philosophers and the poets.

The Chronology, of which only small fragments survive, was granted pride of place on the central table already piled high with books which greeted visitors upon first entering Gray's rooms, hence the volume's description as the inescapable 'Wonder & Amazement' of Gray's several guests. The tome was often left open, ready always to be admired and consulted, or even to receive any carefully considered additions to its painstaking and sublimely accreditive reconstruction of the past. As a document that attempted to bring a grand and visible order to a (potentially) maddeningly diverse and complex array of cultural information, Gray's Chronology was cut from very much the same cloth as his Commonplace Book and other notebooks he kept in the course of his life. All such projects were titanic and on-going efforts dedicated to the slow accumulation and synchronization of knowledge, and need never – and this is of course a significant point when dealing with anything Gray wrote – come to any kind of definitive conclusion. All were potentially and by their very nature endless. Each was a physical and physically impressive tool by means of which the poet strove to achieve some sense of sustained epistemological and ontological clarity. Much in the same manner that Samuel Johnson would only slightly later in the century attempt to combat the onset of severe depression and a chaos of mental anxiety by turning to the safety and indisputable *factual* nature of mathematical calculations (Mrs. Thrale one day discovered him in the midst of determining whether the national debt 'would, if converted into silver, serve to make a meridian of that metal for the globe of the whole earth'), Gray similarly consoled the recurring symptoms of his own sense of isolation and depression with the order he found – or forever sought to find – in a comprehensive view of the larger patterns and cycles of nature, of history, and of intellectual certitude.[2] No matter how diverse or distinct from one another the material of Gray's readings or his learn-

---

[2] Hester Lynch Piozzi, *Anecdotes of the Life of the Late Samuel Johnson, L.L.D*, ed. G. B. Hill, *Johnsonian Miscellanies*, Volume 1 (Oxford: Oxford University Press, 1897) 200.

ing in general seemed to be at first glance, all of that material could be organized and tabulated clearly within the pages of his Commonplace Books or would, similarly, find an appropriate place within the discrete and aesthetically pleasing columns of his Chronology. The indices generally prefaced to such Commonplace Books typically used the artificial patterns of language and linguistic order to separate and to codify experience, in much the same way that the governing structure of the Chronology as a whole rested on the culturally determined patterns and (now antiquated) divisions of the Olympiads.

Gray initially attempted to keep his notebooks in the manner first recommended by the philosopher John Locke in his writings on education. According to Locke's method, subjects were filed in an index prefixed to each volume by, respectively, first letter and then first vowel. Thus the page number indicating an entry on Aristotle, for example, would be filed under 'A', and then under a subdivision 'i'; an entry on Athenaeus under 'A' and then 'e', and so on. Such a system allowed the note-taker to move fluidly between his daily readings, devoting his attention to any number of different authors, subjects, or volumes in the course of the day, while at the same time permitting him to keep close track of the precise location of his various notes. Rooting their own sifting of the myriad possibilities of human experience and of human nature in such schemes of language, number, order, and design, it should by now be clear that lifelong projects such as the Commonplace Books and the Chronology formed for Gray no antithesis to his other writing and poetry. Indeed, Gray's scholarly obsessions, far from having served as a drain on his time and attention – time and attention, as critics since Gibbon and even Walpole himself have never tired of lamenting, which might far better have been devoted to his own imaginative endeavours – formed the necessary concomitant to those endeavours. The one could not even have been attempted, let alone completed, without the other. If the Commonplace Books and the Chronology had not been able to provide Gray with the semblance of order and design in his studies, in history, and in the world at large, it is possible that he would never have been able coherently to formulate or to write any poetry at all. He likewise no doubt enjoyed the fact, again, that the eternal and inviting open-endedness of such projects – always waiting to be tweaked or modified one last time – defied the necessary conclusions required of his published poetry. The essentially private nature of such documents insured that there was simply less *pressure* on Gray when he was writing as a scholar. Thus the more scholarly aspect of Gray's life in many ways provided, in a very basic and comprehensive sense, the structures and blueprints from and within which he was able more carefully to construct his verse.

Since first beginning the Chronology in the winter of 1746–47, then, Gray had largely been content in his reading and in the generally uneventful progress of his day-to-day life at Cambridge. From this point forward the assertion that one survives best in this world simply by focusing energy and attention outside of one's *self* becomes something of a refrain in his correspondence. In his short account of Gray's life, David Cecil nicely summarized the approach to religion and spirituality that seemed from the poet's middle years to characterize the manner of his devotions. Describing the tone of Gray's belief as 'a sober straight-forward Anglican sort of religion', Cecil wrote:

> He did not have mystical visions; and his mind was too unmetaphysical to appreciate the significance of dogmatic theology. But his poetical temperament, responsive as it was to the appeal of the ancient and the mysterious made him unsympathetic to purely rationalist interpretations of the universe, and also susceptible to the religious sentiment. He readily accepted the creed in which he was brought up; and his faith in it was confirmed by that awe-inspiring sense of divinity that came to him at such times as his journey up to the Grande Chartreuse. Nor was his belief shaken by melancholy. On the contrary, melancholy made him cling to it, Was not religion the only sure gleam of hope in a dark and disillusioning universe?[3]

The gradual approach of middle age – he was, after all, now thirty years old – also brought home to Gray the psychological necessity of, as he would later put it, 'to always have something going forward'. 'To be employed', as he wrote simply and memorably on one occasion, 'is to be happy' (and although he would in time grow to fear and even to despise Voltaire, Gray's constant reiterations that one can find fulfilment or contentment only in selfless or self-denying *action* echo nothing so much as the French thinker's similar conviction that 'one must give one's self all the occupation one can to make life supportable in this world', or, yet again and even closer to Gray's own sentiments, 'not to be occupied, and not to exist, amount to the same thing'. Expectations – particularly expectations centred on individuals and their loyalties or generosity – were advisedly to be kept to a minimum, and an honest and heart-felt gratitude for the simpler pleasures in life was, conversely, always to be encouraged. Grumbling complaints were sometimes made – more often than not to Wharton – regarding the frustratingly slow pace of change within the University, but such complaints seem often to have been voiced merely from the vague and almost obligatory sense of self-flagellation and self-criticism so often endemic to closed, academic environments. In actual fact, Gray enjoyed the measured pace of life at the University (its caution perfectly suited his own temperamental need

---

[3] Cecil, 128.

carefully and painstakingly to move through his studies) and he felt comfortable enough about his own rate of progress in his several and various projects to joke about the enervated nature of his environment with Wharton. 'The spirit of Lazyness (the Spirit of the Place)', he wrote of Cambridge to his friend in April, 1749, and recalling the playful *Hymn to Ignorance*,

> begins to possess even me, that have so long declaimed against it: yet it has not so prevail'd, but that I feel that Discontent with myself, that *Ennuy*, that ever accompanies it in its Beginnings. Time will settle my Conscience, Time will reconcile me to this languid Companion: we shall smoke, we shall tipple, we shall doze together. we shall have our little Jokes, like other People, and our long Stories; Brandy will finish what Port begun; & a Month after the Time you will see in some Corner of a London Evening Post, Yesterday, died the Revnd Mr. John Grey, Senior-Fellow of Clare-Hall, a facetious Companion, & well-respected by all that knew him. his death is supposed to have been occasion'd by a Fit of an Apoplexy, being found fall'n out of Bed with his Head in the Chamber-Pot. (*CTG* 317–18)

The continuing '*Ennuy*' of Gray's life and obscurity, as he describes it in this passage to Wharton, however, was soon to be seriously disturbed. No sooner had the poet begun to settle down and reconcile himself to the fine and private pace of life within the walls of his college, than the languid tranquility of his place in that scholarly world began to show signs of the turbulence – unsought, un-looked for, and intensely public – which was to come. Far from being inappropriately eulogized (as the 'Revnd Mr. John Grey') in some obscure corner of the London newspapers for the comic or ignoble manner of his death, as he only half-jokingly speculated he would be in the letter quoted above, Gray was very soon to exchange the advantages of such obscurity for a fame and a celebrity his own modest ambitions had led him never to covet, nor even to entertain. He would spend a great deal of time and personal energy in the remaining years of his life fending off the consequences of a Faustian bargain with posterity that he had really never willingly undertaken to negotiate in the first place.

*

The ceremonies surrounding the Installation of the Duke of Newcastle as Chancellor of the University on 1 July 1749, in many ways heralded precisely the kinds of public 'Magnificences' that were so suddenly and so unexpectedly to characterize the latter half of Gray's own life. They formed a prelude of sorts to the life of fame, a taste of such greater things as were yet to come. Newcastle was installed in an elaborate ceremony that began with a procession from Clare Hall, where the Duke was then staying, to the Senate House, where the constituent members of the University had assembled in all their considerable regalia. After being greeted by a congratulatory speech given by the Vice-Chancellor, Newcastle was invested with the various trappings of his new position; the Senior Proctor, clasping Newcastle's right hand in his own, administered the oath of office. A public oration was then read (in Latin) to the assembled crowd, above whom Newcastle now presided in an elegant chair of State. The Installation Ode required by the occasion had been written by Gray's friend William Mason, and set to music by Boyce, who was then 'Composer to His Majesty'. The assembly then moved *en masse* to the hall and Master's lodge of Trinity College, where a feast had been prepared for no fewer than eight hundred guests. Nor were the festivities to end there. Services were held in St. Mary's Church on Sunday morning, Monday saw the conferral of honorary degrees (again at the Senate House), and Tuesday witnessed the Commencement ceremony itself. Not until Wednesday 5 July was Newcastle finally free to leave the University and return to London. Walpole had written to Mann in Florence describing the anticipation and frankly strong-armed enthusiasm that Newcastle himself had made certain would characterize the installation ceremonies. 'The whole world goes to it', Walpole wrote of the extravagances at Cambridge, 'he [Newcastle] has invited, summoned, pressed the entire body of nobility and gentry from all parts of England'. 'His cooks', Walpole added, somewhat impressed in spite of his own better judgement of Newcastle's personal and political character, 'have been there these ten days'.[4]

Gray had himself included a lengthy description of the Installation in a letter sent to Wharton only a few days after the ceremonies were concluded. The 'Week of Wonders', as he facetiously christened the extended affair in his account, had been characterized by a great deal of hubbub and confusion, but ultimately rewarded the alternately solemn and frantic efforts of its participants with very little of any real substance. 'Every one, while it lasted', Gray summarized concisely, 'was very gay, & very busy in the Morning, & very owlish & very tipsy at night'. Mason's celebratory Ode, he added in the spirit of generous loyalty, was 'the only Entertainment, that had any tolerable Elegance'. (Many years later, when he would be compelled to write a similar ode for precisely such an installation ceremony at Cambridge, Gray was to feel far more forcefully and for himself the pressures of writing occasional verse on a subject largely uncongenial to his own feelings and beliefs.) Gray concluded his account of University affairs with an expression of hope that

[4] WC xx.71.

Mason's own recent appointment to a college Fellowship, when taken together with Tuthill's election and the determined leadership of their mutual friend and ally James Brown, would at least soon 'bring Pembroke into some esteem'. 'But then', he conceded, 'there is no making Bricks without Straw. They have no Boys [i.e. undergraduate students] at all, & unless you can send us a Hamper or two out of the North to begin with, they will be like a few Rats straggling about an old deserted Mansion-House'.

Gray had been especially looking forward to his friend Henry Tuthill's return to Cambridge in the Michaelmas term of 1749. Tuthill's brief visit to Pembroke that summer to witness Newcastle's Installation for himself had reminded the poet just how much he enjoyed the young man's company and irrepressibly 'high Spirits'. The flicker of life which followed Tuthill's arrival that autumn, however, was not yet to be kindled into the lively flame of genial companionability. On 7 November, Gray received a letter from his mother, informing him that his aunt, Mary Antrobus, had died at Stoke Poges two days earlier. Her death – at the comparatively young age of only forty-six years old – was sudden and unexpected. Gray immediately wrote to his mother, consoling her on the loss of a close and beloved sister. He attempted as best he could (and with a genuine sincerity almost incomprehensible to most modern readers) to reconcile such a passing within the inscrutable plans of a merciful God. Mary Antrobus's final days must have been painful ones, and the onset of the illness that finally took her life was swift; Gray could only suggest that it was better for all concerned that her death had come as suddenly as it had. 'Perhaps, if we reflect upon what she felt in this life', he wrote to his mother feelingly,

> we may look upon this as an instance of his goodness both to her, and those that loved her. She might have languished many years before our eyes in a continual increase of pain, and totally helpless; she might have long wished to end her misery without being able to attain it; or perhaps even lost all sense, and yet continued to breathe; a sad spectacle to such who must have felt more for her than she could have done for herself. However you may deplore your own loss, yet think that she is at least easy and happy; and has now more occasion to pity us than we her. I hope, and beg, you will support yourself with that resignation we owe to him, who gave us our being for our good, and who deprives us of it for the same reason. I would have come to you directly, but you do not say whether you desire I should or not; if you do, I beg I may know it, for there is nothing to hinder me, and I am in very good health. (CTG 324–25)

Gray throughout his life often gave voice to his fears regarding the possibility of a lingering death – of dwindling into a sad and pathetic 'spectacle' – either for himself or for those he loved; the poet who most compellingly articulated the very human desire for perpetuation and remembrance was, rather oddly, one who at the same time prayed fervently that death accomplish its inevitable purpose as swiftly as possible, and one who likewise would have shunned almost any attempt at extreme or extraordinary measures to prolong an existence better returned to God's mercy. While it may seem a little strange or even out of character for Gray not immediately to have rushed to his mother's side to comfort both her and her surviving sister, Anne, Gray – still so very close to his mother in spirit and temperament – apparently knew best just what sort of comfort Dorothy Gray herself desired on such an occasion. He may instinctively have realized that in order to come to terms with her sister's death, his mother stood more in need of silence and room for meditation and prayer, than of the solace of sustaining or diverting conversation. Whatever his mother's immediate response to his letter of condolence, however, Gray would not stay away from Stoke for very long. Just over two weeks after receiving word of his aunt's death, Gray returned to Buckinghamshire. Interrupting his stay only with an occasional, brief trip into the city, he remained at West End House well into the first week of the new year.

Visiting London that December, Gray was particularly eager to see Walpole, who had only the month before just barely escaped being killed during an attempted robbery in Hyde Park. An account of the attack had been printed in the *London Evening Post* for 9–11 November. Returning from Holland House one evening, and guided on its way only by the light of the moon, Walpole's coach had suddenly been approached by two highwaymen obviously intent on robbing its occupants. The pistol of one of the robbers went off accidently (such misfirings were shockingly common) and its bullet sped past Walpole's face, grazing the skin beneath his eye. The shot was close enough actually to have left a residue of gunpowder on Walpole's cheek, and he confessed himself considerably stunned by the encounter. 'If I had sat an inch nearer the left side [of the coach]', Walpole later recalled with some drama in the *Short Notes* on his life, the bullet 'must have gone through my head'.[5] As it was, a sound but shaken Walpole typically made much of the incident. When one of the robbers (the celebrated 'gentleman highwayman' James Maclean) was finally apprehended and tried at the Old Bailey just one year later, Walpole's refusal to testify against the 26-year-old career criminal earned him an 'honourable mention' in the Grub Street ballad soon being circulated on the subject – a reference with which he was delighted (Walpole's silence ultimately did the young Scotsman little good; Maclean was executed at Tyburn on 3 October, 1750).

---

5 WC xiii.23.

Gray, like his friend, was also quick to recognize the peculiar glamour attached to one who had escaped so narrowly from such a potentially deadly encounter. He was very soon joking with Walpole about how it must feel 'when one returns from the very Brink of Destruction'. Once Gray had made certain for himself that Walpole was indeed still to be found in one piece at Arlington Street, he probably returned as soon as possible to Stoke. For all of Walpole's fuss, Gray knew where his care and reassurance were needed most. Only gradually did he even allow his attention to be turned once again to the substance of the scholarly routine that had by now become second nature to him. Having spent Christmas and his birthday quietly with his mother and his aunt at Stoke Poges – the absence of Mary's face around the familiar hearth must have left a gaping hole in their acknowledgement of the season – Gray returned to Cambridge well before the beginning of term. He stayed in residence without absences of any kind for an unusually long stretch of time – until 3 June, when he once again returned directly to the family at Stoke.

No correspondence survives either to or from the poet immediately subsequent to his own letter to Walpole just after the latter's accident (and written about ten days before Gray's own departure for Stoke and London the previous November) or prior to a letter – again to Walpole – dated from Stoke on 12 June, 1750. While any numbers of documents written in the nearly seven-month interval that separates those two letters to Walpole may have been lost to us over the years, there are other reasons that could just as easily account for this slightly unusual gap in Gray's correspondence. He had, to put the matter simply, some far more important things on his mind.

*

The death of a close relative or a loved one can very often, weeks, months, and even years after the event itself, provide eerie, fleeting glimpses of the mortality – of the stunningly proximate existence of death itself – which daily haunts each of our own lives. The transitions of those near to us in spirit, or even of those to whom we only sense a spiritual or emotional attachment, seem invariably to underscore the simple and unavoidable fact that Death, too, is never very far from us, lurking just beneath the feeble protection of our conscious minds or, in the words of Philip Larkin, as 'a small unfocused blur' just beyond the range of our vital peripheral vision.

Depending largely on the mood and the personality of the bereaved, such glimpses of our inevitable end necessarily vary both in their forms and in their effects. For some, such moments raise the spectre of a taboo subject – a subject simply too unspeakable directly to be confronted or addressed. The depiction of the fear of the soldiers who encounter the ghost of Hamlet's father in the opening scene of Shakespeare's tragedy touches many of us as it does precisely because it so effectively mirrors the response of denial – because it so artfully captures the near-antic posture of resistance. Shakespeare's representation is all the more effective for including the audience in the dread anxiety that lurks for all of us in the watches of the night. Others, however, would agree with the French writer Marguerite Yourcenar, in her assertion that death is simply a passage which we must learn somehow to welcome and embrace. 'We should think of death as a friend', Yourcenar has written, 'even though we feel a certain instinctive repugnance to do so'.[6] Having once overcome this 'repugnance', such a view contends, we can perhaps in time grow to regard the contemplation of mortality as an essential if paradoxical cornerstone of the *vitam beatam* – of the happy life. With the 'surprise' of his Aunt Mary's death yet exerting its lingering influence on his consciousness, and with the concerns of his unfinished poem on Education, Government, and the virtues of posterity still relatively fresh in his mind, Gray attempted to bring some sense of meaning to recent events by once again, as in the past, at least attempting to adopt and maintain the resolution of the latter approach. Doing so would involve completing a set of verses he had begun literally years before.

As we have already seen, it is not too much of an exaggeration to suggest that the progress, uniformity, and simple sense of order which Gray sought to capture both in his Chronology of Ancient Greek History and in the notes of his Commonplace Books led Gray to search for just such an order – precisely such a design – within the patterns and rituals of his own life. In a manner similar to his poetic heir, Robert Frost, Gray was a writer who looked everywhere for the 'portent in little'. If not exactly having been returned from 'the very Brink of Destruction' himself, Gray yet imagined, as he once again experienced the intoxicating rebirth of an English spring, what it might be like to return and to enquire after his own fame and reputation once he had been consigned to the grave. How would his memory be kept? Of what would his practical legacy consist? Who, if anyone, would be left to mourn him? Always of a melancholy temperament, Gray may have felt that his own life had of late become too crowded with death, change, and decay, and too empty of any corresponding sense of renewal, restoration, and rebirth.

Within the last few years so much seemed – for better or for worse – to have been taken *from* Gray, and so little seemed to have been granted

---

[6] Marguerite Yourcenar, from *With Open Eyes* (Boston: Beacon Press, 1984), excerpted in *The Grim Reader: Writings on Death, Dying, and Letting Go*, eds. Maura Spiegel and Richard Tristman (New York: Doubleday, 1997) 64.

in return. The recapitulation of his losses is formidable. Richard West had died, in pain and alone. William Antrobus had also been reft from his family. Both Gray's own father and the father of his best friend had passed away within months of each other, also in pain and suffering (the fact that Philip Gray's practical legacy consisted largely of financial chaos, and that his death had been marked only by a collective sigh of relief on the part of his family and relatives was in itself far from reassuring). The recent, terminal illnesses of both his uncle Jonathan Rogers and of his Aunt Mary had introduced death into the very house at Stoke Poges which his mother now called home. His own childhood home in Cornhill, for that matter, had burned to the ground in a matter of hours, taking with it so much that was known and familiar, if not necessarily reassuring, and leaving only a vain and smoking pile of expensive rubble and ashes. The quarrel with Walpole, too, still weighed heavily on Gray's mind. The poet had yet to come to terms with what their mutual disagreements and bad faith had cost them both in the way of affection, and of intimacy. What if, Gray must have asked himself, Walpole had indeed been killed by a highwayman's bullet in the park that night? How, again, would *he* have been remembered? And by whom? The aristocracy – even the Whig aristocracy – had a rather different way of handling such things, but even they, for all their pomp and ceremony (and here the memory of the elaborate spectacle of the trial of the Scottish Lords in Westminster Hall and their executions may have passed through his mind), had still to face the inevitable end. With so much suffering and (seemingly) so little compensation in this world, what was the point of it all? Were talents and abilities lent to men only to rust wasted – untried and unused? Were the reassuring rituals of domestic and familial life of any value if they, too, were doomed to die? – not merely to die, in fact, but ultimately to pass away as unremembered and unknown as if they had never existed at all. And finally (although it is a matter which for the most part lies far beneath the surface of Gray's work), what was the value of one's life in soteriological terms? What if, on his own deathbed, he was to be faced only with prospect of the buzzing, white noise of eternity? The poet of Gray's *Elegy* is admittedly no Hamlet, but haunting even his anxious speculations concerning the persistence of personal achievement and memory in the face of disintegrating time are the spectres of those same eternal questions that deter the melancholy prince of Denmark from taking his own life, or even, for so long, attempting to take the lives of others.

Throughout the spring of 1750 such questions must have crowded within Gray's mind, contriving at times to push all other thoughts aside. In attempting to formulate some sort of answer to them, the poet returned to some lines he may have begun writing down very soon after the death of Richard West eight years earlier. When he had finally completed the verses – just eight days after his arrival at Stoke Poges on 3 June – he folded them up, and left them to be sent on to Walpole later that same afternoon. For any hopes he may have entertained regarding his friend's opinion of the piece, and for any faith he genuinely possessed in his own abilities as a poet, Gray could hardly have anticipated the larger response his work was eventually to receive. In the quiet, melancholy stillness of the Stoke Poges spring, Gray had simultaneously put an end to – and initiated the critical beginning of – what would in time become one of the most popular poems in the English language. Although, in the pages that follow, we will be focusing our attention rather more intently and specifically on the *Elegy*'s connection to the death of West and to the poetry already written by Gray as he mourned the loss of that friendship, we would do well to keep some of these larger questions and concerns in mind. A deceptively 'straightforward' and accessible poem in many ways, the *Elegy* – as the most cursory glance at its critical history demonstrates – is by no means a simple poem. It is a work which lends itself to an unusually wide range of readings – and one that can be put to an equally diverse number of uses. Gray's *Elegy* is numbered high among the very greatest poems in the English tradition precisely because of its simultaneous accessibility and inscrutability.

II. The Voice of Nature

In his letter to Walpole of 12 June, Gray was remarkably coy regarding the possible merits of the poem he enclosed for his friend. 'As I live in a place', he began with an apparent reference to Cambridge, but with a sidelong glance perhaps, too, at Stoke Poges itself,

> where even the ordinary tattle of the town arrives not till it is stale, and which produces no events of its own, you will not desire any excuse from me for writing so seldom, especially as of all people living I know you are the least a friend to letters spun out of one's own brains, with all the toil and constraint that accompanies sentimental productions. I have been here at Stoke a few days (where I shall continue good part of the summer); and having put an end to a thing, whose beginning you have seen long ago. I immediately send it you. You will, I hope, look upon it in light of a *thing with an end to it*; a merit that most of my writings have wanted, and are like to want, but which this epistle I am determined shall not want. . . . (*CTG* 326–27)

Adding a post-script which noted that Thomas Ashton's *Dissertation* – a polemic against the theological writings of their mutual acquaintance

Dr. Conyers Middleton – had recently been published in London, Gray concluded: 'So much for other people, now to *self* again. You are desired to tell me your opinion, if you can take the pains, of these lines'.

A reader unfamiliar with Gray's correspondence (one at the same time almost impossibly unaware of the *Elegy*'s subsequent popularity) might certainly be forgiven for bestowing no more than a cursory glance on this particular letter, and on its casual, deliberately unspecific reference to 'these lines', before moving on. Gray's words were perfunctory, even trivializing. The poem that was very soon to transform his life – and to transform or at least profoundly affect the development of lyric poetry in English – is here, on the occasion of its first introduction to the world, dismissed with considerable, seeming modesty on the part of its author. The *Elegy* is twice referred to in the letter as little more than a 'thing'; 'it' is a 'thing', moreover, the chief merit of which is said to consist in the simple and terminal fact of its completion: a *thing with an end to it*. Yet Gray's letter, when brought together with the reminiscences of his friends and acquaintances, offers a number of important hints regarding precisely when, where, why, and for whom – if anyone, in particular – the poem was 'originally' written. Before focusing our attention more closely on the *Elegy* itself, we first need briefly to address the still vexed questions that surround the compositional history of Gray's most famous poem.

Sending a copy of the *Elegy* to Walpole on 12 June, Gray observed in passing that he has 'put an end to' the poem only very recently, apparently even within the past 'few days' that had followed on his arrival at Stoke just over one week earlier. Such an observation seems strongly to support (though it does not confirm) the perception that the church-yard at Stoke Poges itself played a significant role in the conclusion, if not the inception of the *Elegy*. Gray almost certainly, on the Sunday following his arrival in Buckinghamshire, attended regular services at the parish church, where both he and his mother would have had the opportunity to pause and pay their respects at the grave of Mary Antrobus (the situation of the tomb itself would have made such a visit virtually unavoidable). Gray, in any event, seems from his own accounts of his long, meditative walks in the Buckinghamshire countryside, often to have found the melancholy quiet of the church-yard profoundly soothing. The actual sight of his aunt's tomb may well have been the spur that re-awakened within Gray's mind the elegiac impulse to which he had several times attempted to give a coherent voice within the past few years. It is of crucial importance to remember that Gray's own mother had had the tomb built for her aunt and herself not very long before this time, and that Gray no doubt – as early as 1750 – suspected if not absolutely knew for certain that it was destined eventually to hold his own remains as well. In paying his respects at the vault which already housed the body of his aunt and that was later to house that of his mother, Gray could not help but have been aware that he was standing before the grave which would, surely and in time, be his own. The sensations experienced on such a bizarrely proleptic and apophatic moment must have been for him uncanny. How, indeed, can one describe the thoughts of an individual who has the opportunity of confronting the physical reality of his or her own grave while still alive? Who, Gray would again have found himself asking in the summer silence of the church-yard, might be found standing in his own stead in the years following his death, and what would be their thoughts? How would he be mourned in this worthy place, how remembered? What, if any, were the lessons to be learned from the fact of one's own mortality? Gray's *Elegy*, a poem which would in time become famous most for its seeming transcendence and universality, was for its author a work firmly rooted in some grimly real and quite frankly practical questions concerning the worth, the value, and the significance of his own life. It had been a relatively common practice among poets and writers of the classical world, as Gray no doubt knew, to composed their own epitaphs while yet alive. Still, the scene the *Elegy* would eventually recreate, in which the 'forlorn' poet in some sense revisits his own grave to inquire after his reputation and legacy (not necessarily his poetic legacy, we should remember, but his larger and more comprehensive legacy as an educated and devout human being) was for Gray himself no mere fanciful narrative convention – no incidentally useful and literary trope. He had actually been there. He had already experienced how it felt. He knew.

*

We need once again to return briefly to the questions that surround the *Elegy*'s composition. If we know that Gray put the last, finishing touches on the poem sometime in the first and second weeks of June, 1750, when might he actually have begun writing the work? The events that took place in the autumn and winter of 1749 and the spring of 1750 seem clearly to have prompted Gray to complete the *Elegy* and to introduce it, through Walpole, into the world at large. But where are we to locate the very heart of its beginnings? Mason in his *Memoirs* suggested that the summer of 1742 – the period following the death of West that had seen the burst of creative activity which produced the 'Sonnet', the *Adversity* Ode, and the *Eton Ode* – had likewise witnessed the composition of some of the earliest portions of the *Elegy*. 'I am inclined to believe' Mason wrote after Gray's death, 'that the Elegy in a Country Church-yard was begun, if not concluded, at this time [August 1742] also: Though I am aware that as it stands at present, the conclusion is of a later date; how that was originally I shall show in my notes on the poem'.[7]

The most substantial piece of evidence Mason produced which might eventually support what remains at best and in his own words little more than a carefully qualified 'inclination' towards a conjecture, was the draft of the poem that is today known as the 'Eton Manuscript' (currently, as its name suggests, in the possession of Gray's old school). In this unique manuscript draft of the poem – a draft containing elements that clearly pre-date the version of the work first sent to Walpole in 1750 – the poem is not only given a slightly different title ('Stanza's wrote in a Country Church-Yard'), but is also preserved in the very act of becoming. The Eton manuscript is not so much a 'version' of the *Elegy*, in fact, as it is a document that captures the poem in the actual process of being written, rewritten, and revised for some form of private or public audience. In so doing, it offers readers a distant mirror of the mind of the poet himself, as he grappled with painstaking care, with the various, possible solutions to the questions raised within the poem about memory and desire.

The series of verses that Gray copied into his Commonplace Book from the August of 1742 capture the poet in the very act of attempting – in a progression of lyrics, each of which employed different rhetorical strategies, and which ranged in their responses to West's death (and to death, in general) from vain denial to coy excuse – to come to terms with the loss of West, and with the impact of that loss on his own life. The *Elegy* of the Eton Manuscript bears witness to the same hard-fought battle with loss and mourning, only the various doctrinal and emotional solutions to his problem are in this second instance contained rather within the ambitious scope of a single document. The Eton Manuscript is in some respects little less than a palimpsest of Gray's grief. Its language shows us the slow and painful progress of his emotions as surely and as clearly as the rings of a tree harden, in time, to preserve a record of its maturation and growth.

In fact three versions of the *Elegy* in Gray's own handwriting exist. The first of these is the Eton Manuscript version. The second is a later draft of the poem copied into the second volume of the poet's Commonplace Book. Finally, there is the draft sent to Wharton on 18 December 1750, and now in the British Library (the version sent to Walpole and subsequently circulated in manuscript does not survive). Gray's final draft of the *Elegy* – or, to put it differently, the poem most often reprinted and read by today's readers – contains thirty-two stanzas: the twenty-nine stanzas of the poem proper, and the concluding three stanzas of the

---

[7] Mason, *Memoirs* (1775) 157.

'Epitaph' that complete the work. The version of the Eton Manuscript, in contrast, contains an earlier draft of the poem in only twenty-two stanzas, the last four of which were later bracketed for omission by Gray himself. To what remained of what appears to have been this 'original' or first draft of the poem (lines 1–72 of the published work), Gray then 'added' an additional sixteen stanzas, bringing the total length of the Eton version – including the four bracketed stanzas – to roughly thirty-five stanzas. Any line or word count of the *Elegy* is necessarily compli-cated by the fact that Gray's extended version of the poem included a transitional stanza that then incorporated material drawn from the 'cancelled' stanzas of the Eton manuscript. In the final, published version of the *Elegy*, some of the stanzas added to the first draft in the Eton Manuscript would be dropped, and several significant emendations in word choice and vocabulary would also be made. The draft of the *Elegy* in the Eton Manuscript, it should further be noted, preserves almost throughout the text the division of the individual verse quatrains of the poem – each consisting of four lines of rhymed iambic pentameter – into discrete and separate verses. In the draft of the poem eventually sent to Wharton in December 1750, by contrast, the verse stanzas of the poem were written continuously; no space separates one quatrain from the next.

Why should these complications and discrepancies between the three original, holograph versions of the *Elegy* – the fine distinctions of which, arguably, belong more properly within the provenance of the bibliogra-pher or textual editor – be of interest to a reader of Gray's life? The simple fact of the matter, again, is that in the absence of any explicit and indisputable reference to the *Elegy* in Gray's correspondence before he finally sent the version to Walpole in June, 1750, the internal evidence provided by such documents becomes an invaluable source of informa-tion for dating the poem, and thus for tracing the unusually complicated history of its composition. Only if textual scholars can tell us approxi-mately *when* Gray wrote the poem, can we feel confident in answering the more intriguing question that asks *why* he wrote it, and – in the event that such a concern even remains relevant – for whom.

Given the existing evidence, two basic scenarios regarding the poem's compositional history have been postulated by scholars over the years. The first such scenario returns us once again to Mason. Relying pri-marily on the evidence of the Eton Manuscript as 'the first manuscript copy', Mason suggested that Gray had originally intended the poem to end with the four stanzas later marked for cancellation in the margin of that manuscript. Quoting those sixteen lines, Mason then observed, 'And here the poem was originally intended to conclude'. So far, so good. The Eton Manuscript does indeed appear to constitute an earlier and tentatively *complete* draft of the poem, a draft which, in fact, is in some ways and for some readers, more balanced and coherently structured than the later, published version of the work. As Gray's editor Roger Lonsdale has observed:

> The three opening stanzas brilliantly setting the poet and the poem in the churchyard, are followed by four balanced sections each of four stanzas, dealing in turn with the lives of the humble villagers; by contrast with the lives of the great; with the way in which the villagers are deprived of the opportunities of greatness; and by contrast, with the crimes inextricably involved in success as the 'thoughtless world' knows it, from which the villagers are protected. The last three stanzas, balancing the opening three, return to the poet himself in the churchyard, making clear that the whole poem has been a debate within his mind as he meditates in the darkness, at the end of which he makes his own choice about the preferability of obscure innocence to the dangers of the 'great world'.[8]

Lonsdale supported his observations regarding the coherency and the lucidity of Gray's initial design for the work by citing several of the classical parallels that the poet clearly had in mind when he set about composing the poem – well-known passages from Virgil's *Georgics*, for example, and from Horace's second *Epode*. Mason's suggestion that the first twenty-two-stanza draft of the *Elegy* constituted an early, coherent, and complete 'version' of the poem can thus be supported with relative ease by a close reading of the work as it exists in that same form; precedents in the writings of classical antiquity further support the view that such an elegy might certainly have been read by an educated, contemporary audience as finished, self-contained, and in every sense 'complete'.

Mason's stated belief that this finished, Eton Manuscript draft of the poem was not only begun but also completed in August 1742, however, is not so easily supported by the surviving textual evidence. Nor is such an account consistent with the memories and speculations of Gray's other friends – most notably those of Walpole himself. Mason, it will be remembered, did not make Gray's acquaintance until 1747, and nowhere in the frequent correspondence that was to result from their friendship would any reference be made to the compositional history of the *Elegy* which would in any way support the view subsequently advanced by Mason himself – i.e., that the poem was a direct response to the death of West in 1742. In fact, presenting such a conjecture to Walpole many years later, when preparing his *Memoirs* of Gray for the press in 1773, Mason very quickly received a letter from Walpole in return, correcting what he immediately perceived to be a mistake in the dating of

---

[8] Lonsdale, *PTG*, 114.

the postulated composition of the poem. Contesting Mason's chronology, Walpole wrote: 'The *Churchyard* was, I am persuaded, posterior to West's death at least three or four years, as you will see by my note. At least I am sure that I had the twelve or more first lines from himself above three years after that period, and it was long before he finished it.'[9]

Later that same month Walpole again wrote to Mason, who had apparently presented him with an argument that furthered and advanced at greater length and in greater detail his own position, and withdrew his opposition to the latter's outlines of events. 'Your account of the Elegy', he wrote simply and tantalizingly to Mason on 14 December, 'puts an end to my criticism.'[10] Yet, as one of the editors of Gray's correspondence, Leonard Whibley observed, Walpole was often more polite than genuine when pretending to agree with his correspondents. His deferral to Mason would seem to constitute precisely one of those instances in which Walpole's sense of truth may have been sacrificed to his overriding sense of epistolary decorum; Gray's oldest surviving friend may also have felt somewhat delicate about questioning the literary judgement of the man whom the poet had himself chosen to serve as his literary executor.

In the absence of the hard evidence of Mason's counter-argument to Walpole (his 'account' has unfortunately since been lost to us) we are left with a second possible scenario for the composition of the *Elegy*. According to the anecdotal evidence provided by Walpole's own memory, Gray had by as late as 1746 (the period following their reconciliation in November, 1745) written only the very beginning of the poem – 'the twelve or more first lines'. Even given Gray's notoriously dilatory rate of poetic composition, it would be hard to imagine the poet unable for nearly four years to move beyond the opening two or three stanzas of the work. While such an account in no way eliminates the possibility that Gray had begun to think about the larger issues and concerns (and had perhaps even begun to shape the narrative and imagery) which would eventually come to characterize the *Elegy* in both its manuscript and its published versions very soon after West's death, its terms effectively place the *terminus a quo* for the actual composition of the work closer to 1745–46, than 1742. In letters dating from the period immediately following the reconciliation of the two friends and Walpole's removal to Windsor in the autumn of 1746, it will be remembered, several references had been made on Gray's own part to the exchange of writings which had begun once again to take place between the two men. Walpole's account suggests that even by August and Sep-

9   WC xviii.117–18.
10 WC xxviii.123.

tember of 1746, when Gray had resumed writing poetry in English for
the first time since the isolated *floriut* of 1742, he may barely have begun
work on the *Elegy*.

Gray's own few references to the *Elegy* – and to the vaguely designated verses that appear, in time, to have taken shape as the *Elegy* –
would seem to support Walpole's unrevised, memorially based account
of the poem's history. His letter to Walpole of 12 June 1750, quite specifically confirmed Walpole's account that he had seen the opening lines of
the poem several years earlier: 'Having put an end to a thing, whose
beginning you have seen long ago, I immediately send it you.' Gray's
'long ago', remember, must necessarily have been no earlier than the very
end of 1745, when he was reconciled with Walpole at Arlington Street;
his specific reference is more likely to have been to the late summer
months of 1746, when he pointedly noted in a letter to Wharton that
he had once again begun writing poetry in English. Gray's only possible
reference in his surviving correspondence to the *Elegy* as a work-in-
progress is found in a letter to Wharton dated 11 September of that same
year. Having first noted that he had been amusing himself with the study
of Aristotle, he concluded: 'this & a few autumnal Verses are my Entertainments during the Fall of the Leaf'. As one twentieth-century editor
of the poet's correspondence (Whibley, himself following the lead of his
predecessor Duncan C. Tovey) concluded, we recognize in this reference
to 'a few autumnal Verses' of 'no poem except the *Elegy* to which Gray
could be alluding'.[11]

*

The complex cluster of evidence, assertion, and counter-assertion that
I have been attempting only briefly to sketch in these past few pages
leaves us, once again, with no definitive answer to the question of exactly
when Gray wrote the *Elegy*. We do at least know for certain when and
how the poem was *not* composed: it was not written in a single 'sitting',
nor was it the product of several hours or even several days or weeks,
but rather of many, many months and even many years of work. Almost
fifty years after Gray's death, the poet John Keats would memorably
express in a letter to his publisher John Taylor his own belief that 'if
poetry comes not as naturally as the Leaves to a tree, it had better not
come at all'.[12] Keats's statement has often been quoted out of context,
and accepted by generations of post-Romantic readers (of whom we still
form a part) as an incontestable and even universal maxim on the

[11] See *CTG* Appendix I, 'The Composition of the Elegy' (1214–16).
[12] *The Letters of John Keats*, ed. Hyder Edward Rollins, 2 vols. (Cambridge: Harvard
University Press, 1958) i.238–9.

composition of lyric poetry. Gray, however, like so many other poets writing in the eighteenth century – poets for whom constant and theoretically endless revision and rewriting were considered to be essential parts of the poetic process itself – felt otherwise. For Gray, to paraphrase the critic Harold Bloom's comment on the Renaissance poet and dramatist Ben Jonson, art was *'hard work'*.[13] It was the kind of hard work, moreover, which could take a great deal of time; Gray – a well as, for that matter, Thomson, Pope, or even Johnson – would have found the language of Keats's easy, organic metaphor quite frankly absurd.

Throughout his correspondence, Gray would several times comment on his own sporadic methods of composition. 'You apprehend too much from my resolutions about writing', he wrote on one occasion, 'they are only made to be broken'. He would emphasize his inability to exert any real, conscious control over his own creative faculty. 'I by no means pretend to inspiration', he would write to Wharton several years after the publication of the *Elegy*,

> but yet I affirm, that the faculty in question is by no means voluntary. it is the result (I suppose) of a certain disposition of mind, which does not depend on one's self, & which I have not felt this long time. you that are a witness, how seldom this spirit has moved me in my life, may easily give credit to what I say. (*CTG* 571)

Gray himself, as he is ready to admit in this passage, treads a fine line between more traditional, received ideas about poetic 'inspiration', on the one hand, and what he characterizes as a rather more idiosyncratic and (for modern readers) psychologically plausible if still imprecise, 'disposition of mind', on the other. Gray, it will be remembered, had been ready playfully to experiment with the figure of the poetic Muse who provides the writer with guidance and inspiration in such poems as the early *Ode on Spring*. He knew from hard experience that the very concept of the inspirational Muse was far more than a simple or straightforward rhetorical trope. He also knew, however, much like the poet Sir Philip Sidney before him, that the most moving and emotionally resonant poetry came not from without, but from within; that in order to give a truly convincing voice to his thoughts and emotions, he needed not only to 'dispose his mind' to composition, but to 'look within his heart' and write.

The *Elegy*, then, while it may have been prompted by the inspirational stirrings of occasional circumstance that were, in Gray's own words, somehow beyond 'one's self', by no means sprang full grown

---

[13] Harold Bloom, *The Anxiety of Influence: A Theory of Poetry* (London: Oxford University Press, 1973) 27.

from the head of its creator. He approached the *Elegy* over the years with the diligence of a poetic Flaubert; Gray would no doubt have sympathized with that later author when he compared his own patient and painstaking process of writing to that of a workman turning delicate napkin rings on a lathe, noting that he persisted in writing if only because 'it gives me something to do, and it affords me some private pleasure'.[14] 'To be employed', Gray would write in 1757, 'is to be happy'.

The valuable evidence of the Eton Manuscript, while it does not fully support Mason's inclination to believe that a tentatively 'finished' draft of the poem was completed as early as August 1742, does lend substantial credence to the belief that the *Elegy* was composed in at least two major bursts of creative activity on Gray's part. The first version of the poem ends with a clear and unambiguous determination voiced by the poet to 'pursue the silent Tenour of [his] doom' – that is to say, to throw in his lot with the obscure villagers who have little if anything to do with the 'Majesty', 'Success', 'Power', and 'Genius' so fruitlessly pursued by the world at large. The second version of the poem shuns the familiar stoicism of this original ending to insist on the indisputable *naturalness* of the human desire for memory and memorialization and, rather than ending the poem with a solemnly easy assurance of the 'eternal Peace' that lies beyond the grave, extends the work with a substantially more complicated narrative which imagines the death of the poet himself, and ends with a representation of what appears to be his own, admonitory epitaph within the language of the poem. The first poem, much like the *Adversity* Ode, attempts to rest content within the traditional consolations of Christianity; the second, bearing instead a closer thematic relationship to the advances of the *Eton* Ode, pursues the issues raised by the varieties of human mourning and memorialization to what some interpret to be considerably more anxious and temporary conclusions.

Mason's desire to interpret the first draft of the *Elegy* as having been written at the same time as the *Sonnet* on the death of Richard West, the *Eton Ode* and the *Ode to Adversity* is in many respects a natural one. Few readers who have spent any time with the narrative of Gray's life, it should by now be clear, can underestimate the impact of West's death on the poet's state of mind; the fundamental similarity of subject and purpose that unites all four poems would likewise seem to demand that we look as closely as possible for those elements – and the chronology of their composition is surely relevant here – which might connect them. While we admittedly possess no hard evidence that the poems

---

[14] Gustave Flaubert, as translated by Geoffrey Braithwaite for Julian Barnes, in *Flaubert's Parrot* (New York: McGraw-Hill, 1984) 30.

were indeed written at the same time, the conceptual or 'practical' argument most often maintained by those who would wish to deny such a possibility – i.e. the notion that Gray, having only just begun to write poetry in English, could not possibly have been so productive within such a short space of time – is equally untenable. For all the intensity of thought and feeling that all four poems together work to articulate and to crystallize, they are all notably – even notoriously – short works. The 'spirit' that moved Gray to write poetry, and the desperate need he felt throughout the summer of 1742 to make some sense of his loss, could very easily have resulted in the creation or at least the inception of all four works in a remarkably short period of time. Gray, again, often took months and years to polish his work to a perceived perfection, yet we should be careful always to keep in mind that the extended genesis of poems such as the *Eton Ode* and, more particularly, the *Elegy* in no way precludes the possibility that an initial, intense moment of creativity resulted in a manuscript the essential outline of which was to remain largely unchanged.

If we accept Walpole's recollection of having initially been shown 'the twelve or more first lines' of the *Elegy* some time in 1745 or 1746, we can nevertheless still entertain the hypothesis that the poem was an outgrowth if not a direct result of the emotional crucible – the painful productivity of which historical moment is beyond dispute – which followed hard upon the death of West in 1742. With the exception of the (by all accounts) hastily written *Ode on the Death of a Favourite Cat*, all of Gray's other poetry in English (and, it should be remembered, the fragment of Book II of *De Prinicipiis Cogitandi* as well) had thus far been prompted by the circumstances surrounding his friend's death. It is by no means too far-fetched to suppose that the *Elegy* owes something of its initial impulse to the summer of 1742 as well. As Jean Hagstrum wrote in a ground-breaking and what can only be described as lovingly perceptive essay on Gray's 'sensibility' first published in 1974: 'Vastly more influential than any literary model or cultural trend, more intimately related to his mind and heart than the trial and sentencing of the rebel Scottish lords in London, the friendship with West was the soil from which the "Elegy" grew, a traditional view that needs reviving'.[15] Hagstrum's immediate reference here, incidently, is to a by now largely forgotten, 1946 scholarly essay by W. M. Newman, which had attempted to argue that Gray's immediate 'source' and inspiration for the *Elegy* had been the trial and execution of the Lords in the August of 1746; London, Newman suggested, not Stoke, had provided the real background to the poem, and the concluding epitaph of the final draft had been added to the Eton Manuscript version only because the

---

[15]   Hagstrum in Downey and Jones, 15.

memory of the events in Westminster themselves had 'faded' with time. As has been intimated, there is no reason to suppose that the tragic and admittedly spectacular events of 1746 might *not* have played some small role in Gray's imagination when writing the poem; Hagstrum's impassioned advocacy of an emotionally rooted reading of the *Elegy* which in so many ways precedes and eclipses such, more biographically tenuous source and background studies, however, is doubtlessly closer to the truth. Hagstrum's is likewise and rather peculiarly a reading that tends often to constitute one's initial reaction to the poem. If the reader knows anything about Gray's personal history, the impulse to read the *Elegy* as a testament to the poet's affection for West is very close to spontaneous. Second thoughts may lead one eventually and more soberly to deem the work, as Cleanth Brooks so memorably argued, not so much an 'artless tale', as a complex, ironic, and verbally sophisticated artefact. Yet final reconsiderations seem invariably and inescapably to return one to what Frank H. Ellis many years ago described as the 'biographical problem' of the *Elegy*. Something about the language of the poem itself, paradoxically, demands that we look beyond its status as 'text' – that we pass beyond a predictably modern 'reading' of the work as, exclusive of all other factors, a socially or culturally constructed document – in the effort to discover the human roots of its emotional intensity and the raw, compelling power of its vision. The intuition of critics such as Hagstrum and others who look to West for the source of that emotion may, again, defy or even ignore certain, contemporary critical obsessions, but such an intuition just as surely sounds the note of truth in almost any reader who takes the time to illuminate Gray's life for him or her self by what André Maurois characterized as 'the bright light within' – the sympathetic flame that alone makes literature and its interpretation relevant and actually valuable to our lives.

On the personal level, then, the *Elegy* fulfilled both for West and for its author the role specifically played in ancient religious ceremonies of mourning and farewell by the keening lament of those women who remained behind, and who prepared the corpse of the loved one for the tomb or for the funeral pyre. Such songs and laments lay at the center of the ancient funeral ceremony because they represented 'the expression of love made memorable by form'.[16] The *Elegy* is also a formal expression of love – the poem is what the Greeks would have called Gray's γοός or 'goós' for West, a song that testifies to the depth of the spiritual connection between the two friends, and at the same time sounds a heart-felt lament bewailing the bitterness of their parting. When the character of Odysseus, in the eleventh book of Homer's

---

[16] Emily Vermeule, *Aspects of Death in Early Greek Art and Poetry* (Berkeley: University of California Press), excerpted as 'A Very Active Dead' in *The Grim Reader*, 265.

Odyssey, evokes the shade of Agamemnon at the entrance to the underworld, he is moved to tears by the account of his comrade's homecoming, and by the unthinkable treachery of Clytemnestra. Both men are
appalled by Clytemnestra's 'foul and dreadful' deceit, but they are no
less stunned by her treatment of her husband's body in death. 'That
whore', as Agamemnon refers angrily to his wife and assassin, had not
even has the common decency to 'close my two eyes as my soul swam
to the underworld, or shut my lips'. In ancient Greek culture, where the
preparation of the corpse for burial was a particularly sacred ritual
(the body would normally be bathed and anointed, and – its eyes closed
and its jaw firmly shut – displayed with its feet towards the open entryway), such neglect was profoundly abhorrent and sacrilegious. Gray,
who had never had the opportunity of visiting West in his final days
and hours, and who had been deprived the opportunity of seeing for
himself that the rites and ceremonies of interment had been properly
performed (his distrust of West's family and 'friends' inclined him to
doubt that they had been), enacted for West, in the *Elegy*, a proper
burial. The *Elegy* is Gray's personal πρόθεσις ('prothesis') and ἐκφορά
('ekphora') for West – a formal ceremony of remembrance, and a slow,
mournful passage to the tomb itself. In the absence of having cradled
West's head in his own arms, and with his own hands having ministered
to his extreme needs, Gray voiced in the *Elegy* a sense of an intimate,
personal involvement in his friend's death, and recognized the possible
implications such a loss had for his own life – a life seemingly grown
sear even in the passage of his youth, and in the earliest years of middle
age.

                                        *

   The opening stanzas of Gray's *Elegy* memorably situate the poem's
solitary observer among the sights and sounds of a rural church-yard:

> The curfew tolls the knell of parting day,
> The lowing herd wind slowly o'er the lea,
> The ploughman homeward plods his weary way,
> And leaves the world to darkness and to me.
>
> Now fades the glimmering landscape on the sight,
> And all the air a solemn stillness holds,
> Save where the beetle wheels his droning flight,
> And drowsy tinklings lull the distant folds;
>
> Save that from yonder ivy-mantled tower
> The moping owl does to the moon complain
> Of such as, wandering near her secret bower,
> Molest her ancient solitary reign. (*PTG* 119–20)

The poet of the *Elegy* is remarkably alive to almost everything around him. The specific details and sensations on which he focuses in the poem's opening stanzas – be they aural (the tolling of the evening curfew, the sounds of the 'lowing herd', the 'solemn stillness' of the air, the 'droning flight' of the beetle, the 'drowsy tinklings' of the distant sheep, the complaints of the 'moping' owl, etc.) or visual (the dropping of the daylight in the west, the movement of the herd across the nearby meadow, the weary 'plodding' of the ploughman, the fading of the 'glimmering' landscape, the eminence of the church's 'ivy-mantled tower', the intimation, even, of the owl's 'ancient' and 'solitary' bower) – all are remarkably vivid and *present* to his conscious observation. He forms the center of all he sees: the 'glittering landscape' fades on his sight only, the church's tower is 'yonder' only by virtue of its situation vis-à-vis the speaker himself. Alone in the gloaming – and the opening stanza's 'leaves the world to darkness and to me' underscores both a privileged as well as an imperiled isolation – the poet–figure and his recorded observations alone confer some sense of order on the landscape. These things would never have been brought together, the voice of the elegist seems to say, had it not been for the isolated and emphatically monosyllabic 'me'.

Once again, as in almost all of Gray's earlier work, one immediately recognizes the specific influence in the poem's opening lines of the philosophy of John Locke. 'The objective quality of Eighteenth-Century literature', as Kenneth MacLean observed, 'is certainly owing in part to the fact that Locke's demonstration that all ideas originate in sensation induced writers to give almost undue attention to the external world'.[17] Yet the speaker of the *Elegy*, however emphatically proprietary he may appear to be in the poem's opening stanzas regarding the natural or 'outside' world, will be compelled in time to acknowledge some hardly learned lessons concerning the nature of all human understanding. The *Elegy* begins with a catalogue of the phenomena of the 'external' world, but moves on eventually to explore the limits of that world – daring even to approach the shifting borders of a new one.

In her analysis of the 'greater lyric' in eighteenth-century poetry (the 'greater lyric' having been defined as a lyric poem that 'concerns abiding issues about man, nature, and human life which have always occupied serious poets in their most ambitious work'), the modern critic Anne Williams perceptively observed that, in sharp contrast to other poets of the so-called 'graveyard school', Gray appears actually to go out of his way in these opening lines to avoid the kinds of self-consciously 'terrific' effects such poems looked more typically to create. In his own *Elegy*, Gray, as Williams observed, 'avoids any effort to express or arouse

---

[17] MacLean, *John Locke and English Literature of the Eighteenth Century*, 13.

terror, the hallmark of the tradition he evokes'.[18] Wandering among the
tombstones, the poet of the *Elegy* notices different objects, and gives
voice to other, less sensational concerns. Pursuing his careful observations of the rural scene, the elegist continues to follow his thoughts
among the tombs, once again taking sharp notice of the smallest, intimated details:

> Beneath those rugged elms, that yew-tree's shade,
> Where heaves the turf in many a mouldering heap,
> Each in their narrow cell for ever laid,
> The rude forefathers of the hamlet sleep.
>
> The breezy call of incense-breathing morn,
> The swallow twittering from the straw-built shed,
> The cock's shrill clarion or the echoing horn,
> No more shall rouse them from their lowly bed.
>
> For them no more the blazing hearth shall burn,
> Or busy housewife ply her evening care:
> No children run to lisp their sire's return,
> Or climb his knees the envied kiss to share. (*PTG* 120–22)

The imaginative consciousness of the elegist extends itself both beneath
the 'mouldering heaps' of the burial plots and into the 'narrow cells' of
the dead villagers, recreating even, in the process of its conjectures, the
domestic scenes and situations of their past lives.

Yet in some far more fundamental respects, the elegist of Gray's poem
is markedly unobtrusive and even evasive. Prompted only by the movement of its own, ordering consciousness, the mind of the elegist certainly
withdraws from some of the less picturesque aspects of his surroundings, and in doing so avoids some of the more threatening implications
embedded (quite literally) within those surroundings. The voice of Gray's
Elegy, as Williams put it, is that of a psyche 'persistently defending itself
against intense emotions'. These 'defenses', Williams argues, 'appear in
numerous ways':

> through the cautious indirection of verbal expression, through rhetorical
> questions, descriptions by negation and describing what is *not* there;
> through the limited emotional range the speaker seems to permit himself
> . . . avoiding the conventional terrors of the graveyard meditation as well

---

[18] Anne Williams, *The Prophetic Strain: The Greater Lyric in the Eighteenth Century*
(Chicago: University of Chicago Press, 1984) 108.

as the ritualized, hyperbolic expressions of grief indigenous to the pastoral elegy. What we find instead is gentle nostalgia, poignant memories,
and resignation.[19]

The details of Gray's poem warrant precisely such an observation. The
most famous images in the poem look to present the reader with quiet
intimations of such things as can never fully be seen or realized – things
which, by the very terms of human existence, will never have the chance
to impress themselves on the human subject. Having first considered the
possible advantages and disadvantages of a life of country obscurity (and
illiteracy) from the vantage of what we, as humans, leave behind us in
the shape of testaments and memorials, Gray's elegist broaches the larger
and potentially more troublesome issue of nature's profligacy (the essentially democratic philosophy of the poem at this point again finds much
of its origin in Locke's writings). The possibility that 'Chill Penury'
had frozen the 'genial currents' of the villagers' souls prompts the poet's
well-known articulation of the inescapable *fact* of aesthetic, political,
intellectual, and emotional waste:

> Full many a gem of purest ray serene
> The dark unfathomed caves of ocean bear:
> Full many a flower is born to blush unseen
> And waste its sweetness on the desert air.
>
> Some village-Hampden that with dauntless breast
> The little tyrant of his fields withstood;
> Some mute inglorious Milton here may rest,
> Some Cromwell guiltless of his country's blood.
>
> The applause of listening senates to command,
> The threats of pain and ruin to despise,
> To scatter plenty o'er a smiling land,
> And read their history in a nation's eyes,
>
> Their lot forbade: nor circumscribed alone
> Their growing virtues, but their crimes confined;
> Forbade to wade through slaughter to a throne,
> And shut the gates of mercy on mankind,
>
> The struggling pangs of conscious truth to hide,
> To quench the blushes of ingenuous shame,
> Or heap the shrine of Luxury and Pride
> With incense kindled at the Muse's flame. (*PTG* 127–30)

[19] Williams, 108.

The resignation of Gray's speaker in the face of such seeming 'inequities' lies at the heart of the *Elegy*. 'Resignation', as Williams has observed, 'is one of Gray's many euphemisms for death, but more broadly it indicates an attitude toward life, the world, and experience that the speaker displays throughout the poem: his stoic acceptance of the inevitable'.[20]

Gray's speaker would seem to confront death directly, even audaciously, in the narrative of the *Elegy*'s closing stanzas. Having first reflected that all human beings seem to desire the tribute of remembrance from those they leave behind, Gray turns the poem at its ninety-fifth line to displace the voice of his elegist, and traces instead the story of that same speaker's own death and burial. The shift is not an entirely fluid one, but the poet's intention in introducing the 'hoary-headed swain' of the twenty-fifth stanza is clear enough. The remaining lines of the *Elegy* trace the final days and hours of the very same poet whose graveyard meditations have thus far formed the substance of Gray's work. As the swain patiently informs the curious reader:

> 'There at the foot of yonder nodding beech
> 'That wreathes its old fantastic roots so high,
> 'His listless length at noontide would he stretch,
> 'And pore upon the brook that babbles by.
>
> 'Hard by yon wood, now smiling as in scorn,
> 'Muttering his wayward fancies he would rove,
> 'Now drooping, woeful wan, like one forlorn,
> 'Or crazed with care, or crossed in hopeless love.
>
> 'One morn I missed him on the customed hill,
> 'Along the heath and near his favourite tree;
> 'Another came; nor yet beside the rill,
> 'Nor up the lawn, nor at the wood was he;
>
> 'The next with dirges due in sad array
> 'Slow through the church-way path we saw him borne.
> 'Approach and read (for though can'st read) the lay,
> 'Graved on the stone beneath yon aged thorn.' (*PTG* 136–38)

The famous, three-stanza epitaph that follows and concludes Gray's *Elegy* recounts the blighted achievements of a poet 'unknown' either to fortune or to fame. Although, unlike the villagers among whose graves he has been wandering, educated in the traditions of 'Fair Science', this same poet was 'marked' by fortune temperamentally to be melancholic and withdrawn. Unable to give himself enthusiastically or wholeheart-

---

[20] Williams, 108.

edly to the affairs of the world, both his merits and his frailties were circumscribed by the governing circumstances of his life, much as they are now and forever circumscribed by and contained within the larger, inscrutable intentions of 'his Father and his God'.

Gray's displacement of the self in the concluding lines of the *Elegy* has prompted much debate over the years. Although seeming directly to confront the fears implicit throughout the poem (i.e. fears of an early death or of youthful promise unfulfilled), Gray has carefully and only after great consideration redirected such fears so that they seem originate not from within himself, but from within the youth of the epitaph – the 'youth to fortune and to fame unknown'. In the earlier, cancelled conclusion to the *Elegy*, Gray seemed to suggest that we should all resign ourselves to our fate. His 'original' four-stanza conclusion read:

> The thoughtless World to majesty may bow
> Exalt the brave, & idolize Success
> But more to Innocence their Safety owe
> Than Power & Genius e'er conspired to bless
>
> And thou, who mindful of the unhonour'd Dead
> Dost in these Notes thy artless Tale relate
> By Night & lonely Contemplation led
> To linger in the gloomy Walks of Fate
>
> Hark how the sacred Calm, that broods around
> Bids ev'ry fierce tumultous Passion cease
> In still small Accents whisp'ring from the Ground
> A grateful Earnest of eternal Peace
>
> No more with Reason & thyself at strife;
> Give anxious Cares & endless Wishes room
> But thro' the cool sequester'd Vale of Life
> Pursue the silent Tenour of thy Doom. (*PTG* 130–31)

Although differing in the tone and structure of its resignation, the final conclusion to Gray's poem stands, as Williams has observed, as the appropriate culmination of 'a pattern of reticence, indirection, or disguise that the speaker has manifested all along.' As Williams further noted, 'The vicarious, indirect mode of [the epitaph's solution] is completely in character with all we have seen of his tendency to avoid the spontaneous. A modern critic is unavoidably tempted to read the image of burial as a sign of repression; certainly speaking often of one's self in the third person may be a kind of linguistic defensiveness.'[21]

---

[21] Williams, 108.

Yet the final ending of Gray's *Elegy*, for all its participation in the repression that has characterized the poem as a whole, is oddly optimistic. Resignation has given way to what might perhaps best be described as a healthier form of relinquishment – of temporary and perhaps even permanent surrender to an ordering consciousness which exists *beyond* the poetic subject himself. The concluding lines of the epitaph suggest that while the poet may not yet perceive the patterns of his own destiny within the noisy activities of the living, he has at least come to recognize the truth of the 'trembling hope' in which he must finally place his faith. Gray returns us, in fact, quite pointedly to Locke and to the *Essay Concerning Human Understanding*. Having begun the poem with a demonstration of the workings of the senses – with an articulation of the sights, sounds, and sensations of the speaker in the church-yard at twilight – Gray concludes the poem with a narrative demonstration of the caution issued by the philosopher even as he outlined the possibilities and the limits of our capacity to understand 'the vast Extent of Things'. In this sense, the *Elegy* rather nicely picks up where the earlier *Eton Ode* leaves off. The latter poem ends with a recapitulation of the benefits of a limited human understanding; the *Elegy* takes the suggestion of blissful ignorance one step further – one step higher. 'If we can find out', as Locke himself had written in the opening pages of his *Essay*, 'how far the Understanding can extend its view; how far it has Faculties to attain Certainty; and in what Cases it can only judge and guess, we may learn to content ourselves with what is attainable by us in this State'.[22] The *Elegy* is aware that the destiny of man remains unfathomable. In the very teeth of this awareness, he has come to the church-yard still. What he has found there has perhaps best been expressed in our own century by Gray's direct poetic descendent, Philip Larkin, in his masterful 1955 poem, *Church Going*. Of a similar parish church and graveyard, Larkin's poem muses:

> A serious house on serious earth it is,
> In whose blent air all our compulsions meet,
> Are recognized, and robed as destinies.
> And that much never can be obsolete,
> Since someone will forever be surprising
> A hunger in himself to be more serious,
> And gravitating with it to this ground,
> Which, he once heard, was proper to grow wise in,
> If only that so many dead lie round.[23]

---

[22] Locke, 45.
[23] Philip Larkin, *Collected Poems*, ed. Anthony Thwaite (London: Faber and Faber, 1988) 98.

We must content ourselves, Larkin's lines seem to imply, not with absolute knowledge itself, but with the barest intimation of such knowledge – with the intimations and the hunches, even, of a hasty interloper on the greater scene of humanity. In the second book of his *Essay*, Locke himself had written:

> The infinite wise Contriver of us, and all things about us, hath fitted our Senses, Faculties, and Organs, to the conveniences of Life, and to the Business we have to do here. We are able, by our Senses, to know and distinguish things; and to examine them so far as to apply them to our Uses, and several ways to accommodate the Exigencies of this Life. We have insight enough into their admirable Contrivances and wonderful Effects, to admire and magnify the Wisdom, Power and Goodness of their Author. Such a Knowledge as this, which is suited to our present Condition, we want not Faculties to attain. But it appears not that God intended we should have a perfect, clear, and adequate Knowledge of them; that perhaps is not the Comprehension of any finite Being. We are furnished with Faculties (dull and weak as they are) to discover enough in the Creatures, to lead us to a Knowledge of the Creator, and the Knowledge of our Duty; and we are fitted well enough with Abilities to provide for the Conveniences of the living; These are our Business in this World.[24]

The *Elegy* is in many ways nothing less than a narrative demonstration of Locke's own insights regarding the decorum that separates the 'Business' of this world, from the greater, more comprehensive knowledge promised each of us in the next.

*

Apropos some of the observations noted earlier in this chapter, conventional schoolbook explanations of the *Elegy* often begin by pointing out that Gray's poem is technically (at least according to many traditional definitions) not really an 'elegy' at all. Refusing to limit his meditations on the transience as well as the stubborn (though not necessarily self-centred) egoism of human life to any one individual, such explanations observe, Gray's *Elegy* stakes its claim to wider territories of poetic form and substance – territories that consequently lift the poem beyond the conventions and generic limitations of a 'proper' (i.e. personal and occasional) elegy. Such an attitude can inform even the most sophisticated readings of the poem. Early in his provocative and chronologically wide-ranging survey *The English Elegy: Studies in the Genre from*

[24] Locke, 302.

Spenser to Yeats, for example, the modern critic Peter M. Sacks paused to observe:

> There is some question as to whether Gray's 'Elegy Written in a Country Churchyard' in fact belongs to the kind of elegy I have been defining, namely, a poem of mourning occasioned by a specific death. Gray had originally entitled the poem 'Stanzas Wrote in a Country Church Yard', and the later title was his friend William Mason's suggestion. Mason recognized the alternatingly rhymed iambic pentameter quatrains as the form used by such 'elegists' as Hammond and Shenstone, poets who were reviving the license of a merely formal definition to write so-called elegies on subjects of love or philosophical reflection.[25]

'And yet', Sacks hastened immediately to acknowledge, 'Gray's poem is, of course, a poem of mourning'. The question of generic distinction at least heightens the reader's awareness of the manner in which the *Elegy* transcends and occludes some of the more 'standard' or easily discernable boundaries of poetic form. Gray's lines 'of course', as Sacks concedes, constitute a poem of mourning and, consequently, substantively earn the right to be defined as elegiac.

The years immediately following the death of West and what might without exaggeration be described as the catastrophic personal losses suffered by Gray in the early and mid 1740s prompted the poet on several occasions to search for a way out of the chaos of meaning and emotion through the patient crafting and recrafting of certain traditionally valued poetic tropes, and through the reverentially (or at least respectfully) resonant language of cento, imitation, and parody. The lengthy gestation of the *Elegy* itself reflects the simple notion that time alone grafts meaning and coherence onto the tender shoots of memory. As a trained and ardent classicist, Gray was of course familiar with the dual literary and iconographic traditions in western culture that posit 'Time', on the one hand, as an insatiable devourer of human youth, human experience, and even human emotions, while recognizing on the other the potential for the same passage of Time to reveal truth and understanding. *Tempus edax rerum* – time devours all things; yet at the same time, *Veritas filia temporis* – truth is the daughter of time. In the wake of his omnivorous destruction, Χρόνος (or Time) bestows a glancing blessing on his race of victims. The *Elegy* is in some respects Gray's simple tribute to and articulation of the balm of temporal perspective afforded by the simple fact of man's embodied existence.

But, of course, it is far more than just that. Hagstrum, in the analyses quoted earlier, further compared the wound that had been inflicted

---

[25] Peter M. Sacks, *The English Elegy: Studies in the Genre from Spenser to Yeats* (Baltimore: Johns Hopkins University Press, 1985) 133.

on Gray's creative psyche by the shock of West's death to that suffered by the legendary Greek hero, Philoctetes. Incapacitated by a snake bite while *en route* to Troy, Philoctetes, who possessed the bows and arrows of Hercules that could alone kill Paris and so bring about the end of the Trojan war, was brought back to Asia Minor by Odysseus and Diomedes. 'Unlike the wound of Philoctetes', Hagstrum writes,

> Gray's was a guilty one – or so he regarded it – and it did not permit him often to draw his bow. But when he did, the strength of his arm and the accuracy of his aim are owing to his suffering. He arouses an echo in every bosom because in his best serious poetry he knew himself a man. At the heart of his humanity was his sensibility; at the heart of his sensibility was his melancholy; at the heart of his melancholy – to continue opening this Chinese next of boxes – lay his friendships, enlivening at first but finally inhibited; and at the heart of each love frustrating its fulfillment was. . . . But who can go deeper?[26]

Recent academic scholarship on Gray has in fact taken up the implicit challenge of Hagstrum's final query with a vengeance. George Haggerty has argued that Gray's 'fears about his own dark and troubled sexuality are everywhere apparent in his poetry'. Robert Gleckner, too, though focusing his critical attention more intensely on Gray's Pindaric Odes, has contended that one of the personal histories which motivates and is dramatized within Gray's writing is his 'heroic struggle to come to terms with his own sexuality, with his love for West . . . [and] with his all-absorbing grief at West's early death'.[27]

The truth and the focus of the arguments presented by critics such as Haggerty and Gleckner, it should by now be clear, are incontestable. The fundamental paradox of the *Elegy*'s continued and virtually uninterrupted popularity, however, is – by virtue of the elaborate textual substrata which, such reading argue, underlie the poem – transformed into an even greater enigma than ever before. For if, as critics such as Haggerty have so persuasively argued, Gray's fears regarding his sexuality are 'everywhere apparent' in his work, why then have those 'fears' remained largely undetected, or at least undiscussed, until now? If the 'meaning' of the *Elegy* is rooted so deeply in the specific social, cultural, and linguistic circumstances that shaped and governed homoerotic or homosocial behaviour in the early and middle years of the eighteenth century – if we are only *now*, in other words, permitted openly to discuss and to analyze the elaborately coded language that shrouds and encrypts the poem's deepest biographical contexts and resonances – why then has

---

[26] Hagstrum in Downey and Jones, 17.
[27] Gleckner, 7; the observations of George Haggerty are quoted from an unpublished essay in Gleckner, 13.

the poem been granted its near unprecedented status in the canons of literature for well over two hundred years? Does a clear and unapologetic elucidation of the *Elegy*'s homoerotic subtext not suggest that we have for years been 'misreading' the poem, or catching only very partial and fragmentary reflections of a lustre deliberately dimmed and darkened by the hand of its creator? The *Elegy* – should the trend of contemporary criticism that seeks to gloss its legitimate meanings with reference to the deliberately obfuscated text of Gray's own life continue – may, despite the arguably conservative nature of its religious, doctrinal, and spiritual meanings, ultimately achieve the un-looked for status of being one of the most 'radical' and transformative poems in the English tradition.

III. The Peeress Comes

Having dispatched a completed draft of the *Elegy* to Walpole early in June, Gray, now comfortably settled at Stoke for the remainder of the summer, was well aware of the fact that manuscript copies of the poem would very soon be passing among (and, in time, beyond) Walpole's select circle of friends and acquaintances. Gray would also have known that some of those same individuals would be transcribing his lines into their own commonplace books – books that often took the form of neat, quarto-sized, keepsake volumes or scrapbooks in which bound sheets of hot-pressed paper could be fixed within sturdy cardboard covers. Mason, in his *Memoirs*, graciously observed that Walpole's own good taste was 'too much charmed' with the piece to 'withhold the sight of it from his acquaintances'. Gray, for his own part, eventually professed himself dismayed by the attention the poem had been receiving that summer. Although he wrote a lengthy letter to Wharton on 9 August (in which he noted, in passing, the recent death of Conyers Middleton with the observation: 'for my Part I find a Friend so uncommon a Thing, that I can not help regretting even an old Acquaintance'), he made no mention of the *Elegy*, nor did he refer to the poem's increasingly wide circulation among fashionable London society. Only at the end of the year, in fact, on 18 December, would Gray even send Wharton himself a copy of the poem from Cambridge, prefacing the stanzas with the first of several decorous if not entirely convincing rhetorical attempts to distance himself both from the *Elegy*'s value as a piece of poetry, and from its ever-increasing fame. 'The Stanza's, which I now enclose to you', he wrote,

> have had the Misfortune by Mr W:s Fault to be made . . . publick, for which they certainly were never meant, but it is too late to complain.

they have been so applauded, it is quite a Shame to repeat it. I mean not
to be modest; but I mean, it is a shame for those who have said such
superlative Things about them, that I can't repeat them. I should have
been glad, that you & two or three more People had liked them, which
would have satisfied my ambition on this head amply. (*CTG* 335)

Whatever grain of truth of there might have been in Gray's protestations
to Wharton, it was pretty clear from the start that Walpole, at least, had
far grander ambitions for his friend's work. Comfortably ushering Gray's
poem into the finest and most fashionable London parlours, Walpole
essentially saw to it that everyone who was anyone was reading and
talking about the *Elegy*.

One of those who chanced to encounter the *Elegy* in manuscript form
in the summer of 1750 was the Dowager Viscountess Cobham. Lady
Cobham was the widow of Sir Richard Temple, first Viscount Cobham,
and the daughter of Stoke Poges native Edmund Halsey. Her father had
purchased the Manor House at Stoke from the previous owners, the
Gayer family, some time shortly after Gray's own birth, in about 1720.
Following her husband's death in 1749, Lady Cobham left her former
home at Stowe and took up residence at the Manor House. In
the summer of 1750, she lived there with her 22-year-old niece (by
marriage), Miss Henrietta Jane Speed. Miss Speed, the daughter of
lieutenant–colonel Samuel Speed in Gore's Regiment of Dragoons
and a lineal descendent of the well-known geographer John Speed
(1552–1629) had been born at Holyrood. Since the death of her brother
in 1747, she had been residing with her aunt, who had taken upon
herself the responsibilities of raising and educating the young woman
and introducing her into society. Destined clearly to stand as sole heir
to Lady Cobham's impressive estate, Miss Speed added to the beguiling
charms of property and liquidity a personality by all accounts notable
for its cheerfulness, native intelligence, and simple, unaffected charm.
Unfortunately, surviving portraits of Miss Speed – most notably the well-
known painting executed by Peter Falconet many years after her marriage to Joseph Marie de Viry, Baron de la Perrière, afterwards created
Comte de Viry, Sardinian Minister at the Hague, London, and Paris –
offer us no very clear glimpse of the young and vivacious woman first
encountered by Gray in 1750. In a sketch of Miss Speed's character
written after her own death by the second Earl Harcourt, she is described
as having possessed

the most brilliant parts, she was good humoured, full of vivacity, and had
an inexhaustible fund of original and engaging wit; strong sense, united
with observation, and penetration the most acute more than supplied the
want of literary knowledge, for which she had not the least relish; and,
without having ever given herself the trouble of learning anything, she

appeared to know everything. . . . Her person was tall but not slender, her complexion dark, and, although she had no pretensions to beauty, yet an easy and graceful air, with fine eyes and teeth, united to render her altogether extremely pleasing.[28]

The later-life Comtess de Viry was corpulent if yet good-humoured. Despite the Earl's casual reference to her 'want of literary knowledge' in the account quoted above, Miss Speed appears to have retained a genuine affection both for Gray as an individual and for his works, even in the years following his death.

The Manor House in which Lady Cobham and her niece were living in 1750 was a handsome property, situated immediately adjacent to the Church of St. Giles and the churchyard at Stoke. The original structure had been substantially rebuilt by Henry Hastings, Earl of Huntingdon, in the mid-sixteenth century. The property was heavily mortgaged towards the end of the Earl's lifetime (about 1580), during which period it was reported by tradition to have been occupied by the Lord Chancellor, Sir Christopher Hatton. Queen Elizabeth herself was entertained at the property shortly before her death, in 1601, by which date the Manor House was leased under the crown to the Lord Chief Justice, Sir Edward Coke. Gray, as we shall see, was very much aware of the property's participation in the pageant of the Tudor court. He was likewise aware of the rich potential presented by the estate to any poet willing to exploit or at least cleverly to parse into a greater meaning the mythological possibilities inherent in its history.

Also spending the summer with Lady Cobham in 1750 was a woman rather closer to her own age, Lady Schaub, a woman whose history was summarily represented by Walpole as 'a French widow of Nismes [sic], and a Protestant, and remarried to Sir Luke Schaub'. The latter was a native of Switzerland who had early in his ambassadorial career served as secretary to the late Lord Cobham, hence the subsequent connection between their spouses. Lady Schaub, who would in time maintain a set of apartments comparatively nearby at Hampton Court Palace, enjoyed a reputation for being, as Walpole phrased it, 'very gallant'. She was socially active and not easily intimidated. Taken together, the three women at the Manor House formed a formidable if not absolutely daunting company. Their easy and elegant combination of beauty, wit, and feminine 'gallantry' in some respects confronted Gray with precisely the kinds of social and fashionably intellectual challenges for which his increasingly comfortable life at a Cambridge college had done nothing whatsoever to prepare him.

---

[28] *The Harcourt Papers*, ed. Edward William Harcourt (privately printed) viii. 1–3; reprinted in *CTG* 332 n.1.

The circumstances of Gray's first contact with Lady Cobham, Miss Speed, and Lady Schaub has, thanks almost entirely to the poet's own self-parodic and in this particular instance self-mythologizing impulses, actually been presented as something of a representative encounter between the would-be 'private' poet and his insistent, even invasive audience in the mid-eighteenth century. If one can picture Gray in the place of the weary and exhausted Alexander Pope of the 'Epistle to Arbuthnot', and likewise envision the women of the Manor House as the hoard of self-serving admirers in whose face Pope's servant John emphatically shuts the door, one forms a pretty sound idea of the manner in which their initial, missed encounter is often interpreted. The facts of the incident and of the subsequent intimacy between the two parties would seem, however, to suggest otherwise.

Lady Cobham was by all accounts delighted to learn, from the Reverend Robert Purt, that the author of the *Elegy* then being shown and read in every fashionable London drawing room was even then residing with his mother and his aunt at their residence in Stoke Poges. It was likewise, no doubt, something of a social coup to learn that the tolling curfew of the *Elegy*'s first stanza was none other than the very same church bell which sounded each evening in such close proximity to her own home. Lady Cobham accordingly dispatched Lady Schaub and Miss Speed to make their way across the fields and down the narrow country lanes one late summer afternoon, with instructions formally to introduce themselves to the man who was responsible for such compelling poetry. The social exertions of her subalterns were not immediately to be rewarded, however; Gray was not at home when the two ladies arrived at his aunt's house. Lady Schaub – who may already have met Gray in the company of Walpole, who had in turn first encountered Lady Schaub herself almost nine years earlier at a London ball – hastily scribbled a note on some of Gray's own papers; the papers lay within easy view on a table in the ground-floor parlour in which the poet often read and studied. Such evidence of the ladies' call obliged Gray to return the visit, which he appears to have done almost immediately. Gray found himself to be very much at ease in the company of these elegant society ladies, the three of whom were in time more than ready to reiterate their admiration for his poetry, and to find even his casual conversation – so memorably derided by Walpole and others as tedious and aridly pedantic – as little less than captivating. The easy rapport that arose between Gray and Lady Cobham (and her guests) in many ways comes as no real surprise. Gray's experience and conversation with his own mother and his two aunts over the years had ensured that he develop some considerable ability in maintaining his own in the polite conversation of fashionable (and, by the standards of the day, well-educated) female society. The early weeks of October found the poet on several occasions invited to dinner at the Manor House. Some time very soon after first calling on Lady Cobham, he commemorated the circumstances of their eventual meeting and subsequent intimacy in a short and hastily written comic ballad, which he entitled *A Long Story*.

*

A Long Story begins with a description of the Manor House at Stoke Poges:

> In Britain's isle, no matter where,
> An ancient pile of building stands:
> The Huntingdons and Hattons there
> Employ'd the power of fairy hands
>
> To raise the ceiling's fretted height,
> Each panel in achievements cloathing,
> Rich windows that exclude the light,
> And passages that lead to nothing. (*PTG* 144–45)

The playful and carelessly paradoxical combination of geographical imprecision ('In Britain's isle, no matter where . . .') and exact, historical reference ('Huntingdons and Hattons') in these opening stanzas immediately sets the tone for the light-hearted and inconsequential narrative which follows. The poem's metre, likewise, instantly alerts the reader to its status as a piece of humorous verse. *A Long Story* is written for the most part in rhyming, iambic tetrameter; on some few occasions Gray uses a nine-syllable line to further the comic effect (he similarly and deliberately pushes his double or feminine rhymes in the poem close to their Byronic breaking points, throwing off pairs such as 'imbroglio'/'folio', 'old tree'/'poultry', etc.). The normative force of verse forms and rhyme-schemes in English poetry is surprisingly strong, and even today it would be enormously difficult if not close to impossible to write anything *other* than comic verse in the metre Gray chose to work in here.

Following a further, brief recapitulation of the history of the Manor House, Gray describes its three, current occupants as 'a brace of warriors' outfitted not in the 'buff' leather jackets that might more properly have signaled their status as dangerous and conquering enchantresses and 'Amazons', but dressed rather from head to foot in bonnets, aprons, and a rustling of 'silks and tissues'. Having learned that a 'wicked imp' of a poet is living nearby, the three fairy queens decide to search the neighbourhood and find him out:

The heroines undertook the task;
Through lanes unknown, o'er styles they ventured
Rapped at the door, nor stayed to ask.
But bounce into the parlour entered

The trembling family they daunt,
They flirt, they sing, they laugh, they tattle,
Rummage his mother, pinch his aunt,
And upstairs in a whirlwind rattle.

Each hole and cupboard they explore,
Each creek and cranny of his chamber,
Run hurry-scurry round the floor,
And o'er the bed and tester clamber. (*PTG* 147–48)

The Muses, however, have secreted their poet in the garden. The spell left by the visitors upon the parlour table nevertheless compels him soon to pay his respects at 'the great house', where he is introduced to the countess and her friends. The poet is so impressed that his imaginative and expressive powers fail him, and he is left speechless:

... [S]oon his rhetoric forsook him,
When he the solemn hall had seen;
A sudden fit of ague shook him,
He stood as mute as poor Macleane.

Yet something he was heard to mutter,
'How in the park beneath an old tree,
'(Without design to hurt the butter,
'Or any malice to the poultry),

'He once or twice had penned a sonnet;
'Yet hoped, that he might save his bacon:
'Numbers would take their oaths upon it,
'He ne'er was for a conjurer taken.' (*PTG* 150–51)

The spirits or 'ghostly Prudes' that haunt the property are outraged by the cordial hospitality extended to this 'sinner' of a poet. Before betraying anything of substance concerning his actual contact with Lady Cobham and her guests, Gray breaks the poem off with the casually scrupulous, parenthetical notation that the five hundred stanzas that would have constituted the body of its narrative have inadvertently been 'lost'.

Typically and constantly allusive, *A Long Story* draws much of its poetic strength from its mock-heroic reference to what Mason later described as the works of 'the old romance writers'; the poem seeks to advance an elaborate compliment to Gray's newly discovered, near neighbors at Stoke with reference to the imaginative topography of a peculiarly native, British 'fairyland'. Indeed, the very notion that one might at any moment be subject to an unsolicited 'visitation' by the powers or forces that regularly operate, unperceived and unregarded, beyond the bounds of the natural and rational universe of mankind is in itself fairy-tale-like. The genially 'supernatural' world of *A Long Story* shares the borders of its own fantasy land on the one side with a fantastic kingdom of old English myths and legends – the land of 'all the Nurse and all the Priest have taught', and inhabited by the likes of Robin Goodfellow, Oberon, and the denizens of Spenser's own land of faerie – just as surely as it stakes its imaginative, territorial claims on the other as far as the Rosicrucian world of elemental spirits that motivates Pope's *The Rape of the Lock*.

The vaguely pseudo-Spenserian conceit of the poem (and one remembers with reference to *A Long Story* Norton Nicholls's otherwise implausible comment that Gray 'never sat down to compose poetry without reading Spenser for a considerable time previously') suggests, again, that Gray is himself a 'wicked imp' of a poet whose powers are incapable of withstanding the charms of a greater and more powerful enchantress such as Lady Cobham. Throughout the poem the local landscape of Buckinghamshire is mythologized, and both its inhabitants and their activities appropriately 'enchanted'. The hastily scribbled note actually left for Gray by Lady Schaub, for example, is in the poem transformed into a magical spell 'left ... upon the table'. When faced with the peeress herself, Gray's powers of speech fail him (in a reference unusual in the poem to contemporary British society, he compares such speechlessness to the notorious silence of the highwayman James Maclean, when called upon to apologize to his victims for his crimes).

Like Horace Walpole's own, later collection of *Hieroglyphic Tales*, *A Long Story* is for the most part a determinedly erratic and pointedly occasional *jeu d'esprit* – 'a wild and fantastic farrago', Mason would call it – written in a casual and playful manner. In suggesting that the verse stanzas which would have constituted the body of the poem have inadvertently been 'lost' to modern audiences (a stretch of narrative that would of course have dwarfed the 'surviving' thirty-six stanzas) Gray resorts to what was to some degree a perfectly acceptable trope in mid and late eighteenth-century literature; both poets and novelists throughout the period – Richardson, Mackenzie, Sterne, Macpherson, Chatterton, to name only a few – had recourse at one point or another in their writing to the conceit of the found, unfinished, or fragmentary text. Yet it is still worth noting that the stanzas immediately preceding the abyss of annihilation at the inconclusive 'conclusion' of *A Long Story* (the poem, even in its title, delights in the structural paradoxes of its form) create a curious counterpart to the end of the recently completed *Elegy* itself. There are, on closer observation, several peculiar points of comparison between the two works. The 'daemon' poet of *A Long Story*, for example, offers in the stanzas quoted above an *apologia* for his poetic practice remarkably similar to the account related to readers of the *Elegy* by the 'hoary-headed swain'. Both poets have been seen from time to time in the rural countryside near Stoke – near a 'favourite tree' in the *Elegy* and 'in the park beneath an old tree' in *A Long Story*; in both poems the poet–persona attempts to offer some justification for himself by protesting the essentially harmless and inoffensive nature of his activities. The poet in the *Elegy* is silenced finally and conclusively by his interment in the grave; the carved epitaph of his tomb alone documenting – yet at the same time, of course, obscuring and deflecting attention away from – the mortal legacy of his lived life. The comic abysm or aporia of *A Long Story* self-parodically mimics, in its tremendous oblivion of sustained narrative and meaning, the blank and voiceless silence of death itself. Having only recently wound its way towards a satisfactory conclusion to the more heartfelt and serious work, in other words, Gray's imaginative energy would seem to have dictated that the *Elegy*'s own resolution in oblivion manages to make itself felt and to exert its shaping, teleological power even in such a deliberately comic and lighthearted work as this.

Both Lady Cobham and – particularly, it would appear – Henrietta Speed were suitably flattered to find themselves the latest subjects of Gray's poetry. Completed (as the poem's reference to the trial and sentencing of the highwayman Mackenzie makes clear) sometime in the first or second week of October, *A Long Story* was itself soon being circulated in manuscript among a wide circle of readers. Thanking him for the verses, Miss Speed wrote to Gray soon after receiving them:

Sir,
I am as much at a loss to bestow the Commendation due to your performance as any of our modern Poets would be to imitate them; Every body that has seen it, is charm'd and Lady Cobham was the first, tho' not the last that regretted the loss of the 400 stanzas; all I can say is, that your obliging inclination in sending it has fully answer'd; as it not only gave us amusement the rest of the Evening, but always will, on reading it over. Lady Cobham and the rest of the Company hope to have yours' tomorrow at dinner.

I am your oblig'd & obedient
Henrietta Jane Speed. (*CTG* 331–34)

Readers outside of Lady Cobham's own circle, however, stumbled over the poem's detailed references to the particular history of the Manor House, and were for the most part thoroughly mystified by the myriad of private jokes and references in the work. The fact that such a casual and deliberately light-hearted – and yet at the same time highly esoteric – effort had been allowed to occupy a place as the immediate 'sequel', as it were, to the perceived solemnity and transcendence of the *Elegy* (already being praised precisely for its supposed universality and accessibility) could hardly have helped matters any. Then again, the ease and facility with which Gray could turn his hand to light and satiric verse was rarely, if ever, to be recognized by the larger reading public in his own lifetime.

By 18 December *A Long Story* had travelled on the *Elegy*'s substantial and generous coat tails at least as far as Durham. Gray wrote to Wharton, who had obviously read the poem, from Cambridge at the end of the year:

> [T]he Verses you so kindly try to keep in countenance were wrote to divert a particular Family, & succeeded accordingly. but, being shew'd about in Town, are not liked there at all. Mrs French, a very fashionable Personage, told Mr W: that she had seen a Thing by a Friend of his, wch she did not know what to make of, for it aim'd at every Thing, & meant nothing. (*CTG* 335)

It was in this same letter that Gray himself enclosed the draft of the *Elegy* to Wharton, noting in conclusion: 'I have been this Month in town . . . diverting myself among my gay Acquaintance; & return to my Cell with so much the more Pleasure'. The extent of Gray's 'gay Acquaintance' had now been extended to include not only Walpole and his increasingly wide circle of friends, but of course Lady Cobham, Henrietta Speed, and many of *their* friends as well. Although Gray clearly enjoyed spending time in the company of these women and was flattered by the many compliments to which their patronage exposed him, the suggestion that his attentions to Miss Speed herself were anything more than strictly social and convivial has absolutely no basis whatsoever in fact. The possibility of a romantic attachment between the two may well have been invented by a later generation of critics in order to flesh out the notion that Gray was a poet habitually, as the *Elegy* would have it 'crossed in hopeless love'. Gray had, as we have seen, indeed been 'crossed in hopeless love', not only by Walpole, but – in his affection for West – by Death itself. His feelings for Henrietta Jane Speed could hardly have been placed in the same category as those two earlier and passionately romantic friendships. 'A fine Lady', Gray winked to a knowing Wharton in his letter of 18 December, was 'the

last Thing in the World' capable of throwing his 'house' – or indeed his
heart – 'into Tumults'.

IV. Inflicted Honour

Gray's remark to Wharton in his letter of 18 October that he looked
forward to a return to his quiet 'Cell' in Cambridge 'with so much the
more Pleasure' for having remained for such a long time in Stoke and
London was apparently genuine. Resuming his residence at Peterhouse
after an absence of some six months, Gray settled down to an extended
stay in Cambridge, a stay that was to continue – with only the briefest
of visits to Stoke in the late winter – well into the new year.

These months were not, however, to be a very restful time for Gray.
If 1742 can to some extent be regarded as the early *annus mirabilis* of
his activity as a poet, 1751 was to be no less miraculous for the transformations it would effect in Gray's life and reputation both within and
beyond the small collegiate community he now regarded as home. Gray's
self-described 'few autumnal verses' were about to change the course of
English poetry. His own ambitions – and we have no real reason to doubt
him when he protests that they were circumscribed by the recognition
of his growing yet still necessarily narrow bounds of his own friends and
social acquaintance – were about to be gratified well beyond the point
of satiety; the youth of the *Elegy* who had until now passed a life of
semi-rural retirement 'to fortune and to fame unknown', was very soon
to find his professedly modest desires crowned by an overwhelming and
close to unprecedented frenzy of renown. At the age of thirty-four,
Thomas Gray was about to succeed to the unofficial laureateship left
vacant by Alexander Pope seven years earlier, and reluctantly to assume
the mantle of fame and notoriety worn properly and exclusively by 'the
most famous living poet' in England.

Toward the beginning of February, Gray indirectly received word
from London that a copy of the *Elegy* had fallen into the hands of the
publishers of a comparatively new and – to the poet's own mind – disreputable periodical, the ostentatiously redundant *Magazine of Magazines*. The *Elegy*, the publishers informed Gray, was about to be included
in the February number of their second volume. Copyright laws in the
modern sense, of course, would not even begin to develop in England
until the landmark decisions handed down in the cases of Millar vs.
Taylor (1769) and Donaldson vs. Beckett (1774) – both of which cases,
though tried in different courts, concerned James Thomson's *The
Seasons*. The Statute of Anne of April 10, 1710, by simply acknowledging the individual author as the source of literary protection and pos-
tulating the adoption of a limited time of legal protection on public

works, had, nevertheless, at least begun to effect some shift in the conceptual and theoretical notion of copyright itself. The relative point is
that under existing laws Gray had no way of preventing the *Magazine
of Magazines* from publishing his poem nor, even, could he block its
publishers from attributing the work to him or – for that matter – to
anyone else.

Gray's best and, quite frankly, his only recourse was to turn for assistance to Walpole himself. Accordingly, just days before the *Elegy* was
set to appear in print without Gray's consent or cooperation, he wrote
to Walpole from Cambridge, explaining the situation and asking his
friend to pull whatever strings he could to rectify things. 'As you have
brought me into a little Sort of Distress', he began,

> you must assist me, I believe, to get out of it, as well as I can. yesterday
> I had the Misfortune of receiving a Letter from certain Gentlemen (as
> their Bookseller expresses it) who have taken the *Magazine of Magazines*
> into their Hands. they tell me, that an *ingenious* Poem, call'd, *Reflec-
> tions* in a Country-Churchyard, has been communicated to them, which
> they are printing forthwith: that they are inform'd, that the *excellent*
> Author of it is I by name, & that they beg not only his *Indulgence*, but
> the *Honor of his Correspondence*, &c: as I am not at all disposed to
> be either so indulgent, or so correspondent, as they desire; I have but
> one bad Way left to escape the Honour they would inflict upon me. &
> therefore am obliged to desire you would make Dodsley print it
> immediately (which may be done in less than a Week's time) from your
> Copy, but without my Name, in what Form is most convenient for
> him, but in his best Paper & Character. He must correct the Press himself,
> & print it without any Interval between the Stanza's, because
> the Sense is in some Places continued beyond them; & the Title must
> be, Elegy, wrote in a Country Church-yard. If he would add a Line or
> two to say it came into his Hands by Accident, I should like it better.
> (*CTG* 341–42)

'If you behold the Mag: of Mag: in the Light that I do', Gray concluded,
'you will not refuse to give yourself this Trouble on my Account, which
you have taken of your own Accord before now'. One final post-script
warned Walpole to act on this request as soon as possible. 'If Dodsley
don't do this immediately', Gray wrote with chastening brevity, 'he may
as well let it alone'.

As matters turned out, Dodsley was in fact able to do all that Gray
requested with a promptitude that went far to rectify the possibility of
any ill feelings. On 15 February, just one day before the *Magazine of
Magazines* published a version of the *Elegy* predictably replete with
copying errors and typographical changes inimical to Gray's personal
vision, the *Elegy* was officially published in a quarto pamphlet priced at

six-pence. Prefaced to the poem were the following lines, signed 'The Editor' and written by Walpole himself:

> The following POEM came into my hands by Accident, if the general Approbation with which this little Piece has been spread, may be call'd by so slight a Term as Accident. It is the Approbation which makes it unnecessary for me to make any Apology but to the Author: As he cannot but feel some Satisfaction in having pleas'd so many Readers already, I flatter myself he will forgive my communicating that Pleasure to many more.[29]

The original printing of the *Elegy*, though yet containing a number of *errata* the presence and legacy of which were understandably to annoy the poet, is – particularly given the haste with which it was necessarily delivered from the press – a surprisingly elegant quarto pamphlet. The text of the poem is clearly presented in well-spaced lines; the wide margins of its presentation and the comfortable amount of space both on the top and at the bottom of each page offer the reader a pleasant sense of a swift, fluid, and yet still gracefully paced movement through Gray's lines (modern readers who have first encountered the *Elegy* within the cramped pages and strait-jacketed columns of a classroom anthology or burdened by the weight of many footnotes in a heavily annotated edition, will be struck not only by the typological decorum of the original printing, but by its luxurious sense of *spaciousness*). Gray's words are further adorned in the quarto by a number of traditional (by the mid-eighteenth century) *memento mori* emblems such as woodcuts of death's heads and cross bones. Although strikingly primitive – particularly when compared with the later illustrations to the poem provided by Bentley and Blake – these modest illustrations are suitably if rather surprisingly effective; their blunt outlines form an appropriately spare and unapologetically unsophisticated graphic counterpart to the *Elegy*'s advancement of the inherent value of 'the short and simple annals of the poor'. Gray's expressed desire that his own name not appear anywhere on the pamphlet itself was hono ured by Dodsley. The poet was to have no such luck influencing William Owen, the publisher of the *Magazine of Magazines*, who was within days promoting the sale of his own periodical by advertising its contents in the *General Advertiser*, and calling particular attention to the inclusion in its forthcoming number to a work written by 'the very ingenious Mr Gray of Peterhouse'.

Gray was pleased with the result of Walpole's timely intervention. His pride, which could have been injured by the multitude of errors Owen's unsupervised printing might conceivably have attributed to him, was

---

[29] Reprinted in Lonsdale, *PTG*, III.

placated. On 20 February he once again picked up his pen to write to his old friend in London, this time rather more firmly in a spirit of reconciliation and even thanks:

> You have indeed conducted with great decency my little *misfortune*: you have taken a paternal care of it, and expressed much more kindness than could have been expected from so near a relation. But we are all frail; and I hope to do as much for you another time. Nurse Dodsley has given it a pinch or two in the cradle, that (I doubt) it will bear the marks of as a long it lives. But no matter: we have ourselves suffered under her hands before now; and besides, it will only look the more careless, and by *accident* as it were. I thank you for advertisement, which saves my honour, and in a manner *bien flatteuse pour moi*, who should be put to it even to make myself a compliment in good English. (*CTG* 342–43)

The references in this letter to Dodsley as the 'Nurse' or midwife who has effectively facilitated the birth and early sustenance of Gray's 'misfortune', and the poet's reference to Walpole as the proper individual to bestow a 'paternal care' on the work – when taken together with his earlier letter's reference to the poem's public conception and appearance (at least in the *Magazine of Magazines*) as an 'Accident' and 'Sort of Distress' – work metaphorically to situate the *Elegy* as an illegitimate child, the bastard product of a romantic and inescapably erotic union between Gray and Walpole himself. The language of birth and nascence is used commonly enough to describe a writer's relationship to and emotional bond with his or her own work, yet few authors refer so easily and with such seeming levity to literary conception as an illicit or miscalculated encounter with a strumpet-muse – an 'accident' or 'misfortune' that needs to be 'taken care of'. Gray looks to shrug off the *Elegy* as a near-abortive birth saved only by the discrete ministrations of 'so near a relation' as Walpole himself. His language betrays an extreme and complex state of confusion and anxiety regarding the *Elegy* in print – the poem is a shameful child, the secretive and huddled birth of which has come very close to destroying its author's sense of 'honour' and decency.

Yet, for all the anxiety and trepidation that clearly attached itself to so spectacularly public a debut for the *Elegy*, Gray appears at least very quickly to have resigned himself to the simple *fact* of the pamphlet's appearance and even, indeed, to the poem's slightly more mangled presentation in the *Magazine of Magazines*. Would he have preferred that the *Elegy* never have been published at all? The relatively quiet and uncomplicated inclusion of his earlier, shorter works in volumes such as Dodsley's *Collection* would seem, a first glance, to argue against a profound and prohibitory antagonism on Gray's part to the public expo-

sure and consumption of works equally personal, at least, in their conception and execution. Perhaps Gray felt that the indirection and near-
Baroque allusiveness of the poetic voice in the *Elegy* was – if not
absolutely impenetrable – at least so finely honed and polished as to
secure him from the deeper proximity of personal reference in the work.
Accepting the publication of the *Elegy* as a *fait accompli*, Gray was able
to do the most he could to secure its initial and continued accuracy in
print. The most prolific and public of poets in the late seventeenth and
early eighteenth centuries – both Dryden and Pope of course among
them – were alive to the easy comparisons to be made between the indiscrete and coarsely motivated display of the prostitute, on the one hand,
and the equally indiscrete surrender of authority and control experienced
by the published author, on the other. To commit one's writing to the
press, as John Wilmot, the Earl of Rochester, put it in a poem written
shortly after the Restoration of Charles II (but one nevertheless still relevant to Gray's own predicament), was effectively to make one's self 'the
Fiddle of the town' – a 'fiddle' to be fingered, plucked, and played upon
by any self-appointed critic, imitator, parodist, or plagiary who happened to pick it up.[30] Rochester's near contemporary, Edmund Waller,
similarly rejuvenated familiar tropes regarding the possible 'career' of
the poetic document once it has passed from the hands of its creator (his
'On Saint James' Park', for example, opens with the question, '. . . who
knows the fate / Of lines that shall this paradise relate?').[31] Such matter-
of-fact admissions of the uncertainty regarding the fate (and, for that
matter, the value) of one's poetry became increasingly prominent
throughout the period.

*

Gray had moved on in his letter to Walpole of 20 February, 1751, to
note that he would soon be sending to London 'the beginnings of a
drama, not mine, thank God, as you'll believe, when you hear it is finished, but wrote by a person whom I have a very good opinion of'. The
drama in question was Mason's *Elfrida*, and appears to have been the
means by which Gray effected an introduction between his oldest childhood friend and the fellow poet who was eventually to serve as his own
literary executor. Mason and Walpole – if only to suit Gray's own sense
of the personal symmetry and idiosyncratic pattern he felt (or needed to
feel) was a part of his own life – needed to get to know one another.

[30] *The Poems of Thomas Wilmot, Earl of Rochester*, ed. Keith Walker (Oxford: Basil
Blackwell, 1984) 83.
[31] 'On Saint James' Park' in *The Poems of Edmund Waller*, ed. G. Thorn Drury, 2 Vols.
(London: George Routledge and Sons, 1893) ii.40.

Already by the beginning of March the growing tremors and rumblings of the *Elegy*'s popular success had begun to be felt even in Cambridge. In the first week of that month, Gray once again wrote to Walpole, noting some few of the errata that had, not surprisingly, crept into the unsupervised and unauthorized printing of the poem. Gray actually began keeping a record of the several proper appearances of the poem with some detail and precision. On the Pembroke manuscript of the *Elegy*, for instance, he noted that the work 'went thro' four Editions; in two months; and afterwards a fifth, 6th, 7th, and 8th, 9th, and 10th, and 11th'. 'I do not expect any more editions', he had written mistakenly to Walpole that March, 'as I have appeared in more magazines than one'. Although this last joke about having been published 'in more magazine than one' is probably a punning glance at the very title of the 'Mag: of Mag:', Gray would not, in truth, have very long to wait before other piratical printings of the poem began to appear. A version of the *Elegy* was almost immediately included in a number of the *London Magazine* for that same March, 1751 (the periodical was actually published in the first week of April).

Walpole was of course from the start delighted with Gray's popular success – a popular success which, by no means incidentally, redounded ultimately to the credit of his own perceptive taste and cultivation. He naturally found the position of patron a congenial one, and to be the patron of such a poet – of particularly such a poem as Gray's *Elegy* was now looking to become – could only compound the praise of his own discernment and fine taste. Some recent developments within Gray's own family actually stood Walpole in consolatory need of the *Elegy*'s reflected glory. The death of his eldest brother (Robert Walpole, second Earl of Orford) on 20 March had been followed by the unsettling revelation that he had willed almost all his property ('prodigious spoils', a disgruntled Horace called the estate) to individuals outside of his own family. The Earl's firstborn son, Horace's nephew George Walpole (now third Earl Orford) was hit hardest by the blow; Horace himself, however, was thrown by the terms of his brother's will. Of even greater concern to him than his own personal welfare was the potential damage such a legacy now inflicted on the maintenance of his father's hard-won reputation. 'It is no small addition to my concern' he wrote Horace Mann just one week after learning the news, 'to fear or foresee that Houghton and all that remains of my father's glory will be pulled to pieces'.[32] Almost alone among the Walpoles, it seems, Horace had at least appreciated what the accumulation and ostentatious magnitude of Houghton had really meant to his father – the kind of success it symbolized to a man born into the world as the son of a family of great antiquity, but

[32]   WC xx.239.

still essentially Norfolk farmers – particularly in the years just preceding and subsequent to his final fall from political power. To be forced to stand idly by and without any recourse as his father's treasures were scattered across (and eventually out of) the country, and ineffectually to watch the fabric of Houghton Hall itself succumb so soon to the ravages of time and fortune, was a grim development not only for Horace himself but – could they only be made to understand the depth of such a domestic and dynastic tragedy – the entire, extended Walpole family as well.

Gray understood his old friend's state of mind. Closing a letter to Walpole written on 16 April, he commented with genuine sympathy on this recent 'Alteration' in the Walpole family, observing at the same time, 'You were very good, when you found Time to let me know, what I am interested in, not barely from Curiosity, but because it touches you so nearly'. Perhaps because of Walpole's manifest uneasiness concerning the consequent disruption in his own family, Gray allowed him to proceed with a project he might well not otherwise have countenanced, let alone in any way encouraged. Some time very soon after the extent of the *Elegy*'s success as a published poem had begun to be evident to him, Walpole came up with yet another scheme to further Gray's success. Richard Bentley – since 1748 a close friend of Walpole's and, it will be remembered, a privileged member of the Triumvirate that constituted Strawberry Hill's select Committee of Taste – had somehow, in the course of his prodigious academic childhood and youth and even in his subsequent years as a disreputable and debt-ridden itinerant on the continent, managed to nurture his considerably native talents as a graphic artist. It was in fact owing almost entirely to Bentley's skills as an artist and draftsman, and to his peculiar ability to translate into the solid substance of visual design the airy, architectural daydreams (some would say nightmares) of Walpole himself, that the latter was able to construct at Strawberry Hill a residence consonant with his idiosyncratic inner vision. The two men – Bentley's constitutional indolence feeding off of Walpole's energy and enthusiasm – encouraged one another. Walpole now decided that what was needed to enhance Gray's reputation as a poet even further, was an edition in which his friend's several published works were brought together with some fugitive pieces that had until then circulated only in manuscript – such as *A Long Story* – and, to add the distinctive and crowning touch to such an endeavour, all the poems would then be illustrated by Bentley. The *Elegy* and the three odes included anonymously in Dodsley's 1748 *Collection* – the *Ode on the Spring*, the *Eton Ode*, and the *Ode on the Death of a Favourite Cat* – would form the centrepiece of what was to remain a decidedly slim volume, but Gray would have to provide some other works to fill out the volume.

Gray, with some slight hesitation, but showing himself still unusually amenable to Walpole's scheme, accordingly sent to him by that September a copy of the *Hymn to Adversity*, which he had transcribed verbatim with some few slight changes in spelling and punctuation from the version recorded in his Commonplace Book almost ten years earlier. Taken together with *A Long Story*, the *Adversity Ode* brought the number of Gray's poems only to an even half-dozen. He instructed Walpole to tell Dodsley, who at about the same time was likewise looking for material to furnish a fourth volume of his popular *Collection*, that he 'had nothing more, either nocturnal or diurnal, to deck his Miscellany with'. Gray similarly had 'nothing more' that he could have sent to Walpole to swell the size of an effort that he still personally felt, in his less optimistic moments, would open him to charges of authorial vanity.

Work on the illustrated edition continued sporadically throughout the ensuing winter months at Bentley's usually slow pace. By July, 1752 – well over one year after the possibility of such a volume had been approved by Gray – the poet was only just beginning to receive the first proofs for the collection at Stoke. Both the death of his friend Wharton's father that April and a sudden illness which had then overtaken his own mother had diverted Gray's attention away from the project throughout much of the late spring and early summer. Having been sent one of the first proof prints from London, however (the Cul de Lampe representing the village funeral that was to appear at the conclusion of the *Elegy*'s 'Epitaph'), Gray was undisguisedly astonished at the quality of the workmanship. The plates based on Bentley's original drawings had been expertly engraved by Johann Sebastian Müller. Those which were to illustrate the *Elegy* were executed by Charles Grignion, who obviously bestowed a great deal of care on the work, and perfectly captured the pseudo-Gothic sensibilities of Bentley's originals. Referring to the proof of the Cul de Lampe yet at the same time crediting Bentley with having provided an inimitable graphic incentive to the painstaking work of the engravers, Gray wrote Walpole on 8 July:

> I am surprized at the Print, which far surpasses my Idea of London Graving. The Drawing itself was so finished, that I suppose, it did not require all the Art I imagined to copy it tolerably. My Aunts [Mrs. Rogers and Mrs. Oliffe, then staying at Stoke] just now, seeing me open your Letter, take it to be a Burying-Ticket enclosed, & ask, whether any body has left me a Ring? and so they still conceive it to be, even with all their Spectacles on. Heaven forbid they should suspect it to belong to any verses of mine; they would burn me for a poet. (*CTG* 362–63)

The excellence of the engraving having thus fired even its author's timorous enthusiasm for the project, Gray undertook to provide Bentley with an original sketch in his own hand of the Stoke Manor House, to be used as the basis for one of the illustrations eventually included with *A Long Story* (although, he demurred to Walpole, 'Mr Bentley . . . will catch a better Idea of Stoke-House from any old Barn he sees, than from my Sketch').

At about the same time, Gray also set about composing the text of some few short 'Stanzas' addressed to Bentley, which he appears to have intended to serve as a complimentary, verse preface to the volume. These unfinished 'Stanzas' began:

> In silent gaze the tuneful choir among,
>   Half pleased, half blushing, let the Muse admire,
> While Bentley leads her sister-art along,
>   And bids the pencil answer to the lyre.
> See first their course, each transitory thought
>   Fixed by his touch a lasting essence take;
> Each dream, in fancy's airy colouring wrought,
>   To local symmetry and life awake!
> The tardy rhymes that used to linger on,
>   To censure cold and negligent of fame,
> In swifter measures animated run,
>   And catch a lustre from his genuine flame.
> Ah! could they catch his strength, his easy grace,
>   His quick creation, his unerring line;
> The energy of Pope they might efface,
>   And Dryden's harmony submit to mine. (*PTG* 153–54)

Many have criticized Gray's praise of Bentley's skill in these lines as inappropriate and almost ludicrously excessive. Taking note of the fragment when it first appeared in print in Mason's *Memoirs* in 1775, John Langhorne, writing in the *Monthly Review*, suggested that readers move from Gray's self-professed 'transitory thoughts' to the supposedly 'lasting essence' of Bentley's designs, and 'bid defiance to risibility if you can'. Few have commented on the fact, however, that Gray is clearly having a great deal of fun in these lines – fun both at his own expense as well as Bentley's. The outrageous hyperbole of his poetic compliment and *envoi* is almost certainly intentional. It is no accident, for example, that the only poets mentioned in the line of descent which leads to Gray's own 'meaner gems' are – in addition to Dryden and Pope, mentioned above – Shakespeare and Milton. Gray would never seriously have compared the tiny body of his own work to the prolific output of any one of those poets, much less to that of all four. The closing lines of the 'Stanzas' – the final rhymes of which were unfortunately lost when a corner of the original manuscript was torn and then apparently discarded – would seem even, when the essentially humorous nature of their intent is at last acknowledged, to provide some clue as to precisely why Gray decided ultimately to abandon the idea of including such prefatory verses to the volume. Only shortly after the lines quoted above, Gray wrote:

> Enough for me, if to some feeling breast
>   My lines a secret sympathy [   ]
> And as their pleasing influence [   ]
>   A sigh of soft reflection [   ] (*PTG* 155)

In suggesting that his 'lines' (and the poet almost certainly had the *Elegy* in mind here) contained within them the power to inspire a 'secret sympathy' in the 'feeling breast' of 'some' – if not all – readers, Gray may well have felt that his light verses had suddenly and unintentionally grown solemn. The passing admission, even in the course of such a casual *jeu d'esprit*, that his poetry contained emotional and quite frankly homoerotic subtexts unavailable to the average reader was, after the briefest of reconsiderations, a bit too candid for Gray's own comfort here. Having begun the lines in a lighthearted vein, Gray was alarmed at the personal, confessional direction in which they had so swiftly carried him. Better, he no doubt thought, to let both the poetry and the engravings speak to each other and for themselves.

As it turned out, Gray's authorial anxieties regarding the joint-venture with Bentley – so markedly absent from his earliest references to the volume – began within the next few months to surface openly. His initial enthusiasm predictably gave way to some equally predictable fears and worries. Gray received the first proofs for the project towards the end of December, at which time he noted merely that he was surprised the book was to be printed as a folio, rather than a smaller and more common quarto volume (he appears actually to have been mistaken in this regard); he observed too that the 'Stanzas' – i.e. the *Elegy* – were numbered, 'which', he added coldly, 'I do not like'. By the time he wrote to Dodsley in the second week of February, 1753, he was evincing a degree of alarm which – had it not perforce entailed the arrogant cancellation both of Bentley's and of Walpole's efforts on his own behalf as well – might easily have prompted Gray to back out of the project altogether. He began his letter to Dodsley abruptly:

> I am not at all satisfied with the Title. to have it conceived, that I publish a Collection of *Poems* (half a dozen little Matters, four of which too have already been printed again & again) thus pompously adorned would make me appear very justly ridiculous. I desire it may be understood (which is the truth) that the Verses are only subordinate, & explanatory

to the Drawings, & suffer'd by me to come out thus only for that reason. . . . you need not apprehend, that this Change in the Title will be any prejudice to the Sale of the book. a showy title-page may serve to sell a Pamphlet of a shilling or two; but this is not of a price for chance-customers, whose eye is caught in passing by a window. . . . (*CTG* 371)

Gray insisted that the volume be titled, instead, *Designs by Mr R. Bentley, for Six Poems by Mr T. Gray*. Dodsley, confident that the collaboration would make its way in the world regardless of whose name received precedence on the title page, was amenable to the change.

No sooner had Gray's fears regarding the title of the book been laid to rest than he received another and even more formidable shock. Immediately after sending off his response to Dodsley, Gray sat down to a letter from Walpole which informed him that his portrait by Eccardt was even then serving as the model for an engraving of his head and shoulders that was in turn to be used as the frontispiece to the volume. Faced suddenly with the prospect not only of being accused of exceptional vanity in publishing such a slim collection of poetry in his proper name in the first place, but of then having the hubris likewise to preface that collection with his own picture, Gray positively shook with mortification and anger. 'Sure you are not out of your Wits!' he shrieked to Walpole,

this I know, if you suffer my Head to be printed, you infallibly will put me out of mine. I conjure you immediately to put a stop to any such design. who is at the Expence of engraving it I know not; but if it be Dodsley, I will make up the Loss to him. The thing, as it was, I know will make me ridiculous enough; but to appear in proper Person at the head of my works, consisting of half a dozen Ballads in 30 pages, would be worse than the Pillory. I do assure you, if I had received such a Book with such a frontispiece without any warning, I believe, it would have given me a Palsy. (*CTG* 372)

'I am extremely in earnest', he repeated to Walpole, '& can't even bear the Idea!' Walpole responded almost immediately, protesting that the design of prefacing a copy of Gray's portrait to the collection had been Dodsley's idea, and not his own, and that he had already warned the publisher that such an engraving might not coincide Gray's own wishes. 'The Head', he assured Gray succinctly, 'I give up'.

The collected volume of poems – or rather, as it was now to be called, Bentley's *Designs* – was finally published on 29 March, 1753. The thirty-six-page edition was in the end printed as what was then known as an 'imperial' quarto, a volume consisting of $15 \times 10^{1}/_{2}$ sheets, in which both the plates and the poems were printed only on one side of the page.

The price of half a guinea was perceived as placing the *Designs* just slightly beyond the reach of many purchasers, who were willing to spend that much on such volumes only if they were voluminous and ostentatiously 'rich and showy' (Gray himself, to offer some idea as to just how much the price of the volume would have been in practical terms, insisted at about this same time on spending no more than half a guinea for a full week's lodging in central London).

Those who did purchase the collection, however, were reassured that they had, indeed, received far more than their money's worth. Bentley had not only designed for all six of Gray's poems one full-page illustration, but he had likewise included carefully executed headpieces and tale-pieces to compliment each work. The layout of his stunning illustrations was partly indebted to the now-famous Albrizzi edition of Tasso's *Jerusalem Delivered* (1745). Although Bentley's engravings attracted a few negative criticisms in Gray's lifetime, few if any readers today would deny the incomparable elegance of his effort. Not only had the artist set himself the task of providing graphic counterparts to the narrative and imagery of Gray's work, he had likewise, as the engravings included in the final product so clearly demonstrate, read and understood those poems with a truly sympathetic mind. While one work – the *Ode on the Death of a Favourite Cat* – demanded and received from Bentley a drawing that managed somehow to capture its own sly and feline (and vaguely, in the eighteenth-century perception of the term, 'oriental') sense of humour, another – the *Elegy* – summoned from the artist an equally appropriate (though not overly solemn) depiction of the startling finality and indiscrimination of death. Writing of the illustrations for the comic feline elegy, the critic Irene Tayler has commented:

> Bentley . . . worked up small hints from the language of the poem, making from Gray's mere mention of a Chinese vase a complete oriental setting with costumed cat, and of the 'wat'ry God' and 'malignant Fate' robust imitations of Greek architectural statuary. The picture is thus a paradigm of Bentley's techniques; the household cat surrounded in mock solemnity by the rich culture of fashionable eighteenth-century England, its deference to Classical tradition, its vogue of Chinoiserie, its decorous but pervasive accolade to the artist as gentleman-maker.[33]

Bentley confronted the mood of each of Gray's poems with equal care and skill. His flawless *Elegy* illustrations graphically implicate the reader in the inescapable mortality of the poem's world; the shadow of the individual that falls, corpse-like, across the grave being pointed out by the hoary-headed swain, each reader is meant to realize with a sudden,

---

[33] Irene Tayler, 'Two Eighteenth-Century Illustrators of Gray: Richard Bentley and William Blake' in Downey and Jones, 121.

dizzying shock, is nothing less than a sly intimation – a pointed fore-shadowing – of their *own* inevitable death and burial. Almost every nuance of Gray's comparison in the poem that matches the display and 'pomp' of 'power' against the fecundity of the world of those who pursue the 'noiseless tenor of their way' finds a place in Bentley's depiction. The illustrations are technically noteworthy as well; Bentley's clean and precise execution approaches perfection.

In fact, Bentley's full-page engravings for both the *Elegy* and the *Ode on the Death of a Favourite Cat* arguably stand head and shoulders above any rival artistic conceptions as the best illustrations of either of those works ever published. William Blake, who would be drawn to his predecessor's lifelong depiction of the painful confrontation between innocence and experience in the narrative of human history, and who would likewise evince a deep sympathy for Gray's eventual interest in the bardic origins of English poetry, was himself, later in the century, to undertake a unique series of illustrations for Gray's poems. His innovative technical interpretation would be to place copies of the printed text of Gray's verses in the centre of folio sheets, and then surround the language of the earlier poet by the often stunning colour of his own watercolour images. 'Blake's intention . . . throughout his entire series of illustrations to Gray', as Tayler has commented, would be 'on the one hand to correct by pictorial emphasis what he felt to be a rather morbid turn in the poet – his pallid caution, his melancholy, his retreat from life – and on the other hand pay homage to his very great if sometimes latent poetic power.'[34] Blake's graphic interpretations of Gray's work (he would complete 116 separate illustrations for the personal library of the wife of his friend and patron, John Flaxman) are themselves fascinating and sporadically inspired; yet, as his biographer Peter Ackroyd has conceded, 'Blake's particular ability to conjure . . . monumental images within so small a space has the consequence, intended or unintended, of lending an air of strangeness, and even on occasions monstrousness, to his creations'.[35] Bentley's illustrations, by contrast, were meant not so much to provide corrective or supplementary images to Gray's texts, as they were to stand as graceful and deferential graphic complements. They are thus, in a very real sense, 'parodies' of the most reverential kind; graphic paeans of praise, working carefully and in harmony with Gray's lines to further, not to occlude or displace, the original language and imagery of the poet himself.

Gray had little if any opportunity to enjoy the volume's success, however. Just one month before its publication, in the final days of

[34] Irene Tayler, 'Two Eighteenth-Century Illustrators of Gray' in Downey and Jones, 122.
[35] Peter Ackroyd, *Blake: A Biography* (New York: Ballantine, 1995) 204.

February, Gray had been abruptly summoned to Stoke Poges by the news that his mother lay ill and close to death. He left Cambridge immediately – on 22 February – and arrived that same evening at Stoke. The next two and a half weeks were agonizing. Gray and his two aunts – Mrs. Oliffe was at that time still staying with Mrs. Rogers at Stoke – must have taken their turns sitting up with Dorothy, and doing whatever they could to ease her final suffering (the precise nature of her ailment remains uncertain, though it may have been some particularly virulent form of cancer). His mother, Gray confessed to Walpole in a hastily written letter of 27 February, hung 'in a condition between Life & Death, tho' (I think) much nearer the latter'. On Sunday, 11 March 1753, at the age of sixty-eight and after 'a long and painful Struggle for life', Dorothy Gray died. She was buried in the tomb at St. Giles that had already, since 1749, housed the remains of her sister Mary. Standing once again before the grave in the Stoke Poges church-yard, Gray might certainly be forgiven if he suddenly felt that he had little use or enthusiasm for Bentley's engravings. One of the central supports of his life had just been kicked out from under him. Though he may to some degree have become reconciled to the idea of his mother's death – she had lived a long life and had, in her final years at least, achieved with her sisters some hard-won degree of ease and contentment – Gray was genuinely grief-stricken by her loss. The *Elegy*, for Gray at least, needed no elaborate engravings to further its more private meanings – the hopes and fears expressed in its lines now made themselves felt along the throbbing pulses of his heart; the *Elegy* had once again been painfully and graphically illustrated for the poet himself by the aching and unavoidable pain of living grief itself.

CHAPTER EIGHT

EXPLORING THE LYRE

The Publication and Early Reception
of the Pindaric Odes
1753–1759

I. Loss and Remembrance

Gray only very slowly reconciled himself to the fact of his mother's death. With the exception of a few days' visit to London, where he was consoled by Wharton, the poet remained at Stoke through the middle of April. He assisted his aunts in whatever arrangements needed to be made regarding the distribution of his mother's property. The remaining members of the Antrobus family seem to have found only in each another the depth of sympathy that could carry them unbroken through such a loss. The practical details that needed to be taken care of in the face of Dorothy's burial helped to provide Gray with some sustaining framework of meaning, and he busied himself in attending to their completion. To find him referring dispassionately in a letter to Wharton written only a few days after his mother's death to the fact that an upcoming visit to London would necessarily be a brief one, if only because he would need almost immediately to return to Stoke in order to pay his aunt Oliffe 'her Arrears' (on the £100 she had loaned him towards the rebuilding of the Cornhill property following the fire of 1748) does not leave the poet – nor, for that matter, does it leave Mrs. Oliffe herself – open to the charge of insensitivity. Such activity was diverting and psychologically necessary for Gray. Only by focusing his attention closely on such seemingly trivial matters as clarifying the minutiae of financial obligations, or in attending to the details of Dorothy's interment and the disposition of her estate, could Gray begin to make his way through the self-described 'misfortune' of having survived his mother's death.

Gray returned to Cambridge on 13 April with little sense of direction and with little idea as to just what he was supposed to do next. From this point on in his life, Gray's physical health began often subtly and more consistently to reflect his inner state of mind. In his correspondence, a seemingly inconsolable sense of melancholy is never far from the surface. He began now routinely to suffer from bouts of near-debilitating mental depression – enduring episodes worse, even, than anything he had experienced as a young man. These attacks – described by the poet as a sudden 'sinking' sensation in his chest and abdomen, or by a feeling of pain and tightness around his heart – followed hard upon the slightest physical exertion. In the years to come, Gray would begin keeping a record in his diaries and pocket notebooks of the onset of these physical symptoms, carefully marking down any return of identifiable ailments, such as rheumatism, or any attack of the gout. He was already aware, of course, of a possible predisposition in his family to the latter illness. He would later in life assert in a letter to Walpole to have 'a better right to this malady' (i.e. the gout) than his friend – a prescriptive 'right' perceived in part to have been the only lasting legacy of his father, Philip. The increasingly familiar agony of the gout and even the secondary symptoms attendant upon the attacks of nervous anxiety often affected him most in his extremities, particularly in the legs and feet.

Not surprisingly, Gray's poor physical health and his correspondingly enervated state of mind began to take their toll on the progress of his studies. His enthusiasm for his 'scholarly' work reached a debilitatingly low ebb; nor, it would appear, was the energy which had fed that enthusiasm very soon to be replaced or in any way superseded by a burning desire to produce new creative work of his own. He toyed with volumes relating to oriental history and travel, and began slowly to cultivate a deeper interest in English history and, eventually, architecture. Unable in the months that followed his mother's death to read or even to think with his usual clarity, Gray seems not, at first, even to have considered turning, as he had turned at such moments in the past, to the solace of creative activity. For all the profoundly felt affection Gray had invested in his mother, her death in 1753 was to trigger in the poet no immediate outpouring of explicitly elegiac verse, as West's death had done in the summer of 1742. Precisely why Gray reacted as he did remains unclear. Perhaps he simply felt that the intensity of the natural relationship between a mother and her son was the emotional token of a bond so universally strong and so generally acknowledged that its force demanded from him no extraordinary articulation. Gray seems on this occasion to have felt no need to 'implore' the passers-by at Stoke Poges for the tribute of their sighs. Such sighs would be freely given and, in any event, could offer the poet little consolation in his loss. For all the intensity of his grief and for all the unarguably great measure of native talent that had been granted to him as a poet, Gray either could not or would not transform the circumstances of his mother's death into the stuff of elegiac poetry. The poetic forms capable of asserting their own rigorous order in the face of such a loss had yet to be recovered by the poet for his own purposes.

In what other directions, then, might he turn at such a time of personal crisis? The answers were slow to come. Throughout the early summer months Gray sought with limited success to lose himself in University business and affairs. An extended visit by the Duke of Newcastle (who was now, it will be remembered, Chancellor of the University) to Clare Hall in the middle of June provided a timely opportunity for such mindless diversion. 'Old Phobus' or 'Old Fibs', as Gray variously referred to Newcastle, may have been a formidable election manager, but his behaviour in the face of certain social occasions could be embarrassingly inept and even infantile. Gray, for his own part, professed a lifelong aversion to Newcastle, and he appears generally to have made little secret of his true opinion of the man. The depth of the poet's animosity is perhaps explained by the fact that Walpole himself regarded the Duke – who had years earlier played some role in his father's downfall – as one of his incontrovertible political enemies; Gray seems likewise, possibly as a result of many a late-night conversation at Strawberry Hill, to have carried in his own judgement of Newcastle's character and abilities some loyal reflection of his friend's political vendettas.

Even so, any social or professional encounter with such a powerful landowner and politician could be a nerve-racking (if, at the same time and in light of recent events, therapeutically mind-focusing) ordeal for someone who was as constitutionally retiring as Gray. And, as Gray knew, such an encounter was sooner or later bound to take place, and so would have to be endured. Gray did not have very long to wait. At a reception for the Chancellor held at Clare Hall soon after his arrival, on 16 June, Gray was formally presented to the Duke. He later wrote to Wharton that he felt he had acquitted himself reasonably well under the circumstances. 'I did not run away from his Grace', he wrote with modest pride in his decorum, 'but follow'd your advice, had a very affectionate squeeze by the hand, & a fine Complement in a corner'. Attempting in retrospect to recall the precise nature of this 'fine Compliment' or even to recollect the general subjects that had been touched upon in the course of their corner conversation, however, Gray claimed to draw a complete blank, professing to recall only that the Chancellor's hand had 'felt warm' in his own, and that he, too, had 'sweated a little' in his nervousness.

It was clear that something a bit more bracing and far more congenial than a nod and a handshake from the University Chancellor would to be needed to shock Gray out of his most recent spell of melancholy indolence. Wharton suspected that he knew precisely what was wanting in his friend's life. Having recently witnessed the birth of his own son Robert or 'Robin', as he was more familiarly to be known, and feeling increasingly secure in his own domesticity and profitably settled in his profession, Wharton invited Gray to travel north to share several of the long summer weeks with him and his growing family at their home near Durham. The spectacle of youth and renewal within the Wharton household, as well as the simple pleasures of an unfamiliar countryside experienced in the verdant fullness of July and August, the doctor reasoned, would do his friend no end of good. Gray, he thought, needed at such a period in his life to be surrounded as much as possible with the sort of care and affection that could quietly reaffirm his own sense of continued value and purpose as an individual.

Gray responded to his friend's proposal with alacrity. Stonhewer, as matters turned out, had already been planning on travelling in the direction of Durham by post-chaise on a visit to his father at nearby Houghton-le-Spring toward the middle of July. Gray could easily accompany Stonhewer on this first leg of the journey and then, punctuating his trip with planned overnight stays at York, Ripon, and Richmond, join Wharton at his home of Elvet House in nearly no time at all. Even the very real threat of civil disturbance on the turnpike roads in Yorkshire (mobs had only three weeks earlier rioted in the county's West Riding, destroying several turnpike bars and houses) was not enough to keep Gray from undertaking the journey. By 24 July he was comfortably settled in front of the Whartons' fireside, having arrived safely on the Sunday evening two days earlier. He soon apprized Brown at Cambridge of his swift and 'very agreeable' journey. 'I can not now enter upon the particulars of my travels', he joked to Brown with what might have been a conscious recollection of the youthful parodies that had once passed between Walpole and himself, 'because I have not yet gather'd up my Quotations from the Classicks to intersperse, like Mr. Addison'. Before one can ever sit down to write properly or 'particularly' on any subject, Gray's protestation implies with a light and disarming candour, one must first have access to such generic models and stylistic precedents as render the transformative power of quotation, imitation, and parodic recollection possible.

Gray's salutary visit to Durham that summer insensibly lengthened into a stay of over two months. He did not leave the Whartons until 28 September. 'Suffice it to tell you', he wrote to Brown of his situation, 'that I have one of the most beautiful Vales here in England to walk in with prospects that change every ten steps, & open something new wherever I turn, all rude and romantic'. 'In short', he added to great bathetic effect, 'the sweetest Spot to break your neck or drown yourself in that ever was beheld'. For all such mildly anxious levity regarding the unfamiliarly rugged landscape which seemed on all sides to confront him, Gray obviously enjoyed the time he spent in the country. The city of Durham itself – never quite the victim of the heavy regional industrialization that would only slightly later in the century darken the skies of its near urban neighbors with a pall of heavy coal smoke, and stain their buildings with a grim and tenacious coat of soot – still retained something of the aspect of its 'hill-island', fortress origins. Described three decades earlier by Defoe in his *Tour* as 'a little compact, neatly contrived city, surrounded almost with the river Wear', Durham yet displayed – from vantage of the footbridges and from the 'Banks' that lined the river's southern edge, in the outlines of its medieval ecclesiastical palace, in its churches, homes, and bridges, in the remnants of its Norman castle and in the great, central tower of the Cathedral – the visible traces of the town's traditionally double aspect as 'half church of God, half castle 'gainst the Scot'. Gray spent the better part of his days enjoying some of the local diversions in the company of his enthusiastic and solicitous host. He twice visited the racetrack near Old Elvet; he attended the Assembly Rooms in the Bailey (the old town's central street); he dined with the new Bishop of Durham himself (Dr. Richard Trevor); he even received a visit himself at Wharton's home of Elvet House from an old acquaintance, Thomas Chapman, Master of Magdalene and a Prebendary of Durham. Surprisingly, Gray made no reference in those letters to Brown which survive from his stay to the great Norman Cathedral itself, although he would certainly have visited the structure, and no doubt spent some of his time exploring its precincts with interest.

Toward the end of September, Gray received some news that compelled him to return to the larger world of his other friends and acquaintances and, for the benefit of those same friends, to forsake for himself the role of the bereaved, and to offer instead the comfort and support expected from the staunchest of companions. At the beginning of the third week of that month, a mutual friend of Mason and of Wharton passed on to Gray the news not only that Mason's half-sister, Anne, had recently been taken seriously ill, but that Mason had likewise, only days afterward (on 26 August) suffered the loss of his father. Gray responded to Mason's misfortune with strong and immediate sympathy. 'I know', he wrote feelingly from Durham,

> what it is to lose a Person, that one's eyes & heart have long been used to, & I never desire to part with the remembrance of that loss, nor would wish you should. it is something, that you had a little time to acquaint yourself with the Idea beforehand (if I am inform'd right) & that He probably suffer'd but little pain, the only thing that makes death terrible. (*CTG* 381)

Rather than meeting up with Mason at Hull, as he had intended originally to do, Gray instead stopped in York on his homeward journey south toward Cambridge. There, on 30 September, he found Mason bearing up as well as might be expected under the weight not only of his sister's illness and the loss of his father, but also, as Gray soon discovered, the recent passing of his 'most intimate friend' – a Dr. Marmaduke Prickett, whom Mason had been nursing through a fever even in the days immediately following his father's death. Adding terrible insult to his grievous personal misfortune, Mason's clergyman father had effectively disinherited his eldest son by leaving his entire estate to his second wife – Mason's stepmother – and then entailing it to her daughter. 'He has absolutely no support at present but his fellowship', Gray wrote, relaying the news of Mason's situation to a concerned Wharton,

> yet he looks more like a Hero, than ever I knew him, like one that can stare poverty in the face without being frighted, & instead of growing little & humble before her [the second Mrs. Mason], has fortified his Spirit & elevated his brow to meet her like a Man. (*CTG* 385)

Gray himself drew some strength from the sheer force of Mason's dignity on this occasion. The language of his letter suggests a slight recollection of his own *Adversity Ode* (in that poem's expressed desire to feel what others feel and thence to 'know [himself] a man'). Mason now faced each day with a profound uncertainty regarding his own future. His hands trembled uncontrollably, and his 'spirits' were liable at any moment to drop into a depth of despair. Yet those same spirits, as Mason had written Gray just before the latter's visit to York, had 'supported [him] hitherto supprizingly'. Mason's fortitude seems to have extended even to provide an emotional support and a model for the poet himself.

Still, misfortune followed on misfortune. No sooner had Gray returned to Peterhouse, than he learned that his aunt Oliffe had recently suffered a stroke. Stopping in Cambridge only overnight to attend to his most urgent business there (he had planned originally to remain in College for an entire week), Gray pressed directly on to Stoke. He arrived on 4 October to find his aunt 'recover'd surprisingly from the greatest danger'. Mrs. Oliffe's speech remained slightly slurred and indecipherable to strangers, but the spectacle of her swift recovery at such an age – she was already well past seventy – left Gray thankful. He recognized at the same time, however, that her sister (his aunt, Mrs. Rogers) would benefit both practically and emotionally from his continued presence in the household, and he soon declared his intention of spending the remainder of the autumn and early winter in the company of both his aunts at Stoke.

The months passed slowly. Increasingly as the autumn weather gave way to a drear and chilly November, Gray found his summer's hoard of renewed spirits and vitality slowly slipping away. Several weeks after his initial return to Stoke, he had felt himself up to sending Wharton a detailed account that traced his progress from Durham all the way down into Buckinghamshire. He described with the affectionate precision of observation he shared only with his Durham friend all the details of the seasonal English landscape. Even toward the end of October he cheerfully closed one letter with a post-script which declared delightedly: 'Every thing resounds with the Wood-Lark, & Robin; & the voice of the Sparrow is heard in our land'. Only shortly later, however, in a letter written on 5 November, he confessed to Mason,

> Stoke has revived in me the memory of many a melancholy hour, that I have pass'd in it, & tho' I have no longer the same cause for anxiety, I do not find myself at all the happier for thinking, that I have lost it. as my thoughts now signify nothing to any one but myself, I shall wish to change the scene, as soon as ever I can. (*CTG* 388)

Mason, who was then in London and who had managed to work himself out of the depression surrounding his father's death by securing a position as private secretary to Lord Holdernesse (a Yorkshire nobleman serving at the time as a Secretary of State in Pelham's government), promptly assisted Gray in locating some suitable rooms in Jermyn Street where he could stay while in London. Mason understood that if Gray was ever truly to reassert himself and allow himself to be recalled to life in the wake of his mother's death, he would need to be prepared to spend more time than he had yet attempted to spend far away from the scenes and from the familiar environments which, even in their lighter aspects, concealed but never fully erased the shadow of Dorothy's memory.

*

The early months of 1754 found Gray at least beginning to turn more regularly to his old pastimes – to the diversions of his books and to his local friends – in his attempts to move at a more measured pace through the final stages of mourning. The popular success of the *Elegy* and the generally positive response to Bentley's collected volume of *Designs* may even have suggested to Gray the possibility that – if only he set his mind properly to the task – he might actually be able to gain some substantial reputation as a published (if never a prolific) poet. With an eye towards nurturing and cultivating the 'two or three Ideas more' he claimed still to have in his head, Gray began researching the history of English prosody with greater diligence than he had ever done in the past. He asked that Brockett, at Trinity, procure him a number of volumes of early Tudor and Elizabethan verse. Included among his requests were copies of the work of Samuel Daniel, Frances Meres, and Henry Howard, Earl of Surrey. He had begun rereading Chaucer and John Lydgate, and had taken to drafting in his Commonplace Book and other notebooks various lists and catalogues of 'British Poets', and tables of different metres.

The months and years ahead were to find Gray sporadically but persistently at work on a planned history of English poetry and its origins. Work on this contemplated history grew in time almost completely to displace his former scholarly interests – his comprehensive survey of Greek history, his often painstaking reading of classical authors, and his patient study of ancient and modern travel accounts were all, from this point in his life, almost completely suspended. All his attention was devoted instead to the background and development of the English poetic tradition.

In the years immediately following the poet's death, Mason claimed considerable credit for having first suggested the topic of such a history to Gray's mind. In July, 1752, William Warburton had passed on to Mason a manuscript sketch for a history of English verse which he had discovered among the papers of Alexander Pope. Mason later wrote:

> Mr. Gray was greatly struck with the method which Mr. Pope had traced out in this little sketch; and on my proposal of engaging with him in compiling such a history, he examined the plan more accurately, enlarging it considerably, and formed an idea for an introduction to it. In this was to be ascertained the origin of Rhyme; and specimens given, not only of the Provençal Poetry, (to which alone Mr. Pope seemed to adverted) but of the Scaldic, British, and Saxon; as, from all these different sources united, English poetry had its original.[1]

Gray promptly copied Pope's outline into the second volume of his Commonplace Book, and so his new obsession began slowly to take root. His subsequent devotion to the topic was as sincere as it was wildly ambitious. His typically meticulous research into such subjects as the distinguishing characteristics of English metre, and the roots of English poetry in the 'Gothic' rhythms of Anglo-Saxon, Old High German, Old Norse, and Welsh verse would eventually, as critics such as William Powell Jones have so patiently demonstrated, inform the metrical experimentation of works such as *The Progress of Poesy* and *The Bard*, no less than it would shape the Norse and Welsh imitations of the early 1760s. As his studies progressed, Gray was to grow increasingly convinced that the origins of rhyme in English poetry were Celtic, and so he turned more and more to a study of Welsh poetry and language to untangle the particular history of English verse measures. Although he would never complete his planned volume on English poetry, Gray demonstrated even in the writing of his notes and in his essay-fragments on the project, in the words of Powell Jones, 'a combination of critical

---

[1]   Mason, *Memoirs*, 277.

approach and scholarly knowledge of the subject that he would have made of his projected history and outstanding creative work'.[2]

Even as Gray began this newest project, he remained willing to put his skills as a researcher to work in the interests of his closest friends. Responding to a plea from Walpole for some historical information relating to the marriages of Henry VI and Henry VII – information which Walpole hoped would assist him in identifying some of the figures included in two paintings he had recently purchased for Strawberry Hill – Gray was no less thorough and enthusiastic than when addressing his own interests. He diligently sent Walpole an extraordinarily lengthy letter on the subject, at the end of which he wrote mischievously and in the style of a medieval copyist, 'This is all at present complyed by the paynful hand & symple engyne of your honour's pour bedesman, T: G:'. Lest Walpole should imagine him to be completely 'buried in the dust of an old Chronicle', Gray reminded his friend that he maintained an interest not only in matters 'that happen'd 300 years ago', but kept himself abreast of contemporary political events as well. The recent general election (a contest prompted by the death of Henry Pelham on 6 March) had seen the establishment of a new government administration led by Newcastle (Pelham's brother); the election had also once again seen the return of Walpole to the House, this time as Member for Castle Rising. 'I am still alive (I'd have you know)', Gray wrote Walpole, '& tho' these events are indeed only subjects of speculation to me, [I] feel some difference still between the present and the past.'

At the end of May, Gray had the opportunity to congratulate his old friend John Chute on having finally (upon the death of his estranged and unreliable brother, Anthony) passed into possession of the stunning estate of The Vyne, near Basingstoke in Hampshire. Dating from the early sixteenth century, Chute's new home was even by the standards of the day a proud and enviable property, having already passed through a period of unusually tasteful renovation while in the hands of John Webb in the years just prior to the Restoration. Many of the more aesthetically appealing portions of the older structure (most notably the brick entrance belonging to the original Tudor mansion, and the chapel from the same period, ornamented with rare Flemish glass and tiles) were left standing much as they were, and newer additions were made only after judicious and careful consideration. Gray visited Chute at the Vyne early in July and although, as he would write the following month in a letter to Wharton, the year was not 'behaving itself well' and the weather had continued unseasonably cool and rainy throughout the summer months, the two men enjoyed the time spent in one another's

---

[2] Powell Jones, 89.

company. Together they travelled the short distance to Twickenham to pay Walpole a visit, at Strawberry Hill.

Gray had begun so much to enjoy even such short journeys in and around England (and he seems so much to have savoured the happy memory of his previous summer's comfortable visit to Wharton near Durham) that from this point on in his life he made a point of undertaking, whenever possible in warmer weather, extended vacations from Cambridge. With his mother no longer an anchoring presence at Stoke Poges and with his friends and former colleagues finally settling down to pursue their lives in locations that seemed at times to extend to all four corners of the Kingdom, Gray felt that he was entitled likewise to do as he pleased, and to travel throughout the country and make such visits as might happen to take his fancy. He began to feel freer and less constrained by circumstances than he had ever felt in the past, and his native curiosity increasingly prompted him to experience the world around him as fully as he could. The remarkable diversity of the English countryside, too, began increasingly to interest him far more than he had ever thought possible; as his interest in such subjects as natural history and botany ripened in the years of his early middle age, he was delighted to find that he could be as much at home and as intellectually comfortable examining the local flora in the fields and along the pathways of rural England, as he would otherwise have been reading the volumes of history which remained piled high on his tables at Peterhouse – volumes which, after all, would always and patiently be awaiting his attention whenever he chose to return to Cambridge.

Pausing in mid-summer to look in on his Aunt Rogers at Stoke only briefly, Gray soon after his stay with Walpole embarked on the second of the grand summer circuits that were typically to constitute his method of travel and sightseeing in the years to come. In the summer of 1754 his curiosity set him off in the direction of the Midland counties. He first visited the great house of Stowe in Buckinghamshire (in Gray's day the impressive mansion and estate of the Temple and the Grenville families). He then made his way to Woburn Abbey in Bedfordshire (the seat of John Russell, the Duke of Bedford and home to an impressive collection of paintings), before visiting Wroxton Abbey in Oxfordshire (home to Francis North, first Earl of Guilford), and then finally reaching the town of Warwick. Warwick itself ('a place worth seeing', he wrote succinctly but without much enthusiasm to Wharton) impressed Gray with the situation of its castle. He was sadly disappointed, however, with the effect of the improvements that had recently been carried out on that property by its owner, Lord Brooke. The late summer found Gray as far afield as the southernmost tip of Northamptonshire, where he was probably joined in his rambles by his Cambridge acquaintance Frederick

Montagu, whose brother George was then in residence at his house of Greatworth, near Brackley.

Gray wrote Wharton a lengthy letter detailing his summer's itinerary shortly after his return to Stoke in mid-September. His description of Guy's Cliffe – 'a very agreeable rock' situated north of Warwick on the route to Coventry and famous for its associations with the legendary Guy of Warwick – was among the first of many such careful vignettes Gray would, in the years to come, include in his letters to Wharton. 'I had heard often of Guy-Cliff two miles from the town', he wrote on this occasion,

> so I walked to see it; & of all improvers commend me to Mr. Greathead [Samuel Greathed], its present Owner. he shew'd me himself, & is liter-ally a fat young Man with a head & face much bigger than they are usually worn. it was naturally a very agreeable rock, whose Cliffs cover'd with large trees hung beetleing over the Avon, which twists twenty ways in sight of it. there was the Cell of Guy, Earl of Warwick, cut in the living stone, where he died a Hermit (as you may see in a penny History, that hangs upon the rails in Moorfields) there were his fountains bubbling out of the Cliff; there was a Chantry founded to his memory in Henry the 6th's time. but behold the Trees are cut down to make room for flower-ing shrubs, the rock is cut up, till it is as smooth & as sleek as sattin; the river has a gravel-walk by its side; the Cell is a Grotta with cockle-shells and looking-glass; the fountains have an iron-gate before them, and the Chantry is a Barn, or a little House. Even the poorest bits of nature, that remain, are daily threatned, for he says . . . he is determined, it shall be *all new*. These were his words, & they are Fate. (*CTG* 409–410)

In his barely contained outrage at the liberties taken with such natural and historic sights as Guy's Cliffe – an outrage tempered only by a sus-tained perception of the ineluctably ludicrous propensities in human nature – Gray in many ways anticipated the disappointed reaction of the modern tourist who has long looked forward to enjoying a particular sight or prospect, only to find that same location damaged or destroyed by a vulgar desire tastelessly to exploit and so to profit from its attrac-tions. The aesthetically and historically inappropriate atrocities wrought upon Guy's Cliffe by the Greatheds eventually became something of an enduring, private joke among Gray's own circle of friends and corre-spondents. 'Did you go to Guys' Cliffe', Walpole would ask Lady Ossory in a letter written many years later, 'and see how Lady Mary Greathead painted it straw-colour, and stuck cockle-shells in its hair?'.[3] Walpole's self-conscious and temporary Gothic experimentation at Strawberry Hill was one thing; the misguided architectural 'improvements' typically

---

[3]   WC xxxii.353.

inflicted by the aesthetically impaired Lord Brookes of this world, Gray
and his correspondents would clearly have agreed, were a different
matter altogether.

Returning once again to Stoke at the end of September, Gray was
pleased to learn that Wharton had not only acted on his plans temporarily to leave Durham and set up his medical practice in London, but
that he had already begun to settle his family into their new accommodations in Coleman Street. Wharton, who had himself only recently
visited Strawberry Hill, and who had returned to the City completely
besotted by Walpole's fanciful Gothic project, had caught something of
Walpole's contagion and was already considering just what 'Gothic
ornaments' would be appropriate to his own new residence in town.
Although he professed himself pleased that his friend had thus whole-
heartedly entered 'into the Spirit of Strawberry-Castle', Gray was at the
same time quick to caution Wharton that such ornamentation was a task
that demanded unusual discrimination and taste, and could easily be
taken too far. Such fanciful additions were far from appropriate to every
residence, and should be undertaken only with the greatest care. 'If you
project anything', he warned Wharton, 'I hope it will be entirely within
doors; & don't let me (when I come gaping into Coleman-street) be
directed to the Gentleman's at the ten Pinnacles, or with the Church-
porch at his door.'

By the end of the month Gray had left Stoke to spend the long and
largely uneventful winter of 1754–55 in Cambridge. With the exception
only of a brief absence that bracketed the Christmas holiday and his
birthday (a melancholy week that he that year almost certainly spent
with his aunt at Stoke), Gray remained in unbroken residence at Peterhouse until the end of April. One communication seems at least to have
held the possibility of enlivening the passage of those winter months at
Cambridge, though it resulted in a proposal to which Gray himself paid
little attention. Walpole recorded in his very brief *Memoir of Gray* the
following concise anecdote: 'In the winter of 1755, George Hervey, Earl
of Bristol, who was soon afterwards sent Envoy to Turin, was designed
for Minister of Lisbon; he offered to carry Mr Gray as his secretary, but
he refused it'. George William Hervey, second Earl of Bristol, was indeed
– as Walpole's note asserts – appointed Envoy to Turin in 1755. He was
shortly afterwards (in 1758) sent as Ambassador to Madrid. No significant evidence relating to Gray's possible appointment as the Earl's personal secretary exists today, nor does Gray himself anywhere in his
surviving correspondence mention such an offer (the poet's only reference to the Earl, in a letter to Brown, relates exclusively to Bristol's eventual recall from Madrid in 1761, just prior to the war with Spain). The
fact that he chose not to accept nor even, apparently, ever seriously to

have considered such an offer should come as no real surprise. Gray, with considerable justification, no doubt considered himself far above any such situation; even if he had entertained the possibility of accepting such a post, Gray would have realized that there were in his case far too many practical considerations easily to be overcome. The poet, now approaching forty years of age, would for one thing have considered himself far too old to be entering the world of ambassadorial politics; he had grown accustomed to having his own way – *in* his own way – and he would certainly have found the prospect of taking orders from anyone, much less from the Earl of Bristol, an intolerable imposition. Moreover, he had never been all that comfortable in the heat of Florence or Rome, and Portugal promised summers no less humid and unpleasant than those of the Italian peninsula. And could he even consider leaving his aunt Rogers entirely alone at Stoke or, for what that matter, leaving Walpole and their mutual friends at Strawberry Hill, or abandoning a Wharton only newly settled in nearby London? No, Gray reasoned. Cambridge was now his home, and the incentives that once again saw him entertaining the prospect of remaining on continental soil for any length of time would need to be far more enticing than they were that winter. He was increasingly aware (and this was a private development he had thus far kept to himself) that there were paths which led, as he was soon to put it, 'beyond the limits of a vulgar fate'. He was beginning once again and to his own surprise to acknowledge that there was poetry still to be written and – even more remarkably – poetry still to be published by the man who was fast becoming the most famous elegist in English.

II. High Pindaricks

In December 1754, Gray enclosed in a letter to Wharton some remarkable stanzas that he had entitled in his own Commonplace Book transcription simply as an 'Ode, in the Greek Manner', and which he noted with some imprecision as having been 'Finish'd in 1754'. These were the same verses to which he had referred well over two years earlier, in a letter to Walpole, as the 'high Pindarick upon stilts', which he claimed even then to have been close to completing. 'It wants but seventeen lines of having an end', Gray had written of the poem as early as July, 1752, adding doubtfully, 'I don't say of being finished'. Gray later acknowledged that the 'Ode' was written only 'by fits & starts at very distant intervals'. He claimed that December to be sending the 'Ode' to Wharton, in London, merely as a diversion. 'If this be as tedious to You, as it is grown to me', he wrote,

I shall be sorry that I sent it you. . . . my Taste for Praise is not like that of Children for fruit. if there were nothing but Medlars & Blackberries in the world, I could be very well content to go without any at all. . . . I desire you would by no means suffer this to be copied; nor even shew it, unless to very few, & especially not to mere Scholars, that can scan all the measures in Pindar, & say the Scholia by heart. (CTG 416)

A little over two months later, Gray again wrote to Wharton, slightly qualifying the anxiety of these last remarks. 'In truth', he confessed, 'I am not so much against publishing, as against publishing *this alone*'. Gray further disclosed that he had 'two or three Ideas more' in his head, 'Ideas' that in time developed into the equally experimental and metrically complex, *The Bard*, and in the unfinished *Ode on the Pleasure Arising from Vicissitude*. The verses Gray sent to Wharton at the end of the previous year constituted a completed draft of the first of his efforts 'in the Greek Manner', and the same lines eventually appeared in print as *The Progress of Poesy*. Gray was to withhold publication of this first of his Pindaric odes until he completed work on *The Bard* some two years later, in the summer of 1757.

In his late nineteenth-century biography of the poet, Edmund Gosse observed that the Pindaric odes 'marked a third and final stage in Gray's poetical development'. 'In the *Elegy*', Gosse observed with reference to this development,

he had dared to leave those trodden paths of phraseology along which the critics of the hour, the quibbling Hurds and Warburtons, could follow him step by step, but his startling felicities had carried his readers captive by their appeal to a common humanity. He was now about to launch upon a manner of writing in which he could no longer be accompanied by the plaudits of the vulgar, and where his style could no longer appeal with security to the sympathy of the critics. He was now, in other words, about to put out his most original qualities in poetry.[4]

Gosse's suggestion that Gray was purposefully attempting in these later poems to avoid 'the plaudits of the vulgar' gave succinct voice to a manner of reading the perceived complexity of the odes as a matter of self-obfuscation which had already greatly influenced critics over the years. Gray's Pindarics have most often been read as rhetorically reactionary responses to the general availability and accessibility of his earlier poetry and, specifically, to the enormous popularity of both the *Eton Ode* and, of course, the *Elegy*. Gray's modern editor Roger Lonsdale concisely recapitulated such a view in his own edition of Gray's poetry when he wrote: 'Perhaps embarrassed by the great popularity of

---

[4] Gosse, 177–18.

the *Elegy*, [Gray] seems to have been determined to puzzle all but the most learned of his readers, as is clear from the brief motto from Pindar's *Olympian Odes* ii. 85, which he himself translated as "vocal to the Intelligent alone" . . . prefixed to the *Odes*'.[5]

Lonsdale's remarks – summing up a response to the *Odes* that had been repeated in various forms by a number of Gray's critics throughout the nineteenth and twentieth centuries – appeared over thirty years ago. There are a number of good reasons still to argue such a position today. For one thing, it describes a response which seems to have been accepted as a legitimate reaction to and explanation of the poems in Gray's own lifetime. Almost all those individuals included among Gray's close circle of friends and correspondents claim to have been taken aback both by the referential obscurity and by the metrical and stanzaic peculiarities of the *Odes*. Walpole, who was eventually to send off copies of both *The Progress of Poesy* and *The Bard* ('two amazing odes of Mr. Gray') to Horace Mann in Italy, would confess to his old correspondent when he did so, 'they are Greek, they are Pindaric, they are sublime – consequently I fear a little obscure'. 'I could not persuade him to add more notes,' Walpole further wrote to Mann of their author, 'he says whatever wants to be explained, don't deserve to be'.[6] Gray, who would in time submit to including in a later (1768) edition of his poetry extensive notes to both poems, originally – as Walpole's comments remind us – resisted providing any such textual or editorial assistance to readers of the two odes. Although he continued to protest that there were few references in either poem that could not be understood by any reasonably educated reader who took the time patiently to read the lines, Gray had clearly and deliberately presented even to the most loyal of those readers works that stood in marked contrast to his earlier poetry. The fundamental and defining characteristic of the odes, Gray's denials to the contrary notwithstanding, remains to this day the striking contrast they seem to form – structurally, metrically, stylistically, linguistically, and substantively – to his previously published poems.

*

Odes written in the Pindaric manner had been wildly popular in the years immediately following the restoration of Charles II in 1660. Critics such as Eric Rothstein have speculated that the form's ability easily to be manipulated by those seeking to write panegyrics on a wide variety of individuals and historical events, as well as its generic capacity likewise easily to include in its stanzas some of the methods of competing,

---

[5] Lonsdale, *PTG*, 157.
[6] *WC* xxi.120.

heroic narratives, rendered it a particularly useful tool for the poets of the final decades of the seventeenth century. 'With it, unlike narrative,' Rothstein points out of the Pindaric model, 'poets could choose whether or not to build on any historical event. Fashion and practicality declared for it.'[7] Abraham Cowley was easily the most prominent of those poets who exploited the form to its fullest extent. In works such as his 1660 'Ode upon the Blessed Restoration', and also, even earlier, in the 'Pindarique Odes' included in his 1657 collection of *Poems*, Cowley reintroduced the irregular ode as one of the most popular forms of occasional, panegyric poetry. His most memorable odes participated in an enthusiastic and at times confusingly jumbled play-space of praise and paean. There is something peculiarly Augustan in the gleeful and circumambient inclusivity of Cowley's odes. Although the actual prosodic structures which governed Pindar's original Greek odes would not properly be analyzed and described until the early nineteenth century, Cowley and his many imitators both in his own and in later generations – Dryden, Congreve, Prior, and Pope all prominently among them – attempted as best they could to capture something of Pindar's formality, something of his structural and architectonic solidity, and something also of his peculiarly allusive and what some have described as 'gnomic' manner of reference to mythical history.

The tail end of the seventeenth century, however, had already witnessed a decline in the popularity of the form; Congreve, for example, eventually, in his 1705 *Discourse on the Pindarique Ode*, repented his own attempts at the kind, condemning both Cowley and his Pindaric models as 'a Bundle of rambling incoherent Thoughts, express'd in a like Parcel of irregular Stanzas'. 'I believe those irregular Odes of Mr. Cowley', Congreve elaborated, 'may have been the principal though innocent occasion, of so many deformed Poems since, which instead of being true Pictures of Pindar, have (to use the Italian Painters Term) been only Caricatures of him, Resemblances that for the most part have been either Horrid or Ridiculous.'[8] The blissful and breathless enthusiasm that both prompted and, more often than not, found itself featured in Congreve's earlier, Cowleyan models was likewise deemed excessive and unwarranted. Poets throughout the period might still from time to time be found experimenting with the form, but few poets writing in the early or mid-eighteenth century would have attempted to follow up the success of a poem such as the *Elegy* with odes written in a mode that had long been dismissed by many as too obscure, too formulaic, and

---

[7] Rothstein, 4.

[8] William Congreve, 'A Discourse on the Pindarique Ode' in *The Complete Works of William Congreve*, ed. Montague Summers, 4 vols. (New York: Russell and Russell, 1964) iv.82;85.

simply – to eyes and minds unused to its structural complexity – too difficult to read.

Why, then, was this the rhetorical move which Gray now chose – and chose only after the careful consideration of years – to make? Lonsdale's assertion that the poet had been 'embarrassed' by his former popularity, and that he consequently desired to 'puzzle' his readers surely holds at least one possible key to Gray's motives; it is the precise nature of this 'embarrassment' that must be examined. By the middle years of the 1750s, the barely concealed sub-texts of much of Gray's earlier, published poetry had begun already to give him pause. As we have seen, it was one thing to have documents expressing (and to his own eyes very *clearly* expressing) his continuing love for and indebtedness to West circulating among his nearest friends and colleagues; it was quite another to see those same documents being clapper-clawed by the palms of seemingly every vulgar poetaster, or praised in rapturous language by all the 'People of Qualitie' in the kingdom. Gray on one level felt that in turning such poems as the *Eton Ode* and the *Elegy* over to the public, he had lost both the physical and the rather less tangible intellectual possession of something that had once *belonged* to him, of something which, indeed, was little less than a part of himself – an emanation, for all its own richness of allusion, of his own private emotional and spiritual life. That a testament such as the *Elegy*, once linked to Gray himself, could even possibly be read as a transparent statement of affection and desire on the part of the poet – a blueprint to his private state of mind – came very close to terrifying him. Gray soon also began to realize that poems such as the *Eton Ode*, similarly written in direct response to West's death, now revealed to his own eyes far too much about his state of mind than he would ever be comfortable with. Gray's continued resistance to the criticism that his Pindaric odes needed editorial glossing in order fully to be understood by his readers begins to make sense only when we take him at his word. Given his recent and anticipated experience with the 'reader–response' criticism to poems such as the *Eton Ode* and the *Elegy* in the form of reviews, imitations, and parodies, Gray seems genuinely to have felt that the last thing his readers needed from him was any further assistance in interpreting or deciphering his poetry. True, he had written in a mode known for its 'difficulty', and part of him was proud simply to have produced the kind of poetry that he felt better reflected his status as a scholar; yet another part honestly dreaded to learn what he may inadvertently have revealed about himself even in such densely and at times obscurely referential works.

In order for us more fully to understand this element of Gray's design in following up the *Elegy* with the more rigorously allusive odes of 1757, it will be necessary for us to jump ahead in the narrative of Gray's life for one moment – to the year 1763. At that time, a parody of the *Eton*

Ode was published that provides us with a glimpse of everything that Gray, transforming his poetic style in the mid-1750s, feared most from a remorselessly curious and at times dangerously perceptive reading public. The Pindaric odes of 1757 would famously attract their own parodists and imitators, to be sure, but in so doing they would further draw attention away from the more personal poetry in which, Gray himself now realized, he had – for all his attempts at parodic and allusive deflection – spoken out far too clearly.

*

The *Eton Ode*, it will be recalled, had first been published as a folio pamphlet by Dodsley in 1747 and was only subsequently included, in January, 1748, in that same publisher's popular *Collection of Poems . . . By Several Hands*. Like the *Elegy*, the *Eton Ode* attracted the close attention of imitators and parodists throughout Gray's lifetime. The anonymous 'Ode on Ranelagh, Addressed to the Ladies', first published in 1763, was only one of several professed imitations of the *Eton Ode*, imitations that in actual fact often constituted scrupulously precise textual parodies of Gray's original. Central lines from the original *Eton Ode* are retained nearly unchanged in these parodies, and the relationship connecting such 'imitations' to what some would call their 'target text' remained at all times clearly delineated and in the foreground. The 1763 'Ode to Ranelagh' was to be especially noteworthy, however, for the manner in which it managed to retain such threats as it perceived to be central to the *Eton* ode – particularly the threats of time, experience, and the dangers inherent in the fact of a peculiarly masculine maturity – yet at the same time redirected the relentless movement of Gray's original. If Gray's poem begins in sunshine and ends in the inevitable darkness of human maturity, the anonymous Ranelagh parody constructs an ostensibly less tragic song of experience by beginning in the night and false illusion of the pleasure gardens in Chelsea to move towards a more 'enlightened' experience in the world at large.

Many mid-century novelists and critics of the masquerade attacked Ranelagh and Vauxhall as the haunts of the vulgar and the unscrupulous, and the venues for indiscreet assignations. William Whitehead's popular 'Song for Ranelagh Gardens', emphatically depicted the 'frolicsome Round' of the Rotunda as the province of 'Flirts' and 'pert Little Things' who sought to reappropriate phallic authority and, in a gesture similar to that which distressed Justice Fielding and the Middlesex magistrates so much in the increasingly popular masquerades, confound societally sanctioned gender boundaries. In her 1986 study of the reversals of social and sexual hierarchies accomplished in the 'collective metamorphoses' of the eighteenth-century masquerade, the critic Terry Castle

placed particular emphasis on the erotic inversions possible in the intoxicating realms of Heiddegger's Haymarket assembly room, Cornelys's
Carlisle House, and – by mid-century – Ranelagh's Rotunda. By oblit-
erating (or at least obscuring) the 'distinguishing Mark of the Sexes', the
proprietors of masquerades and other festivals in the carnival space of
Ranelagh gardens initiated a sexual chaos that could lead not only to
the dreadful extremes of effeminacy and actual homosexual intrigues
and 'abominations', but to an equally threatening confusion and viola-
tion of imposed heterosexual roles. The transformative powers of the
masquerade could – at the very worst – result in the establishment of a
'feminocracy', the masquerade venue itself temporarily metamorpho-
sized into 'a gynesium'[9]. Roy Porter has similarly observed: 'Masked
balls, such as those staged in Soho by Casanova's one-time-lover Mrs
Cornelys, were well-known fronts for pick-ups – "the whole Design
of the libidinous Assembly seems to terminate in Assignations and
intrigues." '[10]

Both Whitehead's Ranelagh 'Song' and the parody of the *Eton Ode*
which followed in its metrical footsteps picked up on this popular
presentation of the masquerades at Ranelagh as the gender-less or at
least gender-confused arena of sexual intrigue, erotic chaos, and emasculation. The threat was made particularly clear in Whitehead's short
'Song':

> Ye Belles! and ye Flirts! and ye pert Little Things!
>   Who trip in the frolicsome Round,
> Pray tell me, From whence this indecency springs,
>   The Sexes at once to confound?
> What means the cocked hat, and the masculine Air;
>   With each motion designed to perplex?
> Bright eyes were intended to languish: – not stare!
>   And softness, the test of your Sex . . .
>
> The VENUS, whose statue delights all Mankind,
>   Shrinks modestly back from the view;
> And kindly should seem, by the Artist designed,
>   To serve as a model for you!
> Then learn, with her beauties, to copy her Air;
>   Nor venture too much to reveal!
> Our fancies will paint what you cover with care;
>   And double each charm you conceal.

[9] Terry Castle, *Masquerade and Civilization* (Stanford: Stanford University Press, 1986)
254.
[10] Roy Porter, *English Society in the Eighteenth Century* (London: Penguin, 1982; 1990)
264.

The blushes of Morn, and the mildness of May,
  Are charms which no art can procure!
O, be but yourselves! and our homage we'll pay;
  And your empire is solid and sure!
But if, Amazon-like, you attack your Gallants,
  And put us in fear of our lives;
You may do very well for Sister and Aunts!
  But believe me, you'll never be Wives!

The gardens at Ranelagh here become the dangerous playground – the forum for parodic expression – for the female assumption of a confounding semiotic system that blurs and occludes the empowering distinctions of masculine authority. The assumption by the females of a particular masquerade libertinism, sexual formulations, immodest costume, martial prowess: *all* the carnivalesque violations emphasized as threatening to masculine authority are here. The predatory females at Ranelagh forsake the imposed sexual and social distinctions – the required behavioral patterns – which would allow them some place in the male hierarchy. By assuming the clear eyed 'Masculine air' of their suitors and potential husbands, they not only displace those masculine figures, but (they are told) put themselves in danger of securing only the subsidiary and marginalized female roles of chaste sisters and maiden aunts. They not only jeopardize their sexuality, they are denied *real* sexual identity, by their assumption of a sexually aggressive or even sexually active role. They are to be punished, bullied, ridiculed, and teased into submission. The central female place in the patrilineal hierarchy – that of the heir-producing wife – is refused them, and reserved for another less threatening, less demanding feminine type – a type who knows enough to follow the imposed patterns of an aesthetic, mythological, and sexual tradition the very aim and purpose of which is to delight '*Man*kind'. Henry Fielding had condemned the sites of the masquerades (sites such as Ranelagh) as 'in Reality the Temples of Iniquity', and places which the Middlesex magistrates declared to promote 'the Corruption of the Morals of both Sexes'. Whitehead's 'Song' echoes Fielding's moral condemnation of Ranelagh and, in its warning against the 'Amazon-like' women who frequent the Rotunda similarly calls to mind Fielding's earlier description (in his 1728 poem *The Masquerade*) of female masquerade participants as an 'Amazonian race'.

The 'Ode on Ranelagh' begins with a description of the great hall and the surrounding pleasure gardens in Chelsea that is a precise parody of the opening stanzas of the *Eton Ode*. Yet whereas Gray's original strikes a confident tone of calm and nostalgic reminiscence that is maintained until the structural turning point of the poem between the fifth and sixth stanzas, its parodic counterpart is much more tentative in establishing its ethos towards the target text:

> YE dazzling lamps, ye jocund fires,
>   That from yon fabric shine,
> Where grateful pleasure yet admires
>   Her Lacy's great design:
> And ye, who from the fields which lie
>   Round Chelsea, with amazement's eye,
> The gardens, and the dome survey
>   Whose walks, whose trees, whose lights among,
> Wander the courtly train along
>   Their thought-dispelling way.[11]

This first stanza seems to suggest an affectionate nostalgia similar to Gray's original. 'Dazzling', 'jocund', 'grateful pleasure': the language of the parody reinforces a playful attitude towards Gray's poem, as does the comically inappropriate substitution of James Lacy's Rotunda for the bronze statue of Henry VI – 'Henry's holy shade' – which stands in the centre of the Eton School-Yard. Only the reference to the 'thought-dispelling' walks in the stanza's final line prepares the reader for the derisory tone that begins to creep into the second and third stanzas:

> Ah, splendid room! ah, pleasing shade!
>   Ah, walks belov'd in vain!
> Where oft in happier times I stray'd,
>   A stranger then to pain:
> I feel the gales, which from you blow
>   A momentary bliss bestow,
> As waving fresh their gladsome wing,
>   They seem to sooth my famish'd soul,
> And redolent of tea, and roll,
>   To breath a second spring.
>
> Rotunda, say, for thou hast seen
>   Full many a sprightly race,
> In thy bright round with step serene,
>   The paths of pleasure trace;
> Who chiefly now delight to lave
>   Green hyson in the boiling wave,
> The sable coffee which distill?

---

[11] 'Ode on Ranelagh. Addressed to the Ladies', in *The Poetical Calender*, ed. Fawkes and Woty (London, 1763) v. 93–97.

> What longing progeny are found,
> Who stroll incessant round and round,
>   Like horses in a mill?

The 'gales redolent of tea and roll', the 'Green hyson', the miniaturiza-
tion of the 'boiling wave' and the luxurious 'sable tea' all recall the
mock-heroic status granted to the material paraphernalia gathered
around Belinda in Pope's *Rape of the Lock*. Yet the gentle affection and
even fascination that temper Pope's account of feminine pleasure and
coquetry and which, ultimately, provide him with an opportunity for a
more complicated satiric critique of sexual behavior and contemporary
courtship rituals is absent from the Ranelagh parody. The harsh description of the Ranelagh women as horses incessantly circling the rotunda
anticipates Squire Bramble's depiction of the tedium of Ranelagh's entertainments in Smollett's *Humphry Clinker*.

The trivialization of the gardens at Ranelagh (in the fourth stanza the
more significantly metaphorical 'unknown regions' of the *Eton Ode* are
transformed into the garden's maze that offers an opportunity for sexual
assignation and recrimination) is in fact preparatory to a trivialization
of the threat of masculine maturity itself, and the shifting of the responsibility for a tragic and ultimately inescapable self-knowledge ready to
strike the Eton childhood, to a sought after (and, one is led to suppose,
well-deserved) misery on behalf of the Ranelagh 'ladies'. The fourth
stanza derides the 'gravely stupid' concentration that passes for thought
among such women, but also stresses the very real danger of being
caught in an illicit assignation:

> Alas! regardless of their doom,
>   The lovely victims rove;
> No sense of sufferings yet to come
>   Can now their prudence move:
> But see! where all around them wait
>   The ministers of female fate,
> An artful, perjur'd cruel train;
>   Ah! show them where in ambush stand,
> To seize their prey, the faithless band
>   Of false deceitful men!
>
> These shall the lust of gaming wear,
>   That harpy of the mind,
> With all the troop of rage and fear,
>   That follow close behind:
> Or pining love shall waste their youth,
>   Or jealousy with rankling tooth
> That gnaws bright Hymen's golden chain,

Who opens wide the fateful gate,
For sad distrust, and ruthless hate,
    And Sorrow's pallid train.

Ambition this shall tempt to fix
    Her hopes on something high,
To barter for a coach and six
    Her peace and liberty.
The stings of Scandal shall these try,
    And Affectations haughty eye,
That scowls on those it us'd to greet;
    The cutting sneer, th'abusive song,
And false report that glides along
    With never-resting feet.
        . . .

To each her suff'rings: all must grieve,
    And pour a silent groan,
At homage others charms receive,
    Or slights that meet their own:
But all the voice of truth severe
    Will suit the gay, regardless ear,
Whose joy in mirth and revels lies!
    Thought would destroy this paradise
No more! – Where ignorance is bliss,
    'Tis folly to be wise.

In both the *Eton Ode* and the parodic 'Ode on Ranelagh', the threat that is being articulated is a specifically masculine one. The children on the playing fields of Eton are yet ignorant they *are* men, and are thus 'little victims, regardless of their doom'. In a similar manner, the false and deceitful men who lie in wait just beyond the dazzling lamps of the Rotunda are a threat to the females in 'Ranelagh'. In the parody, however, the threat is perceived to be an external one – the postlapsarian condition is one that might well be avoided, but is instead actively sought after and courted. Men may be 'false' and 'deceitful', but the women work to bring their fate upon themselves. In the *Eton Ode* masculinity signifies maturity, adversity, responsibility, and inescapable care; in 'Ranelagh' the threat is localized to the consequences of sexual aggression and internecine feminine jealousy. The great cares of masculine maturity are transformed into the petty and pointedly avoidable woes of female love, jealousy, mistrust, and marital ambition. The final, epigrammatic line of Gray's poem – 'Where Ignorance is bliss, 'tis folly to be wise' – is itself transformed from a temporary blessing into a strikingly nasty dismissal of feminine capacity for change.

The fact that these tensions involving gender are typically picked up by the parodists of Gray's poem – and the very fact that the calm and unruffled surfaces of Gray's verse could be stirred up with such vigor by a contemporary audience – was something that a man of Gray's temperament found particularly threatening. Gray's original *Eton Ode* had confined itself to the world of *masculine* pleasures – the homoerotic intensity of schoolboy attachments – and to the world of *masculine* cares. Any reference to the overtly feminine was repressed or otherwise carefully blocked from the vision of the poet. Gray's parodists, however, chose to make central to their work precisely those 'feminine' elements that the poet himself had purposefully pushed to one side – precisely those 'female' elements which he had repressed. The ultimate ethos of the 'Ranelagh' parody is dismissive and misogynistic, yet it again seems on some level to 'understand' its target text more fully than the most superficial thematic analysis might be willing to concede. The exclusion of feminine power and identity from Gray's original – the boundaries of gender which Gray had taken care *not* to articulate on the surface level of his poem's meaning – is precisely the focus of the parodic response to the *Eton Ode*. The threat of such an awareness in parody formed one of the motivating elements in Gray's growing desire himself to control the responses of his readers to his work.

*

When Gray first sent the copy of his 'Ode in the Greek Manner' to Wharton on his thirty-seventh birthday in 1754, he claimed at one and the same time to be bored with the piece, while still expressing a familiar anxiety lest the poem pass from Wharton's own hands and into those of a larger audience. Although already contemplating both the form and the subject matter of those pieces he would be working on in the coming year (i.e. *The Bard* and the unfinished *Ode on the Pleasure Arising from Vicissitude*), Gray was yet undecided as to the manner in which such short and potentially baffling works might best be presented to a wider though still select audience. As Lonsdale and other critics have speculated, the most obvious solution to Gray's problem was to withhold publication of the 'Ode' until he had himself completed enough poetry to justify a separate – if still small – volume. By the spring and early summer of 1755 Gray appears to have given the piece a new title, referring to the work in a letter to Bedingfield for the first time as 'The Powers of Poetry'. He seems also throughout the course of that year, even as he continued work on his unfinished verses, to have grown increasingly less satisfied with the first of his Pindaric efforts. Mason asked to be sent a copy, but Gray chose on this occasion to leave his friend's curiosity unsatisfied. To Bedingfield he had first written: 'I have been already threatened with publication, tho' there is no more than three copies of it in the world. To abate your curiosity I assure you it is very incorrect, & being wrote by fits and starts at very distant intervals is so unequal that it will hardly admit of individual corrections'. By the end of the year he sent Bedingfield the opening stanza of the poem, dismissing the whole effort as 'no favourite of mine'.

Although, again, many of Gray's earliest readers professed themselves puzzled by the supposedly intricate organization of the poem, its construction was surprising or dramatic only to the degree that it attempted rigorously and rationally to conform to the Pindaric mode. *The Progress of Poesy*, as Gosse was to note precisely, was 'a poem of three stanzas, in an elaborately consistent verse-form, with forty-one lines in each stanza. The length of these periods is relieved by the regular division of each stanza into strophe, antistrophe, and epode . . .'.[12] Further commenting on Gray's ability to recreate 'the Greek quality of structure in his lyrical work', Gosse finally observed of the odes: 'His poems, whatever they are, are never chains of consecutive stanzas; each line, each group of lines, has its proper place in a structure that could not be shorter or longer without a radical re-arrangement of ideas'. Gray, in other words, tried as best he could to recreate the rhythms of his Greek originals within the formal confines of English prosody. The complex but regular and highly structured pattern of his original model is copied in his own, clear repetition of strophe, antistrophe, and epode. The strophes and epodes are written in such a manner so as to reflect their ostensible purpose of being sung to the accompaniment of music and dancing.

Yet *The Progress of Poesy* was not only, as later critics such as Gosse were quick to point out, a piece that sought by structural and stylistic means to reproduce the feel and the lyric movement of the triumphal odes or *epinikia* of Pindar; it was likewise a piece which (finally) identified itself even in its title as a 'progress' poem. The first of Gray's Pindaric *Odes*, therefore, as Lonsdale has commented,

belongs to one of the most popular poetic genres of the seventeenth and eighteenth centuries, a genre which flourished as the Augustans developed a historical perspective that established them as the heirs in a direct line of succession from the civilizations of ancient Greece and Rome. The purpose of the progress poem was to expound this genealogy, tracing back their arts and virtues to Greece and then describing the continuous historical and geographical progress westward to Britain. The route could show minor variations, but usually proceeded through Rome and medieval Italy. . . . Only in Britain was true liberty to be found, according to the Augustans, so that the arts had inevitably settled there.[13]

[12] Gosse, 118.
[13] Lonsdale, *PTG*, 160.

Gray's poem sets out to argue that poetry is nothing less than a gift from the gods. The music of the lyre can soothe the cares of mankind and inspire the individual with heaven-sent joy. The celebration of an aesthetic function is combined with a nationalist purpose – the latter of which would appear incidently to voice its author's own ambition to be ranked high among the most celebrated poets of the English tradition.

Gray's *Progress of Poesy* opens with a memorable epigraph from the second of Pindar's *Olympian Odes*:

φωνᾶντα συνετοῖσιν ·ἐς
δὲ τὸ πᾶν ἑρμηνέων χατίζει

The quotation, once translated into English, cautions readers that the verses that follow are properly 'vocal to the intellect' or 'to those who understand', only; 'all others [will] need interpreters'. In this particular instance, an awareness of the precise context from within which Gray extracted these lines might possibly add something to the significance of his epigraph. Pindar's original reads:

πολλά μοι ὑπ᾽ ἀγκῶνος ὠκέα βέλη
ἔνδον ἐντι φαρέτρας
φωνᾶντα συνετοῖσιν ·ἐς δὲ τὸ πᾶν ἑρμηνέων
χατίξει. σοφὸς ὁ πολλὰ ⲉἰδὼς φυᾷ· μαθόντεϛ δὲ λάβροι
παγγλωσσίᾳ κόρακεϛ ὥς, ἄκραντα γαρύⲉτον
Διὸς πρὸς ὄρνιχα θεῖον.[14]

[I have many more such arrows as this in the quiver beneath my arm, many arrows that will be understood only by those who understand; the crowd will need interpreters. The true poet is one whose gift has been bestowed upon him by nature; but those who possess merely a formal knowledge of song are like grappling crows, cawing vainly in the face of the god-like bird of Zeus.]

The immediate context of Pindar's original lines underscores the fact that Gray was indeed defying the interpretive abilities of his critics in his latest poetry, yet they manage at the same time to suggest something of the poet's anxiety that his recourse to such a rigorous poetic form might be regarded by some as the revelation of his own 'true' nature as a writer given to correctness and scholarly precision, but one who lacked true inspiration. The epigraph is meant defiantly to signal to Gray's most learned readers – those whose opinion meant most to him – that he was a poet of divine inspiration no less than he was a craftsman of impeccable style and form; that he was, in fact, a poet by nature as much as

[14] Pindar, Olympian II (For Theron of Acragas) ll.149–58.

he was a poet by art. The contest between artistry and inspiration figured in Pindar's lines seems further to highlight the connection of such a seemingly impersonal (or at least personally unrevealing) poem, to its deep and genuine subtext as an expression of Gray's mourning for his mother.

The opening lines of Gray's poem spectacularly invoke the sacred and classical sources of poetic inspiration. They are among the most exhilarating and exuberant lines Gray would ever write:

> Awake, Aeolian lyre, awake,
> And give to rapture all thy trembling strings.
> From Helicon's harmonious springs
> A thousand rills their mazy progress take:
> The laughing flowers, that round them blow,
> Drink life and fragrance as they flow.
> Now the rich stream of music winds along,
> Deep, majestic, smooth, and strong,
> Through verdant vales and Ceres' golden reign:
> Now rolling down the steep amain,
> Headlong, impetuous, see it pour:
> The rocks and nodding groves rebellow to the roar. (*PTG* 161–63)

The 'mazy progress' of Gray's imagery and rhythm leads to an oddly onomatopoeic effect in the stanza's final line, by which point the vital fecundity of lyric poetry – a force which feeds the very music of life in its impetuous progress – threatens to escape the poet's control. Having once established the 'headlong' and 'impetuous' power of the twin springs of Helicon sacred to the muses, Gray deftly directs the reader's attention in the next stanza to the power of harmony to quiet and to calm 'the turbulent sallies of the soul'. Jove himself, the poet notes, has on memorable occasions been compelled to submit to the seductive charms of the Muses. Mars, too, has been calmed by music. In its open acknowledgement of the seemingly paradoxical 'powers' of poetry, the passage recalls the rhetorical query of John Dryden's 1687 *A Song for St. Cecilia's Day*: 'What passion cannot music raise and quell?' Gray's lines emphasize the view that the harmony of the lyre – the 'Sovereign of the willing soul' – alone possesses the ability to 'produce all the graces of motion in the body'. Pindar's golden lyre awakens the dance and emboldens the voice to sing the praises of Venus 'with antic Sports and blue-eyed Pleasures'. Now swiftly, now slowly – 'Frisking light in frolic measures; / Now pursuing, now retreating' – inspired by cadences of the poet, the graces dance their evanescent attendance on the goddess. The force of the dance and the patterned harmonies of the music give birth and then nurture 'the bloom of young desire and the purple light of love'.

Having thus emphasized the necessary participation of the lyre and the poet–musician in the grand and universal dance of love, Gray begins the poem's second triad with a strophe that abruptly recalls the mortal darkness which concluded his own *Eton Ode*. In so doing he moves the reader to consider both the potential and the actual role of music and 'poesy' in human society:

> Man's feeble race what ills await,
> Labour, and penury, the racks of pain,
> Disease, and sorrow's weeping train,
> And death, sad refuge from the storms of fate!
> The fond complaint, my song, disprove,
> And justify the laws of Jove. (*PTG* 167)

The deliberate recollection of the theological and ontological imperatives articulated in the opening lines of Milton's *Paradise Lost* would seem to underscore Robert Gleckner's contention that throughout the middle years of his poetic career, Gray continued to be profoundly engaged with – not to say haunted by – the near-inescapable poetic achievement of his epic predecessor. The form of the traditional epic question that follows, however, is phrased in such a manner so as to render its 'answer' something of a forgone conclusion: 'Say', Gray asks of the disposition of Jove, 'has he given in vain the heavenly Muse?'. The response, of course, is an emphatic 'No'. At least not if Gray has anything to say about it. The remaining verses of Gray's poem together trace the civilizing influence of poetry across an exquisitely imagined landscape of 'ice-built mountains' and 'boundless forests'. The epode (II.iii) describes the displacement of poetic genius from Greece to Italy in the classical period. The eventual 'progress' of the Muses to English soil contains some of the most lyrically concise and subtly referential lines Gray ever composed:

> Woods that wave o'er Delphi's steep,
> Isles that crown the Aegean deep,
> Fields that cool Ilissus laves,
> Or where Maeander's amber waves
> In lingering lab'rinths creep,
> How do your tuneful echoes languish,
> Mute but to the voice of anguish?
> Where each old poetic mountain
> Inspiration breathed around:
> Every shade and hallowed fountain
> Murmured deep a solemn sound:
> Till the sad Nine in Greece's evil hour
> Left their Parnassus for the Latian plains.

Alike they scorn the pomp of tyrant-power,
And coward Vice that revels in her chains.
When Latium had her lofty spirit lost,
They sought, oh Albion! Next thy sea-encircled coast. (*PTG* 170–72)

The third strophe follows the progress of the 'Mighty Mother' in her new island home. Gray's description of Shakespeare as a poet who, though he stands as a direct heir to the classical tradition, nevertheless remains first and foremost the fond and untutored 'darling' child of Nature, reflects a long-standing disinclination to acknowledge the determining role of art or craftsmanship in the dramatist's works. In a response to the gift of the Muses that seems little more than infantile, Shakespeare is described as a playful innocent, entrusted with a mighty and powerful gift – a gift which is possibly beyond his means of control:

To him the mighty Mother did unveil
Her awful face: the dauntless child
Stretched forth his little arms and smiled.
'This pencil take,' (she said) 'whose colours clear
Richly paint the vernal year:
Thine too these golden keys, immortal boy!
This can unlock the gates of joy;
Of horror that and thrilling fears,
Or ope the sacred source of sympathetic tears.' (*PTG* 172–73)

The antistrophe that follows celebrates the achievements of Milton ('. . . second he, that rode sublime / Upon the seraph-wings of Ecstasy, / The secrets of the abyss to spy') and Dryden, whose 'less presumptuous car' rode 'Wide o'er the fields of glory'. Having thus summoned the most illustrious and inviolable of his predecessors, Gray is careful not to lay particular stress on the legitimacy of his own place in the line of succession he has so exclusively outlined above; the final epode of his poem, looks rather to articulate a modest regret that the lyre once handled by Shakespeare, by Milton, and – more recently – by Dryden, should now have passed into such supposedly unworthy hands:

Oh! lyre divine, what daring spirit
Wakes thee now? Though he inherit
Nor the pride nor ample pinion,
That the Theban eagle bear
Sailing with supreme dominion
Through the azure deep of air:
Yet oft before his infant eyes would run
Such forms of glitter in the Muse's ray

With orient hues, unborrowed of the sun:
Yet shall he mount and keep his distant way
Beyond the limits of a vulgar fate,
Beneath the Good how far – but far above the Great. (*PTG* 176–77)

*

It should at once be stated that Gray's artful and painstaking recreation of the Pindaric mode in English easily assures *The Progress of Poesy* a well-deserved place among the most truly remarkable poetic achievements of the age. The ode stands as one of the most ambitious products a literary culture which considered itself most noteworthy not so much for its generic innovations in prose fiction, nor, even, for its groundbreaking achievements in such areas as literary biography or narrative history, but rather, for its unprecedented poetic self-consciousness; the eighteenth century was a period which, however predictably unreliable any of its other, contemporary attempts at comprehensive self-definition may eventually have proven, prided itself most and with greatest accuracy on its generic awareness. Insofar as Gray's ode constituted a thorough-going revitalization of both form and substance in the history of English poetry, it was the quintessential product of precisely this cultural knowledge. In its final form, the ode comprised within the economic yet still elegantly architectonic movement of its three, linguistically precise triads a startlingly pure revisioning of an absolute potential for some of the most radical and hitherto unexplored, synchronic possibilities of style and meaning in English verse. As such, it stands as no mean accomplishment. Indeed, *The Progress of Poesy* asks to some extent be read as an exuberant and exhilarating manifesto. The elegant and allusively structured alternation of its patient strophes, antistrophes, and epodes lends the ode an air of classical dignity that is very nearly unprecedented in the English tradition. The implicit challenge of its design – the gauntlet its innovation proudly throws down before the tired conventions and the threadbare tropes and genres that seemed increasingly to constitute the self-satisfied banality of mid-eighteenth-century English poetry – announces the appearance of an informed and innovative generic experiment. Gray's ode demands that its readers stand up and take notice of its reclamation of poetic form and meaning. It insists that they pay attention to a timely reiteration that poets and poetry *per se* have important jobs to do. Gray's self-consciously ambitious engagement with many of the most difficult aspects of his Theban predecessor's intricate and technically sophisticated hymns pulled no punches in its acknowledgement of and practical confrontation with the dazzlingly complex history of the lyric impulse in the western tradition. *The Progress of Poesy* at the same time attempted to incorporate an intellectual comprehension of generic form and translation theory into a new and delightfully vital artistic creation, and so stands by any stretch of the imagination as a truly astounding achievement. In terms of its dazzling technical proficiency, and with due regard the sheer pride and effort it displays in the resultant spectacle of an active and eager poetic genius at work and at the height of his powers, *The Progress of Poesy* in some respects surpasses even the inevitable touchstone of the *Elegy* as the most impressive of Gray's achievements as a poet.

In the many years that have passed since *The Progress of Poesy* was first printed in 1757, the early glow of its novelty gradually faded away; the work's subsequent status as a bemusing if curiously self-indulgent experiment in prosody and poetic form slowly ossified into a tendency on the part of general readers to regard the ode as a designedly abstruse and unfortunately anaemic metrical curiosity. The condemnation of critics such as Samuel Johnson resulted finally in a critical neglect that rendered the bold and unapologetic intellect of the poem's artifice prey, finally, to the disregard of the most vociferous of Gray's modern critics. For many years the poem attracted little critical attention. The deeper causes that motivated this neglect remain uncertain. The ode, together with its eventual companion piece, *The Bard*, were to stand head and shoulders above any of the other poetry to published in that same year; the innovation of its design only further highlighted the imitative nature of the efforts of poets such as William Whitehead and William Wilkie. John Dyer's Virgilian didactic poem celebrating England's wool trade, *The Fleece*, was likewise perhaps ambitious in scope, but unremarkable and derivative both in design and execution.

Gray himself claimed never to have held out much hope for the popular success of the ode. His friends also, as we have seen, expressed their concern regarding the work's supposed obscurity. They continued to press him to provide some sort of textual apparatus for his readers, but the poet refused for a long time to add even the most basic explanatory glosses. 'I do not love notes', he wrote to Walpole, 'They are signs of weakness and obscurity. If a thing cannot be understood without them, it had better be not understood at all'. Such comments formed Gray's response to his friend's protestation that both *The Progress of Poesy* and *The Bard* were arresting but inscrutable. Bedingfield, for his part, was to confide that he had overheard three fashionable members of society discussing the Pindaric *Odes* while at the York races, and passed on their judgement that the verses were 'impenetrable & inexplicable'. 'They wish'd I had told them in prose', Gray perceived, 'what I meant in verse'.

*

Throughout the autumn and winter of 1755, Gray's health grew increasingly precarious. As early as July he had perceived that he was 'not quite right'. He began to suffer from repeated and debilitating attacks of gout, and derived little if any benefit from a regimen of medicine that seemed on occasion to comprehend the entire stock-in-trade of an Apothecary's shop. He wrote to Chute, detailing the variety of his complaints:

I have had *advice*, & have been bloodied, & taken draughts of salt of Wormwood, Lemons, Tincture of Guiacum, Magnesia, & the Devil. you will immediately conclude, they thought me rheumatic & feverish. no such thing! they thought me gouty, & that I had no fever. all I can say is, that my heats in the morning are abated, that my foot begins to ach again, & that my head achs, & feels light and giddy. (*CTG* 431)

Gray spent weeks laid up at Stoke throughout the autumn months, further troubled by a combination of aches and soreness in his legs and feet, persistent light-headedness, 'broken and unrefreshing sleeps', chronic headaches, a skin rash, and chest pains. 'These symptoms', he demurred to Wharton, 'are all too slight to make an illness; but they do not make perfect health. That is sure.' In the course of the preceding summer Gray had paid another visit to Chute. His host was only beginning to recover from the shock of having lost his heir and nephew, and the recent death of his old travelling companion Francis Whithed cast a melancholy gloom over Gray's stay at the Vyne. He remained with Chute for only a few days before undertaking an excursion to Southampton, Winchester, Portsmouth, and Netley Abbey, returning to Stoke on 31 July. He continued there in 'a very listless, unpleasant, & inutile state of Mind'.

Even in the face of such setbacks, Gray continued to work sporadically on his own original compositions. Work on *The Bard* was apparently suspended for a period of several months; although two-thirds of the poem existed in draft, any attempts to bring the second 'odikle' to a conclusion were temporarily abandoned. Gray was reported to have been working on yet another Pindaric ode, a composition celebrating 'The Liberty of Genius'. This project came to nothing, and only a fragment of the poem's argument remains. 'All that men of power can do for men of genius' Gray had intended to argue, 'is leave them at their liberty, compared to birds that, when confined to a cage, do but regret the loss of their freedom in melancholy strains, and loose the luscious wildness and happy luxuriance of their notes, which used to make the woods resound'.

Gray did manage, at about this time, to make some further progress on a poetic fragment that has since become known as the *Ode on the*

Pleasure Arising from Vicissitude. In his pocketbook for the year 1754, Gray had jotted down what appear to have been his first ideas for the poem, suggesting that it might effect a 'Contrast between the Winter past & coming spring'; he further noted that this contrast could lead nicely to a contemplation of 'Joy owing to that vicissitude. Many that never feel that delight. Sloth, envy Ambition. How much happier the rustic that feels it though he knows not how.' The form of the fragment we possess today suggests that the poet may have planned as many as nine, eight-line stanzas to have constituted the finished work. Gray managed to compose only the first few stanzas of this ode, however – roughly fifty-nine lines.

In sharp contrast to the more rigorously constructed stanzas and the self-consciously weighty rhythms of the two Pindaric *Odes*, the *Vicissitude Ode* is surprisingly light in tone and movement. The stately pentameters and hexameters of the Pindarics are replaced here by lighter tetrametres and trimetre lines. The opening verses may recall the classical language of Lucretius, but they are infused as well with a peculiar freshness and immediacy:

> Now the golden Morn aloft
> Waves her dew-bespangled wing;
> With vermeil cheek and whisper soft
> She wooes the tardy spring,
> Till April starts, and calls around
> The sleeping fragrance from the ground;
> And lightly o'er the living scene
> Scatters his freshest, tenderest green.
>
> New-born flocks in rustic dance
> Frisking ply their feeble feet;
> Forgetful of their wintry trance
> The birds his presence greet:
> But chief the sky-lark warbles high
> His trembling thrilling ecstasy
> And, lessening from the dazzled sight,
> Melts into air and liquid light. (*PTG* 202–03)

The awakening vitality of the 'tardy' spring morning is all the more striking when contrasted with the grim winter months from which it has so suddenly and magically emerged:

> Yesterday the sullen year
> Saw the snowy whirlwind fly;
> Mute was the music of the air,
> The herd stood drooping by:
> Their raptures now that wildly flow,

> Nor yesterday nor morrow know;
> 'Tis man alone that joy descries
> With forward and reverted eyes. (*PTG* 203–04)

The essence of Gray's humanism here focuses the reader's attention on man's unique abilities to remember and to interpret the past and to anticipate the future. The poet appears likewise to suggest, however, that in thus inescapably rooting his 'joys' outside of the lived and present moment – in rooting his happiness either in an act of retrospection or in a posture of grateful anticipation – man effectively defeats his own purposes. Present contentment, paradoxically, seems to be possible only when one is occupied in critically re evaluating the past or optimistically contemplating the future. All is not lost, however; armed with these twin weapons of 'Reflection' and 'Hope', Gray suggests, man can turn even his most painful experiences into the stuff of wisdom:

> Smile on past Misfortune's brow
> Soft Reflection's hand can trace;
> And o'er the cheek of Sorrow throw
> A melancholy grace;
> While Hope prolongs our happier hour,
> Or deepest shades, that dimly lower
> And blacken round our weary way,
> Gilds with a gleam of distant day. (*PTG* 204–05)

The turning of the poem's fifth stanza suggests the manner in which Gray planned further to contemplate this vision of man's interpretive vantage:

> Still, where rosy Pleasure leads,
> See a kindred Grief pursue;
> Behind the steps that Misery treads,
> Approaching Comfort view:
> The hues of bliss more brightly glow,
> Chastised by sabler tints of woe;
> And blended form, with artful strife,
> The strength and harmony of life. (*PTG* 205)

The last completed stanza of the poem concisely and concretely develops this vision of man's happiness as the result of the humble acknowledgment of the dramatically paratactic but still benevolent nature of all human experience:

> See the wretch, that long has tossed
> On the thorny bed of pain,
> At length repair his vigour lost,

And breathe and walk again:
The meanest flowret of the vale,
The simple note that swells the gale,
The common sun, the air and skies,
To him are opening Paradise. (*PTG* 205–06)

After this last, vivid stanza Gray's poem breaks down into less coherent fragments. The poem was transcribed by Mason into the second volume of Gray's Commonplace Book, where it was entitled 'Fragment of an Ode found amongst Mr. Grays papers after his decease and here transcribed from the corrected Copy'. Mason first printed the poem in his 1775 edition of Gray's *Works*.

*

The project that continued sporadically to occupy most of Gray's creative attention throughout this period, however, remained the Pindaric ode which was to develop in time into *The Bard*. Since putting the finishing touches on *The Progress of Poesy* in 1754, Gray had begun to delve deeper than ever before into the historical origins of English prosody. Whereas the first Pindaric *Ode* had unabashadly celebrated the shaping influence of the Classical and Italian traditions on English poetry, Gray's subsequent researches prompted him increasingly to consider the role played by alternate and frequently devalued poetic traditions. How did the practices and characteristics of Romance prosody (with its use of accentual–syllabic verse and rhyme), of German poetry (with its traditional alliterative verse form), and – increasingly more intriguing for Gray – of the 'bardic' Celtic poetry composed in Welsh, Cornish, and Breton, or the Gaelic verse of Ireland, Man, and Scotland, or even the Skaldic or Court poetry of Old Norse contribute to the traditions of modern English poetry?

The Bard recounts the circumstances of a legendary confrontation between the last of the ancient Welsh bards and the army of King Edward I on Mount Snowden. The incident was said to have taken place following Edward's subjection of the Welsh in 1283. Edward's nationalistic vision in the earliest years of his reign for a union of the British peoples, Gray expected his readers to remember, had been repeatedly frustrated by continued resistence both in Scotland and in Wales. In the latter kingdom, Prince Llewelyn ap Gruffydd, grandson of Llewellyn the Great of North Wales, led two separate rebellions against English overlordship, the first in 1277, the second just five years later. By 1284, Edward appeared decisively to have defeated the Welsh forces. He oversaw the imposition of English laws on the Celtic enemy, and set about dividing the conquered principality into shires on the English model. The construction of massive and costly castles at Conway, Carnarvon, Beaumarais, and Harlech served to proclaim English supremacy over the House of Llewelyn. Welsh resistance would continue throughout the middle years of the King's reign, however; Edward's rule was to be challenged by a further rebellion in 1287, and by yet another failed uprising in 1294–95. Each uprising against the English resulted only in more brutal repression of the Welsh rebels. In 1301, Edward felt secure enough to extend his claims in the area to include direct control over the feudal Marcher Lords (i.e. the lords of the Welsh 'march' or borderlands), and pointedly conferred upon his son, Edward, the title of Prince of Wales.

Gray's interest in the origins of rhyme in English poetry, as we have seen, had led him deeper and deeper into the study of Welsh poetry and language. Throughout the early and mid-1750s, he became increasingly convinced that the measures of English poetry 'not improbably might have been borrowed from the Britons, as I am apt to believe, the rise of Rhyme itself was'. The second volume of his Commonplace Book preserves a full seven folio pages of meticulous notes under the heading 'Cambri'. The particular incident that formed the narrative basis of Gray's *Bard* finds its immediate source in Thomas Carte's tremendous three-volume *History of England* (1747). Following Edward's subjection of the Welsh in 1283, Carte wrote:

> The onely set of men among the *Welsh*, that had reason to complain of *Edward*'s soverignty were the *Bards*, who used to put those remains of the antient *Britains* in mind of the valiant deeds of their ancestors: he ordered them all to be hanged, as inciters of the people to sedition. Politicks in this point got the better of the king's natural lenity: and those, who were afterwards entrusted with the government of the country, following his example, the profession became dangerous, gradually declined, and, in a little time, that sort of men was utterly destroyed.[15]

As critics of Gray's scholarship have repeatedly observed, it is more than likely that Gray was aware even as he read this description of Edward's persecution of the bards that Carte's account was not only unsubstantiated, but very close to fictional. 'In this instance, as in many others', Powell Jones wrote, 'Gray showed plainly that he was both historian and poet. The poet in him, however, was wise enough to realize that the tradition was far more dramatic than the historical documents.'[16] Gray briefly summarized Carte's account in his own notes, commenting with reference to Edward I:

---

[15] Thomas Carte, *History of England*, 3 vols. (London, 1747) ii.196.
[16] Powell Jones, 96.

he is said to have hanged up all their Bards, because they encouraged the Nation to rebellion, but their works (we see), still remain, the Language (tho' decaying) still lives, & the art of their versification is known, and practiced to this day among them'.[17]

Gray had completed the first two sections of his ode by the late summer of 1755, but his design of expressing the degree to which 'men shall never be wanting to celebrate true virtue and valor in immortal strains' faltered in his attempts to demonstrate the continuity of bardic inspiration not only in his own era, but in the products of the sixteenth and seventeenth centuries. Gray found himself unable to work on the poem for a period of well over twelve months.

Sometime in May, however, the famous 'blind harper' John Parry, of Raubon, North Wales, arrived in Cambridge. Parry, who was totally sightless, maintained a position as harper to Sir Watkin Williams Wynne of Wynnstay (he had served Sir Watkin's father before him). For more than ten years, Parry had been offering demonstrations of his talents as a musician in rather more public venues – and to considerable acclaim. He first caught the attention of the public after winning a harp-playing contest with one Hugh Shon Prys of Llanddervel. In April 1746, he travelled to London, where his performances at Ranelagh caused something of a sensation. Yet Parry was no mere performer. He treated both his instrument and the music that constituted its legacy with the seriousness of the scholar and the historian. As early as 1742, he had collaborated with Evan Evans in assembling a reliable collection of *Antient British Music*. It was the first of three such collections of Welsh music to which Parry was eventually to lend both his name and his expertise.

Gray, for one, was absolutely delighted with Parry's performance in Cambridge that spring. 'Mr. Parry has been here', he wrote with excitement to Mason toward the end of May,

& scratch'd out such ravishing blind Harmony, such tunes of a thousand year old with names enough to choak you, as have set all this learned body a'dancing, & inspired them with due reverence for *Odikle*, whenever it shall appear. (*CTG* 502)

He added: 'Mr. Parry (you must know) it was, that put Odikle in motion again'. Gray included a draft of the conclusion to 'Odikle' – or *The Bard* – in the very same letter to Mason. In the weeks to come, he continued to revise the stanzas. By 11 June, he had grown confident enough in the achievement of the poem to share a corrected version of the work with Wharton in London. The electricity of Parry's performance had pushed

[17]   Reprinted in Lonsdale, *PTG*, 181.

him finally to finish the poem on which he had been working, on and off, for years.

*

Gray's poem opens abruptly, as Edward and his army are confronted by the last of the Welsh bards among the mountainous tract of *Craigian-eryie* – the highlands of Caernarvonshire and Merionethshire:

> 'Ruin seize thee, ruthless king!
> 'Confusion on thy banners wait,
> 'Though fanned by Conquest's crimson wing
> 'They mock the air with idle state.
> 'Helm nor habuerk's twisted mail,
> 'Nor even thy virtues, tyrant, shall avail
> 'To save thy secret soul from nightly fears,
> 'From Cambria's curse, from Cambria's tears!'
> Such were the sounds, that o'er the crested pride
> Of the first Edward scattered wild dismay,
> As down the steep of Snowdon's shaggy side
> He wound with toilsome march his long array.
> Stout Gloucester stood aghast in speechless trance:
> 'To arms!', cried Mortimer and couched his quivering lance.
>   (*PTG* 183–84)

The second stanza describes the figure of the Bard – 'Robed in the sable garb of woe' – as he denounces the effects of Edward's campaign. The pictorial details of Gray's representation, by the poet's own admission, were borrowed 'from a well-known picture of Raphael, representing the Supreme Being in the vision of Ezekiel:

> With haggard eyes the poet stood;
> (Loose his beard and hoary hair
> Streamed, like a meteor, to the troubled air)
> And, with a master's hand and prophet's fire,
> Struck the deep sorrow of his lyre. (*PTG* 185–86)

The epode that follows sets out the bard's lament for his murdered companions. His agonized litany is cut short by the appearance of the ghosts of those same bards, ranged along the nearby cliffs:

> 'Cold is Cadwallo's tongue,
> 'That hushed the stormy main:
> 'Brave Urien sleeps upon his craggy bed:
> 'Mountains, ye mourn in vain

'Modred, whose magic song
'Made huge Plinlimmon bow his cloud-topped head.
'On dreary Arvon's shore they lie,
'Smeared with gore and ghastly pale:
'Far, far aloof the affrighted ravens sail;
'The famished eagle screams and passes by.
'Dear lost companions of my tuneful art,
'Dear as the light that visits these sad eyes,
'Dear as the ruddy drops that warm my heart,
'Ye died amidst your dying country's cries –
'No more I weep. They do not sleep.
'On yonder cliffs, a grisly band,
'I see them sit, they linger yet,
'Avengers of their native land;
'With me in dreadful harmony they join,
'And weave with bloody hands the tissue of thy line.' (*PTG* 186–89)

Together, the bard and his spectral companions begin to prophesize the fate of the Royal line from Edward himself to Richard III:

"Weave the warp and weave the woof,
"The winding-sheet of Edward's race.
"Give ample room and verge enough
"The characters of hell to trace.
"Mark the year and mark the night,
"When Severn shall re-echo with affright
"The shrieks of death, through Berkeley's roofs that ring,
"Shrieks of an agonizing King!
"She-wolf of France, with unrelenting fangs,
"That tear'st the bowels of thy mangled mate,
"From thee be born who o'er thy country hangs
"The scourge of heaven. What terrors round him wait!
"Amazement in his van, with Flight combined,
"And Sorrow's faded form, and Solitude behind. (*PTG* 189–90)

The epode of the second ternary that follows offers a grim and huddled catalogue of English history from the reign of Richard II, through the 'long years of havoc' of the Wars of the Roses and the murder of the princes in the tower. Having traced the history of Edward's line to its end in Richard III, the chorus of ghostly bards vanishes among the mountain crags. In their stead, however, the bard is granted a vision of the manner in which the Welsh line, through the Tudors, will be restored to the English throne following the defeat of Richard III and Bosworth. The reign of Queen Elizabeth is singled out for particular praise. Taliessin is called upon to celebrate the inevitable victory of the bards over Edward's barbarism. Of Elizabeth, the bard proclaims:

'Her eye proclaims her of the Briton-line;
'Her lion-port, her awe-commanding face,
'Attempered sweet to virgin-grace. (*PTG* 197)

And the revival of poetry in Elizabeth's reign is figured as a re-animation of the very spirit that Edward had attempted so brutally to exterminate:

'What strings symphonious tremble in the air,
'What strains of vocal transport round her play!
'Hear from the grave, great Taliessin, hear;
'They breath a soul to animate thy clay.
'Bright Rapture calls and, soaring as she sings,
'Waves in the eye of heaven her many-coloured wings. (*PTG* 197–98)

The final stanza summarizes the achievements of the poets of Elizabeth's reign and of those who were to follow in their footsteps. The lines deliberately invoke the language of Spenser, Shakespeare, and Milton. Thus reassured of the eventual triumph of poetry, the bard turns from Edward and his forces, and plunges headlong to his death:

'The verse adorn again
'Fierce war and faithful love,
'And truth severe, by fairy fiction dressed.
'In buskined measures move
'Pale Grief and pleasing Pain,
'With Horror, tyrant of the throbbing breast.
'A voice as of the cherub-choir
'Gales from blooming Eden bear;
'And distant warblings lessen on my ear,
'That lost in long futurity expire.
'Fond impious man, think'st thou yon sanguine cloud,
'Raised by thy breath, has quenched the orb of day?
'Tomorrow he repairs the golden flood,
'And warms the nations with redoubled ray.
'Enough for me: with joy I see
'The different doom our fates assign.
'Be thine despair and sceptered care;
'To triumph, and to die, are mine.'
He spoke, and headlong from the mountain's height
Deep in the roaring tide he plunged to endless night. (*PTG* 198–200)

*

In an unusually concise and perceptive essay on the state of poetry and criticism in Britain in the decades following the death of Alexander

Pope in 1744, the twentieth-century critic Arthur Johnston nicely reminded his readers that as early as 1726 – the year in which Thomson published the first version of the first section of what was in time to become *The Seasons*, and a year that likewise saw the earliest appearance of John Dyer's influential landscape poem 'Grongar Hill' and the pirated printing of Jonathan Swift's remarkable *Cadenus and Vanessa* – English poets had already begun to betray signs of fatigue and anxiety when confronted, as they correctly perceived themselves to be, by the constant and pressing need to define themselves against the achievement of their late seventeenth- and early eighteenth-century predecessors.[18] Dryden may have been among the first poets in English explicitly to express something of the excitement inherent in the realization that the world was 'past its infant age' – that an 'old age' had finally passed away for good, and that the time had come 'to begin anew'. Yet the weary Dryden was equally successful in intimating a concomitant realization that in the footsteps of Shakespeare, Jonson, and Milton, it was not going to be at all easy for the poets of the new century to find new subject matter for their verses, or for them to devise new ways of addressing it. Minor poets of the period such as Joseph Warton (in works such as his 1744 nature poem, *The Enthusiast*) and Mark Akenside (most notably in his wildly ambitious *The Pleasures of Imagination*, also published in 1744) pointedly attempted to write verse on subjects traditionally considered to be inherently 'unpoetic'. They desired most of all to be innovative – to make it *new*. As Akenside wrote in the first book of his own epic project:

> . . . the love
> Of nature and the muses bids explore,
> Thro' secret paths erehwile untrod by man,
> The fair poetic region, to detect
> Untasted springs, to drink inspiring draughts;
> And shade my temples with unfading flowers
> Cull'd from the lauretate vale's profound recess,
> Where never poet gain'd a wreath before.[19]

Or, as he had demanded with similar ambition in his earlier 'Hymn to Science', published in 1739, when he was only seventeen years old:

> Say from what simple springs began
> The vast ambitious thoughts of man,
>   Which range beyond controul,
> Which seek Eternity to trace,

---

[18]   Arthur Johnston, 'Poetry and Criticism After 1740' in *Sphere History of Literature*, Vol. 4: *Dryden to Johnson*, ed. Roger Lonsdale (London, 1971; 1986) 313–49.
[19]   Mark Akenside, 'The Pleasures of Imagination', Book I, ll. 48–55.

Dive thro' th'infinity of space,
And strain to grasp the whole.[20]

The poets of the mid and later eighteenth century each, to some degree, strained to grasp and to express their own perception of this same 'whole'. Akenside's lines echo Thomson's earlier insistence that the art of poetry be constantly replenished and rejuvenated, inspired by heaven so as to 'please, instruct, surprise, and astonish'. The poets of the period aimed for the Longinean sublime, and many of their efforts retain to this day a joyous faith and vitality in the unexplored *possibilities* of poetry as a social, political and aesthetic means of action.

The poets of the latter half of the century were no less determined in their own particular ways and on their own particular terms to be innovative. 'One of the main characteristics of the poets writing between 1740 and 1780', Johnston observed, was 'their desire to restore poetry "to her ancient truth and purity"'. 'And to do this', he added, 'they sought new models – genres, styles, dictions, prosodic devices that had been used by writers they admired – as an aid to being different, new, and serious.'[21] It was this last characteristic – the emphasis on the thoughtful or earnest aspect of the poetic enterprise – which seemed most to distinguish the generation of Collins, Smart, and Churchill from their immediate predecessors. Eric Rothstein expressed much the same perception as earlier critics such as Johnston when he observed of the period, 'What was most distinctive about the verse of these years was, I think, a *posture*, an *attitude*. The controlling attitude was one of sympathy, a call for fellow-feeling.' Yet, as Rothstein further notes, the poems of the middle and later years of the eighteenth century 'increasingly appeal to non-rational faculties in the reader, so that they tend to explore passions and sensory impressions but almost never explore ideas'.[22] One might take issue with this last element of such an overview – Gray's poetry, at least, though passionate, was also from start to finish relentlessly intellectual and scholarly, and to some degree obsessed with the very nature of 'ideas' – but Rothstein's general characterization holds true. Both Johnston and Rothstein emphasized the fact that when Robert Lowth (whom Gray met and apparently admired) succeeded Joseph Spence as Professor of Poetry at Oxford in 1741, he boldly devoted his lectures to the non-traditional subject of Hebrew poetry, laying particular emphasis on its essential simplicity of form, as well as pointing out its deeper connections to the more familiar, classical rhetorics of Greece and Rome antiquity. The poets of the later eighteenth century, in

[20] Mark Akenside, 'Hymn to Science', ll. 31–36.
[21] Johnston, 315.
[22] Rothstein, 120–21.

other words, had new models to follow, new poets to admire and to imitate. Virgil and Horace were not necessarily replaced, but they made room along the shelf and on the table for an eclectic array of daring and exotic newcomers. The traditionally literary or poetic 'canon', as it were (lest we be inclined to think that earlier ages were any less troubled than our own), was turned on its head, and in the process of being reconstituted and reformed. The 'original' Pindar was rediscovered; Milton's minor poems were now embraced as exemplars of what poetry ought properly to accomplish; the uniquely resonant legacy of Edmund Spenser – in the work of poets such as Thomson, Beattie, and Akenside – was similarly redefined.

It was in the midst of this upheaval, that Thomas Gray sat down to write *The Progress of Poesy* and *The Bard*. On a personal level, Gray's Pindaric models allowed him to address such emotional issues as the loss of his mother with a rigorous and vehement assertion of poetic *form*; on the aesthetic level, they announced themselves as the avatars of a new poetic era, defining monuments of a larger cultural project that argued for the vital importance of passionate, lyrical endeavour – a return to origins and to the explosive and miraculous energy inherent in the very act of creation itself – a uniquely sophisticated assertion of order and life in the face of darkness. Johnston's assessment of the place of Gray's Pindarics within the larger ambitions of this same cultural moment bears repeating. Although, he began:

> Nothing in the period better indicates the difficulty for a poet of finding something to write *about*, if observed facts of the natural and social world were not sufficient inspiration. Nothing in the period better indicates the need of the poet to examine the nature of poetry and its function, to be aware of his own sensibility and to probe and portray it, to adopt poetic styles and startling roles in order to discover what he might be, and so discover who he is.[23]

Drawing a necessary connection between the achievement of the *Odes*, on the one hand, and the sustained popularity of Gray's earlier lyrics, on the other, Johnston observed that whereas Gray in his own persona in the *Elegy* admitted to or presented himself as being ineffectual – 'a good man, poor, proud, without ambition, but with a power of emotional attachment and a faith superior to those about him' – the bard is not isolated and alone, but rather 'the mouthpiece of an order natural and supernatural that will ensure, in time, the destruction of the corrupt and the restoration of the good'.[24] By becoming the bard, in other words, Gray could say things he could not say as the elegist, Thomas Gray.

---

[23] Johnston, 329.
[24] Johnston, 330.

Once again, Eric Rothstein's observations in his generous reassessment of the achievement of Gray's later poetry nicely complement Johnston's claims. 'Neither antiquarian nor arrogant about capturing the "soul" of a dead poet', Rothstein wrote of the *Odes*, 'they recreate Pindar's art in a new way just as their content gives voice to a cyclical, yet always differing pattern of history'.[25] Although it would be a matter of centuries before the critics began truly to gauge the significance of the poet's *Odes*, already, in the summer of 1757, Gray had redefined the parameters of poetry itself, no less spectacularly than he had redefined the parameters of his own status as England's greatest and most innovative living poet.

*

It has often been observed that the antiquarian impulse of much late eighteenth- and early nineteenth-century poetry was to have an obvious political or 'nationalistic' relevance, even though, as one critic of the nascent, 'Romantic' movement in the period has written, 'the scholars and clergymen who collected the manuscripts, broadsides, and oral performances, and who travelled over the countryside like the geologists, botanists, and bird-watchers were not especially political creatures'. As Marilyn Gaull further observed:

> The courtly tradition, originating in Southern France and Italy, idealized that aristocratic political system disrupted by the Revolution of 1688 in England. . . . The folk tradition, on the other hand, was based mainly on an idealization of agrarian and even pastoral societies, populated with innocent, spontaneous, simple, virtuous, intuitive, innately musical and wise peasants who lived in tune with their natural environment and in close proximity to the faeries and demons that were the major source of their charm.[26]

Works such as *The Bard* – particularly when read alongside poems such as William Collins's as yet unpublished 'Ode on the Popular Superstitions of the Highlands of Scotland' (1749) – anticipate the interest of the early Romantic poets in this 'folk tradition' – a tradition supposed to have been preserved in the lore of the ancient bards and the fantastic narratives of Celtic romance. The distinction between the study of chivalry and the courtly tradition – as manifested in works such as Richard Hurd's 1762 *Letters on Chivalry and Romance* – on the one hand, and in the line of lyric development as preserved in the contem-

---

[25] Rothstein, 95.
[26] Marilyn Gaull, *English Romanticism: The Human Context* (London: W.W. Norton and Co., 1988) 257.

porary oral traditions of lays, romances and ballads, on the other, was a significant and consequential one. Scholars such as Gray were far less interested in the paternalistic vision of courtly society than they were in the construction of a native tradition of a rawly powerful and untutored poetic genius. *The Bard* in some significant respects merely extends the antithesis first outlined in the *Elegy* into the antiquarian past. Where the earlier poem had sought to contrast the pomp and power of the wealthy with the short and simple annals of the poor, the later work likewise contrasted the authority of a brutally established, paternal hierarchy with a generalized, indigenous Welsh bard and his ghostly though still vocal progenitors. As the critic Morris Golden observed:

> Within the strictest classical confines of form, the bards are Gray's attempt to present directly the voice and character of savage rhapsody, of the soaring soul unhampered by the restrains of civilization; . . . They are the magicians, addressing something deeper in man than the surface that fears death and fights for rule. They have a deep association with the underlying forces of nature – as witness their participation in the workings of destiny – and the assurance that their appeal to humanity is indestructible and will revive in spite of temporary repression.[27]

Gray's latest effort in the Pindaric mode seemed also and not incidentally to return to some of the very same questions regarding the possible limits of human knowledge and experience that the poet had so patiently explored in the *Elegy*. *The Bard*, in other words, continues to manifest Gray's fascination with issues of perception, intuition, and poetic authority as such issues had been addressed and to some extent answered in Locke's *Essay Concerning Human Understanding*. The *Elegy* seemed to agree with Locke's assertion that some final perspective on the condition of mankind would always be wanting within the terms of human endeavour itself. Towards the end of his *Essay* Locke had asked his readers:

> What shall we say then? Are the greatest part of Mankind, by the necessity of the their Condition, subjected to unavoidable Ignorance in those Things, which are of greatest Importance to them? (for of those, 'tis obvious to enquire.) Have the Bulk of Mankind no other Guide, but Accident, and blind Chance, to conduct them to their Happiness, or Misery? Are the current Opinions, and licensed Guides of every Country, sufficient Evidence and Security to every Man, to venture his greatest Concernments on; nay, his everlasting Happiness, or Misery? Or can those be the certain and infallible Oracles and Standards of Truth, which teach

---

[27]   Morris Golden, *Thomas Gray: Updated Edition* (Boston: Twayne Publishers, 1988) 86.

one Thing in *Christendom*, and another in *Turkey*? Or shall a poor Countryman be eternally happy, for having the Chance to be born in *Italy*; or
a Day-Labourer be unavoidably lost, because he had the ill Luck to be
born in *England*? How ready some Men may be to say some of these
things to be true, (let them chuse which they please;) or else grant, That
GOD has furnished Men with Faculties sufficient to direct them in the
Way they should take, if they will but seriously employ them that Way,
when their ordinary Vocations allow them the Leisure. No Man is so
wholly taken up with the Attendance on the Means of Living, as to have
no spare Time at all to think of his Soul, and inform himself in Matters
of Religion. Were Men as intent upon this, as they are on Things of lower
Concernment, there are none so enslaved to the Necessities of Life, who
might not find many Vacancies, that might be Husbanded to this Advantage of their Knowledge.[28]

The Bard may on some level have represented an attempt by the poet
to push beyond the natural limits of a merely 'human' understanding –
to anticipate the state in which a greater knowledge of the divine scheme
would, in fact, be made available to the poet and his audience. Writing
on what he described as our complex ideas of 'Substances', and attempting to account for the seemingly universal human intuition of divine
structure, Locke had observed:

In the Discovery of, and Assent to these Truths, there is no Use of the
Discursive Faculty, *no need of Reasoning*, but they are known by a superior, and higher Degree of Evidence. And such, if I may guess at Things
unknown, I am apt to think, that Angels have now, and the Spirits of just
Men made perfect, shall have, in a future State, of Thousands of Things,
which now, either wholly escape our Apprehensions, or which, our short-
sighted Reason having got some faint Glimpse of, we, in the Dark, grope
after.[29]

The Bard stands in some respects as Gray's anticipation of this 'future
State' – an anticipation by the poet, in this world, of the power of such
truths as we will all apprehend in the assured and future state of death.

III. A Sort of Aera

The passage of years had done nothing to alleviate Gray's constitutional
fear of fire. The destruction of the Cornhill property in the disastrous
City blaze of 1748 seemed only to have lent a deeper legitimacy to the

[28] Locke, 707–08.
[29] Locke, 683.

poet's lifelong anxiety. Gray began now to speculate openly among the college Fellows that it was simply a matter of time before the ready fabric of Peterhouse also fell victim to such a disaster. The whole of Cambridge, for that matter, was one huge tinderbox – a catastrophic conflagration just waiting to happen. Members of the university, Gray cautioned, needed to maintain a constant vigilance against the possibility of some drunken toper accidentally knocking over a candle in the night, or even of a more sober collegian failing properly to extinguish their hearth fire before turning in one evening, and thus burning the entire college down about their heads.

In the first week of January 1756, Gray happened to notice in one of the London newspapers an advertisement announcing the sale of rope ladders at the shop of one Ephraim Hadden, near Hermitage Stairs, Wapping. He immediately wrote to Wharton, asking him to purchase such a device and send it on to him at Peterhouse. 'I never saw one', Gray admitted of the article in question, 'but I suppose it must have strong hooks, or something equivalent, a-top, to throw over an iron bar to be fixed withinside of my window'. He further specified: 'It must be full 36 foot long, or a little more, but as light and manageable as may be, easy to enroll, & not likely to tangle'. Wharton promptly sent such a 'machine' to Cambridge – complete, apparently, with 'Firebags' designed to carry one's hastily-gathered valuables to safety as well – and Gray at once set about attaching the contraption to his bedroom window. To this purpose, he affixed an iron bar outside his second-storey, north-facing window, which looked into the church-yard of little St. Mary's. Attached to the stonework of the building by means of two stout props or stanchions, the bar projected well beyond the lines of the windowsill itself, so that the rope ladder, when fully extended, would hang free and clear of the side of the building. An occupant alerted to the danger of a fire needed simply to hook the ladder to the bar, fling the coil from the window, and then shin or rappel themselves along the rope to the safety of the yard below. The bar that Gray attached outside the window of his rooms is still, today, clearly visible from Trumpington Street.

Preparations of this sort could hardly be made without attracting some degree of attention and comment within the comparatively small academic community. Gray's inadvertently public disclosure of his fears and his apparent willingness to go to any lengths to protect himself in the event of a fire unfortunately and in no time at all instigated some of the rowdier elements of the university to have some fun at the poet's expense. Less than two months were to pass before Gray found himself with reason profoundly to regret his foolishness in ever having hoped that such a means of escape could provide him simply with some measure of security in the face of an unexpected alarm.

Early one morning in the first week of March, a group of students
(described in one later account as 'some rakish Fellow-Commoners . . .
in a freakish mood') happened to be passing beneath Gray's bedroom in
the pre-dawn darkness when their attention was suddenly drawn to the
contraption affixed outside the window above them.[30] According to the
most reliable of the several accounts that were later to emerge describing the incident, the undergraduates were that morning 'going a
hunting', and had opportunely paused outside the building merely to
'have a little sport before they set out'. Prominent among the ring-
leaders of these mischief-makers, it seems, was Viscount Percival, then
a Fellow-Commoner of Magdalene College; Percival was egged on by a
number of Petrenchians – several of whom must surely themselves have
had some personal contact with Gray in the past, and almost all of
whom would have been familiar with the poet's growing reputation for
'delicacy'.[31] Other accounts would maintain that the party that night
was made up of the sort of 'high-coloured young gentlemen' among
whom Gray was 'by no means a favourite', and that the group was actually on its way home, and bringing their drunk and roaring evening to
a close when the fire-escape happened to catch their eyes. Whatever the
case, one member of the party was sent around to the wooden stairs
which led up to Gray's chambers. Once there, he began loudly and fran-
tically to raise the alarm with shouts of 'fire'. The other students gathered beneath the window and waited to see how Gray would respond
to such a hue and cry. They hoped that the terrified poet would be so
frightened as to begin descending by means of the rope; then, just as he
was about to reach the safety of the ground beneath his feet, the young
fellows planned to '[whip] the butterfly up again'. In one version of
events, the students went so far as to place a tub of water directly under
the window, thereby rendering a quick climb back up the rope to the
building's second floor the only means of avoiding the spectacle of public
humiliation, to say nothing of the chill which was sure to follow the
frenzied panic of such an exertion. According to this more elaborately
malicious account, the plan of humiliation succeeded 'only too well'.
'Gray', it was reported, 'without staying to put on his clothes, hooked
his rope ladder to the iron bar, and descended nimbly into the tub of
water, from which he was rescued with shouts of laughter by the unman-
nerly youths'. He was rescued in earnest only when Stonhewer appeared
on the scene and, wrapping the shocked and shivering poet in the coat
of a passing watchman, carried him back into the safety of the college.
A second and rather more trustworthy version of the affair records that
the commotion succeeded only in bringing Gray as far as the window

---

[30]   See *CTG* Appendix J, 'Gray's Removal from Peterhouse to Pembroke' (1216–20).
[31]   Gosse, 125.

ledge, from which vantage the tip of his delicate white night-cap was seen to peak fearfully into the darkness below, before its owner realized the nature of the prank and withdrew again to the warmth and safety of his 'couch'.

However much Gray exposed himself physically that morning, the simple fact that he had been singled out as the target of such a humiliating prank left him speechless with mortification. He nowhere recorded his own version of events in any detail, and he seemed disinclined personally to allude to the specifics of the incident among even his closest friends. He wrote briefly to Wharton immediately after the commotion:

> Tho' I had no reasonable excuse for myself before I received your last letter, yet since that time I have had a pretty good one, having been taken up in quarreling with Peter-house, and in removing myself from thence to Pembroke. this may be look'd upon as a sort of Aera in a life so barren of events as mine, yet I shall treat it in Voltaire's manner, & only tell you, that I left my lodgings, because the rooms were noisy, & the People of the house dirty. this is all I would chuse to have said about it. . . . (CTG 458)

Quite apart from having been cruelly tormented on the night in question, Gray also smarted from the lingering embarrassment attached to the public spectacle of his humiliation. The thoughtless cruelty of the students left him numb with indignation. Mason, who was in residence at Pembroke at the time, eventually offered his own readers a markedly spare version of the prank. He seems to have been anxious to stress the fact that such callous horseplay only added the final straw to a burden of disregard and impertinence on the part of the college that had long since become intolerable. Mason would write:

> Two or three young Men of Fortune, who lived in the same stair-case, had for some time intentionally disturbed him with their riots, and carried their ill behaviour so far as to frequently awaken him at midnight. After having borne with their insults longer than might reasonably have been expected from a man of less warmth of temper, Mr Gray complained to the Governing part of the Society. . . .[32]

The end result of all this unseemly commotion was Gray's abrupt departure from Peterhouse and his immediate removal across Trumpington Street to Pembroke. The Peterhouse Butler's Book notes that Gray was in residence during the week ending 5 March; his name had been entered as usual to the list for the following week as well, but was later scored through by the Butler's pen. The Pembroke Admission Book at

---

[32] Mason, 241n; see also CTG Appendix J.

the same time contains the concise entry, 'Thomas Gray, LL.B. admissus est ex Collegio Divi Petri. March 6, 1756'. Gray's defection from Peterhouse, in other words, was a transition accomplished in a matter of days, perhaps even a matter of hours. He was to remain a member of the college until his death fifteen years later.

*

Gray's long-standing ties to Pembroke and the deep personal connections he had for so many years maintained with its members helped to make the transition between colleges an easy one. He was placed first in the chambers of one of the junior Fellows of the college, Edward Hussey Deleval, who was not then resident. These rooms were situated on the first floor of the seventeenth-century Hitcham building, on the south side of what was then known as the New Court – the innermost court of the college today called Ivy Court. Begun in 1659 and finished just two years later, the western portion of Hitcham building presented a clean, classical facade. Gray told Wharton that his rooms were comfortable and spacious. They are also private. 'I am for the present extremely well-lodged here', he wrote soon after his arrival, and, he added – evoking a momentary but telling recollection of the Grand Tour he had made so many years earlier – 'as quiet as at the Grand Chartreuse'. Some time later, in June 1758, Gray moved to a more spacious set of chambers, adjacent to the Hall and at the westernmost end of the Hitcham building. From these rooms, which he was to occupy until his death, Gray enjoyed a view of Ivy Court to the north, and looked out upon the Master's garden, to the south. They were handsome accommodations, consisting of a large sitting room, a bedroom, and a small 'closet' or study. In the central parlour, the three large windows which faced onto the inner courtyard were ornamented with generous clusters of mignonette; the grey-green flowers flourished in the light on the deep window sills, and filled the room with their rich flagrance. The perfume of other sweetly scented plants lingered in all three rooms. Pots of fresh blossoms, ornamental vases holding cut flowers, and bowls of heady potpourri were placed throughout. A pair of tremendous Japanese vases commanded attention in the sitting room. The polished wood of the elegant harpsichord on which Gray entertained himself with the toccatas of Scarlatti and Pergolesi sparkled in the spring sunlight. The leather-bound volumes of the poet's ever-increasing library were stacked neatly on little tables, or ranged precisely along free-standing bookshelves. The fine wooden paneling on all sides and the lines of a new stone chimney-piece which ornamented the hearth at end of the main room, added the finishing touches of luxury to the set.

Gray had timed his defection from Peterhouse well. The disputes regarding academic appointments and admissions that had driven such a dramatic wedge between the majority of the Fellows and the Master of the college, Roger Long, several years earlier, were now pretty much a thing of the past. Soon after Gray's arrival at the college Roger Long – who was then in his seventy-sixth year – was taken ill. For several months it seemed likely that the mastership would fall vacant. Gray exerted his own efforts at the time in support of the possible candidacy of his old friend James Brown, then President and Senior Fellow of the college, and recruited Mason ('who', he suggested, 'is himself qualified to be Master') in his campaign to 'do every thing to further Mr Brown's election'. Long made a full and unexpected recovery, however (he would live to be ninety years old), and before much time had passed internal affairs at Pembroke returned to normal.

The society into which Gray now found himself admitted was more than congenial to him. Some familiar faces, it was true, were now gone. Mason had recently resigned his Fellowship following his appointment as domestic chaplain to Lord Holdernesse; he had subsequently received the living of Aston, in Yorkshire. Christopher Smart had packed his bags for London some six years earlier. Smart's subsequent history was to be a harrowing one. Early in 1756 he fell ill; his convalescence in the months that followed was marked by a sudden commitment to a markedly more 'enthusiastic' form of religious worship. Suddenly taking the biblical injunction to 'pray without ceasing' literally, Smart was likely to fling himself down in the middle of a busy street to pray. He pressed his friends (a dwindling number of individuals on whom he was likely to call at any hour of the day or night) to join him in these conspicuous fits of worship, thus prompting Johnson's memorably loyal comment that he would 'as lief pray with Kit Smart as with anyone else'.[33] Despite such testaments of affection, Smart found his mental health deteriorating further. In May 1757 he was admitted to St. Luke's Hospital for the Insane. It was during this incarceration that he would compose the fragments of his *Jubilate Agno*. Smart lived on until 1771, the year of Gray's own death.

Twenty years before he formally joined the society of Pembroke, Gray had predicted that Smart 'must come to a Jayl, or Bedlam, and that without any help, almost without pity'. Still, he gained no satisfaction from that fact that he had lived to see his prophecy fulfilled. Although contemporary accounts were almost unanimous in their assertions that Gray and Smart had little time for one another and that were never even on comfortable terms, Gray was among those who contributed something for Smart's support. The most famous anecdote connecting the two poets suggests that Smart was not beyond venting his own

---

[33]   Boswell, *Life of Johnson*, 281.

troubled spirit in unsavoury witticisms at Gray's expense. 'Gray *walks* as if he fouled his small-clothes', Smart is supposed to have remarked, 'and *looks* as if he smelt it'. If the comment is indeed Smart's, as one recent historian of the college has written rather desperately, 'the school-boy tittering about "smalls" does at least hint at that eye for the little and the hidden, which both poets enjoyed.'[34]

In addition to his relationship with James Brown, Gray had maintained close contact with his old friend Henry Tuthill, and soon demonstrated himself eager to make new acquaintances within the college. With the exception of the 47-year-old Brown, the average age of the rest of the Pembroke Fellows at the time of Gray's arrival was a startlingly low 30. Gray appears to have had good relations with nearly all the Fellows; he even, eventually, established some degree of intimacy with figures such as Francis Mapletoft, whose silhouette 'portraits' of Gray and Mason still hang in the college; also close were Humphrey Senhouse (elected Grindal Fellow of Pembroke not long after Gray's admission), Richard 'Dick' Forester, and Joseph Gaskarth or 'Gaskyn'. The experimental philosopher Edward Hussey Delaval, whose elder brother had been sent down from the college several years earlier, was perhaps the most playful and energetic of the junior Fellows, and one whose company was consistently cheerful. Gray referred affectionately in his letters to the busy activities of 'Deleval the loud' or 'Mr Delly', as he had playfully dubbed him, and very soon joined the rest of the college in its enjoyment of Delaval's performances on his novel and celebrated set of musical glasses. Other Fellows – Thomas Axton, John Bedford, Thomas Milburn – figure only vaguely in Gray's correspondence. 'Doctor' Samuel May alone among his new colleagues, it would appear, demonstrated in his dealings with others the sort of 'dirty spirit' for which the poet constitutionally had little or no patience.

Prominent among the very few Fellow–Commoners in the college at the time of Gray's arrival was John Lyon, ninth Earl of Strathmore. Strathmore was by all accounts a charming and intelligent young man. As Lord Chesterfield had occasion to comment on the death of Strathmore's father – the eighth earl – just three years earlier, the younger man demonstrated himself even as schoolboy to be 'a good classical scholar . . . with a turn to learning'.[35] Gray described him to Wharton soon after his arrival as 'a tall genteel figure in our eyes', and noted with approval that he seemed to get along smoothly both with his college tutor, Brown, and with Tuthill, who served him in the capacity of a private instructor. Strathmore probably owed his presence at Pembroke to the influence of

---

[34]   A. V. Grimstone, ed. *Pembroke College, Cambridge: A Celebration* (Cambridge: Pembroke College, 1997) 90.
[35]   Quoted in *CTG* 417.

the Durham natives Stonhewer and Wharton. Both men had long been acquainted with the earl's mother, who had a generation earlier herself been one of the most sought-after heiresses in that county. Strathmore's younger brothers, John Philip Lyon and Thomas Lyon, were to follow their brother to Pembroke in the coming years. Gray enjoyed the company of all three men. He would eventually pay a visit to Strathmore – 'the Thane of Glamis' – at his castle in Scotland.

Finally, William Palgrave, the son of an Ipswich physician who joined the college as a Fellow–Commoner in 1757, would also make some small claim on Gray's attentions; so too would the Gloucestershire native, Edward Southwell. This latter gentleman was the only son of Edward Southwell, who had served as Principal Secretary for the State of Ireland for thirty-five years, and who has also been M.P, for Bristol City from 1739 to 1754. He was a tall and well-spoken young man, although Lady Mary Wortley Montagu – who was to meet him in Venice in the course of his Grand Tour in 1759 – later claimed to have been deprived of an entire night's sleep as the result merely of the sight of his face. 'He has neither visible nose nor mouth', Lady Mary would write to her daughter: 'He appears insensible to his misfortune, and shows himself everyday on the Piazza, to the astonishment of all the spectators'.[36] Southwell would remain in touch with Gray following his return to England, at which time the poet was pleased to report to Mason that he was 'no more a cockscomb than when he went from hence'.

For all such pleasant company, the wrangling between Long and the Fellows at Pembroke had taken a dramatic toll on the college in the years immediately preceding Gray's arrival. In the thirty-seven-year period dominated by the mastership of the outspoken Norfolk Tory, the total number of undergraduate enrollments amounted to only 193 entries. In 1748 only one pensioner was admitted to the college; the following year saw the admission of two Sizars. Even by 1756, Pembroke counted among her number only six Fellow–Commoners; the addition of lesser scholars and bachelors left the total number of undergraduates still short of thirty students. Building activity, which in the previous century had resulted in the proud achievements of the tudor-style Ivy Court and Wren's elegant chapel, had by mid-century slowed to a complete standstill. Conscious of the college's dwindling reputation, Gray, Brown, and others could only look forward to the revitalization of the college resources which they hoped would follow the end of Long's tenure as Master. Until that time, however, few changes of any real significance could be made.

*

[36] See Lady Mary Wortley Montagu, *Complete Letters*, ed. Robert Halsband (Oxford: Clarendon Press, 1965–67) iii.224;228.

In the summer of 1756 – perhaps as a result of the unanticipated disruption and commotion that had characterized the spring months – Gray decided not to embark on the sort of peripatetic summer tour to which he had gradually grown accustomed in recent years. Such a break in habit and custom, however advisable it may have seemed at the time, left him at loose ends. Toward the end of the second week of June Gray journeyed to London to visit Frederick Montagu – the 23-year-old cousin of Walpole's friend and correspondent George Montagu – who had recently left Trinity to read for the bar. His stay in town was plagued by persistent attacks of gout, and he soon left the city for the comparative comfort of Stoke.

Even the country retreat in Buckinghamshire, however, refused to work its usual, soothing magic. Gray's physical aches began slowly to subside, but by the end of July he confessed himself to Mason nearly immobilized by an attack of deep and intractable melancholy. 'You know I am at Stoke', he wrote to Mason, at Tunbridge, on 23 July,

> hearing, seeing, doing, absolutely nothing. not such a nothing, as you do at Tunbridge, chequer'd & diversified with a succession of fleeting colours; but heavy, lifeless, without form & void; sometimes almost as black as the *Moral* of Voltaire's Lisbon, which angers you so. I have had no more pores & muscular inflations, & am troubled only with this depression of mind. you will not expect therefore I should give you any account of my *Verve*, which is at best (you know) of so delicate a constitution, & has such weak nerves, as not to stir out of its chamber above three days in a year. (*CTG* 466)

Gray's allusion in this passage to the primordial chaos described in the opening lines of the Hebrew book of Genesis ('The earth was without form and void, and darkness was upon the face of the deep') underscores the unusually debilitating blackness of his melancholy that July. The numbing stasis of the poet's scholarly and creative inactivity that summer was further undermined by a terminal sense of emptiness – by the heaviness of a void which, quite unlike the darkness of the Old Testament's *tohu* and *bohu*, held little if any promise of creation. The wind and spirit of Gray's own inspiration was for the time being completely and utterly becalmed.

At the beginning of August he attempted to shake his depression with a visit to 'poor Mr. Chute', who had himself been suffering from an unusually severe attack of gout in London. When Chute's symptoms had subsided enough so that he could make the journey by carriage to the Vyne, Gray joined him in Hampshire. Very soon after his arrival, however, a further attack left Chute 'nailed to his bed'. The unprecedented virulence and extent of these visitations alarmed even Gray, who was himself, of course, no stranger to the illness. At the end of the first week of September he wrote in concern to Walpole:

> Poor Mr. Chute has now had the Gout for these five days with such a degree of pain & uneasiness, as he never felt before. whether to attribute it to Dr. La Cour's forcing medecines, or to a little cold he got as he came hither, I know not, but for above forty hours it seem'd past all human suffering, & he lay screaming like a Man upon the rack. the torture was so great, that (against my judgement & even his own) he was forced to have recourse to [an] infusion of Poppy-heads, which Cocchi used to give him, & in [half] an hours time was easy, fell into a gentle perspiration, [&] slept many hours. This was the night before last, & all yesterday he continued cheerful and in spirits. at night (as he expected) the pain returned, not so violent, but in more places, for now it is in one foot, both knees, & one hand, and I hourly dread it will increase again to its former rage. (*CTG* 479)

Gray confessed himself at a loss in these circumstances. The local doctors were of no use. With the exception the servants and of Walpole's friend and protégé, the German painter John Müntz, the poet found himself alone at the Vyne. However much he wished to escape the duties of a nurse and comforter, he was trapped. 'As [Chute] had no other company in the house', he later wrote to Wharton, 'it was impossible to leave him in that condition'. Gray did his best to convince his host to return to London for treatment, or possibly even to Bath, but Chute seemed 'rather set against' such a removal.

The arrival of some additional guests toward the end of September finally shifted some of the responsibility for his friend's health from Gray's shoulders. By the time he was finally able to leave the Vyne in the first week of October, he left Chute well enough to sit up in his chair by the fire 'with no great pain'. The burden of having nursed Chute through the 'cruel fit' of the preceding five weeks, however, appears eventually to have exacted a heavy toll on the friendship between the two men. Although Gray would continue to meet Chute as a frequent visitor to Walpole's home in future, he was never again himself to stay as a guest at the Vyne. He even intimated in a letter to Wharton, in September 1757, that he welcomed an invitation to visit the latter if only because it furnished him with a suitable excuse 'for not going into the country to *a place, where I am invited*' – a reference, apparently, to Chute's Hampshire home. In much the same vein, he confided pointedly to Walpole in July 1758, that if his friend was journeying in the direction of The Vyne, he should be 'glad to attend [him] thither, and *back again*'. In both instances Gray took care quite literally to underscore his cryptically expressed disinclination to spend any length of time in Chute's company. Apart from the possible friction and discomfort that resulted from the extended intimacy of their contact in the late summer and early autumn of 1756, there were no discernable reasons for such a breach.

Gray divided the remainder of the year aimlessly between Stoke, Strawberry Hill, and London, returning to Cambridge only toward the end of December. The Christmas and New Year holidays, spent in the company of friends and among familiar surroundings, passed smoothly enough. The opening weeks of 1757, however, found the small community of Fellows and students at Pembroke suddenly and without warning rocked by a potentially disastrous scandal. At some point in early January, Gray's friend Henry Tuthill – who had migrated from Peterhouse to Pembroke in 1746, and who had in recent years served the college in offices including Chaplain, Junior Treasurer, and even Dean – abruptly left Cambridge, never to return. On 5 February, the following entry, signed by Roger Long, James Brown, and others, was made in the College Register:

> This day the Master in the presence of 5 Fellows, declared Mr. Tuthill's fellowship to be vacant, he having been absent from the College above a month contrary to the Statutes which [inflict] this punishment upon such absence.

A second, unsigned entry immediately followed this declaration:

> Since Mr. Tuthill's absence common fame has laid him under violent suspicion of having been guilty of great enormities; to clear himself from which he Has not made his appearance and there is good reason to believe he never will.

The exact nature of these 'great enormities' was deliberately left unclear. The matter was effectively hushed up by the society at Pembroke, and although it is likely that Gray wrote about the scandal to Mason and to Wharton that February, any of those letters that may have contained detailed or extended reference to the Tuthill affair were later destroyed. Ketton-Cremer was no doubt correct in assuming that Tuthill had been 'accused of some homosexual offense'; the oblique wording of the second entry leaves room for few other interpretations.[37] The notation of '*violent* suspicions' and 'great *enormities*' operated as something of a code among Gray's contemporaries.

---

[37]   Ketton-Cremer, *Thomas Gray*, 148.

Gray was badly shaken by the affair and its possible aftermath. In the first of the letters he wrote in the immediate wake of Tuthill's deprivation still to survive, Gray's cryptic references to the scandal betray his anxiety in the face a possible public scandal. His correspondence also suggests that he was particularly frustrated by his own powerlessness to effect any change for the better. 'I cannot interpose at present', he wrote to Wharton on 17 February, 'lest I make the matter worse'. In the weeks to come, and in spite of his own supposed impotence with regard to the matter, Gray nevertheless made a point of personally consulting with Wharton, Mason, and Walpole in the hope of outlining some possible strategies for dealing practically and sanely with the situation within the University, without abandoning Tuthill completely to his fate. Some suitable explanation for the Fellow's abrupt departure from Cambridge, at the very least, would need to be floated among the University community at large. More pressingly, some provision needed likewise to be outlined in private for Tuthill's personal and professional future; his academic career, clearly, was over. Gray was determined at least to offer whatever practical assistance lay within his means, and he contributed financially to the disgraced man's support.

His anxiety regarding Tuthill's ultimate fate, unfortunately, appears to have been well founded. Mitford was to go on record in 1828 with the assertion that Tuthill eventually 'drowned himself', though he offered no details or corroborating evidence to support such a claim. 'If he lived on in difficult circumstances', Leonard Whibley has written of Tuthill in our own century, 'it is possible that Gray helped him, and Mason's allusion to Gray's "private charity when his means were lowest" may refer to Tuthill as one of the recipients.' Whibley further observed that Gray's direction in his will for his executors to 'apply the sum of two hundred pounds to the use of a charity, which I have already informed them of', may very well have been a provision designed for Tuthill's benefit even after the poet's own death.[38]

In the event, Pembroke emerged from the Tuthill scandal relatively unscathed. Any fears that rumors of the affair would prompt an exodus of Fellow–Commoners were unfounded. Lord Strathmore (Tuthill's pupil, it will be remembered) and his brother, who had together left Cambridge at the beginning of January, returned about 10 February, and were soon seen to be going about their business as usual. Edward Southwell, who left the college on 14 February, apparently made a point of reassuring Gray before his own departure that he would be absent for no more than a week; true to his promise, Southwell returned to Pembroke on about the 25th of that month. Even so, Gray's distress over the manner in which the entire episode was handled subsided only very

---

[38] See *CTG* Appendix G 'Henry Tuthill' (1206–10).

slowly. Mitford even suggested that the habitual melancholy that already darkened the poet's life now deepened into a gloom which was the enduring characteristic – and the direct result – of 'the misbehavior and misfortune of one whom he had called his friend'; this 'friend', of course, being Tuthill.

Throughout the period in which his attentions were thus focused on the internal affairs of the college, Gray made little progress on the few pieces of poetry that lay still unfinished among his papers. 'Odikle is not a bit grown', he had written jokingly of *The Bard* to Mason just before the Christmas holiday, 'tho' – he added teasingly – 'it is fine mild open weather'. The unexpected appearance of a number of visitors in the early months of the New Year left Gray with even less time than usual to devote to his own poetry. Mason's friend George Simon Harcourt, Viscount Nuneham, arrived in April. Lord Nuneham would later in life prove himself a reliable patron and friend to Mason. Gray confided to Wharton that Nuneham struck him as 'a sensible, well-bred young man, a little too fine for me, who love a little finery'. In a letter to Mason, Gray was more carefully positive. 'Stonhewer has done me the honour to send me your friend Lord Newnham hither with a fine recommendatory letter (written by his own desire) in Newmarket-week', he wrote:

> do not think he was going to New-Market. no! he came in a Solitaire, great Sleeves, jessamine-powder, & a large Bouquet of Jonquils within twelve miles of that place on purpose not to go thither. We had three days intercourse, talk'd about the Beaux-Arts, and Rome, & Hanover & Mason, whose praises we celebrated *a qui mieux mieux*, vowed eternal friendship, embraced, & parted. I promised to write you a thousand compliments in his name. I saw also Ld Villiers and Mr. Spencer, who carried him back with them, *en passant*. they did not like me at all. (*CTG* 499)

'Here has been too', Gray announced in the same letter 'the best of all Johns (I hardly except the Evangelist and the Divine) who is not to be sure a bit like my Lord N, but full as well in my mind'. He was referring to Lord John Cavendish, who had formerly been one of Mason's students at Peterhouse. He was a quaint and methodical little man (George Selwyn apparently captured the general effect of his appearance when he described him 'a learned canary bird'), whose company and manner Gray found unusually congenial. Other prominent visitors to Cambridge that spring included the Duke of Bedford and his son, Francis Russell, as well as Richard Rigby, one of the Duke's more unscrupulous supporters, and who later in his career served as Paymaster of the Forces. Gray's old acquaintance Nicholas Bonfoy also dropped in on Gray briefly at this time, apparently undertaking his visit to ensure means for the continued support of Tuthill.

*

The time had at last come, Gray felt that summer, for the two Pindaric odes to be published. Mason had been pressuring him to print the poems for some time, and the poet finally negotiated the matter with Dodsley, who undertook to pay him forty guineas for the copyright for both works. Gray further consented that Walpole print the quarto volume at his own Strawberry Hill Press; accordingly, two thousand copies were turned out within a period of three weeks, from 16 July to 8 August (a vignette of Strawberry Hill appeared on the title page). The *Odes by Mr. Gray* was priced at one shilling. In this original printing, neither ode was individually titled; the two poems appeared merely as *Ode I* and *Ode II*. Gray, then staying at Stoke, arranged for several copies of the volume to be sent directly to Brown at Cambridge, where they were to be judiciously distributed among the Master and the Fellows of Pembroke, and among other, select members of the University community. Copies 'of the Bard & his Companion', as Gray put it, were also dispatched to Bedingfield for distribution among his friends and family.

The *Elegy*, is will be remembered, had found its way into print only incidently, having first circulated for months in manuscript among the fashionable members of a select social circle dominated by Walpole. Had Gray not been faced with imminent prospect of the poem's mangled appearance in the disreputable *Magazine of Magazines* in the early winter months of 1751, the publication history and very probably the reception of the *Elegy* (and the narrative of its subsequent critical history and reputation) might have followed a markedly different course. The publication of the two Pindaric odes in 1757, by contrast, was an event that was far more carefully orchestrated under the watchful eyes of the poet himself. More than one year before the appearance of Dodsley's slim quarto, Gray had written to Bedingfield, promising to share the ode he was then calling the *Powers of Poetry* only when they had the chance to meet in person. The poet appeared then to give voice to some of his anxieties regarding the exposure of the odes – anxieties very similar to those he experienced prior to the formal publication of the *Elegy* in 1751. Bedingfield had been informed of the existence of the new poems by Mason, and Gray once again sensed that even before he had fully prepared himself to deal with the practical consequences of such public exposure, his verses were slipping beyond his control. The trepidation he had expressed with regard to the presentation of Bentley's *Designs* just four years earlier was still fresh in his mind and, again, particularly

in light of his own perception of the intimate subtexts that necessarily (and even in the case of the odes) connected his poetry to his personal life, Gray perhaps rightly on this occasion distrusted Walpole's
flare for self-promotion and drama. Gray did not want the publication
of the *Odes* to be an emphatically public affair. He carefully tried to
steer clear of promoting any notion that the celebrated author of the
church yard *Elegy* had written what might by some be perceived to be
a kind of 'sequel' to that earlier poem. 'I should very readily shew you
[the ode]', he had written cautiously to Bedingfield from Cambridge in
April, 1756, 'whenever we meet, & be glad to ask your opinion of it:
but I can convey it to you no other way than by the Post, which is not
to be depended upon, & I have already been threatened with publication, tho' there are no more than three copies of it in the world'. Gray
then seemed immediately to qualify much of what he had just written
by admitting candidly to Bedingfield: 'I find myself still young enough
to taste the sweets of praise (and to like the taste too) yet old enough
not to be intoxicated with them. To own the truth, they give me spirits,
but I begin to wonder, they should hurt any body's health, when we can
so easily dash them with the bitter salutary drop of misery and mortality, that we always carry about us.'

When the two *Odes* were finally published in August 1757, Gray took
some care to solicit friends such as Walpole, Brown, and Bedingfield to
report back to him on the tenor of their reception. Protesting first that,
as the individual responsible for the physical appearance of the work,
Walpole would himself 'forgive [the] vanity of an Author, as the vanity
of a Printer is a little interested in the same cause', he then asked Walpole
to relate to him 'what you hear any body say, (I mean, if any body says
anything).' Brown, to whom Gray wrote from Stoke, was requested to
concern himself primarily with the reception of the works within the
University community, and to tell him, as he put it, the views of *'mes
Confrères*, the Learned,' who could be relied upon 'at least to find fault,
if not commend'. In his letter to Brown, Gray maintained the pretense
that he solicited such opinions only as a matter of amateur curiosity, and
even pretended to apologize for his interest. Having sent him the
'present' of 'Dodsley's packet' to Cambridge and heard nothing from
him for over a week, he wrote: 'you will not wonder, therefore, at my
curiosity, if I enquire of you, what you hear said'. To Bedingfield Gray
wrote jauntily: 'I have order'd Dodsley . . . to send you piping hot from
the Press four copies of the Bard & his Companion'. Bedingfield was to
distribute the copies among some friends and acquaintances of the poet
instructed to pay particular attention to local report, so as to tell Gray
'what the North sayd either in good or bad'. 'As to the South', he added
with conscious self-deprecation, 'it is too busy and too fastidious to
trouble its head about anything that has no wit in it'.

Although students of literary history have tended until only recently to accept the notion that the publication of the *Odes* marked a failure in Gray's professional career as much as it signaled a fatal misstep in his own, idiosyncratic development as a poet, a number of dedicated professional critics have worked hard in recent years to set the record straight. Gray's *Odes*, from the moment the volume was first published until at least the time of the poet's death in 1771, was in no way and by no measure either a critical or a popular failure. True, the remarks of Arthur Onslow, then Speaker of the House of Commons, may have voiced the initial reaction of some of the poems' earliest readers when he casually dismissed *The Bard* (at least) as 'a pretty good tale, but nothing to the *Churchyard*'. Gray himself, of course, was more than sufficiently aware of the fact that much the same objection would be voiced by a large number of readers. There remained an audience, however, which valued the poet's brave attempt to do something different – to branch out in new directions. Not everyone was alive to what Gray was actually attempting to accomplish in the odes, but those who sensed something of his greater design were ready to applaud. The new *Odes* were greeted with enthusiasm by many, and Gray's fellow poets were significantly to be counted among the admirers of his work. Lord Lyttelton (to whom Thomson had dedicated *The Seasons*, and whose own pieces had appeared in the second volume of Dodlsey's 1748 *Collection*) wrote to Walpole, praising what he described as 'the bright and glorious flame of poetical fire' that manifested itself in the odes. William Shenstone, who had assisted Dodsley in the editing of the *Collection*, and who was to work with Percy in assembling his *Relics of English Poetry*, also thought them worthy efforts. Warburton told Gray that he liked them 'extremely', and ventured to say that 'the World never passed so just an opinion upon anything as upon them'. Hurd made a point of writing to Gray from Cambridge that 'every body here, that knows anything of such things, applauds the Odes. And the readers of Pindar dote on them'. Hurd also suggested, however, that part of their perceived success among 'the Learned' was owing to Gray's already unshakeable reputation within the university community both as a scholar and a poet. 'Every body would be thought to admire' the poems, he confessed in the same letter, although ' 'tis true, I believe, the greater part don't understand them'. Dr. John Brown, of St. John's College, Cambridge, yet another contributor to Dodsley's *Collection* and soon to be widely known for his popular volume, *An Estimate of the Manners and Principles of the Times*, was overheard to remark that Gray's efforts in the Pindaric mode were the best in the language. Friends and acquaintances ranging from the actor David Garrick, then at the height of his fame as a performer, to Henrietta Jane Speed, all reassured Gray with their support. Of the latter, Gray wrote to Wharton: 'Miss Speed seems to understand [the poems]; and to all such as do not, she says φονατα συνετοισι [or 'vocal to the intellect alone'] in so many words'.

The notices in some of the professional journals and magazines were slightly less kind, but, again, many of the reviewers seemed to pay less attention to the material that Gray had actually presented to them, than they did to such poetry as he so pointedly had *not* undertaken, on this occasion, to provide. They refused to engage the *Odes* on their own terms, and spent much of their time bemoaning the absence of the spectral 'Gray's Elegy, Continued' that they seem to have expected from Gray's pen. While the response of the professional critics should not be ignored, we would do well to remember that the reviews and journals at this period did not yet possess quite that degree of critical authority which they were to exercise in the decades to come. Reviewers such as John Gibson Lockhart and John Wilson Croker, who were to wield such authority in the romantic period, had yet to be fully unleashed upon the critical world. Oliver Goldsmith, who was only just beginning to establish his own reputation in the London literary scene, and who would later in life, in a conversation with John Craddock, casually assert that he could 'mend' Gray's *Elegy* by "leaving out an idle word in every line', notably observed of *The Bard* in the *Monthly Review* for September, 1757, that 'the Author seems to have taken the hint for this subject from the fifteenth Ode of the first Book of Horace'.[39] Far from being shamed by the intimation of such a debt, Gray wrote to Wharton that he particularly 'admired' the connection drawn by Goldsmith between the prophecy of Nereus in his predecessor's work, and the bard's condemnation of Edward in his own, though the advice of the same author that he 'be more an *original*, & . . . cultivate the native flowers of the soil, & not introduce the exoticks of another climate', is relayed to Wharton in the same letter in a spirit of gentle tolerance. Unsigned, positive notices on the *Odes* also appeared in the *Critical Review* (in a piece mistakenly attributed to Dr. Thomas Francklin, the Professor of Greek at Cambridge) and in the *Literary Magazine*.

Samuel Johnson's influential criticisms of the *Odes* in his 'Life of Gray' would be published only ten years after the poet's death. Much in the manner of his objections to Milton, Swift, and the disdainfully 'metaphysical' Cowley, Johnson's dismissal of Gray's *Odes*, in particular, is likely to strike the modern reader as unnecessarily rash and unfair. Quite apart from his caviling with individual stanzas and imagery, Johnson finally and famously pronounced with reference to both poems:

These odes are marked by glittering accumulations of ungraceful ornaments: they strike, rather than please; the images are magnified by affec-

---

[39] *Monthly Review*, xvii (1757) 242.

tation; the language is laboured into harshness. The mind of the writer seems to work with unnatural violence. 'Double, double, toil and trouble'. He has a kind of strutting dignity, and is tall by walking on tiptoe. His art and his struggle are too visible, and there is too little appearance of ease and nature.

To say that he has no beauties would be unjust: a man like him, of great learning and great industry, could not but produce something valuable. When he pleases least, it can only be said that a good design was ill directed.[40]

The design of the *Odes* was not so 'ill-directed' on the occasion of their first appearance in the world so as to miss the audience for whom they were intended. More than two-thirds of the original edition of two thousand copies had been sold within the first month of printing. The fact, too, that the poems immediately prompted several popular parodies – Robert Lloyd's *Two Odes* (1760) among them – may have alarmed the author by the presumption of their intrusion and appropriation, but they served no less emphatically to underscore the fact that the poems were being read and were prompting discussion and debate, both about the nature of poetic diction and about the role of the poet in society, in general. Gray on several occasions expressed his resignation to the simple fact that the poems, though well-received, would never rival the *Elegy* or even the *Eton Ode* in terms of general popularity; but such resignation does not necessarily signify any disappointment with their reception. With the publication of the *Odes*, Gray had indeed managed once again to taste the 'sweets of praise', and he was, perhaps to his own surprise, content to discover that such sweets, however strong, no longer had the power very heavily to intoxicate him.

IV. Voluntary Gloom

On 12 December 1757, the actor, dramatist, and theatrical manager Colley Cibber – having served in the office of poet laureate for twenty-seven years – died. Cibber, whose personal vanity both on the page (most notably in his proleptic and much maligned 1740 autobiography, *An Apology for the Life of Mr. Colley Cibber, Comedian*) and whose behaviour in the world at large unfortunately attracted the talents of a singularly talented and influential band of detractors (Pope and Fielding among them), had arguably been no more ineffective in the post than his immediate predecessors, Laurence Eusden and Nicholas Rowe. Cibber's occasional court productions – rewarded as they were by an

---

[40] Johnson, *Lives of the English Poets*, iii. 440.

emolument consisting of an allowance of 'canary wine' or sack – were slight and easily forgettable. Writing to order is never an easy task for an imaginative author; few poets welcome the constraint of being expected to present, on demand, tailor-made and invariably laudatory or lachrymose verses in praise of state occasions.

Mason instantly saw in the vacancy created by Cibber's death a moment of rare opportunity – if not for himself, then perhaps at the very least for his friend Gray. In his *Memoirs*, Mason was to write of the laureateship: 'this place the late Duke of Devonshire (then Lord Chamberlain) desired his brother (Lord John Cavendish) to offer to Mr. Gray; and his Lordship had commissioned me (then in town) to write to him concerning it'.[41] Mason passed on this information to the poet almost immediately; although the better part of the mid-December correspondence between the two friends no longer survives, Gray outlined his reasons for declining any such position at length in a letter to Mason that must have followed hard on the heels of his more formal refusal. Gray wrote on 19 December:

> Tho' I very well know the bland emollient saponaceous qualities both of Sack & Silver, yet if any great Man would say to me, 'I make you *Rat-Catcher* to his Majesty with a salary of 300 £ a-year & two Butts of the best Malaga; and tho' it has been usual to catch a mouse or two (for form's sake) in publick once a year, yet to You, Sr, we shall not stand upon these things'. I can not say I jump at it. nay, if they would drop the very name of the Office, & call me *Sinecure* to the Kg's majesty, I should still feel a little awkward, & think every body, I saw, smelt a Rat about me: but I do not pretend to blame any one else, that had not the same sensations. for my part I would rather be Serjeant-Trumpeter, or Pin-Maker to the Palace. nevertheless I interest myself a little in the History of it, & rather wish somebody may accept it, that will retrieve the credit of the thing, if it be retrievable, or ever had any credit. Rowe was, I think, the last Man of character that had it. as to Settle, whom you mention, he belong'd to my Ld Mayor, not to the King. Eusden was a Person of great hopes in his youth, tho' at last he turned out a drunken Parson. Dryden was as dis-graceful to the Office from his character, as the poorest Scribler could have been from his verses. [In sh]ort the office itself has always humbled the Pos[sess]or hitherto (even in an age, when Kings were somebody) if he were a poor Writer by making him more conspicuous, and if he were a good one, by setting him at war with the little fry of his own profession, for there are poets little enough to envy even a Poet-Laureat. (*CTG* 543–45)

The sentiments expressed in Gray's last sentence here might be construed as a thinly veiled attack on Mason's own vanity; Gosse, at least, would

---

[41]   See *CTG* 543.

assert that Mason 'raged with disappointment' when he realized that he would not, following Gray's first refusal, be offered the post himself. In any event, the laureateship was within only a matter of days offered to the Cambridge-educated poet and dramatist William Whitehead, who gladly accepted the position.

Gray's correspondence in the early months of 1758 found him calmly but determinedly fending off further responses to his odes, and dealing in an equally level-headed manner with the flood of solicitation and advice demanded of him by Mason. His spirits throughout the close of winter and the early spring months were unusually low, and the generally poor state of his health was further exacerbated by a succession of debilitating head colds that he seemed incapable of shaking off, and a state of depression which the leaden gloom of the season did little to cheer. 'My spirits', he confessed with typical candour to Wharton at one of his lowest points that February, 'are very near the *freezing point*'. On 8 March he wrote again to Wharton, who had recently taken up residence in Southampton Row near Bedford House (which stood on the north side of what is today Bloomsbury Square), regarding his continuing depression, and of the manner in which it seemed both to deter and yet at the same time exert a determining influence on his scholarly pursuits:

> It is indeed for want of spirits, as you suspect, that my studies lie among the Cathedrals, and the Tombs, and the Ruins. To think, though to little purpose, has been the chief amusement of my days; and when I would not, or cannot think, I dream. At present I find myself able to write a Catalogue, or to read the Peerage book, or Miller's Gardening Dictionary, and am thankful that there are such employments and such authors in the world. Some people, who hold me cheap for this, are doing perhaps what is not half so well worth while. As to posterity, I may ask (with some body whom I have forgot) what has it ever done to oblige me? (*CTG* 565–66)

It was at about this time that Gray filled in the last ninety pages of the second volume of his Commonplace Book with notes under the headings *Sepulchra* and *Ecclesia*; the first selection catalogued the monuments of the Royal Family and the places of Residence of the Nobility, the second detailed facts and observations on a selection of twenty-eight Welsh and English cathedrals. Throughout the spring he kept himself further occupied by annotating the blank leaves in a copy of Kitchen's English Atlas, *A Catalogue of the Antiquities, Houses, &c., in England and Wales*. In spite of such determined and self-consciously busying occupations, he seemed still to remain trapped in the stasis of a hopeless melancholy. As he had written with unusual precision to Mason at about this time:

> A Life spent out of the World has its hours of despondence, its inconveniences, its sufferings, as numerous, & as real (tho' not quite of the same sort) as a life spent in the midst of it. the power we have, when we will exert it, over our own minds, join'd to a little strength and consolation, nay, a little pride, we catch from those, that seem to love us, is our only support in either of these conditions. (*CTG* 561)

The persistence and the sense of guilt betrayed by Gray's despondency throughout the late winter and spring may have been exacerbated by the fact that he was increasingly aware that, in actual terms, he had little if any thing to complain about. His financial situation was more secure than it had ever been before. Some time shortly after his mother's death, he sank a large portion of his property in an annuity, so that he could enjoy a larger regular income. Such solid investments meant that money matters were no longer uncertain or likely to change radically for the worse.

Gray did his best to remind himself that despite his sense of depression, his personal situation was in reality far less dismal than it might have been. The grief and misfortunes of others underscored his own prosperity. Toward the end of January he had sent to Edward Bedingfield a copy of an epitaph he had 'just wrote' for inscription on the tomb of his friend John Clerke's wife. Mrs. Clerke had died in childbirth on 27 April, 1757, at the age of only thirty-one. Her husband, once a contemporary of Gray's at Peterhouse, had for many years since practiced as a physician at Epsom. Gray's epitaph on Mrs. Clerke was eventually inscribed on a tablet in St. George's Church at Beckenham, in Kent, where Clerke's father had served as Rector. Its commemoration is simple, conventional, and direct:

> Lo! where this silent marble weeps,
> A friend, a wife, a mother sleeps:
> A heart, within whose sacred cell
> The peaceful virtues loved to dwell.
> Affection warm, and faith sincere,
> And soft humanity were there.
> In agony, in death, resigned,
> She felt the wound she left behind.
> Her infant image, here below,
> Sits smiling on a father's woe:
> Whom what awaits while yet he strays
> Along the lonely vale of days?
> A pang, to secret sorrow dear;
> A sigh; an unavailing tear;
> Till time shall every grief remove,
> With life, with memory, and with love. (*PTG* 208–09)

Gray's lines look to dwell with gentle dignity on the eventual recovery of that individuality which would otherwise seem to have been lost in the moment of death; the dissolution of mortality at once disperses and encapsulates the individual, rendering her mortal remains static but open to that temporal multivalency which is the result of the defining, personal relationships of this world (Lo, where this little marble weeps, / A Friend, a Wife, a Mother sleeps'). Only within the redemptive structures of Christian belief, Gray's lines suggest, will each of us be re-integrated and recognized as our 'essential' selves. Writing the 'Epitaph' for Mrs. Clerke, Gray could not help but recall the death of his own mother; the death 'agony' that threatens to unbalance the restraint of Gray's commemoration at its seventh line might even have brought to bear the earliest and most vivid memories of the poet's own childhood – of the pain and 'agony' experienced by his own mother in her many experiences of childbirth – on the task of memorializing his friend's wife.

Nor was this the only epitaph that Gray would be compelled to write at this period. In early April he received word at Cambridge that Wharton's eldest son – the familiarly nick-named Robin – had died. The letter he wrote to his grieving friend reveals just how closely the two men had come to rely upon each other for emotional strength and support at precisely such times of difficulty. Gray wrote to Wharton that April:

> I am equally sensible of your affliction, & of your kindness, that made you think of me at such a moment. would to God, I could lessen the one, or requite the other with that consolation, which I have often received from you, when I most wanted it! but your grief is too just, & the cause of it still fresh, to admit of any such endeavour. what indeed is all human consolation, can it efface every little amiable word or action of an object we loved, from our memory? can it convince us, that all the hopes we had entertain'd, the plans of future satisfaction we had form'd, were ill-grounded & vain, only because we have lost them? the only comfort (I am afraid) that belongs to our condition is to reflect (when time has given us the leisure for reflection) that others have suffer'd worse, or that we ourselves might have suffer'd the same misfortune at times & in circumstances, that would probably have aggravated our sarrow. (*CTG* 569–70)

And again, in June:

> I am much concern'd to hear the account you give of yourself, & particularly for that dejection of spirits, which inclines you to see everything in the worst light possible, and throw a sort of voluntary gloom not only over your present, but future days, as if even your situation now were not preferable to that of thousands round you, & as if your prospect

hereafter might not open as much happiness to you, as to any Person you know. the condition of our life perpetually instructs us to be rather slow to hope, as well as to despair, & (I know, you will forgive me, if I tell you) you are often a little too hasty in both, perhaps from constitution. (CTG 570–71)

The lines Gray wrote as an epitaph for young Robin Wharton look in a similar manner of consolation to focus the attention of the bereaved not on the joys and opportunities that will be missed in the course of a natural life, but rather on the childhood innocence that can never, now, be sullied by the experience of the outside world and maturity:

> Here, freed from pain, secure from misery, lies
> A child, the darling of his parents' eyes:
> A gentler lamb ne'er sported on the plain,
> A fairer flower will never bloom again.
> Few were the days allotted to his breath;
> Now let him sleep in peace his night of death. (PTG 210)

The Epitaph's insistence that Wharton 'let go' of his grief for his son implicitly reiterates the sentiments of the *Eton Ode* in its suggestion that the 'night of death' is nothing more than a reprieve from the 'pain' and the certain 'misery' of adulthood.

*

In the second week of June Gray left Cambridge briefly to undertake a 'little expedition' into the Fens. 'I have been exercising my eyes', he wrote to Mason, 'at Peterborough, Crowland, Thorney, Ely, &c; and am grown a great Fen-Antiquarian'. As was by now his well-established practice, Gray took a number of architectural notes on the abbeys and castles he visited in the course of his week-long tour; he protested to Wharton that the diversion had not been a heavy undertaking, but had merely served to affect a change of scenery which 'amused' him 'a little'.

Shortly after returning from this tour, Gray received word from his aunt Mrs. Oliffe at Stoke that Mrs. Jonathan Rogers, Dorothy Gray's eldest sister, had lately been 'very ill' and now looked to be in increasingly poor health; Jane Oliffe added that she was far from being in the best of shape herself. Gray soon travelled to Stoke, where he stayed for much of the summer, undertaking extended visits to Strawberry Hill, and accompanying Lady Cobham and Henrietta Speed to Hampton Court, and to the seat of the Earl of Northumberland, Syon House, near Isleworth. In August, Lady Cobham was visited at Stoke Manor House by the Garricks, and although Gray made a point of being present for his

friends nearly every day for an entire week, he confessed himself no
longer capable of exerting the kind of energy necessary for such social
situations to be in any way enjoyable. 'They are now gone', Gray wrote
of the Garricks at the end of the month, '& I am not sorry for it, for I
grow so old, that, I own, People in high spirits & gayety overpower me,
& entirely take away mine.' Despite the sound nature of his own advice
to Wharton, Gray was himself plagued by low spirits as the summer
drew to its close. In September he ended a letter to Brown with the observation that he had little to complain of with regard to his physical health,
but 'as to my spirits they are always many degrees below changeable,
& I seem to myself to inspire every thing around me with ennuy & dejec-
tion'. Watching as his aunt moved through the final stages of a painful
illness did nothing to lighten his mood. He wrote of his aunt's condition
to Wharton. 'I have not been a step out of the house for this fortnight
or more past',

> for Mrs. Rogers has been at the point of death with a disorder in her
> stomach accompanied with continual & laborious reachings, & a total
> loss of appetite, that has reduced her to the weakness of an infant, I mean,
> her body, tho' her senses are still perfect, & (what I think remarkable)
> she has recover'd the use of her speech . . . & pronounces almost as plain,
> as she ever did. (*CTG* 589)

'The approaches of death are always a melancholy object' Gray now
wrote, '& common humanity must suffer something from such a spectacle'. Mrs. Rogers died at the end of September, and Gray devoted much
of the autumn to tying up her financial affairs. According to the terms
of his aunt's will, which was proved by Gray and Mrs. Oliffe, as joint
executors, in the first week of October, Gray himself was left £500, in
addition to certain house property. The cottage at Stoke Poges – the
house that had for so many years provided the poet with a certain shelter
and comfort – was put up for sale. Gray himself returned for the time
being to Cambridge, but, as events proved, his restless spirit was no
longer content to remain there for very long.

CHAPTER NINE

INTERLUDE

Bloomsbury and Studies in Norse and Welsh Poetry
1759–1761

I. A Season of Triumph

Some time toward the beginning of July 1759, having finally settled the details of his aunt's estate, Gray decided abruptly to abandon the new chambers at Pembroke into which he had moved the previous year (and in which he had spent precious little time since) and take up temporary residence in London. He hired a set of rooms in Southampton Row, in a property owned by a Mr. Jauncey. The poet's seemingly impulsive decision to forsake the seclusion of academic life – for however short or undetermined a period – and move to Bloomsbury was based on a fortuitous combination of circumstances. Earlier that spring, Wharton had succeeded to the country manor and estate of Old Park, near Durham, and the ensuing vacancy of his friend the Doctor's old rooms made the transition a relatively smooth and convenient one for him to make. Much of the furniture, china, and linen that Gray had inherited from his aunt had already been entrusted to Wharton's care several months earlier, so there was much less physical upheaval or disturbance than might otherwise have been expected. There were, to be sure, some minor drawbacks to the situation. His new rooms were located directly above a bakery (he jokingly referred in his letters to Wharton to their shared nickname for the residence as the 'Oven'), and Gray expected that summer to be 'baking with the heat all the summer'. Having left Stoke for good, and having at least completed the generally unsettling business of his co-executorship with Mrs. Oliffe, the time no doubt seemed right for such a change. The prospect of returning to Cambridge as the long and solitary summer vacation was only just beginning, at least, could not possibly have held any more attraction. The recent opening of the British Museum just a short walk from the poet's new residence, on the other hand – with all its 'manuscripts and rarities by the cart load' – held tremendous promise for a scholar of Gray's temperament, and he looked forward to the time he would spend at work in the new facility as his 'chief amusement'. Moreover, Gray's financial situation had once again improved – so much so that he could now afford such amenities as would render his residence in London rather smoother and less personally stressful than it might have been at any other time in his life. From this point on, Gray engaged a manservant to attend to his personal needs, though he found it necessary to terminate the services of at least two uncongenial employees (he referred to one, John, as 'a lad that cannot do any earthly thing') before settling on a suitably fastidious assistant in the person of Stephen Hempstead. Hempstead was to remain loyally in the poet's service for the remainder of his life.

Even from London, Gray wrote to Wharton of the weather and the various floral fortunes of the season, though his personal observations were now limited to the state of the jessamine he could glimpse within the prospect of his 'new territories' overlooking Bedford Gardens, and to speculations based on the composition of the nosegays he purchased at flower market in Covent Garden. He still detailed the accounts of the harvests and the rural calendar – the stuff of which he continued to copy into personal journals – yet his records to Wharton were rather more punctuated than they had ever been before by qualifying apologies ('I think'. 'I hear', 'I am told') with respect to the second-hand nature of his information. Be that as it may, the area in which he now lived had yet to become all that urban. The new Museum itself still very much stood as one of the northernmost landmarks of the metropolis. Gray was, as he noted in a letter to Palgrave, within comparatively easy striking distance of 'all the fields as far as Highgate and Hampstead . . . so rus-in-urbe-ish that I believe I shall stay here, except little excursions and voyages, for a year to come'. To Wharton, however, he soon confessed, 'I do not see much myself in the face of nature here', but, he added, 'I enquire'.

As expected, the better part of Gray's time in these summer months was spent in the new Museum. Its library, he wrote to Brown, had soon become his 'favourite Domain', where, he continued,

> I often pass four hours in the day in the stillness & solitude of the reading room, which is uninterrupted by anything but Dr Stukeley the Antiquary, who comes there to talk nonsense, & Coffee-house news. the rest of the Learned are (I suppose) in the country; at least none of them come here, expect two Prussians, & a Man, who writes for Ld Royston. when I call it peaceful, you are to understand it only of us Visitors, for the Society itself, Trustees, & all, are up in arms, like the Fellows of a College. the Keepers have broke off all intercourse with one another, & only lower a silent defiance, as they pass by. (*CTG* 632–33)

Life in London, it seems, was proving in certain respects to be not so very much different than life in college, after all.

In spite of such squabbling, Gray was more than satisfied with the manuscript material in the Harleian and Cottonian collections that now lay at his disposal. The entire summer was spent in the happy pursuit of scholarship. 'I live in the Museum', he wrote to Wharton in September,

> & write volumes of antiquity, I have got (out of the original Ledger-book of the Signet) K: Richards 3d's Oath to Elizabeth, *late calling herself Queen of* England; to prevail upon her to come out of Sanctuary with her 5 Daughters. his Grant to Lady Hastings & her Son, dated 6 weeks after he had cut off her Husband's head. a Letter to his Mother; another to his Chancellor, to persuade his Sollicitor General not to marry Jane Shore then in Ludgate by his command. Sr Tho: Wyat's Defence at his Tryal, when accused by Bp Bonner of high-treason; Lady Purbeck & her Son's remarkable Case, & several more odd things unknown to our Historians. (*CTG* 642–43)

Still more material demanded Gray's attention when he returned to his rooms in the evenings. Walpole's relation Lord Hertford had in the preceding year turned over to his antiquarian cousin an impressive cachet of the state papers and private correspondence of the Conway family dating from the seventeenth century. Edward Conway, first Baron Conway of Ragly and first Viscount Conway, had served as Secretary of State in the early seventeenth century. His grandson Edward Conway, first Earl of Conway, had commanded the same position for a shorter period in the later years of the reign of Charles II. The 'grand heap' that constituted both their private and their public correspondence had been quietly transferred by Walpole to Gray's personal care, and the long summer evenings in Southampton Row were spent reading and deciphering the manuscripts. 'In short', the poet quipped happily to Wharton, 'I am up to the ears'.

Gray's other friends, as usual, made generally welcome claims on his time and attention. Mason's movements and whereabouts throughout the summer months had remained a mystery to him, though by the end of October he expected to see him in the city. Stonhewer's vaguely defined responsibilities as an interpreter and diplomat found him stopping briefly in London on his way to Portsmouth 'to receive a Morocco Embassador'. Walpole's latest additions to the increasingly extravagant follies at Strawberry Hill – the centrepiece of which was modeled on the Holbein chamber in the Queen's Closet at Kennington – were praised by Gray as being 'in the best taste of anything he has yet done'. And Wharton not only kept Gray busy as always with his scrupulous accounts of the weather and natural history, but also sought his assistance in purchasing wall-hangings and tapestries for refurbishment at Old Park. Brown, comfortable in Cambridge, similarly solicited Gray to keep an eye out for some hard-to-find theology texts that he hoped might be available at John Nourse's bookshop in the Strand.

*

Generally reticent and at times close to cryptic in his references to contemporary political and military affairs, even Gray could not help but be caught up that year in the general enthusiasm which surrounded recent English victories under the leadership of William Pitt in the conflict with France that would later be dubbed the Seven Years' War. The war, which began in 1756, had initially been an unmitigated disaster for the English. On the continent, Hanover was compelled to surrender to French forces; in North America, the armies of the enemy looked to follow their earliest victories in New York with further triumphs in Pennsylvania and the Mid-Atlantic colonies. Meanwhile, in India, the surrender of a British garrison to the nawab of Bengal had resulted in the horrific death by suffocation of nearly all the prisoners in the tiny holding cell that was soon infamously known throughout the world as the Black Hole of Calcutta (only twenty-three of the 146 prisoners pressed into the room's confines emerged alive). Only when Pitt emerged as Minister in charge of war in the struggle for power that had followed the inefficiency of a short-lived coalition government would the tide begin to turn in favour of the British. First bolstering the financial support of Frederick II and the Prussian Army, and of Prince Frederick of Brunswick's Hanoverian forces on the continent, Pitt then turned the superior power of the British navy to its best advantage in an attempt to cripple the French at sea and wreak havoc on their commercial trade. The appointment of James Wolfe and William Howe as leaders of newly organized and more efficient expeditionary forces galvanized not only the troops themselves, but seemed to unite the entire country in a surge of renewed commitment and patriotism.

The brightness of such prospects notwithstanding, these continued to be tense months for the British, and even within the closeted quiet of the Museum, at least one heart beat with anxiety regarding the lingering possibilities of a French invasion of England. As Gray wrote:

> Every body continues as quiet about the Invasion, as if a Frenchman, as soon as he set foot on our coast, would die, like a Toad in Ireland: yet the King's Tents & Equipage are order'd to be ready at an hour's warning. no body knows positively, what is the damage, that Rodney has done, whether much or little: he can only guess himself; & the French have kept their own secret, as yet. of the 12 Millions, raised for the year, eight are gone already, & the old Party assures us, there is no more to be had for next year. You may easily guess at the source of my intelligence, & therefore will not talk of it. News is hourly expected of a Battle in Westphalia, for Pr: Ferdinand was certainly preparing to fight the French, who have taken Minden by storm. (*CTG* 628)

Even as Gray wrote this letter, however, the winds of change were in the air. The expedition of George Rodney's squad against the French at

Le Havre, the outcome of which Gray had so nervously anticipated in the passage above, succeeded in its almost total bombardment of the supplies and of the flat-bottomed transport boats that had been assembled at the port city in preparation for a full-scale invasion of England. Admiral Hawke's victory against the Brest Fleet at Quiberon Bay compounded the French humiliation. Although other raids on the French coast at St. Malo and Rochefort were to prove costly failures, the Battle of Minden, in August, was likewise a great success for the English and Hanoverian forces; the triumph of Ferdinand and his British allies in Germany, as the historian Paul Langford has written, guaranteed the preservation of the Electorate by 'rendering French victory in the German war improbable'.[1] By 8 August Gray could write with relief to Brown:

> The season for triumph is at last come; I mean for our Allies, for it will be long enough before we shall have reason to exult in any great actions of our own, & therefore, as usual, we are proud for our neighbors. Contades' great army [at Minden] is entirely defeated: this (I am told) is undoubted, but no particulars are known yet; & almost as few of the other victory over ye Russians, which is lost in the splendor of this great action. (CTG 632)

Gray was correct in supposing that the British forces would soon enough have 'reason to exult' in great actions of their own. Walpole was soon gleefully joking in his letters that 'one is forced to ask every morning what victory there is, for fear of missing one', and pretending to bewail the fact that the parish church bells of England had been 'worn threadbare with ringing for victories'. In India, Robert Clive defeated the nawab of Bengal at Plassey; Admiral Boscawan likewise bested the French Toulon Fleet off Cape Lagos, and British forces triumphed in Dusquene; the capture of Louisburg – a key garrison on the St. Lawrence – proved in time to have been a watershed victory. The success of British forces in the North American Lakes led General Wolfe famously to attack Quebec, a settlement critically situated along the route to Montreal; Wolfe crushed the French troops under Montcalm on the Plains of Abraham, a victory that cost him his life.

The circumstances surrounding Wolfe's heroic death that fateful September day were forever to be linked in cultural memory to Gray's own *Elegy* by means of an anecdote later repeated on several occasions by a member of Wolfe's expedition, a young midshipman aboard the *Royal William* by the name of John Robison. Eventually a Professor of Natural Philosophy at the University of Edinburgh, Robison in

---

[1] Langford, *A Polite and Commercial People*, 337.

later years offered a recollection of Wolfe's demeanour and behaviour on the night before the battle. His anecdotal memory is preserved in at least two written versions. The first such account was passed on to the poet Robert Southey by Sir Walter Scott many years after the event. 'On the night when Wolfe crossed the river with his small army', Scott reported,

> they passed in the men-of-war's long boats and launches and the General himself in the Admiral's barge. The young midshipman who steered the boat was John Robison. . . . I have repeatedly heard the Professor say that during part of the passage Wolfe pulled out of his pocket and read to the officers around (or, perhaps, repeated), Gray's celebrated *Elegy in a Country Churchyard*. I do not know if the recitation was not so well received as he expected, but he said, with a good deal of animation, 'I can only say, Gentlemen, that, if the choice were mine, I would rather be the author of these verses than win the battle which we are to fight tomorrow morning.[2]

Scott further suggested to Southey (who was editing some of Wolfe's correspondence at the time) that Wolfe's comment constituted 'a strong way of expressing his love of literature'.[3]

Another version of the incident was recorded by one of Robison's students, James Currie, in a letter written to his father in 1804, within days of having heard the story from the Professor's own lips over the supper table:

> He told me that general Wolfe kept his intention of attacking Quebec a most profound secret; not even disclosing it to the Second-in Command, and the night before the attack nothing was known. The boats were ordered to drop down the St. Lawrence, and it happened that the boat which Professor Robison, then a midshipman, commanded, was very near the one General Wolfe was in. A gentleman was repeating Gray's *Elegy* to the latter, and Mr. Robison heard him (the General) say 'I would rather have been the author of that piece than beat the French tomorrow;' and from this remark guessed that the attack was to be made the next day.[4]

Which of these two early versions of Robison's experience is closer to the actual truth remains impossible to say. The story was later repeated, in slightly different versions, by Henry Mackenzie in *An*

[2] Sir Walter Scott to Robert Southey, 21 September 1830; reprinted in *The Letters of Sir Walter Scott*, ed. H. J. C. Grierson, 12 vols. (London: Constable, 1932–37) xi.392.
[3] Ibid.
[4] Quoted in Ketton-Cremer, *Thomas Gray*, 168.

Account of the Life and Writings of John Home, Esq. (1822) and by William Hazlitt in the *Literary Examiner* in 1823. Alan McNairn has commented:

> The absence of the tale of Wolfe and Gray's *Elegy* in eighteenth-century literature is significant; the story did not conform to the image then being created of the defunct commander. His grand gesture for liberty was unrelated, indeed antithetical, to Gray's ruminations on 'the short and simple annals of the poor' who 'kept the noiseless tenor of their way,' and 'for who, to dumb forgetfulness a prey,' destiny was obscured like a flower 'born to blush unseen, / And waste its sweetness on the desert air.' These lines, never quoted in the narration of Wolfe's last hours, were not useful in heightening the meaning of Wolfe's sacrifice.[5]

There is no reason, however, to doubt the essential substance of Robison's recollection of Wolfe's sentiments. Katherine Lawler, the woman whom Wolfe had intended to marry on his return to England, had pointedly given the general a copy of Gray's poem just prior to his departure for America (the copy, containing Wolfe's own inscription and annotations, still exists in the Fisher Rare Book Library at the University of Toronto). Gray himself, incidently, seems unfortunately never to have received any word of this most celebrated tribute to his poem; no reference even to the victory of Wolfe's forces or to the event of the General's death was made by the poet in his correspondence that summer. Perhaps the greatest and most sincerely felt flattery ever bestowed upon the *Elegy* seems never to have soothed the poet's ear, in life.

II. Idle Notes

Gray had maintained his long-standing interest in the affairs and health of Lady Cobham at Stoke, and continued to profess his polite concern for Henrietta Jane Speed throughout the long summer months in London. Miss Speed was one of those correspondents with whom Gray shared news of international affairs in late August, and she seems to have responded to his continued solicitation with genuine warmth and gratitude. 'I wonder', she wrote on 25 August,

> whether you think me capable of all the gratitude I really feel for the late marks you have given me of your friendship, I will venture to say if you knew my heart you wou'd be content with it, but knowing my exterior

---

[5] Alan McNairn, *Behold the Hero: General Wolfe and the Arts in the Eighteenth Century* (Montreal and Kingston: McGill-Queen's University Press, 1997) 237.

so well as you do You can easily conceive me Vain of the Partiallity you show me; in return for putting me in good humour with myself I will give you pleasure by assuring you Lady Cobham is surprizingly well & most extremely oblig'd to you for the Anxiety you express'd on her account. – we now take the Air ev'ry day and are returnd to our old way of living and hope we shall go on in the same way many Years. (*CTG* 636–37)

Speed invited Gray to abandon the city's heat for the comforts of Stoke Manor House, where, she assured him 'you will find Ev'rything cool but the reception we shall give you – there is always a Bed Air'd for you (and, she added nicely, 'one for your Servant').

Gray took up the invitation to Stoke only late in September, by which time Lady Cobham's health had taken a dramatic turn for the worse. When the ladies decided to return from the country to Lady Cobham's townhouse in Hanover Square, Gray – rather than immediately resettling himself in his own rooms at Southampton Row – remained, at Lady Cobham's particular request, in the same house, forming an integral part of what he referred to on at least one occasion as 'our small Family'. Writing from the Hanover Square residence in late October, Gray related what he knew of the state of Lady Cobham's health in detail to a mutual friend, Mrs. Jennings, of Shiplake, in Oxfordshire. 'I have stay'd thus long', he wrote,

that I might be the better able to say something more determinate on the cause of Lady Cobham's illness & the probability of her recovery: but find myself after all very little wiser in either point. . . . the great malady now is want of sleep, which I can not say she has enjoy'd in a natural way (except for an hour or two at most, & that in the day-time) since we came to Town. she has taken draughts with Laudanum in them over night; but they have succeeded only twice or thrice in procuring quiet slumber, after which the whole following day she had appear'd, as one in perfect health. . . . if any new symptom of consequence should follow, I will take care to inform you. Dr Duncan is still the Man. (*CTG* 647–48)

Gray's apparent optimism with regard to the professional abilities of Dr. William Duncan, who was personal physician to Lord Bute, proved finally to have been ill-founded. Lady Cobham died on 20 March, having endured in the final months of her illness a great deal of pain. The terms of Lady Cobham's will left Gray in possession of a token legacy of some £21, a sum meant to be spent in the purchase of a mourning ring. Miss Speed, named in the will as sole executor and residuary legatee, came into a substantial inheritance of 'at least £30,000 with a house in Town, plate, jewels, china, and old-japan infinite'. Henrietta Jane Speed was now, in fact, an heiress in possession of a considerable private fortune. Precisely how she intended to exercise her new freedom and power remained uncertain; the disposition of so much wealth and the choices to be made among so many possible options, Gray confided with reason and sympathy to Wharton, soon rendered her affairs so complicated 'so that indeed it would be ridiculous for her to know her own mind'.

Gray made a particular point of saying in close contact with Miss Speed in the weeks and months that followed Lady Cobham's death; and, indeed, he stayed in regular contact with her until her eventual marriage to the Baron de la Peyrière in 1762 (a match the wisdom of which he questioned). Immediately following Lady Cobham's death, Gray appears to have spent a fair amount of time in Miss Speed's company. In late June, 1760, he accompanied her on a visit to Grovelands, Shiplake, the home of the same Mrs. Jennings to whom Gray had written in the final months of Lady Cobham's illness. There, in the company of Miss Speed, Mrs. Jennings, and Mrs. Jenning's daughter, he passed what turned out to be an uncongenial three weeks. Soon after his return, he wrote to John Clerke:

> Not knowing whether you are yet returned from your sea-water, I write at random to you. For me, I am come to my resting place, and find it very necessary, after living for a month in a house with the three women that laughed from morning to night, and would allow nothing to the sulkiness of my disposition. Company and cards at home, parties by land and water abroad, and (what they call) *doing something*, that is, racketting about from morning to night, are occupations, I find, that wear out my spirits, especially in a situation where one might sit still, and be alone with pleasure; for the place was a hill like Clifden [i.e., Cliveden], opening to a very extensive and diversified landscape, with the Thames, which is navigable, running at its foot. (*CTG* 692–93)

At some point in their friendship that year – probably shortly during or just after their stay together at Shiplake – Miss Speed is said to have expressed a casual desire to 'possess something from [Gray's] pen, written on the subject of love'. Two slight lyrics, both of them untitled, and referred to subsequently simply as 'Songs', would seem to date from roughly this period of intimacy with Miss Speed. Although both pieces circulated in manuscript in Gray's lifetime, they would be published only after the poet's death. The first 'Song' consists of two short stanzas:

> 'Midst beauty and pleasure's gay triumphs, to languish
> And droop without knowing the source of my anguish;
> To start from short slumbers and look for the morning –
> Yet close my dull eyes when I see it returning;

Sighs sudden and frequent, looks ever dejected,
Sounds that steal from my tongue, by no means connected!
Ah say, fellow-swains, how these symptoms befell me?
They smile, but reply not. Sure Delia will tell me! (*PTG* 241)

The second lyric is similarly little more than a *jeu d'esprit*:

> Thyrsis, when we parted, swore
> Ere the spring he would return.
> Ah, what means yon violet flower,
> And the buds that deck the thorn?
> 'Twas the lark that upward sprung!
> 'Twas the nightingale that sung!
> Idle notes, untimely green,
>> Why such unavailing haste?
>> Western gales and skies serene
> Prove not always winter past.
> Cease my doubts, my fears to move;
> Spare the honour of my love. (*PTG* 242–43)

Both lyrics are bound by tender ties of possible reference to Gray's more serious poetry – the first recalls the dubious nature of blissful Ignorance in the *Eton Ode*, for example, while the second more significantly echoes the *Sonnet* on the death of Richard West. Both songs, too, appear determined to emphasize the indefinable, unknowable nature of any genuinely romantic attachment, and the possibility of loss and disappointment, rather than expressing any explicit affection or attachment to Miss Speed.

*

Gray's main interests through the end of 1759 and into 1760 continued to revolve around the constant flood of news concerning political and military affairs, about which he corresponded with great animation to Wharton and Brown. He also concerned himself with the latest obsessions of the literary world, and with his own, on-going work among the collections in the British Museum. Gray responded with enthusiasm to the earliest volumes of Laurence Sterne's *Tristram Shandy*, of which he observed to Wharton, 'there is much good fun in it, & humour sometimes hit & sometimes mist'. Rousseau's *La Nouvelle Heloïse* – which he was slow in getting his hands on – fared less well in his judgement: 'I was foolish enough to go thro' the six volumes of the *Nouvelle Eloïse*', he wrote to Mason,

> all I can say for myself is, that I was confined for three weeks at home by a severe cold, & had nothing better to do. there is no one event in it,

that might not happen any day of the week (separately taken) in any private family. yet these events are so put together, that the series of them is more absurd & more improbable than Amadis de Gaul. the Dramatis Personae (as the Author says) are all of them good Characters. I am sorry to hear it, for had they been all hang'd at the end of the 3d volume, no body (I believe) would have cared. in short, I went on & on in hopes of finding some wonderful *denouement* that would set all right, & bring something like Nature & Interest out of absurdity & insipidity. no such thing: it grows worse & worse, & (if it be Rousseau, which is not doubted) is the strongest instance I ever saw, that a very extraordinary Man may entirely mistake his own talents. (*CTG* 722)

Gray's most sustained interest throughout the earliest years of the new decade was reserved for the recent examples of Erse poetry that were then beginning to circulate among the London *literati*. Early in the spring of 1760, Walpole's acquaintance Sir David Dalrymple had sent him two species of such poetry. The pieces had been presented to him by the young Scotsman, James Macpherson, as translations of the work of the legendary Highland bard, Ossian, the son of Fingal. Macpherson's 'translations' of this ancient Scots poetry had already been causing something of a sensation in his native country, and Gray's interest in the Erse and Welsh backgrounds of the English poetic tradition led him quite naturally to express a particular interest in Macpherson's supposed discoveries.

From the moment Gray first encountered Macpherson's fragments, his enthusiasm and interest – and very possibly his suspicions regarding their authenticity – were raised. By May, 1760, Gray confessed to Wharton that he was so struck by what he had seen that he had already 'writ into Scotland to make a thousand enquiries'. In June, Gray again wrote to Wharton concerning the poems:

If you have seen Stonhewer he has probably told you of my old Scotch (or rather Irish) Poetry. I am gone mad about them. they are said to be translations (literal & in prose) from the *Erse*-tongue, done by one Macpherson, a young Clergyman in the High-lands. he means to publish a Collection he has of these Specimens of antiquity, if it be antiquity: but what plagues me is, I can not come at any certainty on that head. I was so struck, so *extasié* with their infinite beauty, that I writ into Scotland to make a thousand enquiries. the letters I have in return are ill-wrote, ill-reason'd, unsatisfactory, calculated (one might imagine) to deceive one, & yet not cunning enough to do it cleverly. in short, the whole external evidence would make one believe these fragments (for so he calls them, tho' nothing could be more entire) counterfeit: but the internal is so strong on the other side, that I am resolved to believe them genuine, spite of the Devil & the Kirk. (*CTG* 679–80)

Given the nature of such conflicting evidence, Gray asked Wharton in exasperation, 'What can one do?'

By the time Wharton received Gray's letter, Macpherson had finally published an entire volume of what he presented to the public as translations from original Gaelic. The volume was titled *Fragments of Ancient Poetry, collected in the Highlands of Scotland and translated from the Galic or Erse Language*. Having discovered an enthusiastic and well-positioned patron in his fellow countryman, Lord Bute, Macpherson was to be so much encouraged by the volume's reception as personally to travel to London the following year, at which time he would oversee the publication of another work, *Fingal, an Ancient Epic Poem, in Six Books: Together with several other Poems, composed by Ossian the Son of Fingal. Translated from the Galic Language*. The more thoroughly the Ossian poems were read and examined, however, the greater and more perplexing were the questions that seemed to be raised regarding their authenticity. A genuine public controversy arose around Macpherson's work, though it was a dispute in which Gray himself – having already fully expressed his doubts and uncertainties to his private friends – was disinclined to take any active part.

*

The controversy surrounding Macpherson's translations at least appeared to have had the galvanizing effect of returning Gray's attention to some of his own, recent experimentations with the nascent traditions of English poetry. Gray's scholarly research into the origins of English poetry had resulted in his undertaking a total of six 'translations' (more properly 'imitations' or adaptations) from the Norse and Welsh languages, the three most substantial of which only were published in Gray's lifetime. Gray appears at some stage of the project to have planned to include the fragments in the early portions of his history. The pieces thus formed part of his original and more ambitious design for such a volume, in which he further planned to include translations from 'Old English' or Anglo-Saxon. The 'Advertisement' that eventually accompanied their publication explained these origins, noting of the poet's original intentions: 'In the Introduction to [the History of English Poetry'] he meant to have produced some specimens of the Style that reigned in ancient times among the neighboring nations, or those who had subdued the greater part of this island, and were our Progenitors: the following three Imitations made a part of them'.

By May 1761, Gray had completed translations of two Icelandic lays – *The Fatal Sisters* and *The Descent of Odin* – pieces to which the poet himself referred vaguely as 'odes' (the term lay or 'lai', originally French, had since the sixteenth century been used by scholars and linguists in

England as synonymous with 'song'). In each instance, Gray's originals had been drawn from the Icelandic tradition, though each poem derived from quite different sources: the *Fatal Sisters* formed part of the eleventh century *Darraðar Lióð* (also called *The Lay of Darts* or 'The Song of Darrathor'), whereas the *The Descent of Odin* formed part of the *Vegtams Kviða* or 'The Ballad of Vegtam'.

News of Gray's latest efforts spread quickly. Walpole wrote to Montagu: 'Gray has translated two noble incantations from the Lord knows who, a Danish Gray, who lived the Lord knows when.'[6] Gray's immediate sources for the translations were actually Thomas Bartholin's *Antiquitatum Danicarum De Causis Contemptae A Danis Adhuc Gentilibus Mortis* (1689), the earliest printed source for the Norse sagas, and Thormdus Torfaeus's *Orcades Seu Rerum Orcadensium Historiae* (1697), both published in Copenhagen. Gray's notes from these sources had been carefully copied into his Commonplace Book under the comprehensive heading, 'Gothi'. *The Fatal Sisters* is written in quatrains of trochaic tetrameter; *The Descent of Odin* Gray rendered into octosyllabics couplets.

At about this same time, Gray was also at work on four lays adapted from Welsh, eventually titled, *The Triumphs of Owen. A Fragment, The Death of Hoel, Caradoc*, and *Conan*. All four of these last efforts were in seven-syllable couplets. The first such fragment was drawn from Gwalchmai ap Meilyr's twelfth-century Welsh poem *Ode to Owen Gwynedd*; the ultimate source for the three shorter pieces was the *Gododin* of Aneurin. The more immediate sources for these short pieces, however, were the prose, manuscript translations of Evan Evans, a writer of verse in English and Welsh, and the scholar who had discovered *Gododin*. By 1759, Evans had completed a Latin dissertation on the Welsh bards, *De Bardis Dissertatio*; his chief work, *Specimens of the Antient Welsh Bards, translated into English* was to appear in 1764. As a scholar, Evans had passed on some literal Latin translations of the fragments eventually translated by Gray to Daines Barrington, the fourth son of the first Viscount Barrington, with whom the poet had first become acquainted sometime in late 1759 or early 1760. Although Gray had attempted to acquire some knowledge of the Icelandic tongue to assist him in his work on *The Fatal Sisters* and *The Descent of Odin*, he worked primarily from Latin prose translations. His correspondence reveals that when it came to the specific characteristics of Old English and Norse verse, he at least had some sense of what to aim for, and his various attempts looked to reproduce some of the alliteration and patterns of stressed syllables that he noted as having constituted the defining feature of the original works. Gray does not appear to have

[6] WC ix.364.

known any Welsh to assist him on the four other pieces, and in those fragments from the Welsh he is prone to paraphrase his Latin sources rather than undertake any genuine translations from the original tongue.

The two Norse poems and *The Triumphs of Owen* would eventually be published by Dodsley in the 1768 edition of Gray's *Works*, in which volume they replaced *A Long Story*, a work which, since its original appearance in Bentley's *Designs*, the poet had deemed too anecdotal and personal for the public. The remaining fragments would be published only after Gray's death, in Mason's 1775 edition of the poet's *Works*. Gray wrote to Walpole of the 1768 edition: 'The *Long Story* was to be totally omitted, as its only use (that of explaining [Bentley's] prints was gone: but to supply the place of it in bulk, lest *my works* should be mistaken for the works of a flea or a pismire, I promised to send [Dodsley, the publisher] an equal weight of poetry or prose'.

The Fatal Sisters needed to be conceptualized for Gray's readers by a preface. The poem is a prophecy of the Battle of Clontarf, which had been fought on Good Friday, 1014 (though Gray situates the action on Christmas Day). The battle pitted Sictryg, King of Dublin, and Sigurd, Earl of the Orkneys, against Brian, King of Munster. Both Sigurd and Brian (who happened to be his father-in-law) were killed in the fighting, though the forces of the latter claim a victory. On the day of the battle, Gray further explained:

A native of Caithness in Scotland saw at a distance a number of persons on horseback riding full speed towards a hill, and seeming to enter into it. Curiosity led him to follow them, till looking through an opening in the rocks he saw twelve gigantic figures resembling women: they were all employed about a loom; and as they wove, they sung the following dreadful song; which when they had finished, they tore the web into twelve pieces, and (each taking her portion) galloped six to the north and as many to the south (*PTG* 215–16)

Most readers were impressed by Gray's ability in his imitations to capture something of the quality of 'gothic horror' that they vaguely attributed to his originals. His description of the Valykrie's activities on the day of the battle is grim enough:

> Now the storm begins to lower,
>   (Haste, the loom of hell prepare,)
> Iron-sleet of arrowy shower
>   Hurtles in the darkened air.
>
> Glittering lances are the loom,
>   Where the dusky warp we strain,

> Weaving many a soldier's doom,
>   Orkney's woe, and Randver's bane.
>
> See the grisly texture grow,
>   ('Tis of human entrails made,)
> And the weights that play below,
>   Each a gasping warrior's head.
>
>   . . .
>
> We the reins to slaughter give,
>   Ours to kill and ours to spare:
> Spite of danger he shall live,
>   (Weave the crimson web of war.) (*PTG* 216–19)

An anecdote eventually included in John Gibson Lockhart's 1837–38 *Memoirs of the Life of Sir Walter Scott* told of a clergyman who, in the years immediately prior to Gray's own death, carried a copy of the poet's imitation with him to North Ronaldsha, where he read it 'to some of the old people as referring to the ancient history of their islands. But as soon as he proceeded a little way, they explained they knew it very well in the original'.[7]

The Descent of Odin retells a familiar story from Norse mythology. Frigga, the mother of Balder, protected her son from all potentially harmful elements except, inadvertently, mistletoe. The evil spirit Loki arranged that Balder be struck by a bough of mistletoe held by the blind Hoder. Balder's father, Odin, chief of the Norse gods, undertook a visit to the underworld to learn the fate of his son. It is this incident that Gray's poem sets out to describe. The seer in the underworld named Balder as Hoder's slayer, and further identified Vali, the son of Odin and Rinda, as the step-brother who will avenge Balder's fate. In her address to Odin, the prophetess of the underworld asks some familiar questions (familiar, at least, to readers of Gray's own *Elegy*) of her visitor:

> What call unknown, what charms, presume
> To break the quiet of the tomb?
> Who thus afflicts my troubled sprite,
> And drags me from the realms of night?
> Long on these mouldering bones have beat
> The winter's snow, the summer's heat.
> The drenching dews, and driving rain!
> Let me, let me sleep again.
> Who is he, with voice unblest,

[7] The anecdote is reprinted in Lytton Sells, *Thomas Gray* 198–99, from Starr and Hendrickson, *The Complete Poems of Thomas Gray* (Oxford: Clarendon Press, 1966), 212.

That calls me from the bed of rest?
. . .
   Hie thee hence and boast at home,
That never shall enquirer come
To break my iron-sleep again,
Till Lok has burst his tenfold chain;
Never, till substantial Night
Has reassumed her ancient right;
Till wrapped in flames, in ruin hurled,
Sinks the fabric of the world. (*PTG* 224–28)

The poet's anticipation of the 'Twilight of the Gods' in this prophecy echoes the language of Milton's *Paradise Lost* and Pope's *Essay on Man*, but manages likewise to recall – almost to quote – the lines of his own, early translation of Propertius' *Elegies* ('How flames, perhaps, with dire confusion hurled, / Shall sink the beauteous fabric of the world'). It comes as no surprise that Gray seems to have sympathized with those who say the world will end in fire, rather than ice.

The third of the pieces published in 1768 was the Welsh imitation, *Triumphs of Owen*. The fragment commemorates the victory of Owen, prince of North Wales, over the forces of Henry II in 1157. Once again, Gray emphasizes the perceived aspect of gothic horror in his original material; describing Owen as the 'Dragon-son of Mona', Gray wrote:

Where his glowing eye-balls turn,
Thousand banners round him burn.
Where he points his purple spear,
Hasty, hasty rout is there,
Marking with indignant eye
Fear to stop and shame to fly.
There Confusion, Terror's child,
Conflict fierce and Ruin wild,
Agony that pants for breath,
Despair and honourable Death. (*PTG* 232–33)

The three shorter fragments of Gray's Welsh imitations are written in a similar vein. Each of them, in a manner similar to the far more fully realized *The Bard*, formed part of the poet's attempt in these middle years effectively to combine in his writing an articulation of the rewards of a patient and rigorous scholarship, on the one hand, with a sense of the almost mystic element inherent in 'inspired', bardic poetry, on the other – all attempt to speak in a voice of multivalent authority. The completed fragments seem also, as readers of Gray's work have come by now to expect, to recall some of the themes and rhetorical elements of his earlier poetry. The cursory reader might well be forgiven, for example, for at first mistaking the grim figures of the 'Fatal Sisters' as representations of the dire personifications of the *Eton Ode* somehow translated into or captured in the posture of swift and furious action; the forces of fate are now vigorously and threateningly animated. *Odin* seems likewise to recall the poet's youthful imitation – in his unpublished 'Lines' from the Devil Tavern – of the early eighteenth-century vogue for 'dialogues of the dead'; *Odin* is at the same time a poem which positions its subject as inquiring into the greater, 'divine' causes which motivate and lie beneath the subsidiary tragedies of human experience – Odin, not incidentally, is presented to the reader as engaged in the activity of seeking some explanation for the fact of death.

*

Once again in London, Gray busied himself generally in spending as much time as possible among some of his older friends – Walpole, Montagu, and Henrietta Speed among them. He seems particularly to have enjoyed his regular visits to the opera at this period, and raved no less wildly over the new season's latest sensation (in 1761, a tenor by the name of Filippo Frasi) than he had once done about the latest productions of Metastasio or Purcell. Gray made time for new friendships and enthusiasms as well. Sometime in the early spring, Gray made the acquaintance of Benjamin Stillingfleet. Stillingfleet, who had himself matriculated at Cambridge several years before Gray had even be sent to Eton, shared the poet's enthusiasm for the Linnaean system of Botany; as was often the case in his relations with Wharton, Gray's friendship with Stillingfleet rested in large part on their shared obsession with the minutiae and the changeability of the natural world. Describing his fellow enthusiast to Wharton, Gray wrote from London: 'I have lately made an acquaintance with this Philosopher, who lived in a garret here in the winter, that he may support some near relations, who depend upon him'. 'He is always employ'd,' he added with admiration, 'and always cheerful, and seems to me a very worthy honest man'.

Gray returned to Cambridge at the end of June. With the exception only of a leisurely tour in Suffolk sometime in July – tracing its way among Letheringham, Easton, Wingfield, Burgate, Wortham-Green, and including a visit to Thrandeston, where his friend Palgrave was rector – the poet passed the summer quietly in college. It was at this time that Gray included some of his most significant references to his own late childhood at Eton, by way of advising Wharton on how best to place his nephew in the school. Even as an older man Gray was utterly disinclined in any way to sentimentalize the typical school experience, though he took care in his letters to York to display some concern that the physical introduction of Wharton's nephew to the school be accomplished as smoothly and as painlessly as possible, and particularly stressed the need for the boy to 'have time to familiarize himself to the place, before he actually enters the College'.

Early in September, Gray availed himself of the opportunity to meet with the young scholar and antiquarian Thomas Percy. A graduate of Christ Church, Oxford, Percy had since August been consulting the collection of ballads in the Pepys Library at Magdalene College in Cambridge; the results of much of his research that summer would eventually be displayed in his 1765 collection, *Reliques of Ancient English Poetry*. Gray called on Percy at his rooms in Magdalene, where they together took their tea. Percy shared with Gray some of the transcripts included his growing 'Mss Collection' of ballads, and the two men spent much of the afternoon deep in their conversation exploring the traditions of Welsh poetry, and the *Fragments* of Macpherson. The two, rival scholars appeared that September profitably to pass their time together, though their relationship would later suffer through what appear to have been simple faults of miscommunication and misunderstanding. Powell Jones, in his careful survey of the manner in which Gray's habits as a scholar informed his efforts as a poet, rightly speculated that Percy's visit to Cambridge might very probably have been the event that prodded Gray finally to publish his own, recent Icelandic translations.

At some point in May, 1761, Gray renewed his acquaintance in London with an old companion, Fredrick Montagu. Montagu was a nephew of the first earl of Halifax and a friend of Walpole's whom Gray himself had formerly known as a Cambridge undergraduate; he had since been admitted as a barrister at Lincoln's Inn, and was eventually to follow in his father's footsteps, and serve as MP for Northampton for nearly a decade. Despite their possible connections to one another by means of their respective ties to Walpole, Gray and Montagu were never particularly close. Indeed, the admittedly 'slight' relationship between them would almost certainly have been of little practical significance to Gray's life, had not both men also shared some kind of relationship with still another Cambridge acquaintance, Sir William Williams.

As handsome as he was headstrong, Williams appears by all accounts in life to have cut the kind of dashing and impetuous figure one might otherwise have expected to encounter only within the pages of a romantic novel. Gray was unabashedly captivated by the sight of what he described as the young man's 'fine Vandyke-Head'. Noting that Williams had always manifested a 'wild and extravagant' temperament, William Cole was likewise compelled in a straightforward manner to describe the dashing Baronet of Clapton, North Hants, as, simply, 'one of the prettiest figures of a man that could be seen'; Walpole, no less taken by the features of Williams's character than his friends had been by the features of his countenance, similarly praised the fervour of his ambition, the relentless compulsion of his 'enterprising spirit', and noted with favor the budding promise of his parliamentary career.[8]

That promise perceived by Walpole, however, was very soon cut short; Williams's life was unfortunately destined to end tragically. In the early summer of 1761, by the time Gray had once again met up with Montagu in London, Williams himself had only recently, and in death, attained a morbid kind of celebrity in the international columns of the capital's newspapers. Serving as a captain in John Burgoyne's daring Regiment of Dragoons, Williams had been among those killed in an otherwise successful attack by the British expeditionary force against the French citadel of Bells Isle, in Brittany; although the citadel eventually fell to the British later that same spring, the Baronet had been killed early on in the engagement, on 22 April. His death was later judged to have been 'unnecessary'; the French authorities, when they returned Williams's body to the English for burial, had also returned some £250 in bank notes which had been found among his pockets. Upon learning the news of Williams's death, Walpole had announced simply, 'We have lost a young genius.'

Whereas Walpole took the time that May to lament Williams's death in at least two separate letters (one written to George Montagu, the other – more conscious of the political ramifications of such a loss – to Horace Mann), Gray's passing acquaintance with Williams warranted no such references. Gray more than likely shared some of Walpole's regret that such an exuberant young man had been so needlessly sacrificed before the prime of his life; he may perhaps again have reflected on the democratic indiscrimination of Death, who, choosing at leisure among his gathered horde of victims, was no less likely to consign a baronet to an early grave, as he was to choose for his pleasure a ploughman or a poet. Montagu, however, who had enjoyed a far more intimate relationship with Williams, and who had been appointed to serve as one of the executors to the Baronet's estate, was overwhelmed by the sudden loss of his friend – so much so that Gray expressed some anxiety, to Brown, regarding the manner in which the young barrister was dealing with the 'real affliction' of mourning Williams's untimely death.

The spectacle of Montagu's unabated 'affliction' that summer (Gray, twice, pointedly makes use of that same word in his letters to Mason, in an obvious attempt to convey something of the very real sense of physical pain and torture through which Montagu only slowly appeared to be passing) prompted an unusual response on the part of the poet. Never one to write poetry to order, nor even one typically to be drawn to the composition of poetry as anything other than a highly personal

[8]   WC xxi.505.

if playfully therapeutic, psychic tool, Gray – at Montagu's specific and rather audacious request – agreed to write an epitaph on Williams. The verses were meant to be inscribed on the monument which Montagu planned to erect for his friend at Belle Isle (the project was never completed; several versions of the epitaph, differing from one another only incidentally, were discovered among Mason's papers after his death). Explaining the circumstances of the hasty composition of the epitaph in a letter to Mason later that summer, Gray voiced his own suspicions that Mason had himself encouraged Montagu to make the request; he made no attempt to disguise his dissatisfaction with the task, the effort it demanded of him, and the perceived inadequacy of the final result. 'Montagu (as I guess, at your instigation)', the poet grumbled toward the end of a letter to Mason,

> has earnestly desired me to write some lines to be put on a Monument, which he means to erect as Bellisle. It is a task I do not love, knowing Sir W: W: so slightly as I did, but he [i.e. Montagu] is so friendly a Person, & his affliction seemed to me so real, that I could not refuse him. I have sent him the following verses, which I neither like myself, nor will he, I doubt. However I have shewed him, that I wish'd to oblige him. Tell me your real opinion.

Gray then included in his letter a draft of the following lines:

> Here, foremost in the dangerous paths of fame,
> Young Williams fought for England's fair renown;
> His mind each Muse, each Grace adorned his frame,
> Nor Envy dared to view him with a frown.
>   At Aix uncalled his maiden sword he drew,
> (There first in blood his infant glory sealed);
> From fortune, pleasure, science, love, he flew,
> And scorned repose when Britain took the field.
>   With eyes of flame and cool intrepid breast,
> Victor he stood on Belle Isle's rocky steeps;
> Ah gallant youth! this marble tells the rest,
> Where melancholy Friendship bends and weeps. (*PTG* 239–40)

A transcript in Mason's hand suggests two possible variants on the epitaph's concluding twelfth line ('Where bleeding Friendship oer her alter weeps' or, alternatively, 'Where Montagu & bleeding Friendship weep'); the same transcript preserves a fragment of a 'Rejected Stanza':

> Warrior, that readst the melancholly line
> . . .
> Oh be his Genius be his spirit thine
> And share his Virtues with a happier fate (*PTG* 240)

Not surprisingly, Gray's made-to-order epitaph on Williams has attracted little critical attention over the years; most readers have been content to dismiss the lines as perfunctory; suitable, no doubt, to their immediate purpose as a consolation for Montagu and a memorial for Williams himself, but rhetorically and imaginatively unconvincing. As has so often been the case with Gray's poetry, however, the language and imagery of any supposedly minor effort – as evidenced in this case within the rhymed, iambic pentameters of the 'Epitaph' – seem aggressively to draw the reader's attention to the web of possible links they establish to Gray's more popular, as well as his more polished, work. Recalling – and practically quoting – in the language of its opening quatrain passages from both the *Eton Ode* and the *Elegy*, Gray's lines seem in the second 'stanza' to suggest the antithesis in action of the latter poem's love-lorn subject, even as the uncomfortably gory imagery of its metaphors are apt to remind the modern reader of the poet's Icelandic 'translations'. Here lies an individual, the lines proclaim, of a youth not 'unknown' to Science and to Fortune, but one who willfully spurned such gifts as such forces had to offer, in pursuit of martial glory; Williams may not, in the final analysis, have been guilty of his country's blood, but he was certainly foolhardy in his rush to embrace death, and so scornfully to waste the substantial gifts with which he had been blessed. The *Elegy* can be read as a poem that cautions its readers against waste – waste of time, waste of nature, waste of love – even as it attempts to come to grips with a prevailing meanness of opportunity in human affairs. The *Elegy* then attempts finally to establish in its 'Epitaph' – once again to use words of George Eliot – 'some object which would never justify weariness, which would reconcile self-despair with the rapturous consciousness of life beyond the self'.[9] The epitaph on Williams engages in a far more modest attempt to memorialize a single life of action, while at the same time (much like the *Elegy*) commemorating the enduring bonds of a passionate male friendship; it does so, however, by means of a painfully self-conscious and heavy-handed mode of allusion and literary recollection that is otherwise almost entirely absent from Gray's mature poetry. Gray, as we have had the opportunity to observe over and over again both in his work itself, and in his patient if erratic and often protracted habits of composition, appears to have had little difficulty in reconciling a recognition of poetry as a form or an art – a skill, at which the informed craftsman needed to work and to practice – with a seemingly antithetical reverence for poetry as a sublime and mystical manifestation of the Imagination. On the one hand, poets were labourers who practiced a craft; on the other they were capable of being nothing less than the vatic oracles of the gods. The 'Epitaph' on William underscores the fact that

---

[9]   George Eliot, Middlemarch (Harmondsworth: Penguin, 1965) 25.

for all the emphasis correctly placed by the critical tradition on Gray's reputation as a poet of allusion, parody, cento, pastiche, and imitation, he needed always, still, to maintain some kind of emotional or personal investment in his poetry. In the case of Williams's 'Epitaph', he was conscious not only of having had no such investment of his own in the life of his subject, but was almost certainly aware of the fact that his portrait of Williams as 'foremost' among those who fought 'for England's fair renown', he was woefully misrepresenting the historical truth. The variants of the poem's final lines recorded by Mason only capture the 'Epitaph' itself – rather then being inscribed in monumental marble – in the very act of imploding and disintegrating into dust.

*

Gray returned to London that summer at the beginning of the second week of September. He reached the city on the same day that the new King, George III, was to be married to Princess Charlotte of Mecklenburg-Strelitz. Gray maintained a poise of indifference to the royal wedding, observing to Wharton only that the evening ceremony had happened to take place on 'the hottest night of the year'. The coronation ceremonies later that same month, however, demanded not only Gray's attention, but his active participation as well. Thanks apparently to the efforts of the Duke of Devonshire (to whose brother, Lord John Cavendish, Gray had been introduced), the poet had obtained a seat for the royal pageant in the Lord Chamberlain's 'box' in Westminster Hall. Gray couldn't help but notice that the King's mother, the Princess of Wales, sat in one of the boxes immediately opposite to his own, where she was joined by the company of the 22-year-old monarch's even younger brothers and sisters.

The pomp and ostentation of the coronation ceremonies were unprecedented. For better or worse, the accession of George III was celebrated by many politicians as having signalled the beginning of a new era in English government. The young king made a point of emphasizing, in one of his earliest announcements as monarch, that he 'gloried in the name of Briton'. The abuses in patronage and the ministerial corruption that had characterized his grandfather's seemingly endless reign were declared now to be things of the past; at the very least, the first several years of the reign of George III were to witness significant and far-reaching changes in the manner in which the King dealt with his appointed ministers, and so aimed to fulfil his role as the united kingdom's self-styled, 'Patriot King'. There was the taste of anticipation and the unmistakable flavour of excitement in the air. Once again, an old era had come to its long-anticipated close, and a new period in the country's history was about to begin.

Or so, at least, it seemed to some. While Gray recounted the 'perils and dangers' of the ceremony at considerable length in a detailed letter to Brown, Walpole wrote to Mann in Italy that the occasion was impressive only in its thorough-going and unwarranted wastefulness. 'On this occasion', he noted laconically in an account written shortly after the event, 'to how high water-mark extravagance is risen in England'. Walpole's keen sense of detail and memory, and his lifelong flair for gathering information of all kinds resulted in this instance in some telling comparisons and observations on the seemingly limitless greed and vanity of British society. 'At the coronation of George II', he confided to Mann with an air of anecdotal confidence,

> my mother gave forty guineas for a dining-room, scaffold, and a bed-chamber. An exactly parallel apartment, only with rather a worse view, was this time set at three hundred and fifty guineas – a tolerable rise in thirty years! The platform from St. Margaret's Roundhouse to the church-door, which formerly let for forty pounds, went this time for two thousand four hundred pounds. Still more was given for inside the Abbey. (WC ix.386–89)

'The prebends', he concluded drily, 'would like a Coronation every year.'

Walpole had in fact offered his own account of the actual ceremonies in a detailed letter to George Montagu written only four days earlier, so his feigned concern regarding the inflation evinced by this later coronation may, for him, have provided something in the way of an epistolary diversion. Gray's lengthy letter to Brown at Cambridge painted its own wonderfully colourful picture of the various individuals who participated in the ceremony – the Hall 'throng'd with people head above head, all dress'd, and women with their jewels on' – while still retaining the poet's characteristic sense of humour and perspective. The King's ministers, as he informed Brown, may indeed have been 'mightily dress'd in rich stuffs of gold & colours with long flowing wigs' but even so, as the poet took care to add in an aside, 'some of them' were still 'comical figures enough'. Gray's account of the hasty and huddled luncheon provided by his particular host even as the King himself was being crowned in the Abbey remains a masterful cartoon, capturing as it does the peculiar combination of simultaneous solemnity and absurdity – the uneasy mix of a studied formality, on the one hand, and a manifest ignorance with regard to protocol or procedure, on the other – which so often emerges as the defining feature of such state occasions. 'I should have told you', he paused midway in his description of the participants' chaotic exodus from the Hall,

> that the old Bp of Lincoln with his stick went doddling by the side of the Queen, & the Bp of Chester had the pleasure of bearing the gold paten.

when they were gone we went down to dinner, for there were three rooms below, where the Duke of Devonshire was so good as to feed us with great cold Sirloins of beef, legs of mutton, fillets of veal, & other substantial viands, and liqueurs, which we devour'd all higgledy-piggledy like Porters. after which every one scrambled up again & seated themselves. . . . When [the King and Queen] return'd, it was so dark, that the People without doors scarce saw anything of the procession, & as the Hall had no other light than two long ranges of candles at each of the Peers tables, we saw almost as little as they; only one perceived the [Lords] & Ladies sideling in & taking their places to dine, but the instant the Queen's Canopy enter'd, fire was given to all the Lustres at once by trains of prepared flax, that reached from one to the other. to me it seem'd an interval of not more than half a minute, before the whole was in a blaze of splendour. (CTG 755)

Gray's eye for the elements of bawdy humour inherent in the details and in the moments of confusion and mischance that inevitably occurred on such occasions was as sharp as any other man's. He was clearly delighted to be able to close his narrative to Brown with an anecdote which asserted that the ill-fated Duke of Newcastle had been surprized in closet by one of the Ladies in Waiting, who, 'opening the door to see all was right, found the D:e of Newcastle perk'd up & in the very act of upon the anointed [sic] velvet closestool'. 'Do not think I joke', he protested to Brown, 'it is literally true'. Fastidious Gray might have been, but never can it be said that he was to any degree, among his closest friends and correspondents, a prude.

*

The years were passing quickly. By the autumn of 1761, Gray had already maintained his residence in London for a period of over two years. As early as the second week of May, however, Gray's landlord at Southampton Row had informed the poet of his desire to lease the entire Bloomsbury property to a single individual or family. The only other tenant in the building – a figure referred to by Gray simply as 'the Bishop', and an individual with whom neither Wharton nor the poet had ever enjoyed very cordial relations – had recently vacated the better part of the premises, and Gray only now stood in the way of some more profitable rental arrangement. 'Mr. Jauncey', Gray had written to Wharton that spring, 'means to let his house entire, & in September I shall be forced to look out for another place, & must have the plague of removing'.

Obviously, Gray had intended initially – and despite the considerable disruption that he knew to be entailed by such a move – to stay in London for at least some portion of the ensuing winter, if not to remain there indefinitely. Whether or not, upon learning of Jauncey's plans for the property, he even began seriously to seek alternative accommodations in the same neighbourhood or elsewhere in the city, remains unclear, though an exertion of such a painfully practical nature would clearly never have held any appeal for him. Sometime very soon after the amusing fuss of the coronation ceremony, Gray decided that the time was right for him to return, perhaps permanently, to Pembroke. Perhaps the prospect of once again spending too many of the long and dreary winter evenings alone among his books and papers was too grim even to contemplate; perhaps the novelty and the appeal of the nearby museum and its collections seemed suddenly to have grown cold; perhaps he had come to acknowledge that he genuinely missed socializing with his chosen protégés and companions among the college Fellows, or that he had felt the absence of the comfortable and necessarily social routines of academic life. It is more probable, however, that in spite of his professional accomplishments within the past several years, Gray had felt himself drifting emotionally – had sensed himself to be increasingly aimless or lacking in purpose in the wake of his mother's death. Perhaps, too, he simply needed the light of companionship – of a companion. Such a light, he knew, could be kindled easily enough at Cambridge; could, in fact, best be kindled at Cambridge. To be sure, this new light promised not to dazzle like the blinding blaze of youth, nor would it have very much in common with the cheering activity of a cozy, domestic fireside, nor, even, would it stand comparison to the snug and genial warmth of an elderly couple's well-worn cottage hearth; but its glow was sure and steady, and even though its rays might sometimes falter in their attempts to illumine the darkest and furthermost corners of the room, or ominously throw their antic shadows high upon the ceiling and the paneled walls, they could be counted on still and always to be bright enough, at the very least, for him to read by. Both turning and returning to his friends and acquaintances at Cambridge that autumn, Gray seemed temporarily – if modestly and in his own, peculiar manner – at least to have begun to conquer his lifelong fear of fire, and all that such fires of the heart, for that matter, might be thought to represent.

PART THREE

CHAPTER TEN

IN HARMLESS SOCIETY

Cambridge and Travels
1761–1768

I. A Vast Deal of Good Company

On the morning of Monday, 26 October 1761, a large and heavily laden wagon slowly drew to a halt in front of the gates of Pembroke College. The vehicle was – to resident Cantabrigians, at least – a familiar one. Mr Gillam's regularly scheduled stage wagons could be seen departing punctually for London every Monday, Tuesday, and Thursday, and were just as surely to be heard rumbling into town, having completed the return journey to Cambridge, with even greater frequency – on Wednesdays, Thursdays, Fridays, and Saturdays. Traffic between the university town and the metropolis was increasingly busy, and the regular passage of fellows and students up to the city and back had only recently transformed services such as Mr. Gillam's into highly profitable ventures.

Gillam's charges on this particular occasion included not only the chests and packing crates of those many undergraduates who were only just arriving in Cambridge to begin their first Michaelmas Term, nor merely the smaller baggage and purchases of the driver's more regular 'commuters'; the carrier sat on Trumpington Street that October morning minding nearly thirty parcels of various shapes and sizes that Gray had packed with finicky precision throughout the past few weeks, and which he had finally, the preceding Thursday, seen shipped off from Southampton Row. Gillam had been entrusted with nearly all of the poet's worldly possessions. Among the parcels waiting to be carried through the college gates and through to the second court were boxes of books, feather beds and bedsteads, chairs, tables, washstands, baskets piled high with cushions and pillows, and at least two chests crammed with papers, notebooks, and other items of a personal nature. Of the twenty-eight items listed by Gray on the impromptu invoice sent to Brown, who stood on the receiving end of his friend's shipment in Cambridge, all but three had been marked with crosses indicating that their contents were exceedingly delicate and 'easier to break'. The sturdy back of a large sofa, a heavy settee and some stools, and an unwieldy steel fender alone escaped this scrupulous designation, but only barely; the fire grate itself and its accompanying instruments – sharp-pronged pokers and heavy, metal brushes – were carefully marked by the poet as 'fragile', and to be handled only with the greatest of care. Gray sent a short note to Brown ahead of the delivery, instructing him in precisely what was to be done with his possessions. 'They may all stand pack'd up as they are, & wait till I come, which will be in about 3 weeks, I guess.' 'In the mean time', he felt the need still to add, with a familiar anxiety, 'I beg no fire may be made, nor any body go flaunting in with a candle, for so many mats & so much packing will make it very dangerous.'

Gray returned to the college *in propria persona* by the middle of the third week of November. Having given up his lodgings in London for good, and having officially resumed his residence at Cambridge, the early winter months of 1761 consequently took on for the poet something of the air of a homecoming. The larger pattern of Gray's days and nights had begun to change forever; never again, at least, was he to leave Cambridge for so lengthy a period. By the beginning of December, he was already comfortably settled in his rooms and enjoying the company of friends and colleagues in the university town with a relish he had demonstrated only sporadically in the past. At the beginning of December he dashed off a note to Mason, inviting him to revisit his old haunts, and offering a brief description of what he was likely to find when he arrived:

> Of all loves come to Cambridge out of hand, for here is Mr Dillaval & a charming set of Glasses, that sing like nightingales, & we have concerts every other night, & shall stay here this month or two, & a vast deal of good company, & a Whale in pickle just come from Ipswich. . . . don't talk of the charge, for we will make a subscription: besides we know, you always come, when you have a mind. (*CTG* 766)

The water or musical 'Glasses' Gray describes as being played here were soon to become the height of fashion; the spontaneity of Gray's invitation to Mason works even today to give the reader some idea as to just how novel and unusual such entertainment was at the time, and just how content Gray was to be back in Cambridge.

On the first of December, the *Public Advertiser* announced the imminent publication of Macpherson's *Fingal*. As he had done with his earlier collection of *Fragments*, Macpherson now offered the six-book *Fingal* to the public as a translation of a genuine, ancient 'Epic' poem. He pretended only to have acted as editor to his material, glossing certain historical allusions, and offering selections from Homer and Virgil – and even to the Hebrew Bible – which drew parallels between those founding works of the classical and Judeo-Christian traditions and the work of the blind bard, Ossian. On the authenticity of Macpherson's 'translations', Gray once again, for the time being, withheld his judgement. Of their value as simple, poetical curiosities, he soon confessed to Stonhewer, he was far less undecided. 'For my part', he wrote,

> I will stick to my credulity, and if I am cheated, think it worse for him [the translator] than for me. The Epic Poem is foolishly so called, yet there is a sort of plan and unity in it very strange for a barbarous age; yet what I more admire are some of the detached pieces – the rest I leave to the discussion of antiquarians and historians; yet my curiosity is much interested in their decision. (*CTG* 767)

The new year began with some very welcome news for Mason and consequently with some very hearty congratulations being offered on the part of Gray. Mason's career in the church was flourishing. He had now been serving for several years as rector of Aston, in Yorkshire, and was also a prebendary of York cathedral in addition to his appointment as chaplain to Lord Holdernesse. Three years earlier, in 1757, he had even been appointed one of several 'chaplains in ordinary' to King George II; the appointment had been renewed without question by his successor. Early in January, 1762, the *Gentleman's Magazine* announced the recent death of the Rev. Mr Herring, described in its pages as 'chancellor of the diocese of York, canon residentiary of that cathedral and rector of Carlton, Northumberland'. Thanks largely to the influence of Frederick Montagu (who happened to be brother-in-law to John Fontayne, then Dean of York), Mason was within only days of Herring's death made canon residentiary of the cathedral. The precentorship of the same church was likewise soon obtained for him through the influence of Lord Holdernesse. As the ecclesiastical honours continued to cluster around Mason's shoulders, Gray jokingly wrote to Wharton from Cambridge that he hoped all the attention would induce Mason to 'shut his insatiable repining mouth'. He addressed Mason himself with no less candour. 'It is a mercy', he wrote on 11 January, soon after learning of the first of his friend's appointments,

> that Old Men are mortal, & that dignified Clergymen know how to keep their word. I heartily rejoice with you in your establishment, & with myself that I have lived to see it, to see your insatiable mouth stopt, & your anxious perriwig at rest & slumbering in a stall. The Bp of London (you see) is dead: there is a fine opening. is there nothing farther to tempt you? feel your own pulse & answer me seriously: it rains Precentorships, you have only to hold up your skirt, & catch them. (*CTG* 768–69)

In a letter written only a few weeks later, he joked that Mason was being advanced within the church at such a pace that it now appeared to be necessary for Gray himself, should he wish to learn how properly to address his old friend, to consult the newspapers and magazines. Again extending Mason both his own congratulations and passing on those of Wharton as well, he closed his letter in mock petulance: 'Here, take them, you miserable Precentor! I wish all your Choir may mutiny, & sing you to death.'

Gray's other friends and acquaintances, at least, seemed to be moving through life at a rather more companionable pace. Contact between Gray and Walpole was now as close and familiar as it had been at any point since their reconciliation over fifteen years earlier. Toward the end of February, Gray received from his old friend copies of the first two volumes of Walpole's *Anecdotes of Painting*, which had been printed at the Strawberry Hill Press earlier that month. Gray had already read much of the same work in manuscript (at which time, Walpole wrote to Montagu, his interest in the material grew to such a point that he became quite 'violent about it'), and he now thanked Walpole for the finished product. 'I return you my best thanks for the copy of your book', Gray wrote

> which you sent me, and have not at all lessened my opinion of it since I read it in print, though the press has in general a bad effect on the complection of one's works. The engravings look, as you say, better than I had expected, yet not altogether so well as I could wish. I rejoice in the good dispositions of our court, and in the propriety of their application to you: the work is a thing so much to be wished; has so near a connection with the turn of your studies and of your curiosity . . . that it will be a sin if you let it drop and come to nothing, or worse than nothing, for want of your assistance. (*CTG* 774–75)

Much of Walpole's material from these two volumes had been drawn from the work of a well-known London engraver, George Vertue. Walpole had in 1758 purchased from Vertue's widow a large and chaotic collection of papers, illustrations, manuscript notebooks, and random jottings, and it was only by reading thoroughly through Vertue's material that he had been able to glean much of the substance of his own volume. Gray, who had volunteered a small amount of insight and information from his own researches in the British Museum, felt that his own slight involvement in the project allowed him a voice in subsequent volumes of Walpole's history. 'The historical part', he declared somewhat loftily,

> should be in the manner of Henault, a mere abridgement, a series of facts selected with judgement, that may serve as a clue to lead the mind along in the midst of those ruins and scattered monuments of art, that time has spared. . . . Then at the end of each reign should come a dissertation

explanatory of the plates, and pointing out the turn of thought, the customs, ceremonials, arms, dresses, luxury, and private life, with the improvement or decline of the arts during that period. This you must do yourself, beside taking upon you the superintendence, direction, and choice of materials. (*CTG* 775–76)

Walpole had actually, just earlier that same month, already begun to keep a large memorandum book in which he assembled his material – notes on the history of manners, customs, habits, ceremonies, etc. – in much the same manner suggested in his friend's letter. Gray's tone may seem a little high-handed, but we must keep in mind that he had known Walpole for almost as long as he could remember. Gray would continue to remain in regular contact with Walpole in the years to come, calling on him in London and visiting him for short but frequent stays at Strawberry Hill.

Walpole had only recently arrived at something of a turning point in his own life. In October of the previous year, he had responded emphatically to an enquiry as to his health and affairs by his close friend and cousin Henry Conway's elder brother, Lord Hertford: 'I am an old gouty man that lives in my own manner, and can't tell how the world passes. I have done with it.' Walpole's self-conscious announcement of his own 'retirement' from the active world of political intrigue may have been premature (some of the most bitter and painful incidents in his on-going career as a backstage politician and would-be power broker lay still in the future), yet he did seem rather more intent than ever on concentrating his energies on the Gothic eccentricities of his increasingly beloved Thames-side retreat. When Gray visited Strawberry Hill in this period, he was often greeted by the sight of major, unfinished building projects.

Wharton, meanwhile, had given up the practice of medicine and had left London toward the end of 1759 to settle down to the life of a country squire at his family estate of Old Park. The manor and estate had originally been purchased in the late seventeenth century by Wharton's great-grandfather. The home (since demolished) was in the eighteenth century a quiet, retired spot, where Gray hoped his friend would find 'satisfaction and repose'. Many years after Wharton's death, Robert Surtees described the property in his three-volume *History of Durham*, carefully including the spirits both of its former owner and of Gray in his account. 'The house of Old Park', the antiquarian would write,

stands retired, about half a mile from the Wear, shaded by large elms, and fenced on the South by a moat, beyond which is the *Old Park*, a piece of ground, sloping towards the house. The shell of the old mansion of the Claxtons was repaired (with some additions) in the monastic style, by the late Dr. Wharton. The sequestered situation suits well with the style; the modest quiet front, with its panes of stained glass, and the cross rising in the centre, is seen dimly glimmering through the huge elms. The neglected grounds, once trim as an Abbot's garden, are still sprinkled with the evergreens and matted with periwinkle. The whole neglected spot affords an interesting specimen of the taste of Dr. Wharton, and of his friend the poet Gray, whose genius may, I think, be plainly traced in the style of the building, and in the sequestered character of the grounds.[1]

Throughout these years, Gray seemed to delight more than ever in sending Wharton detailed accounts of the crops and the weather. The most minute chronicles of the slightest changes and fluctuations in temperature, the careful tabulation of precisely which flowers and trees were blooming or turning and dropping their leaves appear to have fascinated them both. Gray took care always to include in his letters to Old Park his respects to Mrs. Wharton, and often to send greetings to the children of his friend's growing family as well. 'My best compliments to Mrs Wharton', Gray closes one letter, typically, 'I hear her butter is the best in the Bishoprick, & that even Deborah [Wharton's third daughter] has learn'd to spin. I rejoice you are all in health . . .'. Congratulating Wharton on the arrival of his second son in June, 1760 (the boy would again be named Robert, in memory of his brother), Gray had taken the opportunity to note that while it may have taken some time to grow used to the quiet retirement of such a place, Wharton seems to have made some headway in acclimatizing himself away from London. 'Another thing I rejoice in', he added, following his congratulations on the addition to Wharton's family,

> is, to know, that you not only grow reconciled to your scene, but discover beauties round you, that once were deformities. I am persuaded the whole matter is to have always something going forward. happy they, that can create a rose-tree, or erect a honey-suckle, that can watch the brood of a Hen, or see a fleet of their own ducklings launch into the water! it is with a sentiment of envy I speak it, who never shall have even a thatch'd roof of my own, nor gather a strawberry but in Covent-Garden. (CTG 677)

Old Park came in time to be regarded by Gray as one of his favourite and most comfortable country retreats – a place where he could leave the sporadic, internecine quarrels of Cambridge far behind him, and where

---

[1]   Quoted in CTG 624–25.

the domestic life of Wharton's family provided something of the familiarity and security he had earlier in his life found at Stoke Poges.

With Stonhewer, Gray appears to have had little extensive contact
at this stage of his life. Stonhewer's activities are often mentioned in
passing in Gray's letters to other correspondents (usually to Wharton),
and although the two men seem to have made a point of regularly
keeping in touch with one another, and although they visited with one
another (most often in London) on a pretty regular basis, Stonhewer's
professional career and responsibilities seem to have been hectic and
time-consuming. He had several years earlier been appointed Histori-
ographer to his Majesty, a position that carried a stipend of £200 a year.
Another court appointment – that of Knight Harbinger (an officer in the
royal household) had followed in 1756. At some time just prior to 1759
he had what Gray characterized as the 'good fortune' to receive the post
of Interpreter of Oriental Languages, and was spending the better part
of his time in London. This last position, at least, entailed some interesting duties. In a letter to Wharton written in the spring of 1759, Gray
reported that Stonhewer had to travel down to Portsmouth officially to
receive an Ambassador from Morocco.

The winds of change and maturity seem likewise to have blown
many of Gray's other Cambridge friends and acquaintances to all
four corners of the kingdom. William Palgrave, who was admitted
Bachelor of Laws in 1759, was in June of that same year ordained as
Deacon of Norwich, and soon after settled down to a comfortable
life as Rector of Thrandeston, in Suffolk (where Gray had already
visited him). Gray's fellow Cosin and Hale scholar, John Clerke, was
throughout these years still practicing as a physician at Epsom, in Surrey,
where Gray in 1763 was to pay him a brief visit. Lord Strathmore,
who would in 1767 marry the heiress Mary Eleanor Bowes was
generally kept busy with the management of his properties both in
Durham and in Scotland, where Gray, as we shall see, was soon to pay
him a visit. Strathmore's youngest brother, Thomas Lyon (to whom Gray
referred casually and with affection as 'Tom') had been admitted as a
Fellow–commoner at Pembroke in June, 1758, and elected a Fellow just
over two years later. Lyon would continue at Pembroke until 1767,
at which point he was to begin a decade-long career as parliamentary
representative for Montrose Burghs. Lord John Cavendish, who was
among Gray's youngest friends and to whom he endearingly referred as
'the best of all Johns' was, along with his friend Frederick Montagu,
likewise returned to Parliament in the General Election of 1761.
Cavendish would in later years twice serve as Chancellor of the Exchequer; Montagu was to be Lord of the Treasury in 1782 and 1783.
Political appointments did little to put the pair beyond the reach of
Gray's humour, however. Informing Mason in the summer of 1761 that

'Lord John' had finally recovered from a recent illness, Gray observed that his friend,

> answers me very chearfully, as if his illness had been but slight, & the Pleuresy were no more than a hole in one's stocking. he got it (he says) not by scampering, & racketing, & heating his blood, as I had supposed: but by going with Ladies to Vauxhall. he is the picture (& pray tell him, if you see him) of an old Alderman, that I knew, who after living 40 years on the fat of the land, (not milk & honey, but arrack-punch and venison) & losing his great toe with mortification, said to the last, that he owed it to two grapes, which he eat one day after dinner. he felt them lie cold at his stomach the minute they were down. (*CTG* 745–46)

The 'old Alderman' to whom Gray referred in the letter was Alderman Thomas Nutting of Cambridge, the father of Gray's aunt by marriage, Mrs. William Antrobus. Gently poking fun at Strathmore, Gray silently but significantly and at the same time makes sure that he is likewise taking neither his own family – nor himself – too seriously.

Gray continued to make and to cultivate new friends following his return to Cambridge in 1761. Christopher Anstey, who had been a scholar at Eton before moving on to become a Fellow of Kings from 1746 to 1754, had in the autumn of 1761 undertaken a translation of the *Elegy* into Latin; his *Eligia Scripta in Caemeterio Rustio Latinè Reddita* was published anonymously in February, 1762, almost precisely eleven years after the publication of the original. His translation prompted from Gray some observations on the difficult task of translation itself, and some familiar ideas concerning the decorum appropriate to poetic language. 'Every language' Gray had written to Anstey,

> has its idiom, not only of words and phrases, but of customs and manner, which cannot be represented in the tongue of another nation, especially of a nation so distant in time and place, without constraint and difficulty; of this sort, in the present instance, are the curfew bell, the Gothic Church, with its monuments, organs and anthems, the texts of Scripture, &c. There are certain images, which, though drawn from common nature, and every where obvious, yet strike us as foreign to the turn and genius of Latin verse; the beetle that flies in the evening, to a Roman, I guess, would have been too mean an object for poetry; 'that leaves the world to darkness and to me', is good English, but has not the turn of a Latin phrase, and therefore, I believe, you were in the right to drop it. (*CTG* 748–49)

The final line of Gray's opening, English quatrain, was in fact rendered by Anstey as 'et solus sub nocte relinquor'. Gray had further suggested to Anstey: 'Might not the English characters be romanized? Virgil is just as good as Milton, and Caesar as Cromwell, but who shall be Hampden?' Anstey decided finally not to rummage the annals for a suitable, Roman replacement; the English names of Gray's original were in the translation simply 'Latinized' as 'Miltonus', 'Cromvellus', and 'Hamdenus'.

London, too, had brought Gray into contact with a number of politically and socially influential individuals with whom he now continued to keep in touch. These included Sir Henry Erskine ('my friend', he confided succinctly to Brown), a Scottish baronet and highly-decorated soldier who had been appointed Keeper of the King's Private Roads, Gates, and Bridges in 1757 and who, during the period of Gray's early homecoming to Cambridge, stood high in the influence of Lord Bute. Another acquaintance was Thomas Pitt, of Boconnoc, in Cornwall ('nephew', as Walpole put it, 'of *the* Pitt'). Pitt would be sent to parliament as Member for the notorious 'rotten borough' of Old Sarum in 1768, and again after Gray's death, in 1774–84; he was the son of a Lord of the Admiralty, and was much later in life created Baron Camelford. In the years to come, Pitt was to settle at Twickenham, where his enthusiasm and his talents as an amateur architect would have considerable influence on the increasingly eclectic Gothicism of Strawberry Hill. Closer in his affections than either of these two men to Gray, however, was the friendship of the Reverend William 'Billy' Robinson. Gray may have known Robinson, a Yorkshire man and a Fellow of St. John's, by sight and general reputation as early as 1752; the period of their intimacy, however, dated from the time of their introduction to one another at the home of Conyers Middleton sometime shortly after Robinson's ordination in 1754. Robinson was brother to the famous 'blue-stocking', the educated reformer and patron Elizabeth Montagu. Gray was regularly in touch with Robinson following the latter's marriage (to a woman the groom himself described as 'of his own age' and 'not handsome') in July, 1760; he would later visit the couple at Denton, near Canterbury, where Robinson served as rector.

It was early in the summer of 1762, however, that Gray initiated a friendship which would have a profound and lasting impact on the rest of his life. On Friday, 11 June, Gray had stepped across the road to take his afternoon tea with William Lobb, a recently appointed Fellow of Peterhouse. Lobb, a casual acquaintance whose own presence did not loom at all that large in Gray's Cambridge social life, happened on that occasion to be entertaining another individual as well, a considerably younger man named Norton Nicholls. Nicholls had been admitted as a Pensioner to Trinity Hall only two years earlier. The account of the first encounter between Gray and Nicholls is best given in a letter Nicholls himself almost immediately dashed off to a close friend of his in London

– William Johnson Temple – who had only recently been sorely disappointed in a similar encounter with yet another literary lion, Samuel Johnson. 'My dear Temple', Nicholls scrawled in his excitement,

> Now I give you leave, nay insist on it, that you Envy me! Last Friday I had the Happiness of drinking Tea with the great Mr Gray at Lobb's Room. I assure you after the first Quarter of an hour which was quite little enough for me to compose my Spirits, and get Courage enough to be happy I was as much so as it is possible for you to conceive me in such Circumstances. I did not find him as you found Johnson, surly, morose, Dogmatical, or imperious. But affable, entertaining and polite. He had no other opportunity of shewing his superior abilities but such as naturally presented itself from the subject of Conversation, which however he never propos'd.
>
> Conceive if you can how happy I find myself when he told me he hop'd to have the Pleasure of my Company some Afternoon at Pembroke. He has not yet fix'd on any. I am under a thousand Anxieties whether or no he will. But Lobb assures me I may depend on more of his Acquaintance. I assure you the whole afternoon, and ever since I have been employ'd with this Idea. That I should be acquainted with one of the greatest Men who ever existed in the World! That he should (as it is probable he may) visit me in my own Room!
>
> We had some Discourse about Dante and he seem'd very much astonished that I should have read any of it. He speaks of it in the highest Terms, and particularly desir'd me to read one part of it, the Story of Count Ugolino; as you may imagine, I read it the next morning, and found it what I expected one of the finest Things I had ever read in my life. (*CTG* 1303–04)

'What I could chiefly observe in him', Nicholls concluded in further compliment to his new acquaintance, 'was vast politeness, great Good-nature, and the most elegant accuracy of Phrase in the World.'

Even across time and in this first, wildly enthusiastic product of the relationship between Gray and Nicholls, one senses something of the younger man's overwhelming charm, openness, and vitality. By almost all accounts, Nicholls's personality as a young man was utterly disarming. Sir Egerton Brydges, it is true, qualified his description of Nicholls by writing in his *Autobiography* that he was 'a very clever man, with a great deal of erudition: but it must be confessed a supreme coxcomb'.[2] Such criticism, however, coming as it does from an author who was himself notoriously self-obsessed, needs to be taken with a grain of salt. The genuine love for Gray which Nicholls developed within the course

---

[2]   Sir Egerton Brydges, *Autobiography*, ii. 88.

of their long and intimate friendship strikes most modern readers of their correspondence as having served as an incomparably valuable and unswervingly faithful guiding light to the poet, particularly in the final years of his life. 'I never saw anybody', James Boswell would write of Nicholls following their first meeting in 1762, 'who engaged me more at the very first meeting than this gentleman'. 'He discovered', Boswell contended, 'an amiable disposition, a sweetness of manners and an easy politeness that pleased me much'.[3]

Years later, in his own *Reminiscences* of Gray (written in November, 1805 and first published in Mitford's edition of the poet's *Works* in 1835–43), Nicholls would offer a slightly more elaborate account of his 'Discourse about Dante' that prompted Gray first to speak with Nicholls. 'Dante', Nicholls recalled, Gray regarded as 'the father of all; to whose Genius . . . he thought it an advantage to have been produced in a rude age of strong, & uncontrouled passions, when the muse was not checked by refinement, & the fear of criticism'.

A mutual and passionate love of Dante, it would soon turn out, was not the only thing that Nicholls shared with Gray. Although radically different from one another in their outward dispositions, the two men in fact came from surprisingly similar backgrounds. Born in 1742, Nicholls, like Gray, was the son of a London merchant. Also like Gray, he came from a broken home; references in the poet's letters to his friend lead one to suspect that Nicholls's father abandoned his mother and his only son very shortly after young Norton's birth. Throughout his life, Nicholls remained alive to the possibility that his father was still alive (he had no substantial information to suggest he was not), and perhaps in need of, at the very least, financial assistance. Both Gray and Nicholls, in other words, were to some degree neglected and subsequently haunted by their fathers. Nicholls's mother, Jane, was the daughter of a Lieutenant–Colonel Charles Floyer of Richmond, Surrey, and it was either in Richmond or in London that Nicholls spent the earliest years of his childhood. He was sent to Eton at the age of twelve. Had he been born just a little over twenty years earlier, his presence at the school might well have transformed the Quadruple Alliance into a union of not four but five such 'bold adventurers'. As it was, Nicholls would in time become not only an intimate of Gray's, but a close and continued friend to Walpole (who affectionately nicknamed him 'the Abbé') as well.

Gray's early friendship with Nicholls was destined in time to flower into one of the most rewarding relationships in the poet's adult life. From

---

[3] James Boswell, *Boswell's London Journal*, ed. with an Introduction by Frederick A Pottle (London: The Folio Society, 1985) 235.

the moment of their first introduction, Gray began instructing Nicholls – informally, of course – in his study and reading, and it was not at all long before Gray could be found, in turn, praising Nicholls in a letter to Mason as 'a young Man worth his weight in gold'. Nicholls, for that matter, delighted in finding himself so soon an intimate of a man whose work – and, it would soon become obvious, whose life as well – he so much valued and respected. He was fairly awestruck at being himself so highly regarded by 'a man who . . . I reverence with the most awful respect for his Sublime Genius, and profound knowledge; and who I am persuaded that I should esteem, love and confide in, for his disposition, and goodness'. They studied together, sat long and late over their evening tea in conversation, and even, in the summer evenings, performed duets together in Gray's rooms, accompanied by the poet himself at the harpsichord. 'And then', Nicholls added gleefully and with the smallest amount of pride in a letter to his London friend, 'we go in great form to the coffeehouse, where we doze over the news and pamphlets till the last stroke of eleven'. Gray felt that he could play with and tease Nicholls in ways he could not indulge with most of his other friends and, as we shall see, he felt that he could, to a certain degree, confide in him regarding feelings and emotions regarding that he would not otherwise even have mentioned to anyone else.

*

Gray remained in Cambridge until 1 July, when he travelled north to spend two weeks with Mason, at York, before moving on to visit Wharton at Old Park. The route along which his journey passed would in time become one of the most familiar of his life. Having passed some three years without being troubled by any major symptoms of the gout, Gray suffered 'two slight attacks' of the illness before leaving college. He was nevertheless in generally good spirits as he prepared to set off on his travels. Mason he found to be 'improved in dignity' consequent upon his appointment as precentor. 'He begins to complain of qualms and indigestions from repose and repletion', Gray reported back to Brown, 'in short *il tranche du Prelat*'. Mason seems to have enjoyed laying out the ecclesiastical red carpet for Gray in all its considerable splendour. 'We went twice a-day to church', Gray noted, 'with our vergers and all our pomp.'

The scene which greeted him upon his arrival at Old Park could hardly have been less formal. Wharton was yet in the midst of some major rebuilding and repairs on the estate. Gray seemed incapable of turning a corner without encountering working clusters of carpenters, upholsterers, labourers, and builders. Wharton's library was not yet ready to accommodate his books, so that its many volumes lay teasingly inaccessible all around the house in unpacked crates and boxes. Two favourite sows – 'Jetty' and 'Fadge' – seemed licenced to wander into the front entryway whenever they felt like it, and just beyond each opened window a 'concert' of poultry stood ready to entertain the distracted guest. Gray claimed that there was but one set of pen and ink in the entire house. The property, in short, was in a state of absolute chaos, so much so that Gray was compelled to compare his friend's building operations with Virgil's description, in Book I of the *Aeneid*, of the building of Carthage. He nevertheless attempted genially to dwell in his letters to Cambridge on the positive advantages of such a situation. 'We take in no newspaper or magazines', he admitted to Brown, sounding for all the world like a citizen of the late twentieth century extolling the calculated deprivations of a rural existence, adding, 'but the cream and butter is beyond compare'.

In fact, Gray so much enjoyed his time at Old Park as to persist in spending the remainder of the summer and much of the autumn with the Whartons. He did not leave Durham until sometime in the first week of November. Rather than return directly to Cambridge, however, he decided to undertake a short tour in Yorkshire and Derbyshire, and then finally to make his way home via London. The weather was cold and rainy but, as usual, the simple fact of journeying through the English countryside lightened Gray's mood. He stopped first at Richmond and then at Ripon, where he made a point of exploring the cathedral both he and Stonhewer had been unable to visit on their earlier trip to the same area in 1753. The sun came out just long enough for him to undertake a patient examination of Fountains Abbey, which lay in the vale of Studley Park, some three miles southwest of Ripon. The dramatic contrast of the sparkling, early winter sunshine cutting through the heavy storm clouds that were still sweeping in from the north must have rendered the scene a beautiful one. Gray took further advantage of the break in the clouds to walk among the picturesque, landscaped gardens of Studley Royal, which had been set out earlier in the century by one-time Chancellor of the Exchequer, John Aislabie.

By the time he reached Leeds later that same day, however, the sky itself seemed to have opened. The downpour was so heavy that Gray could scarcely perceive the buildings of the town from beyond his carriage window. The 'perverse' weather encouraged him not to stop at Leeds, but rather to keep on travelling, first to Wakefield – some thirty miles to the southwest of York – and then on to Wentworth Castle, the country seat of the Earl of Strafford, near Barnsley. He was struck most by the 'rich and cultivated' Yorkshire countryside itself, and when the sun's rays managed once again to pierce through the lowering skies, he admitted the scene to be an unforgettable one. He was considerably less impressed by the Peak district, describing the area to Wharton as 'beyond comparison uglier than any other I have seen in England, black, tedious, barren, and not mountainous enough to please one with its horrors. Yet the 'art of Mr Brown' (Capability Brown, that is), could work wonders even with such natural material as this; Gray was delighted by his visit to Chatsworth house, the seat of the Duke of Devonshire, near Bakewell. 'The house' he wrote, describing the elegant mansion to Wharton,

> has the air of a Palace, the hills rising on three of its sides shut out the view of its dreary neighborhood, & are cover'd with wood to their tops: the front opens to the Derwent winding thro' the valley, which by the art of Mr Brown is now always visible & full to its brim. for heretofore it could not well be seen (but in rainy seasons) from the windows. a handsome bridge is lately thrown over it, & the stables taken away, which stood full in view between the house & the river. the prospect opens here to a wider tract of country terminated by more distant hills: this scene is yet in its infancy, the objects are thinly scatter'd, & the clumps and plantations lately made: but it promises well in time. (CTG 785–86)

Before concluding his tour, Gray visited one last property, that of Hardwicke Hall, near Bolsover. Here he was haunted by the lingering, spectral presence of Mary, Queen of Scots, who had from time to time visited the estate while in the custody of the Earl of Shrewsbury. 'One would think', Gray wrote with a peculiar combination of historical sentiment and a respect untinged by irony unusual to him, that

> Mary, Queen of Scots, was but just walk'd down into the Park with her Guard for half-an-hour. her Gallery, her room of audience, her antichamber, with the very canopies, chair of state, footstool, Lit-de-repos, Oratory, carpets, & hangings, just as she left them. A little tatter'd indeed, but the more venerable; & all preserved with religious care, & paper'd up in winter. (CTG 787)

After passing though Nottingham, where he stayed some three days with Frederick Montagu, Gray boarded a coach and finally returned, by way of main-travelled roads, to London.

*

When Gray arrived in town he learned that the Regius Professor of Modern History, Shallet Turner, had died just two weeks earlier, on 13 November. Although Gray held out some hope that he might receive the appointment to the Professorship himself (his friend Sir Henry Erskine went so far as to suggest his name to Lord Bute), he appears not to have been too much troubled by the rumours then circulating that the position would instead be awarded to Delaval ('next to myself', he wrote Wharton, 'I wish'd for him'). As matters so turned out, the Professorship was awarded before the end of the year to Laurence Brockett, a poor decision that would in only a few years time lead once again to Gray's interest in (or at least involvement with) the post.

Gray's solicitation, via Erskine, of the ministry's regard must in any event have sat uncomfortably with him. Only one year earlier, Gray had jotted down in his pocketbook a few quick lines succinctly describing the modest limits of his own personality and professional duties – lines in which he congratulated himself first and foremost on the 'pride' and self-respect that had thus far prevented him from soliciting or even desiring any high university or government position. In this brief 'Sketch of His Own Character', Gray had pictured himself as follows:

> Too poor for a bribe and too proud to importune,
> He had not the method of making a fortune:
> Could love and could hate, so was thought somewhat odd;
> No very great wit, he believed in a God.
> A post or a pension he did not desire,
> But left church and state to Charles Townshend and Squire. (*PTG*
> 236–37)

The references in the 'Sketch's' final line to Charles Townshend and to Dr. Samuel Squire suggest that the verses were written soon after March or April, 1761; it was in those months that Townshend and Squire had been appointed to serve as, respectively, Secretary of War and Bishop of St. David's. Gray followed Walpole in holding Townshend generally in disdain for his lack of 'common truth, common sincerity, common honesty, common modesty, common steadiness, common courage, and common sense'. Squire he dismissed in a letter to Wharton as a servile 'Devil'. Even if they were written several years before the possibility of his appointment to the Professorship of Modern History in 1762, however, the lines clearly reflect the poet's justifiable pride in never having debased himself by soliciting 'a post or a pension'. To have done so would for Gray have been tantamount to begging. The fact that he in 1762, through his application to Bute, had sullied what had until then been a personal reputation and a sense of self-esteem completely divorced or separate from the vagaries of the larger political world and the taint of ministerial patronage did not sit well with him. Townshend and Squire, as several critics of Gray's poetry have observed, symbolized for the poet everything that was low or servile about political office-seekers and their toadies. Only one year earlier Gray had been able to ridicule such toadies as they deserved; never again, he now felt in the wake of his indecorous eagerness to gain the Regius Professorship, would he ever be able to cast such dangerously self-directed satiric stones.

The new year began quietly for Gray; it was destined to be a comfortably uneventful period for the poet. With Mason he exchanged learned 'dissertations' on the explorations the precentor was then making in and around York Minster; poking about in the ancient structure on his own, Mason had brought to Gray's attention the ruins of a small Gothic chapel located near the northwest end of the cathedral, and the two men began together to bring their learning to bear on the neglected secrets of its original foundation and construction. In February, the writings both of Gray and of Mason were brought to the attention of the Italian author Francesco Algarotti, who was then living in Pisa, and whose compliments were passed on to the pair by William Taylor How, a one-time fellow of Pembroke then travelling in Italy. Algarotti's own work, a text on optics that had in 1739 been translated into English by Elizabeth Carter as 'Sir Isaac Newton's Philosophy Explain'd for the Use of the Ladies', was at the time still quite well known in England, though Gray professed himself privately to Mason equally astonished to find himself 'the particular Friend of a Person so celebrated for his *politezza, e dottrina*, as my Cousin Taylor Howe'. Algarotti would write to Gray later that year, praising him particularly as the Pindar of the English people, and addressing him in his letter as 'Illustrissimo Signor Padrone Colendissimo'. He sent Gray several small treatises of his own – 'thingumterries', Gray called them – on such subjects as the opera ('a good clever dissertation', Gray judged). He was nevertheless on some level flattered by Algarotti's respectful attention, the approbation of which he regarded as something of a balm to the self-inflicted wound of his own recent 'place-seeking'. It was at the very least rewarding to be recognized and congratulated by a fellow (celebrated) author, he decided, 'having no relish for any other fame than what is conferr'd by the few real Judges, that are so thinly scatter'd over the face of the Earth'. On yet another level, however, Gray appears to have been rather baffled by the social and professional niceties demanded by such recognition. His stern injunction to Mason to be 'civil to the Count' when he wrote to Algarotti regarding his self-described *coserelle* reflects his own anxiety concerning just how he ought properly to respond to such praise.

Mason had recently been interesting himself in the affairs of Christopher Smart. Gray, it will be remembered, had himself reluctantly taken up his own pen on behalf of Smart years earlier, when he had requested that Wharton intercede with the Duke of Cleveland on the young man's behalf. In June, 1761, when Mason had begun collecting subscriptions to Smart's *Translations of the Psalms of David*, Gray had put his own name down for two copies. In April, 1763, Smart published his *Song to David* in a quarto volume of twenty-two pages priced at one shilling. Mason had read the latter work, and, he wrote to Gray, 'from these conclude him as mad as ever'. He nevertheless persisted in his attempts to sort through Smart's legal and financial tangles. Gray offered what assistance he could. He seems never to have warmed to 'poor' Smart either personally or, indeed, as a poet. Although Smart's friendships – such as they were – with William Mason, Samuel Johnson, and, later, Dr. Charles Burney would help to sustain him following the dark period of his incarceration for insanity in a private 'hospital' in Bethnal Green, his elaborately constructed, often recondite work received little genuine appreciation until many years after his death in 1771.

Following a short stay in London and 'a little jaunt' to Epsom, to visit his old friend John Clerke sometime in May, Gray settled down to spend the summer of 1763 in Cambridge. He wrote to Wharton at the beginning of August merely to comment on the fact that his recent silence was due only 'to the nothingness of my history'. 'I have been here time out of mind', he wrote, 'in a place, where no events grow.' The torpor of high summer had recently been broken, however, by an unexpected visit from Walpole who, Gray observed to Wharton, 'dined with me, seem'd mighty happy for the time he stay'd, & said he could like to live here'. Walpole's visit to Cambridge, remarkably, was his first in twenty-five years. The 'youthful scenes' revived in his memory by the visit had now to compete with Walpole's very mature and committed interest in Gothic architecture and artifacts. Although he commented in a letter to Montagu that 'the Colleges were 'much cleaned and improved' since his own days at university, he confessed that still, given the choice, he would rather have lived in Oxford. The stormy weather that surrounded Walpole's visit to Cambridge ('we have nothing but rain & thunder of late', Gray wrote Wharton on 5 August), may well have heightened his perception of the stormy Gothicism of Cambridge itself, and thus contributed to the mysterious gestation of *The Castle of Otranto*, which Walpole was to write the following year. As it was, Walpole could talk of little else than the improvements he was even then making to his own Gothic retreat at Strawberry Hill. The stop at Cambridge itself had served only as a momentary interruption in one of Walpole's extended antiquarian tours and shopping expeditions for his beloved property. He had hurried home that evening, Gray wrote, 'to his new Gallery, which is all Gothicism, & gold, & crimson, & looking-glass. He has purchased at an auction . . . ebony-chairs, & old moveables enough to load a wagon'.

Walpole had been accompanied on his tour by his old Eton and Cambridge friend, William Cole. Walpole, with his usual rectitude in epistolary affairs, had kept in closer touch with Cole than had Gray himself, but even so, all three men looked upon one another as old and tried acquaintances. They had known each other so familiarly and for so long as to have become fixtures in each other's lives – the kinds of friends with whom the simple fact of shared, lived experience had formed by now a supple and nearly unbreakable bond. Cole was at this point in his life serving a rector of Bletchley, in Buckinghamshire; he would in 1767 move closer to Cambridge, living first at Waterbeach, and subsequently at Milton. Although not among the most intimate of Gray's adult acquaintances, Cole nevertheless provides us with some of the most intimate details about Gray as he looked and behaved as a mature man. Among the manuscripts Cole left to the British Museum upon his death in 1782 was his collection, *Athenae Cantabrigiensis*, which contained a gathering of anecdotes and biographical data about a great many of his Cambridge acquaintances, including Gray. Cole also jotted down a number of marginalia in his own copy of Mason's *Life* of Gray. In these Cole described Gray as being 'well put together and latterly tending to plumpness' – a description at least partly borne out by a silhouette of Gray cut by Pembroke fellow Francis Mapletoft dating from this period. The silhouette is supposed to be a good one (Mason is said to have used it as a model for the several portraits of Gray he attempted after the poet's death), and we see the slight 'plumpness' of the neck and lower chin. Venturing to compare Gray to his French nemesis Voltaire, Cole wrote: 'I am apt to think [their characters] were very similar. They were both little men, very nice and exact in their Persons and Dress, most lively and agreeable in conversation (except that Mr Gray was apt to be too satyrical) and both of them full of Affectation'.[4] That Gray was satirical and even 'affected' in his conversation should by now come as no real surprise; nor, likewise, should the description which Cole's reminiscences allow us to recreate of Gray's rooms at Pembroke. The poet's exactness with regards to his own person extended, apparently, to his immediate surroundings as well. Flowers filled the window boxes of his rooms and sat in bright clusters in the vases that rested on surfaces piled neatly with books and manuscripts. In other places, elegant oriental jars scented his rooms with a delicate perfume. In fact the essence of Gray's precision, neatness, and delicacy in his early middle age is nowhere better captured than in a recipe for potpourri he was eventually to send to Cole in July, 1764:

> Get some coarse brown Bay Salt: this is the sine quâ non, & (by the way) is not to be had at Cambridge, where under the name of Bay Salt they sell a whitish Kind of Salt, that will never do for our Purpose, & will

---

4   William Cole, quoted in Mitford, xcix.

spoil all: at London the true Sort is common in every Shop, & a Pennyworth of it is enough to make a Bushel of Perfumes. Take a Peck of Damask Roses, pick'd from the Cups, Orange Flowers all you can get, Cloves (the Spice) a Quarter of an Ounce, cut small: scatter them in your Jar mixt in Layers about 2 Inches thick, & thinly sprinkle the Salt over them: repeat this, 'till the Vessel is three Quarters, or more, full: cover it close down, let it stand 2 Days, & then stir it up well with a wooden Ladle or Skimmer: repeat this often, & it is made. If it is always moist to the Touch, it is right: if over-wet, you have only to put in more Flowers, & no more Salt. You may use, if you please, Tops of Lavender, Myrtle-Leaves bruised, Rose-Geranium, Angelica, Shavings of Orrice-Root, or (where Orange Flowers are scarce) young green Oranges sliced, or even the yellow Rind of Seville-Oranges: but of these Things a very little will do, least they overpower the Rest. I can not be particular as to Quantities, because I observed none myself. (*CTG* 1322–23)

The casual and deliberate imprecision expressed in this last sentence, following as it does the excessive care of such a precise and specific formula, is almost comical. Cole, at any rate, was impressed enough by the recipe to set about assembling his own potpourri from the recipe within just two weeks of having received it.

Sometime toward the beginning of October, Gray was surprised by a letter from Mason announcing his friend's decision to marry. That Mason had intended to take a wife had been a well-known bit of gossip within his circle; whether he had already settled on his eventual partner – a Miss Mary Sherman, whom he married on 25 September 1765 – at the time of this announcement to Gray is unclear. Gray's response to Mason's news prompted a reply which very much evinces what Cole characterized as Gray's 'satyrical' side. He wrote Mason:

I rejoice. but has she common sense, is she a Gentlewoman? has she money? has she a nose? I know, she sings a little, & twiddles on the harpsichord, hammers at sentiment, & puts herself in an attitude, admires a cast in the eye, & can say Elfrida by heart: but these are only the virtues of a Maid. do, let her have some wifelike qualities, & a double portion of prudence, as she will have not only herself to govern, but you also, & that with an absolute sway. your Friends, I doubt not, will suffer for it: however we are very happy, & have no other wish than to see you settled in the world. we beg you would not stand fiddleing about it, but be married forthwith, & then take chaise, and come consummating all the way to Cambridge. . . . (*CTG* 821–22)

At least one of Gray's critics has observed that the poet's humour in this letter is 'grossly indecent', and has characterized this response to Mason's news as the 'unkindest' letter Gray ever wrote. But to take deliberate offense at Gray's bawdy and deliberately obscene humour in such a way is simply to miss the point. Mason himself appears not to have taken any offense at the passage, and neither should any of Gray's modern readers. Gray's playfulness may sound a bit too misogynistic in our ears today, but his fooling at least highlights the slightly more caustic side of his character and of his peculiar brand of wit. In the year to come, Gray was to be provided with the opportunity of giving that 'satyrical' side an even freer reign.

II. A Lick of Court Whitewash

With the exception of a two weeks' 'ramble' away from Cambridge at the end of September and the beginning of October, and a month-long stay in London extending through much of November, Gray was content to spend the rest of the year in Cambridge. His 'ramble' was circumscribed not so much by inclination as by the weather and – or so he wrote to Billy Robinson – his dwindling financial resources. 'My conscience' he wrote to Robinson on 10 October, '. . . would (I really think) carry me into Somersetshire [where Robinson was then staying with his old friend and former tutor, a Dr. Ross] did not poverty and winter stare me in the face and bid me sit still'.

The new year began quietly enough. Gray wrote to Walpole from Cambridge toward the end of January, thanking him for a recent remembrance, and reminding him that he had yet to receive a copy of the third volume of the *Anecdotes of Painting*, as well as another volume Walpole had been preparing for the press at Strawberry Hill, on engravers and engraving. Gray hoped that Walpole would soon be able to send both books on from London. He then offered a sample of his opinion regarding the candidates for the High Stewardship of the University, and the possibility that their old Eton acquaintance, John Montagu – now fourth Earl of Sandwich – would be awarded the position. 'Who can damn the Devil?', he asked Walpole of Sandwich,

> he continues his temptations here with so much assiduity, that I conclude he is not absolutely sure of success yet. his leading Partisans, tho' not ashamed of themselves, are yet heartily ashamed of him, & would give their ears, it were any devil, but he. yet he would be chose at present, I have little doubt, tho' with strong opposition, & in a dishonourable way for him. yet I have some gleams of hope, for it is in the power of one Man to prevent it, if he will stand the brunt. . . . (*CTG* 830)

It remains unclear as to whom Gray supposed could prevent the appointment of Sandwich, yet much surrounding the contest – which was soon

to turn into a highly visible and bitterly fought battle on both sides –
was already fraught with rumour, secrecy, and innuendo.

In November of the previous year, the Earl of Hardwicke, who had
served as High Steward of the University for nearly fifteen years, was
taken ill and was expected to die. After the position of Chancellor itself
(a position which had since 1748 been held by the Duke of Newcastle)
the High Stewardship was the most important post held by a University
official. The contest for the succession of Hardwicke's office, however,
was complicated by Newcastle's own recent political misfortunes. Following his accession in October, 1760, King George III made it clear that
he wanted as little as possible to do with Newcastle and his 'dirty arts'.
'I dismissed him before he could dismiss me', the King had recently said
of Newcastle's political crony, the Duke of Devonshire, and he wanted
Newcastle to know that a similar fate lay in store for him and, indeed,
for any other minister or civil servant who did not share the King's own
ideas about the role of the peerage in the new political order. Having
been driven from government power in 1762, Newcastle yet needed, the
King and his ministry felt, permanently to be disabled and disarmed as
a potential threat to their own political hegemony. Newcastle, however,
was not one to give up without a fight. He possessed landed estates in
no fewer than thirteen different counties, and exercised an equally extensive amount of political influence. Moreover, Newcastle still held on to
his position as Chancellor of the University, a position that he had for
the past fifteen years used to his own political advantage; a wealth of
livings, university properties, and lucrative academic appointments had
long been placed at Newcastle's personal disposal.

Newcastle's fall from grace threatened now to limit his influence as
Chancellor. He had hoped immediately to secure the position of High
Steward for Hardwicke's own son, Lord Royston. Toward the end of
November, however, the Earl of Sandwich, who was then serving as Secretary of State for the Northern Department, informed the King that he
himself wished to be considered as a candidate for the position – he even
began canvassing for the post before Hardwicke was even dead. Newcastle, who for all his recent tribulations had expected little if any resistance to Lord Royston's appointment, was consequently forced to dig in
his heels and wage a fierce battle against Sandwich and his ambitions.
The sides were drawn: Lord Sandwich, the candidate of court and of the
new ministry, confronted Newcastle's own determination to maintain his
already tenuous hold over University affairs.

The contest seemed to just about anyone involved either directly or
indirectly in its outcome little less than profoundly bizarre. For one
thing, there was as yet no vacancy to be contested. Following an uncertain period at the end of 1763, Hardwicke's health had actually begun
to improve, and it looked for some time as if a full recovery was not

entirely out of the question. By the time a relapse finally claimed his life the following spring (on 6 March 1764), Hardwicke might well have been forgiven for thinking, at the last, his subsequent interment redundant; he had already been publicly treated as just as good as dead for nearly four months. Even more stunning, however, was the simple fact of Sandwich's own declared candidacy for the post. The Earl's reputation for debauchery was such that when faced with possibility of his appointment to a position of influence in an institution such as Cambridge – the overall purpose of which was dedicated to learning, chaste godliness, and the disinterested, philosophical pursuit of knowledge – most of that same institution's members could only stare, dumbstruck. Sandwich's most recent bit of hypocrisy had even provided him with a nickname – drawn from John Gay's *The Beggar's Opera* – of Jemmy Twitcher. The House of Lords had recently decided to prosecute the 'patriot' John Wilkes for obscene libel. Wilkes, it was alleged, had authored a lengthy parody based loosely on Pope's *Essay on Man*, entitled an *Essay on Women*. The poem – an unrelievedly uninteresting piece of obscenity – had in fact been penned by one of Wilkes's friends and allies, Thomas Putter. Wilkes had written only the 'Notes' to the poem, under the name of Warburton, Bishop of Gloucester. Such details, however, disappeared in the light of Sandwich's bare-faced arrogance. That Sandwich, of all people – a man who, along with Wilkes himself, was a founding member of the Hell-Fire Club (the motto of which was the Rabelaisian tag, 'Fay ce que voudras') – had himself provoked Wilkes was a saturnalian burlesque of the most outrageous and distasteful kind. The contestants knew one another's character too well for the masquerade of justice to be maintained without interruption. When Sandwich proposed that Wilkes would inevitably have to choose between dying on the gallows or dying of the pox, Wilkes famously replied: 'That depends, my Lord, on whether I embrace your principles or your mistress.'

The members of the popular press, it need hardly be added, were having a field day with the contest. Charles Churchill, a long-time friend and supporter of Wilkes, was one of several poets to weigh in publicly with an attack on Sandwich. The work – a satire entitled simply *The Candidate*, first published in May, 1764 – was of a piece with Churchill's other politically occasional poems written that same year. Sandwich, Churchill pretended to argue, was suitable for any number of occupations; the High Stewardship of Cambridge was unfortunately not one of them:

> To whip a top, to knuckle down at taw,
> To swing upon a gate, to ride a straw
> To play at pushpin with dull brother peers,

> To belch out catches in a porter's ears,
> To reign the monarch of a midnight cell,
> To be the gaping chairman's oracle,
> Whilst in most blessed union, rogue and whore
> Clap hands, huzza, and hiccup out Encore![5]

These, Churchill suggested, were achievements far better suited to the Earl's considerable talents, if not as a university official, then as a whoremaster.

Gray wrote regularly concerning the contest both to Wharton (who needed to be kept informed of its general progress) and to Walpole (who had inherited his father's bitter hatred towards Newcastle and all his works). Toward the end of February, when it looked as though Hardwicke's recovery was imminent and assured, and the hasty gathering of the contestants tastelessly immature, Gray wrote to Wharton,

> This silly dirty Place has had all its thoughts taken up with chusing a new High-Steward, & had not Ld Hardwicke surprisingly & to the shame of the Faculty recover'd by a Quack-medicine, I believe in my conscience the noble Earl of Sandwich had been chosen, tho' (let me do them justice to say) not without a considerable opposition. his principal agents are Dr. Brook of St. Johns, Mr Brocket, & Dr Long, whose old Tory notions, that had long lain by neglected & forgotten, are brought out again & furbish'd for present use, tho' rusty & out of joint, like his own Spheres & Orreries. (CTG 832)

In April, following Hardwicke's death and with the contest for the position brought once again to a roiling boil, Sandwich actually paid a visit to Cambridge, where he was entertained by the Master of Trinity, and dined in the College Hall. All but one of the college's undergraduates refused likewise to dine in hall that evening; one group even set about raising a raucous cheer for Lord Hardwicke himself. Following such public humiliation for his guest, the Master of Trinity first insisted that the students sign a document confessing themselves to have been dishonourable both to themselves and to their college. The students, to their credit, pointedly refused to affix their names to any such document. The Master was only two months later compelled to let the matter drop entirely.

It was at the very height of all this emotionally fraught, partizan excitement that Gray decided to write his own satire on Sandwich, a short piece which, like Churchill's longer effort, is today known simply by the title, *The Candidate*. Unlike Churchill's piece, however, Gray's

---

short lampoon was intended apparently to be read only by a few friends and acquaintances. Gray seized on the popular designation of Sandwich as 'Jemmy Twitcher', but he was ready to ring some significant changes on what had by then become a familiar theme:

> When sly Jemmy Twitcher had smugged up his face
> With a lick of court whitewash and pious grimace,
> A-wooing he went, where three sisters of old
> In harmless society guttle and scold.
>   'Lord! Sister,' says Physic to Law, 'I declare
> Such a sheep-biting look, such a pick-pocket air,
> Not I, for the Indies! you know I'm no prude;
> But his nose is a shame and his eyes are so lewd!
> Then he shambles and straddles so oddly, I fear –
> No; at our time of life, 'twould be silly, my dear.'
>   'I don't know,' says law, 'now methinks, for his look,
> 'Tis just like the picture in Rochester's book.
> But his character, Phyzzy, his morals, his life;
> When she died, I can't tell, but he once had a wife.
>   'They say he's no Christian, loves drinking and whoring,
> And all the town rings of his swearing and roaring,
> His lying and filching, and Newgate-bird tricks: –
> Not I, – for a coronet, chariot and six.'
>   Divinity heard, between waking and dozing,
> Her sisters denying and Jemmy proposing;
> From dinner she rose with her bumper in hand,
> She stroked up her belly and stroked down her band.
>   'What a pother is here about wenching and roaring!
> Why David loved catches and Solomon whoring.
> Did not Israel filch from the Egyptians of old
> Their jewels of silver and jewels of gold?
> The prophet of Bethel, we read, told a lie;
> He drinks: so did Noah; he swears: so do I.
> To refuse him for such peccadillos were odd;
> Besides, he repents, and he talks about God.
>   'Never hang down your head, you penitent elf!
> Come, buss me, I'll be Mrs Twitcher myself.
> Damn ye both for a couple of Puritan bitches!
> He's Christian enough that repents and that stitches.' (*PTG* 248–51)

Critics were for a great many years reluctant even to admit that Gray wrote these lines; and, indeed, the poem's textual history is murky enough to warrant some degree of credulity regarding its provenance. Mason frankly admitted that – although he remembered Gray repeating the lines aloud to him – he 'never before saw them in writing', until he was sent a copy of *The Candidate* by Walpole in the autumn of 1774. The poem did not appear in print until February, 1777, when it was published in the *London Evening Post*, with the following preface:

> The following verses are said to be the production of the late celebrated Mr. Gray. They were written on the occasion of Jemmy Twitcher's standing as a candidate for the ——, at ——, and in whose favour the gentlemen of the gown took a very active part. As they are in but a few hands, and I think them too good to be lost, you are at liberty to print them, if you shall think them worth a corner of your paper.[6]

The introductory letter was signed only 'Anti-Twitcher'. The printed version of the poem that then followed contained a number of minor differences from a manuscript text of the work in Gray's own handwriting, the same manuscript which Walpole had discovered among his paper and sent to Mason over two years earlier. 'I thought I never lost anything in my life', Walpole had written of the fugitive copy in September, 1774,

> I was sure I had them, and so I had, and now am I not a good soul, to sit down and send you a copy. . . . I am in a panic till there are more copies than mine, and as the post does not go till tomorrow, I am in terror lest the house should be burnt tonight. I have a mind to go and bury a transcript in the field – but then if I should be burnt too! Nobody would know where to look for it; well here it is! I think your decorum will not hold it proper to be printed in the life, nor would I have it. We will preserve copies, and the devil is in it, if some time or other it don't find its way to the press. My own copy is in his own handwriting. . . . (WC xxviii.168)

Some of Gray's subsequent critics would appear rather to have consigned Strawberry Hill to the flames than see *The Candidate* assume its now comfortable position in Gray's collected works. The startling obscenity of the satire's final line, and the uncompromising and admittedly vicious tenor of the piece as a whole – its gross 'indecency' – seem not to sit well with the apparent, melancholic placidity of some of Gray's more famous poems. When it comes to satire, commentators from Mason onward have often expressed the wish that Gray had taken a small dose of his own advice and – leaving the derisive and nasty business of satiric burlesque to newspaper hacks – himself kept the noiseless tenor of his way.

[6] Reprinted in Lonsdale, *CTG* 246.

If nothing else, however, *The Candidate* stands as something of a verification of the observation once made by Walpole that Gray 'never wrote anything easily but thing of humour'. The brevity of *The Candidate*'s nasty allegory adds to its bite, and while it can certainly be argued that Gray pulls no punches in these lines, he accomplishes just as much – if not more – by way of indirection and association as he does by outspoken indictment. The observation of Law in the poem's third verse stanza that Sandwich's 'sheep-biting look' and 'pick-pocket air' are 'just like the picture in Rochester's book', for example, manages nicely to remind the reader that Sandwich was in fact the great-grandson of the well-known libertine poet John Wilmot, Earl of Rochester, without clumsily hammering home the point. Blessed with such forbears, the shared knowledge of such a commentator winkingly invites us to ask, how could Sandwich have been expected to behave any differently? In the description of Sandwich's physical appearance in the poem's second stanza ('But his nose is a shame and his eyes are so lewd!') Gray similarly alludes only obliquely to the possibility that the Candidate's nose had been damaged by venereal disease. A reference in the next line to Sandwich's gait – 'Then he shambles and straddles so oddly, I fear' – is likewise not merely a jibe at Sandwich's notoriously awkward walk (contemporary observers remarked that he seemed to encompass both sides of the street in a single stride), but also insinuates that Sandwich's venereal complaint has entered its later stages; he seems, at least according to Gray's poem, to be suffering from serious neuropathic symptoms such as tabes dorsalis, or even sabre shins (implying his condition was congenital) which would expose the bowed appearance of his legs.

A surprisingly small number of Gray's critics, however, have commented on the simple fact that, for all Gray's caustic dismissal of Sandwich as an individual, Gray's satire in the poem is aimed far more pointedly at the University faculty itself. His actual target is not so much the hypocrisy of 'Sly Jemmy Twitcher' himself – from whom both the poet and the public had come to expect such behaviour – as it is the hypocrisy of his Cambridge colleagues – of whom the same people had a right to expect better. The fact that the University's capitulation to Sandwich's candidacy is placed not in the mouths of the faculties of Medicine or Jurisprudence, but is sounded rather by that of Divinity herself, heightens the reader's perception of the institution's moral and ethical health. Divinity of course justifies Sandwich's behaviour with reference to that of various prominent figures in the Bible (ll. 23–30), a resort that intensified Gray's larger suggestion that the Cambridge community seems in all the commotion to have forgotten how to read properly. Those very people who ought to be protecting and nurturing learning and encouraging a proper sense of religious devotion, Gray suggests, have capitulated to the enemy; the fact that the poet disliked and distrusted both Newcastle *and* Sandwich affords him a perspective which casts the greatest blame on the corrupt political machinery which operated in either man's favour.

In the end, the outcome of all this controversy could not help but prove anticlimactic. The greatly contested election in the University Senate took place at the end of March, but the result was so close that a final decision had eventually to be referred to the Court of King's Bench (Gray, incidentally, never having received his Master of Arts was not even entitled to vote in the election). It was not until April, 1765 – a full year after the initial vote in the Senate – that Royston, now Lord Hardwicke, was awarded the position. Gray continued to comment in his letters to his friends on the details of the various intrigues and negotiations involved in what had become a seemingly interminable process; as one of his letters put it, his allusions to the contest in all its stages 'are disdainful of the whole proceedings'. Nicholls, in his *Reminiscences*, summarized his own reading of Gray's reaction to the entire affair:

> In the contest for the High Stewardship at Cambridge between Lord Hardwick & Lord Sandwich Mr Gray took a warm, & eager part, for no other reason, I believe, than because he thought the licentious character of the latter candidate rendered him improper for a post of such dignity in the University. His zeal in this cause inspired the verses full of pleasantry & wit which have been published since his death. (*CTG* 1289–90)

Nicholls could have added that however much Gray's 'pleasantry and wit' might momentarily divert one's attention from the profound disservice to the University's 'dignity' engendered by the whole, squalid spectacle of a dirty and hard-fought election, Cambridge itself, in the final analysis, could not help but stand the biggest loser in the affair. Moreover, as Gray wrote darkly in a letter to Wharton, 'the Nation is in the same hands as the University, & really does not make so manful a resistance'.

*

Throughout the earliest stages of the contest for the High Stewardship in 1764, Gray's health had begun increasingly to deteriorate. He began to experience a discomfort quite unlike the familiar aches and pains of his more customary complaints, and his anxiety was high that he was in fact suffering from some sort of rectal fistula or, perhaps, something even worse. He decided to undergo an operation. Wharton was not only quick to offer Gray medical advice, but immediately volunteered to travel down from Old Park to be with him – an offer for which he professed himself thankful but characteristically, when it came to the possibility of drawing attention from among his friends to the state of his own health, declined. On 10 July 1764, he was able to write to Wharton in thanks:

> I do remember & shall ever remember, as I ought, your extreme kindness in offering to be present, & assist me in the *perilous hour*. when I received your letter, I was pleased to find, I had done every thing almost, that you advised. the fault lay in deferring matters too long. upon inspection they found no reason to apprehend a Fistula, but the piles only in an extreme degree, that threaten'd mortification. . . . towards the end of my confinement, during which (you may believe) I lived on nothing, came the Gout in one foot, but so tame you might have stroked it; such a *Minikin* you might have play'd with it. In 3 or 4 days it disappear'd. (*CTG* 836–37)

In addition to receiving Wharton's advice, Gray had consulted the Regius Professor of Physic at Cambridge, Dr. Plumptre. His surgeon was the celebrated Thomas Thackeray, a great-uncle to the novelist William Makepeace Thackeray. Invasive procedures of any kind – however seemingly slight – before the days of sterilization, disinfection, and anaesthesia, could of course be both painful and dangerous. Gray, however, had been in the very best of hands.

Gray's convalescence throughout the long summer months was slow but steady, and not entirely devoid of its own, peculiarly sedentary kinds of entertainment. Nicholls now visited the poet in his rooms as much as possible. His easy-going personality could work transformative wonders on Gray's mood. It was at about this time that Nicholls wrote to William Johnson Temple describing the usual pattern of their evenings:

> I have seen Mr Gray several times, at his own room you may be sure, for I believe he fears some deadly infection in mine. I drink tea there when I please and stay till nine. . . . He has Fitzwilliam's Harpsichord, and we sing Duetts, Marcello's Psalms, in great privacy, an hour or two. . . . Afterwards we sit and talk about what, you know, I never remember, except in scraps (or tatters, or rags, or any word you like better) – and then we go in great form to the coffee-house, where we dose over the news and pamphlets as usual to the last stroke of eleven; I now and then interrupt my own slumbers with a word or two very sensible, solemn nonsense (my fort you know); and Mr. [Theodore Vincent] Gould's incessant, impertinent Babble, will not let me sleep quietly, nor Mr Gray talk, which I should prefer. . . . At the last stroke of eleven we rise, take our lanterns we who have them, Mr. [William] Talbot his galaches, and proceed in procession down stairs (Mr Gould you know stops to talk

bawdy to the Nels in the coffee-room), and so, after leave duly taken at Pembroke gate, home as usual.[7]

The tavern and coffee house referred to in Nicholls's letter cannot accurately have been described as a molly house in the fullest sense of that term; it did not, in other words, cater exclusively or even particularly to a homosexual clientele. Nicholls nevertheless makes it clear in his letter that all the fellows were habitues not only of the coffee-room itself, but were 'regulars' enough to mingle easily with the openly (or at least obviously) homosexual patrons who assembled there nightly. Critics of Gray's poetry, incidentally, would probably have a great deal less trouble accepting the slight (and heterosexually specific) obscenity of *The Candidate*, had we but a sample of the brand of humour to which he was nightly exposed (and clearly, for all his reticence, understood and enjoyed) when surrounded by the effeminate 'Nels' who spent their evenings in the dark and smokey confines of the coffee room.

Walpole had written to Gray on several occasions throughout the late spring and early summer, enquiring after his health. Gray, who not surprisingly had postponed undergoing his minor 'surgery' for as long as possible, had confessed himself to be unwell, but was very soon reassuring his friend that he had 'recover'd in a great degree'. He eventually travelled to London on 16 May and remained there for much of the following month. The better part of the summer was spent in Cambridge; Gray rewarded himself with another, briefer visit to town in September. On both occasions he visited Walpole, who had himself been passing through an eventful and stressful period in his own personal life.

Walpole's beloved cousin, Henry Seymour Conway, had in 1763 endangered his own political career by maintaining his anti-government position on the subject of general warrants – i.e. warrants authorizing the apprehension and arrest of unspecified individuals. Conway's defiance of the King and of the Whig government of Lord Grenville cost him both his civil appointment under the government as Groom of the Bedchamber, as well as his military appointment as commanding officer of a regiment of dragoons. Walpole, whose love for and attachment to his cousin had not lessened over the years, immediately sprang to Conway's defense in the public, pamphlet skirmish that followed Conway's dismissal, and his subsequent defense of his position. The affair had dragged on until the summer of 1764, at which point Walpole's

---

[7] Nicholls's letter was first printed in the *Annual Gazette* of the Pembroke College Society in 1938; the text was reprinted in Ketton-Cremer's *Thomas Gray* (London, 1954) 191.

own position had suddenly and unexpectedly become a humiliating one. His impassioned defense of his cousin was interpreted by government apologists as an inappropriately passionate and only barely concealed declaration of love for his own cousin. 'I should go on to take notice of how extremely personal he grows in the prosecution of his subject', the pamphleteer William Guthrie wrote of Walpole's efforts in Conway's defense in June, 1764,

> How pathetically he dwells on the ingenuous modesty of the general, on his extraordinary humility, on the twenty-seven years that he served, the six regular battles he was engaged in, beside the many bye battles or smaller actions, the heroes under whom he was formed, and the decorum which has graced every period in his fortune, if I did not recollect the unhappy situation of my Author, *C'est une affaire du coeur*: 'Tis his first love who has been so barbarously used.[8]

In the midst of such unseemly public humiliation, Walpole sat down one evening and began writing what was in a very short time to take shape as his generically innovative 'Gothic' novel, *The Castle of Otranto*. The idea for the work, he later claimed, came to him in a dream. He wrote quickly ('one evening I wrote from the time I had drunk my tea', he recalled, '. . . till half an hour after one in the morning, when my hand and fingers were so weary, that I could not hold the pen to finish the sentence . . .'), and by 6 August had finished the novel.[9] It would be published at the Strawberry Hill Press in December, 1764, under the guise of a translation 'from the Original Italian' of one 'Onuphrio Muralto' For a work which was to achieve both an immediate popularity (the first edition of 500 copies was soon followed by a second edition, readied for the press by 11 April the following year; a third edition appeared in 1766) and a lasting influence within the English literary tradition, *Otranto* remained an intensely personal work. Walpole seemed in the novel finally to be working through his own relationship with his powerful father, as well as exploring the ramifications of his own 'forbidden' love for his cousin.

III. So Much Beauty

The autumn and winter of 1764–65 passed quietly for Gray. In late September he undertook a short tour of some of the southern counties

---

[8]   William Guthrie, *Reply to the Counter-Address* (London, 1764) 25.
[9]   WC I.88

in which he had not yet spent much time, travelling by way of London to Winchester, Southampton, Salisbury, Wilton, and Stonehenge. He was profoundly impressed by the country immediately surrounding Netley Abbey. The Abbey (which he had visited once before, almost ten years earlier, and to which he now referred comfortably in a letter to Brown as his 'old friend'),

> stands in a little quiet valley, which gradually rises behind the ruin into a half-circle crown'd with thick wood. before it on a descent is a thicket of oaks, that serves to veil it from the broad day & from profane eyes, only leaving a peep on both sides, where the sea appears glittering thro' the shade, & vessels with their white sails, that glide across & are lost again. . . . the Abbey was never very large. the shell of its church is almost entire, but the pillars of the iles are gone, & the roof has tumbled in, yet some little of it is left in the transept, where the ivy has forced its way thro', & hangs flaunting down among the fretted ornaments & escutcheons of the Benefactors. much of the lodgings & offices are also standing, but all is over-grown with trees & bushes, & mantled here & there with ivy, that mounts over the battlements. (*CTG* 843)

On his way to Southampton, Gray had stopped briefly at Winchester, where he visited the Cathedral, and even dined with the Archdeacon. Otherwise, he was decidedly and contentedly anti-social. 'This place', he wrote disdainfully of Southampton itself, 'is still full of *Bathers*'. 'I know not a Soul', he went on to boast, 'nor have once been at the rooms.' Still, though lodgings were 'very dear', the seafood was abundant and 'very cheap'. From Southampton he travelled quickly on to Salisbury and Stonehenge, where he so far surrendered to his inclinations as a scholar and historian as to take his own measurements of some of the standing stones, and jotted down his notes and calculations of the disposition of the ruins in general. Returning to London, he was once again settled in Jermyn Street by 22 October, 'not at all', he wrote to Brown, 'the worse for my expedition'.

Yet Gray remained in London – to which he was once again referring as a 'tiresome dull place' where 'all people under thirty find so much amusement' (Gray was now approaching his forty-eighth birthday) – only until the end of November, when he returned to Cambridge, where he was to remain for over five months. Toward the end of December Walpole sent him a copy of *Otranto*, and Gray promptly wrote to thank him. 'I have received the C: of O:', he wrote from college, 'and return you my thanks for it. It engages our attention here, makes some of us cry a little, & all in general afraid to go to bed o' nights. We take it for a translation, & should believe it a true story, if it were not for St. Nicholas'. Gray, who had of course been let 'in' on the secret of

Walpole's authorship of the volume (though some attributed the Gothic romance to Gray himself), was being deliberately ironic in his thanks. *Otranto* is on one level a determined if respectful send-up of the excesses of romance narrative, and Gray knew better than anyone that the more solemnly professed pretensions of its narrative were not to be taken all that seriously. He otherwise took the opportunity of the volume's arrival to chide his old friend for not writing in more detail regarding current ministerial crises ('when your pen was in your hand', he scolded Walpole, 'you might have been a bit more communicative'), and expressed his indignation at Walpole's even considering, as he was then doing, a second journey to France; Gray had by now come to detest the growing and pernicious (at least as he saw it) influence of that country's writers and thinkers – particularly of Rousseau and Voltaire – who seemed to him entirely to have captured the imaginations of the English reading public. For his own part, Gray was likewise determined to travel as much as possible, but there would be no more crossing the Channel for him. He was only beginning fully to realize just how much he enjoyed taking shorter and less arduous journeys around England itself, and was intrigued that so much of his own country, and its nearest neighbors, Scotland and Wales, remained yet to be seen.

Toward the beginning of March, Gray was laid up with a mild attack of gout which, though 'very quiet as to pain', still left him for all practical purposes confined to college for nearly six weeks. On 30 April he travelled up to London, where, with the exception of a brief visit to Windsor, he remained for nearly a month. His recent trip to Southampton still fresh in his mind, he had no sooner arrived in town than he began eagerly planning the itinerary of his summer travels. Just before leaving Cambridge, on 29 April, he had written to Wharton at Old Park:

> I have a great propensity to Hartlepool this summer, it is in your neighborhood, & that is to make up for climate & for trees. the sea, the turf, & the rocks, I remember, have merit enough of their own. Mr Brown is so invincibly attach'd to his duties of Treasurer & Tutor, & I know not what, that I give up all hopes of bringing him with me: nor do I (till I have been at London) speak determinately as to myself: perhaps I may find good reasons (against my inclination) to change my mind. (*CTG* 870–71)

He did not, in fact, change his mind. In the last week of May, Gray departed from London for Old Park and 'the remote parts of the Nation', breaking his journey north to visit Mason at York, where he arrived by 29 May. He was glad to be leaving London just as the season was drawing to a particularly dreary close, and just as it seemed everywhere 'teeming with prodigies' (among other things, the Regency

Bill had been introduced that spring, and the ensuing controversy regarding the possible exclusion or inclusion of the Princess of Wales – the King's mother – from its provisions still raged high; earlier in the month a mob of weavers from Spitalfields who had rioted on Ludgate Hill was dispersed only when fired upon by soldiers). Gray stayed with Mason for about two weeks. Only two or three days after his arrival, he again had the misfortune to suffer a mild attack of the gout, which left him confined to the house for most of his visit. Still, he managed to pass the time pleasantly. Old acquaintances such as Edward Bedingfield stopped by for tea, and Gray may also on this occasion have met Mason's intended bride, Mary Sherman, the daughter of a garrison storekeeper at Hull.

Despite having recently experienced some trouble with his eyes, Mason busied himself in Gray's company by undertaking to annotate an interleaved copy of Shakespeare. His glosses may have been intended to support a future edition of the playwright's work; if so, however, they were never published. Very soon after leaving York for Old Park, Gray sent Mason a short poem, nominally addressed to the precentor's servant, Mrs. Anne. 'Willy' – for so Gray comically refers to Shakespeare – complains of Mason's attempts at editing. 'Much have I born from Cankered critic's spite', Willy observes,

> From fumbling baronets and poets small,
> Pert barristers and parsons nothing bright:
> But what awaits me now is worst of all.
> . . .
>
>   Better to bottom tarts and cheesecake nice,
> Better the roast meat from the fire to save,
> Better be twisted into caps for spice,
> Than thus be patched and cobbled in one's grave. (*PTG* 253–55)

'Tell me, if you don't like this', Gray joked to Mason, '& I will send you a worse.' Although read by some as a semi-serious deprecation on Gray's part of Mason's project of producing yet another edition of Shakespeare's works, the verses are far more significant for what they have to say about Gray's attitude towards his own writing. The fear of being 'patched and cobbled' in one's grave – expressed so disarmingly in this poem – is intimately related to the fear of being 'patched and cobbled' (both critically and parodically) while one was yet alive. The shared danger in both cases was the danger of exposure, and the resignation of interpretive authority into the hands of a popular audience. Mason, as matters turned out, was delighted with Gray's lines. 'As bad as Your Verses were', he wrote to Gray from Aston towards then end of July, 'they are Yours, & therefore when I get back to York I'll paste them carefully in the first page of My Shakespeare to enhance its Value for I intend it to be put in My Marriage Settlement as a Provision for my Younger Daughters'.

Gray arrived at Old Park on about 12 June. Within days of his arrival, he travelled the short distance to Hartlepool, on the Cleveland coast. It was the first of two such visits he would make while staying with Wharton that summer. Hartlepool was still, in Gray's day, a relatively small seaside community. The town as yet bore little resemblance to the larger port and ship–building centre into which it would develop in the next century. To Gray, the area seemed quaint and untouched – a perfect place to drink the waters or sample the efficacy of a sea-cure. 'I am delighted with the place', he wrote lightheartedly to Mason. 'There are the finest walks & rocks & caverns, & dried fishes, & all manner of small inconveniences a Man can wish.' Gray took copious notes on the teeming natural life of the seashore itself, and was just as much impressed by the seemingly fine health and vitality of the local inhabi-tants – a health they seemed to enjoy despite the paucity of their diet ('they live on the refuse of their own fish-market), and the conspicuous absence of fresh bread or water. 'Nowhere have I seen a taller, more robust or healthy race', he wrote with some disbelief to Brown, at Cam-bridge, following his second visit to the coast, 'every house full of ruddy, broad-faced children'. 'Nobody dies but of drowning or old age', he decided judgementally, 'nobody poor but from drunkenness, or mere laziness'.

At some point during his two-month stay with Wharton, Gray was joined at Old Park by Lord Strathmore (Strathmore's younger brother, Thomas Lyon, it will be remembered, was a Fellow of Pembroke). Strathmore was then planning to leave his Durham property of Hetton-le-Hole in order to spend some time at his ancestral home at Glamis, in Scotland. Gray, along with Thomas Lyon and his cousin, one Major Lyon, was invited to accompany Strathmore on his northward journey, and to stay as his guest in Scotland. Gray naturally leapt at the chance to experience the land of Ossian for himself, and the trio departed from Hetton on 19 August. They headed directly for Edinburgh, covering – by Gray's own calculations – a rather remarkable seventy-seven miles of their journey on their first day, and travelling a further fifty-three miles in the course of their second morning and afternoon. The unaccustomed speed with which Gray was hurtled through the countryside, and the unavoidable fatigue that followed hard upon the constant bouncing and jolting of such a long and unbroken journey, may well have contributed to Gray's subsequent disenchantment with Edinburgh itself, a city that he very soon dismissed to Wharton as 'the most picturesque (at a dis-tance) and the nastiest (when near) of all capital Cities'. Physically exhausted as well as mentally spent by the bustle and confusion of the journey, Gray asked only to be allowed to retire to his own rooms and to bed soon after dinner.

The presence of Thomas Gray in Edinburgh was not an occasion so easily to be ignored, however. Despite his protestations of fatigue, Gray was compelled on the night of his arrival to endure a dinner party arranged in his honour and hosted by Dr. William Robinson, a former historian and – at the time of their meeting – Principal of Edinburgh University. Also present at the dinner were a small group of Edinburgh intellectuals and 'literati', among them Alexander Carlyle and William Wight; the well-known physician and Professor of Medicine, Dr. John Gregory, had graciously placed his own home at the disposal of both Robinson and his guests. The dinner was not a success, however, and Gray sorely disappointed his somewhat over-enthusiastic Scottish hosts. His spirits were such that even an attempt to compliment him by praising the popularity of the *Elegy* backfired. Gray apparently replied to Robinson's complimentary remarks on the poem by snapping that the *Elegy* owed its extensive popularity only to its subject, and suggesting that 'the public would have read it as well if it had been written in prose' – a remark which, in a better humour, even Gray himself would admit to have been a gross and unfairly self-deprecating exaggeration. Robinson subsequently told Norton Nicholls that Gray impressed him only negatively – as 'the idea of a person who meant to pass for a very fine gentleman'. Dr. Carlyle later apologized that Gray, on the occasion, 'had not justice done him', for, as Carlyle further explained, 'he was much worn out with his journey, and retiring soon after supper, proved that he had been taken at a time when he was not fit to be shown off'.[10] Gray's growing realization throughout the meal's heavy formalities that, however genuinely well-intentioned his hosts may have been, he was being treated in the manner of a rare and captive specimen ('to be shown off', as Carlyle put it) to the assembled company only further increased his constitutional reluctance to participate in such celebratory and ultimately egocentric displays. Be that as it may, the poet retired to his rooms that evening having made no great impression on his several hosts.

Knowing that he was scheduled to spend only two nights in Edinburgh, Gray paid hasty visits to the some of the city's principal attractions – including the Castle, Holyrood House, and Arthur's Seat – none of which seemed very much to interest him. On the morning that followed the near-disastrous dinner party at Dr. Gregory's, he and his travelling companions rose early, ready to undertake the final stages of their journey to Glamis. They crossed the Firth of Forth in an open and

---

[10] *Autobiography of Alexander Carlyle of Inveresk, 1722–1805*, ed. John Hill Brown, with a new Introduction by Richard B. Sher (Bristol: Thoemmes, 1990) 485.

sailless, four-oared yawl. The weather was blustery and the waters of the firth choppy and rough; Gray – never all that comfortable on smaller bodies of water, let alone on one which led so spectacularly towards the threatening chaos of the open sea – queasily confessed himself to have been 'tossed about rather more than I should wish to hazard again'. Perhaps he recalled his similarly disquieting Channel crossing so many years before. From Perth, where they spent the night, they were ferried across the Tay ('a very noble river'), and by dinner time on the 22 had been deposited at Glamis.

Gray was much impressed by Strathmore's residence and the area surrounding it. 'The Castle', he wrote to Wharton,

> stands in Strathmore (i.e. the Great Vally) which winds about from Stonehaven on the East-Coast of Kincairdinshire obliquely as far as Stirling near 100 miles in length, & from 7 to 10 miles in breadth, cultivated every where to the foot of the Hills on either hand with oats or bere-barley, except where the soil is mere peat-earth (black as coal) or barren sand cover'd only with broom & heath, or a short grass fit for sheep. (*CTG* 888–89)

The grounds, he wrote, were a pleasant combination of long and noble avenues, small groves, and walled gardens 'full of broad-leaved elms, oaks, birch, black-cherry-trees, Laburnums, &c: all of great stature and size'.

Gray was also impressed by Strathmore's personal involvement in and commitment to the various improvements being undertaken on the estate. Strathmore, whom he described admiringly as 'the greatest Farmer in the neighborhood',

> is from break of day to dark night among his husbandmen & labourers; he has near 2000 acres of land in his own hands, & is at present employ'd in building a low wall of 4 miles long; & in widening the bed of the little river *Deane* . . . both to prevent inundations, & to drain the Lake of Forfar. this work will be 2 years more in compleating; & must be 3 miles in length. all the Highlanders, that can be got, are employ'd in it; many of them know no English, & I hear them singing Erse-songs all day long. (*CTG* 890)

The Gaelic singing of the Highland natives must have struck Gray as an appropriately authentic touch. The mild weather (it continued 'generally very fine & warm') encouraged Strathmore's guests to sit long into the evenings by the castle's open windows. The prospect that lay before them was stunning. Now and then in the twilight sudden showers and gusts of wind would sweep down from the mountains, and shake the heavy trees which shaded the valley's crystal-clear trout streams. 'A very little art', Gray confessed, with a nod to his host's continuing efforts, 'is necessary to make all this a beautiful scene'.

There were even more beautiful and awe-inspiring scenes yet to come. On 11 September, Strathmore's cousin, Major Lyon, volunteered to accompany Gray on a short journey into the Highlands. An expedition of only five days, the trip was to serve for Gray as something of a whirl-wind tour of the region, offering him a taste – if not a thorough-going familiarity – with some of the country's more impressive, natural sights, and touching on some of the social customs and traditions of its inhab-itants. From Glamis the two men first passed westward through the small market town of Meigle, crossing the river Isla near 'Cowper of Angus' or Cupar Angus, and spending their first night at Dunkeld ('If I told you how', he wrote cryptically to Wharton, 'you would bless yourself'). Their next day's goal was Taymouth, an overland journey some twenty-seven miles to the west; the dramatically shifting prospects glimpsed through the rocky mountains along the route – for brief moments brightly and uniformly illuminated – impressed Gray deeply, and the activity of travelling itself was pleasant. 'In short altogether', he decided, 'it was one of the most pleasing days I have passed these many years'. Having reached Taymouth (or Balloch) as planned, the travellers were the next day well situated to admire She-khallian (the immensity thus comfortably dubbed 'the Maiden's Pap' by locals, but deemed by Gray to be nothing less than a 'monstrous creation of God'), which lay to the north, while at the same time contemplating the 'awful height' of Beni-More ('the great Mountain'), to the west. The heights of the latter peak, Gray noted, were said to look down upon the grave of Fingal, near the village of Killen, at the southwest end of Loch Tay.

Within two days the travellers were approaching the Pass of Kil-liecrankie. The entire landscape here seemed to Gray only recently to have emerged untouched from the shrouded and primeval mists of the time. The oak-covered hills near the pass – throughout which were scat-tered grotesque masses of rock – appeared to rise 'like the sullen coun-tenances of Fingal & all his family frowning on the little mortals of modern days'. The tremendous mists and roar produced by the fall of the river Tummel, just south of its confluence with the 'black river' Garry, left him close to speechless, as did Beni-Gloe and the 'Rumbling Bridge', which spanned a deep chasm carved among the rocks by the river Bran. 'In short since I saw the Alps', Gray wrote to Wharton, 'I have seen nothing sublime till now'.

Returning to Glamis Castle, Gray found awaiting his arrival a letter from James Beattie, who was then serving as Professor of Moral Phi-losophy and Logic at Marischal College in Aberdeen. News of Gray's presence in Scotland had been passed on to Beattie by his colleagues in Edinburgh, and he had written the poet in order graciously to extend to him an invitation to visit Aberdeen. Beattie's letter fairly glowed with its author's generous and deeply felt appreciation of Gray's achievements as a poet. 'It was yesterday I received the agreeable news of your being in Scotland', he had written to Gray on 30 August,

> and of your intending to visit some parts of it. Will you permit us to hope, that we shall have an opportunity, at Aberdeen, of thanking you in person, for the honour you have done to Britain, and to the poetic art, by your inestimable compositions, and of offering you all that we have that deserves your acceptance, namely, hearts full of esteem, respect, and affection? If you cannot come so far northward, let me at least be acquainted with the place of your residence, and permitted to wait on you. Forgive, sir, this request; forgive me if I urge it with earnestness, for indeed it concerns me nearly. (CTG 885)

Gray could not, in fact, quite muster the energy to journey 'so far north-ward' as Aberdeen. Lord Strathmore cheerfully acquiesced to Gray's receiving Beattie at Glamis, however, where the established poet and his young admirer spent a comfortable two days together. Gray offered Beattie, who candidly confessed his own ambitions as a poet, some pro-fessional advice (he later wrote to say that he hoped he had not in any way discouraged Beattie from pursuing such a path), and the latter was in turn impressed by the effortless combination – the calm and easy balance – which Gray seemed to effect between his profound learning and scholarship, on the one hand, and his engaging spontaneity, on the other. He wrote to his close friend William Forbes: 'I . . . found him as easy in his manner, and as communicative and frank, as I could have wished.' Beattie further cemented his friendship with Gray by sending him, following his departure from Glamis, two books on the popular superstitions of Scotland ('very silly ones indeed', he confessed, 'but the best that could be had'). Beattie's home institution, Marischal College, Aberdeen – acting, no doubt, on his own, enthusiastic recommendation – extended Gray an invitation to accept an honorary degree as Doctor of Laws, an honour Gray decided finally to decline. He had neglected to finish his course and claim his Doctor's degree at Cambridge, he wrote from Glamis on 2 October, 'judge therefore, whether it will not look like a slight & some sort of contempt, if I receive the same degree from a Sister-University. I certainly would avoid giving any offense to a set of Men, among whom I have pass'd so many easy, & (I may say) happy hours of my life.'

At the end of the first week of October, Gray left Glamis and began the long journey southward by way of Sterling (rather than again undertaking to cross the Firth of Forth). He spent a further two weeks at Old Park before completing his journey to London. He would have preferred to have met Mason in York as well, but, he confessed, 'the finances were at so low an ebb, that I could not exactly do what I wish'd'. Nor, he frankly and rather tactlessly admitted to his old friend, did he particularly relish the prospect of spending any time in the company of Mason's wife. Mrs. William Mason had been taking extra care to make her new home clean and comfortable, and Gray – used to having his own way in matters of domestic comfort – took offense at her newly laid down household laws. Expanding on this second reason for having passed by the Minster Yard at York to pursue a more direct route to the capital, Gray complained uncharitably: 'I do not love confinement, & probably by next summer may be permitted to *touch* whom & where & with what I think fit without giving . . . any offence.' By the end of the month he was once again comfortably ensconced in familiar surroundings in Jermyn Street, where he took up rooms above the shop of the hosier and hatter, Mr. Roberts, and where he need have no compunction about touching 'whom and where and what' he pleased. He was both wonderfully refreshed, mentally, yet at the same time close to physically exhausted by his travels. Despite any such fatigue, he remained eager to share with his closest friends the particulars of this most recent of his journeys.

Sometime the following year, Gray went so far as to jot down some 'Advice to a friend travelling in Scotland'. The material – which traced his own itinerary from Durham to Glamis – was drawn almost entirely from the notebooks he had kept while pursuing that same journey in 1765. The 'Advice' was intended particularly for the use of Brown, who intimated to Gray that he was considering soon undertaking such a journey himself. Gray's pointers are for the most part of a practical nature, indicating distances, for example, and pointing out principal sights and attractions. In the days before guidebooks and maps had become quite so ubiquitous as they are in today's tourist and travel culture, the material would have stood any of the more adventurous of Gray's companions, Brown among them, in reasonably good stead; he is for the most part carefully accurate, solidly practical, and – though a trifle negative regarding the larger cities along his route – encouraging and often enthusiastic. Regarding accommodation and sustenance in Scotland, however, Gray offered his reader only the following general advice and caveat:

See your sheets air'd yourself. eat mutton or hard-eggs. touch no fried things. if they are broil'd, boil'd, or roasted, say that from a child you have eat no butter, & beg they would not rub any over your meat. there is honey, or orange-marmalade, or currant-jelly, which may be eaten with toasted bread, or the thin oat-cakes, for breakfast. dream not of milk. ask your Landlord to set [i.e. sit] down, & help off with your wine. never scold at any body, especially at Gentlemen, or Ladies. (*CTG* 1246)

*

Gray remained in London throughout the entire month of November. He attempted within his first week back in town to visit Walpole at Arlington Street, but found his effort rewarded only with the disheartening spectacle of an empty house and an equally disheartening and 'uncomfortable' account of his friend's situation. Walpole had recently suffered an attack of gout ('in both feet'), and had left England for France early in September, hoping that the simple change of scenery might effect an improvement in his health. His discomfort only increased, however, when a bad cold caught during the brief crossing compounded his illness. He made it only as far as Paris, where he remained confined to his rooms. At the hazard of 'being called an old woman', Gray offered his friend some advice as to how he might minimize his pain – advice that clearly reflects the poet's own experience and continuing struggle with the same disease:

> I will take upon me to desire, when the fit is actually upon you, that you will make no sudden changes in your diet, I do not say in quantity, but in quality. That when you are recovering & the pain is gone, but has left behind it a weakness in the joint, you will not be too indulgent to that weakness: but give yourself so much of motion & exercise, as you can well endure. above all, keep your legs warmer at all times, whether you are well or ill, in bed or up, than you have commonly used to do, & as far as may be, always in the same temperature. the quantity of wine you have commonly used has been so inconsiderable, that I do not believe it ever did, or will hurt you: but if you leave it off, mix a little quantity of spirit, brandy or whatever else is palatable to you, with your water.... my prescriptions are simple, but they are such as I use myself, who am a Fellow-sufferer with you, about your own age, have (unhappily for me) a better right to this malady than you, begun to feel it earlier, & yet have hitherto felt it mildly, & never in my stomach or head. I only say, they are better than French Nostrums, or People of Qualitie's receipts. (*CTG* 900–01)

Gray added in closing that his recent journey to Scotland had pleased him far more than he had ever expected it would. Passing on the briefest of gossip (three imminent separations rumoured in 'the married world'), he conjured Walpole to take care of himself, and looked forward to the news of his improved condition from his servants.

Walpole responded almost immediately to Gray's unsolicited advice, writing to him from Paris only days later, on 19 November. His most recent attack, he confessed rather uncharacteristically, had been a dramatic one. 'Nine weeks passed before I could even walk with a Stick', he grumbled from across the Channel,

> yet the state of Convalescence, as it has been in my second fit, was much worse & more uneasy than the heigth of the pain, from the constant sickness at my Stomach. I came hither, mended miraculously with the Sea & the journey, but caught cold in a fortnight, & have had six weeks more of pain in both feet, and such sickness that I have been very near starved: besides such swelled legs, that they were as much too big for my body, as before they would have been too little for any other person's alive. I have now got the better of every thing but the weakness, & am only thrown or tumble down ten times a day. For receipts, you may trust me for making use of none; I would not see a physician at the worst, but have quacked myself as boldly, as Quacks treat others. (*CTG* 902–03)

'So much for the Gout!' Walpole concluded, dismissing the topic as cheerfully as he could. Paris, he went on, seemed either to have changed dramatically in the past twenty-five years, or (a far more likely possibility) to have possessed the power somehow to have shielded him from its 'ugliness' on his first visit in 1739. 'I cannot conceive', he wrote, recalling his first visit to the city in Gray's company all those years ago, 'where my eyes were':

> It is the ugliest, beastly Town in the Universe. I have not seen a mouthful of verdure out of it, nor have they anything green but their treillage & window shutters. Trees cut into fireshovels & stuck into pedestals of chalk, compose their country. Their boasted knowledge of Society is reduced to talking of their suppers, & every malady they have about them, or know of. (*CTG* 903)

Walpole's opinion of Parisian society would of course change dramatically as the months went by. He very soon managed to insinuate himself into the salon of the (now blind and aging) Marie du Deffand, Marquise de Chastres, on the rue St. Dominique. Although she was twenty-one years his senior, Madame du Deffand became in time one of Walpole's most intimate and valued correspondents ('mon tuteur', she called him in several of her letters, while he addressed her in turn as 'ma petite'). Many of Madame du Deffand's older allies in Parisian society had recently defected to the salon of her rival and erstwhile pupil and protégé, Julie de Lespinasse, so young Horace's attentions to her came at a most opportune time, and were warmly welcomed. What exactly appealed to Walpole about the relationship is slightly more difficult to determine, though his attraction to the older woman's whimsical eccentricities seems only further to have whetted his insatiable, chronicler's appetite for fast-disappearing tidbits of social gossip and historical anecdote. Perhaps, too, as one of Walpole's biographers has suggested, he viewed his newfound friend and correspondent as a kind of latter day Madame de Sévigné, and valued the simple fact that he had established himself on a level of epistolary intimacy with her.[11]

*

By the beginning of December Gray had returned from London to Cambridge, where he soon settled himself in to pass what Walpole, in his 'long and lively' letters from Paris, had taken to calling 'this Siberian winter'. The weather throughout Europe early in the year was bitterly cold, and the fronts sweeping across the Continent brought unusually heavy amounts of snowfall to both France and England; Gray imagined his friends Mason and Wharton in the North to be 'buried under the snow'. Even at Cambridge there fell in February a 'deep snow' that threatened to delay the early and eagerly watched-for blooming of the hepatica, the primrose, and the crocus.

The often blustery conditions made little practical dent in Gray's own daily routine, however. Snug in his college rooms, Gray passed the months neatly transcribing the observations he had scribbled into various pocket notebooks throughout his summer tour into an interleaved, three-volume copy of Linnaeus's *Systema Naturae*, which he had purchased in London in October, 1759. We remember that the poet's obsession with the close observation of natural history was in part the legacy of his uncle Robert. Yet Gray's careful observation of the natural world was also a compulsive response to the perceived threat of a disordered imagination, and as such it is intimately related to Gray's other scholarly and creative endeavours. Such meticulous attention to the details of the world of nature puzzled Gray's friends in the poet's own lifetime; none of his long-time companions – with the exceptions of Wharton and (perhaps) Nicholls – appear to have understood the soothing and calming effect that the order, system, pattern, and predictable, seasonal repetition of these observations had on his psyche. 'Mr Gray often vexed me', Walpole would write to Lady Ossory some few years after his friend's death, 'by finding him heaping notes on an interleaved

---

[11] Timothy Mowl, *Horace Walpole: The Great Outsider* (London: John Murray, 1996) 217.

Linnaeus, instead of pranking on his lyre'. Not that the pages of the *Systema Natura* were incapable of moving Gray to poetry; alongside his carefully scripted observations on the activities of hermit-crabs, butter-flies and beetles (he at one point typically records a very precise descrip-tion of the larvae deposited by a scavenger beetle in the body of a dead mole he had uncovered in Cambridge), Gray eventually transcribed into his interleaved *Linneaus* a series of technical verses in Latin on the 'Orders of Insects'. Additional lines describing the orders of insects were discovered among the poet's papers years after his death. Even into material as scientific and as (normally) prosaic as this, however, Gray managed to breathe the faintest, enlivening wisp of poetry. One such description – of the second of the six orders catalogued by Gray, the Coleoptera (the name was first used by Aristotle to describe a particular kind of beetle) – reads:

> Cassida sub clipei totam se margine condit.
> Chrys'mela inflexa loricae stringitur ora.
> Gibba caput Meloë incurvat, thorace rotundo.
> Oblongus frontem et tenues clipei exerit oras
> Tenebrio. Abdomen Mordellae lamina vestit.
> Curta elytra ostentat Staphylis, caudamque recurvam. (*PTG* 338; 340)

[Cassida hides itself completely beneath the rim of its shield. Chrysomela is drawn in tightly by the inflexible edge of its leathern armour. Hunchbacked Meloë bends in its head, with a rounded thorax. Oblong Tenebrio juts out its head and the thin margins of its shield. Plating covers the abdomen of Mordella. Staphylis displays shortened sheaths and a backward-curving tail.]

Translating the stuff of Linneaus into verse is a difficult and dubious task; the most devoted reader of Gray's poetry or correspondence can be forgiven for dismissing these lines as marginally interesting, at best. Yet, without exaggeration, even Gray's versified notes on natural history betray the slightest outline of the impulses which elsewhere compelled him to the craft of genuine poetry. Gray here crystallizes as ordered and comprehensible the seemingly incomprehensible diversity and com-plexity of the world around him; by imposing order in the smallest matters of nature, he insinuates a certain degree of order into its larger mysteries as well. The martial vocabulary – through which the very distant spirits of Virgil and (indirectly) Homer are conjured ever so slightly – further adds a faint aura of the mock-heroic to the lines, transforming these slight-est of Gray's verses themselves into the distant, playful descendent of ancient works such as the pseudo-Homeric *Batrachomyomachia*.

As the unusually harsh winds of winter gave way finally, by the beginning of March, to the unseasonably mild temperatures of an equally unanticipated, pleasant spring, Gray wrote to Wharton that with regard to general health and spirits, he had little of which he could really complain. He had spent the cold winter months in comparative isolation and comfort; his physical health was surprisingly robust, and his state of mind was for the time being balanced on a nicely even keel – neither overly optimistic nor excessively dour. 'As to me', he confessed of the past few months to his 'dear Doctor' Wharton, 'I have been neither happy, nor miserable: but in a gentle stupefaction of mind, & very tolerable health of body hitherto'.

The change of seasons offered Gray a green-leafed incentive towards the accumulation of newer and even more unusual experiences (particularly in his increasingly adventuresome capacity as a wide-ranging and voracious traveller) and, in general, a fresh-breathed opportunity for change. The spring was, as always, the best time for Gray to rouse himself and to shake off the 'gentle stupefaction of mind' that had thrown its warm and comfortably numb mantle of genial indolence over the months of his long winter's hibernation. The first thing he needed to do was to leave Cambridge as soon as possible. Gray this spring decided to spend the latter part of April and the first two weeks of May at his customary lodgings in Jermyn Street before undertaking a visit to his old acquaintance Billy Robinson and his wife at Denton, near Canterbury. He probably broke his journey into Kent by remaining for a few days in the neighborhood of the cathedral town with a distant cousin – one Alderman Gray, a grocer – to whom he was related on his father's side (the connection was not a particularly strong one, and we hear little from the poet himself or, indeed, from any of his Gray or Antrobus relations about his Canterbury cousins). Exploring the area both on foot and from the vantage of coaches and carriages, Gray was pleasantly surprised by the cultivated landscape around Denton. 'The country', he wrote describing the landscape of Kent to Nicholls later that same summer, 'is all a garden, gay, rich, & fruitful, & (from the rainy season) had preserved . . . all that emerald verdure which commonly one only sees for the first fortnight of the spring'. He visited Margate and Ramsgate (the former of which struck him even then as Bartholomew Fair '*flown* down' from London; the latter of which he viewed without comment), and took advantage of the exceptionally fine weather to make a quick but thorough tour of the entire coast to the southeast of Deal, passing Sandwich, Deal, Dover, and the decaying coastal defenses at Folkestone, on his way towards the tiny and picturesque seafront town of Hythe. The feeling of having been placed on an isthmus between the local rivers and their several tributaries, on the one hand, and the great, sweeping passage of the sea, on the other, was for Gray exhilarating, if only in its bold and busy presentation of even further, as yet untapped possibilities of travel and discovery. Both the towering silhouettes of the great, three-masted naval ships – their magnificent sails billowing to taut, white expanses of canvas in the powerful Channel winds – as well as the outlines of the smaller, square-rigged, merchant brigs set clearly against the vividly contrasting background of the earth and sky, moved Gray nearly to poetry. 'In the west part of it from every eminence' he wrote, 'the eye catches some long winding reach of the Thames or Medway with all their navigation. In the east the sea breaks in upon you, & mixes its white transient sails & glittering blew expanse with the deeper and brighter greens of the woods and corn' ('This last sentence', Gray paused self-consciously but also self-parodically to observe in his letter to Nicholls, 'is so fine I am quite ashamed. But no matter! you must translate it into prose').

Gray returned briefly to London in July, but much of the summer – excepting only a short break at the end of that month and the beginning of August – was spent in Cambridge. His most recent expedition had inspired him so far as to bring him to suggest to Nicholls that they together travel through Wales the following summer. Gray was even more than usually enthusiastic about such a tour, and Nicholls himself appears to have raised little if any objection against such a scheme. Gray wrote to Wharton at Old Park in August, recommending to him Christopher Anstey's *New Bath Guide*, which had just been published (Gray found the 'new and original kind humour' of Anstey's volume infectiously entertaining), and endearingly sending to Wharton's children – and most particularly to his ten-year-old daughter, 'Miss Debo', whom he had neglected to mention in an earlier letter – his love and kisses. To Mason, however, he revealed an altogether different aspect, confessing that same month that he was 'in no spirits, & perplex'd beside with many little cares', but joking, too, that he would not trouble his friend with any of his own worries and anxieties. 'I have always consider'd the *Happy*, that is, new-married People' such as Mason and his wife, he joked, 'as too sacred, or too profane, a thing to be approach'd by me'. Although he still teased Mason about his new domestic partner, he took care as well to enquire about her health, which he thought at the time to be improved.

In the early autumn Gray travelled into Suffolk to spend a few weeks with Palgrave at Thrandeston, turning briefly out of his way to visit Sir Robert Walpole's home at Houghton for the first time. The younger Walpole himself, as it turned out, was to be much on Gray's mind that same month. Even as he was on the road to Houghton, Gray was startled by a report in the newspapers that his friend had been struck down by a 'paralytick disorder'. His mind raced ahead, envisioning a nightmare scenario for his friend's health. 'He may live in this state', he scribbled in his panic to Nicholls, 'incapable of assisting himself, in the hands of servants or relations, that only gape after his spoils, perhaps for years to come.' 'Think', he concluded morosely, 'how many things may befall a man far worse than death.' By late September he at last received a letter from Cole informing him that 'thank God! the worse part of the news was false', and that Walpole had endured merely yet another (albeit debilitating) attack of the gout.

The report of Walpole's poor health, which had cast something of a cloud across Gray's autumn excursion, was only the first of several pieces of bad news that ushered in yet another excessively harsh winter. Shortly after his return to Cambridge at the end of September, Gray received from Stonhewer news that Dr. John Brown, for a great many years a Fellow of St. John's, had committed suicide at his residence in Pall Mall by slashing his throat with a razor. Brown had been no particular acquaintance of the poet, but the news of his grisly suicide was complicated by the fact that he appeared to have taken his own life at least partly in response to a recent, satirical poem about his political activities written by Mason and published anonymously in the *St. James's Chronicle*. Gray wrote hurriedly to a panicked and remorseful Mason, who was then staying in London, assuring him that Brown had apparently at no point prior to taking his life made any mention of Mason or, indeed, of the satire itself. If the poem had contributed to Brown's instability of mind, Gray reassured his friend, 'he would have talk'd or raved about it, & the first thing we should have heard of, would have been this, which (I do assure you) I have never heard from anybody.' Gray knew better than anyone that one's poetry, once submitted to public scrutiny, effectively passed beyond the control of its author.

Of even greater concern to them both, however, were Mason's reasons for having travelled up to London in the first place. Mrs. Mason's health, poor to begin with, had since her recent marriage deteriorated even further. She was clearly suffering from tuberculosis, although both she and her husband seemed reluctant to admit this to be the case. Gray, who had finally met Mrs. Mason in person that autumn and who appears to have been rather surprised, not to say discomfited, to have found her 'a pretty, modest, innocent, interesting figure', hoped in a letter to Mason that the 'change of air' might in itself accomplish 'more than medicine'. London in the early winter, however, was no place for consumptives to look to recover their health, and Mrs. Mason's illness continued to pursue its grim and inevitable course. Gray, himself suffering from a persistent and worsening sore throat that had been aggravated by three continuous weeks of 'Lapland weather' ('I have had for these six weeks a something growing in my throat ... which will, I suppose, in due time stop up the passage'), wrote to Mason toward the end of January enquiring after his wife's health, and tried as best he could decorously and solicitously to make light of her condition; since meeting with Mrs. Mason personally, his casual teasing of her and of Mason himself had sounded on a new, more genial and genuinely affectionate note. 'If she has withstood such a winter & her cough never the worse', he wrote, paraphrasing his catechism, 'she may defy the Doctors and all their works'. 'Pray, tell me how she is', he added gently, 'for I interest myself not merely on your account, but on her own.' The worst of the winter weather seemed to have passed even by the end of January, and Gray hoped that the 'vernal & mild' air which followed and now held the promise of an early spring would facilitate Mrs. Mason's swift recovery.

Mason responded to Gray's queries almost immediately, writing a heart-felt letter from his lodgings in Pall Mall. 'No, alas,' he cried,

> she has not withstood the Severity of the Weather. It nipt her as it would have done a flower half witherd before, & she has been this last month in a most weak condition. Yet this present fine season had enabled me to get her three or four times out into the air, & it seems to have had some good effect, yet not enough to give me any substantial hopes of her recovery. There are few Men in the world that can have a competent Idea of what I have of late felt, & still feel, yet you are one of those few, & am sure will give me a full share of your pity. Was I to advise Stonehewer to a Wife it should certainly be to a fine Lady, It should not be to one he could Love to the same degree that I do this gentle, this innocent creature. (*CTG* 950)

The doctor attending Mrs. Mason appears only that month to have broken the news to her husband that, for all her claims to have been feeling 'something better', she was 'irretrievably gone'. Gray supported Mason as best he could, suggesting that his wife might benefit from 'sea-air', and advising a journey to the Kentish coast he had himself so recently enjoyed. Responding to the more personal tone that had entered Mason's letter, he wrote:

> There are a few words in your letter, that make me believe, you wish I were in Town. I know myself, how little one like me is form'd to support the spirits of another, or give him consolation: one that always sees things in their most gloomy aspect. however be assured, I should not have left London while you were in it, if I could well have afforded to stay there till the beginning of April, when I am usually there. this however shall be no hinderance, if you tell me, it would signify any thing to you, that I should come sooner. (*CTG* 952)

Unfortunately, Mason would not be given the chance to avail himself of the solace of Gray's company in his darkest hours. Mary Mason's disease only grew worse. On 27 March – just as the blasts of the long winter looked finally to be giving way to the warmth of spring – she died. Gray broke in upon his friend's grief to express his sorrow and regret at such a loss in a note the language of which Mason himself described as seeming 'to breathe the voice of Friendship in its tenderest & most a pathetic note'. 'I have long understood', Gray had added touchingly at the end of his letter, 'how little you had to hope.' Mason received Gray's condolences just as his wife was being laid to rest in Bristol, on 1 April. 'I cannot express the State of my Mind or health', he confessed, 'I know not what either of them are.' He was able to pass through Cambridge on his return journey to York later that week, at which time he and Gray were able finally and together to confront the loss of his wife, and to contemplate the path of Mason's personal future without her. Mason returned home with the assurance that Gray would within weeks pay him an extended summer visit at Aston.

*

Gray seemed that same year to make a particular point of enjoying the social possibilities of the spring season even more thoroughly than usual. He arrived at Jermyn Street for a stay of nearly two months in the capital on 20 April. He visited, as always, with old friends such as Stonhewer, Hurd, and Palgrave, and briefly renewed his acquaintance too with Frederick Augustus Hervey – an ambitious young clergyman and graduate of Corpus Christi – whose friendship he had long shared with Mason. Hervey was the younger brother of that same Lord Bristol who had in 1754 advanced the possibility of Gray's appointment as his private secretary. Thanks to his brother's continued success (Lord Bristol had recently been appointed Lord Lieutenant of Ireland), Hervey had himself become Bishop of Cloyne; he would shortly be created Bishop of Derry, and would in 1779 succeed his brother as fourth Earl of Bristol. 'I have seen his lordship of Cloyne often', Gray joked to Mason that spring, 'He is very jolly and we devoured four raspberry-puffs together in Cranbourn-alley [in Leicester Square] standing at a pastrycook's shop in the street.' Within the same period, Gray made brief excursions to the Duke of Devonshire's residence in Chiswick and to the Duke of Northumberland's Syon House, at Isleworth, as well as undertaking his usual visit to Walpole at Strawberry Hill. Despite – or rather because of – continued heavy rains, the hues of the lush and verdant landscape were especially intense and compelling. 'Be assured', he wrote Brown in Cambridge, 'the face of the country looks like an emerald, if you love jewels.'

Gray had particular reasons for wishing to convince Brown that the countryside was especially inviting that spring; Brown had promised to accompany him on the journey north to visit Mason, and Gray was eager to finalize their travelling plans. 'Where are you?', he began a letter on 2 June to Brown petulantly, 'for I wrote to you last week to know how soon we should set out, and how we should go. Mason writes to-day, he will expect us at Aston in Whitsun-week; and has ordered all his lilacs and roses to be in flower.' Gray returned to Cambridge for the briefest of week-end visits in mid-June. The two men set out in a hired chaise in the direction of Bawtry, near Doncaster on the Yorkshire border, on 15 June; 'we shall find our way from Bawtry', Gray wrote to Mason, 'very cleverly.' Less than a week later Gray was relating Mason's rapturous descriptions of his own home at Aston, to Wharton at Old Park. 'Here we are, Mr Brown & I', he joked, 'in a wilderness of sweets, an Elysium among the coal pits, a terrestrial heaven'. The three men soon left this Eden among the collieries, however, for a quick visit to the limestone ravine of Dovedale and 'the Wonders of the Peak'. After a very brief visit to Mason's new residence at York (where Mason was taking up his appointment as Canon Residentiary and Precentor), Brown and Gray returned to Old Park.

The two men remained with Wharton and his family through much of July. Together they ventured on further, brief excursions to the eponymous fortress ruin at Barnard Castle, to Rokeby Park (the Palladian home built by Sir Thomas Robinson in 1735 and the inspiration for Sir Walter Scott's poem 'Rokeby'), and to the ancient market town of Richmond. The enjoyment they derived even from such tame sights as these and from a subsequent jaunt to Hartlepool, prompted Wharton and Gray to begin considering a more extended, adventurous excursion into the Lake District; a busy Mason declined an invitation to accompany them, and Brown had already made certain plans to travel north into Scotland. After first fulfilling some genuinely agreeable social obligations (such as meeting Lord Strathmore's new bride at one of the couple's Durham properties), and after enduring some rather less rewarding visits (the frequency and necessity of which, Gray complained to Mason, was nothing less than 'the ruin of all [his] country-expeditions'), Gray and Wharton left Old Park and headed in the direction of Westmoreland and Cumberland on 29 August.

They travelled first to Newcastle and then on to the ancient market town of Hexham, where it began to rain heavily. Persevering through an almost uninterrupted downpour, they reached Keswick two nights later, having attempted some cursory sightseeing in Carlisle and Penrith. At Keswick they began at least to glimpse, through the veil of rain, some of the natural attractions already beginning to draw large numbers of tourists to the region; most noteworthy was the tremendous mountain of Skiddaw, the soft if lofty contours of which belied its name, which in English means 'craggy' or 'rugged hill.' During their overnight stay at Keswick, however, Wharton suffered a serious asthma attack. Despite his manifest discomfort, both he and Gray decided still to push on the following morning over the 'stupendous hills' as far as Cockermouth. Yet it very soon became clear that Wharton's condition was only growing worse, and that the combination of extremely wet weather (which showed no sign of letting up) and the physical exertion their planned walking tours would necessarily have entailed, together rendered such arduous excursions out of the question. Accordingly they retraced their route back to Old Park through heavy thunder showers, having been afforded only the barest and dampest glimpse of the natural scenery that had motivated their trip in the first place. Gray's own disappointment was surprisingly minimal. 'Now you will think from this detail', he wrote to Mason, after recounting the final leg of their homeward journey through yet another, interminable downpour, '. . . that we had better have staid at home. No such thing! I am charm'd with my journey, & the Dr dreams of nothing but Skiddaw, & both of us vow to go again the first opportunity.' Their vow again to undertake such an expedition would be kept – although, as we shall see, Wharton was destined never to experience the natural beauty of the Lake District in Gray's company.

*

Gray and Wharton's abortive expedition to the Lakes that autumn was productive of one very slight burlesque by the poet. Sometime before reaching Penrith on the second day of their journey, the two men had stopped briefly along their route to inspect the local church in the small town of Appleby. There, they encountered the early seventeenth-century tomb of Margaret Clifford, Countess of Cumberland. On the tomb they read the following epitaph, which had been written by her daughter, Anne, Countess of Dorset, Pembroke, and Montgomery, in 1716:

> Who Faith, Love, Mercy, noble Constancy
> To God, to Virtue, to Distress, to Right
> Observed, expressed, showed, held religiously
> Hath here this monument thou seest in sight,
> The cover of her earthly part, but passenger
> Know Heaven and Fame contain the best of her.[12]

---

[12] Reprinted in Lonsdale, *PTG* 256.

Playing on the rather curious historical fact that the Countess responsible for the confusing and subsultory syntax of this epitaph had lived
at each one of her six castles in succession (residing, respectively, at
Skipton, Appleby, Brougham, Brough, Pendragon, and Bardon Tower),
Gray composed an impromptu epitaph appropriate to the final resting
place of the versifying Anne Clifford herself:

> Now clean, now hideous, mellow now, now gruff,
> She swept, she hissed, she ripened and grew rough,
> At Broom, Pendragon, Appleby and Brough. (*PTG* 257)

Gray's parodic epitaph nicely combines a sharp, satiric jab at Clifford's
seemingly pointless, peripatetic lifestyle, with a critical swipe at the
halting and overly convoluted syntax of her lines. The poet likewise, one
suspects, toys with the familiar and classical *siste viator* trope clumsily
employed in his parodic model comically to memorialize its author – a
'wayfarer' who, in life, was herself apparently incapable of 'stopping' or
remaining at any one location for very long.

The wheezing and difficulty in breathing that Wharton had experienced at Keswick had not, as it turned out, been a harbinger of any
serious or extended asthmatic episode. Gray remained at Old Park following their return for about another two weeks. He passed the days
pleasantly with Wharton's family, of which he was now – if not an equal
member – at least a familiar and unremarkable fixture, functioning
somewhat in the capacity of an affectionate and watchful, bachelor
uncle. When, for example, the Doctor's sixteen-year-old daughter Peggy
began that month to manifest an interest in drawing, it was Gray who
took it upon himself to solicit Mason to search out an able and appropriate instructor for the teenager ('he must be elderly, & if ugly and ill-
made, so much the better'). Physically, too, Old Park had by now become
a second home to him, and the afternoons were passed in casual comfort
both in and out of doors; 'the peaches & grapes send forth a good smell',
he wrote cheerfully toward the end of his stay, '& the voice of the Robin
is heard in our land'. (Gray's casual though seasonally inappropriate
allusion in the latter half of this sentence – to *Song of Solomon*, ii.12:
'The flowers appear on the earth . . . and the voice of the turtledove is
heard in our land' – was perhaps prompted by a sub-conscious recollection of the slightly more relevant line immediately preceding it in the
Biblical text: 'the rain is over and gone'.)

On 24 October, Wharton accompanied Gray to York, where they
enjoyed a few, last days together in Mason's company. Even Gray's
lengthy country excursions, however, had sometime to come to an end.
On 2 November the poet accomplished the return journey to Jermyn
street at break-neck speed ('Don't I go galloping five hundred [miles],

whenever I please?', he had only recently asked Mason boastfully), and had quickly settled into his regular accommodations to spend a further six weeks in London, before finally returning to Cambridge on 14 December. Enlivening this visit to the city was news of Norton Nicholls's recent presentation to the livings of Lound and Bradwell, in Suffolk. Nicholls's uncle, William Turner, had purchased the livings; the death of the incumbent at the end of October paved the way for his recently ordained nephew to fill the positions. Gray sent Nicholls his hearty congratulations as soon as he learned the news, joking that he hoped soon to visit his friend only to find him 'snug in the rectory, surrounded with fat pigs and stubble-geese'.

Throughout the last two months of the year Gray's health was plagued by 'many and various maladies'. He suffered from 'regular' attacks of the gout ('first in one, then in the other foot') as well as enduring the recurrent pains of neuralgia and rheumatism. Although he dismissed his discomfort to his friends as little more than 'troublesome', he was for all practical purposes confined to his rooms in college until the end of the year. Still, his holiday letter to Old Park was long and cheerful, and obviously reflected his recent intimacy not only with Wharton himself, but with each and every member of the family. 'Does Miss Peggy rival Claude Lorraine yet', he began his systematic inquiry into the progress of their several occupations and interests,

> & when does she go to York? Do Debo [Deborah] & Betty [Elizabeth] tend their Chrysalises, & their samplers? is Kee's [Catherine's] mouth as pretty as ever? does Robin read like a Doctor, dance like a Fairy, & bow like a Courtier? does Dicky [Richard] kick up his heels, & study Geography? please to answer me as to all these particulars. (*CTG* 988)

The illness and subsequent death of Wharton's brother Jonathan in London that February cast a temporary gloom over Gray's adopted family. The poet reiterated his affection for Wharton and all those connected to him by extending to his friend not only his personal support and sympathy throughout the crisis of Jonathan Wharton's health, but by attempting likewise to offer whatever self-professedly modest assistance he could in the way of legal advice on the settlement of the younger Wharton's will.

*

Sometime between two and three o'clock in the morning of 18 January, Gray was roused from his sleep by a respectful but persistent hammering on his door. The voice which – for all its deference and understatement – then whispered urgently from the stairway again sounded the alarm the poet had dreaded his entire life. 'Don't be frighted, Sir!', he heard through the panels, 'but the college is all of a fire.' Gray's consternation can only be imagined. He hurriedly gathered his clothes around him and rushed into the chill, open air of the college's second court. His instinctive sense of panic must almost instantly have been quieted by the absence of any visible flame or smoke in or around his own rooms. The fire, as it turned out – far from engulfing 'all' the college – was confined to the recently vacated rooms of Tom Lyon. Lyon's chambers (which had only just been designated to receive Mason) were located directly opposite Gray's own, on the middle floor of the court's north side. Brown's rooms, which were in the same wing and separated from Lyon's by only by a single intervening set of chambers, had been in considerably more danger from the fire than Gray's own. The fire – successfully contained within its point of origin – took about an hour and a half to quell completely. The woodwork within the rooms was completely destroyed, and the faint morning sun must have revealed them now to the still-excited Fellows gathering in the courtyard to be a charred and blackened shell. Things could have been much worse. The college owed its preservation on this occasion, as Gray later recounted to Nicholls, to the scrupulously rigorous prayers of some local Methodists. As Gray recounted: 'two Saints, who had been till very late at their nocturnal devotions, & were just in bed, gave the first alarm to the college & the town'. The rigorous discipline of Methodism, it seemed, had in this particular instance at least combined with the sect's call to social duty and action in such a way as to preserve the new court, and perhaps to save the entire college from a fiery demise as well.

The constant banging and hammering of reconstruction and repair that throughout the next few weeks reverberated from across the court-yard seems, surprisingly, to have distracted Gray only slightly from his consideration of the details of a major project which now demanded his personal attention (although, in general, one feels that the poet would whole-heartedly have agreed with the German philosopher Schopen-hauer's contention in the next century that such noise was 'a torture' to all intelligent people). At some point in the previous year, Gray had met with James Dodsley – younger brother to Robert Dodsley, who had retired in 1759 and died five years later – in London, and agreed to the production of a collected edition of his poetry. Shortly thereafter, Gray's admirer in Scotland, James Beattie, approached the poet with a similar but entirely separate proposition that a complete volume of his poetical works be printed by Robert and Andrew Foulis, the Glasgow booksellers and printers who had already gained a considerable reputation in the publishing world for their handsome and remarkably well-crafted editions of the works of classical authors including Homer, Horace, and

Cicero. Although Gray had some initial fears that two such editions might reflect a conflict of interests, or in some way work to 'cancel' one another out, it was eventually decided by the poet himself that both printers would go ahead with the project as a cooperative and genially competitive joint – venture ('It is Mr *Foulis of Glasgow*, that prints them in Scotland', Gray informed Dodsley, 'I have desired, he would not print a great number, & could wish the same of you.')

At the beginning of February Gray sent precise instructions to both Dodsley and – through Beattie – the Foulis brothers, specifying the order in which the poems were to appear in the edition, and carefully stating his desires with regard to the general disposition and presentation of his works in the proposed volume. The title of the collected edition, he noted – although this new volume was for the first time to include explanatory notes to the poetry – was to be simply and only *Poems by Mr Gray*. Whether the explanatory glosses themselves appeared in the form of footnotes or endnotes appears to have been of little consequence to him (Dodsley in fact printed the notes at the bottom of each page). Gray's most pressing concern, as always, was that the texts of the poems themselves be free of any sloppy misprints or casual, typographical errors. As he wrote to Dodsley that February:

> all I desire is, that the text be accurately printed, & therefore whoever corrects the press, should have some acquaintance with the Greek, Latin, & Italian, as well as the English tongues. let the order stand thus, unless you have begun to print already: if so, it is indifferent to me.
>
>   1. Ode. (Lo, where the rosy-bosom'd, &c:)
>   2. Ode, on the death of a favourite Cat.
>   3. Ode, on a distant prospect of Eton-College.
>   4. Ode, to Adversity.
>   5. The progress of Poësy, a Pindaric Ode.
>   6. The Bard, a Pindaric Ode.
>   7. The Fatal Sisters.
>   8. The Descent of Odin.
>   9. The Triumphs of Owen, a fragment.
> 10. Elegy, written in a country church-yard.
>
> You will print the four first & the last from you own large edition (first publish'd with Mr. B:s plates) in the 5th & 6th you will do well to follow the edition printed at [Strawberry Hill]. I mention this, because there are several little faults of the press in your Miscellanies [i.e. in Dodsley's *Collection*]. (*CTG* 999–1000)

'Remember', Gray cautioned in closing these general instructions, 'the *Long Story* must be omitted.'

Gray himself seems to have had considerably mixed emotions regarding the two major 'innovations' of the edition – the inclusion in the volume of the three, hitherto unpublished imitations – *The Fatal Sisters*, *The Descent of Odin*, and *The Triumphs of Owen* – and the significant addition of explanatory notes to the poems. To Beattie (though not, apparently, to Dodsley) he confessed that he had agreed to the first of these additions only 'to make up (in bulk) for the omission of that *long story*'. He wrote similarly to Walpole after the volume's publication that he had only included those same efforts 'lest *my works* should be mistaken for the works of a flea, or a pismire'. 'As to the notes', he wrote revealingly to Beattie, 'I do it out of spite, because the Publick did not understand the two odes (which I have call'd Pindarick) tho' the first was not very dark, & the second alluded to a few common facts to be found in any six-penny History of England . . .'. Like T. S. Eliot's notoriously unhelpful and at times even misleading notes to *The Wasteland*, Gray's self-confessedly 'spiteful' glosses – though purportedly elucidating certain matters of historical fact and at times pointing out noteworthy sources of indebtedness to his poetic predecessors ranging from Virgil and Dante, to Dryden and Matthew Green – are to some degree to be treated only as condescending sops to the unusually dense Cerberus which stood, in his mind, for the public taste.

Gray seems never truly to have reconciled his professed incomprehension of the inability of his general reading audience simply to grasp the narrative meaning of his later poetry with his deeply felt conviction that truth and genuine understanding will always be *paucorum hominim*. Responses such as Beattie's to Gray's annotations must only have confirmed the poet in his opinion that the inclusion of such notes, if not an absolute mistake, was only a necessary evil – a comment less on Gray's own style and vocabulary than on the ever-diminishing literacy of the so-called 'common' reader. 'I think You have condescended to Your Readers inattention even more than was necessary:', Beattie wrote from Aberdeen soon after receiving Gray's instructions for the press,

> for my own part, I never found any difficulty in understanding Your poetry. The first of the Pindaric odes is so perspicuous, that I could hardly conceive it possible for any person of Common sense to misunderstand it. If there be any obscurity in *the Bard*, it is only in the allusions; for the style and imagery are clear distinct and strong. But readers now-a-days have nothing in view but amusement; and have little relish for a book that requires any degree of attention. (*CTG* 1011)

T. S. Eliot's own comments, in his essay on the Elizabethan dramatist Philip Massinger, concerning the complex and at times seemingly

inscrutable relationship that perforce exists between the 'original'
achievement of any single writer, on the one hand, and that same writer's
necessary indebtedness to various literary sources, models, and predecessors, on the other, are surely relevant to Gray's own, uniquely
labyrinthine combination in his poetry of borrowings, allusions, and
cento-like 'cuttings'. 'One of the surest tests is the way in which a poet
borrows', Eliot memorably declared: 'Immature poets imitate; mature
poets steal; bad poets deface what they take; and good poets make it
into something better, or at least something different.'[13] Like *The Wasteland* itself, much of Gray's poetry – and certainly the later odes and
the imitations from Norse and Welsh – are best understood as exciting
and in many ways radically innovative experiments in poetic *form*;
like *The Wasteland*, too, they are not only 'something different' from
their sources, they are very often – if not invariably – 'something
better'.

The volume of *Poems by Mr Gray* was published by Dodsley in
London on 12 March 1768, in an edition of 1,500 copies, each priced
at half a crown; a second printing, of a further 750 copies, was called
for before the end of the year. The superior Glasgow edition produced
by the Foulis brothers – a handsome quarto priced economically at only
five shillings – soon followed on 4 May. Gray was especially pleased
with the latter volume, and soon wrote to Beattie that he 'rejoiced' in
the careful attention that the brother artisans had bestowed on the
project. The clean, large type of their edition had been especially
designed for the project by the brothers' long-time patron, Alexander
Wilson; the Glasgow *Poems* strikes one even today as having been conceived and executed less as a commercial venture, than as a genuine
labour of love and respect.

Walpole, it might be remarked, rather surprisingly played no role
whatsoever in the publication of the *Poems* in 1768. Indeed, not only
had Gray seen no reason to consult with him regarding the on-going
preparation of the volume throughout the preceding months, but he had
not even alerted him to the publication of the book that spring. Walpole
was left to learn of its appearance through a February announcement in
the *Public Advertiser*. He felt Gray's neglect all the more keenly since he
had himself been soliciting the poet's advice and criticism regarding the
historical accuracy and persuasiveness of his own, recently completed
Historic Doubts on the Life and Reign of King Richard the Third. Why,
he must have puzzled to himself, had Gray not likewise consulted with
him on the *Poems*? Had Walpole's enthusiasm not singled out Gray's
work earlier in their lives, after all, there may well not have been
cause for any such volume in the first place. As Walpole wrote on 18

[13]   T. S. Eliot, *Selected Essays* (London: Faber and Faber, 1932) 206.

February – less than a week after sending a copy of his own work to Gray at Cambridge, and only five days after the publisher's earliest announcement in the London newspapers:

> . . . I am extremely out of humour with you. I saw *poems* by *Mr. Gray* advertised: I called directly at Dodsley's to know if this was to be more than a new edition? He was not at home himself, but his foreman told me he thought there were some new pieces, and notes to the whole. It was very unkind, not only to go out of town without mentioning them to me, without showing them to me, but not to say a word of them in [your] letter. (*CTG* 1013)

Walpole moved on in the same paragraph to apologize for not always sharing his own 'hasty trifles' with Gray, but protested at the same time that he himself constantly forgot his own works 'in a very short time after they are published'; Gray's poetic productions, he intimated, were always to be treated otherwise. Yet the very ease with which Walpole moved between the subject of taking credit and earning fame for himself as a result of his *own* writing, on the one hand, and that of assisting Gray in circulating and promoting *his* poetry, on the other, may itself reflect precisely the sort of proprietary attitude which Walpole habitually demonstrated towards the poet's work – a claim to ownership Gray now wished rather to avoid than to encourage. Gray dismissed his friend's complaint of neglect as nothing more than a 'friendly accusation', and made light of the matter in his next letter to Walpole. His easy explanation of the way in which the project only inadvertently grew into an entirely 'new' edition provided the opportunity for some of his more memorable observations on the nature of his own creative powers; it was in his response to Walpole on this occasion that he spoke of writing when he 'liked' to only because it made him feel better, and dismissed the entire project of the complete edition as having provided simply a necessary sense of an ending. 'What has one to do, when *turned of fifty*', he now wrote, 'but really to think of finishing?'

*

That spring Gray left Cambridge early in April, once again, as in 1766, undertaking a leisurely tour through 'different parts of Kent' before returning to spend the better part of July and August in London. He appears to have remained for some portion of June at Ramsgate, and then to have moved on to visit Billy Robinson at Denton Court until roughly the middle of the following month. It was on this second visit to Denton that Gray composed his short burlesque verses on Lord Holland's villa at Kingsgate – lines to which he referred later that same

year only as his *Arcanum Arcanorum* or 'Secret of Secrets'. On his previous visit to Denton just two years earlier, Gray had made a particular
point of *not* visiting Kingsgate precisely because, as he explained to
Nicholls, 'it belong'd to my Lord Holland'. The appearance in May,
1767 of a privately printed broadsheet containing Lord Holland's own
verses, *Lord Holland Returning from Italy, 1767*, may have prompted
Gray to change his mind, and to undertake his own maliciously critical
visit to the property.

Lord Holland (the former Henry Fox, Secretary of State under Newcastle in 1755–56 and shortly afterwards created Paymaster General and
eventually, with the assistance of Lord Bute, Leader of the House of
Commons) had begun constructing his fantastic and fanciful residence
– inspired supposedly by Cicero's Formian villa at the now long-
vanished coastal city of Baiae in Campania – near Margate in 1763.
Even in their inception, however, the several structures of Holland's villa
were intended to resemble nothing so much as an architecturally eclectic collection of ancient ruins. As Walpole was to write many years later,
describing the scene which greeted visitors at Kingsgate to his close
friend Mary Berry, the grounds contained 'scattered buildings of all
sorts, but in no style of architecture that ever appeared before or has
since, and with no connection with or to one another, and in all directions . . .'.[14] It was thanks almost entirely to Walpole himself that Gray
possessed the animus against Fox necessary to write such lines in the
first place; the former must often, over the years, have underscored with
the force of personal insight and anecdote the minister's already notorious and close to unparalleled reputation for having often resorted to
strong-arm tactics and bribery in order to achieve his own considerable
political ambitions.

Although the unscrupulous machinations and Machiavellian tactics
of the villa's owner attract some attention in Gray's verses (Lord Holland
is introduced in the poem's first line as 'Old and abandoned by each
venal friend', and his retreat is very soon described as the 'congenial
spot' he has chosen 'to mend / A broken character and constitution'),
the poet's fiercest criticism is apparently reserved for the masturbatory
architectural folly – the pointless, stylistic macaronics – of the 'ruins'
themselves. Having first described the natural desolation indigenous to
the Kentish coast near the treacherous sandbanks of Goodwin Sands,
Gray adds:

> Yet nature cannot furnish out the feast,
>   Art he invokes new horrors still to bring.
> Now mouldering fanes and battlements arise,

[14]   WC xii. 100.

> Arches and turrets nodding to their fall,
> Unpeopled palaces delude his eyes,
> And mimic desolation covers all. (*PTG* 262–63)

Yet the 'mimic desolation' of these manufactured ruins, the reader soon discovers, is in truth only a modest reflection of the genuine and thorough-going destruction (Gray suggests) its owner had once dreamed of visiting on the capital itself. Had his former political allies – such as Bute, Shelburne, Rigby, and Calcraft – been 'true' and loyal to his own ambitiously self-serving plans, Lord Holland might well have achieved his egotistical dreams of destruction and control. He might, as Gray puts it in his closing lines, have 'realized the ruins' he can now, in his dotage, only 'feign':

> Purged by the sword and beautified by fire,
> Then had we seen proud London's hated walls:
> Owls might have hooted in St Peter's choir,
> And foxes stunk and littered in St. Paul's'. (*PTG* 264)

The slight, allusive echo contained within Gray's last line (to ll. 70–71 of Pope's *Windsor Forest* – 'The Fox obscene to gaping Tombs retires, / And savage howlings fill the sacred Quires' – and referring to the murderous desolation effected by England's Norman conquerors in the eleventh century) suggests that Holland's political designs looked likewise completely to destroy this allegorical or symbolic, English countryside. It remains striking that even within so incidental and occasional a satire as this, it is the topographical potential of his material which Gray seeks, almost intuitively, to emphasize and to underscore. His lines 'On Lord Holland's Seat near Margate, Kent', as these verses have come to be known since their initial (and as far as Gray was concerned, unintentional) publication in 1769, typically and in this case satirically address not only the actions of an individual, but the moral and ethical resonance of a precise, physical space.

Gray personally appears to have had little if any regard for these verses. He even left his original copy of the lines in the drawer of a table that sat in his dressing-room at Denton. Only after returning to Cambridge was the draft returned to him by Robinson. Gray himself eventually took the time to copy out and send copies on to both Nicholls and Mason; the latter promptly passed yet another draft on to Palgrave, in Suffolk. Within a very few months, Gray's 'stanzas on a decayed statesman' were being widely circulated, and his own name was for better or for worse inextricably linked to the production. Walpole successfully discouraged Mason from including them in his collected *Works*;

only a few years later, however, Stephen Jones included them in his 1799 edition of Gray's poetry.

Gray had meanwhile returned to spend the dog days of summer in London. Having only recently expressed to Walpole his supposed desire to devote his time quietly to the thought of 'finishing' (like Shakespeare's Prospero he seems to have been determined that from this point on in his life he would turn an inordinate portion of his thoughts over to the peaceful contemplation of his own, supposedly imminent end), Gray was blissfully unaware of the personal and professional challenges which yet lay ahead of him. And in this case, indeed, it may have been foolish to be any more the wiser with regards to what the future held in store. Soon to enter his fifty-third year, Gray was likewise about to undertake one of the most troublesome professional responsibilities he could ever have imagined. As a scholar, as a poet, and as a caring individual, Gray's life – for all his intuitions to the contrary – was far from over.

CHAPTER ELEVEN

GILDED HORRORS

The Professorship of Modern Poetry, the Ode for Music, and the Tour of the Lake District
1768–1769

I. A Reward and a Credit

The Huntingdon road – the main artery leading northwest out of Cambridge since the Romans first set out the line of the Via Devana in the first and second centuries AD – is a route extraordinarily rich in local, literary, and even national history. Travellers seem no sooner to have left the outermost ring of the University colleges behind them (Fitzwilliam College, New Hall, and Girton College – all modern foundations – line the red-bricked outskirts here) before they are passing through the tiny town of Fenstanton, once home to the famous landscape gardener Capability Brown. Just a few miles beyond Fenstanton, a lesser road veers off to the east, leading to St. Ives – a settlement only slightly larger than its near neighbour, where Oliver Cromwell spent five years of his life – and eventually depositing travellers at the fifteenth-century church where the novelist Laurence Sterne, author of *Tristram Shandy*, held his first curacy; the nearby manor house at Hemingford Grey stakes an impressive claim to being the oldest continually inhabited house in the entire country. Before arriving at Huntingdon, one passes the Roman settlement of Godmanchester, a town along the Great Ouse boasting several sixteenth- and seventeenth-century era thatched and half-timbered houses. The old county seat of Huntingdonshire itself, which William Cobbet would in the early years of the next century compellingly describe as 'one of the places that tend to lengthen life and make it happy', was Cromwell's birthplace. Visitors to Huntingdon today can pay their respects to the revolutionary hero (should their politics incline them to do so) either at his birthplace on the High Street, or at the old grammar school (now a museum) which both he and the diarist Samuel Pepys once attended as boys. The poet William Cowper had boarded in a house on the same High Street as recently as 1767. George Street, angling off the High Street to the southwest, leads to Hinchingbrooke House. The site of Hinchingbrooke, originally occupied in the early thirteenth century by a Benedictine nunnery, had been turned over to the Cromwell family shortly after the Dissolution. It was here that the Protector's great-grandfather, Sir Richard Cromwell, in the sixteenth century constructed a magnificent Tudor country retreat. The property was subsequently sold, in 1627, to Sir Sidney Montague. The residence had been significantly altered and rebuilt in 1660, when Edward Montague was created first Earl of Sandwich. In the 1760s, Hinchingbrooke House was home to Gray's former Eton schoolfellow, John Montague, fourth Earl of Sandwich, the subject of Gray's satirical poem, *The Candidate*. On a sweltering summer night in 1768, the road that connected Huntingdon and Cambridge – a transit which, thanks to Sandwich's wrangling some four years earlier had already figured to some degree in the on-going university saga that linked academic positions to ministerial patronage – was destined to play a small but significant role in the drama of Gray's own life, and in what were to prove the final chapters both of his professional and of his poetic career.

Laurence Brockett, the Professor of Modern History at Cambridge, had been spending the evening of Thursday, 21 July at Sandwich's estate. The Earl's notorious behavior had not improved since his dramatic (and dramatically public) exposure in the contest for the High Stewardship some four years earlier. As usual, the two men had been drinking heavily over their dinner. The postprandial scene can well be imagined. Sandwich's extraordinary reputation for excess encourages one even to picture a tableau of diurnal, domestic debauchery that would not have been out of place in the novels of Henry Fielding, earlier in the century, or in some of the more scathing of Hogarth's satirical engravings. The table cloth long since removed, the wine bottles and tankards of ale having perhaps given way to glasses of wine or pure West Indian punch, the two men sat conversing in their armchairs deep into the night. By the time they decided to part for the evening, Brockett's judgement was badly impaired by drink. Nevertheless, as the late evening drew to its early morning close, he undertook to mount his horse and, accompanied only by his servant, begin the return journey of about twenty miles from Hinchingbrooke back to Cambridge.

Brockett had not travelled very far along the road before he tumbled from his mount and injured himself. Possessed of all the stultifying oblivion to physical pain of the true alcoholic, the fuddled Brockett insisted on remounting his horse and continuing his journey. He had not made very much progress before a second fall injured him even more severely than the first. Quite apart from having inflicted upon himself a very bad bruising, Brockett must have sustained in this second tumble some serious and painful internal injuries as well. The road both before and behind stretched dark and deserted into the night, and it no doubt took some time for Brockett's man to seek out assistance. The consequent jostling of Brockett's bruised and bloated body as he was carried to safety can only have aggravated his injuries further; his drunken stupor did nothing to facilitate his recovery. For nearly three days Brockett lay injured and largely insensible. By the evening of Sunday, 24 July, he was dead.

Gray, only just returned from his several weeks' vacation in Kent, had been staying in Jermyn Street at the time of the incident. He learned of 'poor Brockett's' death only indirectly, in a letter from his Cambridge cousin, 'Molly' Antrobus. The official account of events eventually offered in the *Cambridge Chronicle* for 30 July was understandably circumspect. Gray was left to fill in some of the details regarding Brockett's injuries only by listening carefully to the gossip that was soon being circulated among his academic friends and colleagues. The university community was small, and Gray had of course known something of Brockett ever since he had first been appointed a Fellow of Trinity (where he had earlier completed his undergraduate degree) in 1744. Brockett had been an active plotter and intriguer in university affairs ever since his earliest days in Cambridge; like most such 'players', he inspired few emotions in the breasts of his professional colleagues other than those of distaste and distrust. Nearly twenty years earlier, Gray had worried in a letter to Wharton that because he appeared to fit so easily into the pocket of Edward Keene, Brockett would 'by main Force' be created a Fellow of Peterhouse. Gray's anxiety on that earlier occasion proved to have been unfounded. One is nevertheless compelled to agree that for someone who would later in life be infamous for living 'a free and luxurious' existence, Brockett had managed for almost two decades to enjoy a remarkably successful career within the university. He had been appointed to the Professorship of Modern History hard upon the death of the previous occupant, Shallet Turner, in 1762 (at which time Gray had himself confessed a hope that his own name might be put forward for the post); Brockett's success in being granted the chair was due largely to the fact that he had once served as private tutor to Sir James Lowther, afterwards (1784) first Earl of Lonsdale, and nephew to Lord Bute, who personally favoured his nomination. Brockett, for all his excesses, must throughout his life have possessed an ease of manner and conversation that at least brought him to the attention of those in positions of political and institutional power. When Robert Smith, the Master of Trinity died in February 1768 – only the winter before Brockett's own death – Brockett's name was once again one of only two immediately brought forward by Cambridge gossips as his possible successor.

*

The Regius Professorships of History at both Oxford and Cambridge had originally been founded by King George I in 1724. The endowments were established at least partly out of a sense of xenophobia; the King's statement to the Vice-Chancellors of both Universities on the occasion of the foundation professed dismay that 'the Education and Tuition of Youth both at home and in their Travels' had too often been left in the hands of 'Persons of Foreign Nations'. The Crown consequently announced its determination 'to appoint two Persons of Sober Conversation and prudent Conduct, of the Degree of Master of Arts or Bachelor of Laws, or of Some higher Degree in one of the Said Universitys, Skilled in Modern Languages, one for the University of Cambridge, and the other for that of Oxford, who Shall be obliged to read Lectures in the Publick Schools, at Such time as shall hereafter be appointed'.[1] The practical responsibility of these teachers would be to instruct students in the writing and speaking of modern languages; the aim of the foundation was essentially to prepare young men for careers in public and civil service, by insuring their competence in at least two such languages. The stipend attached to each of the Professorships was a generous £400 a year (before the deduction of customary fees and taxes). Prior to Brockett's tenure, the position at Cambridge had been occupied only by Shallet Turner and Samuel Harris, both of whom had been Fellows of Peterhouse.

Gray was now eminently qualified to hold such a position. He may well have anticipated his appointment to the Professorship from the moment he first heard of Brockett's death. His name, it will be remembered, had already been brought forward on the occasion of Turner's death in 1762, and Gray had many years earlier – possibly as early as 1748 – observed of the post: 'I certainly might ask it with as much, or more Propriety, than any one in the Place.' In 1768, his name was suggested to the Duke of Grafton by his old friend Stonhewer, who was then serving as Grafton's secretary. Thanks largely to the Earl of Chatham's recent illness, Grafton had by 1769 not only attained the headship of the treasury, but had effectively been serving as first minister since Chatham's withdrawal from active politics in the spring of 1767. Grafton within days recommended Gray to the King, and wrote to the poet on Wednesday, 27 July, to offer him the Professorship.

Gray's response to Grafton's offer was prompt, concise, and effortlessly elegant. 'My Lord', he wrote on about 27 July from London,

> Your Grace has dealt nobly with me; and the same delicacy of mind that induced you to confer this favour on me, unsolicited and unexpected, may perhaps make you averse to receive my sincerest thanks and grateful acknowledgments. Yet your Grace must excuse me, they will have

---

[1]   Reprinted in *CTG* Appendix S 'Gray and the Professorship of Modern Poetry', 1253.

their way: they are indeed but words; yet I know and feel they come from my heart, and therefore are not wholly unworthy of your lordship's acceptance. I even flatter myself (such is my pride) that you have some little satisfaction in your own work. If I did not deceive myself in this, it would compleat the happiness of,

My Lord,

Your Grace's

Most obliged and devoted servant. (CTG 1034)

Within only days of receiving Grafton's letter and extending this reply, Gray found himself kissing the hand of his monarch at the King's levee. He appears to have been both pleased and genuinely embarrassed by the court ceremony. That the King himself as well as the entire Cabinet-Council had approved his nomination 'in words of great favour' was a circumstance he found particularly gratifying, and one that he instructed all his correspondents, should they refer to the appointment, to repeat; Gray was yet aware that he owed much to the personal influence of Stonhewer, to whom he referred in a letter to Wharton as the 'inside' of the matter. To Nicholls alone he confessed with unaffected modesty that the day of the reception 'was so hot & the ceremony so embarrassing to me', that although the King made several gracious speeches, he could hardly recollect a word of what had been said to him.

Gray – not without some justification – regarded the post as a sinecure. Brockett, after all, had not delivered a single public lecture during his tenure. His immediate predecessor, Shallet Turner, had maintained the chair for twenty-seven years in a similar manner. 'As to reading lectures', William Cole wrote laconically of Turner shortly after his death, 'he never thought it incumbent upon him to do so'. Gray, however, was compelled both by his own conscience and by outward circumstances to feel rather differently about the matter. In the September following Gray's appointment, the Vice-Chancellor and the Heads of Houses at Oxford had submitted a memorandum to the King, in which it was suggested that the Regius Professor of Modern History conform to a certain number of requirements each term. These requirements included the delivery of a course of no fewer than fifty lectures each year, and residence in full term. Anxious to live up to what he now felt to be the responsibilities of his new position thus implied by the resolutions of his sister university, Gray eventually submitted to Grafton a proposal for a number of methods for choosing the pupils to be tutored by him. 'Notwithstanding his ill-health', Mason wrote of the poet, he 'constantly intended to read lectures'.[2] Gray's conscience was to remain

[2] Ibid., 1259.

sorely troubled, as we shall see, by 'the sense of [his] duty, which [he] did not perform'.

The scope and ambition of Gray's proposals, at least, were impressive. He suggested, for example:

1. That the Professor shall apply to the several Heads of Colleges, & desire them to recommend one or more young Gentlemen, who shall be instructed without expence in some of the modern languages, & attend such lectures as He shall give. the number (if each smaller College send one, and the larger two) will amount in the University of Cambridge to nineteen.

2. That the Prof:r shall nominate and pay two Praeceptors, qualified to instruct these Scholars in the French and Italian tongues.

3. That he shall reside the half of every Term at least in the University (which half-terms at Cambridge make about a hundred & ten days, almost one third of the year) & shall read publickly once at least in every Term a lecture on modern History to his Scholars, & any others, that shall be present.

4. That He shall besides at short & regular intervals give private lectures to his Scholars on the same subject, prescribe a method of study, direct them in their choice of Authors, & from time to time enquire into the progress they have made in the Italian & French tongues.

5. That if he neglects these duties, he shall be subject to the same pecuniary mulcts, that other Professors are according to Statute. (*CTG* 1256)

Mason later recalled that Gray drew up and submitted to Grafton no fewer than three different 'schemes for regulating the method of choosing pupils privately to be instructed by him' – though he may well have mistaken the several documents which were essentially drafts towards one single proposal for a series of independent 'schemes'.[3]

In the meantime – always able and confident when it came to beginnings, outlines, and schema – Gray set about composing an impressive inaugural lecture. The speech could be delivered either in English or in Latin. Gray characteristically chose to write in the latter language. He got so far only as to complete a fragment of the Exordium, as well as tracing both the necessary 'Preparations and accompanyments' for the study of history, and a list of possible 'Sources of History' (e.g. Public

---

[3]   Mason *Memoirs* 397; see also *CTG* 1257.

Papers, Treaties, Letters, Memoirs, etc.). Of the third and most promisingly speculative section of the speech – 'Of History Itself' – only the
title is given.

II. Ancient Aversions

Gray continued to feel nervous and ill at ease regarding the responsibilities of his new position. Toward the end of 1768, however, political
circumstances worked to present the poet with an opportunity at least
publicly to show his gratitude to Grafton and, indirectly and perhaps
more importantly, to Stonhewer himself. In November, 1768, Grafton
was elected to the position as Chancellor of Cambridge University.
Grafton was elected to the Chancellorship primarily on the strength of
his status as First Lord of the Treasury. He would of course be expected
to use his position to influence the dispensation of royal ecclesiastical
patronage in the form of prebends, livings, and bishoprics in favour of
the Cambridge divines. He could anticipate, in turn, the support of the
Cambridge academic community for his ministry. Just how close the
relationship between national politics and the University could be had
been demonstrated in the years immediately preceding Grafton's
appointment by the Duke of Newcastle. Newcastle (an active and
aggressive patron who had maintained the Chancellorship for nearly
twenty years) had effectively strengthened Whig influence in the colleges
through the office of Chancellor and had, in return, used his ministerial
position to secure for members of the University by far the better portion
of those livings in the gift of the Crown.

On the occasion of Grafton's election as Chancellor the University
Senate – gambling, as always, on the erratic and unpredictable popularity of Minsters of State – seemed to have had its eye on a particularly
propitious future. Thanks to the Earl of Chatham's recent illness Grafton
had by 1769 not only attained the headship of the treasury, but had
effectively been serving as first minister since Chatham's withdrawal
from active politics in the spring of 1767. Here, the delighted Cambridge
clergymen must have thought as they voiced their unanimous approval
of Grafton's appointment, lay the high-road to ecclesiastical preferment.
The University had continued under Newcastle's strong-handed if
often materially rewarding Chancellorship since his fall from political
power in 1762 and was understandably eager to initiate this auspicious
new order. The Installation ceremony, which had already promised to
be an impressive display, was accordingly being treated as a gala event
in Cambridge. Instructions were given that no expense was to be spared
to render the occasion memorable.

*

The Installation ceremony itself was to take place on the morning of 1 July 1769. The festivities for the reception of Grafton as Chancellor were to be patterned after Newcastle's installation exactly twenty years earlier. They would include a formal procession to the Senate House, a congratulatory greeting by the Vice-Chancellor and the presentation of the Patent of Installation, a Latin speech by the Public Orator and – the spectacular set-piece of the ceremony – the performance of a 'grand anthem' or Installation Ode.[4] Grafton's ode was to be written especially for the occasion by Gray – now invariably touted as 'the author of the celebrated Elegy in a country church-yard' – and set to music by John Randall, who was then Professor of Music at Cambridge. Once the proceedings at the Senate House were concluded, the Chancellor and the representatives of the University were to adjourn in the early evening to Trinity College Hall where, again following the precedent of Newcastle's installation in 1749, they were to dine 'in a very splendid manner'. The entertainment was scheduled to continue well into the evening, and would include a debate in Trinity Chapel 'on the question whether the Conqueror came in by conquest or consent of the people', and a performance of Handel's *Acis and Galatea* at the Senate House. Guests on the occasion were to include the Archbishop of Canterbury, the Duke of Bedford, marquis of Gransby, Lord Sandwich, the Bishop of Lincoln, and, as the *Gentleman's Magazine* informed its readers, 'a great many of the principal nobility, foreign ministers, and gentlemen of the first distinction'.

Expectations for such a spectacular affair proved in the event to be too overwhelming for the excited Cambridge populace. The small university town was hopelessly over-burdened with the many visitors who had come up from London as sightseers to witness the proceedings, and the morning of the ceremony found the cool, rococo splendour of Gibbs's Senate House, according to one witness, 'a scene of riot and mobbing'. 'The doors were ordered to be opened at ten', wrote Richard Gough, a London antiquary, recounting events to a friend,

> but there were such numbers waiting without, that they rushed in at the door and windows in one body, without regard to tickets. The proctors cleared first the body of the house of all strangers, and then endeavored to clear the galleries of gentlemen, but in vain. One lady lost her shoes; Lady Griffith a diamond pin for recovery of which she paid twelve guineas.[5]

[4] A description of the Installation ceremony was included in the *Gentleman's Magazine* 33 (1769) 361.
[5] John Nichols, *Illustrations of the Literary History of the Eighteenth Century* (London, 1828) v.216. Richard Gough's account of the 'hustle and bustle' of the Installation Ceremony is recounted in a letter to the Rev. Benjamin Forster, 6 July 1769.

Order was eventually restored, but not before £30 worth of damage was done to the theatre windows, which were smashed in the near-riot that preceded the arrival of the Chancellor's train. Several of the windows of Great St. Mary's church, over against the Senate House on King's Parade, were also shattered as the crush of eager spectators pressed to gain entrance to the ceremony. It was obviously not without reason that Grafton was described on the occasion as fearful of being 'pressed to death by people who never saw a Duke before'.

The guests were not the only ones to have difficulties with the festivities or to disrupt the dignity of the proceedings. The ceremony itself seems to have gone wrong from the start. His Grace the Duke was already distracted by the mutinous rancour of party politics in the metropolis, and can hardly have been said to have had his mind upon the matter at hand. The attacks on his administration by the vituperative 'Junius' had begun appearing in the *Public Advertiser* in January, 1769, and by midsummer the vilification of Grafton and his policies had reached such proportions that the Chancellor himself, according to one close friend, was said to have experienced 'neither pleasure nor comfort' from the elaborate ceremonies surrounding his installation.[6] In his letter to the *Public Advertiser* of 30 May, Junius had made a point of attacking Grafton's private character ('sullen and severe without religion, profligate without gaiety, you live like Charles II, without being an amiable companion, and, for aught I know, may die as his father did without the reputation of a martyr').[7] The letter sounded a new note of hostility and animosity in the attacks on Grafton, and signalled a willingness to engage the Chancellor's personal and private character, as well as his public record.

To make matters worse, Grafton had been further troubled on the morning of Grafton's installation by a number of minor disagreements with the University authorities – disagreements that extended to such annoyingly trivial details as what fashion of wig might be suitable to the occasion (the long, flowing wig and 'abundant curls' worn by the Duke of Newcastle were not in keeping, it seems, with Grafton's 'youthful appearance').[8] More significantly, the Duke had been unable to deliver his own prepared speech when faced with the compliments of the Public Orator and Vice-Chancellor in the middle of the ceremony, and had been forced to reply in an extemporaneous manner which displayed his own

---

[6] Grafton's remarks are recorded in Joseph Cradock's *Literary and Miscellaneous Memoirs*, 4 vols. (London, 1826) i.106.

[7] *The Letters of Junius*, ed. John Cannon (Oxford: Clarendon Press, 1978) 69.

[8] Cradock, *Literary and Miscellaneous Memoirs*, 105.

rhetorical skills in a less than flattering light. Following the ceremony Grafton (who later confessed that he 'never was so flustered'), censored the Vice-Chancellor – Dr. Hinchcliffe, Master of Trinity College – for not apprizing him of the custom of the compliments.[9] Hinchcliffe merely noted that he had assumed that the Prime Minister, of all people, might have been able to 'collect a few sentences together' should occasion dictate.[10] 'I never', one associate later admitted of the new Chancellor's performance in the Senate House, 'heard him speak or saw him appear to greater disadvantage'.[11]

In spite of Grafton's diverting – if slightly ominous – ineptitude throughout the installation ceremonies, the highlight of the morning's entertainment remained the performance of Thomas Gray's 'Installation Ode'. Grafton had himself had the opportunity to read (and, one assumes, to approve) the *Ode* in manuscript in early June. According to Gray himself, the piece had been rehearsed 'again and again' in the weeks immediately preceding the ceremony. The structure of such celebratory odes was, in any event, predictable, and Gray – who had on more than one occasion made known to his friends his 'ancient aversion' to such 'state poems' – seemed to have made little effort to alter the traditional pattern of praise demanded by the occasion. Gray, we remember, had attended Newcastle's Installation twenty years earlier and had declared William Mason's *Ode* on that occasion to be 'the only Entertainment that had any tolerable Elegance'. As we shall see, Gray appeared to have written his own *Ode* with Mason's work particularly in mind. When writing the *Ode* for Grafton's Installation, Gray presented himself to his friends and correspondents as having little desire to draw any attention to the piece. It was already bad enough, he commented at one point, that he should have had to take upon himself the invidious task of 'praising [Grafton] to his face'.

Political circumstances worked to make the poet even more circumspect. Although public expectations regarding Gray's piece seem to have run pretty high (at least one Cambridge bookseller expected the published *Ode* to 'sell prodigiously'), the parodies and burlesques which now invariably greeted any attempts at birthday odes, New Year odes, and other occasional pieces were an additional incentive to draw attention away from Gray's effort, and keep the increasingly empowered critical reviews and periodicals as far away from the ceremony as possible. The likelihood of being caught up in the newspaper controversies of the *Public Advertiser* – and of being thus implicated in the exposure,

---

[9]   John Nicholls, *Illustrations*, v.316.
[10] Cradock, *Literary and Miscellaneous Memoirs*, 106.
[11] Ibid.

slander, and 'catchpenny contrivances' that seemed invariably to be a part of the contemporary political contest that surrounded Grafton's ministry – held no appeal for the poet. The anxieties of parody were in this instance, at least, explicitly tied to the inescapabilities of public political commitment and revelations of explicit immorality, as well as to the more usual fears of exposure, self-revelation, and resignation of poetic authority. Parodies, which find their origin in the English tradition within the contexts of the political activity and political commitment of the Civil Wars and Restoration period, have the potential of placing the private individual in a public context, and then ruthlessly scrutinizing him; they work to connect the spheres public and the private. For Gray, it was precisely this threat of personal revelation within the confines of ostensibly political attack that makes the parodies so dangerous. The attacks of Junius on Grafton's extramarital liaisons and sexual indiscretions can only have served as a further warning to Gray to keep as low a profile as possible in the inevitable journalistic scuffles which would follow the installation ceremonies.

The composition of the *Ode for Music* in the spring of 1767 was a task which Gray, in a decidedly uncharacteristic gesture, volunteered to undertake. Nicholls later suggested that Gray's unusual alacrity on this particular occasion may have been prompted by his desire that he might 'offer with a good grace what he could not have refused had it been asked of him'. Although Gray was perhaps glad that the University Chancellorship was finally out of the hand of 'that old fizzling Duke', Newcastle, he felt little personal loyalty either to Grafton or to his ministry (Gray's politic leanings we remember, were – as he once put it – those of a '*true* and *rational* Whig'). He essentially regarded the composition of the *Ode* as the settling of a score. 'I thought myself bound in gratitude to his Grace', he wrote following the ceremony in July, 'unasked to take upon me the task of writing those verse, that are normally set to music on this occasion'. Nicholls recalled that the actual composition of the ode was 'a task to which he submitted with greatest reluctance', and one that he was anxious to keep a secret. Gray himself wrote to Wharton only a few months before the ceremony, calling it of all his current employments, simply, 'the worst'.

There are several reasons for Gray's particular aversion to the task of writing the *Ode*. The spring of 1769 saw him in an increasingly precarious state of health. He suffered from unusually frequent attacks of gout, 'which', he noted, 'tho weakly and not severe, were at least dispiriting, & lasted a long time'. He complained as well of melancholy and 'want of spirits', and found it increasingly difficult to get any work done at all. The very task of writing was for Gray, as we gave seen, one effective method of staving off his constitutionally 'leucholic' temperament – a manner of fighting off that feeling which lay heavy upon the unoccupied mind as something 'lifeless, without form and void'. It was a weapon, as Gray's deliberately biblical language implied, against a genuine chaos of emotion and imagination, a means of combating mental oblivion. Throughout his correspondence, Gray several times commented on his sporadic method of composition ('you apprehend too much from my resolutions about writing; they are only made to be broken'), and, as we have seen, referred on several occasions to his inability to control his own creative faculty.

As might have been expected, Gray waited until the last minute even to begin writing the piece, and thus allowed a number of unfortunate circumstances to complicate matters even further. The *Ode* was originally to have been set to music by Dr. Charles Burney. Mason had in fact written to Burney in February 1769, warning him that Gray had not yet begun the composition – 'tho', he added with some hesitancy, 'he seems to have intended it'. Burney's own offer to compose the Installation ode had been accepted several months before the ceremony was to take place. He was eventually discouraged from the task by the expense of transporting the carefully chosen London musicians necessary to his composition to Cambridge, and eventually resigned the commission. The composition of the ode eventually devolved upon Randall 'to the astonishment', Burney would later recall with some bitterness, 'of all the musical profession'.[12]

The constrained circumstances of the production, failing health, and a chronically reluctant poetic temperament thus all contributed something towards Gray's delay in completing the *Ode*. Yet added to these anxieties that only helped augment Gray's habitual hesitancy was one which, although it had always been present to some degree in the past, Gray was now openly acknowledging: the anxiety of parody. Gray knew – particularly in light of the recent Junius epistles – that his reasons for writing the *Ode* would be held up to a ruthless public scrutiny. He knew as well that he would quickly be denounced for being a servile and sycophantic hireling whose motives in preparing the piece were less than honourable. Gray acknowledged these fears even as he composed the *Ode*. 'I must comfort myself with the intention', he wrote to Wharton in April, 'for I know it will bring abuse enough upon me'. Worse still was the suspicion – well-confirmed by popular poetic practice and Gray's own experience – that the *Ode* was to be parodied even before it was printed and presented to the public in its proper form. 'I expect', Gray wrote to Nicholls shortly before the ceremony, 'to see it torn piece-meal in the

[12]   Roger Lonsdale, *Dr. Charles Burney: A Literary Biography* (Oxford: Clarendon Press, 1965) 77–78.

North Briton before it is born. The musick is as good as the words; the former might be taken for mine and the latter for Dr. Randall's'. Although Gray was, as we have seen, inclined on occasion to using the language of nascence and birth to describe his own poetical compositions, the terminology of literary abortion in this particular instance remains striking. As always, Gray attempts to distance himself from his own creation – disparaging it, dimunifying it, calling it his 'odikle' just as he had called *The Bard* eight years earlier and, most significantly, pretending that any longevity permitted his own work would depend at least as much on those parodies which prolonged its existence in the popular journals as any merits it might possess on its own. A few weeks following the installation Gray wrote to Beattie from Cambridge, noting of his own verses:

> I do not think them worth sending you, because they are by nature doom'd to live but a single day, or if their existence is prolong'd beyond that date, it is only by means of news-paper parodies, & witless criticism. this sort of abuse I had reason to expect, but did not think it worth while to avoid it. (*CTG* 1070)

It is striking that Gray dismissed his own verses as ephemera – the parodies themselves, his anxious protestations imply, are themselves potentially more stable and enduring. Gray could of course be prepared for the parodies of the *Ode for Music* if only because of his previous treatment at the hands of the popular press. Although generally acknowledged as one of the most popular poets of the mid-eighteenth century, Gray's work had never escaped the hands of literary parodists before, and there was every reason to expect that a piece as potentially volatile as the *Ode* would attract even more attention.

The *Installation Ode* which Gray prepared for Grafton's ceremony was written not in the form of the regular Pindarics of 1757, but was structured rather as a secular cantata – that is, an occasional work for several voices with orchestral accompaniment, consisting of a succession of contrasting sections in which solos and semi-choruses are interspersed. While the *Ode for Music* is perhaps less regular that Gray's earlier efforts in the Pindaric mode, it remains in many respects as metrically complex, allusively rich, and syntactically evasive as its predecessors. In Gray's piece the personified forces of revelry, sin, and disruption ('Comus and his midnight-crew', 'Ignorance', 'dreaming Sloth', 'Mad Sedition', 'Servitude', 'painted Flattery', 'Envy base', and 'creeping Gain') are dismissed from the academic gathering at the poem's memorable injunction: 'Hence, avaunt, 'tis Holy ground'. Praise is then granted in the first three verse stanzas (or Air, Chorus, and Recitative, as Gray categorizes them), to the place where '[f]irst the genuine

ardour stole' upon the opening poetic and intellectual souls of great
British geniuses such as Milton and Newton. Gray's opening is confident and powerful, and clearly and economically develops the
fundamental dramatic situation of the *Ode*: the ever-vigilant sons of
Cambridge keep a constant watch on those precincts exclusively set aside
for the advancement of 'bright-eyed' Science and the development of
'sacred' poetry.

Milton – 'the bard divine' – begins to praise the physical setting
of Cambridge in the Air that follows. Newton rests comfortably
on a celestial cloud at the poet's side and 'nods his hoary head and
listens to the rhyme'. The passage is – given the fact that its supposed
speaker is Milton himself – an appropriately complex pastiche of lines
from the *Ode on the Morning of Christ's Nativity* (from which it
derives its complicated verse stanza), *Il Penseroso*, *Lycidas*, *Comus*, and
Paradise Lost:

> 'Ye brown o'er-arching groves,
> 'That Contemplation loves,
> 'Where willowy Camus lingers with delight!
> 'Oft at the blush of dawn
> 'I trod your level lawn,
> 'Oft wooed the gleam of Cynthia silver-bright
> 'In cloisters dim, far from the haunts of Folly,
> 'With Freedom by my side, and soft-eyed Melancholy.' (*PTG* 269–70)

Gray's lines seem even more deliberately than usual to invite the
question of precisely how original the poet is being here. The obvious
Miltonic echoes (to which we will return in a moment) are of course
clues to one source of indebtedness. Just how conventional or derivative
the specific topographical element of this sort of praise appears to be
may be seen by comparing Gray's lines with a similar passage in the
Installation Ode written by William Mason and set to music by William
Boyce for Newcastle's Installation in 1749. In Mason's ode, Cambridge
was similarly characterized as 'Majestic Granta' and 'learning's richest
shrine'. Mason likewise emphasized the actual physical setting of
Cambridge as a place particularly blessed by the 'genuine British Muse',
describing the fenland, rather comically, as a 'happy plain' – a suitable
setting for the anticipated re-enactment of Attic glories. Cambridge is
the 'genial soil' upon which Emulation spreads her 'bright beams' and
upon which Science sheds her 'kindliest dews'. Gray's lines in fact recall
Mason's other odes on Cambridge with even more linguistic specificity.
In a piece written to commemorate his leaving St. John's College in 1746,
Mason had written lines in which he solicited Memory, with reference
to the language of Thomson's *Seasons*, to:

... teach th'ideal stream to flow
Like gentle Camus, soft and slow;
Recall each antique spire, each cloister's gloom,
And bid this vernal noon of life re-bloom.[13]

The tone of Gray's later *Ode for Music* is anticipated in phrases such as 'gentle Camus', 'antique spire', and 'cloister's gloom'. A piece to which Gray is even more obviously indebted, however, is Mason's *Ode* describing his imminent return to Cambridge, as Fellow of Pembroke Hall, in 1747:

Lo, where peaceful CAMUS glides
   Through his ozier-fringed vale,
Sacred Leisure there resides
   Musing in his cloyster pale.
Wrapt in a deep solemnity of shade,
   Again I view fair Learning's spiry seats,
Again her ancient elms o'erhang my head,
   Again her votary contemplation meets,
Again I listen to AEolian lays,
   Or in those bright heroic portraits gaze,
That, to my raptur'd eye, the classical page displays.[14]

While this is not particularly good poetry (there is something unusually uncomfortable, for example, in the image of Learning's 'spiry seats' and in the pendant threat of the next line's faintly Damoclean elms), the imagery and personifications which characterize Mason's lines (which in turn echo Milton) were obviously on Gray's mind when he wrote his own *Ode*. 'Cloyster pale', for example, works with the earlier 'cloistered gloom' to prefigure 'cloister dim'. The 'AEolian lay' becomes an 'indignant lay'. 'Oe'rhanging elms' are happily transformed into 'O'er-arching groves', and a 'gentle ... ozier-fringed' Cam is exchanged, in Gray's later effort, for a 'willowy' Camus. These are minor transmutations. Gray seems, again, almost to have been writing his own *Ode for Music* with Mason's work spread out before him on his desk.

   Gray's verses thus deliberately and predictably mimic, imitate, echo, and parody the works in the peculiar occasional and topographical tradition in which he was working. Yet, paradoxically, it is in allusive passages such as these that Gray begins to make the musical ode his own, as it were, and tempers the solemnity and sincere patriotism of

[13] 'On Leaving St. John's College, Cambridge' in William Mason, *Works*, 4 vols. (London, 1811) I. 27.
[14] Mason, *Works*, i.31.

similar efforts with an element of elaborately disguised humour and self-parody. It is tempting to think, for example, that when writing this supposedly sincere and solemn praise of Cambridge, Gray recalled the verses he himself had written sometime in the spring or summer of 1742, when he found himself returning to Peterhouse as a Fellow–Commoner, following his return from the Grand Tour. The same Ignorance who is banished in the opening line of the 1769 *Ode for Music* had been created, in Gray's earlier verses, the local deity or 'genius of the place'. Gray's lines amusingly anticipate the physical and inspirational structures described in the opening lines of the *Ode for Music* complete with melancholic bowers, Gothic turrets and cloisters, and a lone and reverential Cantabrigian. The opening lines of the later *Ode for Music* ('Hence, avaunt, 'tis Holy ground'), had even been foreshadowed in the Miltonic opening of the early *Hymn to Ignorance* ('Hail, horrors, hail! ye ever-gloomy bowers, / Ye gothic fanes and antiquated towers, / Where rushy Camus' slowly-winding flood, / Perpetual draws his humid train of mud'). In the *Ode for Music* a 'willowy' river Cam 'lingers with delight'. In the earlier *Hymn to Ignorance* a sluggish, 'rushy', and 'slow-winding' Camus carries its 'humid train of mud'. In the *Ode* a solitary poet is surprised by an 'indignant lay' on the holy ground of Cambridge; in the *Ignorance* fragment the lone and isolated poet invokes not Milton or Newton, but the guardian of 'leaden' Ignorance. It is difficult, too, to read Gray's later description of the 'empyrean Day' that lights the Cambridge setting of the later poem without surmising that he himself recalled the 'native darkness of the sky' and 'damp cold touch' of the fogs in the earlier fragment.

While Gray thus appears at times to be writing the *Ode for Music* with an imitative eye towards Mason's earlier topographical poetry, while at the same time making self-parodic references to his own work, other elements of humour and parody enter the poem at a level that would almost certainly have been accessible to *all* his listeners and readers. One need hardly look any further than the most obvious textual cues for the kind of referential game Gray is playing with his auditors; the passage already quoted provides some excellent examples of a parodic–allusive technique which extends beyond self-parody to parodies of other works and of other authors.

Gray's stanzas, as Roger Lonsdale noted, deliberately and most explicitly echo lines 61–67 of *Il Penseroso* in their recollection of a verdant, rural solitude conducive to contemplative melancholy. Yet there are echoes as well (in phrases such as 'silver-bright', 'haunts of Folly', 'soft-eyed Melancholy') of poets as diverse as Shakespeare, William Drummond, Joseph Hall, Alexander Pope, and David Mallet. Why include such a wide range of allusive reference?

Is there a particular reference here, or has Gray finally and completely lost control of his notoriously kleptomaniacal poetic temperament?

There are a number of possible explanations. Perhaps the controlled tetrameter couplets of Milton's original verses were almost *too* delicately balanced for the expansive and exuberant tone Gray is seeking to establish here. Milton, far from being a pensive and isolated scholar, is described by Gray as '[r]apt in celestial transport' and surrounded by the 'choral warblings' of his fellow Cantabrigians – he is the absolute centre of dramatic and poetic attention. In any event, the allusive momentum of Gray's verse quickly moves the lines beyond Milton's own poetic utterances, and draws in the entire tradition of English poetry which *surrounds* Milton's work. Gray's Milton, in other words, is in these lines echoing not only himself and the writers of the generation which preceded his own poetic activity, but (given the historicity of the poet 'John Milton'), enunciating an anachronistically impossible, proleptic echo of the poets of the early and mid-eighteenth century as well.

If there is something startlingly hubristic about the ventriloquistic presumption of putting poetry in Milton's mouth in the first place, such hubris is perhaps mitigated by the subtly comic suggestion that Milton, in the hereafter, is himself as voracious, appetitive, and appropriative a poet as he had ever been in life. Although, again, the general significance of Gray's allusions has often been debated among critics, there is much to be gained in this particular instance by recalling the original setting of Milton's verses a bit more closely.

Readers will recall that in *Il Penseroso* Milton had described the life of a young poet in the 'studious cloister's pale' (a phrase explicitly and parodically echoed here by Gray) who is devoted to the task of gaining the wisdom and self-discipline necessary to the creation of a truly 'prophetic' strain of poetry. Gray himself, as the modern critic Clarence Tracy observed, had at times cultivated a similar kind of poetic melancholy that was not so much an affliction, as an enabling creative power.[15] In the opening lines of the *Ode for Music*, however, Gray's attitude towards this Miltonic aim of melancholia, as outlined in *Il Penseroso*, is qualified by a gentle irony. While Gray readily grants Milton the desired authority and rhetorical power of the prophetic poet, Milton's verses in Gray's poem remain *not* vatic and oracular, but derivative and parodic. If Milton, as Harold Bloom has argued, *is* the 'great Inhibitor', the producer of all that anxiety which blocks creativeness in subsequent generations of poets, he is here put in the unique position of having to confront not only his progenitors and his *own* creations but

[15] Clarence Tracy, 'Melancholy Marked Him for Her Own' in Downey and Jones, 38.

the creations of later English poets in the other world.[16] The Miltonic penchant for devouring other authors turns Gray's fictional 'Milton' into something of a poetic-celestial Uroboros, his own textual tail hanging obtrusively from his mouth.

The Recitative that follows Gray / Milton's initial praise of Cambridge contains a description of the '[h]igh potentates and dames of royal birth' who had been the major benefactors and benefactresses of the University in the course of its long history: Edward III, Mary de Valentia (Countess of Pembroke), Elizabeth de Burg (Countess of Clare), Margaret of Anjou, Elizabeth Widville (wife of Edward IV), Henry VIII, and, finally and most conspicuously, the 'venerable Margaret', the countess of Richmond and Derby, founder of St. John's and Christ's Colleges. This impressive assembly is described (again, rather comically) as 'pacing forth, with solemn steps and slow' to get a better look at the Senate House festivities.

The gathered nobility offer a modest justification of their gifts in the Quartetto which follows the *Ode*'s second Recitative.

> 'What is grandeur, what is power?
> 'Heavier toil, superior pain.
> 'What the bright reward we gain?
> 'The grateful memory of the good.
> 'Sweet is the breath of vernal shower,
> 'The bee's collected treasures sweet,
> 'Sweet music's melting fall, but sweeter yet
> 'The still small voice of gratitude.' (*PTG* 272)

The passage obviously recalls Gray's earlier *Elegy* in its evocation of the possibilities – and the inherent instability – of human memory and recollection. Here, it seems, the nobility can at least hope for the 'frail memorial' of institutional gratitude. The song of the nobility gently reminds its listeners that while the 'boast of heraldry' and the 'pomp of power' may indeed lead to the ubiquitous and unavoidable graves of the country church-yard, the beneficence of the aristocracy has, nevertheless, at least presented the occasion for the pealing anthem of Gray's own poem. If, as William Empson once suggested, the implied politics of the *Elegy* complacently justify a social arrangement that permits the aristocracy to exist in the first place, that complacency is explicitly emphasized in the middle of Gray's *Ode for Music* by the nobility's solicitation not only of recognition, but of thanks and gratitude.

---

[16]   Bloom, *The Anxiety of Influence*, 32.

In the closing stanzas of the poem Margaret of Anjou – 'leaning from her golden cloud' – praises the initiation of Grafton's Chancellorship on the 'festal morning' of his inauguration, and detects in his pedigree (Grafton was, among other things, a descendant of an illegitimate son of Charles II), a talent to bring to light the as yet undiscovered geniuses which will prove a credit to the university:

> 'Thy liberal heart, thy judging eye,
> 'The flower unheeded shall descry,
> 'And bid it round heaven's alter shed
> 'The fragrance of its blushing head:
> 'Shall raise from earth the latent gem
> 'To glitter on the diadem. (*PTG* 273)

The recollection of the *Elegy*'s language and imagery (the 'blushing, 'unheeded' flower, the 'latent gem') is again striking. Yet again, however, the imagery of the earlier poem seems to be invoked with a sense of parodic distance. The suggestion that the indiscrete and intemperate Grafton will single-handedly be able to correct the inequities of nature and society which remain unresolved in the *Elegy* is, in its own way, as comic as the implication that Milton – the great Protestant poet – cannot help, in the hereafter, imitating and echoing the verses of a disenfranchised Roman Catholic such as Alexander Pope.

Gray's poem ends by praising the new academic harmony to be had by the university under the guidance of the 'star of Brunswick', that is the leadership of George III and, as Roger Lonsdale has pointed out, the House of Hanover in general:

> 'Lo, Granta waits to lead her blooming band,
> 'Not obvious, not obtrusive, she
> 'No vulgar praise, no venal incense flings;
> 'Nor dares with courtly tongue refined
> 'Profane thy inborn royalty of mind:
> 'She reveres herself and thee. (*PTG* 273)

The moral as well as the academic fate of the University is in shakier hands than Gray seems openly to acknowledge here. Although the poet had, in a private letter to Grafton written in July 1768, pretended to admire Grafton's 'delicacy of mind', it is difficult to believe that Gray could sincerely praise before the public the 'inborn royalty of mind' of a man who had recently been guilty of a number of glaring political and social indiscretions, including appearing publicly at the theatre with his mistress, Nancy Parsons.

The performance of Gray's *Ode for Music* lasted just under one hour. Much of the humour, irony, and subtle self-reference seems to have passed unnoticed by Gray's initial auditors. The main criticisms of Gray's *Ode* (in many ways a surprising one given the poem's seeming narrative simplicity) concerned themselves with the 'complexity' and 'difficulty' of the work. The piece was, as Gough later reported, 'well set and performed, but charged with obscurity'.[17] Gray himself was content to let the occasion pass without much comment, and allowed Nicholls to speculate that 'the Ode was sung, and played, and applauded (all but) as it deserves'. Once the ceremony was over Gray hurried off to his friends in the north of England and embarked on a tour of the Lake District and Yorkshire. Although Richard Gough ventured to suggest that the *Ode* 'was not equal in part of beauty or sublimity to any of Mr. Gray's finer pieces', reception of the piece was generally favorable.[18]

Following the ceremony the guests exited from the Senate House in a markedly more decorous manner than they had first entered, and repaired to Trinity College Hall, where they were regaled on 'seven turtles and a number of haunches, with plenty of Claret, Champagne, and Burgundy'. Another account credited the Trinity Kitchen with providing no less than 'twenty turtles . . . and fifty haunches of venison', but it is doubtful, by that point in the evening, whether anyone was counting.[19]

*

The Installation Ode or *Ode for Music*, as it has since come to be known, was Gray's last major poetic production. Although Samuel Taylor Coleridge later saw fit to praise the work as 'very majestic', and seems genuinely to have preferred it to Gray's earlier Pindarics (which he characterized as 'frigid and artificial'), the piece has received little sustained critical attention since its initial publication following the Senate House ceremony in 1769.[20] Gosse noted that the work was not in Gray's 'healthiest vein', and regretted that the poet seemed, in this, his final effort, to have attempted a return to 'that allegorical style of his youth from which he had almost escaped'.[21] In our own century some references in the *Ode* have been traced to Christopher Smart's 'Song to David', and James Steele has contended that, given the nature of Gray's

[17] Nicholls, *Illustrations*, v.315.
[18] Ibid., v.316.
[19] Ibid.
[20] For Coleridge's comments see *Specimens of Table Talk*, ed. Henry H. Coleridge (London, 1835) ii. 353–54.
[21] Gosse, 183.

'whiggish' world vision, it is only fitting that he be the poet to write an ode eulogizing the Pittite Grafton.[22] Clarence Tracy argued that poem again attempted a justification of Gray's ethic of withdrawal and non-commitment. In the *Ode for Music*, Gray again struggled to legitimize his life of academic seclusion. Other critics and biographers such as Ketton-Cremer and Morris Golden have echoed what seems to be the general perception that the poem is perversely inscrutable, and lacks real emotional and political commitment, remaining at best a 'competent fulfillment of a debt of gratitude' – 'a good exercise'.[23] Eric Rothstein noted the prevalence of parodies of Gray's work in the mid-eighteenth century, but dismissed those parodic imitations as being of relatively little *literary* importance. Such parodies, he wrote, 'unlike classical imitations of the early eighteenth century, have no significant place in the history of poetry'.[24] One might well argue, however, that there is evidence enough from Gray's own comments in the spring and summer of 1769 regarding the field day the parodists were about to have with his latest production – and the anxieties concomitant to that treatment – to indicate that, at the very least, such parodies merit a 'significant place' in any account of Gray's own poetry. If nothing else, the parodic responses to Gray's work that appeared in the poet's own lifetime and in the years immediately following his death evince a significant degree of sheer poetic energy which *did* play an important role in the history of eighteenth-century poetry, and in fact reveal a significant and complex response to the issues and ideas that lay at the heart of Gray's own concerns as a poet – a response which certainly makes them worthy of closer attention.

The parodic *Ode for Music*, rather than obscuring and disguising the lyric voice by filtering it through various levels of narration, actually highlights and draws attention to that voice. Gray writes of female figures ('Granta' is herself personified as a woman), and writes *in* the female voice to create the 'loud symphonious lay' which moves towards its tremendous crescendo in the Senate House. Although Granta is – much like the poet–narrator of the earlier *Elegy* – pointedly described as 'not obvious' and 'not obtrusive', Gray's self-parodic sensibility in the *Ode for Music* allows him finally to do what he had never attempted to do before – to speak out in a poetic voice with clarity and even indulge in the imaginative luxury of speaking in and through the female voice. It is no accident that the final stanzas of the *Ode for Music* implicitly repudiate the marmoreal inscrutability of the *Elegy*'s epitaph with the

---

[22] Steele in Downey and Jones, 235.
[23] See Morris Golden, *Thomas Gray*, 100–102; Ketton–Cremer, 233–34.
[24] Rothstein, 73.

vigorous 'glad voice' of Cambridge's female protectors. In articulating the first parodic word, Gray paradoxically, with a *coup de grace*, articulated the last.

III. Lap'd in Elysium

Determined to put all controversy surrounding the *Ode* firmly behind him, Gray journeyed northward to visit Mason, who was then in residence at York, sometime in the middle of July. He was accompanied on the journey by Brown, who had decided to travel with Gray at least as far as Wharton's estate at Old Park. The pair had decided to stay with Mason for only a very few days before travelling on to Darlington (Mason had himself, by the end of August, decamped to Hartlepool). Even so, Gray must have thought to himself as the carriage carried the two men towards each of their friends, it was already something of a blessing to be moving so swiftly through the high summer scenery and away from the dusty torpor that would very soon again be settling on Cambridge. The first leg of their journey – along what Gray himself was comfortable calling 'the common northern road' – was by now a pleasantly familiar one. Gray had further declared his intention of pursuing some physical exercise while on his vacation. 'I am so fat', he confessed candidly to Wharton shortly before the visit, 'that I have suffered more from heat this last fortnight, than ever I did in Italy'. And this was no summer to be carrying any extra weight; in the heat of the midday sun the thermometer at Cambridge is said to have recorded a staggering temperature of 116 degrees Fahrenheit. The very prospect of later that autumn carrying out the tour of the Lakes that had been interrupted by Wharton's attack of asthma two years earlier, seemed even in its anticipation softly to cross Gray's mind like a refreshing breath of fresh air from the green fields, and even from the lowering summer skies.

Gray and Brown reached Old Park on about 26 July. They remained as Wharton's guests for over two months. Gray broke his stay on at least one occasion to undertake (on horseback, no less) the roughly twenty-mile journey across Sherraton Moor, to visit Mason at Hartlepool. An unbroken spell of wet and stormy weather in the Northeast had transformed the still-primitive roads in the district into a quagmire described by Gray as 'next to impassable'; even the roads heading towards and through Durham were close to unnegotiable. Brown appears to have begun the homeward journey back to Cambridge sometime toward the end of the second week of September; although Gray later noted in a letter that his friend had 'deviated a little from the common track' in his progress towards the south, Brown was safely back in his rooms in college by the 23 of the month. On 29 September, Gray and Wharton left Old Park themselves to set out on their long-anticipated journey to the Lake District. Wharton planned to travel with Gray at least as far as Keswick.

Their trip began disastrously. The two men undertook to travel on their first day's journey only as far as the tiny village of Brough, just over the Durham border in Cumbria (or what was then Westmoreland). The town boasted the ruins of a castle that had originally been built in the twelfth century within the remains of the ancient Roman fort of Verterae. The traveller's arrival that autumn likewise coincided with a heavily attended cattle fair; Gray would later comment that the tremendous herds gathered together on the hills just beyond the town resembled nothing so much as 'a great army encamp'd'. Wharton, however, was destined not to be vouchsafed a glimpse even of these modest, local attractions. Soon after the two men settled into their accommodations for the night, Wharton was again seized with a violent and debilitating fit of asthma. His breathing was apparently so laboured that he feared aggravating his condition any further and – much to the regret of both men – decided to return home to Old Park early the following morning. Gray, as some of his subsequent observations on the tour would make abundantly clear, deeply regretted the prospect of having to undertake this long-anticipated journey by himself. He almost certainly offered, at the very least, to accompany Wharton back home, and it is likely, given the depth of their friendship, that he likewise offered once again to defer his own tour of the Lakes and Yorkshire. Yet Wharton, who best knew the state of his own health, managed somehow to convince Gray otherwise. He may have done so, however, only after extracting from his friend a promise – a promise that Gray keep him informed of his own progress on the journey, by writing down an extended and scrupulously precise account of his travels.

True to his word, and almost from the moment Wharton left him at Brough, Gray began keeping a continuous account of his travels. Not since he had written his extensive and colourful letters from the Continent so many years earlier, when accompanying Walpole on the tour of France and Italy, had Gray attempted, even indirectly, such a precise and detailed journal or travel narrative. Indeed, although, as we have seen, Gray was in the habit of scribbling short notes and *aides-memoirs* regarding his previous journeys throughout England and Scotland, not since he had kept his own little, personal diary during those same months in France, had he had reason to devote an entire notebook to such an extensive account of one single such trip. That the account was originally intended for Wharton's own personal amusement there can be no doubt. In many passages, as the editors of Gray's correspondence point out, Wharton is addressed explicitly by his name or by his title, and his

absence is bewailed as the only imperfection to Gray's own enjoyment
(as when, for example, he cries out after his first glimpse of the picturesque expanse of Borrowdale: 'oh Doctor! I never wish'd more for
you'). Whether Wharton suggested that his friend's journal would prove
a salutary amusement to him at Old Park, or whether Gray himself
decided that such a travel account would at least begin to include
Wharton in some of the adventure of the tour remains unclear. Whatever the more particular circumstances of its origin, Gray's *Journal* of
his tour of the Lake District stands among the earliest of written paeans
to the sublime, 'Romantic' beauty of the region; the fact that it was
meant to be a highly personal account (it was emphatically not written
with an eye towards any kind of eventual publication), and the fact too
that its expressed desire was verbally to recreate the scenic landscape for
a sympathetic reader in the language of clear and vivid description, lend
the narrative a peculiar combination of candid authenticity, on the one
hand, and raw, imaginative power, on the other. Gray's *Journal* stands
as a testament to the modern reader that he too, at least, could nurture
the spirit of religious awe in which even the poets of the eighteenth
century from time to time walked with nature.

Gray originally wrote down his observations in two small notebooks.
He then transcribed these original passages and included them in
individual letters to Wharton. He waited until he had begun his
return journey to Cambridge, however, before he began sending these
transcriptions from the original journal notebooks to Old Park. A letter
sent to Wharton from Aston (where Gray was to break his homeward
journey) on 18 October, for example, includes the first portion of the
diary containing Gray's comments and observations for 30 September
and 1 October. A second letter to Wharton, dated 29 October and sent
from Cambridge, picks up the narrative of the tour from 1 to 3 October.
A November letter from Cambridge furthers the account by only two
days (continuing the events of 3 October and adding those of the next
day and evening), while a fourth – dated just after the new year on 3
January 1770 – brings Wharton up to date regarding the events of the
tour as of 8 October. A final section of the journal (the lengthiest individual portion by far, and one that constitutes nearly half the entire
account) Gray neglected himself ever to send to Wharton. This fifth and
final instalment of Gray's tour was eventually copied from his notebooks
by Mason's curate, Christopher Alderson, and sent from Aston by
Mason himself. Gray, as we shall see, was to have other things on his
mind in the spring and summer of 1770. After sending Wharton the
fourth of his own transcripted accounts, he appears to have lost track
of where in his travels he had last left off; once again encountering
Wharton at Mason's house in June, 1770, however, Gray may well have
acquiesced to his friend's request for the last, substantial instalment of

his travel journal, on which occasion the poet then, in all probability, permitted Alderson to copy the original and include it in a final letter to Old Park (Mason commented, when sending this last section of the *Journal* to Wharton, 'I inclose the fragment of the Journal 'which Alderson copied and desired me to forward you with his compliments'). The *Journal* was first published by Mason, as a continuous and uninterrupted document – though with a great many editorial insertions, omissions, and transpositions – in 1775.

*

Gray awoke on the morning of 30 September to a blustery mixture of clouds and sunshine. The winds were still sweeping down across the Lake District from the northwest, and although temperatures remained comfortable enough throughout the day, throughout the course of the afternoon the early morning's sunshine slowly gave way to dark and increasingly overcast skies. Any initial fears Gray might have harboured that his entire holiday would be plagued or even ruined completely by dreary, autumnal weather were not, however, to be realized. Following only one more day of heavy and slightly ominous conditions the winds shifted slightly to the south, carrying with them a series of dazzlingly sunny mornings and afternoons. Only the briefest of isolated showers would mar the perfection of the next few weeks. When writing to Wharton from Aston on 18 October, just after finishing his excursion, Gray would remark that he had been 'so favour'd by the weather, that my walks have never once been hinder'd till yesterday (that is during a fortnight & 3 or 4 days, & a journey of 300 miles, & more'). 'The weather', he would write similarly to Brown from Lancaster, on 10 October, '. . . favoured all my motions just as I could wish'.

Having left the colourful horse and cattle fair at Brough behind him, Gray was very soon passing through the town of Appleby, from which point he planned to follow the valley of the Eden further westward. In the distances to his left the fells of the Lake District could later that day be glimpsed towering in their multitude like 'a hundred nameless hills'. To Gray's right there soon appeared to stretch 'a great extent of black and dreary plains', although the heavy mass of the highest point of the Pennine Chain – Cross Fell, a great many miles to the northeast – could just be glimpsed between the mists and vapours which seemed, with sinister purpose, to hide its summit clearly from sight. Directly beside him the reaches of the Eden itself – 'rapid, clear, & full as ever' – reflected even under an overcast sky compelling views of Appleby's own seventeenth-century castle and Norman keep. Making reasonable progress throughout the morning, Gray crossed the Eden and the river Eamont – which flows north from Ullswater and in the eighteenth century formed

the natural boundary between Westmoreland and Cumberland –
sometime after noon. Gray paused in his journey at Penrith where, following a hearty lunch of trout and partridge, he undertook the first of
his 'walks', climbing a mile or so towards the top of Beacon Hill, whence
he could just glimpse the northernmost reaches of the nearly eight-mile-
long Ullswater.

Gray awoke on the second morning of his tour to overcast skies. The
winds from the southwest remained calm and gentle, however, and the
hovering clouds seem only to have added to the effect of chiaroscuro
that on all sides threw Gray's surroundings into dramatic contrasts of
dazzling light and an equally impressive, bleak, and impenetrable darkness. Gray first travelled the five miles to Ullswater, but soon left the
Keswick road to journey among the shady lanes which angled their way
along the vale of Eamont. By mid afternoon he was again on foot, climbing the 'fine pointed hill' of Dunmallet. 'From hence', Gray recounted
to Wharton, he

> saw the Lake opening directly at my feet majestic in its calmness, clear
> & smooth as a blew mirror with winding shores & low points of land
> cover'd with green inclosures, white farm-houses looking out among the
> trees, & cattle feeding. the water is almost every where border'd with
> cultivated lands gently sloping upwards till they reach the feet of the
> mountains, which rise very rude & aweful with their broken tops on
> either hand. directly in front at better than 3 mile's distance, *Place-Fell*,
> one of the bravest among them, pushes its bold broad breast into the
> midst of the Lake & forces it to alter it's course, forming first a large bay
> to the left & then bending to the right. (*CTG* 1077)

Descending Dunmallet by means of a lesser-used side avenue (which he
commented was 'only not' – i.e. only just barely not – 'perpendicular')
and continuing his journey along the western edge of Ullswater, Gray
late in the afternoon passed through the tiny village of Watermillock
before returning the seven miles to Penrith along the same road he had
first pursued southward earlier in the day.

By the morning of 2 October the clouds had at last fully given way
to a glorious brilliance of sunshine. The peak of Cross Fell alone
remained shrouded in its habitual cloak of high-altitude mists; the outlines of the other, nearer hills and mountains could now be seen 'very
distinct'. At ten o'clock in the morning Gray left Penrith for Keswick,
travelling along the same road that he and Wharton had first
attempted to take two years earlier. The route took him just north of
Threlkeld Common, Flaska Common, and Great Mell fell, and directly
through the towns of Penruddock and Threlkeld; to the immediate northwest loomed the distinctive mass of Saddleback (also called

Blencathra). The furrowed sides of the mountain, Gray wrote, 'were gilt by the noon-day Sun, while its brow appear'd a sad purple from the shadow of the clouds, as they sail'd slowly by it'. Just after midday he passed along the extreme south side of Skiddaw and its smaller 'cub', Latrigg; the former eminence itself – at just over 3,000 feet the highest of the Skiddaw range of fells – was perhaps the first of the mountains encountered on this tour to remind Gray of the Alpine scenery which had so many years ago awed both him and Walpole into the unwilling silence of stark and reverent contemplation. Passing still to the south of these peaks, Gray could then glimpse from a distance of some two miles the 'Vale of Elysium' – the stunningly beautiful stretch of dale along which the River Derwent connects the mass of Derwent Water, to the south, with Bassenthwaite Lake, to the north – 'the sun then playing on the bosom of the lake, & lighting up all the mountains with its lustre'.

Just before two o'clock in the afternoon Gray ate a hasty luncheon at the Queen's Head in Keswick, but was soon again exploring, unac-companied and on foot, among the nearest of the hills and dales. He carried with him on his walks a device that he called his 'mirror' or 'glass' – an instrument known to some as a Claude Lorraine Glass, named after the French landscape painter who perfected one such hand-held mirror in the seventeenth century. Gray's own device, as Mason would later describe it, was a small 'Plano-convex Mirror' some four inches in diameter on a black foil, and bound up in the manner of a notebook so as easily to be carried in a side pocket. The glass was 'a most convenient substitute' for a larger, bulkier camera obscura (liter-ally, a 'dark chamber'), an optical instrument consisting of a large, dark-ened box, into which natural light was admitted by means of a double-convex lens; an image of the external objects focused upon at a distance could then be seen conveniently and coherently recreated on a surface of paper, glass, or some other substance. Gray could thus use his own homemade 'mirror' to draw the frequently immense and close to overpowering vistas that surrounded him on all sides into rather more manageable – if temporary – perspectives. He clearly derived great enjoy-ment from this sense of participating in the construction and interpre-tation of the scenery around him, of himself 'half-creating' both the immensity and the providential design of the natural world. His first day's journey along the thick-hanging woods and long reaches of the Eden, for example, had found him confessing to Wharton 'much employment to the mirror'. The sunny afternoon of 2 October provided even better conditions for the use of Gray's optical glass. So absorbed was Gray in examining his surroundings through the interpretive lens of his pocket mirror that he at one point lost his footing and slipped to the ground, landing on his back 'in a dirty lane with [his] glass open in one hand'. Despite treating himself a nasty scrape which broke the skin across his knuckles, he stayed among the hills that same afternoon long enough to see 'the sun set in all its glory'.

Having already benefitted both mentally as well as physically from his excursions, Gray might later have been forgiven for noting the experiences of 3 October particularly to have constituted a day *creta notanda*. Rising at seven in the morning to what he later described to Wharton as 'a heavenly day', Gray began his explorations from Keswick with a walk to 'Borrodale' or Borrowdale, the aptly named 'Valley of the Fortress', the level expanse of which even then attracted more tourists and sightseers than any other valley in the Lake District. Accompanying Gray was his Keswick 'landlord' and part-time cicerone – probably one Hodgkins, described by Samuel Rogers in his Journal as 'a sensible fellow'. This Hodgkins later described his charge as difficult to please and 'peevish from ill-health'. Although, as we have seen, Gray himself had only one month earlier written of his intention to ride on horseback to visit Mason at Hartlepool, his Lake District guide is recorded as having observed that the poet '*could not* ride on horseback', and grumbled too that Gray had missed out on some of the most sublime views and prospects afforded by the region by refusing to 'go on the water' (although the recollection that Gray's brief Channel crossing years before had prompted him to be violently ill suggests that he may well have possessed – or at least had thought he possessed – sound and legitimate reasons for declining to undertake any boating tours).

Despite his cicerone's testimony regarding his 'peevish' and 'difficult' behaviour, Gray himself appears, from his own accounts, thoroughly to have enjoyed every moment of his tour that day. Having crossed the meadows from the Parsonage at an odd angle, he was soon delighting in the prospects that seemed on all sides dramatically to transform themselves 'at every ten paces'. He sketched the view from the foot of Walla Crag for Wharton as follows:

> opposite lie the thick hanging woods of Ld Egremont, & *Newland*-valley with green & smiling fields embosom'd in the dark cliffs; to the left the jaws of *Borodale*, with that turbulent Chaos of mountain behind mountain roll'd in confusion; beneath you, & stretching far away to the right, the shining purity of the *Lake*, just ruffled by the breeze enough to shew it is alive, reflecting rocks, woods, fields, & inverted tops of mountains, with the white buildings of *Keswick*, *Crosthwait*-church, & *Skiddaw* for a back-ground at distance. (*CTG* 1079–80)

It was after describing this particular view in his *Journal* that Gray exclaimed how much he missed Wharton's company on the journey. The afternoon held even more impressive sights in store, however. The rainy

weather of the preceding three months had swollen the waters of Lodore
Falls to an exceptional degree, and though Gray commented that the
volume of water was still 'not great', he yet enjoyed the privilege of
seeing the normally desultory cascade uncharacteristically 'leaping from
rock to rock, & foaming with fury'. Crossing under Gowder Crag, Gray
was struck by the 'dreadful bulk' of that mountain, and even more
intimidated by the piles of rocky fragments which had clearly – and only
recently – crashed to the base of the road from the shifting and uneasy
sides of the crag itself. 'The place', Gray confessed in his *Journal*,
'reminds one of those passes in the Alps, where the Guides tell you to
move on with speed, & say nothing, lest the agitation of the air should
loosen the snows above, & bring down a mass, that would overwhelm
a caravan'. Quoting a famous line from the third canto of Dante's
Inferno in which Virgil describes those 'wretched souls' who had earned
in their earthly existence neither praise nor blame ('Non rigioniam di
lor; ma guarda, e passa!' – 'Let us not talk of them, but look, and move
one'), Gray notes that having thus recalled his Alpine guides and the
rock falls of so many years ago, he here again 'took their counsel here
and hasten'd on in silence'.

Gray and his guide ended up breaking their journey at the compellingly situated village of Grange. In the fields just outside the town
they encountered 'a civil young Framer' who was overseeing the work
of his hired reapers (the region's crops of oats and barley were only just
then being harvested). The stranger soon led them to a tidy white cottage
in the village itself, where the young man's mother generously welcomed
the visitors to share in a lunch consisting of cold tongue, ale, bowls of
milk, and thin oat cakes on which could be spread some exceptionally
rich and creamy local butter. The farmer, who appears willingly to have
regaled Gray with a wealth of local information and anecdotes, turned
out to have been the same individual who, just one year earlier, had been
lowered down the side of a mountain cliff in order effectively to destroy
an eagle's aerie; Gray appears already to have heard something of the
young man's story from others. In order to prevent eagles from nesting
and breeding in the area (and consequently decimating the fields of
vulnerable young lambs, to say nothing of perpetuating a near holocaust
among the local population of hare, partridge, grouse, and pheasant),
the residents of the dale regularly resorted to destroying any of the brood
or eggs that could be found in the nests and even, when possible,
shooting the parent eagles themselves. The tendency of the surviving parent to find a new mate (probably, Gray speculated, in Ireland)
and then return to breed in the same location, served to make the grim
ritual described by Gray's host a regular and even yearly event. Such
anecdotes not only enlivened Gray's experiences and underscored his
own perceptions regarding the risks entailed by the near-atavistic

conditions governing simple human existence within such an overwhelming physical environment, but likewise appealed to the naturalist
in him; Gray appears to have been nicely satisfied by the fact, for
example, that he was able instantly to recognize from the farmer's
description of the eagle the precise species to which the bird belonged
('the Vultur *Albicilla* of Linneaus in his last edition'), and that he was
capable likewise of recommending not one but two volumes on the
subject to Wharton.

Suitably impressed, not to say intimidated, by the 'aweful ampithe-
atre' of mountains that surrounded Grange, Gray decided that he had
travelled far enough for one day. The sublime and epic grandeur of the
mountains seem to have brought Milton instantly to mind (though the
quotation from Dante, cited above, might indicate that Gray was mentally ranging among several of his favourite poets in search of a language
suitable to describe the overpowering beauty of the scene). Not very far
beyond where he and his guide had stopped at Grange, Gray wrote,

> the dale opens about four miles higher till you come to *Sea-Whaite* (where
> lies the way mounting the hills to the right, that leads to the *Wadd-mines*)
> all farther access is here barr'd to prying Mortals, only there is a little
> path winding over the Fells, & some weeks in the year passable to the
> Dale's-men; but the Mountains know well, that these innocent people
> will not reveal the mysteries of their ancient kingdom, the reign of Chaos
> & old Night. (*CTG* 1088)

The midday sun having long since burnt off the morning hazes and
evaporated the hoar-frost that had once again traced its way skyward
in thin and spidery wisps of bluish smoke, Gray and his guide similarly
retraced their own steps back to Keswick. Displaying a sensitivity to the
subtle transformations constantly wrought upon the colours of the environment by the angle and the intensity of the sun itself that might, alone,
have been worthy of any French Impressionist painter in the next
century, Gray could not help observing that although the features of the
landscape were themselves 'the same in part' as those they had seen
earlier in the day, entirely new aspects and details of the hills and dales
were again revealed to the receptive observer with almost each and every
step of their way. Throughout Gray's afternoon walk of about four miles
back to Keswick, the sun seemed fixedly to hold its place high in the
azure sky, the air was calm and perfectly serene, and the temperature
was as 'hot as midsummer'. Noting that he had thus passed up his best
and perhaps his only opportunity for making the ascent up Skiddaw
itself, Gray nevertheless seemed more than content with the manner in
which he had spent the better part of his day; as he wrote concisely to
Wharton both of the missed opportunity and of his own morning and

afternoon, 'I though it better employ'd'. Only moments later in his account, Gray was once again compelled to resort to the language of Milton (in this instance *Samson Agonistes*) when describing a solitary walk taken shortly after the sun had finally set in the west:

> In the evening walk'd alone down to the Lake by the side of *Crow-Park* after sunset & saw the solemn colouring of night draw on, the last gleam of sunshine fading away on the hill-tops, the deep serene of the waters, & the long shadows of the mountains thrown across them, till they nearly touch'd the hithermost shore. at a distance heard the murmur of many waterfalls not audible in the day-time. wish'd for the Moon, but she was *dark to me & silent, hid in her vacant interlunar cave*. (*CTG* 1089)

Gray spent the next day apparently on his own, exploring nearby Crow Park (which, 'though now a rough pasture' was 'once a glade of ancient oaks') and climbing the easy ascent through the woods of oak, spruce, and scotch-fir which covered Cockshott Hill. He praised the view from the top of the latter, modest rise as superior to that which could be glimpsed from Castle Head, further to the south, 'for', he wrote in the *Journal*, 'I find all points, that are much elevated, spoil the beauty of the valley, & make its parts (wch are not large) look poor and diminutive'. Gray's solitary ramblings kept him busy almost until the fall of evening. Just before returning to his lodgings at Keswick, he turned to catch a view of the setting sun in his 'glass', a view which, he confessed to Wharton, had he been able to transmit it and 'fix it in all the softness of its living colours, would fairly sell for a thousand pounds'. 'This', he wrote of his reflected 'composition' as he closed the first half of his *Journal* and then copied out the last of its passages he would personally transcribe and send to Wharton, 'is the sweetest scene I can yet discover in point of pastoral beauty'; 'the rest', he concluded, 'are in a sublimer style'.

*

The remaining portion of Gray's tour would feature scenes which partook perhaps more than he had at first anticipated in the 'sublimer style' of the District's more massive and, on occasion, shockingly impressive peaks. Gray stayed on a further three days at Keswick, resuming his forward journey only on 8 October, when he angled in a southeasterly direction and pushed towards the old wool and shoe manufacturing centre of Kendal (the son of a cloth merchant himself, Gray may well have been familiar with the eponymous town's once famous and widely distributed serge fabric, 'Kendal Green'). Gray's first day's experiences in and around Keswick and Grange had been close to inimitable, if only with respect to his whole-hearted exhilaration at once again finding himself surrounded by such humbling and awe-inspiring scenery. He nevertheless had little trouble keeping himself occupied. On 5 October he had furthered his pedestrian explorations around Derwent Water itself, crossing to the lake's western shore and continuing south past the village of Portinscale to view the masses of Skiddaw and Saddleback across face of the water, and through a suitably picturesque mixture of clouds and sunshine. A cold wind from the northeast ruffled the surface of the lake, urging its tiny, white-capped waves to break on the thin and rocky strand that divided the body of the Derwent from the trees and undergrowth which seemed on all sides eagerly to crowd about its waters. That same evening Gray once again followed the Penrith road, on this occasion retracing his steps about two miles back towards the northeast in order to inspect the Neolithic stone circle at Castlerigg. Like many of his contemporaries, Gray mistakenly believed the circle to be a relict of the Druids, the priestly caste of the Iron Age Celtic civilization that had flourished in Britain prior to the Roman conquest and consolidation of the region in the first and second centuries AD. Bearing some slight resemblance to its larger and more celebrated Wiltshire cousin, Stonehenge, the prehistoric stone circle at Castlerigg measures some 100 to 110 feet in diameter. Gray numbered some fifty of the circle's ancient, eight-foot-high monoliths lying nearly within reach of the almost preternaturally lengthy shadows cast by the rim of the surrounding mountains; a traveller visiting the sight today would count forty-eight stones – many of them still standing upright after the passage of almost two thousand years – among the circle and its subsidiary structures.

On 6 October Gray once again left his base at Keswick early in the morning, this time to pursue the road that wound directly around the base of Skiddaw some eight miles along the eastern edge of Bassenthwaite Lake. The route at several points dwindled into little more than rough cart roads and 'rugged' country lanes, but the view of the narrow ribbon of the lake itself – unbroken by any islands and stretching well into the northernmost distances of Westmoreland – which eventually broke towards the northwest appears to have repaid any inconveniences encountered in the course of the journey. Stopping to eat his lunch at a public house near a bridge that crossed the slight width of the river Derwent, Gray contented himself with 'sauntering a little by the waterside' before once again returning 'home'. Several small showers had moved across the fells in the course of the afternoon, but Gray was far more intrigued (and apparently almost childishly delighted) to learn from a fellow traveller that snow had actually fallen – so early in October! – on Cross Fell earlier that same morning.

Gray spent much of his final day in the neighbourhood immediately around Keswick revisiting Crow Park and once again taking an early evening walk along the Penrith road. The possibility of some few, light afternoon showers seem to have kept him close to the village itself; 7 October was, in any event, Keswick's market-day, and Gray's usual comments on his activities for the morning and afternoon include on this occasion some more general and speculative observations regarding the diet, economy, and natural history of the indigenous population – precisely the kind of information, in other words, which he could most easily have gleaned from casual conversations with and among the inhabitants themselves. Gray likewise concluded his journal entry for the same day with an 'excellent' (though to modern readers unnecessarily complicated) local recipe for the preparation of perch – a recipe which he directed explicitly to the attention of Mrs. Wharton.

On the morning of 8 October Gray began to travel by way of the Ambleside road the not inconsiderable distance south towards Kendal. Following the well maintained road that passed under the hovering mass of Helvellyn and skirted the eastern side of a placid Thirlmere, Gray reached the southern end of that narrow lake just in time to see the congregation of the small chapel at Wythburn leaving their Sunday morning services. Having soon passed the 'wild confusion' crowning Helm Crag, on his right, Gray nevertheless paused to capture the impressions of his first view of Grasmere in a language worthy of its situation and beauty. Just beyond Helm Crag, he wrote,

> opens one of the sweetest landscapes, that art ever attempted to imitate. (the bosom of [the] mountains spreading here into a broad bason) discovers in the midst Grasmere-water. its margin is hollow'd into small bays with bold eminences some of rock, some of soft turf, that half conceal, and vary the figure of the little lake they command, from the shore a low promontory pushes itself far into the water, & on it stands a white village with the parish-church rising in the midst of it, hanging enclosures, corn-fields, & meadows green as an emerald with their trees & hedges & cattle fill up the whole space from the edge of the water & just opposite to you is a large farm-house at the bottom of a steep smooth lawn embosom'd in old woods which climb half way up the mountain's side, & discover above them a broken line of crags, that crown the scene. not a single red tile, no flaring Gentleman's house, or garden-walls, break in upon the repose of this little unsuspected paradise, but all is peace, rusticity, & happy poverty in its neatest most becoming attire. (*CTG* 1098–99)

Gray had intended originally that Sunday to travel only as far as Ambleside. The town's best available accommodations proving upon closer inspection to be 'as dark & damp as a cellar', however, Gray in

turn 'grew delicate', and decided to persevere and travel the further fourteen miles to Kendal that same afternoon and evening. By the time he
entered the town that night, it was so dark that he mistook the many
rows of 'tenters' – the large wooden frameworks upon which the locally
manufactured cloth was stretched to dry in the open air – for actual
houses. His inn at Kendal looked at first to offer accommodation only
marginally better than that which he had declined to engage at Ambleside earlier that same day, yet the landlords quickly showing themselves
to be 'civil sensible people', Gray decided to remain in the town not one
but two nights.

His next day was spent – rather in the nature of a brief hiatus from
his recent outdoor excursions – poking around the village's large parish
church. He described in his *Journal* for Wharton a number of the individual chapel monuments; an altar tomb dating from the thirteenth
century and ornamented with brass arms and quarterings – still to be
seen to this day – was singled out has having been worthy of particular
notice. An after-dinner ramble took him along the Milnthrope turnpike
to see the river Kent and Sizergh Castle, the ancestral home of the Strick-
land family. The following morning found him moving even further to
the south, interrupting the twenty-two-mile journey to Lancaster only
once, at the small town of Burton. Lancaster itself he found in the midst
of its own harvest fair, but Gray busied himself rather among the great
castle, portions of which dated as far back as the twelfth century. On
the next day he crossed the river Lune and spent the morning listening
to the anecdotes of an old Cockler, whom he had found mending fishing
nets along the strand, related in a dialect strange to Gray's ear.

Within the next few days, Lancaster, Hornsby, and the small market
town of Settle were each explored in turn, before Gray's progress to the
south brought him once again in closer proximity to the mountain landscape. The distant and truly awe-inspiring view of the level summit of
Ingleborough – one of the most impressive and popular of the Yorkshire
hills – compelled the poet to refer to the eminence in his *Journal* in vital,
pantheistic terms; 'that huge creature of God', Gray called the mountain. His next day's visit to the tremendous ravine of Gordale Scar,
however, came very close to rivalling anything Gray had yet encountered
in his travels. Leaving the village of Malham on foot and clambering
towards the rough cliffs of the upper valley, Gray wrote:

> I followed my guide a few paces, & lo, the hills open'd again into no
> large space, & then all farther way is bar'd by a stream, that at the height
> of about 50 feet gushes from a hole in the rock, & spreading in large
> sheets over its broken front dashes from steep to steep, & then rattles
> away in a torrent down the valley. the rock on the left rises perpen-
> dicular with stubbed yew-trees & shrubs, staring from its side from the

height of at least 300 feet. but these are not the thing! it is that to the right, under which you stand to see the fall, that forms the principal horror of the place. from its very base it begins to slope forwards over you in one black & solid mass without any crevice in its surface, & overshadows half the area below with its dreadful canopy. when I stood at (I believe) full 4 yards distance from its foot, the drops which perpetually distill from its brow, fell on my head, & in one part of the top more exposed to the weather there are loose stones that hang in air, & threaten visibly some idle Spectator with instant destruction. it is safer to shelter yourself close to its bottom, & trust the mercy of that enormous mass, wch nothing but an earthquake can stir. the gloomy uncomfortable day well suited the savage aspect of the place, & made it still more formidable. I stay'd there (not without shuddering) a quarter if an hour, & thought my trouble richly paid, for the impression will last for life. (CTG 1107)

The morning of 14 October found Gray travelling towards Skipton, and then pushing farther to the southeast through the Wharfe valley to Otley. By the time he reached the 'smoky ugly busy town of Leedes', however, his vacation was effectively over, and he 'drop'd all farther thoughts' of keeping his journal. Making his homeward journey by way of Aston, Nottingham, Leicester, and Huntingdon, Gray finally reached Cambridge on 22 October. He seems already – before he had even begun to settle back into his academic life at Cambridge – to have begun planning his next summer's excursion to Wales.

*

Gray's *Journal*, again, was not published in his own lifetime, nor, indeed, would the poet ever have considered such a private and occasional memoir to have been in any way suitable for a larger, public audience. Yet, as one recent critic of Gray's travel writing has asserted, Gray – 'without ever intending it' – was paradoxically 'destined to become one of the first significant British travel writers'.[25] There are several possible explanations for such an odd development, some of them rather obvious, others perhaps not quite so apparent to nor so readily discernable by modern readers.

The most plausible explanation for Gray's eventual inclusion among the ranks of the most respected and influential English travel writers – for the easy and appropriately natural impulse to place his *Journal* high in the same category with such works as, say, Arthur Young's *Six Month's Tour Through the North of England* (1770), Dorothy

[25] William Ruddick, 'Thomas Gray's Travel Writing' in Hutchings and Ruddick, 127.

Wordsworth's *Journals*, or, even more tellingly, William Wordsworth's own *Description of the Scenery of the Lakes in the North of England* (1810) – is quite the simplest: it belongs there. At their best, Gray's travel narratives and his descriptions of the natural scenery in the Lake District, in particular, anticipate and even rival those offered by the region's better-known popularizers among the next two generations of English writers. Wordsworth himself, so often portrayed as Gray's poetic and stylistic nemesis, appears actually to have credited Gray's abilities as a poet – to which he refers as his 'Author's powers of mind' – with having provided his predecessor both with the perception and with the compositional skills to describe the area 'with distinctness and unaffected simplicity'.[26]

Subsequent readers, even those thoroughly familiar with Wordsworth's poetry and prose, have likewise rarely failed to acknowledge the arguably unprecedented achievement of Gray's travel writing – the apparently seamless combination in many passages in the *Journal* of a careful, responsible, and authentically precise description of the natural world, on the one hand, with an ability at the same time accurately and unaffectedly to gauge the transformative *power* of that landscape on the individual human imagination. One twentieth-century critic, William Ruddick, has perceived in many of Gray's mid- and later-life travel writings an even more powerful synergy between this first aspect of his descriptive prose – his habitual tendency towards 'exact' and 'constantly specific' observation – with 'a spatial and potentially pictorial sense of natural beauty in a landscape which Gray does not seem to have possessed as a younger man'.[27] Not only, in other words, is Gray capable of describing what he sees in the Lakes with care and precision, he possesses a rare ability likewise to concentrate the most prominent features of that perceived landscape into an aesthetically pleasing and organized whole; like a skilled painter, Gray recreates the fundamental reality of what he observes – its forms, colours, tones, contrasts, and natural presence – at the same time that he draws it together and spatially 'composes' it within the framed canvas of his patient, considered prose. His habit of pausing whenever possible to view the natural environment through the lenses of his hand-held 'glass' must surely have facilitated this ability to draw the various and disparate elements of the greater landscape into a perceptual whole – to make them, if only for a single and carefully preserved moment in time, cohere.

[26] *Wordsworth's Guide to the Lakes*, ed. E. de Selincourt (Oxford: Oxford University Press, 1970) 69; quoted in Ruddick, 'Thomas Gray's Travel Writing' in Hutching and Ruddick, 142.
[27] William Ruddick, 'Thomas Gray's Travel Writing' in Hutchings and Ruddick, 134.

A simple recognition of this participatory, creative component of Gray's travel writing – only partially constitutive yet nonetheless vital to the overall effect of his account – leads one soon to isolate some of the other distinguishing characteristic of the *Journal* which may also have contributed to its influence and success. Despite the fact, for example, that Gray was himself an avid and lifelong reader of travel narratives (both ancient and modern), he seems rarely to have felt the need, in his own travel writing, ever to refer to those earlier works; this last feature of writings such as the *Journal* forms quite a contrast, of course, to Gray's all-pervasive habits of parodic reference and allusion in his poetry and in his regular correspondence. Unlike all of his verse and most of his surviving prose, Gray's descriptive travel accounts – which for the most part pointedly eschew the unremitting sub-strata of literary reference that characterizes his other writing – often appear very close to spontaneous, or even 'artless'. Perhaps the generically dictated nature of the travel writer's act of immediate and unmediated *participation* within the landscape itself discouraged any sustained or possibly intrusive reference to 'literary' sources extraneous to the very moment of perception. Gray carried a great many texts in his head, and we should never forget that the allusive habits of his writing lifetime were very close to instinctive, spontaneous, and at times subconscious; yet the generic imperatives of the travel narrative which demanded, first and foremost, a scrupulously accurate description of the world that exists beyond the embodied self of the author seem on some level to have mitigated (at least in later accounts such as the *Journal*) against such reference. Having said this, it should at the same time be noted that Bruce Redford has suggested that the scope of Gray's literary reference in his Lake Country *Journal* is in actual fact no less wide-ranging or persistent than in his other correspondence. Quoting a much criticized passage from the poet's description of 'the jaws of Borodale', Redford observed that the account is presented to its reader as a deliberately composed 'georgic setpiece'. Even in the travel writing, as Redford noted, 'Gray's instinct for compression in all aspects of the letter – narrative, judicial, descriptive – teaches him to rely on allusion for the array of tones and details he chooses not to supply directly.'[28]

Gray's immediate audience in the *Journal* likewise exerted a profound influence on his style and, consequently, contributed to the power and subsequent influence of the narrative itself. Gray's letters to Wharton are for the most part no less playful, allusive, or stylistically complex than those he wrote to his other regular correspondents; in particular, his letters to Wharton participate in the semi-coded language peculiar

[28] Redford, *The Converse of the Pen*, 95–106.

to the small, collegiate society to which they had both, originally, belonged, and in which their earliest acquaintance had been rooted. In the *Journal* narrative, however, Gray's primary aim is neither to flavour his latest, gossipy serving of University news with the spice of wit, nor, in this particular account, is he all that concerned to convey under the cover of other 'languages' and other texts a hidden or elaborately encrypted meaning. He desired rather immediately and viscerally to recreate for Wharton – who for the second time in the space of less than three years had been denied the opportunity of experiencing such environments for himself – the details and the emotional and spiritual effects of his surroundings. Generic, literary allusions and embedded references to the pictorial conventions of the graphic arts had there place in such a personal and specifically directed account, but they needed – in order for the *Journal* to accomplish its occasional purpose – prudently to be kept to a minimum. The layered density of coded reference that works always to add meaning and resonance to Gray's verse is, again, largely absent in the Lake District *Journal*; the resultant prose is often sparer, crisper, clearer. It is at the same time, quite frequently, rather more emphatically plastic than much of Gray's other writing – whatever rethinking, rewriting, and recrafting there is to the *Journal*'s substance and style occurs much more than is usually the case in Gray's published writing on the surface of the work. In his description of his passage through the wild Craven scenery between Lancaster and Settle on 12 October, for example, Gray writes:

> The nipping air (tho' the afternoon was growing very bright) now taught us, we were in Craven. the road was all up & down (tho' no where very steep). to the left were mountain-tops (Weryside), to the right a wide valley (all inclosed ground) & beyond it high hills again. in approaching Settle the crags on the left drew nearer to our way, till we ascended *Brunton-brow*, into a chearful valley (tho' thin of trees) to *Giggleswick* a village with a small piece of water by its side covered with coots. (*CTG* 1106)

The qualifications articulated here – 'tho' the afternoon was very bright', 'tho' no where very steep', 'tho' thin of trees' – appear largely unpremeditated and spontaneous. The language is similarly easy-going and idiomatic: the 'nipping air', the 'up and down' road, the 'chearful village' with its 'small piece of water'. Less polished by far than Gray's poetry, the narrative of the *Journal* nevertheless resolves itself into a style which is, in its own way, bracingly casual and intimate.

One additional advantage of the fact that the *Journal* was intended for the private audience of a close and confidential friend, of course, was

the often unselfconscious inclusion by its author of incidents and observations of a highly personal nature. Many passages in the account as
it was eventually published – even in Mason's earliest, bastardized
version – would surely have been excised from a more designedly public
document. Gray's ignominious slip in the muddy lane near Keswick, his
conversation with the young farmer on 3 October (through which,
perhaps, shines the slightest of romantic infatuations?), his chat with the
cockler on the sands near Pooten, on Morecambe Bay, even the recipe
included for the benefit of Mrs. Wharton: all these moments remain vital
to Gray's account precisely because they present to readers a unique
combination of general observation and undisguisedly personal anecdote. Gray – as much as is ever possible in his writing – by addressing
his account to Wharton came close to letting his epistolary and stylistic
guard down.

Finally, the *Journal* may unintentionally have managed to strike a
sympathetic chord in subsequent visitors to and chroniclers of the Lake
District in its determined avoidance of the obviously 'picturesque'. Gray,
in his account of his travels, wants as little as possible to do with the
burgeoning Cumbrian tourist industry. Although we have long tended
to credit (or to blame) the first generation of Romantic writers – writers
such as Wordsworth, Coleridge, Southey, DeQuincy, and Mary Robinson – with having 'discovered' and truly popularized the Lake District,
we tend likewise to forget that the sustained and arguably catastrophic
explosion of the region's tourist industry in the very late eighteenth and
early nineteenth centuries was due, at least in part, to the incentive
created by the on-going war with France for a growing middle class to
vacation at home rather than abroad. The proselytizing topography of
Wordsworth's poetry and the summer invasions of the urban bourgeois
which, by even by the second decade of the nineteenth century, had
already transformed the local culture and industry of the region almost
beyond recognition to living memory, in reality only reaped a foul
harvest sown some few generations earlier. Years before Gray had even
considered a trip to the Lakes, poets such as John Dalton had celebrated
the area's sublime and 'awful' scenery as worthy of a thoughtful contemplation; John Brown, Arthur Young, and William Gilpen in the
1770s and 1780s were only following and exploiting a trend already
established by their predecessors. Gray, as William Ruddick has emphasized, constantly avoided those 'views' and obligatory stations (what we
would today refer to as the 'tourist traps') which were surrounded by
the local industry already lying in wait to entertain and to exploit
unwary visitors to the region. As a salutary corrective to the interpretations usually advanced to explain the tour-guide Hodgkin's recollections
of Gray's 'timid' reluctance to take to the water on his Lakeland tour,
Ruddick observes:

Gray may well have felt nervous about venturing on the water, as his early detractors claimed, but it seems equally likely that he did not relish the prospect of submitting himself to the attentions of the Keswick boatmen, who would have given him what had already developed into the stock ride round the lake, stopping off at recognized places to savor the correct impressions of sublimity (on the way out towards the head of the Lake and Borrowdale) and beauty (on the return). An eagerly-anticipated experience of discovery would have turned into what we might think of as a 'theme park' experience . . .'.[29]

What Gray would think of the Lake District could he see it today is perhaps better left unimagined. Readers touring the area with a copy of his *Journal* in their pockets or their rucksacks today, however, cannot help but detect beneath the surface of Gray's honest admiration of the Lakes the stirrings of an anxiety which may well have suspected that he was to count himself among the last generation of visitors vouchsafed a view of the region's beauty before it became so thoroughly overrun and commodified that it threatened to disappear entirely. Those same readers, turning from the bare and well-worn paths of packed dirt beneath their feet, from the traffic and the tea rooms and the stands of Beatrix Potter postcards, and from the ubiquitous motor-launches whining and sputtering in a haze of bluish exhaust on the surface of the lakes themselves, are likely to lose their thoughts in the sympathy of imaginative retrospection and, understanding its impulse, quietly read on.

[29] William Ruddick, 'Thomas Gray's Travel Writing' in Hutchings and Ruddick, 136.

CHAPTER TWELVE

AMOROUS DELAY

Charles Victor de Bonstetten
1769–1770

I. Entering the *Nemorum Nox*

Toward the end of November 1769, Gray received a letter from Norton Nicholls, who was then close to winding up his own, extended autumn vacation from his parish duties with a two-week visit to Bath. Nicholls's progress towards the increasingly fashionable spa town from his rectory at Bedingfield had been a leisurely one. Having first travelled to Southampton, from which vantage he passed three days exploring the Isle of Wight, Nicholls then spent a relaxing six weeks with a cousin in Dorset before finally heading north into Somerset. The mild weather, which at the beginning of Nicholls's rambles had only just begun to tinge the fields and woods with, as he put it, 'a 1000 beautiful varieties of colour', provided an entire pallet of transient and mournfully delicate, autumnal backdrops to the suitably unexacting drama of his own sporadic sightseeing.

Nicholls lingered briefly at Stourhead, the elegant home of the banker Richard Hoare near Stourton, in Wiltshire. He was duly impressed by the improvements that had only recently been effected in the property's landscape gardens by the architect Henry Flitcroft. Hoare was among the first Englishmen to permit his gardens to forsake the grand, geometrical formations patterned after the French manner of Le Nôtre, and so allow them instead to pursue a more sinuous, irregular, and calculatedly 'natural' design. The valley's small and undistinguished meres had been transformed, in the process, into picturesque lakes, bordered by elegant, ornamental trees and shrubbery. While in the neighborhood, Nicholls informed Gray, he had also visited 'Persfield' or Piercefield, the country seat and gardens of one of their mutual acquaintances, a Mr. Morris.

The city of Bath itself had even come as something of a surprise to Nicholls; the town had undergone some impressive changes in recent years. For a visitor such as Nicholls, John Wood the Elder's stunningly elegant renovation of the ancient Roman city of Aquae Sulis into a Palladian playground for the rich, the fashionable, and the famous, was impressive if only in its thorough-going uniformity. The distinctive, honey-coloured stone of the local quarries seemed, by the time Wood was through with it, gracefully to stretch and to wind itself around every curve of the Avon valley's steep hills. 'It was so new a sight to see a town built of hewn stone', the London native confessed, 'instead of ragged dirty brick, and streets and parades on a regular plan, and above all the circus, instead of the confused heap of building of all shapes and sizes which compose every other town in England'. In the distances beyond the circus and the still-emerging Royal Crescent (the stunning sweep of the latter would not be completed by the younger Wood for another four years), the neighbouring country appeared to rise with a watercolour grace toward the sky, its sportive hedges broken strategically by the shade of fine old trees, its cultivated fields likewise divided into discrete and tidy parcels by the intervening blankets of its woods.

Nicholls's most pressing reason for writing to Gray, apart from the simple fact that it seemed to him like 'an age' since he had last received any word from his friend, was to alert him to the fact that he had, while staying in Bath, taken the liberty of placing a letter of introduction to Gray in the hands of a new acquaintance, a vibrant and excitable young man from Switzerland by the name of Charles Victor de Bonstetten. Only a few nights earlier, as Nicholls explained to Gray, he had attended a ball that had been held at the town's new Assembly Rooms. The rooms had very soon become crowded to the point of immobility. Cramped and unable even to see who was dancing with whom, the energetic and improvisational Nicholls decided suddenly to scramble onto the top of a nearby table, thereby providing himself with the height and the perspective that afforded a sweeping view of the social activity taking place below. No sooner had Nicholls mounted the table-top, however, than he found himself being joined there by Bonstetten, who had in a similar manner leapt to the surface as he sought a temporary refuge from the press of the crowd. As the crush of spectators on all sides threatened still to jostle them from their perch, the two men found themselves clinging together precariously for the pretense of stability. Their impulsive and spontaneous embrace, as Bonstetten would write many years later, signalled the exuberant beginning of a lasting friendship. At the time, Nicholls himself wrote with considerably more reservation to Gray that he had purposefully picked Bonstetten out 'from among the mob in the rooms here'. It would have been far more honest for him to have confessed, from the start, that the two men had literally been thrown into each other's arms.

For all of Nicholls's slightly coy reticence with regard to the precise circumstances of this first meeting with Bonstetten, his enthusiasm for his new acquaintance fairly bubbled over in the letter he soon wrote to Gray – a letter in which he described his new acquaintance at length. 'I shall be a little disappointed', he confessed to the poet,

> if you do not think him better than common for his age, and very little spoiled considering that he is the only son of the treasurer of Berne, and

of one of the six noble families which bear the chief sway in the aristocracy. He was first at the university of Lausanne; afterwards his father sent
for him home; then he went to Leyden, but thought Holland a most triste
pays, and begged to be released, so he had leave to cross over to England;
he seems to have read, and to be unwilling now to waste his time if he
knew how to employ it; I think he is vastly better than any thing English
(of the same age) I ever saw; and then, I have a partiality to him because
he was born among mountains; and talks of them with enthusiasm –
of the forests and pines which grow darker and darker as you ascend,
till the *nemorum nox* is completed, and you are forced to grope your
way; of the cries of eagles and other birds of prey adding to the horror;
in short, of all the wonders of his country, which disturb my slumbers in
Lovingland. (*CTG* 1085–86)

Although Nicholls refers with natural familiarity to the Suffolk district
in which he was then living – Lothingland (from nearby Lake Lothing,
and sometimes called by the locals 'Lovingland') – the more humourous,
metaphorical connotations of his confession that his 'slumbers in Lovingland' have recently been 'disturbed' by such sublimely erotic dreams
lie only just beneath the surface of his fanciful epistolary prose. Both
Nicholls and Gray were about to tumble into one of the most emotionally fraught – and for Gray, at least, one of the most emotionally painful
– romantic friendships of their lives. For the past several years – at least
since the production of the Pindaric *Odes* and the experiments in Norse
and Welsh poetry – Gray had successfully deflected or avoided the deeper
impulses of his emotional or sexual life. His focused, scholarly projects
at Cambridge, no less than his regular travelling had served, as Jean
Hagstrum suggested, as 'socially and personally acceptable substitutes
for the more dangerous passions'; with the appearance of Bonstetten, as
Robert Gleckner has further observed, 'all of the conflicting, largely
repressed feeelings involved in Gray's intense relationship with West
... surged to the surface'.[1] The *nemorum nox* or 'dark and gloomy
wood' that Nicholls here appropriately if unintentionally describes as
having constituted the 'selva oscura' of Gray's own later years was
an autumnal labyrinth which would in time lead to the unlooked-for
revelation of some disturbing personal and sexual truths.

*

By the time he had precipitated himself into Nicholls's ready arms
in the autumn of 1769, Bonstetten was already a man with something
of a past – if, indeed, such a thing is possible for a young man only

---

[1] Hagstrum in Downey and Jones, 8; Gleckner, 181.

twenty-four years old. As Nicholls had faithfully reported to Gray, Bonstetten had been born into one of the small but still powerful families of the Swiss aristocracy. His father was 'Trésorier' or the treasurer of the canton of Berne. Even as a very young man, Bonstetten had enjoyed a reputation for possessing, as his father would later recall, an 'esprit ardent et inconstant' – a 'spirit' or personality both impassioned and erratic in its romantic, aesthetic, and social impulses. He had been educated, again as Nicholls noted in his letter to the poet, both at Geneva and Lausanne, but such formal education appears to have had little if any effect on his volatile and eagerly mercurial temperament. The intellectual currents of the day seemed often, at that time, to carry fashionable young men into certain calculated and even predictable directions; a sketch of Bonstetten's career suggests that as a very young man he had religiously followed every dip and eddy of the well-established routes those currents had carved in the often posturing walls of an impressionable, European youth. He professed an early, intellectual passion both for Rousseau and for Voltaire, although – much like Boswell before him – he came eventually to dismiss the former thinker, at least, as having been guilty of certain 'deficiencies in his understanding'. Like Boswell, too, Bonstetten paid his respects to Rousseau in person; he also visited Voltaire. It was not Boswell but Edward Gibbon whom he resembled, however, when he evinced a rather more corporeal passion while in Lausanne for Suzanne Curchod (later Madame Necker) who, as Gibbon would write in his *Memoirs*, possessed the same, rare combination of personal attractions 'embellished by the virtues and talents of the mind', upon which later observers would often seize as the defining characteristic of Bonstetten himself.[2] Gibbon's renunciation of the future Madame Necker is well known; a similar termination to Bonstetten's imitative infatuation was, consequently and in time, only to be expected.

Bonstetten was to remain throughout his long life a dedicated follower of fashion. He claimed to have been born with the heightened and often mournful sensibility of the era's increasingly fashionable model of male generosity and fraternity – the hyper-sensitive and often excessively lachrymose 'Man of Feeling'. The vogue for the pose of Romantic sensibility was already on the rise. Taking their cue in England from the work of popular philosophers like Anthony Ashley Cooper, Third Earl of Shaftesbury, and from poets such as Thomson, Blair, and Young (and even, to some extent, from Gray himself), a younger generation of thinkers and writers sought actively to cultivate a heightened susceptibility to delicate feelings, an emotional responsiveness often

---

[2] Edward Gibbon, *Memoirs of My Life*, ed. Georges A. Bonnard (London: Thomas Nelson and Sons, 1966) 84.

and best expressed by the flow of sympathetic tears. Bonstetten himself claimed that he had once, while still a boy, been so overwhelmed by the misfortune attendant even the happiest of mortal lives as to have gone through the motions of committing suicide, much in the manner of Goethe's Werther. The romantic sight of a pendant moon breaking through the scudding night clouds was alone enough, he would later intimate, to sway him from his purpose. In fact, Bonstetten's seemingly histrionic melancholy anticipated the larger cultural phenomenon of 'Wertherism' to an uncanny degree. Had he been born only a few years later, Bonstetten might very well have ended up as one of the seeming multitude of prematurely self-slaughtered corpses – dutifully clad in their yellow breeches and blue coats – which were rumoured eventually to litter the European countryside.

Bonstetten's own destiny, for better or worse, had led him instead to England. When Nicholls first encountered him at Bath, Bonstetten had only recently crossed the Channel from Holland where, with his father's permission, he had supposedly been continuing his education. The ostensible object of his visit to Britain was to learn the English language. After a very short stay in London, Bonstetten chose to lodge himself with a clergyman's family in Berkshire – a family characteristically and with unerring charm impossibly designated by Bonstetten himself as belonging to a 'Mr. Schmidith'. With the manic and erratic diligence so typical of his personality, Bonstetten had quickly set himself to his work. He soon wrote to his father that he was charmed by the English people. 'Oh! le bon pays que l'Angleterre!', he gushed soon after his arrival, 'qu'il est doux de vivre chez un peuple où les hommes sont généreux, bons, humains, et les femmes belles et modestes...' ('Oh, what a wonderful country England is! How sweet it is to live among a people where the men are generous, good-hearted, and humane, and the women both beautiful and modest').[3] Not very much time passed, however, before word of the increasingly lavish entertainments and seasonal pastimes that were to be enjoyed at Bath reached the young man's ears. There was little harm, Bonstetten no doubt reasoned, in supposing that one could learn the language as well – if not better – from the members of the *beau monde* as from a rural curate and his family. And so it came to pass that Bonstetten, one late November evening, found himself clutching the energetic rector from Suffolk on a table-top in the public rooms in Bennett Street.

Within only weeks of his first encounter with Nicholls, Bonstetten left the social whirl of Bath and made his way once again to London.

---

[3] Reprinted in Marie-L. Herking, *Charles Victor de Bonstetten 1745–1832, Sa vie, ses Œuvres* (Laussanne: Imprimerie La Concorde, 1921) 64.

Nicholls – not at all alone in being impressed by the young man's character and undeniably handsome appearance – was nevertheless determined on taking the lead in facilitating the traveller's progress through
English society. By the time Bonstetten once again set foot in the capital,
Nicholls had been sure to provide him with letters of introduction not
only to Gray, but also to such individuals as Thomas Pitt of Boconnoc,
Cornwall (the eldest brother of William Pitt, Earl of Chatham, a friend
of Walpole's and eventually, in his own right, Baron Camelford), and
to Pitt's society acquaintance and confidant, Mrs. Hay. Bonstetten was
officially presented at Court where, in general and unsurprisingly, as
Nicholls put it, he 'succeeded very well'. The Court presentation was a
formal affair (the rank of Bonstetten's father as an aristocratic professional appears to have fulfilled the necessary requirements of status), and
the young man made quite an impressive showing in an elegant outfit,
complete with the knee-breeches and buckle shoes required by the
occasion, his sword hanging by his side, his mouth judiciously, if only
momentarily, shut.

Meanwhile back in Cambridge, Gray had been so impressed by his
friend's eager description of Bonstetten that in early December, just a
few weeks after receiving Nicholls's letter, he travelled up to London
with the sole purpose of meeting this fascinating young man for himself.
Gray's first few days in town yielded few amusements. The weather was
gloomy, and the 'reigning diversion' of the season was an exhibition of
the Italian Fantoccini's at Hickford's Rooms in Pariton Street – a puppet
show that Gray dutifully attended and which he in fact appears to have
found mildly entertaining. Gray, who had for a number of weeks had
some reasons for being concerned regarding his old friend, Dr.
Hurd, was able to set his mind partly to rest regarding his fears for the
latter's health. Together the two men spent an hour of one overcast
morning walking in and around Lincoln's Inn Fields. Stonhewer, too,
was in town, as were Mason's acquaintances – Viscount Newnham
and the optician Jesse Ramsden – with each of whom Gray passed some
time.

Finally, he was brought together with Bonstetten. Although no
account of the precise circumstances surrounding their first, face-to-face
meeting has been preserved, the encounter must certainly have been for
both parties a pleasant one. Bonstetten was himself so impressed and
even overwhelmed by the great poet that he appears almost immediately
to have decided once again to forsake the social activity of London for
the opportunity of indulging in somewhat more studious pastimes. For
his own part, Gray was struck to the point of infatuation; no one he
had met in recent years possessed half the charm, vitality, and seeming
diligence as this elegant young man from Berne. Some few days were
spent in seeing the sights of what was still, it must be remembered, Gray's

native city, yet the main force of attraction between the two men lay largely in the substance of their conversations. Bonstetten unaffectedly drank in the judgements and opinions of the man to whom he was soon referring in his dutiful letters home as the premier poet in England; he basked in the warm affection so liberally offered by his celebrated guide. For his own part, Gray found the respectful attention of so compelling an individual very close to intoxicating. The earliest days of their friendship were marked, at least on Gray's side, by the same giddy sense of infatuation which had characterized his earliest romantic attachments. The encounter with Bonstetten was for the poet, for lack of any better expression, a matter of love at first sight. The gloom of the weather and of the season had suddenly been dissipated; in its place Gray felt an enthusiasm and a thirst for life – a vital sense of purpose – of a sort that he could not remember having experienced for a great many years. He felt, as close as one can experience such a feeling at all, a return of youth, a 'second spring'.

A great many years after Gray's first meeting with Bonstetten, Sir Egerton Brydges would write in his *Autobiography* of having personally been told an anecdote by Bonstetten relating to his stay in London, and to his earliest days in Gray's company. The new friends had supposedly been making their way along the crowded city streets one afternoon when Gray discerned lumbering ahead of them the large and erratic figure of Dr. Samuel Johnson. 'Look! look! Bonstetten!' Gray is said to have cried as he pointed out the figure to his companion, 'the great bear – there goes *Ursa Major!*'.[4] While Bonstetten is unlikely completely to have fabricated such an anecdote, we know that the nickname of 'Ursa Major' was independently and sneeringly bestowed on Johnson by Lord Auchinleck only some few years later, when Johnson undertook his famous journey to the Hebrides, and on which occasion both he and Boswell stayed with the latter's father in Ayrshire. And although the appearance of scorn or bitterness inherent, too, in Gray's supposed remark is disconcerting, one only reluctantly dispenses as anachronistic with the only recorded encounter which brings the two figures – one the most influential and respected poet of his age, the other perhaps the most personally authoritative literary arbiter of all time – together at all. Gray had admittedly confessed to Nicholls that he had once gone so far as actually to decline the advantage of Johnson's personal acquaintance, commenting at the same time that he considered the Doctor's prose style to be 'turgid' and 'vicious'. Yet Gray was considerably less censorious of – and even impressed by – what he on at least once occasion commended as Johnson's innate 'goodness of heart'. 'I have heard him say', Nicholls would recall of the poet, 'that Johnson would go out in London

---

[4] Samuel Egerton Brydges, *Autobiography*, ii.111.

with his pockets full of silver, and give it all away in the streets before he returned home.'

Johnson, in turn, dismissed much of Gray's poetry – with the notable exception of the *Elegy* – as dreary or unhappy 'trifles'. Boswell, in his *Life of Johnson*, records several of Johnson's influential pronouncements on Gray's work, including the following notorious exchange, which took place at the dinner table of Mr. and Mrs. Thrale just three and a half years after Gray's death:

> He [Johnson] attacked Gray, calling him a 'dull fellow'. BOSWELL. 'I understand he was reserved, and might appear dull in company; but surely he was not dull in poetry.' JOHNSON. 'Sir, he was dull in company, dull in his closet, dull every where. He was dull in a new way, and that made people think him GREAT. He was a mechanical poet'. He then repeated some ludicrous lines, which have escaped my memory, and said, 'Is not that GREAT, like his Odes?' Mrs. Thrale maintained that his Odes were melodious; upon which he exclaimed,
> 'Weave the warp, and weave the woof'; –
> I added in a solemn tone,
> 'The winding-sheet of Edward's race'. '*There* is a good line'. 'Ay, (said he,) and the next line is a good one', (pronouncing it contemptuously:)
> 'Give ample verge and room enough'. –
> 'No, Sir, there are but two good stanzas in Gray's poetry, which are in his *Elegy in a Country Church-yard*'. He then repeated the stanza,
> 'For whom to dumb forgetfulness a prey', &c. mistaking one word; for instead of *precincts* he said *confines*. He added, 'The other stanza I forget'.[5]

Boswell's account is of course at least as interesting for what it tells us about its writer's own opinions regarding Gray's poetry as it is for its professed reportage of Johnson's admittedly more influential judgement on the *Elegy* and the Odes. (In times of spiritual tribulation, Boswell looked to the poet of the *Elegy* as a model and a pattern for his own behaviour in the face of adversity, and earnestly reminded himself in his journal on such occasions simply to 'Be Gray'.) Whatever prejudices might have prevailed between the two men, had the normally vivacious Bonstetten possessed either the impetuosity or the presence of mind that winter afternoon to have disengaged his arm from Gray's own and plucked Johnson by the sleeve, we would probably now possess the record of an extended encounter between them; judging from what we now know about Johnson's own bouts with melancholy and depression – and the often ritualistic means by which he sought throughout his life to combat such fits of despondency – he and Gray may well have had

[5]   James Boswell, *Life of Johnson*, ed. Pat Rogers (Oxford 1904; 1980) 600–1.

a great deal more in common with one another than either man could ever reasonably at the time have supposed.

*

When Gray returned to Cambridge just before Christmas – on 21 December – he took Bonstetten with him. For the earliest part of his stay, the poet's guest was lodged in the coffee house that stood near the gates of Gray's own college; within only two weeks, however, he appears to have moved into a set of rooms within Pembroke itself. Gray's old friends eagerly welcomed their colleague's young 'find' into their otherwise staid little circle. William Cole, now living four miles north of Cambridge at Milton, dined at Pembroke just after the Christmas holiday, and was duly introduced to Bonstetten, whom he described (in a journal he happened then, for the benefit of his own proficiency in the language, to be keeping in French) as 'un jeune Homme d'une grande Beauté et beaucoup de merité comme un Ecolier' ('a young man of considerable beauty, and of equal worth as a scholar'). Michael Tyson, an antiquarian and Fellow of Corpus (and a long-time acquaintance of Walpole, Cole, and Mason) joined Cole and Bonstetten at a New Year's Day sermon in Trinity College chapel, where they went expressly to hear the organ. The pretense that there was some serious work to be done, however, could not be dispensed with entirely. In a letter written to Nicholls in the very first week of the new year, Bonstetten recounted in his lively if still broken English the pattern of his days and nights while in Gray's company:

> *Hence vain deluding Joys* is our motto hier, written on every feature, and ourly spoken by every solitary Chapel bel; So that decently you cant expect no other but a very grave letter. I realy beg you pardon to wrap up my thoughts in so smart a dress as an in quarto sheet. I know they should appear in a folio leave, but the Ideas themselves shall look so solemn as to belie their dress. – Tho' I wear not yet the black gown, and am only an inferior Priest in the temple of Meditation, yet my countenance is already consecrated. I never walk but with even steps and musing gate, and looks commercing with the skyes; and unfold my wrinkles only when I see mr. Gray, or think of you. Then notwithstanding all your learnings and knowledge, I feel in such occasions that I have a heart, which you know is as some others a quite profane thing to carry under a black gown.
>
> I am in a hurry from morning till evening. At 8 o Clock I am roused by a young square Cap, with whom I follow Satan through Chaos and night. He explained me in Greek and latin, the *sweet reluctant amorous Delays* of our Grandmother Eve. We finish our travels with a copious breakfast of muffins and tea. The apears Shakespair and old Lineus strugling together

as two ghosts would do for a damned Soul. Sometimes the one get the better sometimes the other. Mr. Gray, whose acquaintance is my greatest debt to you, is so good as to shew me Macbeth, and all witches Beldams, Ghost and Spirits, whose language I never could have understood without his Interpretation. I am now endeavoring to dress all those people in a french dress, which is a very hard labour. (*CTG* 1110–12)

Gray added the following, telling post-script to Bonstetten's effort:

I never saw such a boy: our breed is not made on this model. he is busy from morn[ing] to night, has no other amusement, than tha[t] of changing one study for another, like[s] nobody, that he sees here, & yet wishes to stay longer, tho' he has pass'd a whole fortnight with us already. his letter has had no correction whatever, & is prettier by half than English. (*CTG* 1112)

Exactly one month later, Bonstetten recorded in a letter to his mother the intensity of his attachment to Gray. 'I eat every day in his rooms', he wrote of Gray on 6 February, 'he lives in great retirement, and is so kind as to show pleasure in seeing me. I call on him at any hour, he reads with me what I wish, I work in his room; we read natural history for amusement'.

Although he had planned originally to leave Cambridge early in February and stop in London only briefly before returning home, Bonstetten's departure from England was constantly deferred. He did, in fact, take his leave of Gray on Monday, 12 February, but rather than heading on to Dover from London, he retraced his steps and returned to Pembroke, where he spent an additional month in Gray's company. Together the two men went ahead in their reading of Shakespeare and Milton, and Bonstetten amiably continued his study of botany and 'old Lineus' [sic] under the personal tutelage of the curator of the physic garden at the University, a Mr. Miller.

As Bonstetten's short visit to Cambridge lengthened that winter into an extended stay of nearly three months, Gray's attraction to the young man deepened. The difference of over thirty years that ought to have separated them seemed, touchingly, only to draw them closer to one another – to inspire that peculiar kind of confidence which seems to exist only between the very young and the very old, or at least those aware of the approach of old age. Gray felt himself stirred to a depth of feeling which, as he would have been the first to admit, he had not experienced in many years; such feeling touched on emotions which he had hardly been prepared ever really to experience again. He was understandably reluctant to see his protégé return home. His days had begun once again to have a purpose – Bonstetten's disarming youth and beauty had worked their nostalgic and slightly painful magic well.

Bonstetten recalled later in life that on those few occasions on which he attempted to question Gray about his own writing, the poet only demurred, intimating that there was what his protégé described as an 'impassible gulf' between the emotions and events which had inspired that poetry so many years earlier, and the interests and activities of his current, retired existence. The young man mistakenly credited such reticence on Gray's part – such a seeming inability to talk openly about the emotional energy which lay very close to the surface of his most memorable poetry – to the simple 'fact' that Gray had himself never been 'in love'. Gray's undeniably lively heart and sensibility, Bonstetten reasoned, had never found the appropriate objects of their affections. Bonstetten at the same time, however, apparently recognized the extent of his own, recent conquest of Gray's heart, and he appears rather touchingly to have been embarrassed by it. A great many years later, compiling his *Souvenirs* as an old man in 1831, Bonstetten was able to write with engaging frankness about his relationship with the poet (at a distance of – remarkably – more than sixty years). The account of their friendship that he eventually included in his otherwise casual autobiography repays close attention:

> Ma gaieté, mon amour pour la poésie anglaise que je lisais avec Gray, l'avaient comme subjugué, de manière que la grande différence de nos âges n'etait plus sentie pour nous. J'étais logé À Cambridge dans un café, voisin de Pembrokhall; Gray y vivait enseveli dans une espèce de cloitre, d'où le quinzième siècle n'avait pas encore déménagé. La ville de Cambridge avec ses colléges solitaires n'était qu'une réunion de couvens, où les mathématiques et quelques sciences ont pris la forme et la costume de la théologie du moyen âge. De beaux couvens, à longs et silencieux corridors, des solitaires en robes noires, de jeaunes seigneurs travestis en moines à bonnets carrés, partout des souvenirs de moines à côté de la gloire de Newton. Aucune femme honnête ne venait égayer la vie de ces rats de livres à forme humain. Le savoir prospérait quelquefois dans ce désert du coeur. Tel j'ai vu Cambridge en 1769. . . . Gray, en se condamnant à vivre à Cambridge, oubliait que la génie du poète languit dans la sécheresse du coeur.
>
> La génie poétique de Gray était tellement éteint dans le sombre manoir de Cambridge, que le souvenir de ses poésies lui était odieux. Il ne se permit jamais de lui en parler. Quand je lui citais quelques vers de lui, il se taisait comme un enfant obstiné. Je lui disais quelquefois: *Voulez-vous bien me répondre?* Mais aucune parole ne sortait de sa bouche. Je le voyais tous les soirs de cinq heures à minuit. Nous lisions Shakespeare qu'il adorait, Dryden, Pope, Milton, etc., et nos conversations, comme celles de

l'amitié, n'arrivaient jamais à la dernière pensée. Je racontais à
Gray ma vie et mon pays, mais toute sa vie à lui était fermée
pour moi; jamais il ma parlait de lui. Il y avait chez Gray entre
le présent et le passé un abîme infranchissable. Quand je voulais
en approcher, de sombres nuées venaient le couvrir. Je crois que
Gray n'avait jamais aimé, c'était le mot de l'enigme, il en était
résulté une misère de coeur qui faisait contraste avec son imagination ardente et profonde qui, au lieu de faire le bonheur de sa
vie, n'en était que le tourment. Gray avait de la gaieté dans
l'ésprit et de la mélancholie dans sa caractère. Mais cette mélancholie n'est qu'un besoin non-satisfait de la sensibilité. Chez Gray
elle tenait au genre de vie de son âme ardente, reléguée sous le
pôle arctique de Cambridge.[6]

[My cheerfulness, my love for the English poetry which I read
with Gray, so conquered him that the substantial difference in
our ages was no longer even felt by us. I was housed, in Cambridge, at an inn in the vicinity of Pembroke Hall; Gray himself
lived in a kind of cloister, where it still seemed to be the fifteenth
century! The city of Cambridge itself, with its isolated colleges,
was little more than a cluster of medieval cloisters, in which
mathematics and several of the sciences still retained the habits
of the middle ages – the beautiful cloisters, the long and silent
halls, the lonely figures in their black college gowns, the young
men disguised as monks in their square caps, and above all the
shades of monks side by side with the glories of Newton. There
were no honest women to cheer up the life of these book-rats in
human form, [but] knowledge thrives in this desert of the heart.
In such a manner did I view Cambridge in 1769. . . . Condemned
to live in Cambridge, Gray forgot that poetic genius becomes
enervated in such parched and unemotional environments.
   Gray's poetic flame was so snuffed by the sombre environments of Cambridge that the very memory of his poetry had
become odious to him; he would permit no one even to speak of
it. When I quoted some of his verses to him, he pursed his lips
like an stubborn child. I asked him several times: *Why don't you
give me a proper answer*? But he wouldn't so much as utter a
single word! I saw him every evening from five o'clock until mid-
night. We read Shakespeare (whom he loved), Dryden, Pope,
Milton, etc., and our friendly conversations never came to any
final conclusions. I told Gray about my life and my country, but
all of his life was for me a closed book. He never spoke of
himself. There was, for Gray, an impassable chasm between the
past and the present. Whenever I tried to cross it, dark and
sombre clouds darkened my way. I think that Gray was never in

[6]   Charles Victor de Bonstetten, *Souvenirs, écrits en 1831* (Paris, 1832) 117–18.

love – that was the answer to the riddle – and he was, as a result, a miser of the heart; [this] formed a sharp contrast to his profound and burning imagination which, instead of imparting happiness to his life, gave him only torment. Gray had a certain cheerfulness in his soul, but melancholy, too, formed part of his character. But this melancholy was only the result of some unsatisfied need in his sensibility. With Gray one led a kind of ardent life of the soul, always tempered, however, by the arctic spiritual weather of Cambridge.]

Bonstetten's ever-watchful father, however, seems to have cared little for the considerable attention his son had so easily been garnering in England. The fact that almost everyone in Cambridge – from the Vice-Chancellor of the University to the lowliest undergraduate – seems, thanks largely to his friendship with Gray, to have taken to distinguishing Bonstetten with their attention, meant less than nothing to the Trésorier. Once again, he peremptorily recalled his son home to Switzerland.

On Wednesday, 21 March, Gray accompanied Bonstetten on what was now assuredly the young student's final, farewell journey from Cambridge to London. Remaining in town for less than two days, Bonstetten embarked for France that same Friday, having first accepted as a parting gift from the poet a 'loan' of £20. Gray, reluctant to spend even one minute away from the side of his departing friend, personally handed Bonstetten into the Dover coach at four o'clock in the morning. As he watched the carriage rumble off into the early morning darkness, Gray was not only down-hearted, but decidedly angry. Bonstetten's 'cursed' father, he had explained to Nicholls before leaving Cambridge,

> will have him home in the autumn, & he must pass thro' France to improve his talents & morals. . . . I have seen (I own) with pleasure the efforts you have made to recommend me to him. *sed non ego credulus illis*, nor I fear, he neither. he gives me too much pleasure, & at least *an equal share* of inquietude. you do not understand him so well as I do, but I leave my meaning imperfect, till we meet. I have never met with so extraordinary a Person. God bless him! I am unable to talk to you about anything else, I think. (*CTG* 1114)

It was in such a mood – silent, knowing, and reluctant – that Gray waved his last farewell to his friend, and attempted with an unaffected ease to turn his back on the disquieting events of the past three months.

II. In Insulam Relegatum

Gray returned first to London, where he spent ten days before heading back to Pembroke. The normally restful and familiar return journey to

Cambridge, however, must on this occasion have been one of the loneliest such trips he had ever undertaken. For all the promise of the burgeoning spring, the university town seemed, to Gray, cold and lifeless without his young and irrepressibly enthusiastic companion by his side. Left to pass his evenings alone or in the company of his academic colleagues, Gray was morose and generally out-of-humour with almost everything around him. However much he may have been aware that the feelings of desolation and even abandonment he was experiencing would fade with time, Gray in his heart yet harboured an aching pain for Bonstetten's enthusiasms; he genuinely missed the younger man's slightly fractured sense of wide-eyed discovery and delight. Having within such a relatively short space of time grown accustomed to seeing his old world through new and youthful eyes, the effect for Gray of Bonstetten's sudden absence was very much like being stripped of a pair of rose-tinted spectacles; the vision that resulted was one which soon faded into its former dull and inescapably familiar outlines.

A letter from Bonstetten – who had stopped briefly at Abbeville on the road to the French capital – struck a momentary light in the gloom, yet the feeling of darkness soon returned. On 4 April, Gray wrote to Nicholls complaining both of his loneliness and of a less familiar, restless anxiety. The letter was the first he had sent to his friend at Blundeston since his return from London. 'At length, my dear Sr', he began,

> we have lost our poor de B:n I pack'd him up with my own hands in the Dover-machine at 4 o'clock in the morning on Friday, 23 March, the next day at 7 he sail'd & reach'd *Calais* by noon, & *Boulogne* at night. the next night he reach'd *Abbeville*, where he had letters to Mad: Vanrobais, to whom belongs the famous manufacture of cloth there. from thence he wrote to me, & here I am again to pass my solitary evenings, which hung much lighter on my hands, before I knew him. this is your fault! pray let the next you send me, be halt & blind, dull, unapprehensive & wrong-headed. for this (as Lady Constance says) *Was never such a gracious Creature born!* & yet – but no matter! burn my letter that I wrote you, for I am very much out of humour with myself & will not believe a word of it. you will think, I have caught madness from him (for he is certainly mad) & perhaps you will be right. oh! what things are Fathers & Mothers! I thought they were to be found only in England, but you see. (*CTG* 1115)

The critic Bruce Redford has convincingly argued that Gray's seemingly slight allusion to Shakespeare's *King John* in this letter carried an enormous amount of weight. Redford has further demonstrated that it is only through the close reading of such allusions that we can begin to understand the effect of Bonstetten's departure on Gray. 'Though he only quotes one line', as Redford observed,

> Gray manages to convey the full weight and substance of Constance's lament for her son. He will not, like Constance, rave extravagantly or tear his hair; but he will adjust his habitual manner to conform to his heightened emotional state, and imply a sense of loss by conjuring up her frantic wail. Allusive variation permits Gray to suggest that he feels both a parent's love for Bonstetten and, like Constance's attachment to Arthur, more than a parent's love.[7]

Along much the same lines, Robert Gleckner has convincingly demonstrated that the language of Gray's surviving letters to Bonstetten frequently echo the language of the poet's earlier letters to Richard West, in particular those written towards the beginning of their intense relationship following Gray's return from the Grand Tour in the summer of 1741.[8]

While yet in London, Gray attempted to secure an English translation of the Swiss naturalist Gottlieb Sigmund Gruner's three-volume *Die Eisgebirge des Schweizerlandes* – a work no doubt suggested to him by Bonstetten, and one which could further whet his appetite for a possible visit to Switzerland. He had immediately ordered the volumes from his bookseller in town, but was disappointed to learn they would not be available for at least a month. Until then, he asked Nicholls plaintively, how was he to pass the time? He concluded the letter by once again referring to his own loneliness at Pembroke, and by echoing almost instinctively, in his language, Nicholls's own description of the *nemorum nox* that he had earlier described as hanging so threateningly over Bonstetten's native land. 'This place never appear'd so horrible to me', Gray shivered as he looked around him in Cambridge, 'as it does now. Could not you come for a week or fortnight? It would be sunshine to me in a dark night!'

Bonstetten continued dutifully to write to Gray throughout his visit to Paris. His stay in that morally perilous city threatened now to extend throughout the entire summer. Gray, needless to say, looked forward to each of the young man's letters, at the same time that he professed a growing trepidation with regard to his protégé's well-being. All of Bonstetten's letters to Gray dating from this period were unfortunately lost or destroyed after the poet's death, and only three of Gray's responses to his young friend survive. These three letters were first printed by a friend of Bonstetten's, Friedreich Matthison, in his *Auserlesene Gedichte*,

---

[7] Redford, *The Converse of the Pen*, 110–11.
[8] See Gleckner, 184.

where they were included in the notes to some verses on Lake Geneva in which a reference had been made to the figure of Gray himself; they were eventually translated from the German and reprinted by Anne Plumptre in a collection of continental correspondence first published in 1799. The letters contain some of the most revealing and touching prose that Gray ever wrote, each of them giving a different turn to the poet's expression of the growing anxiety and heartache which haunted his separation from Bonstetten.

The first of these letters was sent from Cambridge on 12 April, in immediate response to Bonstetten's own report from the French capital. 'Never did I feel, my dear Bonstetten', Gray began,

> to what a tedious length the few short moments of our life may be extended by impatience and expectation, till you had left me: nor ever knew before with so strong a conviction how much this frail body sympathizes with the inquietude of the mind. I am grown old in the compass of less than three weeks, like the Sultan in the Turkish Tales, that did but plunge his head into a vessel of water and take it out again (as the standers-by affirm'd) at the command of a Dervish, and found he had pass'd many years in captivity and begot a large family of children. The strength and spirits that now enable me to write to you, are only owing to your last letter, a temporary gleam of sunshine. Heaven knows, when it may shine again! I did not conceive till now (I own) what it was to lose you, nor felt the solitude and insipidity of my own condition, before I possess'd the happiness of your friendship. (*CTG* 1117–18)

The oriental tale which Gray mentions in this letter was originally included in the *Turkish Tales* – a collection of 'eastern' fables resembling the *Arabian Nights' Entertainments* and originally translated into English from the French of François Petis de la Croix in 1708. The specific story to which Gray refers was one of the most popular oriental fables of the eighteenth century, and one to which writers of the period often referred casually, certain that their readers or correspondents would be familiar with any allusion to the tale (Horace Walpole, some few years earlier, had off-handedly suggested in a letter to Lord Stafford that one of their mutual acquaintances was 'like the sultan in the Persian Tales'; his reference was to the very same story to which Gray calls Bonstetten's attention in his own letter). Following its earliest publication in the original collection published by Tonson in 1708, the story had famously been retold by Joseph Addison, who, in his *Spectator* No. 94, confessed to finding it an instructive and 'very pretty' story. Gray appears pointedly in his own letter to draw attention to the subjective perception of the passing of time which the story invites its readers to consider, but it is worth remembering too, that in referring to a collection such as the *Turkish Tales*, Gray was reaching as far back as possible into the extensive memories of his own readings as a child and a young adult. In fact, the last occasion on which Gray had extended recourse· to the often parodic narratives and language of the eastern tale, was when he first expressed the anxiety of separation from Walpole himself when he first came up as an undergraduate to Cambridge over thirty-five years earlier. Echoes of that early love – once felt so deeply and sincerely – as well as that of his subsequent relationship with West, would appear to have been awakened by Bonstetten's recent stay in Cambridge. Gray may even subconsciously have been recalling the reaction of the sultan in the story, once he has removed his head from the basin of water. As Addison recounts the fable: 'He [the sultan] immediately upbraided his teacher for having sent him on such a Course of Adventures, and betray'd him into so long a state of marriage and servitude; but was wonderfully surprised when he heard that the state he talked of was only a Dream and a Delusion; that he had not stirred from the Place where he then stood; and that he had only dipped his Head into the Water, and immediately taken it out again'. 'The Hours of a wise Man', Addison concluded the tale,

> are lengthened by his Ideas, as those of a Fool are by his Passions: The Time of the one is long, because he does not know what to do with it; so is that of the other, because he distinguishes every Moment of it with useful or amusing Thought; or in other Words, because the one is always wishing it away, and the other always enjoying it.[9]

Gray's letter to Bonstetten raises the appalling possibility that the poet himself, while all the time appearing to advance within the quiet precincts of his college to 'Knowledge and Wisdom', had in fact grown old in 'Ignorance and Folly' – that he had betrayed the deepest impulses of his heart, and had consequently led a life ultimately as barren and as fruitless as the prospect offered in Addison's tale. Had Bonstetten perhaps, inadvertently, taught the ageing poet that to have led one's life without having fully experienced a mature, romantic passion was tantamount to having endured a living death? In alluding to what he calls the 'larger Addisonian context' in this letter, Redford, at least, concedes that 'the result is to imply that longing for Bonstetten has not only disrupted his quite scholarly routine and upset a precarious mental equilibrium, but that it has caused him to doubt the truth of the very conviction that he had previously shared with Addison –

[9]   Joseph Addison and Sir Richard Steele, *The Spectator* (London, 1945; 1970) i, 293.

a belief in the supreme value of "Study, Reading, and the Pursuit of Knowledge" '[10]

Pulling himself up with a painful shock, and reminding himself that it was he who was meant to be playing the role of mentor in this relationship and not Bonstetten, Gray returned to his Commonplace Book to transcribe into the same letter – almost word for word – some notes he had made on the Book VI of Plato's *Republic* many years before. 'I must cite another Greek writer to you', he wrote,

> because it is very much to my purpose. He is describing the character of a Genius truly inclined to Philosophy. It includes (he says) qualifications rarely united in one single mind, quickness of apprehension and a retentive memory; vivacity and application, gentleness and magnanimity: to these he adds an invincible love of truth, and consequently of probity and justice. Such a soul (continues he) will be little inclined to sensual pleasures, and consequently temperate; a stranger to illiberality and avarice being accustom'd to the most extensive views of things and sublimest contemplations, it will contract an habitual greatness, will look down with a kind of disregard on human life and on death, consequently will possess the truest fortitude. Such (says he) is the Mind born to govern the rest of Mankind. But these very endowments so necessary to a soul form'd for philosophy are often the ruin of it (especially when join'd to the external advantages of wealth, nobility, strength, and beauty) that is, if it light on a bad soil; and want its proper nurture, which nothing but an excellent education can bestow. In this case he is depraved by the publick example, the assemblies of the people, the courts of justice, the theatres that inspire it with false opinions, terrify it with false infamy, or elevate it with false applause: and remember, that extraordinary vices and extraordinary virtues are alike the produce of a vigorous Mind: little souls are alike incapable of one or the other.
>
> If you have ever met with the portrait sketch'd out by Plato, you will know it again: for my part (to my sorrow) I have had that happiness: I see the principle features, and I foresee the dangers with trembling anxiety. . . . Go on, my best and amiable Friend, to shew me your heart simply, and without the shadow of disguise, and leave me to weep over it (as I now do) no matter whether from joy or sorrow. (*CTG* 1118–19)

If it accomplished nothing else, Gray's extended reference to Plato's description in the *Republic* of the proper education and discretion of a 'Genius truly inclined to Philosophy' would have reminded Bonstetten

---

[10]   Redford, *The Converse of the Pen*, 109.

– much as it reminds us today – of the degree to which the obsessions which haunted his poetry were rooted in and derived from his scholarship and reading in the classics. Yet, as Jean Hagstrum has so rightly pointed out, these lines betray 'a return to Gray of the stoicism 'of the forties, and the circumstances appear to be dramatic. The 53-year-old poet has been overmastered by a passion that is driving him past the line of decorum to the brink of madness'. The ideal man of the *Republic*, as Hagstrum further observed:

> is introduced in the middle of a letter that begins and ends in passion. . . . The last paragraph of the letter . . . is a cry of the heart: Gray wants the young man, about to be exposed to Continental and urban gaieties, to 'shew me your heart simply and without the shadow of disguise, and leave me to weep over it'. . . . Undoubtedly, of the several virtues Plato recommends it is moderation and temperance that Gray wishes most to enforce on the young friend who has so discomposed his spirits – that quality in the soul of a good man that keeps him but 'little inclined to sensual pleasures'. Gray is in such anguish that it is difficult to regard the teaching of sensual discipline as merely disinterested instruction. . . . In brief, Gray is sexually jealous.[11]

Two days after sending this letter off to Bonstetten at Paris, Gray wrote to Nicholls, who had himself professed to a great wonder that the remarkable innocence of the young Bernese had been 'so little spoiled' as a result of his extended contact with the world. Nicholls, like Gray, worried that the considerable seductions of Parisian society would soon push his memories of his English hosts from his mind, and wondered too whether he or Gray would ever in fact hear from Bonstetten again. 'What you say of poor B: is so true', he wrote Gray on 14 April, '& (let me add) expresses so well my own feelings, that I shall transcribe your words and send them to him: were I in his place, I should be grateful for them!'.

*

Toward the end of April, Gray travelled to Blundeston to spend a few days with Nicholls. He interrupted his journey to Suffolk only briefly to visit Palgrave, who was now serving as Rector at Thrandeston. Before leaving Cambridge, Gray once again wrote to Bonstetten (on 19 April), striking in his letter much the same note as he had in his earlier correspondence:

---

[11]   Hagstrum in Downey and Jones, 10.

Alas! how do I every moment feel the truth of what I have somewhere read: *C'est n'est pas le voir que de s'en souvenir*, and yet that remembrance is the only satisfaction I have left. My life now is but a perpetual conversation with your shadow. – The known sound of your voice still rings in my ears. – There, on the corner of the fender you are standing, or tinkling on the Pianoforte, or stretch'd at length on the sofa. – Do you reflect, my dearest Friend, that it is a week or eight days, before I can receive a letter from you and as much more before you can have my answer, that all that time (with more than Herculean toil) I am employ'd in pushing the tedious hours along, and wishing to annihilate them; the more I strive, the heavier they move and the longer they grow. I can not bear this place, where I have spent so many tedious years within less than a month, since you left me. I am going for a few days to see poor Nicholls invited by a letter, wherein he mentions you in such terms, as add to my regard for him, and express my own sentiments better than I can do myself. (*CTG* 1127)

Gray's purpose in visiting Nicholls that April, as his letter makes clear, was to escape Bonstetten's lingering presence in Cambridge. The fact that he rather obviously looked forward while at Blundeston to pursuing his obsession with the young man – if in conversation only – does not appear to have struck him as in any way self-defeating. Gray proceeded in his letter to quote the language of 'poor Nicholls's' correspondence, passing on to Bonstetten a passage that can only further have fuelled the flames of that young man's ego. 'I am concern'd (says he)', Gray transcribed,

that I can not pass my life with him. I never met with any one that pleased and suited me so well: the miracle to me is, how he comes to be so little spoil'd, and the miracle of miracles will be, if he continues so in the midst of every danger and seduction, and without any advantages, but from his own excellent nature and understanding. I own, I am very anxious for him on this account, and perhaps your inquietude has proceeded from the same cause. I hope, I am to hear, when he has pass'd that cursed sea, or will he forget me thus *in insulam relegatum*? If he should, it is out of my power to retaliate'. (*CTG* 1127–28)

There appears on the face of it actually to have been very little danger that Bonstetten would even encounter much less succumb to any of the threats – either philosophical or sexual – from which both Gray and Nicholls seem so anxious, in their letters, to protect him. The young man's acquaintance with the Duchess d'Enville and her daughter-in-law, both of whom he had met in Geneva some few years earlier, ensured him an entry into those circles of Parisian society which, far from giving rise to gossip and scandal, were eminently respectable. Once he had left

Paris, Bonstetten was to travel slightly south along the Seine to stay with the Duchess at La Roche Guyon, the chateau of the La Rochefoucauld family, where the author of the 1665 *Maximes* had completed much of that work. Yet, again, Gray was at this point less concerned that Bonstetten would imbibe any of the French moralist's (at times dangerous) Senecan reflections, than that he would surrender himself to the more dangerous, hedonistic doctrines of the 'Philosophes' – the collective name applied to the generally anti-religious writers and thinkers of the French enlightenment, such as Voltaire, Diderot, Buffon, Condillac, d'Holbach, and Helvétius.

As he had himself grown older, Gray's distaste for the tenets of such skeptics had likewise grown more pronounced. Only a few weeks after he sent his anxious advice to Bonstetten in France, Gray received from James Beattie a copy of that author's latest, eight-volume prose work, an *Essay on the Nature and Immutability of Truth, in Opposition to Sophistry and Skepticism*. 'If you should at any time do my book the honor to look into it', Beattie wrote Gray, 'I hope that you will favour me with your opinion of the style' – 'as to the doctrine', he added knowingly, 'I dare say we are of the same mind'. Beattie's 'metaphysical' work followed the manuscript he had sent to Gray some few months earlier from Aberdeen of Book I of his proto-Wordsworthian *The Minstrel*, in which the 'progress of poetical genius' is traced in Spenserian stanzas through the figure of one 'Edwin'. Gray read both of Beattie's works early that summer, and concurred with their author that they were, indeed, 'of the same mind'. Of *The Minstrel*, in particular, he wrote:

> The truth is, I greatly like all that I have seen, and wish to see more. The design is simple, and pregnant with poetical ideas of various kinds, yet seems somehow imperfect in the end. Why may not young Edwin, when necessity has driven him to take up the harp, and assume the profession of a Minstrel, do some great and singular service to his country? (what service I must leave to your invention) such as no General, no Statesman, no Moralist could do without the aid of music, inspiration, and poetry. (*CTG* 1140)

Gray admitted in the same letter that he has been able to give the *Essay . . . on Truth* only the most cursory reading, but he seems entirely to approved of Beattie's attack on Hume. 'I will not enter at present into the merits of your *Essay on Truth*', Gray wrote,

> because I have not yet given it all the attention it deserves, though I have read it through with pleasure; besides I am partial; for I have always thought David Hume a pernicious writer, and believe he has done

as much mischief here as he has in his own country. A turbid and shallow stream often appears to our apprehensions very deep. A professed sceptic can be guided by nothing but his present passions (if he has any) and interests; and to be masters of his philosophy, we need not his books and his advice, for every child is capable of the same thing, without any study at all. Is not that *naivité* and good humour, which his admirers celebrate in him, owing to this, that he has continued all his days an infant, but one that has unhappily been taught to read and write? That childish nation, the French, have given him vogue and fashion, and we, as usual, have learned from them to admire him at second hand. (*CTG* 1141)

Gray's distrust of 'that childish nation, the French', returns us once again to his anxiety regarding the state of Bonstetten's mental and moral health. Once again, the poet's continuing uneasiness concerning his young friend's susceptibility to the supposedly infantile obsessions of the Parisian *beau monde* of course betrays as much, if not more, about Gray's own state of mind in the late spring and early summer of 1770. Gray was indeed jealous of Bonstetten's affections, and he was equally troubled by his own impulses to surrender to what he could not help but regard as the 'vulgar caresses' of his own desire, or indulge in 'vain remorse'. This last sentiment was particularly troubling to him. 'Chronic remorse', the twentieth-century novelist Aldous Huxley once wrote, 'is a most undesirable sentiment. . . . On no account brood over your wrongdoing. Rolling in the muck is not the best way of getting clean'.[12] And Gray was here rolling in the muck with a vengeance, and that, too, over the self-perceived 'wrongdoing' of what was on some level merely the heartfelt gesture of a generous emotion.

Gray's professed purpose in visiting Nicholls at Blundeston that April was, again – and this he freely admitted to his friend – to divert his attention away from his increasingly obsessive thoughts about Bonstetten. If such was in fact the case, no journey could have been more ill-conceived or misdirected. Sitting in the quiet of the garden at Blundeston with the one person who could do least to dispel his sense of abandonment and self-pity, Gray's own contribution to their conversations must rarely have departed from the object of their mutual affections. He had carried Bonstetten's letters with him from London to Suffolk, and the two men together reinforced each other's melancholy. When they were not actually reminiscing about the events of Bonstetten's recent visit to England, they were busy planning their own trip to Switzerland – a trip which Bonstetten, in his correspondence

---

[12]   Aldous Huxley, 'Foreword', *Brave New World* (London: Grafton Books, 1977) 7.

with Gray, continued rather recklessly to encourage. The crisp spring air heightened Gray's sense of loss, and his solitary walks among the shells and pebbles of the tide fed the aching, romantic longing that touched the deepest recesses of his heart.

Returning to Cambridge at the beginning of May, Gray was delighted to find yet another lengthy letter from France already awaiting him. He wrote back to Bonstetten less than two days later, announcing,

> I am return'd, my dear B., from the little journey I made into Suffolk without answering the end proposed. The thought, that you might have been with me there, had embittered all my hours. Your letter has made me happy; as happy as so gloomy, so solitary a Being as I am is capable of being. I know and have too often felt the disadvantages I lay myself under, how much I hurt the little interest I have in you, by this air of sadness so contrary to your nature and present enjoyments: but sure you will forgive, tho' you can not sympathize with me. It is impossible with me to dissemble with you. Such as I am, I expose my heart to your view, nor wish to conceal a single thought from your penetrating eyes. – All that you say to me, especially on the subject of Switzerland, is infinitely acceptable. It feels too pleasing ever to be fulfill'd, and as often as I read over your truly kind letter, written long since from London, I stop at these words: *La mort qui peut glacer nos bras avant qu'ils soient entrelacés.* (*CTG* 1132)

Yet another letter from Paris, written about 16 May, however, elicited a decidedly cooler response on the part of Gray, and prompted him even to rethink the effusive epistolary 'happiness' with which he had responded to the letter received earlier that same month. 'When I return'd to Cambridge', he wrote to Nicholls on 22 May,

> I found a long letter from De B: expressing much kindness, but in a style *un peu trop alambiqué* [a bit too oversubtle], & yesterday I had another shorter, & making bad excuses for not writing oftener: he seems at present to give into all the French nonsense & to be employ'd much like an English boy broke loose from his Governor. I want much to know, whether he has wrote to you yet: if not, I am seriously angry, tho' to little purpose. (*CTG* 1133)

Gray's language in the passage suggests that, as spring ripened finally into summer, the intensity of his emotional attraction to Bonstetten had begun finally to run its necessary course. Professing a displeasure with what he characterized as Bonstetten's 'French nonsense' and (given his months-long stay within the confines of a celibate Cambridge college, rather understandable) adolescent behaviour, the older man was on some level simply disappointed with his correspondent's juvenile tastes and weaknesses. As Bonstetten's letters arrived in England with less and less frequency, and as they continued more prominently to feature an affection and over-subtlety of manner that the poet claimed to find morally as well as rhetorically offensive, Gray began to entertain some second thoughts regarding his emotional investment in the relationship. Time and distance, which he knew from hard experience could help to heal the most stubborn wounds of the heart, had begun finally to work in his favour. Only one year after writing the letter quoted above, as Gleckner has observed, 'even to Nicholls (who was in Paris with Bonstetten) Gray ceases all mention of Bonstetten, this abortive 'affair' (almost certainly one-sided) apparently too traumatic for mere words, though nonetheless indelibly inscribed on his memory'. 'Possibly', Gleckner rightly concluded of Gray, ' his adamance was fueled by Bonstetten's having become something other than the West redevivus Gray had first imagined him to be.'[13]

*

Other circumstances helped also to ironize the unequal nature of this most recent attachment, shedding a clearer light on its inherent and inevitable instability. Following his return from Suffolk, Gray spent only three days in Cambridge before again mounting a coach – one now facing towards London. Comfortably settled in his usual lodgings in Jermyn street by the evening of 10 May, he began more successfully than he had at Thrandeston (or 'Lovingland') to allow his attentions to be diverted by matters completely unrelated to Bonstetten's recent visit. He did so, now, by being especially focused and practical. He busied himself in the Haymarket, attempting to procure a microscope for Nicholls from the well-known optician, Jesse Ramsden, and he sounded a far more characteristic note than had been heard in his correspondence of late when he complained of Ramsden – to whom he pointedly referred as 'Mason's favourite', and not his own – as a dilatory 'Lyar and Fool'. He followed some events then underway in Westminster relating to the business of the University, and duly reported back to Brown at Cambridge regarding the details of their progress. For good measure, he also passed on the latest gossip relating to a scandalously disputed seat in the House of Lords. He enjoyed a casual breakfast with Lord Strathmore and his brother Thomas Lyon (a one-time fellow of Pembroke), and appears on the occasion even to have enjoyed the company of Lyon's infant daughter. He travelled the short distance one afternoon to Hampton

---

[13]   Gleckner, 184.

Court to dine with Stonhewer, whom he delighted to find in excellent health; Stonhewer soon returned the courtesy, and visited the poet in town. Gray spent much of his time, in other words, among old friends. The very comfort of their camaraderie highlighted the easy fit of their fellowship. His infatuation with Bonstetten seemed, conversely, increasingly more inappropriate, and even absurd.

One episode in particular may have helped to effect a shift in Gray's perspective on recent events. Shortly after his arrival in London, Gray was visited by yet another young foreigner – a Frenchman – who, like Bonstetten, was visiting England ostensibly to improve his proficiency in the language. On this occasion, it was a certain Marquis de Villevieille, from Provence, who had been pushed in Gray's direction by the French ambassador in London, Louise Marie Florent. He seemed 'a quiet good sort of young Man', Gray wrote to Nicholls. 'He knows and tried to speak English, & has *translated me* by way of exercise.' Gray was flattered enough by the Marquis's attentions to repeat his description of the young man to Brown in Cambridge, but he seems also to have raised his guard against such homage; he was not going to allow himself once again – and so soon – to have his affection engaged by a transient young foreigner, however charming he might be, or however diligently he paid court to the poet's fame.

Gray's recent conversation with his old friends still echoing in his mind, the poet set his sights rather on his anticipation of his departure from London, and a planned visit to Mason at Aston. Gray looked forward to the possibility that Nicholls would accompany him on the journey to Yorkshire. 'Now if you like to accompany me, you will meet me at Camb: & we pursue our way together, trees blooming and nightingales singing all around us. let me know your mind & direct to me at Camb:ge.' Gray, it seems, had finally begun to recover some of the spirits he had so recently and so abjectly lost to Bonstetten.

Gray reached Aston by the first week of June, having broken his travel northward to stop for only two days at Cambridge. Nicholls had not been present at Cambridge, nor were there any letters from him awaiting Gray's arrival at the college. Gray consequently undertook the journey to Aston on his own. Nicholls had contacted him just prior to his departure from London with some rather unwelcome news. Their mutual acquaintance William Temple, now living at the rectory of Mamhead, near Exeter in Devonshire, had decided to separate from his wife. Temple had written to Nicholls, asking the latter to pass on a request to Gray to provide him with some reading matter which might distract his attention from his own unhappy domestic situation (he confessed his marital and professional troubles to James Boswell, as well). 'You will see best from his own words what he wants', Nicholls wrote, and I am sure you will feel his situation; any instance of attention and kindness from you will be a medicine to his distress; his spirits require to be raised, and I know nothing so likely to raise them; if you should write yourself it would be an act of charity indeed! he has no other refuge or consolation than his books, when his mind is unbent from that attraction he sinks into despair. In short his letter is too painful a portrait of his mind, and I send it to you because I think you are interested in his fate. What must I say to him about that resolution of separating which he seems to speak of seriously? Will it pass off of itself? or should I dissuade it? or what can it mean? separating only from her bed? . . . I would do the best, but am quite at a loss. I am sure your heart will prompt me to advise me. (*CTG* 1136–37)

Gray took advantage of his brief stop-over in Cambridge to respond to Nicholls's request. As it was, he was stunned and even outraged by what he interpreted to be his friend's unfeeling indiscretion in suggesting that Gray himself would 'feel [Temple's] situation' because of his own recent separation from Bonstetten. Gray wrote back to Nicholls in a tone of unaccustomed bitterness:

I would wish by all means to oblige & serve T: in any way I am able, but it can not be *in his way* at present. he & you seem to think, that I have nothing else to do but transcribe a page from some common-place book on this head: if it were so, I should not hesitate a minute about it. but as I came from Town only on Thursday last, have only two days to pass here, & must fetch all the materials from my own recollection, he must excuse me for the present. let him begin with Ld Bacon's Henry 7th & Ld Herbert's Henry 8th, & by that time I return to Aston (wch will be in 3 weeks or less) perhaps I may be able to help him onwards a little. I keep the letter till we meet, least it be lost. I would reply nothing to the article of *separation*. (*CTG* 1137–38)

The passage that follows this last remark is heavily scored through and illegible. One nevertheless glimpses something of the extent of Gray's injured pride in the simple recommendation that a man passing through the depressive agonies of a marital separation would do well to pick up a copy of Herbert's 1649 *Life and Reign of King Henry VIII* as a restorative to a healthier frame of mind.

The two weeks Gray spent in Yorkshire were for the most part uneventful. The quiet of Mason's country retreat provided perhaps too stark a contrast to the recent activity of his London visit, and his anxiety began slowly to return. He told Mason that he was considering resigning the Professorship of Modern History because he was unable to perform the duties outlined in his memorandum; only with great difficulty did Mason dissuade him from taking such a drastic step. Wharton may well have visited Aston while Gray was a guest there; if he did so, the meeting would have been their last. However much progress Gray seemed to be making when it came to personal matters, it is striking that even after returning to Cambridge on 23 June, the unlikely possibility that a letter from Bonstetten (who was still in Paris) had been misdirected and consequently lost after being forwarded to Yorkshire from Cambridge, quickly heightened the poet's state of nervous anxiety.

III. A Six Weeks' Ramble

Gray's summer travels were far from over, however. On the day immediately following his return to Pembroke he dashed off a quick note to Nicholls, suggesting that they meet on the first or second of July either at Huntingdon or at the Wheat-sheaf Inn – which lay just over five miles further along the Great North Road, at Alconbury Hill – to begin a projected tour 'thro Worcestershire, Shropshire, & other of the midland counties for about three weeks'. Once met at Huntingdon or at Alconbury Hill, the two could plan a more precise route for their tour. Gray disliked having to remain in Cambridge during the University Commencement (which fell that year on 3 July), and he was clearly anxious to begin the journey. He was prepared to wait out Nicholls's arrival at Alconbury Hill, even if that meant remaining on his own for one or even two days.

Before leaving Cambridge, Gray busied himself in tidying up a number of loose ends. It was at about this time that he wrote to Beattie, thanking him for *The Minstrel*. He confessed himself recently to have been in low spirits, and professed a hope that his forthcoming journey would help to dispel his depression. 'That forced dissipation and exercise we are obliged to fly to as a remedy, when this frail machine goes wrong', he wrote, 'is almost as bad as the distemper we would cure.' On the same day he wrote to Beattie – 2 July – he signed his will, engaging three fellows of Pembroke as witnesses (Richard Baker, Thomas Wilson, and Joseph Turner). The document appointed William Mason and James Brown to act as the poet's Joint-Executors.

The journal for this latest tour – the last such excursion Gray was ever to undertake – was unfortunately maintained not by Gray himself, but by Nicholls. The account appears subsequently to have been lost or destroyed. The pair began their journey, as arranged. by meeting up at the Wheat-sheaf Inn, from which point they drove across the midland counties into Shropshire and Worcestershire. They then veered further to the south, following the descent of the river Severn into Gloucestershire. They broke their journey to spend a week at the popular inland resort of Malvern Wells, in Worcestershire, where Nicholls met up with some old friends and acquaintances. While staying at Malvern, Nicholls later wrote in his *Reminiscences*, Gray was 'delighted' with the extensive view from the Hertfordshire Beacon, from which vantage he could easily trace the division of the Severn Plain from the undulating countryside around Hereford. Gray must have felt both his physical health and his general spirits to be improving, since the two friends spent the high summer mornings and afternoons walking the many trails and paths that ran along the high-lying hills, ranging from West Hill, to the north, to Ragged Stone and the Gloucester Beacon (or Chase End), to the south. Gray was considerably less delighted, however, by the prospect of socializing with Nicholls's friends. As far as the scenery went, Nicholls recalled, Gray was happy, 'but', he continued,

> certainly not so with the numerous society assembled at the long table where we dined every day; tho' he staid there a week, most obligingly on my account, as I found some acquaintances whom I was glad to meet. He had neither inclination to mix much in conversation on such occasions, nor I think much facility, even if he had been willing. This arose perhaps partly from natural reserve, & what is called *shyness*, & partly from having lived retired in the University during so great a part of his life, where he had lost as he told me himself 'the versatility of his mind'. (*CTG* 1299)

Gray's 'versatility of mind', it hardly needs pointing out, had in no way suffered from his many years at Cambridge. His social skills, however, (and one recalls Walpole's criticisms of Gray's 'conversation' many years earlier) were now emphatically of a sort that shone to better advantage in academic surroundings; he might easily have been perceived by individuals who, themselves, generally moved outside of such comparatively cloistered environments as curt, opinionated, argumentative, and even rude. More to the point, Gray's by now constitutional disinclination to compromise his own behaviour on the smallest points of personal comfort – a disinclination which the habits of a near lifetime had unquestioningly supported and underscored – mitigated against an accommodating social conversation.

Malvern, as it turned out, provided at least one pleasantly unexpected surprise for the poet. Oliver Goldsmith's *The Deserted Village*, which had been published only a very few months earlier, was drawn to Gray's attention while the two friends were staying at the resort. Gray requested that Nicholls – for their joint enjoyment – undertake to read the poem aloud. 'He listened with fixed attention', Nicholls recalled, '& soon exclaimed – "That man is a poet"'. The impromptu exclamation constitutes Gray's only recorded judgement on Goldsmith, a poet with whose works his own writing was destined, in time, often to be coupled and compared.

From Malvern Wells, the two travellers moved on to the pleasant town of Ross, which sits above the East bank of the river Wye. From Ross, they undertook the forty-mile journey to Chepstow by boat, following the course of the river itself. The descent proved for Gray to be the scenic highlight of their tour. 'The very light, & principle feature of my journey was the river *Wye*', he wrote to Wharton shortly after his return to Cambridge,

> which I descended in a boat for near 40 miles from Ross to Chepstow: its banks are a succession of nameless wonders: one out of many you may see not ill-described by Mr. Whatley in his *Observations on Gardening* under the name of the *New-Weir*: he has also touch'd upon two others, *Tinterne-Abbey* and *Persfield* (Mr. Morris's). both of them famous scenes; & both on the Wye. Monmouth, a town I never heard mention'd, lies on the same river in a vale, that is the delight of my eyes, & the very seat of pleasure. (*CTG* 1142)

The journey home included brief stops at the town of Abergavenny – nestled in the impressive scenery of south Wales – and at the small estate of Leasowes, at Halesowen in Worcestershire, where the poet William Shenstone had been born, and where he died in 1763 (Gray had twice in his correspondence noted Shenstone's approval of his own Odes in 1757, and seems to have acknowledged the latter's wish that they were 'a little clearer' with no comment). Also on the way home, Gray paid what was to prove the only visit of his life to Oxford, where he noted merely to have 'past two days . . . with great satisfaction'.

The weather throughout the tour had continued very hot, but generally serene. London, where Gray spent a fortnight before returning to Cambridge, seemed by contrast to leave one stewing in the humid, urban heat. When Gray finally escaped back to Pembroke in the third week of August, the university was still in the midst of the 'dead quiet' that preceded Michaelmas Term. Many of the college fellows had not yet returned from their own summer expeditions. At Pembroke, even as August gave way to September, the stultifying calm of the long vacation was broken only by the scratching of Gray's own pen in the hush of the late summer afternoons; James Brown was the only other Fellow in residence.

As always, Gray did his best to carry some of the enthusiasm and some of the fresh air of his summer travels with him into the new academic year. In mid-September, he wrote to Walpole (who was himself laid up in Arlington Street with a severe fit of gout) hoping to console him on his illness, and commenting as well on the state of his own health. His overall buoyancy of mood, although smacking of what some might interpret as a certain Rouchefoucauldian discrimination or lack of sympathy, he credited to his recent expedition, and to the simple and straightforwardly beneficial effect of physical exercise. 'The smartness of the pain you undergo', he paused to observe to his friend, 'is an undoubted sign of strength and *youth*, & the sooner it will be over'.

Walpole was to remain ill for many weeks, and Gray's own improved health was to prove temporary; the neurasthenia soon returned as the weather grew wetter and chillier, and his own reprieve from the pain of the gout was, as we shall see, destined soon to come to an end. He attempted to focus his attention on matters which extended beyond his own health and spirits, and looked around for something to which he might turn his hand. Earlier in the year he had sent an outline – comprising an introduction and four separate sections – to Thomas Warton, who was then in the midst of planning his *History of English Poetry*. Warton had either been told by Hurd that Gray himself had gone so far as to have drawn up a plan for precisely such a work, or, indeed, he may already himself have seen the *Advertisement* prefaced to the Norse and Welsh odes in the 1768 edition of the *Poems*, and requested that Hurd, in turn, pass on 'any fragments, or sketches of a design' for the work on to him. Gray's reply to Warton, in any event, was an extended and careful one, constituting, as William Powell Jones put it, 'a beautiful gesture, for he had really abandoned the project when he took up English architecture and antiquities in the spring 1758 as a prelude to an intense study of English history for the next three or four years'.[14] 'You may well', he wrote Warton,

> think me rude or negligent, when you see me hesitating for so many months, before I comply with your request, and yet (believe me) few of your friends have been better pleased than I to find this subject (surely neither unentertaining, nor unuseful) had fallen into hands so likely to do it justice, few have felt a higher esteem for your talents, your taste, & industry. in truth the only cause of my delay has been a sort of diffidence, that would not let me send you anything so short, so slight, & so imperfect, as the few materials I had begun to collect, or the observations I had made on them. A sketch of the division & arrangement of the subject however I venture to transcribe, and would wish to know, whether it corresponds in any thing with your own plan, for I am told your first volume is already in the press. (*CTG* 1122–23)

The plan that Gray appended to the letter was thorough in its intention of studying the cultural background of English verse, and the origin of rhyme in Latin, French, Italian, and eventually English verse:

[14]   Powell Jones, 107.

INTRODUCTION

On the poetry of the *Galic* (or Celtic) nations, as far back as it can be traced.

On that of the Goths: its introduction into these islands by the Saxons & Danes, & its duration. on the origin of rhyme among the Franks, the Saxons, & Provençeaux. some account of the Latin rhyming poetry from its early origin down to the 15th Century.

P: 1

On the School of Provence, which rose about the year 1100, & was soon followed by the French & Italians. their heroic poetry, or romances in verse, Allegories, fabliaux, syrvientes, comedies, farces, canzoni, sonnets, balades, madrigals, sestines, &c:

Of their imitators the *French*, & of the first *Italian* School (commonly call'd the Sicilian) about the year 1200 brought to perfection by Dante, Petrarch, Boccace, & others.

State of Poetry in England from the Conquest (1066) or rather from Henry 2d's time (1154) to the reign of Edward 3d (1327).

P: 2

On *Chaucer* who first introduced the manner of the Provençaux improved by the Italians into our country. his character & merits at large; the different kinds in which he excell'd. Gower, Occleve, Lydgate, Hawes, G: Douglas, Lindsay, Bellenden, Dunbar, &c:

P: 3

Second Italian School (of Ariosto, Tasso, &c:) an improvement on the first, occasion'd by the revival of letters the end of the 15th century. The lyric poetry of this & the former age introduced from Italy by Ld Surrey, Sr. T. Wyat, Bryan, Ld Vaux, &c: in the beginning of the 16th century.

Spenser, his character. Subject of his poem allegoric & romantic, of Provençal invention: but his manner of [treating] it borrow'd from the Second Italian School. Drayton, Fairfax, Phin: Fletcher, Golding, Phaer, &c: this school ends in Milton. . . .

P: 4

School of France, introduced after the Restoration. Waller, Dryden, Addison, Prior, & Pope, which has continued down to our own times. (*CTG* 1123–24)

Warton confessed himself 'infinitely obliged' to Gray for the document, and articulated his regret 'that a writer of [Gray's] own consummate Taste' had not had the opportunity of executing it for himself. He maintained his differences with Gray on a number of points both major and minor (he eventually felt compelled to admit that dramatic verse – omitted from consideration in his own original plan as well as left unconsidered in Gray's outline – 'necessarily fell into [his] general design'), but concluded his correspondence with the poet with a profound and sincerely felt compliment. 'I cannot take my Leave', he wrote, 'without declaring, that my strongest incitement to prosecute the *History of English Poetry* is the pleasing hope of being approved by you; whose *true genius* I so justly venerate, and whose *genuine Poetry* has ever given me such sincere pleasure'.

Warton had not, of course, been the only one to whom it occurred to seek Gray's advice as an author on matters 'poetical'. For all his attempts to distance himself from the general flow of society both in Cambridge and in London, Gray was still capable of striking up new friendships – some of them with unlikely or unexpected subjects. One such relationship was initiated in this, the final year of Gray's life, with Richard Farmer, a Fellow of Emmanuel College. Gray had probably known Farmer as a casual acquaintance for several years; although he is never mentioned by name in any of Gray's earlier letters, Farmer shared the poet's keen interest in old English literature. Several years earlier, the antiquarian Thomas Percy had been in contact with Farmer with regards to the *Reliques of Ancient English Poetry*, an anthology of older English verse which Percy eventually published in three volumes in 1765. Percy had apparently asked Farmer to solicit Gray's opinion about the collection. When Gray did not respond immediately to Percy's request for information, the latter took offense (Percy knew Gray only slightly, having met with him in September, 1761, while taking tea with him in his chambers). A few years later Percy again approached Farmer for advice – on this second occasion with respect to the work of Henry Howard, Earl of Surrey – and again Farmer appears to have suggested Gray's friend Mason as a possible resource. Percy this time wrote back openly to Farmer, 'I would rather go a hundred miles in search myself, than ask a single question either of him or his brother Gray'.[15] Farmer nevertheless seems finally, in 1770, to have met Gray in a slightly more amicable situation; the two dined together one evening, in the company of a Mr. Oldham, at Peterhouse. The writers' interests could not help but – within the confines of such a small academic community – bring the two men together (although, despite their shared passion for poetical antiquities, the two men were

---

[15]   See *CTG* Appendix N, Gray and Thomas Percy (1229–34).

strikingly dissimilar in their appearance and demeanour). William Cole recalled:

> It must have been about the Year 1770; as the first Time they ever met to be acquainted together, was about that Time, I met them at Mr. Oldham's Chambers in Peter House to Dinner. Before, they had been shy of each other; and tho' Mr. Farmer was then esteemed one of the most ingenious men in the University, yet Mr Gray's singular Niceness in the Choice of his Acquaintance made him appear fastidious to a great Degree to all who was not acquainted with his Manner. Indeed there did not seem to be any Probability of any great Intimacy, from the Style & Manner of each of them: the one a chearful, companionable, hearty, open, downright Man, of no great Regard to Dress or comon Forms of Behaviour; the other, of a most fastidious & recluse Distance of Carriage, rather averse to all Sociability, but of the graver Turn: nice & elegant in his Person, Dress & Behaviour, even to a Degree of Finicalness & Effeminacy. So that Nothing but their extensive Learning & Abilities could ever have coalesced two such different Men: & both of great Value in their own Line & Walk. They were ever after great Friends, & Dr Farmer & all of his Acquaintance had soon after too much Reason to lament his Loss, & the Shortness of their Acquaintance. (*CTG* 1119–20)

Clouds, as Cole's reflections at the end of his account here suggest, had begun already darkly to gather on the approaching horizon of Gray's life.

CHAPTER THIRTEEN

CONVERSING WITH SHADOWS

Final Months and Death
1770–1771

I. Health and Spirits

Michaelmas Term began badly. A crippling attack of gout left Gray confined to his rooms for the first three weeks of October. He was compelled to spend much of the time resting on his couch or propped up in a sitting position in bed. Visits and physical disturbances of any kind were kept to a minimum. As in the past, the disease affected Gray primarily in the joints of the ankles and the feet, leaving his lower extremities extraordinarily sore and tender to the slightest touch. The mitigating 'compliment' conventionally extended to such sufferers – a saying which intimated that gout, though painful itself, was in truth the 'earnest of a long life' – offered little consolation to one who had come to regard the affliction as merely symptomatic of a larger, systemic pattern of deterioration. 'Life' itself, as Gray had written only half-jokingly in a letter to Walpole one month earlier, was now, he felt, 'only the name of another distemper, of which I know enough already to say, when the gout pinches me, '*tis well, it is nothing else*'. Gray felt himself to be well within his rights in regarding even his day-to-day existence (much as Alexander Pope had done with rather more justification before him) as little more than a 'long disease'.

Gray's illness had on this occasion set in after an extended chill; his attack followed hard on the heels of a fever which the poet had attempted to cure by drinking large amounts of sage tea. Gray's body was now enervated – the physical network which we would today describe as his 'immune system' was weak and compromised – and his recourse to enormous quantities of herbal tea had probably not helped matters any. Gray had at first tried to ward off the gout with a continued regimen of physical exercise. Chastising his friend's tendency towards what he gently characterized as 'Indolence and want of motion', Gray insinuated that Walpole's own near-concurrent attack of gout (he, too, had only recently been laid up with the disease for a period of several weeks) must to some extent be regarded as the latter's own fault. 'Man is a creature made to be jumbled', he wrote in a chiding letter to Walpole on 17 September, '& no matter whether he goes on his head or heels, move or be moved he must'. 'I am convinced I owe my late and present ease', Gray commented on the same occasion, and with apparently no sense of foreboding, 'to the little expeditions I always make in summer'. His summer's lease on good health had proven that year, however, to have had a shorter date than usual. Even by the end of October, Gray would write to Mason that he was only just beginning once again to walk on his own and without any assistance.

Gray's several infirmities left him weak and without interest in his readings. His scholarly and academic routines held no greater charms. No doubt he fingered the pages of a few familiar volumes – his interleaved copies of the works of Linneaus, of William Hudson's stunning *Flora Anglica*, and other collections devoted to natural history could be placed on small tables within easy reach of the invalid – but the slightest physical movement was liable to prompt an intolerable spasm of pain. Even so, Gray attempted to maintain as cheerful a demeanour as possible before his friends and relations, using humour to deflect what he perceived to be an excessive and at times embarrassing solicitation on his own behalf. He observed in a letter to Mason that he would not have bothered even to have mentioned this most recent seizure of his illness at all, had he not already been well persuaded that the latter, too (were he not more careful of his own health and diet), would soon fall victim to such attacks himself. His own illness, Gray gestured with the histrionic sensibility of a comically patient martyr, was meant to stand as a warning to Mason; apropos of his own, latest convalescence, Gray took the opportunity slyly to chastise his correspondent's tendency to 'talk so relishingly of [his] old Port'. For all such casually summoned raillery, there remained a note of genuine querulousness in Gray's comments to Mason. However much he affected to make light about his own suffering, Gray's affliction worked to sour even the memories of such slight and temperate pleasures as were now generally forbidden him by his physicians and colleagues.

The necessary period of Gray's confinement left him little with which to entertain himself other than the internal affairs of his college. He read the local newspapers as usual, and listened to the conversations of those Fellows who were back in residence. Like so many convalescents confined to their beds or otherwise restricted to a limited range of social conversation, he began even more intensely than usual to invest the small world which surrounded him with greater significance than it might otherwise have merited. A letter to Mason dated 24 October was full of the latest gossip and 'University news'. Although the comings and goings of students had long since become a matter of routine for Gray, the events of the recent past were still too strongly present in his memory to leave the spectacle of the simultaneous arrival of so many young men untouched by a lingering sense of nostalgia or regret. Rather than permitting any overtly elegiac note for Bonstetten to creep into his own correspondence, however, Gray sought at once a refuge and a defense in a more light-hearted tone of voice. His pose of epistolary deflection, as usual, was very close to seamless; nothing concerning the behavior of the undergraduates, the voice of Gray's letters insinuates, could come close to surprising him. Lord Richard Cavendish, a son of the Duke of Devonshire, was noted to be leaving Cambridge, 'having digested all the learning and all the beef this place could afford him'. The satiric effect of Gray's casual zeugma is meant to serve as some indication as to just how scholarly Cavendish's inclinations had ever really been in the first place. That same gentleman's 'little Brother George' (Lord George Augustus Henry Cavendish, afterwards created Earl of Burlington) would be taking his place at Trinity. Francis Foljambe, who had matriculated at St John's as Fellow–Commoner in 1768, having first studied as a pupil under Mason's former curate, John Wood, was noted with similar dispassion to have 'resided in college & persevered in the ways of godliness till about ten days ago, when he disappear'd, & no one knows whither he is gone, a hunting or a fornicating'.

Gray reported in passing to Mason that Alleyne Fitzherbert, the youngest son of William Herbert of Tissington, in Derbyshire, had entered St. John's as a pensioner in July. Fitzherbert arrived in Cambridge with a formal letter of introduction to the poet; the young man had nevertheless been surprised one late summer afternoon by the distinction of a personal visit from Gray. The poet was accompanied – or so Fitzherbert himself recalled much later in life – by Dr. Thomas Gisborne, Stonhewer, and Palgrave. 'They walked one after one', Fitzherbert recalled in a reminiscence of the tribute of Gray's visit,

> in Indian file. When they withdrew, every College man took off his cap as he passed, a considerable number having assembled in the quadrangle to see Mr. Gray, who was seldom seen. I asked Mr. Gray, to the great dismay of his companions, what he thought of Mr. Garricks [sic] Jubilee Ode, just published? He answered, He was easily pleased.[1]

This anecdote comes to us at no fewer than three removes. Fitzherbert related the incident to Samuel Rogers, who in turn passed the story on to Mitford, who eventually included it in his edition of Gray's poems. The credibility of the account is consequently open to some question. Would the undergraduates assembled in the second court actually have stood waiting, cap in hand, merely to catch a glimpse of the great poet as he passed by? His recent vacation and imminent confinement to his rooms notwithstanding, was Gray really perceived to be such a recluse

---

[1] Fitzherbert's account is reprinted in CTG 1149.

within the University community – was he really 'so seldom seen', as Fitzherbert puts it – so as to make such an informal, albeit public, visit to another college an event to be treated with such ceremony and reverential awe? The visit (inspection is not, perhaps, too strong a word) appears, in any event, to have been something in the nature of a personal favour; Gray's primary reason for having paid such a public and (potentially) socially indecorous visit to an undergraduate's rooms in the first place was merely to have been able succinctly to report back to Mason (as he indeed did in his letter of 24 October) that 'the little Fitzherbert . . . seems to have all his wits about him'. Most chroniclers of Gray's life have dismissed the anecdote as untrue or, at the very least, exaggerated. Yet Gray's achievements as a poet had long since earned him such attention and respect. Fitzherbert, who later entered the diplomatic service and who would eventually, in 1791, be created an Irish peer, leaves us with an anecdotal glimpse of a Thomas Gray whose very presence in Cambridge was a matter of respect and even veneration.

*

No sooner had Gray begun to recover from his most recent attack of the gout than his weakened system succumbed to yet another miserable cough and cold. The onset of this latest illness was hastened by some of the worst weather the country had seen within living memory. The torrential rains of November 1770 came close to flooding entire counties. The towns and cities which lined the banks of the Severn, to the west, much like those on the Trent, to the northwest, were inundated. The *Gentleman's Magazine* for the month of November reported that in Coventry the local waters had risen unexpectedly in the middle of the night, flooding the lowermost streets of the town and resulting in the deaths of upwards of seventy people. At Bedford, on the river Ouse some twenty-five miles west of Cambridge, the canals and waterways which linked the inland town to other market communities in Bedfordshire, Cambridgeshire, and Norfolk were swollen well beyond their normal capacity. Hundreds of thousands of acres in the Fen Country lay under water. Thousands of heads of cattle had been lost to the rains. Correspondents as far away as Worcester and Gloucester wrote of the necessity of having to pay their visits and to conduct their business amongst one another sailing through the streets from house to house. Nicholls reported of wagons and coaches being violently overturned by the torrents of water near Yarmouth, and noted that the marshes that stretched almost as far as he could see from his own window appeared overnight to have been transformed into 'an Ocean'. Confined as he had been for so long by the gout and aching for some exercise beyond the college walls, Gray had taken advantage of a brief break in the clouds to ride out on the Gog Magogs – the hills that lay to the southeast of Cambridge – for a breath of fresh air. Even such modest exertion, however, now proved too much for him, however. The chest infection that followed this brief excursion again found him confined to his college, this time almost until the end of November.

Gray's subsequent convalescence was rendered no easier by the daily spectacle of his ninety-year-old aunt, Mrs. Oliffe, who was suffering a slow and painful death before his very eyes. Gray had never made any secret of the fact that he had for years dreaded the possibility that he might himself actually live long enough to have to begin taking care of some of his increasingly frail and elderly female relatives. When his aunt Mrs. Rogers had been taken ill in 1758 (the illness that preceded her death at the end of September that same year), Gray had been vaguely informed at the same time that Mrs. Oliffe, too, 'had something' – a 'something' which she took to be a paralytic stroke. 'So that it looks to me', Gray had gloomed to Wharton at the time, 'as if I should perhaps have some years to pass in a house with two poor bed-ridden Women, a melancholy object, & one that in common humanity I can not avoid'.

Mrs. Oliffe had on this latest occasion arrived in Cambridge some-time towards the end of May. She appears in her final weeks to have been lodged very close to Gray, perhaps within the precincts of Pembroke College itself. Gray, again, had never professed any great fondness for Mrs Oliffe. It was she, we should remember, whom he once called 'the Dragon of Wantley's Dam' and 'an old Harridan'. Her character had not improved with age. Mrs. Oliffe's imminent collapse was nevertheless painful even to watch. His aunt's physician, Gray wrote to Nicholls,

> twice a day comes to increase the torture. she is just as sensible & as impatient of pain, and as intractable as she was 60 years ago. she thinks not at all of death, & if a mortification does not come to release her, may lie in this agony for months (at least) helpless & bed-rid. this is what you call a *natural* death! (*CTG* 1151)

His aunt's illness deepened Gray's own sense of hopelessness. In the silences punctuated only by his own racking cough, he was left to consider the inescapable implications of their mutual disintegra-tion. The contrast between having so recently witnessed the display of Bonstetten's youthful energy, and being confronted (as he was now) with such a transparent and diurnal masquerade of mortality was almost too much for him to bear. A 'natural death' as prolonged and as gruesome as that of Mrs. Oliffe, Gray now became convinced, was all that he had left to which he might, himself, look forward.

Mrs. Oliffe appears at the very least to have been gratified in having received the distinction of her nephew's attention. Upon the final event of her death some few months later – and just weeks before Gray's own passing – she left her few possessions not to her nieces, the Antrobuses, who had undertaken the more unpleasant practicalities of caring for her physically throughout her final illness, but rather to Gray himself. Such a gesture was to some extent only to be expected. Gray had taken a great deal of time and trouble over the years ensuring that the several members of his mother's family were comfortable in Cambridge; his Antrobus cousins knew that they could look to their celebrated relation for practical advice, and that they might even, when necessary, press him to put his own personal reputation and authority in the small town to work to their advantage. Although Gray had on at least one occasion protested to his cousin Mary that his connection with 'People in power' was 'very small', he still felt it a responsibility to look to the family interests as best he could. The terms of Mrs. Oliffe's will were not so much a slight to her own, nearer relations, as they were a gesture of acknowledgment – a mark of respect – to the unlikely individual who now stood as the formidable and highly respected *paterfamilias* of the Gray–Antrobus family.

Gray tried his best to shake off the shadows of mortality as the wet and windy autumn afternoons deepened into the unpleasant promise of an even more inhospitable winter. There were now increasingly few consolations to be had, however. Bonstetten, who had been spending some time with his brother at Aubonne, near Geneva, had written once before finally returning home to Berne. The promised oil portrait had still not arrived in Cambridge – 'nor (I suppose) ever will' Gray suspected – but the uncertainty as to its conveyance or even where, precisely, it was to be sent, left open the possibility of its imminent arrival. In his surviving references to Bonstetten (at least in those letters addressed to Nicholls), Gray constantly and carefully sought to distance himself from the young man. The physical pain of the gout, the intractability of his latest illness, the approaching death of his closest living relative and the pervasive damp and chill of the grim winter weather – all these things together worked to persuade Gray that the possibility of any journey to Switzerland in the near future was at best a swiftly dissipating dream.

*

On 16 December, Gray's tenuous health was assaulted by news of yet another death. The cantankerous Dr. Roger Long, having served as Master of Pembroke for as many years as anyone in the college could remember (in fact, since 1733), finally died at the grand old age of ninety. Few if any members of the college were particularly distraught at the news of Long's passing, especially since the vacancy was within days filled by the election of the more amiable James Brown to the post. Together the college Fellows celebrated Brown's election by redecorating the Master's Lodge, quickly dispensing with Long's collection of arcane scientific instruments – his spheres, astrolabes, lyrichords, and orreries – and generally 'brightening' the place up. Its new inhabitant, Gray wrote, taking an evident pleasure in Brown's own excitement and enthusiasm, was 'lost like a mouse in an old cheese'. Fortune seemed suddenly to have smiled upon Brown. In addition to the salary of £150 a year which accompanied the Mastership, he was within weeks also granted the living of Streatham, near Ely. The place brought him an additional £300 per annum. The vacancy had been granted to Brown (with Grafton's support) in the face of some considerable opposition, and Gray was both proud of and happy for his old acquaintance. 'Uncle Toby will have about £400 a year', Gray calculated in a letter to Nicholls, commenting that such remuneration was 'no uncomfortable pittance' for their 'honest friend'.

Long's own eccentricities had worked finally to add a bizarre note to the transition of power and to his own interment. Many years earlier, Long had insisted on constructing and maintaining, in the Master's garden, a kind of basin within which he would from time to time peddle his 'water-velocipede' – a craft designed to provide him with a rigorous if idiosyncratic form of aquatic exercise. Water from the pool had for years slowly been leaking into the vault of the college chapel; the rise in the over-saturated local water table due to the recent flooding must have exacerbated the situation even further. When the time came to lower the late Master's coffin into the ground, the members of the college found themselves depositing Long's remains into a foot or more of muddy, near-freezing water. Long's body had been encased in a wooden coffin before being placed in a larger receptacle of stone – on which were pinned a copy of elegiac verses written by members of the college – but the spectacle still came close to being macabre and disrespectful, not to say indecent.

William Cole, who had travelled the short distance from nearby Milton to attend the service, was among those who professed themselves shocked by the 'slovenliness' of the funeral ceremony. The lesson read for the sermon may have been the right one for the day in question, but it nevertheless remained patently unsuitable to the occasion of Long's interment. Nothing could have prepared the stunned Cole, however, for the sight of Long's coffin only half disappearing into the murky waters beneath the saturated college vault. He made a point of looking around for Gray soon after the ceremony, but was reluctant to draw his friend away from the other Fellows who had together gathered in the Combination Room. 'I wrote the next Day a Note to him', Cole later recalled,

of the unceremonious & indecent Manner of the Funeral, & concluded
by saying, that after what passed in the Chapel to compleat all, they had
taken the poor [Master] from a warm Hall & a noble Fire & flung him
into a Well or Ditch half full of Water. (*CTG* 1155)

To the servant who carried Cole's note Gray only replied mischievously:

How did we know, pray? No Body here remember'd another Burying of
the Kind: shall be proud of your Advice the next opportunity, which (we
hope) will be some Forty years hence. I am sorry you would not send for
me last Night. I shall not be able to wait on you chez vous, so soon as I
would wish, for I go in a few Days to Town, when I shall see Mr. Walpole.
(*CTG* 1155)

The visit to Walpole here mentioned to Cole, taken together with the
rising star of Brown's fortunes, at least had a positive effect on Gray's
spirits. He stayed in London for just over two weeks. By the time he
returned to Cambridge, he was once again eager to offer literary advice
to Nicholls. Having made a note of Nicholls's comments in one of
his more recent letters that he had lately been reading Froissart's
Chroniques, Gray responded with enthusiasm, suggesting a number
of other French histories, such as Monstrelet's *Chroniques de France*,
Villehardoin's *La Conquette de Constantinople*, and Joinville's *Histoire
de Saint Louis*. The patterns of Nicholls's reading may have recalled to
Gray's mind the slightly jumbled and genially haphazard nature of his
own, earliest encounters with some of the same French histories and
romances. 'Our Ancestors', he commented in a letter of 26 January, 'used
to read the Mort d'Arthur, Amadis de Gaul, & Froissart, all alike, that
is, they no more suspected the good faith of the former than they did of
the latter, but took it all for history'. The gleeful indiscrimination with
regard to such texts as Gray described here characterized not only
the habits of his vaguely designated 'Ancestors', but those of his
own youthful reading. Throughout January, in fact, Gray appears to
have been returning to the dim memories of his own earliest years at
Cambridge – memories now tinged with a sort of pleasant melancholy.
Gray may not, as a youth, have confounded history and romance in quite
the same manner he suggests the earliest English historians once did, but
the simple memory of having so easily and eagerly roamed through such
works is still for him, even after such an extraordinary distance of time
and experience, a pleasant one.

The weeks immediately before Christmas had continued unseasonably warm but still wet, with unusually strong winds sweeping down
from the northwest and bringing, as Gray put it, 'vast quantities of rain
instead of winter'. The first snow did not fall in the university town until

Christmas day itself. When the cold weather finally arrived, it did so
with a vengeance. The holidays (and, we should remember, Gray's last,
celebrated birthday on the 26th) were followed by some of the coldest
weather Gray himself had ever seen in Cambridge. The mercury stood
at 16 degrees Fahrenheit the second week of January. At London the
Thames froze over (though the bitter cold seems to have ruled out the
possibility of a frost fair, such as the one which had been celebrated in
December 1683). The freezing weather may well have brought to Gray's
mind the last such 'hard winter' on record – the severe weather of
1739–40 – on which occasion West had even written a Latin poem on
the subject and sent it to Gray, who, then in the midst of his European
tour, had been staying at Bologna. Gray had promptly copied West's
verses into his own Commonplace Book. Then, as now, the city streets
were clogged with snow and ice. Three or four horses were needed to
pull hackney coaches through the near-impassable slush. Coal carts
intent on delivering the heavy fuel which had first been deposited at the
riverside wharves required teams of no less than eight horses to carry
their burden into the city. There were numerous accidents even on the
widest and the most heavily travelled thoroughfares. Pedestrians were
generally kept indoors by the bitterly chill winds which whipped off the
icy river and into the streets.

   Still troubled by his persistent cough, Gray kept to his rooms as much
as possible. The portrait of Bonstetten had finally arrived, but had
proved after so much anticipation to be a disappointment. It no more
resembled its young subject, Gray complained to Nicholls, than he
himself resembled Hercules. 'You would think it was intended for his
Father', Gray grumbled, 'so grave & so composed. Doubtless he meant
to look, like an Englishman or an owl'. Gray continued to pay lip service
to the possibility of undertaking the journey to Switzerland that coming
summer, but he was now careful always to temper the optimism of
Nicholls's increasingly elaborate plans; given the current state of his
health, such a journey seemed to Gray in his more candid moments to
be 'next to impossible'. Nicholls was persistent in his entreaties that they
begin at least to make some practical plans for the trip. Bonstetten too,
Gray's friend maintained, was looking forward to some more concrete
articulations concerning the pair's dates and destinations. Bonstetten
wrote to Nicholls in early March, and the repeated invitation was passed
on to Gray. The advent of some milder spring weather had served only
to whet Nicholls's own increasing appetite for the journey. 'Yesterday I
received a letter from De Bonstetten', he wrote to Gray on 16 March,

   crammed fuller than it could hold, and containing besides two little after-
   thoughts, one three inches by two, the other two by one, which flew out
   when I opened the letter like the oracles of the Sybil. But I like this much

better than any I have received; he intreats us a deux genoux to come, and I you in the same posture and with equal earnestness; if he does not esteem me he is an idiot to take so much pains to persuade me to believe it, because, if he were false, I see no end that it could answer to make a dupe of me at the expense of so much labour and unnecessary dissimulation. He promises, if we come, that he will visit us in England the summer following. Let us go then, my dear Mr. Gray, and leave low thoughted care at the foot of the mountains, for the air above is too pure for it. During the winter, my wandering inclinations are quiet in their hybernacula; but these two or three last glorious days succeeding the rigour of such an unusual season, have awakened them; the animal and vegetable world rejoice, and everything that has life in it begins to shew it. I have lived in the air (being fortunately compelled to attend my garden myself) except during dinner, &c. The effect of this and De Bonstetten's letter is, that I find myself something 'che mi sprona' invincibly to go to Switzerland this summer. A deux genoux, I again intreat you to go with me. (*CTG* 1172)

Nicholls's spring fever prompted him to begin making some practical arrangements for his own departure and absence. He was ready to 'bespeak a curate from the first of June to the last of October', so as to clear his professional desk and have no truly serious excuses for remaining at home.

Gray, however, did not even respond to this latest entreaty on the part of Nicholls. An entire month and a half passed before the latter again took up his pen, once more hoping to prod Gray into some practical course of action concerning the venture. 'It is six weeks since I received De Bonstetten's letter', Nicholls wrote patiently but with increasing pressure on the poet,

in consequence of which I wrote to you; I have long waited for your determination, to enable me to answer it; my own was already made when I wrote to you, only I cannot fix a time till I know yours. I need not say whether it would be agreeable to me to have your company in such a voyage; without it, I shall lose half the pleasure and advantage I flattered myself with the hope of, but I shall go at all events. I should think the first or second week in June, at furthest, is quite late enough to begin the journey; if so, it is high time, I think, to give notice to De Bonstetten. . . . If you don't go with me, I shall go alone. (*CTG* 1183)

The tone of this last letter prompted Gray finally to reply. He could not yet bring to an end the possibility that he might still be well enough soon to undertake the journey to Switzerland as originally planned. Professing not to have realized that Nicholls had been awaiting his own decision before writing to Bonstetten, Gray began,

I can not tell you, what I do not know myself; nor did I know, you staid for my determination to answer B:s letter. I am glad to hear you say, you shall go at all events, because then it is sure, I shall not disappoint you; & if (which I surely wish) I should be able to accompany you, perhaps I may prevail upon you to stay a week or fortnight for me: if I find it will not do, you certainly shall know it. (*CTG* 1184)

Gray had only days before the arrival of Nicholls's entreaty received a 'strange' letter from Bonstetten that he confessed he was yet at a loss fully to understand. In the letter, Bonstetten professed himself to be '*le plus malheureux des hommes*' and informed Gray that he was '*decidé a quitter son pays*'. 'In short', Gray wrote Nicholls, the letter betrayed 'strong expressions of uneasiness & confusion of mind, so much as to talk of *un pistolet & du courage*, & all without the shadow of a reason assigned, & so he leaves me'. 'He is either', Gray reasoned, 'disorder'd in his intellect (which is too possible) or has done some strange thing, that has exasperated his whole family & friends at home, which (I'm afraid) is at least equally possible'.

   Toward the beginning of the final week of May, Gray returned to London, where he lodged in Jermyn street (not, as had hitherto been his practice, with the hosier, Mr. Roberts, but in rooms belonging to an 'oilman', one Mr. Frisby). The stay was to be the poet's last visit to London. Only upon settling into his rooms did he undertake finally to put Nicholls's expectations regarding their travelling together to rest. 'I am but indifferent well', he wrote,

> & think, all things consider'd, it is best not to keep you in suspense about my journey. the sense of my own duty, which I do not perform, my own low spirits (to which this consideration not a little contributes) & (added to these) a bodily indisposition make it necessary for me to deny myself that pleasure, which perhaps I have kept too long in view. I shall see however with your eyes, & accompany you at least in idea. (*CTG* 1187–88)

The 'duty' to which Gray refers again consisted only of the phantas-magoric cluster of professional responsibilities that he felt to have been entailed by his acceptance of the Cambridge professorship. Gray's 'bodily indisposition', however, continued to worsen, and his friends worried that his state of mind could only contribute to his ill-health. Nicholls promptly replied to Gray's letter with a confession that while he was certainly disappointed by the prospect of undertaking his Continental journey alone, he was 'infinitely more concerned' to find Gray as dejected as he appeared to be. With each letter Gray seemed to grow more down-hearted and morose. 'For God's sake', Nicholls finally exploded in a letter of 27 May in exasperation and worry, how can you neglect a duty which never existed but in your own imagination, which catches every alarm too quickly? it never yet was performed, nor I believe expected. I hope your want of health is not so great as you think it. Is it the gout, a return of any former complaint, or what? But you need not answer my question, I am coming to town to be satisfied. I design to be there Wednesday sennight, and you will do me the favour to bespeak for me the story above you at Frisby's or some other lodging near you for a week. (*CTG* 1190)

Nicholls arrived in London, as promised, shortly before his departure for Bonstetten and Switzerland that June. Excited as he was about his summer travels, he had first to make certain that Gray was not, as usual, busy worrying himself to death over nothing.

II. Leaving This World

Yet Nicholls was no doubt troubled – shocked, even – by what he found when he finally arrived in Jermyn street. The poet's health had seriously deteriorated within a matter only of a few months. Gray was waking every morning to chills, fevers, cramps, and nausea, the passing of which left him 'weak & spiritless' for the rest of the day. The neuralgic pain in his head seemed now rarely to leave him. Just about the only productive work he had been able to undertake had been to read through the manuscript of William Gilpin's *Observations on the River Wye*. Having only recently covered much of the same ground as Gilpin, Gray had himself requested to see the latter's self-professed 'remarks' (the two shared a friend in William Mason). As Gilpin later wrote in the preface to his *Observations* (the work was to remain unpublished until 1782),

> the handsome things [Gray] said of them . . . gave them, I own, some little degree of credit in my own opinion; and made me somewhat less apprehensive of risking them before the public. . . . Had he lived, it is possible he might have been induced to have assisted me with a few of his own remarks on scenes which he had so accurately examined; the slightest touches of such a master would have had their effect. No man was a greater admirer of nature than Mr Gray, nor admired it with better taste.[2]

Generous to the last in his comments on and reactions to the writing of contemporary authors whose work he admired, Gray, we remember, had only several weeks before similarly responded at considerable length to

---

[2]   The relevant passage of Gilpin's preface is reprinted in *CTG* 1143.

Book I of James Beattie's poem, *The Minstrel*. 'I shall give you my undisguised opinion of him, as he proceeds', Gray had warned Beattie shortly after receiving the author's gift of a copy of that work, 'without considering to whom he owes his birth, and sometimes without specifying my reasons'. Beattie in turn found Gray's comments for the most part 'perfectly just' and noted them to be 'excellent hints' for any future revision of the work. 'Mr. Gray', Beattie later reflected in his own, judicious review of the poet's written comments to his work, 'has been very particular'. 'I am greatly obliged to him for the freedom of his remarks', he concluded, 'and think myself as much so for his objections as his commendations'.[3]

A visit to Arlington street to see Walpole, who was in the final stages of preparing for his own, imminent departure for Paris, had also provided Gray with some welcome diversion. Yet Walpole, too, was disconcerted by the noticeable alteration for the worse in the appearance and demeanour of his old friend. 'I thought him changed', Walpole wrote with hindsight to Cole later that same month, 'and that he looked ill'. Even so, Walpole credited the unpredictable nature of Gray's by now chronically poor health for his lassitude and poor colour, and appears to have been comfortable enough leaving Gray to care for himself as he once again crossed the Channel to revisit France.

Gray's old friend 'Billy' Robinson also paid a final visit to the poet some time in late May or early June. Robinson, unlike either Nicholls or Walpole, found Gray's mood to be uncharacteristically retrospective and revelatory. Robinson later recalled that he managed to coax Gray into talking about his own career as a poet, and that the author of the *Elegy* voiced some regret that he had not, when possessed of the time and the energy, been more productive. The last year or so had only just begun to find himself in comfortable or, as he put it, 'easy' circumstances, and now, Gray went on to complain with some bitterness, he was to lose his health completely before he was able to accomplish anything of substance. At the last moment, however, Gray checked himself, wearily observing that it would be impious to rail against a providential design the greater structure of which he could not, even as he neared the end of his life, possibly begin to comprehend.

Toward the middle of June, Gray's illness had weakened him to the point that he felt it necessary to call on Doctor Gisborne for a consultation. On Gisborne's advice, he booked a room in Kensington – then still a comparatively small village outside the metropolis – in order to 'take the air' for about two weeks, but soon returned to Jermyn street

---

[3] Reprinted in *CTG* 1171.

with little to show for his semi-rural sojourn. Nicholls also remained with Gray for several days before his own departure for Paris; other visitors in town included both Mason and Stonhewer. In his *Reminiscences*, Nicholls, who memorably lamented the fact that he had kept no very precise record of so many of his conversations with Gray, nevertheless professed to recall his last meeting with his friend in great detail. Their final conversation concerned Gray's anxiety that Nicholls would, on his visit to France, inadvertently contribute to the fame and reputation of Voltaire. 'When I took my leave of him, & saw him for the last time, at his lodging in Jermyn Street, before I went abroad in the beginning of June 1771', Nicholls wrote,

> he said, 'I have one thing to beg of you, which you must not refuse.' – I replied you know you have only to command, what is it? – 'Do not go to see Voltaire' . . . I said I 'Certainly will not; but what could a visit from me signify?' – 'Every tribute to such a man signifies.' – This was when I was setting out for Switzerland to pay a visit to Monsr de Bonstetten in which he would have accompanied me if his health had permitted. (*CTG* 1289)

'I kept my word', Nicholls scrupulously recalled, 'for I passed a month at the Chateau d'Aubonne near Lausanne with Mr de Tcharner Bailiff of the district & did not go to Ferney'. Gray's distrust and even detestation of the power of Voltaire's irreligious views ('No one' Gray had earlier in his life commented to Nicholls, 'knows the mischief that man will do') remained with him till the end; as the consolations of Gray's own religious beliefs made themselves felt with greater force and relevance as his own health failed, so too the antithetical tenets of the renowned atheist of *Les Délices* and Ferney grew ever more distasteful. The notion that reason tempered by scepticism and humour might provide some substantial protection against the evils and sufferings inherent in man's existence was a view for which Gray had less and less patience as he grew older. Only several months earlier, on 17 March, he had written to Walpole:

> Atheism is a vile dish, tho' all the cooks in France combine to make new sauces to it. As to the Soul, perhaps they may have none on the Continent; but I do think we have such things in England. Shakespear, for example, I believe had several to his own share. As to the Jews (tho' they do not eat pork) I like them because they are better Christians than Voltaire. (*CTG* 1175)

For Nicholls, while in France, to have visited Voltaire would not merely have indicated a lack of respect for Gray's own judgement; he would have been putting his very soul in danger. Voltaire – the 'inexhaustible, eternal, entertaining scribbler' of earlier years – had become in time a moral and spiritual troublemaker to be avoided at all costs. '*Il avait le diable au corps*', said Sainte-Beuve of Voltaire; Gray would appear to have felt that Voltaire not only had the devil *in* his body, but possessed something of the eternal adversary's appalling charm as well.

   Before finally feeling well enough to undertake the return journey to Cambridge, Gray also received a formal call from a friend of Nicholls's, one John Clarke, a lieutenant in the royal navy. Soon after his visit Clarke wrote to William Temple describing his impression of the famous poet. 'As much as I admired the man for his Genius', Clarke wrote feelingly, 'so much more did I admire him when I saw him for his benevolence and humanity which I never saw so strong in any body in my Life. It shined out in every word, look, and motion.'[4] Our last image of Thomas Gray as a living, socially active individual is one in which, for all the debilitating weakness of his age and illness, his simple and willing participation in the vital drama of human existence is as strong and as forceful as ever.

*

   Gray returned to Cambridge on Monday, 22 July. He intended his stay to be a brief one; he still planned to set out to visit Wharton at Old Park within a matter of days. That Wednesday afternoon, however, while eating dinner in the College Hall, he suffered from an attack of nausea so overwhelming that he was forced to leave the table and – with the help of some of the college Fellows – retire to his rooms nearby. Brown wrote to Wharton from Gray's rooms that same evening politely conveying his friend's regrets that he was unable to undertake the journey to Durham. Again confined to his couch, Gray was experiencing not only the fatigue, lassitude, and fever which had troubled him throughout the preceding months, but was now liable to be suddenly and violently ill. Travelling the considerable distance to Wharton's home, however welcome the hospitality that awaited at his journey's end, was clearly out of the question. Gray rested that evening and on the following morning Dr. Robert Glynn, a friend of Gray's and at that time the most celebrated physician in Cambridge, was called in to attend the poet. 'This Dr, Glynn', Edmund Gosse would write in his account of Gray's life, 'was conspicuous for his gold-head cane, scarlet coat, three-cornered hat, and resounding pattens for thirty years after Gray's death, and retains a niche in local history as the last functionary of the university

---

[4]   Reprinted in *CTG* 1191–92.

who was buried by torchlight.'[5] Glynn informed Brown that Gray's illness was 'something like a Gout in the Stomach'. The doctor assured him that there were many degrees of the disorder and expressed his professional opinion that Gray might very well recover from the attack within a matter of days. Glynn's diagnosis, however, which rested on an ill-conceived theory of 'retrocedant' gout, which postulated that the disease could leave the joints directly to attack the stomach or heart, was mistaken. Gray was in fact suffering through the final stages of uremia, his increasingly painful symptoms resulting from his body's inability – due to kidney damage – to expel waste products by way of urine, and leading to abnormally high amounts of nitrogenous substances in the blood. Gray's own body, in other words, was slowly poisoning itself.

After passing the evening of the 25th in tolerable comfort Gray, unable even to keep down a small glass of milk, was on the following morning again ill. Dr. Glynn returned, this time bringing with him Dr. Russell Plumptre, the Fellow of Queen's College and Professor of Physic whose medical opinions Gray had so much valued in the past. The two began visiting the patient three and even four times a day. They were still convinced that Gray was suffering from an attack of gout, although they were by this time distressed that they seemed unable to get the better of it. Brown, who confessed more candidly in a letter to Wharton that he was afraid that Gray's friend at Old Park would 'see him no more', had by now alerted Gray's friends and family to the fact that the poet was seriously ill. His faithful servant Stephen Hempstead, who had only a few months earlier left Gray's service to marry and set up his own public house, returned to his former master's side and nursed him with a diligence and care which apparently brought the dying poet a great deal of comfort. Gray's cousin, Mary Antrobus, also arrived to watch and sit with him in the dim, candle-lit room.

Gray himself was by now well aware that his death was imminent. There was even, in the calmer moments which followed upon his fits, a certain tranquility and resignation in his face and demeanour. He at one point turned to his cousin and said simply, 'Molly, I shall die.' He had, beginning Friday and throughout the weekend, suffered violent convulsive fits, and by Monday his mind had grown increasingly disordered. Still, he drifted in and out of consciousness, on one occasion inquiring alertly and almost genially as to the precise nature of his illness, and even paying the doctors himself with money he offered to them from his own purse; at other times he babbled incoherently, racked by convulsions and delirium. He never, Brown later assured both Wharton and

[5] Gosse, 205.

Nicholls, expressed 'the least uneasiness at the thoughts of leaving this world'. On Monday evening Stonhewer arrived with Dr. Gisborne, but after several painful consultations the two returned to London, the physician having resigned any hopes for his patient's recovery. Gray clung to life all throughout the following day, regaining consciousness only indistinctly to instruct those attending him where they might find a copy of his will. By nine o'clock Tuesday evening Brown, sitting in the gathering darkness of Gray's rooms, sensed that the end was near. At around eleven o'clock that night, having slipped into unconsciousness some few hours earlier, Thomas Gray died.

WHERE WE START FROM

A little less than two weeks after Gray was buried in the church-yard at Stoke Poges that August, Brown sat down to write a short note to Thomas Wharton, assuring him that all of their friend's final requests had been attended to as best as possible. The poet's set of rooms at Pembroke had within only a matter of days been emptied of his possessions; the parlour door stood open now as if to receive its new occupant. For Brown, the experience of such a swift transformation was itself disturbing. 'Every thing is now dark and melancholly at Mr. Gray's Room', he wrote Wharton,

> not a trace of him remains there, it looks as if it had been for sometime uninhabited and the room bespoke for another inhabitant. The Papers are in good hands. Mr. Mason carried them with him to York, and his furniture he bequeathed to his Relations here. The thoughts I have of him will last, and will be useful to me the few years I can expect to live. He never spoke out, but I believe from some little expressions I now remember to have dropt from him that for some time past he thought himself nearer his end than those about him apprehended it. (*CTG* 1275)

Mason also wrote to Wharton late that August. The man who had himself been appointed to serve as Gray's literary executor had been distressed to learn of his friend's death only a 'full ten days after it had happened'; once the news had reached him, however, he hurried down to Cambridge, where he spent the better part of a week tidying up the poet's affairs. Brown had insisted that Mason accompany him to London to prove the will, and together the two men had sorted through the poet's effects. Mason's 'first business', he informed Wharton, would be to sift through Gray's letters, 'which', he noted, 'are numerous'. In the months to come, Mason would eventually need to return to London to transfer some of the poet's stocks, and 'to give up the title Deeds of the House in Cornhill'. 'Excuse great Haste & much confusion of mind', he apologized to Wharton in a post-script, 'for I have been hurryed & concerned beyond expression'.

Walpole, it will be recalled, had learned of the death of his lifelong friend not by means of any personal word or message, but through the pages of a newspaper account in Paris about 10 August. Following his return to London and Arlington Street that September, Walpole expressed his regret that no more substantial literary remains had been

found among the poet's papers. As he wrote to Stonhewer from Strawberry Hill following his return from France:

> The loss of Him was a great blow to me, & ought to be so to the World,
> as Mr Mason tells me he has left behind Him nothing finished, which
> might have compensated his death to them, tho not to his Friends. He
> was a Genius of the first rank, and will always be allowed so by Men of
> taste. (*CTG* 1281)

William Cole had conveyed a detailed account of Gray's final days to
Walpole in the last week of August, noting the satisfactory accomplishment of the poet's final wishes, detailing the disposition of his property,
and offering some description of the event of the burial itself. Brown
would eventually write a similar letter to Norton Nicholls, following
Nicholls's final return from his tour of Switzerland and Italy in the early
summer of 1773, informing him of some 'little Presents' and 'Memorials' which Gray had intended to have passed on to his young
friend following his death. Included among these presents was 'a little
picture of [Bonstetten]' – the same portrait the arrival of which Gray
had so eagerly awaited in the final months of his life. 'We thought it
wou'd be acceptable to you', Brown wrote to Nicholls, 'and therefore
with Mr. Mason's full approbation it is sent, and makes a part of
your parcel'.

Certain important facets of Gray's posthumous reputation as a poet
– the myth of the melancholy elegist who otherwise 'never spoke out' –
were already being set in place in the months immediately following
his death. Mason's systematic and devastating bowdlerization of the
materials left at his disposal as literary executor would help fuel the
notion that Gray was (as Gosse was eventually to put it in own his life
of the poet) an emotionally handicapped individual who 'lived, more
even than the rest of us, in an involuntary isolation, a pathetic type of
solitude of the soul'.[1] Mason's censorship of Gray's literary remains,
when taken with Gray's own native reticence and (even more particularly) with his lifelong literary techniques of parodic deflection and ventriloquism, acted as a kind of catalyst that further hastened the living
poet's transformation into a more purely 'literary' or fictional trope.

In a striking instance of synchronicity, Henry Mackenzie's popular
'novel of sentiment' *The Man of Feeling* was first published in April
1771; the second, corrected edition of Mackenzie's genre-defining work
was printed in August of that year – the very same month as Gray's
funeral. In the final chapter-fragment of *The Man of Feeling*, the novel's
ostensible narrator describes the burial of Harley, the hero whose over-

---

[1] Gosse, 210.

whelming and unfailingly charitable sensibility has been documented
in the various vignettes of sentiment and benevolence chronicled
in Mackenzie's tale. The 'Conclusion' to *The Man of Feeling* tells us of
Harley:

> He had hinted that he should like to be buried in a certain spot near the
> grave of his mother. This is a weakness; but it is universally incident
> to humanity: 'tis at least a memorial for those who survive; for some
> indeed a slender memorial will serve; and the soft affections, when they
> are busy that way, will build their structures, were it but on the pairing
> of a nail.
>
> He was buried in the place he had desired. It was shaded by an old
> tree, the only one in the church-yard, in which was a cavity worn by time.
> I have sat with him in it, and counted the tombs. The last time we passed
> there, methought he looked wistfully on that tree: there was a branch of
> it, that bent towards us, waving in the wind; he waved his hand, as if he
> mimicked its motion. There was something predictive in his look! perhaps
> it is foolish to remark it; but there are times and places when I am a child
> at those things.
>
> I sometimes visit his grave; I sit in the hollow of the tree. It is worth
> a thousand homilies! every nobler feeling rises within me! Every beat of
> my heart awakens a virtue! – but it will make you hate the world – No:
> there is such an air of gentleness around, that I can hate nothing; but, as
> to the world – I pity the men of it.[2]

The 'Conclusion' to *The Man of Feeling* reads like a prose translation –
or at least a prose re-visioning – of Gray's famous *Elegy*; the more peculiar similarities to the circumstances of Gray's own death and burial
make such a connection even more remarkable. Harley's sentimental
weaknesses, much like the sentiments of Gray's poem, are seen to be
'universally incident to humanity', and even the most frail or 'slender'
memorial will serve to perpetuate the stuff of such gentle memories.
Later generations of readers would so combine the sentimental 'man of
feeling' and the elegist of Gray's *Elegy* so as almost completely to blur
the distinctions between the two. An air of gentleness still hovers around
the church-yard at Stoke Poges itself; but, as to the world – the time has
long since come not so much to pity the men of it, but better to understand and so, perhaps, to learn from them.

[2] Henry Mackenzie, *The Man of Feeling* (Oxford: Oxford University Press, 1970)
132–33.

BIBLIOGRAPHY

Works by Thomas Gray and Important Editions of Gray's Life, Works, and Correspondence

Commonplace Books. 3 Vols. Pembroke College Library, Cambridge.

The Complete Poems of Thomas Gray. Ed. H. W. Starr and J. R. Hendrickson. Oxford: Clarendon Press, 1935; 1966.

Correspondence of Gray, Walpole, West and Ashton (1734–1771) Chronologically arranged and edited with Introduction, Notes And Index. Ed. Paget Toynbee. 2 Vols. Oxford, 1815.

Correspondence of Thomas Gray. Ed. by Paget Toynbee and Leonard Whibley, with Corrections and Additions by H. W. Starr. 3 Vols. Oxford: Clarendon Press, 1935; 1971.

Designs by Mr. Bentley for Six Poems by Mr. T Gray. London: Printed for R. Dodsley in Pall-Mall, 1753.

'An Elegy Wrote in a Country Church Yard'. Eton College Library, Eton.

Odes, by Mr Gray, Printed at Strawberry Hill. London: R. & J. Dodsley, 1757.

Poems by Mr Gray. London: J. Dodsley and Glasgow: R. Foulis, 1768.

The Poems of Thomas Gray. To Which are prefixed Memoirs of His Life and Writings by W. Mason, M.A. York: Printed by A Ward and sold by J. Dodsley, Pall-Mall, London, and J. Todd, Stonegate, York, 1775.

The Poems of Thomas Gray, William Collins, and Oliver Goldsmith. Ed. Roger Lonsdale. London: Longmans, 1969.

Selected Poems. Ed. Arthur Johnston. London: Edward Arnold, 1967.

The Works of Thomas Gray, [Ed. John Mathias] 2 vols. London, 1814.

The Works of Thomas Gray. [Ed. John Mitford] 4 vols. London: 1835–36.

The Works of Thomas Gray with Memoirs of his Life and Writings by William Mason to which are subjoined Extracts Philological, Poetical and Critical from the Author's original Manuscripts selected and arranged by Thomas James Mathias. 2 vols. London, 1814.

The Works of Thomas Gray; Containing His Poems, and Correspondence with Several Eminent Literary Characters. To Which are added, Memoirs of his Life and Writings, by W. Mason, M.A. London, 1821.

The Works of Thomas Gray in Prose and Verse. 4 vols. Ed. Edmund Gosse. London: 1884.

The Works of Thomas Gray. 2 vols. Ed. John Mitford. London: J. Mawman, 1816.

Secondary Sources

Abrams, M. H. *The Mirror and the Lamp: Romantic Theory and the Critical Tradition*. New York: W. W. Norton and Co., 1953; 1958.

Ackroyd, Peter. 'Biography: The Short Form' in *The New York Times Book Review* (10 January, 1999) 4.

——. *Blake: A Biography*. New York: Ballantine Books, 1995.

Adams, Reginald H. *The Parish Clerks of London*. London and Chichester: Phillimore Press, 1971.

Addison, Joseph. *The Spectator*. 4 vols. Ed. Gregory Smith. London: J. M. Dent and Sons, 1907; 1970.

Akenside, Mark, James Macpherson, and Edward Young, *Selected Poetry*. Ed. S. H. Clark. Manchester: Carcanet Press, 1994.

Albin, Eleazar. *A Natural History of English Insects*. London, 1720.

Arber, Edwards, ed. *English Songs*. London: Henry Frowde, n.d.

Ariès, Philippe. *Western Attitudes Toward Death*. Trans. Patricia M. Ranum. Baltimore: The Johns Hopkins University Press, 1974.

Arnold, Matthew. *The Complete Prose Works of Matthew Arnold*. Volume IX: English Literature and Irish Politics. Ed. R. H. Super. Ann Arbor, Michigan: University of Michigan Press, 1973.

———. 'Thomas Gray' in *Essays in Criticism* 2nd ser., London: Macmillan, 1889, 69–99.

Atkins, J. W. H. *English Literary Criticism, 17th & 18th Centuries* London: Methuen and Co., 1951.

The A to Z of Georgian London. Introductory Notes by Ralph Hyde. Lympne Castle, Kent: Harry Margay, in association with Guildhall Library, London, 1981.

Attwater, A. *Pembroke College, Cambridge: A Short History*. Cambridge: Cambridge University Press, 1936.

Auerbach, Erich. *Mimesis: The Representation of Reality in Western Literature*. Trans. Willard R. Trask. Princeton: Princeton University Press, 1953.

Ausonius. *The Works of Ausonius*. Edited with an Introduction and Commentary by R. P. H. Green. Oxford: Clarendon Press, 1991.

Austen-Leigh, R. A., ed. *Eton College Register: 1698–1752. Alphabetically Arranged and Edited with Biographical Notes*. Eton, Windsor: Spottiswoode, Ballantyne and Co., 1927.

———. *Eton Records*. Eton, Windsor: Spottiswoode and Co., 1903.

———. *An Illustrated Guide to Eton College* (6th ed.). Revised by R. C. Martineau. Eton, Windsor: Alden and Blackwell, 1904; 1964.

Autobiography of Alexander Carlyle of Inveresk, 1722–1805. Ed. John Hill Brown, with a new introduction by Richard B. Sher. Bristol: Thoemmes, 1990.

Bäckman, Sven. *Tradition Transformed: Studies in the Poetry of Wilfred Owen*. Lund: LiberLäromedel/Gleerup, 1979.

Backscheider, Paula. *Reflections on Biography*. Oxford: Oxford University Press, 1999.

Baldwin, Barry. 'Thomas Gray of Posterity' in *Notes & Queries*, 40 (September, 1993) 328–29.

Barker, Hannah, and Elaine Chalus. *Gender in Eighteenth-Century England: Roles, Representations, and Responsibilities*. London: Longmans, 1997.

Baron, Xavier, ed. *London, 1066–1914. Volume I: Medieval, Tudor, Stuart and Georgian London*. East Sussex: Helm Information Ltd., 1999.

Barthes, Roland. *Image – Music – Text*. Trans. Stephen Heath. New York: Hill and Wang, 1977.

Basden, E. B. 'Thomas Gray of Buckinghamshire – Reply' in *Notes & Queries* 13 (1966) 226–27.

Batchelor, John, ed. *The Art of Literary Biography*. Oxford: Clarendon Press, 1995.

Bate, Walter Jackson. *The Burden of the Past and the English Poet*. London: Chatto and Windus, 1971.

Bayne-Powell, Rosamond. *Travellers in Eighteenth-Century England*. London: John Murray, 1951.

Beatty, Bernard. 'Unheard Voices, Indistinct Visions: Gray and Byron' in Hutchings and Ruddick, *Thomas Gray: Contemporary Essays*, 224–47.

Bell, Charles F. 'Thomas Gray and the Fine Arts' in *Essays and Studies* 30 (1944) 50–81.

Bell, W. G. *The Great Fire of London in 1666*. London: John Lane, The Bodley Head, 1920.

Bentley, Richard. *Designs by Mr. R. Bentley for Six Poems by Mr. T. Gray*. London: Printed for R. Dodsley, 1753.

Bentman, Raymond. 'Thomas Gray and the Poetry of Hopeless Love' in *Journal of the History of Sexuality*, 3 (1992) 203–22.

Bill of Eton College and School, 1745. Eton, Windsor: E. P. Willies, 1843.

Black, Jeremy. *The Grand Tour in the Eighteenth Century*. Stroud, Gloucestershire: Sutton Publishing, 1997.

Black, Jeremy, and Roy Porter. *The Penguin Dictionary of Eighteenth-Century History*. London and Harmondsworth, Middlesex: Penguin, 1994.

Blatch, Mervyn. *A Guide to London's Churches*. London: Constable, 1978.

Bloom, Harold. *The Anxiety of Influence*. Oxford and New York: Oxford University Press, 1973.

Bonstetten, Charles-Victor de, *Souvenirs . . . Ecrits en 1831* (2nd ed.). Paris, 1832.

Boswell, James. *Boswell's London Journal*. Ed. with an Introduction by Frederick A Pottle. London: The Folio Society, 1985.

——. *Life of Johnson*. Ed. R. W. Chapman. Oxford: Oxford University Press, 1904; 1980.

Botting, Roland B. 'Gray and Christopher Smart' in *Modern Language Notes*, 57 (1942) 350–61.

Brady, Frank. 'Structure and Meaning in Gray's *Elegy*' in *From Sensibility to Romanticism*. Ed. Frederick W. Hilles and Harold Bloom. Oxford: Oxford University Press, 1965, 177–89.

Braudy, Leo. *The Frenzy of Renown: Fame and its History*. Oxford: Oxford University Press, 1986.

Brewer, John. *The Pleasures of the Imagination: English Culture in the Eighteenth Century*. New York: Farrar, Straus and Giroux, 1997.

Bronson, Bertrand. 'On a Special Decorum in Gray's "Elegy"' in *Facets of the Enlightenment. Studies in English Literature and its Contexts*. Los Angeles: University of California Press, 1968, 153–58.

Brooks, Cleanth. 'Gray's Storied Urn' in *The Well Wrought Urn* London: Dennis Dobson, Ltd. 1947, 96–113.

Brown, Marshall. *Preromanticism*. Stanford: Stanford University Press, 1991.

——. 'The Urbane Sublime' in *ELH* 45 (1978) 236–54.

Browning, Reed. *The Duke of Newcastle*. New Haven: Yale University Press, 1975.

Bryant, Jacob. 'Letter from Jacob Bryant, Concerning Particulars of the Poet Gray' in the *Gentleman's Magazine*, February 1846, i.140–43.

Brydges, Sir Samuel Egerton, *Autobiography*. 4 Vols. London, 1854.

——. *The Ruminator: Containing a Series of Moral, Critical, and Sentimental Essays*. 2 vols. London: 1813.

Burke, Séan. *The Death and Return of the Author: Criticism and Subjectivity in Barthes, Foucault, and Derrida*. Edinburgh: Edinburgh University Press, 1998.

Bygrave, Stephen. 'Gray's "Elegy": Inscribing the Twilight' in *Post-Structuralist Readings of English Poetry*. Eds. Richard Machin and Christopher Norris. Cambridge: Cambridge University Press, 1987, 162–75.

Cantabrigia Depicta: A Concise and Accurate Description of the University and Town of Cambridge. Cambridge, 1763.

Carlisle, Nicholas. *A Concise Description of the Endowed Grammar Schools in England and Wales*. 2 vols. London, n.d.

Carnochan, W. B. 'The Continuity of Eighteenth-Century Poetry: Gray, Cowper, Crabbe, and the Augustans' in *Studies in the Eighteenth Century*, 7, *Eighteenth Century Life*, 12 (1988) 119–27.

Carper, Thomas R. 'Dating Gray's Translations from the Greek Anthology' in *Notes & Queries*. 21 (1974) 255–56.

——. 'Gray's "Orders of Insects": A Mnemonic Device' in *Notes & Queries* 20 (1973) 213–14.

——. 'Gray's Personal Elegy' in *Studies in English Literature* 17 (1977) 451–62.

Carte, Thomas. *History of England*. 3 Vols. London: 1747.

Carter, Philip. 'Men About Town: Representations of Foppery and Masculinity in Early Eighteenth-Century Urban Society' in *Gender in Eighteenth-Century England: Roles, Representations and Responsibilities*. Eds. Hannah Barker and Elaine Chalus. Harlow, Essex: Addison Wesley Longman, 1997.

Castle, Terry. *Masquerade and Civilization: The Carnivalesque in Eighteenth-Century English Culture and Fiction*. Stanford: Stanford University Press, 1986.

Cecil, Lord David. 'The Poetry of Thomas Gray' in *Proceedings of The British Academy* 31 (1945) 43–60.

——. *Two Quiet Lives: Dorothy Osborne and Thomas Gray*. London: Constable, 1948.

Chute, Chaloner. *The History of the Vyne in Hampshire*. London: Simplein, Marshall, and Co., 1888.

Clark, S. H. ' "Pendet Homo Incertus": Gray's Response to Locke' in *Eighteenth-Century Studies* 24 (1991) 273–91.

Collagers v. Oppidans: A Reminiscence of Eton Life [By An Old Etonian]*. London: Simpkin, Marshall, and Co., 1884.

A Collection of Poems . . . By Several Hands. London: R. Dodlsey (vols. i–iii, 1748; vol. iv, 1755; vols. v–vi, 1758).

Colley, Linda. *Britons: Forging the Nation 1707–1837*. New Haven and London: Yale University Press, 1992.

Congreve, William. *Complete Works*. Ed. Montague Summers. 4 Vols. New York: Russell and Russell, 1964.

Cradock, Joseph. *Literary and Miscellaneous Memoirs*. 4 vols. (2nd ed.). London, 1826.

Craik, T. W., 'Gray's Humorous and Satirical Verse' in Hutchings and Ruddick, *Thomas Gray: Contemporary Essays*, 111–25.

Crane, Ronald S. 'Suggestions Toward a Genealogy of the "Man of Feeling" ', in *ELH: A Journal of English Literary History*, 1 (1934) 205–30.

Crompton, Louis. *Byron and Greek Love: Homophobia in Nineteenth-Century England*. Swaffham: GMP Publications Ltd., 1998.

Crouch, Charles Hall. 'Ancestry of Thomas Gray the Poet' in *Genealogist's Magazine*, vol. iii, 74–8.

Cust, Lionel. *Eton College Portraits*. Eton, Windsor: Spottiswoode and Co., n.d.

Damrosch, Leo. *The Profession of Eighteenth-Century Literature: Reflections on an Institution*. Madison, WI: University of Wisconsin Press, 1992.

Daniell, Christopher. *Death and Burial in Medieval England, 1066–1550*. London: Routledge, 1997.

Defoe, Daniel. *A Tour Through the Whole Island of Great Britain*. Ed. Pat Rogers.

Harmondsworth, Middlesex: Penguin Books, 1971.

Dickinson, Emily. *The Letters of Emily Dickinson*. Ed. Thomas H. Johnson. 3 vols. Cambridge, MA: Harvard University Press, 1958.

Dillon, Andrew. 'Depression and Release: The Journey of the Spirit in Gray's *Elegy*' in *North Dakota Quarterly* 60:4 (Fall, 1992) 128–34.

Dilworth, Ernest. 'Landor on Gray's Sonnet on the Death of West' in *Notes & Queries* 15 (1968) 215.

Doherty, F. 'The Two Voice of Thomas Gray' in *Essays in Criticism* 13 (1963) 222–30.

Doody, Margaret Anne. *The Daring Muse: Augustan Poetry Reconsidered*. Cambridge: Cambridge University Press, 1985.

Downey, James, and Ben Jones, eds. *Fearful Joy: Papers from the Thomas Gray Bicentenary Conference at Carleton University*. Montreal, London: McGill-Queen's University Press, 1974.

Draper, John W. *William Mason: A Study in Eighteenth-Century Culture*. New York: New York University Press, 1924.

Dyson, A. E. 'The Ambivalence of Gray's *Elegy*' in *Essays in Criticism*, ed. F. W. Bateson (Oxford), VII (1957) 257–61.

Easson, Angus. ' "A Man of Genius": Gray and Wordsworth' in Hutchings and Ruddick, 205–23.

Eastment, Winifred. *Wanstead Through the Ages*. Letchworth, Hertfordshire: Essex Countryside, 1946; 1969.

Edgecombe, Rodney Stenning, 'Gray, Propertius, and the Games Stanza in the Eton College Ode' in *Notes & Queries* 44 (September, 1997) 319–20.

——. 'Two Sources for Gray's "Eton College" Ode' in *Notes & Queries* 42 (March, 1995) 67–8.

——. *Wonted Fires: A Reading of Thomas Gray*. Salzburg Studies in English Literature, No. 111, Romantic Reassessment, James Hogg and Holger Klein, eds. Salzburg, Austria: Insitut für Anglistik und Amerikanistik, 1992.

Ehrenpreis, Irvin. 'The Cistern and the Fountain: Art and Reality in Pope and Gray' in *Studies in Criticism and Aesthetics, 1660–1800: Essays in Honor of Samuel Holt Monk*. Eds. Howard Anderson and John S. Shea. Minneapolis: University of Minnesota Press, 1967.

Ellis, Frank H. 'Gray's *Elegy*: The Biographical Problem in Literary Criticism' in *PMLA*, LXVI (New York: Modern Language Association of America, December, 1951) 971–1008.

——. 'Gray's Eton College Ode: the Problem of Tone' in *Papers on Language and Literature* 5 (1969) 130–38.

Elton, Oliver. *A Survey of English Literature, 1730–1780*. 2 vols. London: Edward Arnold Ltd., 1928; 1959.

Empson, William. *Some Versions of Pastoral: A Study of the Pastoral Form in Literature*. London: Chatto and Windus, 1935.

Enright, D. J., ed. *The Oxford Book of Death*. Oxford: Oxford University Press, 1987.

Epstein, William H. 'Assumed Identities: Gray's Correspondence and the "Intelligence Communities" of Eighteenth-Century Studies' in *The Eighteenth Century: Theory and Interpretation* 32 (1991) 274–88.

——. 'Professing Gray: The Resumption of Authority in Eighteenth-Century Studies' in *The Profession of Eighteenth-Century Literature*. Madison, WI: University of Wisconsin Press, 1992, 84–94.

Etoniana Ancient and Modern. London and Edinburgh: William Blackwood and Sons, 1865.

Evans, Evan. *Some Specimens of the Poetry of the Antient Welsh Bards, translated into English.* London: R. and J. Dodsley, 1764.

Evelyn, John. *The Diary of John Evelyn.* Ed. E. S. de Beer. 6 vols. Oxford: Clarendon Press, 1955.

Fairer, David. 'Thomas Wharton, Thomas Gray, and the Recovery of the Past' in Hutchings and Ruddick, *Thomas Gray: Contemporary Essays,* 146–70.

Falck, Colin. *Myth, Truth, and Literature: Towards a True Post-Modernism.* 2nd ed. Cambridge: Cambridge University Press, 1989; 1994.

Feingold, Richard. *Moralized Song: The Character of Augustan Lyricism.* London and New Brunswick, NJ: Rutgers University Press, 1988.

Ferguson, John. 'Gray and Catullus' in *Notes & Queries* 25 (1978) 60–1.

Fothergill, Brian. *The Strawberry Hill Set: Horace Walpole and his Circle.* London: Faber and Faber Limited, 1983.

Foladare, Joseph. 'Gray's "Frail Memorial" to West' in Starr, *Twentieth Century Interpretations of Gray's Elegy,* 112–14.

Foucault, Michel. *Histoire de le sexualité, vol. I: La volonté de savoir.* Paris, 1976. English translation, *The History of Sexuality,* vol. I. London, 1979.

Frost, Robert. *Selected Letters of Robert Frost.* Ed. Lawrance Thompson. New York, 1964.

Fry, Paul. *The Poet's Calling in the English Ode.* New Haven and London: Yale University Press, 1980.

Frye, Northrop. *Northrop Frye on Shakespeare.* New Haven and London: Yale University Press, 1986.

——. 'Towards Defining an Age of Sensibility' in *Eighteenth-Century Literature: Modern Essays in Criticism.* Ed. James L. Clifford. New York: Oxford University Press, 1959.

Fussell, Paul. *The Rhetorical World of Augustan Humanism: Ethics and Imagery from Swift to Burke.* Oxford: Clarendon Press, 1965.

Gay, Peter. *The Enlightenment: An Interpretation.* New York: Alfred A. Knopf, 1966.

——, ed. *The Freud Reader.* London: W. W. Norton and Co., 1989.

George, M. Dorothy. *London Life in the Eighteenth Century.* Chicago: Academy Chicago Publishers, 1925; 1984.

Gibbon, Edward. *The History of the Decline and Fall of the Roman Empire,* ed. J. B. Bury. New York: F. Defau and Co., 1906–07.

——. *Memoirs of My Life,* ed. Georges A. Bonnard London: Thomas Nelson and Sons, 1966.

Gilbert, A. N. 'The "Africane" Courts-Martial: A Study of Buggery in the Royal Navy' in *Journal of Homosexuality,* I (1974) 111–22.

Glazier, Lyle. 'Gray's *Elegy:* "The Skull Beneath the Skin"' in the *University of Kansas City Review,* XIX (Spring, 1953) 174–80.

Gleckner, Robert F. 'Blake, Gray, and the Illustrations' in *Criticism* 19 (1977) 118–40.

——. *Gray Agonistes: Thomas Gray and Masculine Friendship.* Baltimore and

London: The Johns Hopkins University Press, 1997.

Glendinning, Victoria. 'Lies and Silences' in Eric Homberger and John Charmley, eds. *The Troubled Face of Biography*. New York: St. Martin's Press, 1988, 49–62.

Golden, Morris. *Thomas Gray*. Updated edition. Boston: Twayne Publishers, 1988.

Gosse, Edmund. *Gray* in 'English Men of Letters', ed. John Morley. London: 1882; 1889.

Gottlieb, Beatrice. *The Family in the Western World, From the Black Death to the Industrial Age*. Oxford: Oxford University Press, 1993.

Granger, James. *Letters . . . with Miscellanies and Notes from Tours in France, Holland and Spain*. Ed. J. P. Malcolm. London, 1805.

'Gray's Elegy and Thanington Churchyard' in the *Gentleman's Magazine*, iii (October, 1857) 661–62.

Greene, Donald. *The Age of Exuberance: Backgrounds to Eighteenth-Century English Literature*. New York: McGraw-Hill Inc., 1970.

——. 'The Proper Language of Poetry: Gray, Johnson, and Other' in Downey and Jones, 85–102.

Griffin, Dustin. 'Gray's Audiences' in *Essays in Criticism* 28.3 (1978) 208–15.

Griffin, M. H. 'Thomas Gray, Classical Augustan' in *Classical Journal* 36 (1941) 473–82.

Grimstone, A. V., ed. *Pembroke College: A Celebration*. Cambridge: Cambridge University Press, 1997.

Groom, Nick. 'Celts, Goths, and the Nature of the Literary Source' in *Tradition in Transition: Women Writers, Marginal Texts, and the Eighteenth-Century Canon*. Alvaro Ribiero, S.J. and James G. Basker, eds. Oxford: Clarendon Press, 1996.

The Guardian. Edited with an Introduction by John Calhoun Stephens. Lexington, KY: University Press of Kentucky, 1982.

Guilhamet, Leon M. 'Imitation and Originality in the Poems of Thomas Gray' in Paul J. Korshin, *Proceedings of the Modern Language Association Neoclassicism Conferences 1967–68*. New York: AMS Press, 1970, 33–52.

Guillory, John. *Cultural Capital: The Problem of Literary Canon Formation*. Chicago: University of Chicago Press, 1993.

Gunn, Thom. *Collected Poems*. New York: Farrar, Straus and Giroux, 1994.

Gursche, Thelma. *The Bishop's Lady*. Cape Town: Howard Timmins, 1970.

Guthrie, William. *Reply to the Counter-Address*. London, 1764.

Haddas, Moses. *A History of Latin Literature*. New York: Columbia University Press, 1952.

Haggerty, George E., ' "The Voice of Nature" in Gray's *Elegy*' in *Homosexuality in Renaissance and Enlightenment England: Literary Representations in Historical Context*. Binghamton, New York: Harrington Park Press, 199–214.

Hagstrum, Jean. 'Gray's Sensibility' in *Fearful Joy*, eds. James Downey and Ben Jones, 6–19. Montreal and London: McGill – Queen's University Press, 1974.

——. *The Sister Arts: The Tradition of Literary Pictorialism and English Poetry from Dryden to Gray*. Chicago: University of Chicago Press, 1958.

Hall, Calvin S. *A Primer to Freudian Psychology*. Harmondsworth, Middlesex: Penguin Books, 1954; 1982.

Hall, Michael. *Cambridge*. Englewood Cliffs, New Jersey: Prentice-Hall Inc., 1980.

Harris, Cyril E. *Thomas Gray, Poet 1716–1771: A Guide to his Life and Works*. Huntingdon, Cambridgeshire: Photo Precision Ltd., 1971.

Harris, John. 'Garden of the Mason School: Stoke Park, Buckinghamshire' in *Country Life* (1985) 940–42.

Harris, R. W. *A Short History of Eighteenth-Century England 1689–1793*. London: Blandford Press Ltd., 1963.

Harrison, Tony. '*V*.' Newcastle-upon-Tyne: Bloodaxe Books, 1989.

Hendrickson, J. Raymond, and Herbert W. Starr, 'Two Poems Attributed to Gray' in *Notes & Queries* 8 (1961) 57–8.

Herking, Maria-L. *Charles-Victor de Bonstetten, 1745–1832, sa vie, ses oeuvres*. Lausanne: Imprimerie La Concorde, 1921.

Hewlings, Richard. *Chiswick House and Gardens*. London: BAS Printers Ltd., 1989.

Hicks, Malcolm. 'Gray Among the Victorians' in Hutchings and Ruddick, 248–69.

Hill, J. W. *A History of Eton College*. London: Hollis and Carter, 1960.

Hinnant, Charles H. 'Changing Perspectives on the Past: The Reception of Thomas Gray's The Bard' in *Clio: An Interdisciplinary Journal of Literature, History and the Philosophy of History* 3 (1974) 315–29.

Hitchcock, Tim. *English Sexualities, 1700–1800*. London: Macmillan, 1997.

Hobday, Charles. *A Golden Ring: English Poets in Florence from 1373 to the Present Day*. London: Peter Owen, 1997.

Hodgson, Godfrey. *A New Grand Tour: How Europe's Great Cities Made Our World*. Harmondsworth, Middlesex: Penguin Books, 1995.

Hollis, Christopher. *Eton: A History*. London: Hollis and Carter, 1960.

Hopkins, Gerard Manley. *The Correspondence of Gerard Manley Hopkins and Richard Watson Dixon*. 2 Vols. Ed. Calude C. Abbot. London: Oxford University Press, 1935;1975.

——. *The Letters of Gerard Manley Hopkins to Robert Bridges*. Ed. Claude Collier Abbot. London: Oxford University Press, 1935.

Hough, Graham. *The Romantic Poets*. London: Hutchinson's University Library, 1953.

Hudson, William. *Flora Anglica*. London, 1762.

Hulme, H. 'The Poet Gray and Knutsford: An Unpublished Pedigree'. Reprinted from the *Knutsford Division Guardian* (July, 1911) n.p.

Hutchings, W. B., 'Conversations with a Shadow: Thomas Gray's Latin Poems to Richard West' in *Studies in Philology* 92:1 (Winter, 1995) 118–39.

——. 'Syntax of Death: Instability in Gray's "Elegy Written in a Country Churchyard"' in *Studies in Philology* 81:4 (Fall, 1984) 496–514.

——. 'Thomas Gray: Past Criticism and Present Volume' in Hutchings and Ruddick, 1–12.

Hutchings, W. B. and William Ruddick, eds. *Thomas Gray: Contemporary Essays*. Liverpool: Liverpool University Press, 1993.

Isbell, Harold. 'Decimus Magnus Ausonius: The Poet and His World' in *Latin Literature in the Fourth Century*. Ed. J. W.

Binns. London and Boston: Routledge and Kegan Paul, 1974, 22–57.

Jack, Ian. 'Gray's *Elegy* Reconsidered' in *From Sensibility to Romanticism: Essays Presented to Frederick A. Pottle*. Eds. Frederick W. Hilles and Harold Bloom. New York: Oxford University Press, 1965, 139–69.

——. 'Gray in his Letters' in Downey and Jones, 20–36.

Jackson, Gabriele Bernhard. 'From Essence to Accident: Locke and the Language of Poetry in the Eighteenth Century' in *Criticism*, 29.1 (1987) 27–66.

Jackson, Wallace. 'Thomas Gray and the Dedicatory Muse' in *ELH* 54 (1987) 277–98.

——. 'Thomas Gray: Drowning in Human Voices' in *Criticism* 28 (1986) 361–77.

Jackson, Wallace, and Paul Yoder, 'Gray's Pindarics: Teaching "The Progress of Poesy" in Christopher Fox, ed. *Teaching Eighteenth-Century Poetry*. New York: AMS Press, 1990, 303–17.

Jarrett, Derek. *Pitt the Younger*. London: Weidenfeld and Nicolson, 1974.

Jefferies, Richard. *The Hill and the Vale*. Oxford: Oxford University Press, 1980.

Jenkins, Simon. *Landlords to London: The Story of a Capital and Its Growth*. London: Constable, 1975.

Jestin, Loftus. *The Answer to the Lyre: Richard Bentley's Illustrations for Thomas Gray's Poems*. Philadelphia: University of Pennsylvania Press, 1990.

Johnson, Samuel. *The Idler and the Adventurer*. Ed. Walter Jackson Bate, John M. Bullitt, and L. F. Powell. New Haven and London: Yale University Press, 1963.

——. *Lives of the English Poets*. Ed. George Birkbeck Hill. 3 vols. Oxford: Clarendon Press, 1905.

Johnston, Arthur. 'Gray's "Triumphs of Owen"' in *Review of English Studies* 11 (1960) 275–85.

——. 'Poetry and Criticism After 1740' in *Sphere History of Literature: Dryden to Johnson*, ed. Roger Lonsdale London: Sphere Reference, 1971; 1986.

——. 'Thomas Gray: Our Daring Bard' in Downey and Jones, 50–65.

Jones, Ben. 'Blake on Gray: Outlines of Recognition' in Downey and Jones, 127–35.

Jones, Myrddin. 'Gray, Jacques, and the Man of Feeling' in *Review of English Studies* 25 (1974) 39–48.

Jones, William Powell. 'The Contemporary Reception of Gray's *Odes*' in *Modern Philology* 28 (1930–31) 61–82.

——. 'Imitations of Gray's *Elegy* 1751–1800' in *Bulletin Of Bibliography* 23 (1963) 230–32.

——. 'Johnson and Gray: A Study in Literary Antagonism' in *Modern Philology*, 56 (1959) 243–53.

——. 'Thomas Gray's Library' in *Modern Philology* 35 (1938) 257–78.

——. *Thomas Gray, Scholar: The True Tragedy of an Eighteenth-Century Gentleman*. Cambridge, MA: Harvard University Press, 1937.

Kallich, Martin. 'Thomas Gray's Annotations to Pope's "Essay on Man"' in *Notes & Queries* 12 (1965) 454–55.

Kaul, Suvir. *Thomas Gray and Literary Authority*. Stanford, CA: Stanford University Press, 1992.

Keats, John. *Letters of John Keats*. Ed. Robert Gittings. London and Oxford: Oxford University Press, 1970.

Keay, John. *The Honourable Company: A History of the East India Company*. New York: Macmillan, 1991.

Kendall, Paul Murray. *The Art of Biography*, with a new Prologue by Stephen B. Oates. London: W. W. Norton and Co., 1965; 1985.

Kermode, Frank. *English Pastoral Poetry*. London: G. Harrap, 1952.

Kernan, Alvin. *Printing, Technology, Letters & Samuel Johnson*. Princeton, NJ: Princeton University Press, 1987.

Kerr, Douglas. *Wilfred Owen's Voices: Language and Community*. Oxford: Oxford University Press, 1993.

Ketton-Cremer, Robert Wyndham. *Horace Walpole*. New York: Longmans, Green, and Co., 1940.

——. *Thomas Gray: A Biography*. Cambridge: Cambridge University Press, 1955.

Kittredge, G. L. 'Appendix – Gray's Knowledge of Norse' in *Selections from the Poetry and Prose of Thomas Gray*, ed. W. L. Phelps. Boston: Ginn, 1894.

Kowaleski-Wallace, Elizabeth. *Consuming Subjects: Women, Shopping, and Business in the Eighteenth Century*. New York: Columbia University Press, 1997.

Krutch, Joseph Wood, ed. *The Selected Letters of Thomas Gray*. New York: Farrar, Straus, and Young, 1952.

Kuist, James M. 'The Conclusion of Gray's Elegy' in *South Atlantic Quarterly* 70 (1971) 203–14.

Laing, Alastair. 'Clubhouse Neo-Classicism: Sculpture at Stoke Poges'. *Country Life* (1983) 186–88.

Lang, J. *Rebuilding of St. Paul's After the Great Fire of London*. Oxford: Oxford University Press, 1956.

Langford, Paul. *A Polite and Commercial People: England 1727–1783*. Oxford: Oxford University Press, 1992.

Lerner, Laurence. *The Uses of Nostalgia: Studies in Pastoral Poetry*. New York: Schocken, 1972.

The Letters of Junius. Ed. John Cannon. Oxford: Clarendon Press, 1978.

Levine, William. 'From the Ridiculous to the Sublime: Gray's Transvaluation of Pope's Poetics' in *Philological Quarterly*, 70:3 (Summer, 1991) 289–309.

Lewis, Wilmarth S. *Rescuing Horace Walpole*. New Haven and London: Yale University Press, 1978.

——. *Thomas Gray, 1716–1771 (R. A. Neil Lecture)* Cambridge: Pembroke College, 1971.

Lillywhite, Bryant. *London Coffee Houses: A Reference Book of Coffee Houses of the Seventeenth and Eighteenth and Nineteenth Centuries*. London: George Allen and Unwin, Ltd., 1963.

Lindsey, Patricia. *The Story of Stoke Court*. Based on research carried out by Joan Philpot, Bayer Plc, 1996.

Litten, Julian W. S. *The English Way of Death: The Common Funeral Since 1450*. London: Robert Hale, 1991.

Locke, John. *An Essay Concerning Human Understanding*. Ed. Peter H. Nidditch. Oxford: Clarendon Press, 1975.

London and Its Environs. Six vols. London: R & J Dodsley, 1761.

Lonsdale, Roger. 'Gray and Johnson: The Biographical Problem' in Downey and Jones, 66–84.

Lonsdale, Roger. 'The Poetry of Thomas Gray: Versions of the Self', *Proceedings of the British Academy*, 59 (1973) 105–23.

Lovejoy, Arthur O. *The Great Chain of Being*. Cambridge, MA: Harvard University Press, 1936.

Lyles, Albert M. 'Historical Perspective in Gray's College Ode' in *Tennessee Studies in English* 9 (1964) 57–61.

Lyte, H. C. Maxwell. *A History of Eton College* (4th ed.). London: Macmillan and Co., 1911.

McCarthy, B. Eugene. *Thomas Gray: The Progress of a Poet*. London: Associated University Presses, 1997.

McDermott, Anne. 'The "Wonderful Wonder of Wonders": Gray's Odes and Johnson's Criticism', in Hutchings and Ruddick, 188–204.

MacDonald, Alastair. 'Thomas Gray: An Uncommited Life' in *The Humanities Association Review* 13 (1962–63) 13–25.

——. 'Gray and His Critics: Patterns of Response in the Eighteenth and Nineteenth Centuries' in Downey and Jones, 172–97.

McGann, Jerome. *The Poetics of Sensibility: A Revolution in Literary Style*. Oxford: Oxford University Press, 1996.

McIntire, Walter T. *Lakeland and the Borders of Long Ago*. Carlisle: Charles Thurman and Sons, 1948.

Mack, Maynard. *Alexander Pope, A Life*. New York and London: W. W. Norton and Co., in association with Yale University Press, 1985.

McKenzie, Alan T. *Thomas Gray: A Reference Guide*. Boston: G. K. Hall, 1982.

Mackenzie, Henry. *The Man of Feeling*. Ed. Brian Vickers. Oxford: Oxford University Press, 1970.

Maclean, Kenneth. *John Locke and the English Literature of the Eighteenth Century*. New York: Russell and Russell, 1962.

——. 'The Distant Way: Imagination and Image in Gray's Poetry' in Downey and Jones, 136–145.

McMurray, William. 'Peterhouse Dinners in the Eighteenth Century' in *Notes & Queries*, XI series, vol. 1 (January–June, 1910) 485.

McNairn, Alan. *Behold the Hero: General Wolfe and the Arts in the Eighteenth Century*. Montreal and Kingston: McGill-Queen's University Press, 1997.

Maddox, Brenda. 'Biography: A Love Affair or a Job' in *The New York Times Book Review* (May 9, 1999) 47.

Malcolm, J. P. *Londinium Redevivum*. 4 vols. London, 1802–1807.

Mandel, Eli. 'Theories of Voice in Eighteenth-Century Poetry: Thomas Gray and Christopher Smart' in Downey and Jones, 103–18.

Manning, Peter J. 'Wordsworth and Gray's Sonnet on the Death of West' in *Studies in English Literature*, 22:3 (Summer, 1982) 505–18.

Marchand, Leslie. *Byron: A Portrait*. London: John Murray, 1971.

Martin, Robert. *Chronologie de la vie et de l'oeuvre de Thomas Gray*. London: Humphrey Milford. Paris: Les Presses Universitaires de France, 1934.

——. *Essai sur Thomas Gray*. Paris: Les Presses Universitaires de France, 1931.

Maurois, André. *Aspects of Biography*. Trans. Sydney Castle Roberts. New York: Frederick Ungar Publications Co., 1929.

Mell, Donald C., Jr. 'Form and Meaning in Augustan Elegy: A Reading of Thomas Gray's "Sonnet on the Death of Richard West"' in *Papers on Language and Literature* 4 (1968) 131–43.

Micklus, Robert. 'Voices in the Wind: The Eton Ode's Ambivalent Prospect on Maturity' in *English Language Notes* 18 (1981) 181–86.

Milton, John. *The Complete Poems*. Ed. John Leonard. Harmondsworth, Middlesex: Penguin Books, 1998.

Mowl, Timothy. *Horace Walpole*. London: John Murray, 1996.

Newey, Vincent. 'The Selving of Thomas Gray' in Hutchings and Ruddick, 13–38.

Newman, Gerald, ed. *Britain in the Hanoverian Age, 1714–1837: An Encyclopedia*. New York and London: Garland Press, 1997.

Newman, W. M. 'When Curfew Tolled the Knell', in *The National Review*, CXXVII (September, 1946) 244–48.

Nichols, John. *Illustrations of the Literary History of the Eighteenth Century*. London, 1828.

Norton, C. E. *The Poet Gray as a Naturalist*. Boston: Harvard University Press, 1903.

Northup, Clark S. *A Bibliography of Thomas Gray*. New Haven: Yale University Press, 1917.

——. 'Addison and Gray as Travellers'. In *Studies In Language and Literature*, 390–439. New York: Henry Holt and Co., 1910.

Oates, Mary I. 'Jonson, Congreve, and Gray: Pindaric Essays in Literary History' in *SEL: Studies in English Literature*, 19 (1979) 387–406.

Observations on the Present State of the English Universities. . . . London: M. Cooper, 1759.

The Official Guide to Burnham Beeches. London: The Corporation of London, 1993.

O'Gorman, Frank. *The Long Eighteenth Century: British Political and Social History, 1688–1832*. London: Arnold, 1997.

Olsen, Kirstin. *Daily Life in 18th-Century England*. London: Greenwood Press, 1999.

Omberg, Margaret. *Scandinavian Themes in English Poetry, 1760–1800*. Stockholm: Almqvist and Wiksell, 1976.

Owen, Wilfred. *Collected Letters*. Eds. Harold Owen and John Bell. London: 1967.

The Oxford Dictionary of Quotations. 4th ed. Ed. Angela Partington. Oxford: Oxford University Press, 1992.

Paglia, Camille. *Sexual Personae: Art and Decadence from Nefertiti to Emily Dickinson*. New York: Vintage, 1990.

Panofsky, Erwin. *Renaissance and Renascences in Western Art*. New York and London: Harper and Row, 1969.

Parini, Jay. *Robert Frost: A Life*. New York: Henry Holt and Co., 1999.

Parrinder, Patrick. *Authors and Authority: English and American Criticism 1750–1990*. New York: Columbia University Press, 1991.

Pattison, Robert. 'Gray's "Ode on the Death of a Favourite Cat": A Rationalist's Aesthetic' in *University of Toronto Quarterly* 49 (1979–80) 156–65.

Pepys, Samuel. *The Shorter Pepys*. Selected and Edited by Robert Latham. London: Bell and Hyman, 1985;1995.

Picard, Liza. *Restoration London*. London: Weidenfeld and Nicolson, 1997.

Pindar, *Odes*. Trans. Richmond Lattimore. Chicago: University of Chicago Press, 1941.

Pinsky, Robert, trans. *The Inferno of Dante*. London, 1996.

Pittock, Murray G. H. *Inventing and Resisting Britain: Cultural Identities in Britain and Ireland, 1685–1789*. London: Macmillan Press Ltd., 1997.

Pope, Alexander. *The Correspondence of Alexander Pope*. 5 vols. Edited by George Sherburn. Oxford: Clarendon Press, 1956.

——. *The Poems of Alexander Pope*. Edited by John Butt. New Haven: Yale University Press, 1963.

Porter, Roy. *English Society in the Eighteenth Century*. Harmondworth, Middlesex: Penguin Press, 1982; 1990.

——. *London: A Social History*. Cambridge, MA: Harvard University Press, 1995.

Porter, Roy and G. S. Rousseau, *Gout: The Patrician Malady*. New Haven and London: Yale University Press, 1998.

Porter, Stephen. *The Great Fire of London*. Stroud, Gloucestershire: Sutton, 1996.

Price, Martin. 'Sacred to Secular: Thomas Gray and the Cultivation of the Literary' in Maximillian Novak (introd.) *Context, Influence, and Mid-Eighteenth-Century Poetry*. Los Angeles: William Andrews Clark Memorial Library, University of California, 1990, 41–78.

Prideaux, W. F. 'Gray and the Antrobus Family' in *Notes and Queries*, 11th series, vi (1912) 461.

Pugh, R. B., General Editor. *The Victorian History of the Counties of England*. London: Oxford University Press, 1959.

Quinney, Laura. ' "Tintern Abbey," Sensibility, and the Self-Disenchanted Self' in *ELH* 64 (1997) 131–56.

Ramazani, Jahan. *Poetry of Mourning: The Modern Elegy from Hardy to Heaney*. Chicago: University of Chicago Press, 1994.

Reddaway, T. F. *The Rebuilding of London After the Great Fire*. London: Jonathan Cape, 1940.

Redford, Bruce. *The Converse of the Pen: Acts of Intimacy in the Eighteenth-Century Familiar Letter*. Chicago: University of Chicago Press, 1986.

——. 'Thomas Gray's Parody of Addison's Ballad Criticism' in *Notes & Queries* 30 (February, 1983) 42–43.

——. *Venice and the Grand Tour*. New Haven and London: Yale University Press, 1996.

Reed, Amy Louise. *The Background of Gray's Elegy*. New York: Russell and Russell Inc. (1924) 1964.

Rhiel, Mary, and David Suchoff. *The Seductions of Biography*. London, 1996.

Rogers, Deborah D. 'The Problem of Copy-Texts for Gray's Epitaph on Mrs. Clerke' in *English Language Notes* 26:2 (December, 1988) 30–34.

Rogers, Pat. *The Augustan Vision*. London: Weidenfeld and Nicolson, 1974.

Rogers, Pat, ed. *The Context of English Literature: The Eighteenth Century*. New York: Holmes and Meier Publishers, Inc., 1978.

Rolph, C. H. *Further Particulars*. Oxford: Oxford University Press, 1988.

Rothstein, Eric. *Restoration and Eighteenth-Century Poetry, 1660–1780*. Vol. 3, Routledge History of English Poetry.

Boston and London: Routledge and Kegan Paul, 1981.

Rousseau, George S. *Perilous Enlightenment: Pre and Post-modern Discourses: Sexual, Historical*. Manchester and New York: Manchester University Press, 1991.

——. 'The Pursuit of Homosexuality in the Eighteenth Century: "Utterly Confused Category" and/or Rich Repository' in *'Tis Nature's Fault": Unauthorized Sexuality During the Enlightenment*. Ed. Robert P. Maccubbin. Cambridge: Cambridge University Press, 1985.

Ruddick, William. 'Thomas Gray's Travel Writing' in Hutchings and Ruddick, 126–45.

Ryskamp, Charles. 'Wordsworth's *Lyrical Ballads* in their Time' in *From Sensibility to Romanticism*, Frederick W. Hilles and Harold Bloom, eds. New York: Oxford University Press, 1965.

Sabor, Peter, ed. *Horace Walpole: The Critical Heritage*. London and New York: Routledge and Kegan Paul, 1987.

Sacks, Peter M. *The English Elegy: Studies in the Genre from Spenser to Yeats*. Baltimore and London: Johns Hopkins University Press, 1985.

Sambrook, A. J. 'Gray's *Elegy* and Thomas Gordon's Tacitus' in *Notes & Queries* 19 (1972) 228.

Scoggins, James. 'The Preface to *Lyrical Ballads*: A Revolution in Dispute' in *Studies in Criticism and Aesthetics, 1660–1800: Essays in Honor of Samuel Holt Monk*, Howard Anderson and John S. Shea, eds., Minneapolis: University of Minnesota Press, 1967.

Sedgewick, Eve Kosofsky. *Between Men: English Literature and Male Homosocial Desire*. New York: Columbia University Press, 1985.

Sells, A. L. Lytton. *Thomas Gray: His Life and Works*. London: George Allen and Unwin, 1980.

Sha, Richard C. 'Gray's Political *Elegy*: Poetry as Burial of History' in *Philological Quarterly* 69 (1990) 337–57.

Shattuck, Roger. 'Nineteen Theses on Literature' in *Essays in Criticism*, vol. xlv, no. 3 (July 1995) 193–98.

Sheppard, Francis. *London: A History*. Oxford: Oxford University Press, 1998.

Sherbo, Arthur. 'Two Notes on Gray's Poems' in *Notes and Queries* 36 (March, 1989) 62.

Sieveking, Giberne. *The Memoir of Sir Horace Mann*. London: Kegan Paul, Trench, Trübner and Co., Ltd., 1912.

Sinclair, F. D. *The Chronology of Gray's Elegy: An Essay on the Origins of the Poem*. Communications of the University of South Africa, 1963.

Sinclair, John D., trans. *Dante, The Divine Comedy 1: Inferno* Oxford: Oxford University Press, 1939;1979.

'The Site of the Churchyard of Gray's "Elegy"' in *Notes & Queries* vol. 157 (July–December, 1929) 193.

Sitter, John. *Literary Loneliness in Mid-Eighteenth-Century England*. Ithaca, New York, and London: Cornell University Press, 1982.

——. 'The Flight from History in Mid-Eighteenth-Century Poetry (and Twentieth-Century Criticism)' in *The Humanist as Citizen*. Eds. John Agresto and Peter Riesenberg. Chapel Hill, NC: National Humanities Center, 1981, 94–116.

Snow, Malinda. 'The Gray Parody in *Brave New World*' in *Papers on Language and Literature* 13 (1977) 85–88.

Snyder, Edward D. *The Celtic Revival in English Literature*. Cambridge, MA: Harvard University Press, 1923.

——. 'Thomas Gray's Interest in Celtic' in *Modern Philology*, 11 (1914) 559–79.

Snyder, Robert Lance. 'The Epistolary Melancholy of Thomas Gray' in *Biography: An Interdisciplinary Quarterly* 2 (1979) 125–40.

Spacks, Patricia Meyer. 'Artful Strife: Conflict in Thomas Gray's Poetry' in *Publications of the Modern Language Association of America*, 81 (1966) 63–69.

——. *The Poetry of Vision: Five Eighteenth-Century Poets*. Cambridge, MA: Harvard University Press, 1967.

Sparrow, John. 'Gray's Spring of Tears' in *Review of English Studies* 14 (1963) 58–61.

Speck, W. A., *Literature and Society in Eighteenth-Century England: Ideology, Politics, and Culture*. London: Longmans, 1998.

Spiegel, Maura and Richard Tristman. *The Grim Reader: Writings on Death, Dying, and Living On*. New York: Doubleday, 1997.

Starr, Herbert W. *A Bibliography of Thomas Gray, 1917–1951*. Philadelphia, 1953.

——. *Gray as a Literary Critic*. Philadelphia: University of Pennsylvania Press, 1953.

——. ' "A Youth to Fortune and to Fame Unknown": A Re-estimation' in *Journal of English and American Philology*, XLVIII, no. 1 (January, 1949) 97–107.

——. ed. *Twentieth Century Interpretations of Gray's Elegy: A Collection of Critical Essays*. Englewood Cliffs, NJ: Prentice-Hall, 1968.

Steele, James. 'Thomas Gray and the Season for Triumph' in Downey and Jones, 198–240.

Stoke Poges: A Concise Account of the Church and Manor, and also of the Poet, Thomas Gray. London: Horace Cox, 1896.

Stoke Poges Church. Slough: C. Luff and Co., 1950.

Stoke Poges Gardens of Remembrance. Published by The Secretary, Church Cottage, Stoke Poges, 1937.

Stokes, H. P. 'Thomas Gray, and His Cambridge Relatives' in *The Cambridge Review*, Vol. XXXVIII, No. 942 (1917) 164–67.

Stone, Lawrence. *The Family, Sex and Marriage in England 1500–1800*. New York: Harper and Row, 1977.

Stow, John. *The Survey of London*. Ed. H. B. Wheatley. London: J. M. Dent and Sons, 1912; 1987.

Suarez, Michael F., S. J. 'Trafficking in the Muse: Dodsley's *Collection of Poems* and the Question of Canon' in *Tradition In Transition: Women Writers, Marginal Texts, and the Eighteenth-Century Canon*. Eds. Alvaro Ribiero, S. J. and James G. Basker. Oxford: Clarendon Press, 1996.

Summerson, John. *Georgian London*. 3rd ed. London: Barrie and Jenkins, 1945; 1978.

Sutherland, James. *A Preface to Eighteenth-Century Poetry*. Oxford: Clarendon Press, 1948.

Sutherland, John H. 'The Stonecutter in Gray's "Elegy" ' in *Modern Philology*, LV (1957) 11–13.

Swearingen, James. 'Johnson's "Life of Gray" ' in *Texas Studies In Literature and Language* 14 (1972) 283–302.

——. 'Wordsworth on Gray' in *Studies in English Literature* 14 (1974) 489–509.

Tasswell, William. Autobiography and Anecdotes by William Taswell, D. D.'. Ed. G. P. Elliott, *Camden Miscellany*, vol. 2, 1853.

The Tatler. Ed. Donald F. Bond. 3 Vols. Oxford: Clarendon Press, 1987.

Tayler, Irene. 'Two Eighteenth-Century Illustrators of Gray: Richard Bentley and William Blake' in Downey and Jones, 119–26.

Terr, Lenore C. 'Childhood Traumas: An Outline and an Overview'. *American Journal of Psychiatry*, 148:1 (January, 1991) 10–20.

Terry, Richard. 'Gray and Poetic Diction', in Hutchings and Ruddick, 73–110.

Thomson, James. *The Seasons and The Castle of Indolence*. Ed. James Sambrook. Oxford: Oxford University Press, 1972; 1984.

Tillotson, Geoffrey, 'On Gray's Letters' in *Essays and Criticism on Research*. Hamden, Connecticut: Archon Books, 1967.

Todd, Janet. *Sensibility: An Introduction*. London and New York: Methuen, 1986.

Tovey, Duncan. *Gray and his Friends*. Cambridge: Cambridge University Press, 1985.

Tracy, Clarence. 'Melancholy Marked Him For Her Own' in Downey and Jones, 37–49.

Treswell, Ralph. *The London Surveys of Ralph Treswell*. Ed. J. Schofield, London: London Topographical Society, 1987.

Trumbach, Randolph. *Sex and the Gender Revolution. Volume 1: Heterosexuality and the Third Gender in Enlightenment London*. Chicago: University of Chicago Press, 1998.

——. 'Sodomitical Subcultures, Sodomitical Roles, and the Gender Revolution of the Eighteenth Century' in *'Tis Nature's Fault: Unauthorized Sexuality during the Enlightenment*. Ed. Robert P. Maccubbin. Cambridge: Cambridge University Press, 1987, 109–21.

Ure, Peter. 'Arnold's "Memorial Verses" and Gray's "The Progress Of Poesy"' in *Notes & Queries* 15 (1968) 417.

Van de Veire, Heidi. 'A Note on Gray's "Adversity"' in *Notes and Queries* 37 (September, 1990) 309–12.

Van Houk, La Rue. 'New Light on the Classical Scholarship of Thomas Gray' in *American Journal of Philology*, 57 (1936) 1–9.

Vernon, P. F. 'The Structure of Gray's Early Poems' in *Essays in Criticism* 15.4 (1965) 381–93.

Virgil. *Eclogues, Georgics, Aeneid I–VI*. With an English Translation by H. Rushton Fairclough, revised by G. P. Gould. London and Cambridge, MA: Harvard University Press, 1999.

——. *Georgics*. Trans. Smith Palmer Bovie. Chicago: University of Chicago Press, 1956.

Walker, Thomas Alfred. *Peterhouse*. Cambridge: W. Heffer and Sons, 1906; 1935.

Walpole, Horace. *Ædes Walpolianæ: or, A Description of the Collection of Pictures at Houghton-Hall in Norfolk*. London, 1747.

——. *Horace Walpole's Correspondence with Revd. William Cole*. Eds. W. S. Lewis and A. Dayle Wallace, Vols. 1 and 2 New Haven: Yale University Press, 1937.

——. *Horace Walpole's Correspondence with George Montagu*. Eds. W. S. Lewis and Ralph S. Brown Jr., Vol. 9. New Haven: Yale University Press, 1940.

Walpole, Horace. *Horace Walpole's Correspondence with Thomas Gray, Richard West, and Thomas Ashton.* Eds. W. S. Lewis, George L. Lam, and Charles H. Bennett. Vols. 13 and 14. New Haven: Yale University Press, 1948.

——. *Horace Walpole's Correspondence with Sir Horace Mann, (I–V).* Eds. W. S. Lewis, Warren Hunting Smith, and George L. Lam, Vols. 17–21. New Haven: Yale University Press, 1954–1960.

——. *Horace Walpole's Correspondence with William Mason.* Eds. by W. S. Lewis, Grover Cronin Jr. and Charles H. Bennett. Vols. 28 and 29. New Haven: Yale University Press, 1955.

——. *Horace Walpole's Correspondence with the Countess of Upper Ossory.* Eds W. S. Lewis and A Dayle Wallace, with the assistance of Edwine M. Martz. Vol. 32. New Haven: Yale University Press, 1965.

——. *Horace Walpole's Correspondence with John Chute, Richard Bentley, The Earl of Stratford, Sir William Hamilton, The Earl and Countess Harcourt, George Hardinge.* Eds. W. S. Lewis, A. Dayle Wallace, and Robert A. Smith. Vol. 35. New Haven: Yale University Press, 1973.

——. *Horace Walpole's Correspondence with the Walpole Family.* Eds. W. S. Lewis, J. W. Reed Jr., with the Assistance of Edwine M. Martz. Vol. 36. New Haven: Yale University Press, 1973.

——. *Horace Walpole's Correspondence with Henry Seymour Conway, Lady Ailesbury, Lord and Lady Hertford, Mrs. Harris.* Eds. W. S. Lewis, Lars E. Troide, Edwine M. Martz, Robert M. Smith. Vol. 37. New Haven: Yale University Press, 1974.

——. *Horace Walpole's Miscellaneous Correspondence.* Ed. John Riely with the assistance of Edwine M Martz and Ruth K.

McClure. Volume 40. New Haven: Yale University Press, 1980.

Walsh, John E. *Into My Own: The English Years of Robert Frost.* New York, 1988.

Warburton, Eliot. *Memoirs of Horace Walpole and his Contemporaries.* 2 vols. London, 1851.

Warner, Sylvia Townshend. *T. H. White.* New York: Viking Press, 1968.

Wasserman, Earl R. 'The Inherent Values of Eighteenth-Century Personification' in *PMLA* 65.4 (1950) 435–63.

Watson, George. 'The Voice of Gray' in *Critical Quarterly* 19:4 (1977) 51–57.

Watson-Smyth, Peter. 'Elegy Written in St. Peter's churchyard Burnham, Sunday, August 28, 1737' in *The Spectator*, 31 (July, 1971) 171–74.

Weber, Carl J. 'The Bicentenary of Gray's "Elegy"' in Starr, *Twentieth-Century Interpretations of Gray's Elegy*, 110–12.

Weinbrot, Howard D. 'Gray's *Elegy*: A Poem of Moral Choice and Resolution' in *Studies in English Literature* 18 (1978) 537–51.

——. 'Gray's "Progress of Poetry" and "The Bard": An Essay On Literary Transmission' in *Johnson and His Age.* Ed. James Engell. Harvard English Studies, 12 (311–32) Cambridge: Harvard University Press, 1984.

Weinfeld, Henry. *The Poet Without a Name: Gray's Elegy and the Problem of History.* Carbondale, IL: Southern Illinois University Press, 1991.

Weinrib, Ben, and Christopher Hibbert, *The London Encyclopedia.* London: Macmillan, 1983; 1993.

Wellek, René. 'The Concept of "Romanticism" in Literary History' in *Comparative Literature* 1 (1949) 1–23.

Whalley, George. 'Thomas Gray: A Quiet Hellenist' in Downey and Jones, 146–71.

Whibley, Leonard. 'The Foreign Tour of Gray and Walpole'. *Blackwood's Magazine*. Vol. 227 (1930) 813–27.

——. 'Thomas Gray at Eton'. *Blackwood's Magazine*. Vol. 225 (1929) 611–23.

——. 'Thomas Gray, Undergraduate' in *Blackwood's Magazine* 227 (1930) 273–86.

White, Daniel E. 'Autobiography and Elegy: The Early Romantic Poetics of Thomas Gray and Charlotte Smith' in *Early Romantics: Perspectives in British Poetry from Pope to Wordsworth*. Ed. Thomas Woodman. New York: Macmillan – St. Martin's, 1998, 57–69.

Whiteley, Paul 'Gray, Akenside, and the Ode' in Hutchings and Ruddick, 171–87.

Widmann, R. L. 'Edmund Malone's Manuscript Notes on Pope and Gray' in *Notes & Queries* 20 (1973) 415–17.

Wilding, Michael. 'The Epitaph to Gray's *Elegy*: Two Early Printings and a Parody' in *Notes & Queries* 15 (1968) 213–14.

Williams, Anne. *Prophetic Strain: The Greater Lyric in the Eighteenth Century*. Chicago: University of Chicago Press, 1984.

Williams, Raymond. *The Country and the City*. New York: Oxford University Press, 1973.

Williamson, Paul. 'Gray's *Elegy* and the Logic of Expression', in Hutchings and Ruddick, 39–72.

Willson, Anthony Beckles. *Strawberry Hill: A History of the Neighborhood*. Richmond, Surrey: Michael Collins, Ltd., 1991.

Wilmot, John. *The Complete Poems of John Wilmot, Earl of Rochester*. Ed. David M. Vieth. New Haven: Yale University Press, 1968.

Wilson, Penelope. '"High Pindaricks upon Stilts": A Case Study in the Eighteenth-Century Classical Tradition' in *Rediscovering Hellenism: The Hellenic Heritage and the English Imagination*. Eds. G. W. Clarke and J. C. Eade. Cambridge: Cambridge University Press, 1989, 23–41.

Winstanley, D. A., *Unreformed Cambridge*. Cambridge: Cambridge University Press, 1935.

Woods, Gregory. *A History of Gay Literature: The Male Tradition*. New Haven and London: Yale University Press, 1998.

Wordsworth. William. *Lyrical Ballads*. 2nd ed. In *Poetical Works*. Vol. 2. Ed. E. de Selincourt. Oxford: Clarendon Press, 1944.

——. *The Prose Works of William Wordsworth*. Ed. W. J. B. Owen and Jane Worthington Smyser. 3 vols. Oxford: Oxford University Press, 1974.

Wright, George T. 'Eliot Written in a Country Churchyard: The Elegy and Four Quartets' in *ELH* 43 (1976) 227–43.

——. 'Stillness and the Argument of Gray's "Elegy"' in *Modern Philology* 74 (May, 1977) 381–89.

Yoder, Paul. 'Wordsworth Reimagines Thomas Gray: Notations on Begetting a Kindred Spirit' in *Criticism* 31 (1989) 287–300.

Young, John. *A Criticism of the Elegy written in a Country Church Yard. Being a Continuation of Dr. J——n's Criticism On the Poems of Gray*. London, 1783.

Zionkowski, Linda. 'Bridging the Gulf Between: The Poet and the Audience in the Work of Gray' in *ELH* 58 (1991) 331–50.

——. 'Gray, the Marketplace, and the Masculine Poet' in *Criticism* 35:4 (1993) 589–608.

INDEX

The struggling Pangs of conscious Truth to hide,
To quench the Blushes of ingenuous Shame,
And at the Shrine of Luxury & Pride
With Incense hallow'd in the Muse's Flame.
                    kindled at

The thoughtless World to Majesty may bow
Exalt the brave, & idolize Success
But more to Innocence their Safety owe,
Than Power & Genius e'er conspired to bless

And thou who mindful of the unhonour'd Dead
Dost in these Notes their artless Tale relate
By Night & lonely Contemplation led
To linger in the gloomy Walks of Fate

Hark, how the sacred Calm that broods around
Bids ev'ry fierce tumultuous Passion cease
In still small Accents, whisp'ring from the Ground
A grateful Earnest of eternal Peace

No more with Reason & thyself at Strife
Give anxious Cares & endless Wishes room
But thro' the cool sequester'd Vale of Life
Pursue the silent Tenour of thy Doom

Far from the madding Crowd's ignoble Strife,
Their sober Wishes never knew to stray;
Along the cool sequester'd Vale of Life
They kept the silent Tenour of their Way.

Yet even these Bones from Insult to protect
Some frail Memorial still erected nigh
With uncouth Rhime, & shapeless Sculpture deckt
Implores the passing Tribute of a Sigh.
Their Name, their Years, spelt by th' unletter'd Muse
The Place of Fame, & Epitaph supply,
And many a holy Text around she strews
That teach the rustic Moralist to die.
For who to dumb Forgetfulness a Prey,
This pleasing anxious Being e'er resign'd;
Left the warm Precincts of the chearful Day;
Nor cast one longing ling'ring Look behind?